Johannes Vermeer

The Netherlands has produced more than its fair share of great painters. Old and modern masters such as Rembrandt, Van Gogh, Appel and, of course, Vermeer are just some of the artists whose names signify not only creative perception and excellence, but also enduring quality. They rightly enjoy a place in the annals of art history. The works of all of these great artists have found their way to the farthest corners of the globe and together they have made a major contribution to how the country of their birth is perceived abroad. As a bank, being able to attach your name to one of these great masters, however fleetingly, is cause for real pride. Although the number of surviving Vermeer works is small – only 35 are recognized as true Vermeers – they are all veritable expressions of the highest form of artistic excellence. And, without exception, they also represent the peak of creative endeavour that characterized our Golden Age in the 17th Century.

The Vermeer retrospective is the glittering result of close cooperation between the Mauritshuis, one of the nation's top museums and home to a unique collection of 15th to 18th-century masters, and Rabobank. Never before have so many works by the old master been brought together in one exhibition. This catalogue will enable you to relive the retrospective again and again. It is also an historic document in the sense that there is little chance an exhibition of this magnitude will ever again be organized.

The organization of this retrospective was preceded by an event which is no less unique. In 1994, two works by Vermeer – *Girl with a pearl earring* and *View of Delft* – were restored. Restorations of this kind are in themselves special and the way they were approached by the Mauritshuis made them even more exceptional. Not only was each carried out under the museum's sole direction, but they occurred literally under the very eyes of the public. Anyone who cared to follow the process was able to look over the restorer's shoulder and see at first hand how this precision work was carried out with love and craftsmanship.

For almost a century, Rabobank has been deeply rooted in Dutch society and has forged close ties with our cultural heritage. Exhibitions such as the Vermeer retrospective increase our awareness that art and culture definitely add value to all of our lives. The fact that we have been able to contribute to the preservation of a small part of that heritage is reason for satisfaction. We are sometimes called the "most Dutch of Dutch banks". It is a designation that appeals to us, especially when, as now, we are able to contribute something of significance to our society.

Herman Wijffels
CHAIRMAN OF THE EXECUTIVE BOARD OF
RABOBANK NEDERLAND

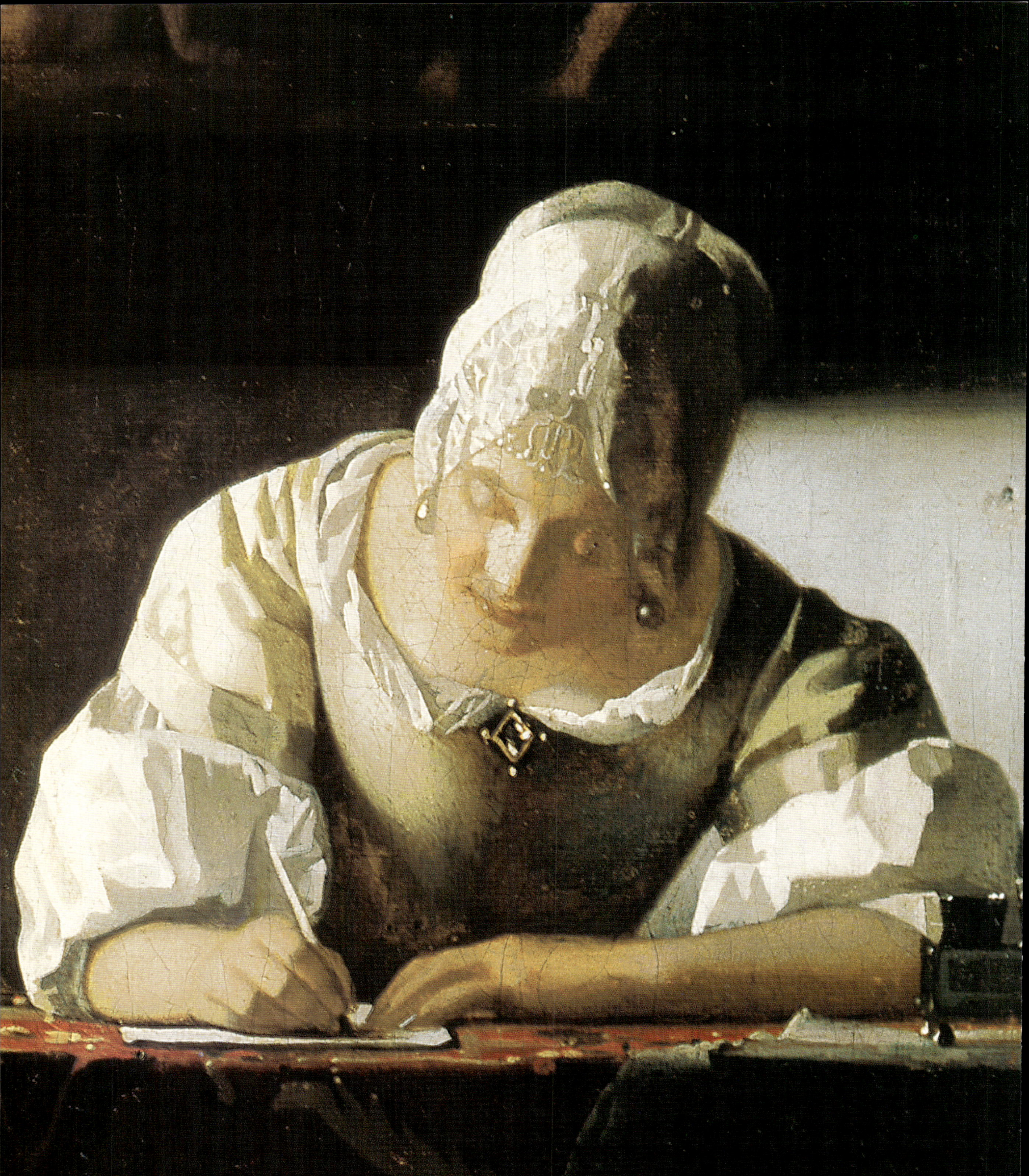

Johannes
Vermeer

ROYAL CABINET OF PAINTINGS MAURITSHUIS, THE HAGUE
NATIONAL GALLERY OF ART, WASHINGTON
WAANDERS PUBLISHERS, ZWOLLE

The exhibition is made possible in The Hague by Rabobank

Rabobank

The exhibition *Johannes Vermeer* is organized by the Royal Cabinet of Paintings Mauritshuis, The Hague, and the National Gallery of Art, Washington.

The exhibition in The Hague is supported by an indemnity from the State of the Netherlands

The exhibition in Washington is supported by an indemnity from the Federal Council on the Arts and the Humanities.

National Gallery of Art, Washington
12 November 1995–11 February 1996

Royal Cabinet of Paintings Mauritshuis, The Hague
1 March–2 June 1996

Curators:
Frederik J. Duparc and Arthur K. Wheelock, Jr.

COVER: *The Geographer* (detail), c. 1668–1669, Städelsches Kunstinstitut, Frankfurt am Main (cat. 16)

BACK COVER: *Young Woman with a Water Pitcher*, c. 1664–1665, The Metropolitan Museum of Art, New York, Marquand Collection, Gift of Henry G. Marquand, 1889 (cat. 11)

FRONTISPIECE: *Lady Writing a Letter with Her Maid* (detail), c. 1670, National Gallery of Ireland, Dublin (cat. 19)

The clothbound English edition is distributed by Yale University Press, New Haven and London, except in The Netherlands, where it is distributed by Waanders Publishers, Zwolle.

Contributors to the catalogue:
Ben Broos and Arthur K. Wheelock, Jr.,
with Albert Blankert and Jørgen Wadum

Editor:
Arthur K. Wheelock, Jr.

Produced by the National Gallery of Art
with the Royal Cabinet of Paintings Mauritshuis
Editor-in-chief: Frances P. Smyth
Copy-edited by Mary Yakush, with Quentin Buvelot, and assisted by Quint Gregory
Translations from the Dutch by Jack Horn
Designed by Chris Vogel, assisted by Wendy Schleicher
Typeset in Van Dijck by General Type, Washington
Printed in The Netherlands by Waanders on 150 grs MC Scheufelen

CIP-GEGEVENS KONINKLIJKE BIBLIOTHEEK, DEN HAAG

Vermeer

Johannes Vermeer / [contributors: Ben Broos ... et al. ; ed. Arthur K. Wheelock]. – Zwolle : Waanders. – Ill.
Uitg. in samenw. met the National Gallery of Art, Washington D.C. en het Mauritshuis. – Uitg. ter gelegenheid van de gelijknamige tentoonstelling 12 november 1995–10 februari 1996 (Washington) en 1 maart–2 juni 1996 (Den Haag). – Met index, lit. opg.
ISBN 90-400-9794-3 geb.
ISBN 90-400-9802-6 (museumeditie) pbk.
NUGI 921/911
Trefw.: Vermeer, Johannes / schilderkunst ; Nederland ; geschiedenis ; 17de eeuw

Contents

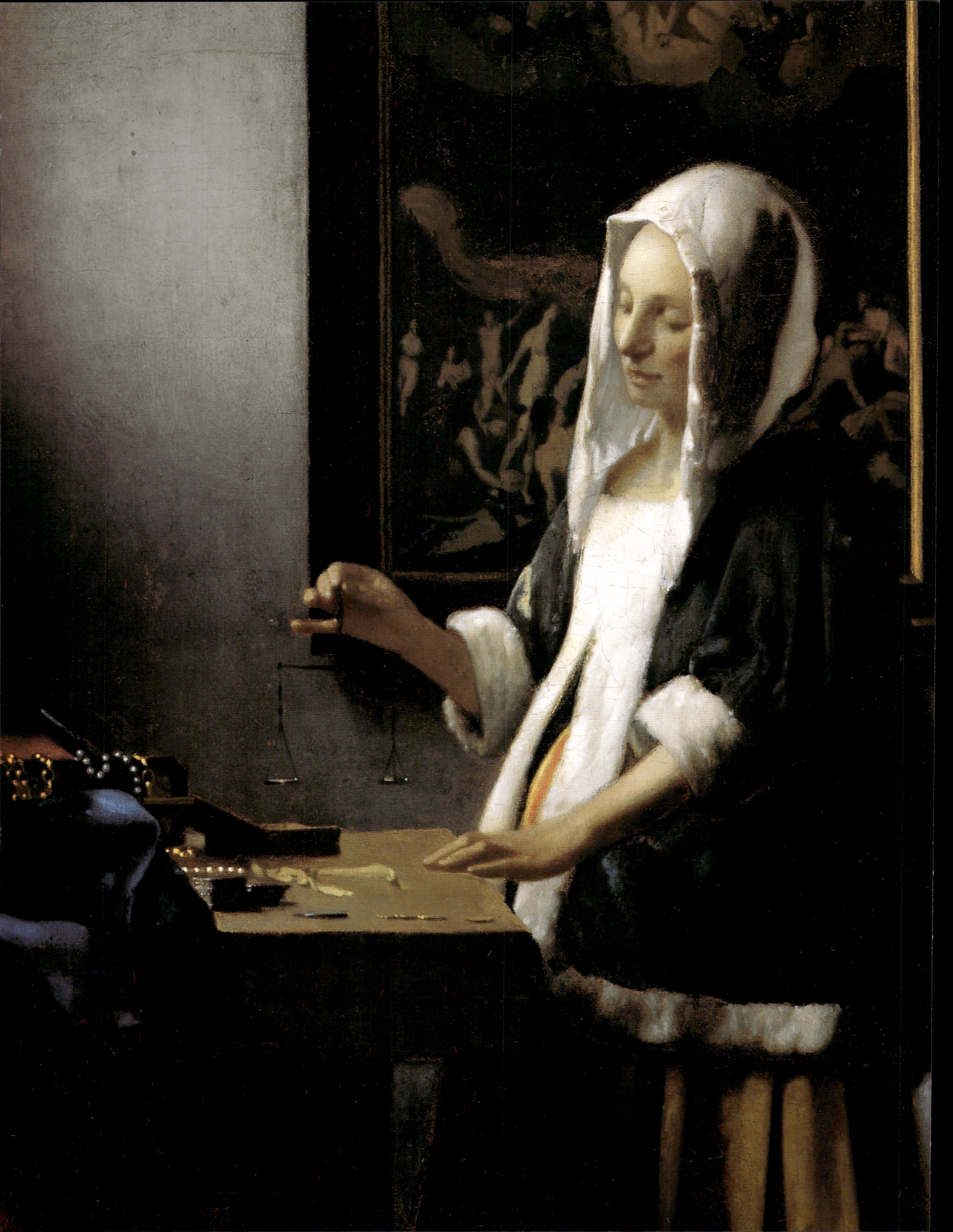

Foreword

The reputation of Johannes Vermeer rests upon a relatively small number of paintings, two-thirds of which are presented in the current exhibition, the first ever devoted exclusively to the art of this remarkable seventeenth-century Dutch master. Many of the themes that Vermeer chose to depict are those he encountered in daily life: a young woman absorbed in reading a letter in the corner of a sunlit room; a girl in a feathery red hat turned toward the viewer, her lips parted and her eyes lit with expectancy; a view of Delft, Vermeer's birthplace and home, with its tiled roofs, church spires, and turreted gates, under an immense sky. In such images, Vermeer found and conveyed values and emotions of lasting concern, transforming reality and reflecting upon the timeless aspects of the human condition. Some of his paintings also have symbolic elements with explicit allegorical connotations. Carefully constructed and rich in meaning, his pictures have intrigued and fascinated viewers over the centuries. We hope that those who have seen the pictures before, individually, will find their pleasure magnified by seeing them brought together, and that newcomers to Vermeer's art will find that the exhibition immeasurably enriches their understanding of Dutch painting.

While a great deal is known about the cultural, social, and political situation in seventeenth-century Delft, relatively little is known of the artist from written records. Neither the facts of his apprenticeship or training, nor the details of any of the commissions that he may have received, is recorded. Yet, the art historical, archival, and conservation studies stimulated by our project have resulted in a far greater understanding of Vermeer's genius and even of the execution and physical structure of his paintings. Visitors to the exhibition will discover anew Vermeer's remarkable mastery of light and texture, and his delicate nuances of color, restored by recent conservation treatments.

The exhibition and accompanying catalogue are the result of a very close and intense collaboration between the National Gallery of Art and the Royal Cabinet of Paintings Mauritshuis. The staffs of both institutions, who will continue to work together long after the exhibition, collectively contributed decades of study to the project. Arthur K. Wheelock, Jr., curator of northern baroque paintings at the Gallery, has brought more than twenty years of accumulated expertise to bear upon his role as a curator of the exhibition and as a principal author and the scholarly editor of the catalogue. Ben Broos, research curator at the Mauritshuis and an expert on the history of collecting, has added an important dimension to the catalogue with his research on Vermeer's changing critical reputation. In an essay by noted Vermeer scholar Albert Blankert, on the nature of Vermeer's 'modern' themes, new insights and interpretations are published. Jørgen Wadum, chief paintings conservator at the Mauritshuis, has provided a study on the artist's use of perspective in which he reveals new evidence of Vermeer's working methods, the direct result of his examination of the paintings exhibited.

In Washington, the exhibition is made possible by United Technologies Corporation, whose continuing contributions to the Gallery's exhibition programs are greatly appreciated. The exhibition in Washington is supported by an indemnity from the Federal Council on the Arts and the Humanities. The Mauritshuis is very grateful that the State of the Netherlands has granted an important governmental guarantee within the framework of the indemnity settlement. In The Hague, Rabobank generously supported the exhibition, and provided funds for the restoration of the Mauritshuis' Vermeer paintings, carried out in full view of visitors to the museum during the summer of 1994. We extend particular

Detail, cat. 10

thanks to United Technologies president and chief executive officer, George David, and Dr. Herman Wijffels, chairman of the executive board of Rabobank Nederland.

Above all else, we are deeply indebted to our lenders for their generosity, cooperation, and good will. We are especially grateful to Her Majesty Queen Elizabeth II for agreeing to lend her rarely exhibited but much-loved Vermeer, *A Lady at the Virginal with a Gentleman (The Music Lesson)*, and to Herbert Beck, Henning Bock, Timothy Clifford, Jan Piet Filedt Kok, Barbara Piasecka Johnson, Raymond Keaveney, Christopher Lloyd, Jochen Luckhardt, Neil MacGregor, Philippe de Montebello, Henk van Os, and Pierre Rosenberg. Each has aided and encouraged this international collaboration and made this long-awaited exhibition a reality.

Frederik J. Duparc
DIRECTOR
ROYAL CABINET OF PAINTINGS
MAURITSHUIS

Earl A. Powell III
DIRECTOR
NATIONAL GALLERY OF ART

Detail, cat. 5

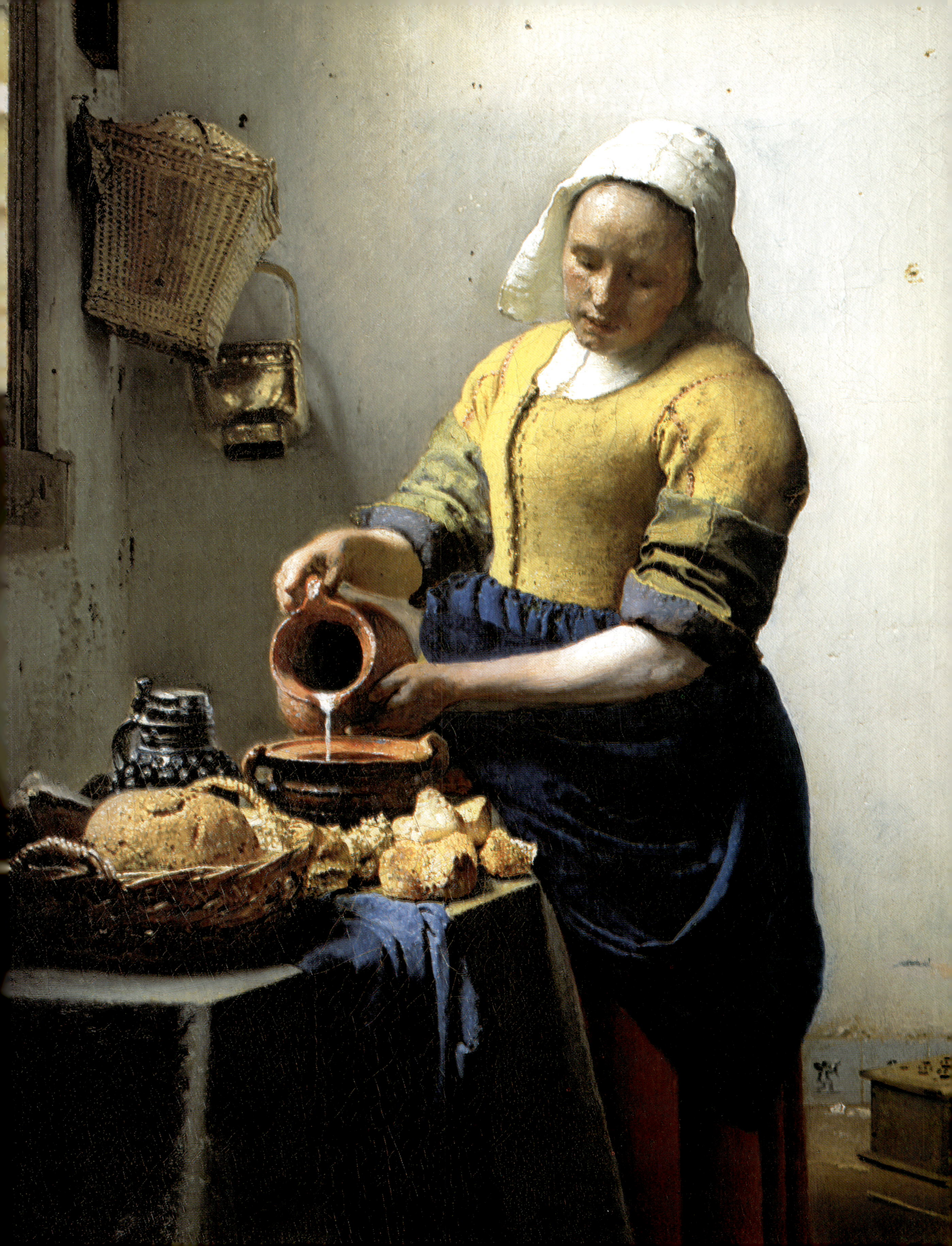

Acknowledgments

From its very inception, *Vermeer* has been a joint project, which benefitted in each and every phase from a close and collegial working relationship between our two institutions. It has been our privilege to collaborate with a team of inspired and motivated individuals on both sides of the Atlantic. As in many important undertakings, ideas take many years to germinate before they are realized. Since 1990, when we agreed to be curators of the exhibition, we have worked together to provide the conceptual underpinning and guidance for all aspects of the project.

To our many colleagues who gave their wholehearted support to our requests for loans, we are enormously grateful: Christopher Brown, Beata Piasecka Bulaj, Michael Clarke, Jean-Pierre Cuzin, Everett Fahy, Bob Haboldt, Roman Herzig, Jan Kelch, Wouter Kloek, Walter Liedtke, Michael Mack-Gérard, Annaliese Mayer-Meintschel, Andrew O'Connor, and Sabine Schulze. We are indebted to Hans Hoetink and Roger Mandle, and to numerous scholars of Dutch art who willingly shared their insights and ideas: Maryan Ainsworth, H. P. ter Avest, J. R. J. van Asperen de Boer, H. Perry Chapman, Daan de Clercq, John Dick, Molly Faries, Jacques Foucart, Bas Dudok van Heel, Kees Kaldenbach, Yme Kuiper, A. Leerintveld, Koos Levy-van Halm, Ekkehard Mai, John Michael Montias, Thera Wijsenbeek-Olthuis, Otto Schutte, and Jaap van der Veen. We also thank the members of the Mauritshuis' advisory committee for their observations on the conservation of *The View of Delft* and *Girl with a Pearl Earring:* David Bomford, Egbert Haverkamp-Begemann, Viola Pemberton-Pigott, Hubert von Sonnenburg, and Ernst van de Wetering.

We are also indebted to the following institutions, whose staffs and resources were essential to the success of our project: Central Research Laboratory, Amsterdam; Centraal Bureau voor Genealogie, The Hague; Iconografisch Bureau, The Hague; Municipal Archives of Amsterdam, Delft, The Hague, and Haarlem; Netherlands Institute for Art History, The Hague; the Rijksarchief, The Hague; Rijksmuseum, Amsterdam, print room; graduate students in art history at the University of Maryland; and students at the Utrecht University art history department. At the National Endowment for the Arts, Washington, Alice Whelihan was especially supportive.

In The Hague, Rik van Koetsveld, deputy director and head of the Vermeer project group at the Mauritshuis, assumed the administrative responsibilities for the exhibition, working with Peter van der Ploeg, curator; Carola Vermeeren, research assistant; conservators Nicola Costaras, who compiled most of the technical descriptions of the paintings, and Luuk Struick van der Loeff; Lieke Vervoorn, head of communications, and her assistant Carola Visser, who implemented the extensive public relations effort for the exhibition; Henk Douna, facility manager, and his staff, who realized the installation; and Albert Verhaar, who, as finance manager, has overseen the complex financial arrangements necessary for such an undertaking.

In Washington, Alan Shestack, deputy director of the National Gallery of Art, and Edgar Peters Bowron, senior curator of paintings, gave their unstinting support, as did numerous other key individuals: D. Dodge Thompson, chief of exhibitions, and his staff who coordinated the administrative details, especially Ann Bigley Robertson, aided by Stephanie Fick and assisted by Megan Teare and Kathryn Haw of the department of northern baroque painting; Ann Leven, treasurer, assisted by Nancy Hoffmann, coordinated insurance; Joseph Krakora, head of the division of external affairs, with Daniel

Herrick, Genevra O. Higginson, and Elizabeth A. C. W. Perry, assisted by Dianne D. Colaizzi and Lisa Claudy, obtained crucial financial support and worked with United Technologies Corporation; Ruth Kaplan, head of the information office, assisted by Deborah Ziska, coordinated publicity; in the conservation division, headed by Ross Merrill, David Bull expertly carried out the restoration of the Gallery's four paintings, for which Melanie Gifford prepared the technical examinations, and Mervin Richard supervised the delicate process of packing and safely transporting all the works; Sally Freitag, chief registrar, assisted by Michelle Fondas, with help from Daniel Shay and Gary Webber, organized and carried out the shipments; in the department of visual services, Rick Carafelli, Barbara Chabrowe, Bob Grove, and Sara Sanders-Buell supplied color transparencies; Gaillard Ravenel, Mark Leithauser, Gordon Anson, and their staff in the department of installation and design are responsible for the beautifully conceived and painstakingly executed design of the exhibition space; in the secretary-general counsel's office, Nancy R. Breuer and Marilyn T. Shaw prepared contracts; and Neal Turtell, executive librarian, and his staff provided invaluable assistance over the years. Supplementary educational materials, made possible through the generous contributions of Mr. Jack Kilgore and Mr. and Mrs. Eijk van Otterloo, were prepared by Susan M. Arensberg, Hugh Phibbs, and Lynn Russell.

Many people worked tirelessly to edit and produce the catalogue. We are especially indebted to the Gallery's editors office, under the leadership of Frances Smyth, for meeting the challenges presented by our project and creating a seamless whole. In particular we would like to thank Mary Yakush, who skillfully organized and edited the manuscript in close collaboration with Quentin Buvelot of the Mauritshuis, and managed the catalogue project, aided by Quint Gregory, who also verified innumerable facts and whose contributions were of critical importance. Meredith Hale compiled major portions of the bibliography, and, together with Aneta Georgievska-Shine, made numerous helpful comments and suggestions for improving the text. Chris Vogel created the elegant design, assisted in the typesetting phase by Wendy Schleicher, and supervised the production of the catalogue. Jack Horn expertly translated portions of the manuscript from the Dutch.

To all those who have helped bring our project to its successful conclusion, we extend our deepest gratitude.

Frederik J. Duparc and Arthur K. Wheelock, Jr.

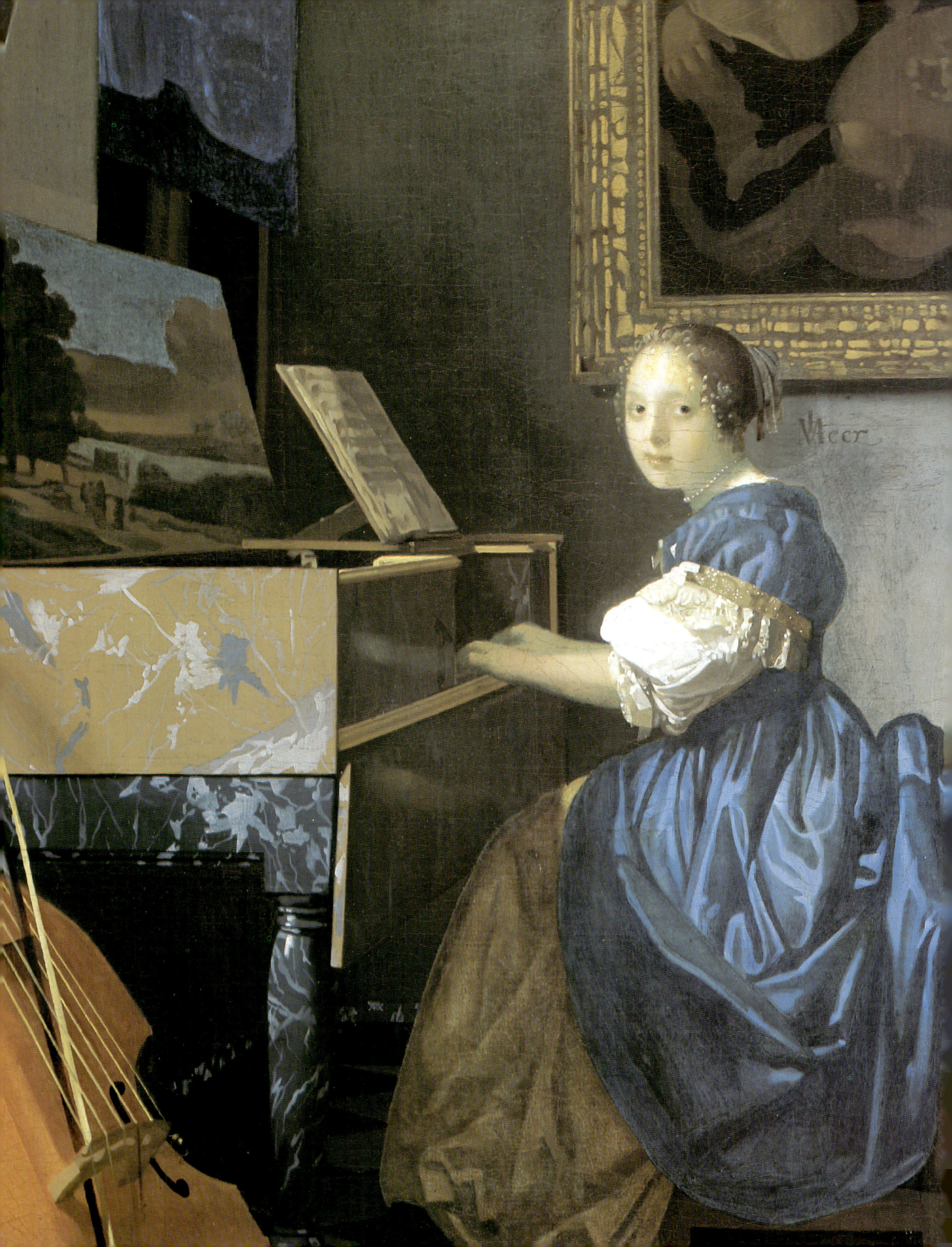

Lenders to the Exhibition

Her Majesty Queen Elizabeth II

Herzog Anton Ulrich-Museum, Brunswick

The Barbara Piasecka Johnson Collection Foundation

Musée du Louvre, Paris

The Metropolitan Museum of Art, New York

National Galleries of Scotland, Edinburgh

National Gallery of Art, Washington

National Gallery of Ireland, Dublin

The Trustees of the National Gallery, London

Rijksmuseum, Amsterdam

Royal Cabinet of Paintings Mauritshuis, The Hague

Staatliche Museen zu Berlin, Gemäldegalerie

Städelsches Kunstinstitut, Frankfurt am Main

Detail, cat. 22

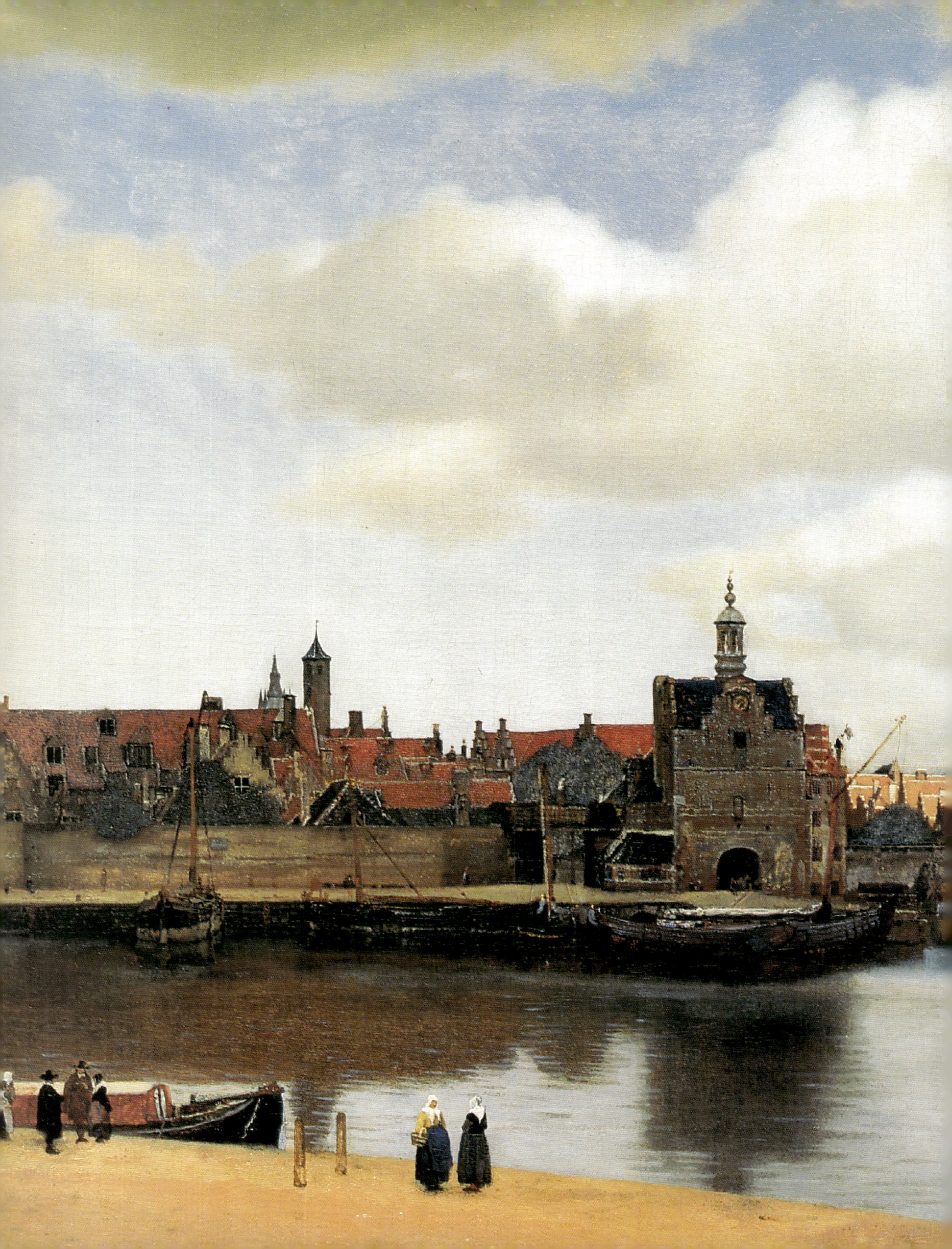

Vermeer of Delft: His Life and His Artistry

ARTHUR K. WHEELOCK, JR.

Vermeer and Delft

BY THE SEVENTEENTH CENTURY DELFT was already a venerable city with a long and distinguished past. The walls and medieval gates of Vermeer's native city, visible in his remarkable *View of Delft* (cat. 7), had controlled traffic over land and water and provided defense for more than three centuries. It was because of these fortifications that Willem de Zwijger (William the Silent), Prince of Orange, chose Delft as his residence during the Dutch revolt against Spanish control.[1] Although the court and the seat of government moved to The Hague at the end of the sixteenth century, Delft continued to enjoy a special status within the province of Holland. While politically allied with the policies of the States General, the city's ties to the House of Orange, through its historical link to William the Silent, remained strong.

The city, with its thriving Delftware factories, tapestry weaving ateliers, and breweries, attracted travelers because of its prosperity and its charm. One Englishman wrote, "Delft has as many bridges as there are days in the year and a like number of canals and streets with boats passing up and down."[2] Most visitors, however, focused upon the imposing tomb of William the Silent, in the choir of the Nieuwe Kerk (New Church). In 1667 the local historian Dirck van Bleyswijck wrote that this tomb, designed and built by Hendrick de Keyser (1565–1628) in 1622, had gained recognition throughout Europe.[3] Not only was it the most magnificent tomb in the Dutch Republic, it also held enormous symbolic importance (see page 19 and note 27).

It was in the Nieuwe Kerk that Reynier Jansz and Digna Baltens christened Johannes ("Joannis"), their second child, and first son, on 31 October 1632. Reynier, a weaver who produced a fine satin fabric called "caffa," had also registered in 1631 in the Delft Saint Luke's Guild as an art dealer, a profession he probably conducted in an inn he had leased on the Voldersgracht.[4] By 1641 Vermeer's father was sufficiently prosperous to purchase a large house containing an inn, the "Mechelen," on the market square in Delft. From this inn Reynier Jansz apparently continued to buy and sell paintings, a business Johannes inherited upon his father's death in 1652. By that time Johannes must have already decided on a career as a painter since only a year later, on 29 December 1653, he registered as a master painter in the Saint Luke's Guild.[5]

Unfortunately, nothing is known about Vermeer's decision to become an artist. The name of his master(s), the nature of his training, the period of his apprenticeship (which must already have begun in the late 1640s), and even the city or cities in which he apprenticed remain mysteries. No written sources indicate whether he was versed in art theory or interested in broad philosophical ideas. Did he ever travel outside of the Netherlands, to Italy, France, or Flanders, to learn about different artistic traditions? Perhaps, but documentation here, as elsewhere, is lacking.

The records also remain tantalizingly vague about Vermeer's relationships with other painters. We know that Leonard Bramer (1596–1674) served as a witness prior to Vermeer's marriage with Catharina Bolnes in April 1653, and that the artist co-signed a document with Gerard ter Borch (1617–1681) two days after his marriage.[6] However, no subsequent contact with either Bramer or Ter Borch can be verified. While Arnold Bon touted Vermeer as the successor to Carel Fabritius' (1622–1654) approach to painting in a poem published in 1667 where he stated that Vermeer, "masterlike, trod his [Fabritius'] path," we know of no specific contact between these two artists. Nor do we have any documents connecting

Detail, cat. 7

Vermeer with Jan Steen (c. 1625–1679) and Pieter de Hooch (1629–1684), both active in Delft in the 1650s. Finally, no documents indicate that Vermeer ever met with painters from other centers, such as Nicolaes Maes (1634–1693) from Dordrecht, or Frans van Mieris the Elder (1635–1681) and Gabriël Metsu (1629–1667) from Leiden and Amsterdam.

Although no sources reveal how Vermeer's paintings were received in the 1650s, by the 1660s he had established a reputation as a serious and innovative artist.[7] Indeed, he was selected to serve as one of the heads of the Saint Luke's Guild in 1662–1663. In 1663 the French traveler and diarist Balthasar de Monconys visited Vermeer, but noted only that his paintings were overpriced.[8] Pieter Teding van Berckhout (1643–1713), a wealthy young amateur, also visited the "excellent" and "famous" Vermeer twice in 1669, the first time seeing "a few curiosities" and the second time "some examples of his art, the most extraordinary and most curious aspect of which consists in the perspective."[9] Further, the 1664 inventory of the Hague sculptor Johan Larson lists a "tronie" by Vermeer, an important indication that by the mid-1660s interest in his works had moved beyond Delft.[10] In 1671–1672 Vermeer was elected once again a headman of the Delft Saint Luke's Guild. In May 1672 he was summoned to The Hague as an expert in Italian paintings – perhaps the most remarkable and suggestive fact as yet discovered.[11]

Despite his respected position within the Delft artistic community, Vermeer fell victim to the disastrous economic climate that followed the 1672 invasion of Holland by Louis XIV of France. Vermeer died three years later, leaving behind a wife, ten minor children, and enormous debts. In a petition of 1677 his widow recounted the difficulties of their last years: "during the ruinous and protracted war [Vermeer] not only was unable to sell any of his art but also, to his great detriment, was left sitting with the paintings of other masters that he was dealing in."[12] In the same year, Catharina Bolnes and her mother, Maria Thins, undertook a heartrending struggle to prevent the sale of the *Art of Painting* (page 68, fig. 2) at a public auction at the Saint Luke's Guild.[13] Given Vermeer's fascination with perspective and optics, it seems relevant that the executor of his estate was the famed Delft microscopist Anthony van Leeuwenhoek, born in Delft in the same year as Vermeer, 1632.[14]

Most of the documents that mention Vermeer pertain to his family. While John Michael Montias admirably analyzed many of them,[15] the importance of Vermeer's mother-in-law, Maria Thins, deserves further mention. The traditional view that Maria Thins resisted Vermeer's marriage to Catharina Bolnes in December 1653 seems somewhat misleading; indeed, all evidence indicates that she and Vermeer had a close and supportive relationship.[16] Before the marriage Vermeer converted to Catholicism, almost certainly in deference to the wishes of his future mother-in-law.[17] By 1656 Maria Thins had loaned the couple 300 guilders, and her 1657 testament treated her daughter very generously,[18] perhaps because Johannes and Catharina had honored her by naming their first child Maria. The young couple eventually lived with Maria Thins, moving into her home on the Oude Langendijk by 1660.

Maria Thins almost certainly had some knowledge of paintings. Through her cousin Jan Geensz Thins, who owned the house in which she lived, Maria was distantly related by marriage to the Utrecht painter Abraham Bloemaert (1564–1651).[19] Moreover, she had a modest collection of paintings from the Utrecht school, which she, together with her brother, and her sister, had inherited from her parents.[20] Vermeer certainly knew those paintings, which were in her home in Delft. At least two appear in the backgrounds of his

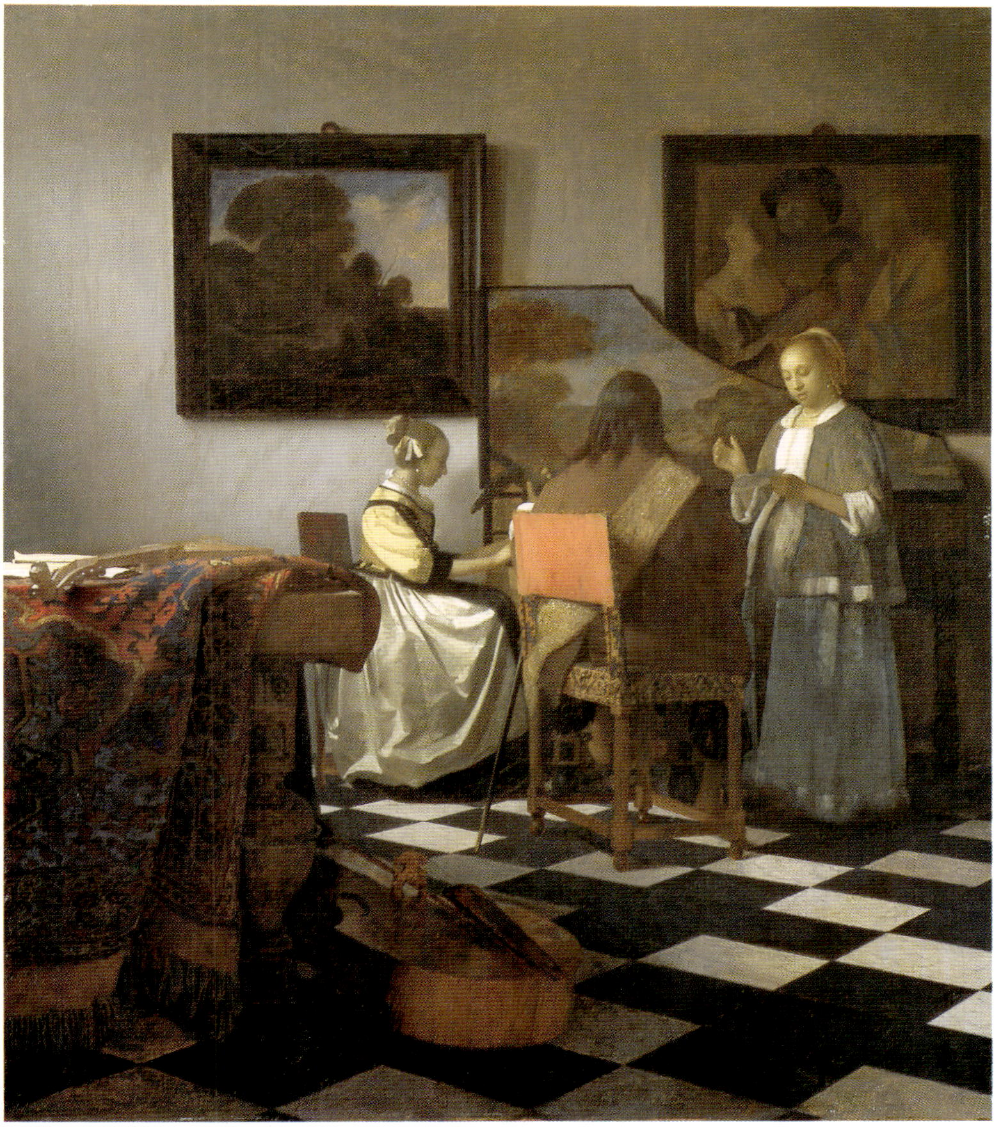

fig. 1. Johannes Vermeer, *The Concert*, c. 1665–1666, oil on canvas, Isabella Stewart Gardner Museum, Boston (whereabouts unknown)

own works: *The Procuress*, by Dirck van Baburen (1590/1595–1624), which he included in both *The Concert* (fig. 1) and *A Lady Seated at the Virginal* (cat. 22, fig. 1), and *Roman Charity*, which hangs on the rear wall of the *Music Lesson* (cat. 8).

Vermeer and Delft Stylistic Traditions

Maria Thins' collection of Utrecht paintings may help explain the character of Vermeer's early works, which do not draw heavily upon Delft stylistic traditions. It is understandable that he found little inspiration in Delft, for during his formative years the city's artistic community was not particularly dynamic. Aside from Bramer, its major artists include the history painter Christiaen van Couwenbergh (1604–1667), the genre and portrait painter Anthonie Palamedesz (1600/1601–1673/1680), the landscape painter Pieter van Asch (1602–1678), and the aged still life painter Balthasar van der Ast (before 1590–after 1660). The arrival of Paulus Potter (1625–1654) in 1646, and his membership in the guild until 1649, must have been a welcome event. Yet, it seems unlikely that any of these painters inspired the young Vermeer or helped determine the direction that his art would take.

While Bramer knew Vermeer well and had numerous contacts with his family in the early 1650s,[21] the precise nature of the older artist's impact remains unclear. Stylistically, the exotic figures in Bramer's small paintings on panel and copper are quite different from those in Vermeer's early religious and mythological scenes. However, Bramer also painted murals, most importantly for the Prince of Orange at the palaces of Honselaarsdijk and Rijswijk. While the murals have almost all disappeared, related drawings suggest that the figures were large in scale and classically conceived.[22] These lost works may have been the key to the stylistic relationship between the two artists.

An artist who traveled widely and who was familiar with Italian art, Bramer would surely have recommended that the young Vermeer expand his horizons with travel as well, perhaps to France and Italy, but certainly to Utrecht and Amsterdam. In Utrecht Vermeer could have met Abraham Bloemaert, Maria Thins' distant relative, who in the late 1640s painted in a broad, classicizing style; in Amsterdam he would certainly have learned something about Rembrandt's manner of painting.[23]

While Vermeer's early style suggests that he received some training outside of Delft, this could only have occurred prior to his father's death in October 1652. It would seem that after that date he would have had to be present to attend to family affairs. He was, in fact, living in the family home "Mechelen" on the Marketplace at the time of his marriage to Catharina Bolnes the following April.[24] By the end of December 1653 he had become a master in the guild.[25]

The close proximity of Delft to The Hague meant that a number of Delft artists active in the 1640s enjoyed the patronage of members of the court. While this source for commissions created a certain degree of economic stability, it also fostered a conservative

LEFT: fig. 2. Gerard Houckgeest, *The Tomb of Willem of Orange*, 1651, oil on panel, Mauritshuis, The Hague

RIGHT: fig. 3. Emanuel de Witte, *Interior of Oude Kerk in Delft*, c. 1650 – 1651, oil on oak, National Gallery of Canada, Ottawa, Purchased in 1983 with the assistance of a grant from the Government of Canada under the terms of the Cultural Property Export and Import Act

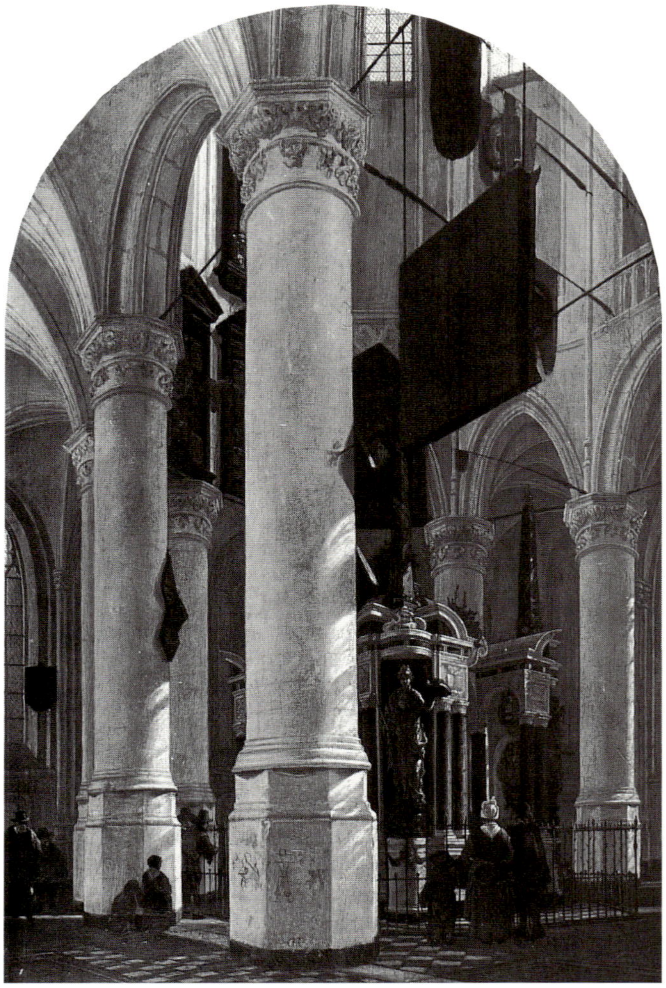

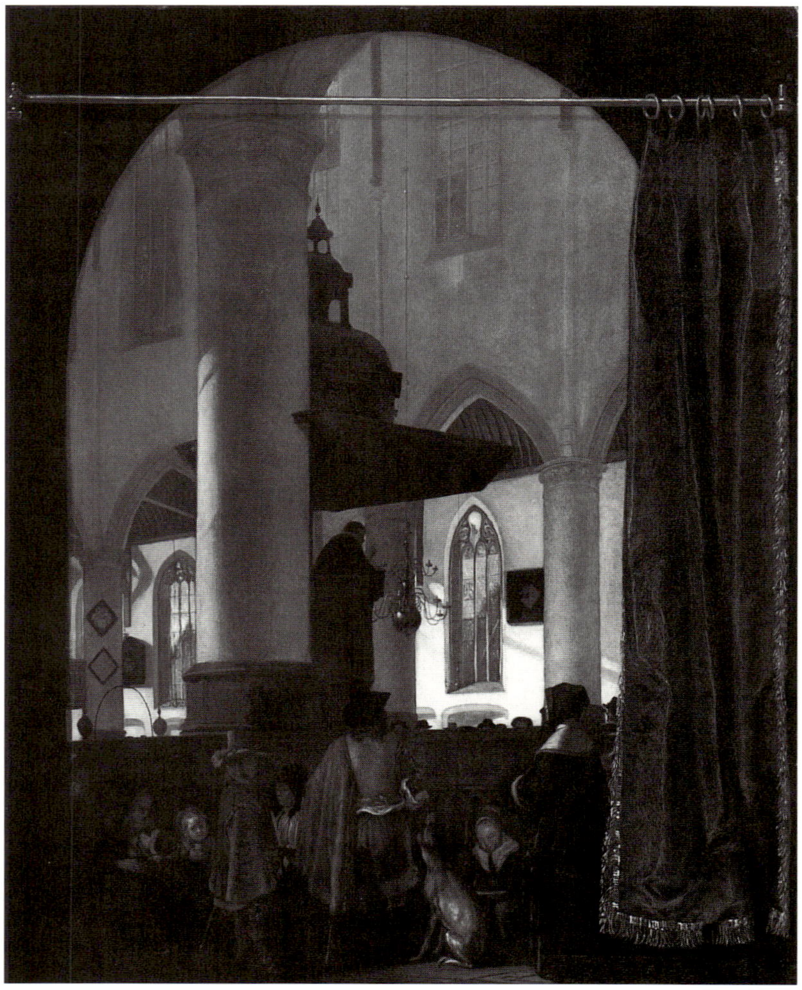

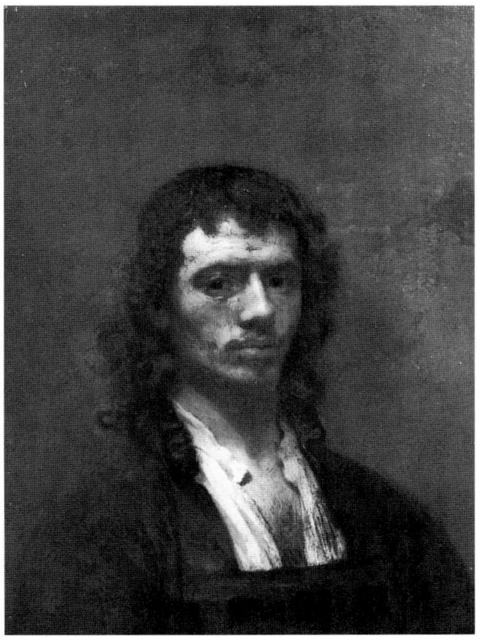

fig. 4. Carel Fabritius, *Self-Portrait*, c. 1648, oil on panel, Museum Boymans-van Beuningen, Rotterdam

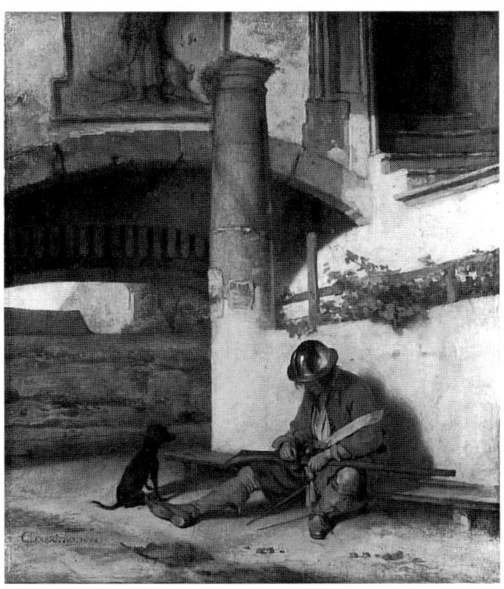

fig. 5. Carel Fabritius, *The Sentry*, 1654, oil on canvas, Staatliches Museum Schwerin

atmosphere, in which established forms of expression were preferred to the stylistic innovations of artists in Haarlem, Amsterdam, and Leiden. Even after the death of Prince Willem II on 6 November 1650, many artists must have continued to believe that large-scale history painting would remain an important artistic current. Indeed, until 1652 a number of classicizing painters were at work on an enormous decorative ensemble for the Oranjezaal in the Huis ten Bosch. Among them were Caesar van Everdingen (c. 1616/1617–1678), Pieter de Grebber (c. 1600–1652/1653), Salomon de Bray (1597–1664), and Gerard van Honthorst (1590–1656), all from Utrecht and Haarlem, as well as the Delft artist Christiaen van Couwenbergh. Several Flemish painters, including Jacob Jordaens (1593–1678), Theodoor van Thulden (1606–1669), and Thomas Willeboirts Bosschaert (1613/1614–1654), added an international flavor to this endeavor. Van Couwenbergh and another (less talented) Delft artist, Willem Verschoor (c. 1630–1678), had also painted classicizing history scenes for public and private patrons.[26]

In 1650, however, a dynamic new style of architectural painting evolved in Delft, which offered an alternative to the conservative artistic traditions that had heretofore dominated the city. Paintings from the early 1650s by Gerard Houckgeest (c. 1600–1661), Emanuel de Witte (c. 1617–1692), and Hendrick van Vliet (1611/1612–1675) depicted the interiors of Delft's two primary churches, the Nieuwe Kerk and the Oude Kerk (Old Church) in ways that emotionally involved the viewer in the scene. They achieved this effect not only through their use of unusual vantage points, diagonal perspective, and strong chiaroscuro, but also by integrating figures in the interior space.

While the reasons for this sudden stylistic development are not entirely understood, they may be related to a change in the country's political fortunes. The unexpected death of the Prince of Orange in November 1650 left the Dutch Republic, for the first time in its history, without the leadership of a Prince of Orange, for Willem II's son, born just eight days after his father's death, was too young to rule.[27] Houckgeest's first architectural paintings in the new style, indeed, depict the tomb of William the Silent (fig. 2), the final resting place of the Princes of Orange. The figures at the tomb pay homage to them, in the process contemplating the inevitability of death. A painting by Emanuel de Witte similarly focuses on figures who listen intently to a sermon (fig. 3), their very presence enhancing the emotional intensity of the scene.

By 1653, Houckgeest and De Witte had both left the city, but the presence of Carel Fabritius both enriched and expanded the artistic legacy accessible to the young Vermeer. To judge from his self-portraits (fig. 4), Fabritius must have been a dynamic individual when he arrived in Delft in 1650, an artist counting among his talents "perspectives" and mural paintings.[28] In the few existing works from his Delft period, among them *A View in Delft with a Musical Instrument Seller's Stall*, 1652 (National Gallery, London), and *The Sentry*, 1654 (fig. 5), Fabritius used perspective to extend the limits of genre painting. In the latter painting, for example, in part through expressive spatial and architectural constructs, he expanded beyond the specific depiction of the sentry's failure to uphold his responsibility for ensuring the city's security, communicating a broad message about human behavior.[29]

The few small-scale paintings remaining from this period of Fabritius' career provide an insufficient basis for assessing his influence on Vermeer, whose early religious and mythological works demonstrate neither an interest in naturalistic settings nor in the laws of perspective. While the brooding melancholia of Vermeer's *Diana and Her Companions*

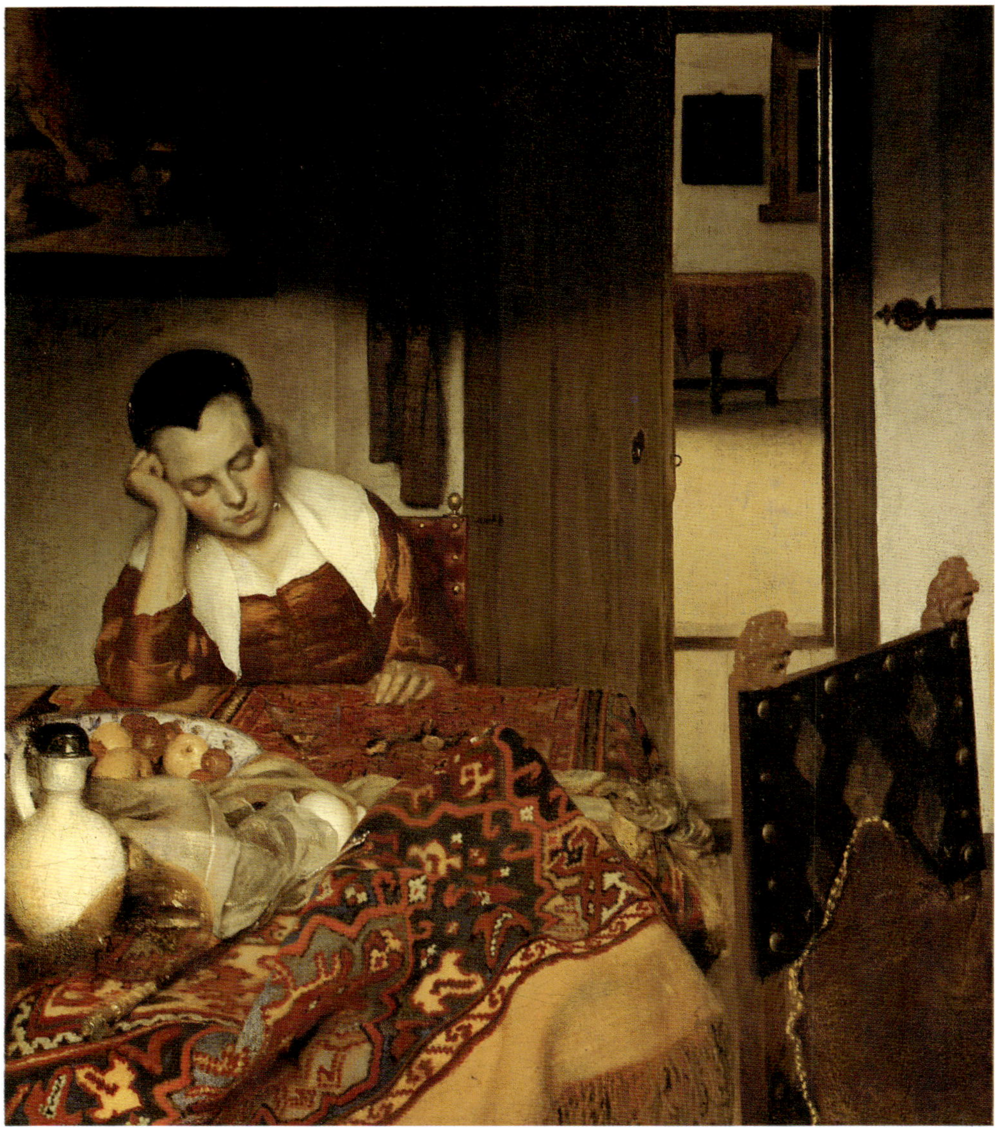

fig. 6. Johannes Vermeer, *A Woman Asleep*, c. 1657, oil on canvas, The Metropolitan Museum of Art, New York, Bequest of Benjamin Altman, 1913

(cat. 3) and *A Woman Asleep*, c. 1657 (fig. 6) recalls the mood of Fabritius' *A View in Delft* and *The Sentry*, Vermeer's full appreciation of Fabritius' expressive ideas developed only later in his career. Whatever its character – personal, stylistic, or thematic – some connection must have existed between the two artists.[30]

Just as Vermeer embarked upon his career in the early 1650s, the artistic character of Delft was undergoing enormous changes. It seems that the importance of history painting in Delft and The Hague around 1650 inspired the young artist to work in this manner, particularly since art theorists placed the depiction of biblical and mythological scenes at the highest echelon in the hierarchy of painting.[31] Vermeer's early paintings *Saint Praxedis*, *Christ in the House of Mary and Martha*, and *Diana and Her Companions* (cats. 1, 2, 3), however, have no clear stylistic ties to Delft's indigenous traditions. He appears to have drawn upon the work of artists from other centers, primarily Amsterdam and Utrecht in Holland, but also Italy and Flanders. Vermeer may have become acquainted with the work of these artists through travels during his apprentice years, through his father, who bought and sold paintings, or through his mother-in-law's collection of Utrecht paintings.

The reasons for Vermeer's shift from biblical and mythological scenes to genre and cityscapes in the latter part of the 1650s are not known. Perhaps he was not entirely comfortable with large-scale figures, or perhaps such works denied him the opportunity to represent naturalistic light and perspective, an interest for which he seems to have had a natural predilection. The arrival in Delft of Pieter de Hooch in 1654, and Jan Steen the following year, may also have led Vermeer in this direction since each artist, in his own

OPPOSITE PAGE

TOP LEFT: fig. 7. Jan Steen, *The Burgher of Delft and His Daughter*, 1655, oil on canvas, Penrhyn Castle (The National Trust)

BOTTOM: fig. 8. Pieter de Hooch, *Players at Tric-Trac*, c. 1654–1655, oil on panel, National Gallery of Ireland, Dublin

TOP RIGHT: fig. 9. Pieter de Hooch, *A Dutch Courtyard*, 1658–1660, oil on canvas, National Gallery of Art, Washington, Andrew W. Mellon Collection

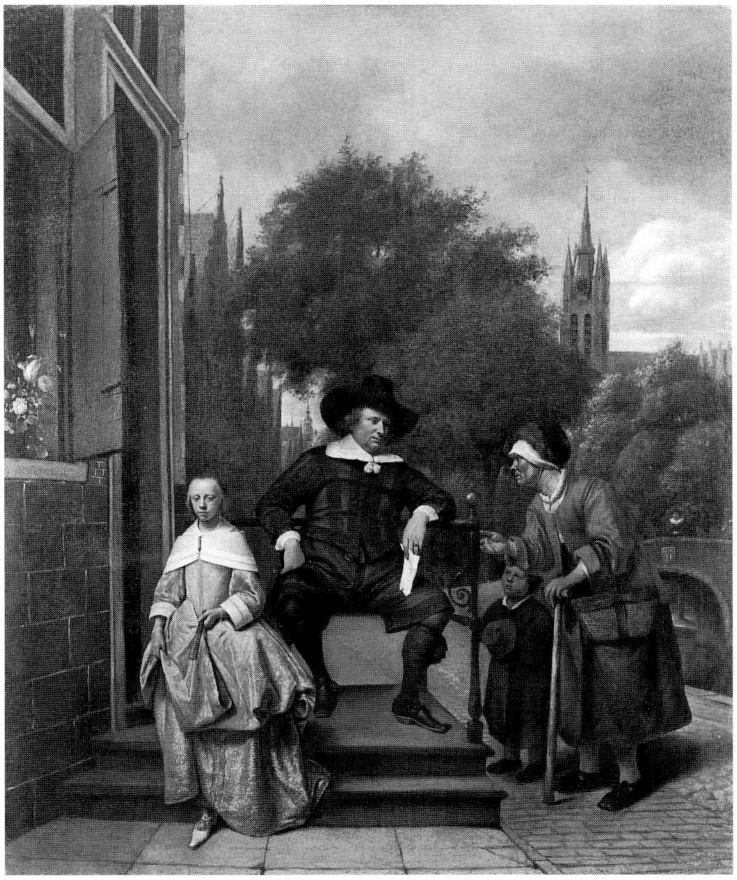

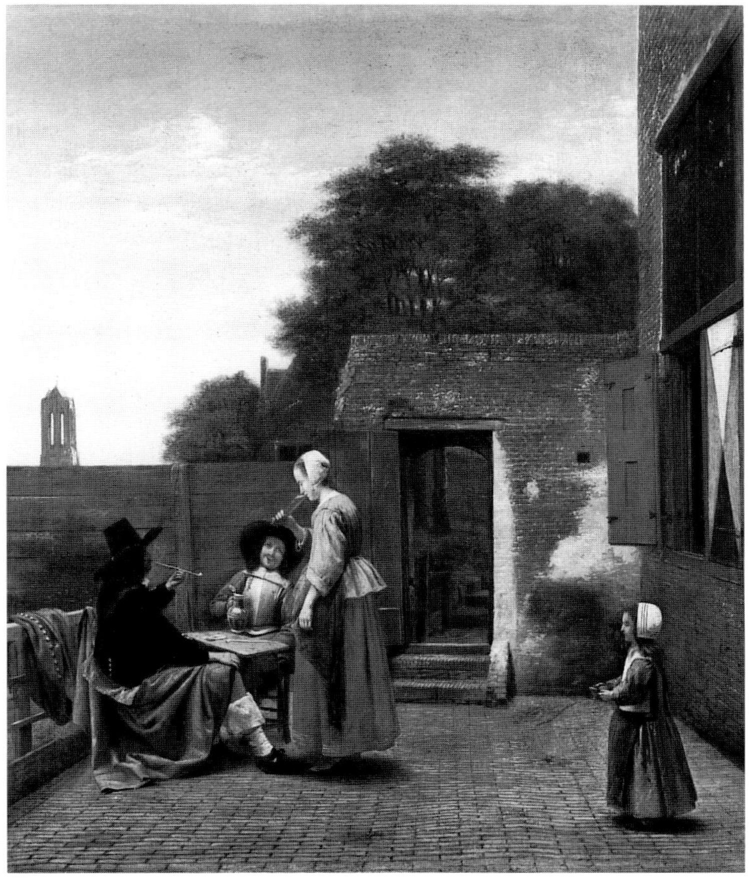

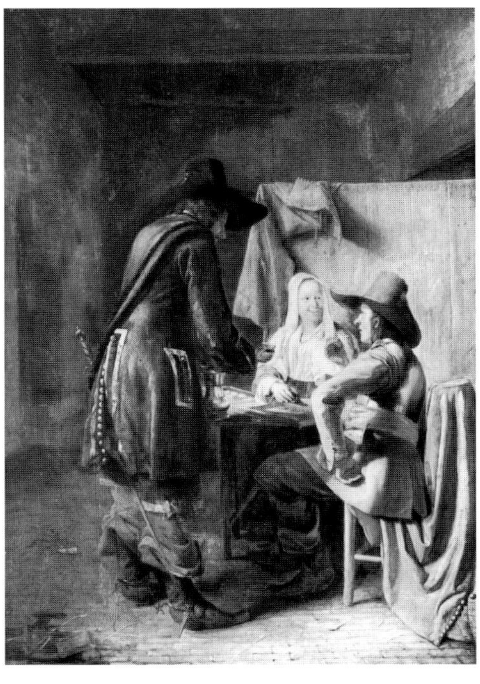

way, demonstrated how effectively architectural and figural elements, drawn from daily life, could be fused to create a new vision of reality. Or perhaps all three of these painters responded to an artistic climate in Delft where artists sought to enlarge upon the conceptual and stylistic innovations of the early 1650s.

The change in style evident in both the work of De Hooch and Steen once they arrived in Delft lends some credence to the latter theory. Steen, who had previously worked in Haarlem, Leiden, and The Hague, had established himself as an innovative genre painter before his brief stay in Delft in 1655. The one painting that clearly belongs to his Delft period, the *Burgher of Delft and His Daughter* (fig. 7), has a restrained compositional structure unlike that of any of his previous works. The burgher's home, and the steps on which he sits, quietly frame his encounter with the beggar woman. De Hooch's response to the artistic climate in Delft, where he resided until about 1660, proves even more essential to Vermeer. De Hooch painted primarily low-life genre and guard room scenes when he first arrived from Rotterdam (fig. 8). His interest lay in the figures and their interrelationships, not in the architectural setting, which he usually indicated in a cursory fashion. Almost immediately after joining the Delft guild, however, De Hooch began to depict middle-class interiors and courtyards in which sunlight played an important role in defining spatial relationships among the figures (fig. 9). Perspective became a primary concern, as did the depiction of texture.

Despite lack of documentation linking Vermeer and De Hooch, the parallels between their works from the late 1650s make it highly probable that the two artists knew one another. Whether one artist inspired the other to alter his subject matter, to sharpen his skills in perspective, and to depict the realistic effects of light and texture, or whether they arrived at their styles simultaneously, are questions that cannot be answered because none of Vermeer's paintings from this period is dated. Vermeer, to modern sensibilities, seems the greater and more innovative artist. Nevertheless, throughout his career, he drew inspiration from the work of others. His genius lay in his ability to transcend his sources with unfailing compositional sensitivity and his gift for conveying an underlying moral tenor to both his history paintings and scenes of daily life. Indeed, after De Hooch left Delft to go to Amsterdam in the early 1660s, Vermeer apparently followed his lead in painting at least two works.[32]

A Patron for Vermeer?

As Vermeer and De Hooch forged, in collaboration or independence, a new style of genre painting in Delft, comparable approaches to genre painting developed in other artistic centers. A widespread preference for delicately executed middle- and upper-class genre scenes emerged in the late 1650s in Dordrecht, with Nicolaes Maes and Samuel van Hoogstraeten (1627–1678); in Leiden with Gerrit Dou (1613–1675), Gabriël Metsu, and Frans van Mieris the Elder; in Deventer with Gerard ter Borch; and in Amsterdam with Jacob van Loo (c. 1615–1670).

The identification of the patrons for whom these artists painted, and the impact of the patrons' wishes on the thematic and stylistic characteristics of their work, proves vexing, particularly for Vermeer. Montias, for example, has proposed that artists such as Vermeer would only have invested the time necessary to paint refined, meticulously rendered genre scenes for specific patrons rather than for the open market. Indeed, the Leiden *fijnschilders* Gerrit Dou and Frans van Mieris the Elder received yearly stipends from patrons in exchange for their highly finished paintings or the right of first refusal for them. Many have speculated about whether comparable arrangements existed for Vermeer and De Hooch. After careful study of Vermeer's relationship to his contemporaries in Delft, Montias has proposed that in 1657, at about the time that Vermeer began to paint genre scenes and cityscapes, he began working for one primary patron, Pieter Claesz van Ruijven (1624–1674), a wealthy patrician collector. Montias argues that Van Ruijven began his arrangement with Vermeer in 1657 as part of a loan agreement and that Vermeer's change from history to genre and cityscape painter resulted from this relationship.[33] According to Montias, the Vermeer paintings in Van Ruijven's collection were bequeathed to his daughter, Magdalena, who married Jacob Dissius in 1680. Indeed, according to an inventory made in 1683 shortly after Magdalena's death, the couple owned, among other works, twenty paintings by Vermeer, none of which is specifically identified.[34]

The hypothesis that Van Ruijven was Vermeer's patron, although appealing, should be cautiously approached, for no document specifies that Vermeer ever painted for Van Ruijven. Moreover, no source confirms that Van Ruijven himself had any Vermeer paintings in his possession. In the agreement for the loan that he made to Vermeer in 1657, which Montias interprets as "an advance toward the purchase of one or more paintings," no such arrangement is stipulated.[35] On the contrary, Vermeer and Catharina Bolnes promised "to return the sum within a year...together with interest...until full repayment shall have been effected." Should they fail to meet their obligation, the couple declared themselves "willing to...be condemned by the judges of this city."[36] The agreement never mentioned paintings as an alternative form of payment.

While Van Ruijven may have acquired paintings from Vermeer, it seems unlikely that he assumed as important a role in the artist's life as Montias suggests. Should Van Ruijven have been Vermeer's patron, one would expect that De Monconys would have visited Van Ruijven in 1663 rather than a baker, presumably Hendrick van Buyten, upon hearing that Vermeer had no paintings at home. Similarly, the Vermeer enthusiast Pieter Teding van Berckhout would also have made an effort to see Van Ruijven's collection in 1669 on his two visits to Delft.

While it is probable that some of the twenty Vermeer paintings listed in the inventory of 1683 came from Van Ruijven, others may have been acquired by Magdalena van Ruijven, Jacob Dissius, or his father, Abraham Jacobsz Dissius, at a sale of twenty-six paintings from Vermeer's estate held at the Saint Luke's Guild Hall on 15 May 1677. No catalogue was made of the sale, hence information about its contents, and the buyers who attended, is lacking.[37] However, as a result of efforts by Vermeer's widow and mother-in-law to prevent the *Art of Painting* from being included in the sale, it is known at least that this one painting by Vermeer was scheduled to be sold at that time.[38] It is probable that other Vermeer paintings were also part of the sale.[39]

An inventory of 1683 lists the mutual holdings of Jacob and Magdalena, which raises the possibility that not all of the paintings in their possession necessarily derived from her side of the family.[40] Indeed, substantial contributions from both sides of the family seem likely given the unusual stipulation in Magdalena's will that Dissius' father, a printer who lived on the Marketplace not far from Vermeer, would share equally in the estate.[41]

After his father's death in 1694, the entire collection became Jacob's property. At some point, one other Vermeer painting must have been added to the Dissius collection, for it contained twenty-one paintings by Vermeer when it was put up for auction after Jacob's death in 1695.[42] The identifiable paintings in this sale, which was held in Amsterdam on 16 May 1696, date from c. 1657 to c. 1673, spanning Vermeer's career from the time he began to paint genre scenes and cityscapes. Whether one patron collected most of these works over time, or supplemented his collection with purchases after the artist's death, is a fascinating but presently unresolvable question.

Vermeer's Artistry

The historical and artistic context in which Vermeer developed as a painter is important for understanding his development as an artist. Indeed, throughout his career Vermeer was remarkably receptive to the stylistic and thematic ideas of others. As discussed by Albert Blankert (see page 31), Vermeer derived most of his genre subjects from well-established iconographic traditions, as for example, in *Girl Interrupted at Her Music* (fig. 10), where he included a wine jug in the context of a musical theme. Similarly, pictorial sources exist for his cityscapes and allegorical paintings. What distinguishes him as an artist, however, are not the connections but the innovative transformations he brought to these traditions.

Because no writings by Vermeer about art have survived, we have no certain under-

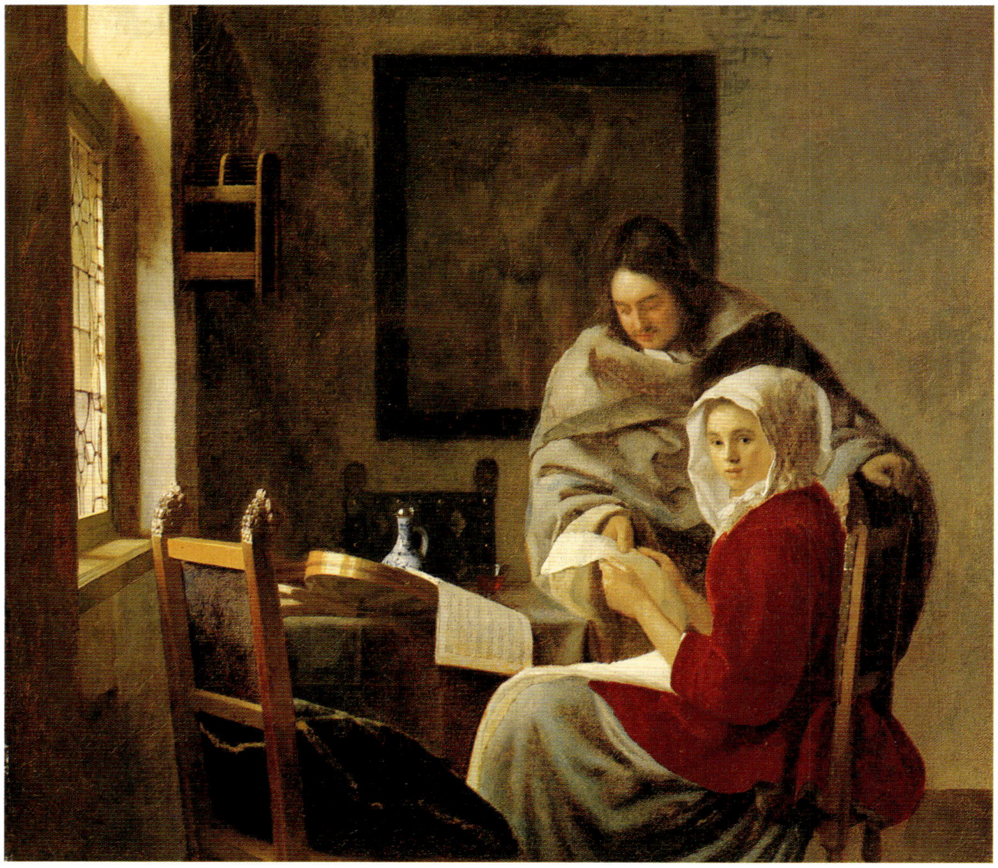

fig. 10. Johannes Vermeer, *Girl Interrupted at Her Music*, c. 1660–1661, oil on canvas, © The Frick Collection, New York

standing of his attitudes about pictorial representation.[43] Nevertheless, somewhere in the course of his training, whether through a teacher or through his own study of literary and pictorial sources, he learned the fundamental principles of painting. He became remarkably adept at layering his paints, not only to create textural and optical effects to simulate reality, but also to enhance a given mood. He also developed a sophisticated awareness of the importance of perspective to create the illusion of a three-dimensional space, and to affect the viewer's perception. Finally, he had an extraordinary awareness of the psychological impact of color.

From the very beginning of his career, explicitly in *Christ in the House of Mary and Martha* and implicitly in *Saint Praxedis* and *Diana and Her Companions*, Vermeer preferred representing quiet, brooding moments that emphasize the meditative side of life. These paintings, in many respects hard to reconcile with Vermeer's later works, indicate a broadness of vision and execution possessed by no "genre" painter of the period. Vermeer's initial impulse to paint large-scale history scenes indicates an early concern with the overall impact of his image rather than with careful rendering of textures and materials. His technique in the early works is relatively free and bold, appropriate to their large compass. While it became more refined and complex in later genre scenes and cityscapes, he always maintained the capacity to suggest rather than describe form and texture.

Once Vermeer began to depict scenes of contemporary life, he used perspective as a major compositional tool, both to create a realistic setting and for its expressive potential. In *A Woman Asleep* of c. 1657 (fig. 6), for example, Vermeer's perspective creates the illusion of a receding space, but, at the same time, the horizon line is placed quite high, so that the viewer looks down on the woman, reinforcing the pervasive sense of melancholy.[44] Vermeer's perspective in this painting, however, is rather intuitive, and not totally accurate. He quickly developed a more scientific approach, perhaps in response to paintings by Pieter de Hooch, Carel Fabritius, and the Delft architectural painters of the early 1650s (see page 19). In *Officer and Laughing Girl* (page 35, fig. 6), for example, orthogonals recede to a single vanishing point midway between the two figures. The placement of the

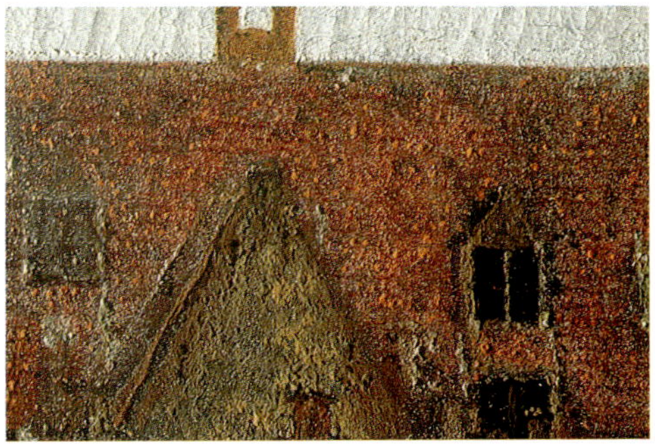

fig. 11. Detail of blue dress, *Young Woman with a Water Pitcher* (cat. 11)

fig. 12. Detail of rooftops, *View of Delft* (cat. 7)

vanishing point here also plays an important psychological function in the composition, for it activates the space between the soldier and girl, intensifying the nature of their relationship. Throught his career Vermeer carefully placed his horizon lines and vanishing points to help establish the particular character and mood he sought for his images.

Vermeer used other, equally important means for creating a semblance of three-dimensional reality. For example, he often placed a chair or table in the foreground of his paintings to establish a barrier between his figures and the viewer. In *Woman with a Lute* (fig. 13), this compositional device not only creates a feeling of depth, it also reinforces the sense of privacy that pervades the scene. Vermeer successfully captured the sense of light filtering through leaded glass windows, and the interaction of light with objects in a room. He paid particular attention to contours, occasionally dissolving them with a diffused stroke of paint, as in the front of the young woman's blue dress in *Young Woman with a Water Pitcher* (fig. 11). Vermeer also had the ability to suggest a vast range of textures, from the translucence of a pearl to the rough-hewn textures of rooftops in the *View of Delft* (fig. 12). He achieved these effects through extraordinary control of his paints and medium, working effectively with both dense impastos and thin glazes. His sensitivity toward color was equally remarkable. Not only did he use the best pigments available, particularly natural ultramarine and lead-tin yellow, which ensured luminosity, but he also understood the optical characteristics of color. For example, in *Woman Holding a Balance* (cat. 10), he painted a thinly applied blue layer over a reddish brown layer, thereby infusing the ordinarily cool blue tones with an inner warmth.

Vermeer was not primarily a realist, though. He frequently modified the scale and even the shape of objects for compositional reasons. The enormous painting of the Finding of Moses that hangs on the rear wall of *Lady Writing a Letter with Her Maid* (cat. 19), for example, appears at a much smaller scale in *The Astronomer* (page 52, fig. 6). He also distorted objects to achieve compositional balance. The bottom edge of the frame of the Last Judgment in *Woman Holding a Balance* is higher before the woman than it is behind her. Indeed, Vermeer often made such adjustments to strengthen patterns of shapes existing around and between his figures, altering, for example, the size of the wall maps in *Woman in Blue Reading a Letter* (cat. 9) and *Young Woman with a Water Pitcher.* He even manipulated light to extend the moment by minimizing the transient effects of shadows. In *The Music Lesson* (cat. 8) and the *Woman in Blue Reading a Letter*, he bathed in light walls that in reality should have been in partial shadow.

Vermeer and the Camera Obscura

The camera obscura functions according to the principle that focused rays of light, whether direct or reflected, will project an image of the source from which they derive. Many camera obscuras were literally darkened rooms into which only a point of light was admitted. The image created would then be focused, perhaps with the aid of a convex lens, on a surface opposite the light source. By the mid-seventeenth century, portable camera obscuras contained lenses and focusing tubes to allow sharp images of objects from various distances.[45] The camera obscura opened a new range of expressive possibilities to many artists at this time by providing a literal frame for their vision and by introducing optical effects not normally visible, such as the halation of highlights, caused by bright lights reflecting off shiny surfaces. Indeed, many found the image of a camera

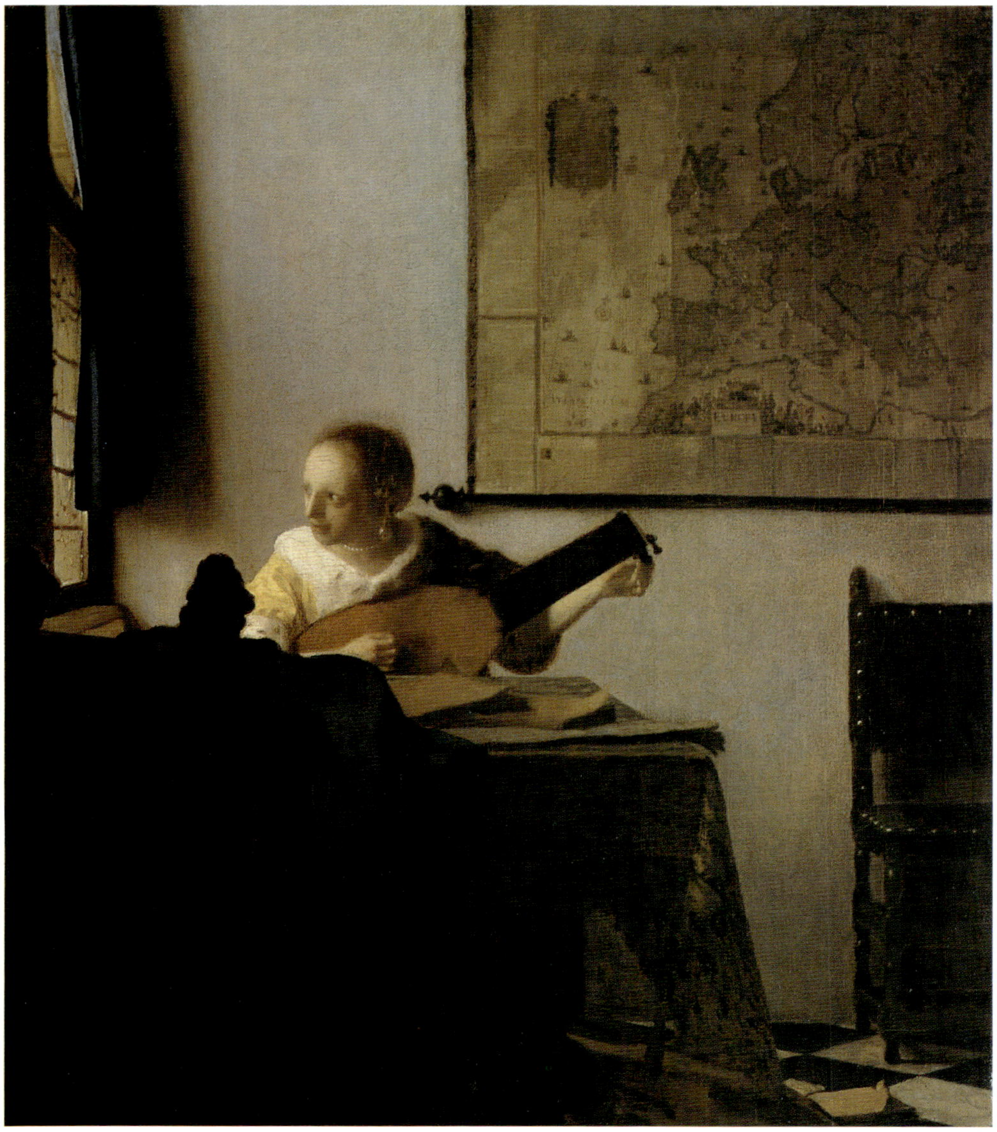

fig. 13. Johannes Vermeer, ***Woman with a Lute***, c. 1664, oil on canvas, The Metropolitan Museum of Art, New York, Bequest of Collis P. Huntington, 1900

obscura superior to the painted image. As Constantijn Huygens (1596–1687), secretary to the Princes of Orange and an art enthusiast, wrote in 1622:

> It is impossible to express the beauty [of the image] in words. All painting is dead by comparison, for this is life itself, or something more elevated, if one could articulate it.[46]

In a period that witnessed the discovery of the telescope and microscope, both optical instruments used to great advantage by Vermeer's Delft compatriot Anthony van Leeuwenhoek (1632–1723),[47] the camera obscura had become "familiar to everyone."[48] It provided both a beautiful image and a means for understanding the underlying laws of nature. Samuel van Hoogstraeten, for example, who erected cameras obscura on at least two occasions, commented:

> I am certain that vision from these reflections in the dark can give no small light to the sight of the young artists; because besides gaining knowledge of nature, so one sees here what main or general [characteristics] should belong to truly natural painting.[49]

Vermeer's interest in the camera obscura and its role in his working process is an extremely complex topic.[50] Since it leaves no physical trace of its use, the only means for establishing Vermeer's use of it is the appearance of comparable optical characteristics in his works, most evidently found in *View of Delft*, *Girl with the Red Hat*, *Art of Painting*, and *Lacemaker* (cats. 7, 14, page 68, fig. 2, and cat. 17). Vermeer probably used the camera obscura as a compositional aid in other paintings as well. While the consistency with which Vermeer modified optical effects in his images indicates that he did not trace the camera obscura image, several intriguing questions related to his use of this device remain unanswered. For example, did the optical characteristics of the camera obscura's image reinforce the artist's own stylistic tendencies, or did they encourage him in new directions? Did Vermeer respond to the camera obscura in different ways at various stages of his career? It is important to understand, however, that Vermeer's interest in the camera obscura seems to have been for its philosophical as well as for its artistic application. While it was a vehicle for revealing optical effects of light and color, in a manner complementary to the science of perspective, it also provided Vermeer with one means for expressing the fundamental concepts essential to his art.

Vermeer's Classicism

Evidence gathered from Vermeer's paintings (see pages 23–27) confirms how carefully Vermeer crafted his compositions. Much as a classicist, he purified and idealized what he saw of the visual world, creating images containing timeless truths of human needs and emotions. Although neither his guiding principles nor his working method are fully understood, the viewer has a keen sense that a profoundly philosophical approach to life underlies Vermeer's work. In its purest form his classicism is revealed in the timeless beauty and elegance of *Girl with a Pearl Earring* (cat. 15). It also occurs in those few paintings that have a portrait-like character, as, for example, *Portrait of a Young Woman* (page 75, fig. 13), whose softly diffused features are comparably executed, and *A Lady Writing* (cat. 13).

Vermeer's philosophy is likely to have had a number of components. Almost certainly its character was affected by religious convictions, evident from his early history paintings to his late work *Allegory of Faith* (cat. 20). To judge from his magnificent *Art of Painting*, it would have included an awareness of the theoretical foundations of pictorial representation. The number of emblematic references in his work indicates that he felt that nature and natural forms can lead to a deeper meaning of human experience. Finally, it would appear that Vermeer had an interest in cartography, music, geography, astronomy, and optics, the study of which inevitably introduced him to Neo-platonic concepts of measure and harmony found in contemporary philosophical thought.[51] Indeed, Vermeer's efforts to achieve these very effects through perspective, proportion, and subtle compositional adjustments indicate that such ideals underlie his depictions of reality.[52]

Vermeer, who began as a painter of large-scale history paintings and accommodated a change of subject matter with a change of style, was unique among Dutch artists in his ability to incorporate the fundamental, moral seriousness of history painting into his representations of domestic life. His genre scenes are likewise concerned with issues fundamental to human existence. Whether conveying the timeless bond between two individuals, the bounty of God's creations, the need for moderation and restraint, the vanity of worldly possessions, the transience of life, or the lasting power of artistic creation, Vermeer's works transmit important reminders of the nature of existence and provide moral guidance for human endeavors.

I would like to thank Meredith Hale and Aneta Georgievska-Shine for their helpful comments and observations about this text.

1. William the Silent lived in Delft from 1572 until his assassination in 1584.
2. Williame Crowne visited Delft in December 1636 at the end of his trip through Germany and Holland with the Duke of Arundel. Springell 1963, 94.
3. Van Bleyswijck 1667, 1: 264.
4. Montias 1989, 63, 70. The inn was called "De Vliegende Vos." Either because of the inn's name, or because of his name "Reynier," which sounds like the French word for fox, "renard," Vermeer's father was known during this period as "Reynier Jansz. Vos." The origin of the name Vermeer, which he first used in 1640, is not known.
5. Montias 1989, 310, doc. 256. The length of apprenticeship was normally six years, although the time period could be shortened if a student produced a "proof" work for the guild. See Montias 1982, 90.
6. For a fuller discussion of the Bramer document see Wheelock 1992, 308. The Ter Borch document was discovered by Montias. See Montias 1989, 102–104, and 308, doc. 251.
7. The first known reference to a painting by Vermeer occurs in the inventory of the Amsterdam art dealer Johannes de Renialme on 27 June 1657. "Een graft besoeckende van der Meer 20 gulden" [A picture of the grave visitation by Van der Meer, 20 gulden]. See Montias 1989, 312, doc. 269. De Renialme, who had also registered as an art dealer in Delft, may have had the paintings as part of his stock. See also page 45.
8. Montias 1989, 318, doc. 294. At the time of De Monconys' visit Vermeer had no paintings to show him. De Monconys then viewed one in the home of a baker, probably Hendrick van Buyten (see note 37), which he felt was worth only one-tenth the amount that had been paid for it. De Monconys arrived with two other Catholics. Montias 1989, 180, identifies the other travelers as "le Pere Leon," the almoner of the French Embassy in The Hague, and Lieutenant Colonel Gentillo. Montias concluded that the trip was connected to the recent arrival and acceptance of a Jesuit Priest in Delft. For a different interpretation of the circumstances of this trip, see pages 48–49.
9. Montias 1991, 48.
10. Montias 1989, 318–319, doc. 298. A "tronie" was a term used to denote a small, bust-length figure study.
11. Montias 1989, 333–334, doc. 341.
12. Montias 1989, 351, doc. 383.
13. See page 23, and note 38.
14. See note 47.
15. Montias 1989.
16. For an analysis of the relationship between the two see Wheelock 1992.
17. Montias 1989, 129.
18. Montias 1989, 311–312, doc. 268.
19. Montias 1989, 106–107, 110, 121.
20. Montias 1989, 122. These are listed in an inventory made after her legal separation from Reynier Bolnes in 1641.
21. For an analysis of the relevant documents, see Wheelock 1992.
22. The only extant murals, albeit in a poor state of preservation, are in the Prinsenhof, Delft.
23. Wheelock 1981, 15, 68, suggested a period of study in Amsterdam. Montias 1989, 105–107, 110, postulated that Vermeer was "apprenticed for the last two to four years of his training in Amsterdam or in Utrecht."
24. Montias 1989, 308, doc. 250.
25. See Montias 1989, 310, doc. 256.
26. For a discussion of this little-known painter, see Sluijter in Delft 1981, 1:175, 2: ill. 173.
27. Willem II was buried in the family crypt underneath this tomb in March 1651. For the political concerns for the future of the Dutch Republic following the death of Willem II, see Wheelock 1975–1976.
28. Fabritius probably came to Delft in anticipation of commissions from the Prince of Orange, only to be thwarted in his ambitions by Willem II's untimely death. See Brown 1981, 159–161.
29. Although Brown 1981, 48, argues that the sentry is not sleeping as he slouches on a bench before the open gate, his attitude is far from alert. Fabritius contrasts his pose not only to the alert dog sitting near him, but also to the bas-relief of an erectly standing Saint Anthony Abbot, who is shown with his attribute of a pig, symbolic of the sins of sensuality and gluttony he is reputed to have overcome.
30. A poem describing Vermeer as Fabritius' successor appeared in Van Bleyswijck 1667, 2, 853–854. As Albert Blankert has discovered, the last stanza of the poem is different in various editions of the publication (Blankert 1975, 90–91, and Blankert 1978, 147–148). Montias 1989, 326, doc. 315, has translated one version as: "But happily there rose from his fire / Vermeer, who, masterlike, trod his path"; and the other as: "But happily there rose from his fire / Vermeer, who, masterlike, was able to emulate him." At his death Vermeer owned at least three paintings by Fabritius. See Montias 1989, 339, doc. 364. For a discussion of these lines and what they reveal about Vermeer's reputation, see page 52.
31. For the theoretical framework of Dutch history painting, see Albert Blankert in Washington 1980, 15–33.
32. See cats. 10, 18.
33. Montias 1989, 246–251.
34. Montias 1989, 359, doc. 417.
35. Montias 1989, 248.
36. Montias 1989, 312, doc. 271.
37. One possible purchaser at that time may have been Hendrick van Buyten, a baker. In 1676 Vermeer's widow appeared with Van Buyten before a notary to state that Van Buyten had accepted two of Vermeer's paintings from Catharina Bolnes as payment for a debt of 617 guilders 6 stuivers. The contract further stipulated, however, that "after being seriously beseeched and upon urgent persistence of the transferrer" (Catharina Bolnes), Van Buyten agreed to return the paintings to Catharina Bolnes once the debt had been repaid. It seems unlikely that Catharina Bolnes would have been successful in her efforts to regain possession of the paintings given the dire state of her finances during these years. In any event, in the 1701 inventory of his collection, "2 little pieces by Vermeer" are noted that may well be those referred to in the above-mentioned document (see Montias 1989, 364–365, doc.

442). Also listed in the inventory, however, are other works that Van Buyten may have bought at the March 1677 sale, including the first item listed, "A large painting by Vermeer." One wonders whether this work could be the *Art of Painting*. Another work that might have been in Vermeer's collection is "a piece of Moses," which may well be the painting seen hanging on the back wall in two of Vermeer's works, *The Astronomer* and the *Lady Writing a Letter with Her Maid*.

38. The documents referred to in this note are printed in Montias 1989. The paintings in this sale were primarily (entirely?) those that were "sold" to Jan Coelenbier for 500 guilders on 10 February 1676 to pay off debts owed by Catharina Bolnes to Jannetje Stevens, a spinster in Delft (doc. 362). Coelenbier, however, appears not to have actually bought the paintings, but rather to have kept them as collateral until which time Catharina Bolnes could buy them back. A year later a suit brought by Jannetje Stevens makes it clear that the debt of 442 guilders still remained outstanding. As a result, Coelenbier agreed to hand over to the executor of Vermeer's estate, Anthony van Leeuwenhoek, the twenty-six paintings for public auction. The agreement reached on that occasion was that Coelenbier would receive the first 500 guilders from the auction and the rest would go to the estate (doc. 377). It seems that among the paintings held by Coelenbier as collateral was the *Art of Painting*. The idea that this work would be sold at public auction, presumably at a low price because of the poor economic climate, induced Maria Thins to try to block its sale by claiming that the painting belonged to her (doc. 379). She asserted that the rights of ownership had been transferred to her by her daughter on 24 February 1676 (doc. 363). Van Leeuwenhoek, however, recognizing that this act of transferral had occurred illegally, since it happened only after the painting had been taken as collateral by Coelenbier, denied Maria Thins' petition. It thus seems that this painting was among those auctioned on 15 March 1677.

39. Most of the paintings were probably part of his stock as an art dealer.

40. Montias 1989, 253, 359, doc. 417. "The inventory listed all the goods, movable and unmovable, accruing to Jacob Dissius both on his own head and as inherited through the death of his wife." That the contents of the estate were considered to be held in common by Magdalena and Jacob Dissius is clear from a subsequent document, dated between 14 and 20 April 1685 (doc. 420), at which time the estate was divided equally between Jacob and his father Abraham Jacobsz Dissius.

41. See Montias 1989, 251–255; 359, doc. 417; 360, doc. 420.

42. Montias 1989, 255–256; 363–364, doc. 439.

43. As Albert Blankert has noted (personal communication) Vermeer's outspoken opinions in 1672 about the Italian paintings in the collection of the Elector of Brandenburg are known. See Montias 1989, 333–334, doc. 341.

44. Similar high horizon lines and complex spatial organizations occur in the paintings of Nicolaes Maes, particularly *The Idle Servant* of 1655 (page 116, fig. 4), which suggest that this artist influenced Vermeer's approach in this early work. The connection with Maes' painting is particularly evident when one examines the x-radiographs of *A Woman Asleep*. See Wheelock 1995, 39–40, fig. 21.

45. Johannes Kepler, for example, used a tent camera obscura when drawing landscapes. See the text of a letter by Sir Henry Wotton, in Potonniée 1936, 25.

46. Huygens 1911–1917, 1: 94. "il ne m'est possible de vous en déclarer la beauté en paroles: toute peinture est morte aux prix, car c'est icy la vie mesme, ou quelque chose de plus relevé, si la parole n'y manquoit."

47. The question of Van Leeuwenhoek's relationship to Vermeer during his lifetime has never been adequately addressed. For the argument that they did know each other and that Vermeer represented Van Leeuwenhoek in *The Astronomer* and *The Geographer* (cat. 16), see Wheelock 1981, 13–15, 136–138.

48. Gerrit Tierie, *Cornelis Drebbel (1572–1633)* (Amsterdam, 1932), 51.

49. Van Hoogstraeten 1678, 263, "Ik ben verzekert, dat het zien van dezen weerglans in 't donker 't gezicht van de Schilder jeugt geen klein licht kan geven; want behalve dat men de kennis van de natuer verkrijgt, zoo zietmen hier wat gros of generael een recht natuerlijke Schildery behoorde te hebben...."

50. The literature on Vermeer and the camera obscura is extensive. See particularly Seymour 1964; Schwarz 1966; Fink 1971; Wheelock 1977A; Wheelock 1977C.

51. See, for example, Palisca 1961, for theories of musical harmonics; and Sonnema 1990, 38–41, for discussions of the philosophical framework for the musical theories of René Descartes and Marin Marsenne.

52. The primary spokesman for Neo-platonic ideals of Beauty was Marsilio Ficino (1433–1499). For the relationship of his theories to art theory see Panofsky 1968, 97–99; 128–141. For a discussion of the impact of Neo-platonism on perspective theory see Wheelock 1977A, 111–116. For the mathematical principles underlying perspective, see Kemp 1986, 237–252.

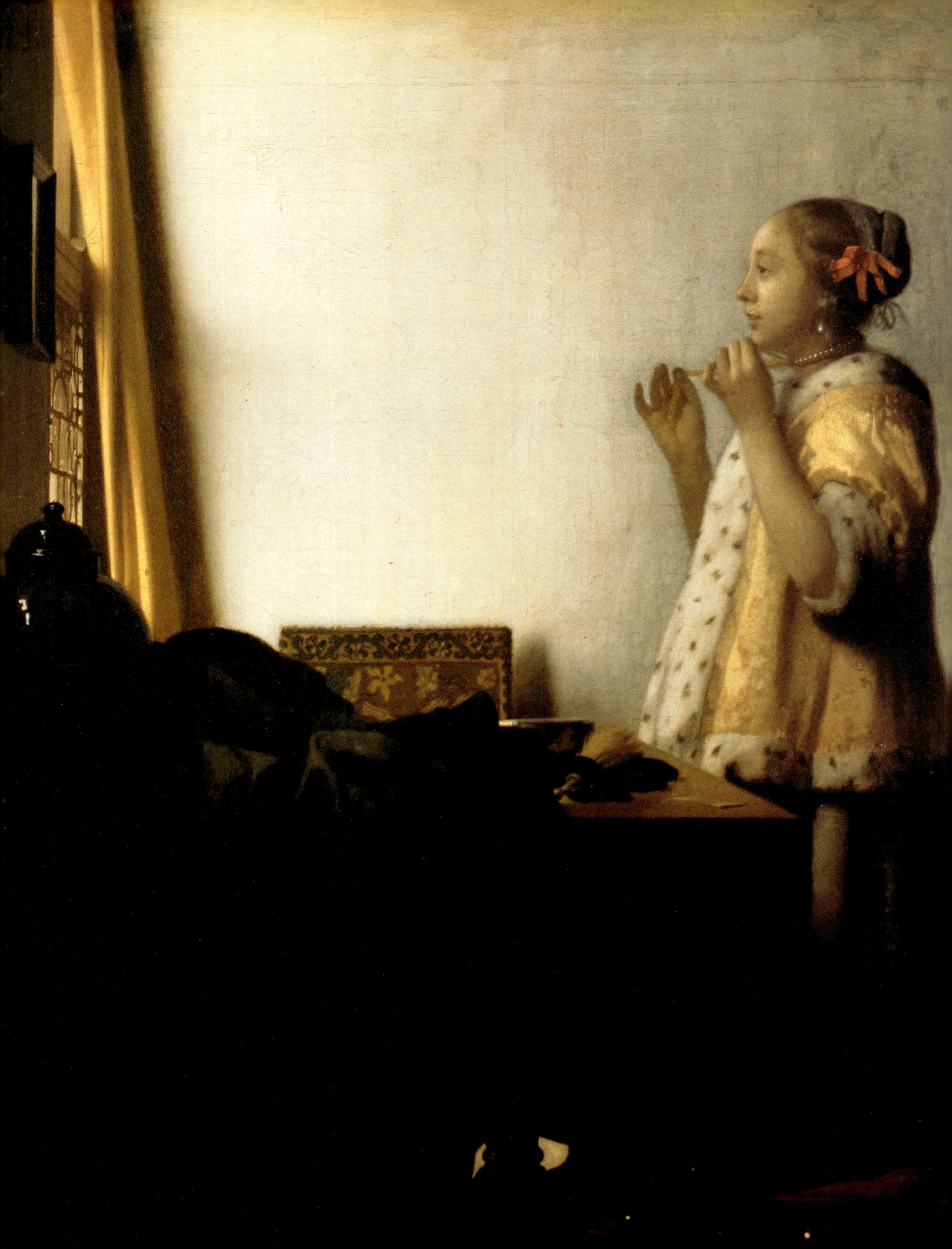

Vermeer's Modern Themes and Their Tradition

ALBERT BLANKERT

"Der liebe Gott steckt im Detail" [God dwells in the detail]
(Aby Warburg)[1]

Antique and Modern

GERARD DE LAIRESSE (1640–1711), WHO WAS only eight years younger than Vermeer, was the most celebrated painter in Amsterdam until he turned blind in 1690. Even after this he remained active in his field, publishing his influential *Groot Schilderboek* (Great Book on Painting) in 1707. His treatise was the first that fully elaborated the concepts now known as "classicistic."

For De Lairesse the subject of the true artist had to be human figures in action. Here he perceived two modes, "the Antique," which he preferred, and "the Modern." "The Antique," he wrote, "persists through all periods, and the Modern constantly changes with fashion." The painters of the modern mode depicted their figures in the dress and setting of their own time. Therefore, according to De Lairesse, "Modern painting is not free," but very limited, for it can "depict no more than the contemporary" and thus "it never lasts, but continually changes and becomes estranged."[2]

De Lairesse's distinction between antique and modern painting is of interest for an understanding of Vermeer since the Delft artist began his career in the antique mode with a biblical and a mythological subject (cats. 2, 3), before becoming a specialist of modern figures. In the important 1740 edition of De Lairesse's treatise, Vermeer himself is cited in one breath with other modern painters, "the old *Mieris, Metzu, van der Meer.*"[3]

Since "Modern paintings vary from period to period," De Lairesse thought it "undeniable [that] their worth will gradually decrease and perish."[4] Such has not turned out to be the historic judgment about Vermeer's work. Nevertheless, the time-bound, "modern" character of most of his paintings presents the viewer with extra problems.

Interpreting the contemporary costumes in Vermeer's modern pictures, for example, is complicated. In our era it has often been claimed that the women in *Woman in Blue Reading a Letter* and the *Woman Holding a Balance*, with their voluminous clothing and bulging bellies, are pregnant (cats. 9, 10). Based on this presumed pregnancy, daring speculations were proposed on the "meaning" of the *Woman Holding a Balance.*[5] If she is not pregnant, these speculations are meaningless.

Another problem regarding the outfit of a woman in a Vermeer arose centuries earlier. His *Guitar Player* was so expertly copied that the copy long passed as the original (figs. 1, 2).[6] The copy is most accurate, except that the woman's long, swinging corkscrew curls were left out. Thus the copy displays a short hairdo, resembling the fashion of the years c. 1690–1700. This indicates that the copy dates from that period, when Vermeer's most fashionable curls of some twenty years before had become unpresentably outmoded. At the time the copy was made, De Lairesse, criticizing "modern painting" for its transitory nature, argued that "the dress of our ancestors [appears] ridiculous and inappropriate in our eyes," so that even their portraits, "though well painted...are viewed with little respect by us."[7] The existence of the copy, with its disrespectfully eliminated curls, seems to underscore his point, yet his criticism also proved to be transitory. With the passing of more time nobody knows or cares anymore whether the model's outfit on an old painting is "inappropriate."

Detail, cat. 12

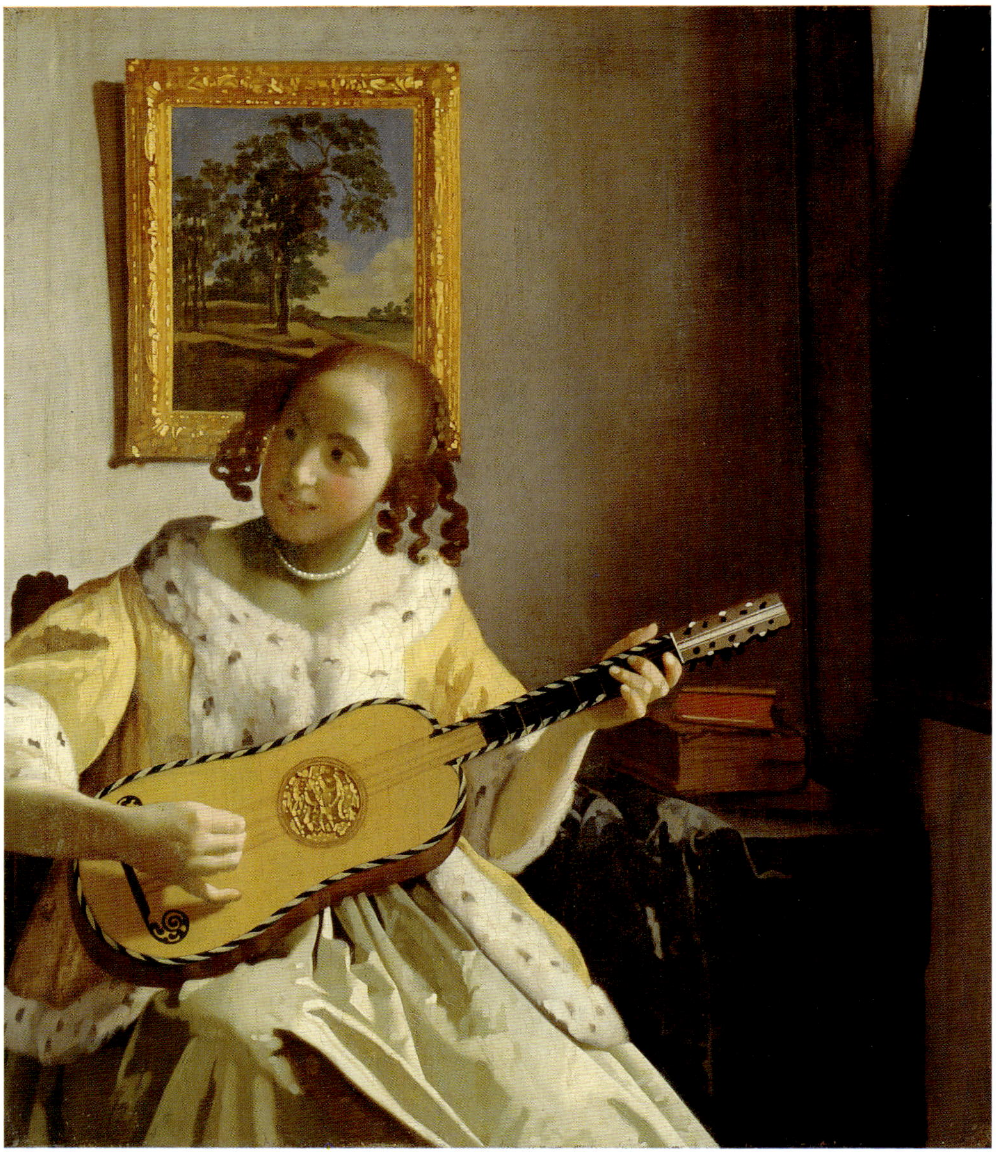

fig. 1. Johannes Vermeer, *The Guitar Player*, oil on canvas, The Iveagh Bequest, Kenwood, London

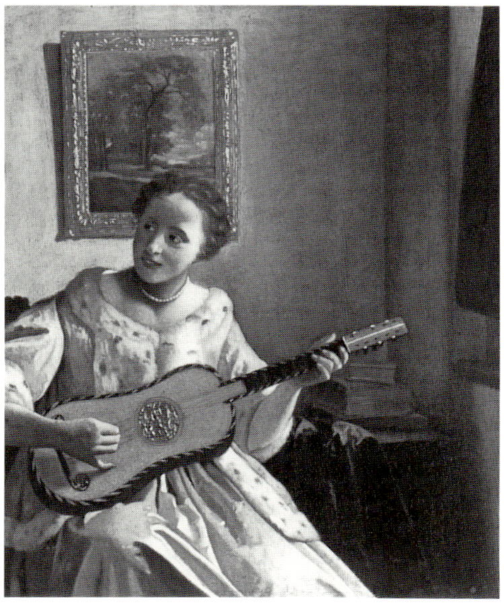

fig. 2. Copy after Vermeer's *The Guitar Player*, oil on canvas, Philadelphia Museum of Art, John G. Johnson Collection

Dandies and Damsels (Jonkers and Juffers)

These are but two of the many instances that demonstrate the difficulty in grasping how Vermeer's contemporaries viewed his work. To understand his own intentions is even harder. To better appreciate his modern scenes it is necessary to compare them to similar subjects depicted by other seventeenth-century Dutch artists. Further, it seems useful to consider carefully the only preserved contemporary characterization of Vermeer's themes, which has been overlooked. It appears in the list of "present-day" painters and their subjects compiled between 1669 and 1678 by Jan Sysmus, city surgeon of Amsterdam: "Van der Meer. Little dandies *[jonkertjes]*...Delft."[8]

What Sysmus meant by "little dandies" becomes clear when we see that he employed the same word to describe the subjects painted by Caspar Netscher (1639–1684) and Eglon van der Neer (1634–1703). Concerning Christoffel van der Laemen (1606–1652) he wrote: "painted foolish little dandies *[pinxit malle jonkertjes]*." The subject matter of Hieronymus Janssen de Danser (1624–1693) he calls "little salons filled with little dandies and damsels *[zaletjes vol jonkertjes en joffertjes]*." Sysmus indicates the themes of Metsu, Ter Borch, and Michiel van Musscher (1645–1705) with just the word *juffertjes*.[9] The subject matter of all these artists is now known as "conversation pieces." "Little" *[-tjes]* undoubtedly refers to their much smaller than life-size dimensions. Sysmus' terms *jonkertjes* and *juffertjes* then are equivalent in meaning to De Lairesse's more theoretically elevated designation modern. Vermeer is unique, but nonetheless fully fits and belongs to this category.

Vermeer's *jonkers* and *juffers*[10] are the young people who appear in most of his works after 1656. Depictions of "dandies and damsels" in inner rooms were a novelty introduced in the 1620s by Dutch artists like Dirck Hals (1591–1656), Willem Duyster (1599–1635), and Pieter Codde (1599–1678). In their work the figures are dressed according to the latest and costliest fashion. They amuse themselves with drinking, eating, music-making, and flirting. The owner and observer of such a painting could delight in the joys of youth.

Cornelis de Bie, in his 1661 book on *The Noble Liberal Art of Painting*, characterized the paintings of Van der Laemen, as did Jan Sysmus after him, as "foolish little dandies." Van der Laemen specialized, says De Bie, in "the very nice depiction" of "courtship, dances, and other pleasurable ways of passing time by foolish little Dandies and Damsels...who are rendered most pleasantly and charmingly." De Bie elaborates in a poem that Van der Laemen's young people are engaged in "foolishness and riotousness," "gorging and a great deal of other craziness," including "teasing and prancing," bass and viol playing, gambling, courting, dancing, "guzzling, swim[ming] in evil, liv[ing] above station," and this "without rule, without moderation *[sonder reghel, sonder maet]*."[11]

Van der Laemen's subjects closely resemble those of Vermeer and other "modern" painters, be it on a more pedestrian artistic level.[12] In one typical Van der Laemen six lavishly dressed young people sit at a table covered with a precious oriental carpet in a room hung with paintings (fig. 3). They are engaged in drinking, smoking, backgammon playing, and music-making. That such activities could be negatively interpreted is apparent from De Bie's poem, but also from various other seventeenth-century texts.[13] These paintings, not unlike films today, offered the spectator deceptively true-to-life images of unattainable things and dubious deeds. He can fully partake in these in his imagination and yet frown on them, always safe in the knowledge that the events before his eyes are not real.

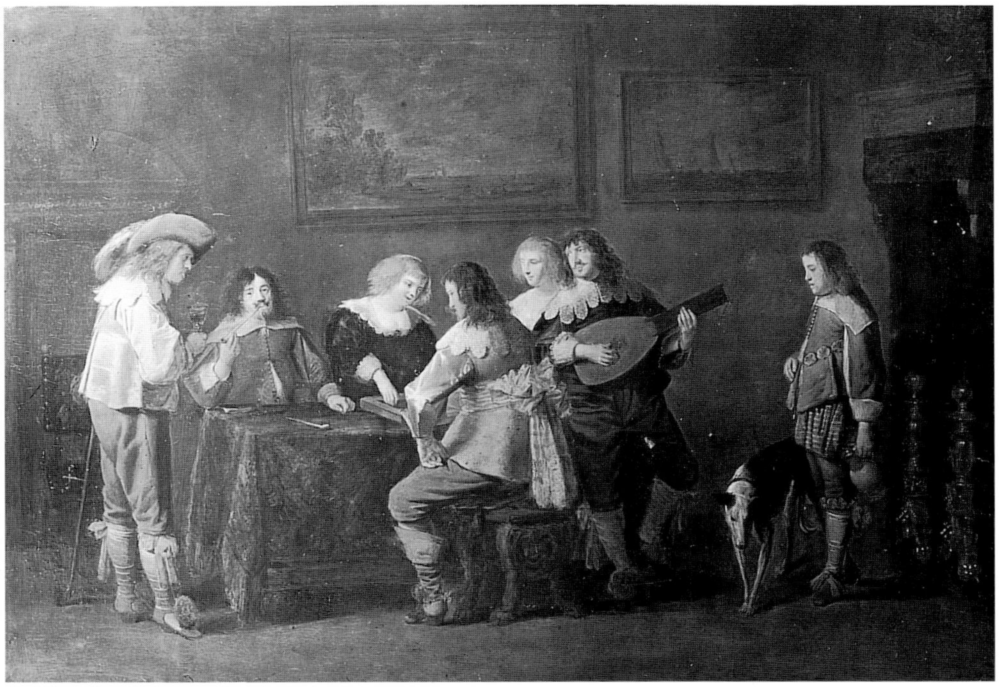

fig. 3. Christoffel van der Laemen, *Merry Company*, 1638, oil on panel, Collection A. Schloss, Paris, before 1940

A Small Episode

The early examples of this genre, from the 1620s, usually depict crowded groups engaged in lighthearted behavior. After c. 1630, a subtler, more reserved conception came to the fore in paintings by Duyster and Codde. They also tended to reduce sharply the number of figures, often to a few or only one. Gerard ter Borch (1617–1681) was the first to perfect this process of refinement and reduction in the 1650s. *The Suitor's Visit* of about 1658 shows a precisely described small episode out of elegant life (fig. 4).[14] A gentleman enters a chamber with hat in hand and makes a submissive gesture to an equally dignified lady. She appears to be sizing him up with some detachment. The event is too minor to attract the attention of the damsel at the table, who is absorbed in trying out on her lute the notes in her music book. The gentleman behind her, who is warming his hands by the hearth, does look back at the new arrival.

Another Ter Borch was known as *The Parental Admonition*, based upon its description by Goethe, until, in our century, its aristocratic "father" was perceived as a customer offering money to a deluxe prostitute (his "daughter") under the scrutiny of a procuress (the "mother").[15] Since then, an "iconological" approach has come in vogue that avoids such mistakes. It uses seventeenth-century texts to interpret specific objects and configurations in Dutch genre paintings as symbols, which thereby reveal the deeper "meaning" of the depicted scene. The anecdotal remains taboo in that approach, as much as it had become with the previously predominant admirers of *belle peinture*. So it is now almost forgotten that Ter Borch and Vermeer painted people engaged in particular actions.[16] In the following pages I will attempt to analyze and define those actions, taking the full risk that I will look as "inappropriate" as when wearing long, corkscrew curls.

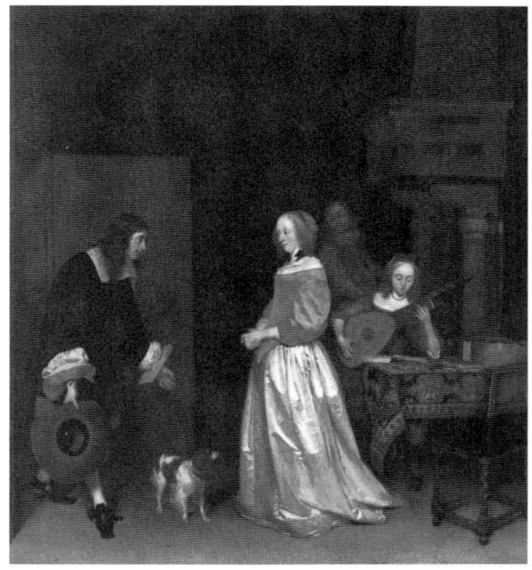

fig. 4. Gerard ter Borch, *The Suitor's Visit*, oil on canvas, National Gallery of Art, Washington, Andrew W. Mellon Collection

Painter of Juffers, Not of the Old, Nor of Gamblers and Dogs

Vermeer's figures play out their actions in the same zone of tension, between dignified and dubious behavior, as those by Van der Laemen and Ter Borch. In fact *juffers*, more than Sysmus' *jonkers*, constitute Vermeer's modern subject matter. Nine of the twenty-one Vermeers in the 1696 auction of his works were listed as a *juffrouw*, another word for *juffer*.[17] Among the thirty-odd Vermeers that survive, sixteen have a damsel, with or without a servant, as their subject. In seven other Vermeers, a damsel in the company of one or more dandies is the central motif. Young women also dominate Vermeer's history paintings of *Diana and Her Companions* and *Christ in the House of Mary and Martha*, and his allegories on *Art of Painting* and *Faith* (cats. 3, 2, and page 68, fig. 2, and cat. 20). A young woman is again the subject of his two bust figures and of *The Milkmaid* (cat. 15, and page 75, fig. 13, and cat. 5). Women are the majority even among the tiny figures on both his *View of Delft* and *The Little Street* (cats. 7, 4). Only *The Astronomer* (page 52, fig. 6) and *The Geographer* (cat. 16), and a lost *Gentleman Washing His Hands* (see page 40), feature male protagonists. Thus Vermeer resembles the painter mocked in De Lairesse's *Schilderboek* who, "trapped by his desire clings to damsels, painting nothing else all his life."[18]

Other Dutch painters of conversation pieces often added old wrinkled people to the young dandies and damsels, thus further emphasizing the beauty of youth (fig. 13). In Vermeer's entire oeuvre an elderly figure appears in only one painting, his early *Procuress* (page 60, fig. 16). Vermeer also differs in that other modern painters used to enliven their scenes with children (fig. 10) or dogs (figs. 3, 4, 9, 10, 12). Vermeer included children only

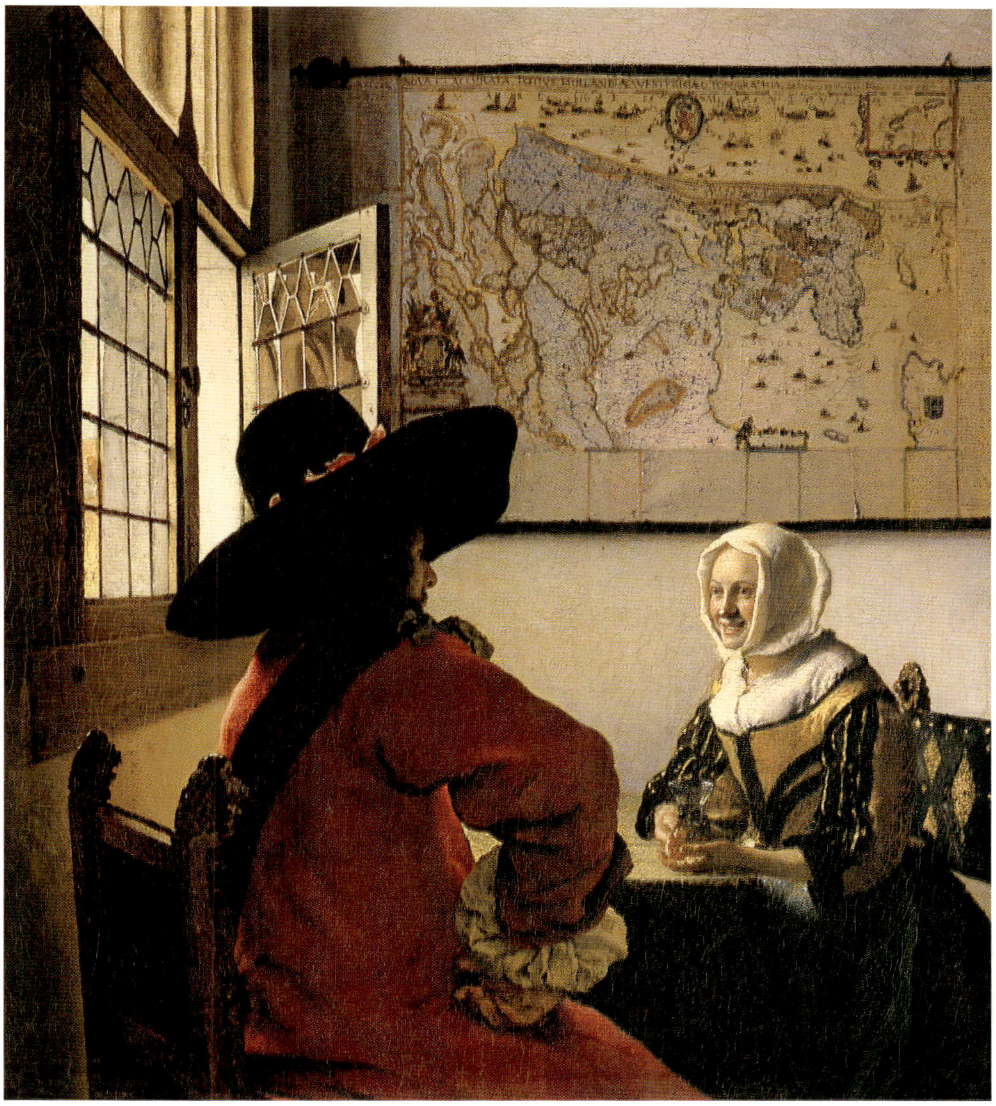

fig. 6. Johannes Vermeer, *Officer and a Laughing Girl*, oil on canvas, © The Frick Collection

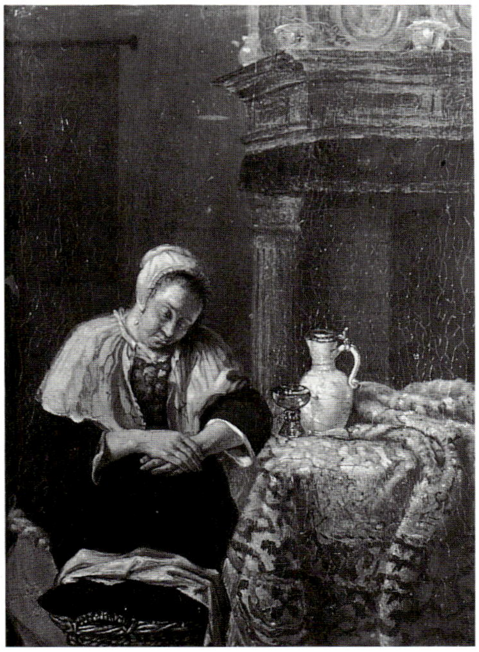

fig. 5. Gabriël Metsu (or copy after?), *Sleeping Girl*, oil on panel, Collection A. Schloss, Paris, before 1940

in *The Little Street*, and his only dog, in *Diana and Her Companions*, is an attribute in a history painting.[19] Vermeer also banned the pipe-smoking and backgammon and card-playing that his colleagues frequently included (fig. 3). In Vermeer's time both activities were often described as most reprehensible. De Bie observed young people gambling in paintings by Van der Laemen, "although this be offending to the Lord God."[20] Was this why Vermeer kept his dandies and damsels from participating? It all fits with De Lairesse's much later "classicist" theories on the need of maintaining "decorum" in painting.

Drinking Wine

Vermeer's earliest modern scene, *A Woman Asleep*, at first sight does not seem to lack "decorum"(page 20, fig. 6). Even so, it has never been doubted that she is the "A Drunken Sleeping Maid at a Table" mentioned in the 1696 sale catalogue. The title itself is proof that this beautiful dreamer is a direct descendent of the undecorously sleeping woman in a dingy inn in earlier paintings by Jacob Duck (c. 1600–1667).[21] Around the same time as Vermeer, Gabriël Metsu (1629–1667) also endowed this theme with a more civilized appearance (fig. 5).[22] Metsu's sleeper, like Vermeer's, sits at a table covered with an oriental carpet, on which we see a wine pitcher and glass. A sewing basket with a "sewing cushion" on top rest neglected at the feet of Metsu's figure. This motif recurs in Vermeer's *The Love Letter* (cat. 18).

That Vermeer's sleeper was called a "maid" [*meyd*] in the 1696 sale catalogue indicates that a major difference in class was discerned between this woman and the many damsels

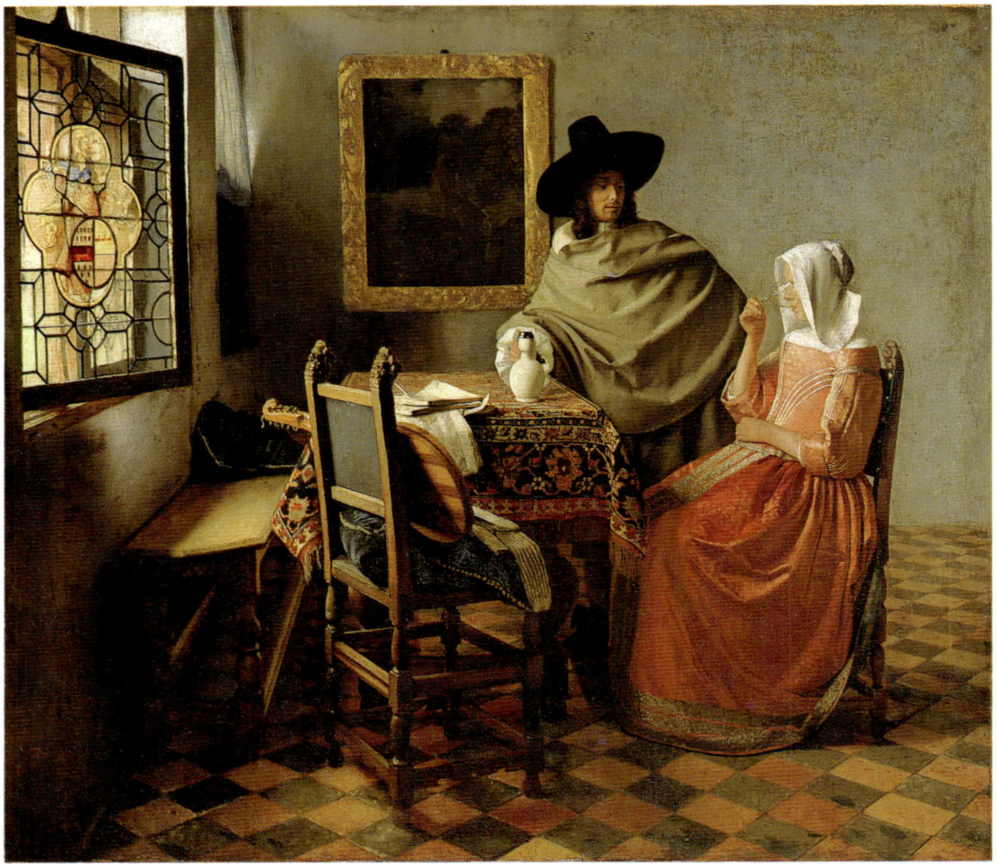

fig. 7. Johannes Vermeer, *The Glass of Wine*, oil on canvas, Staatliche Museen zu Berlin, Gemäldegalerie

in the other Vermeers mentioned. The "Sleeping Maid" does, however, wear precious earrings. This suggests that she is living above her station – a sin that De Bie noted among the types of reprehensible behavior in Van der Laemen's conversation pieces.[23]

Drink also plays an important role in Vermeer's paintings of elegant damsels. When music is being made, a wine jug and glass are within arm's reach (fig. 7) as in many paintings of dandies and damsels by other artists (fig. 3). But Vermeer's *juffers* never imbibe to excess the way the "drunk sleeping maid" did.

Drinking wine is the main motif in the *Officer and Laughing Girl*, in which Vermeer reduced the merry company to one flirting couple (fig. 6). We see the man from behind, and the light directs our attention first to the girl's broad smile and only then to the wine glass she holds.

Vermeer provided another dandy and a damsel holding a wine glass with a much more expansive setting in *The Glass of Wine* (fig. 7). The couple have set their zither and music books aside on a chair and table. Have they been playing and singing, or do they intend to? Now the lady empties her glass while the gentleman watches her. Holding his hand on the pitcher, he appears ready to top her glass up once more. Vermeer thus transformed the old repertoire of the genre painters into a small episode, in the manner of Ter Borch, who may well have directly influenced Vermeer. Its motif of a gentleman watching a drinking lady while keeping his hand on a bottle occurs in the same way in a Ter Borch (fig. 8). In the latter's version, the gentleman puts his arm around the damsel, leaving but little to guess about his intention. Compared to the almost dreamlike stillness of this "episode" in the Vermeer, the version by the generally distinguished Ter Borch seems banal.[24]

Vermeer's *Girl with the Wineglass* (cat. 6) is a variant of his highly restrained *The Glass of Wine*. In the former, Vermeer's dandy, too, is obtrusive. He bows deeply to the damsel, handing her a glass of wine. He concludes his action by touching her hand with his fingertips. She turns her head away from him, allowing only the spectator of the painting to see that the dandy brings a smile to her face. A second dandy at the table in the background has been interpreted as inebriated, or otherwise a rejected lover. Whatever, his

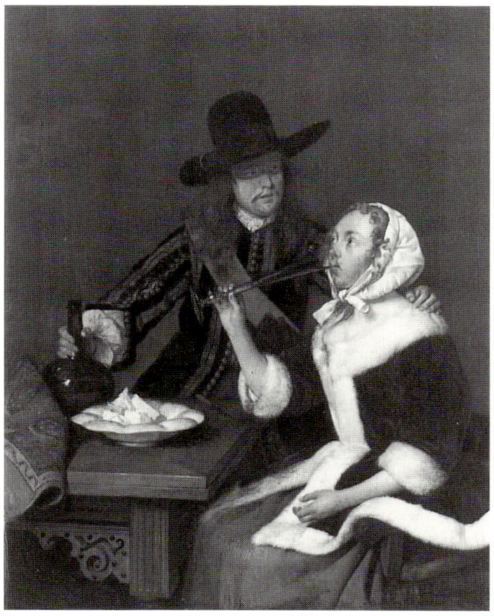

fig. 8. Gerard ter Borch, *A Gentleman Letting a Lady Drink*, oil on panel, The Royal Collection © 1995, Her Majesty Queen Elizabeth II

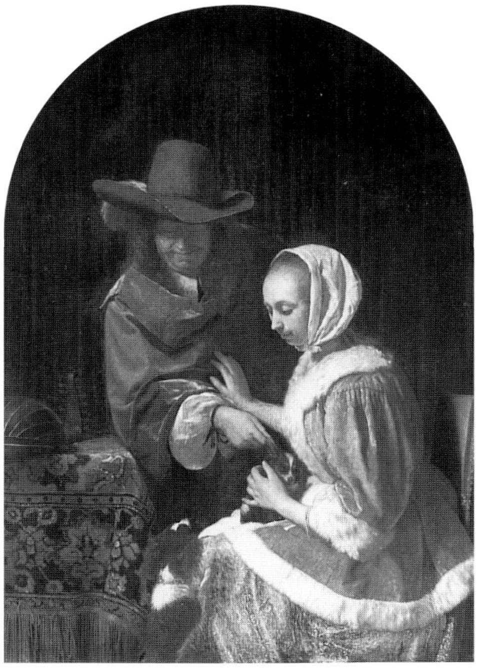

fig. 9. Frans van Mieris the Elder, *Teasing the Pet*, 1660, oil on panel, Mauritshuis, The Hague

action is played out in the margin of the event, much like the zither and music books in *The Glass of Wine* (fig. 7).

It has been observed that the *Girl with the Wineglass* is so reminiscent of slightly earlier works by the Leiden *fijnschilder* Frans van Mieris (1635–1681) that these must have been a source of inspiration to Vermeer.[25] In Van Mieris' small painting of 1660 a damsel sitting in the foreground is similarly courted by a grinning dandy standing behind her (fig. 9). A lute has been put aside for the moment, like the zither in Vermeer's *Glass of Wine*. Van Mieris' damsel fends off the man with one hand, but observes with interest how he caresses the ear of her lapdog between his fingers.[26] With this artful "episode," Van Mieris was the first to give form to an archetype. At least four films contain a scene in which the suitor approaches his darling by caressing her pet.[27] Van Mieris' small dog serves the same function as Vermeer's wine glass in his *Girl with the Wineglass:* the physical connecting link between dandy and damsel.

Whether the drinking and courtship of Vermeer's *Glass of Wine* and *Girl with the Wineglass* will turn into debauchery is not to be inferred from these paintings. A window with a family coat-of-arms is prominent in both. Above both escutcheons, a figure holds a set of reins with bit attached in hand. The bridle, intended to restrain the wild and irrational power of a horse into useful service, had long been the attribute of "Temperantia" or "Moderation."[28] Vermeer must have intended to alert his more attentive spectators, be it inside or outside the painting, to this virtue. This reminds us of De Bie, who characterized the behavior of the "foolish little dandies and damsels" in comparable paintings by Van der Laemen, as being "without rule, without moderation."

Music-making

In other depictions of "little dandies and damsels" Vermeer turned music-making into the central theme. His masterpiece in this genre, *The Music Lesson*, was called "A playing Damsel at a clavecin in a Room, with a listening Monsieur" in the 1696 sale catalogue (cat. 8). A "Monsieur" can be a dignified gentleman of more mature age than a *jonker*, but also a teacher.[29] Vermeer leaves in doubt whether the damsel is receiving instruction or whether the viola da gamba on the floor is meant for the playing of two equal musicians. The gentleman looks at the lady, but nothing tells whether he has more of an eye for her than an ear for her playing. However, the vaguely discernible face of the damsel in the mirror is turned further in the direction of the "Monsieur" than we notice when observing her only from behind.

It seems that Vermeer deliberately left the situation undefined to make it more involving. He thus took a step beyond what Van Mieris had achieved in his *Duet*, an early masterpiece of 1658 that was in many ways Vermeer's precursor (fig. 10).[30] In the Van Mieris a damsel and dandy make music together while a page brings a drink and an extra music book; that is all.[31] The action in Vermeer's *Music Lesson* is even further reduced but, at the same time, more ambiguous and thus more intriguing. The picture's sophisticated restraint is a far cry from the musical instruction displayed in the openly erotic *Flute Lesson* by the much older Dirck Hals (fig. 11).

Closely related to the *The Music Lesson* is Vermeer's *The Concert*, depicting three musicians (page 17, fig. 1). On the wall hangs *The Procuress*, a brothel scene by Dirck Van Baburen (1590/1595–1624) (page 200, fig. 1). This convinced one author that *The Concert*

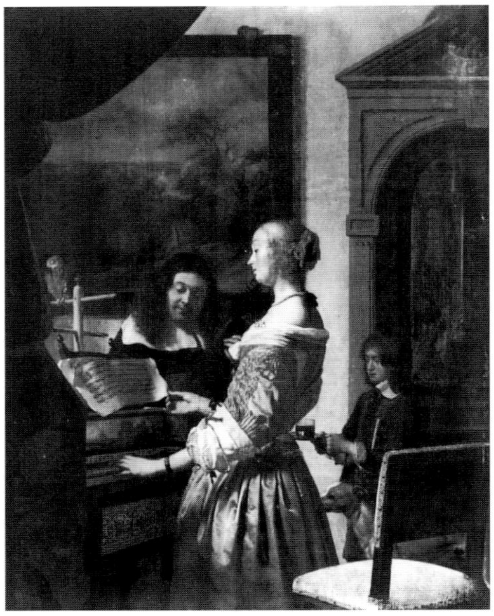

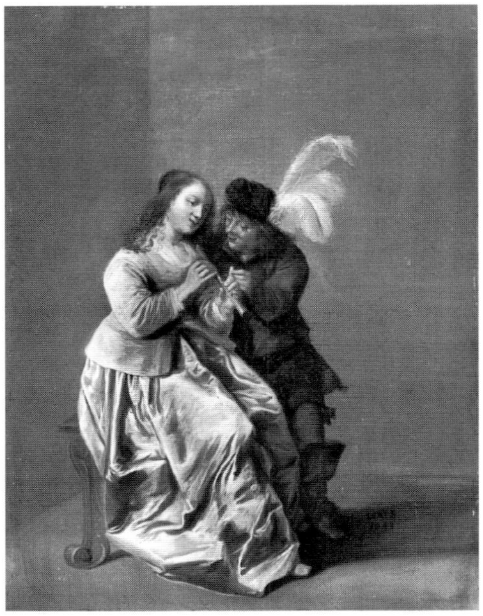

fig. 10. Frans van Mieris the Elder, *The Duet*, 1658, oil on panel, Staatliches Museum Schwerin

fig. 11. Dirck Hals, *The Flute Lesson*, 1646, oil on panel, Niedersächsisches Landesmuseum, Landesgalerie, Hannover

itself also depicts a brothel.[32] Others demurred that the musicians' temperate behavior is rather the opposite of Van Baburen's lascivious scene.[33] Painters of contemporary *jonkers* and *juffers* were obliged also to include the usual paintings on their salon walls. This offered the artist the opportunity to connect his own theme with that of the painting-within-the-painting. He sometimes even made the latter the *clavis interpretandi* [interpretive key] of his picture. Nothing indicates, however, that artists were systematic in linking the paintings they depicted on walls to their main themes. Not in any artist's oeuvre can the consistent use of such a procedure be found.[34] In Vermeer's *The Concert* a landscape is the *Procuress'* equivalent pendant on the wall. Why would it "mean" less to the scene than the *Procuress*, both being just paintings?

The situation is quite different in Vermeer's *Lady Standing at the Virginal* (cat. 21). She looks at us penetratingly, while Cupid in the huge painting right behind her does exactly the same. This can hardly be accidental. Cupid holds up a rectangular piece of paper, which all old descriptions call a letter.[35] Today it is seen as a playing card, and related to an emblem in a book.[36] The most noticeable feature of this paper is, I believe, that it is entirely blank. Thus the young god of love holds out a message to the (male!) viewer, but is it actually intended for him? Still more uncertain is the nature of the message. The expression on the face of the damsel is quite consistent with this uncertainty. Who would dare ascertain if her look is coolly mocking the viewer or inviting him to sit down? Only the empty chair separates him from her.

A variation on this theme is *A Lady Seated at the Virginal* (cat. 22). Her smile seems kinder. The viola da gamba, standing upright, complete with its bow, in the full light of the entryway of the painting, seems an invitation for the viewer to play with the damsel. To the left is the only window in a Vermeer that has its curtain entirely closed, so that any peeking from the outside is ruled out. On the wall Van Baburen's brothel scene *Procuress* is hanging again, this time most prominently. These are but insinuations. Once again Vermeer keeps the viewer guessing as to the intent of the musician's glance.[37]

Letters

Vermeer made six paintings that have as their principal motif a damsel reading, writing or receiving a letter (cats. 9, 13, 18, 19, and page 73, fig. 11, and page 58, fig. 14). Again, it was Ter Borch who first gave a *Woman with a Letter* a most dignified form (page 156, fig. 1). Vermeer's as well as Ter Borch's letters are usually interpreted as love letters, though hard evidence is lacking.[38] In theory, the damsels' letters might concern correspondence with parents or girlfriends. Here again, Vermeer avoids being explicit. X-radiographs have shown, however, that his earliest treatment of this theme, *Girl Reading a Letter at an Open*

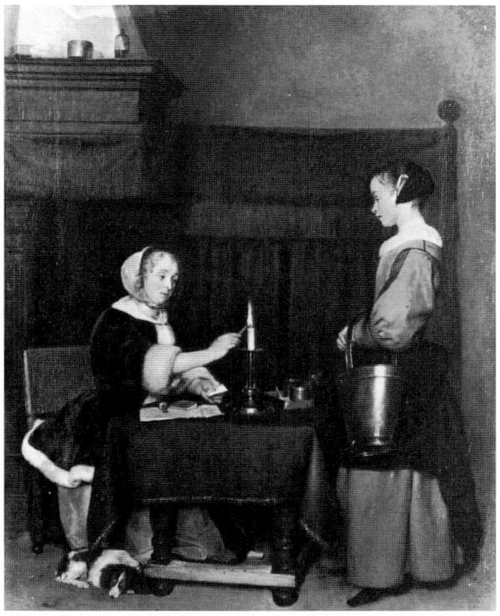

fig. 12. Gerard ter Borch, *Lady Sealing a Letter with a Waiting Servant*, oil on canvas, private collection

Window (page 73, fig. 11), displayed in its first design the same painting of Cupid that is so prominent in *A Lady Standing at the Virginal* (cat. 21).[39] Initially, then, Vermeer did intend an explicit association between the *Girl Reading a Letter* and the young god of love, but in the end he subdued this conspicuous hint and made the white back wall empty.

His later *Woman in Blue Reading a Letter* (cat. 9) was for the first time described in full as "an attractive little lady, standing, reading a letter before her toilet." This "toilet" must be implied by her pearl necklace, which lies before her on the table. The above mentioned idea that this "attractive little lady...before her toilet" is pregnant seems to have originated no earlier than in Vincent van Gogh's 1888 letter to Emile Bernard, from which the notion migrated to Philip Hale's Vermeer monograph of 1913, and has since reemerged repeatedly.[40] No mention of pregnancy occurs in any of the seven extensive descriptions of the *Woman in Blue Reading a Letter* written before 1809.[41] The belly of the virgin goddess Diana, too, looks thoroughly bulbous to twentieth-century eyes (cat. 3).

Vermeer turned the motif of the letter into an "episode" in three paintings. Ter Borch had also paved the way here (fig. 12). In Vermeer's *The Love Letter* a sewing basket and cushion[42] are placed on the floor next to the lady (cat. 18; compare fig. 5). Instead of getting on with this work, she takes a zither to hand. Thinking of her loved one, the damsel is unable to concentrate on her needlework.[43] On the wall behind her hangs a seascape. Iconologists have observed that in the seventeenth century love was sometimes compared to sailing the seas, which can, with equal unpredictability, lead either to shipwreck or safe haven. It is presumably not by accident that a seascape also hangs on the wall in other depictions of damsels with letters.[44]

The central scene of *The Love Letter* focuses on the relationship between the servant, who brings a sealed letter, which has been delivered to the house, to the lady. She takes it in hand and turns her head to the maid, who smiles. We can make what we want of that episode, but to certain limits. The maid may be amused by the lady's embarrassment.

The action of the *Mistress and Maid* in the Frick collection is most similar, but now without any surroundings (page 58, fig. 14). We see the moment at which the letter is handed over. The servant comments with open mouth on the delivery. The lady appears to be impressed. She puts down her pen, suspending her own letter-writing, and looks at the maid. She raises her hand to her chin, perhaps in confusion or, possibly, to indicate merely that she is pondering. We are in any case witness to an abrupt change in the situation.

The opposite is the case in *Lady Writing a Letter with Her Maid* (cat. 19). The damsel writes undisturbed, as the servant whiles away the time looking out the window. The unequalled student of Dutch genre Sturla Gudlaugsson commented on this painting: "The tranquillity of the inner room emanates a peace that humankind cannot find within himself."[45] I wonder whether he paid attention to the floor in front of the table, where we find a seal and rod of wax next to a book with a crumpled cover. In my opinion Vermeer's piece is based on Ter Borch's *Lady Sealing a Letter* of about 1659, in which we see just such a waiting servant (fig. 12).[46] In the Ter Borch a book lies neatly on the table, next to the lady's seal stamp. What can it be other than a volume of model love letters? These were much in use at the time.[47] If so, in the Vermeer such a book has been tossed on the floor as useless. The lady has commenced (once more?) writing on a clean sheet. The maid will need patience before she can deliver the final version of the letter. The "tranquillity" is thus disturbed and the scene seems quite human after all.[48]

The Toilet

Another recurrent motif with painters of damsels is their primping before a mirror. The existence of someone for whom her endeavor is intended is again tacitly implied. A picture by Gabriël Metsu, done shortly after 1655, shows a young lady in a luxurious room, making much of her prettification (fig. 13).[49] The mirror into which she gazes, with its opened wings, resembles a devotional triptych. Vermeer's *Woman with a Pearl Necklace* is a marvel of simplicity within this tradition (cat. 12). It depicts the moment at which the damsel inspects herself in the mirror to decide whether to tie the ribbons of the pearl necklace. Similar simplicity had earlier been practiced by Ter Borch around 1650 in a picture of a girl who looks in a mirror while fastening a jewel to the top of her bodice (fig. 14).[50] A young servant brings the girl a pitcher on a basin for washing. They are precious pieces of silver.

A similar set of a silver pitcher and basin appears in Vermeer's masterly *Young Woman with a Water Pitcher* (cat. 11). Although it would seem that this woman too is at her toilet, various authors have noticed that her action is, or appears to be, inexplicable. Why does this woman stand still with one hand on the pitcher and the other on the window, which she could be opening or closing?[51] With its lack of clarity of action the picture is unique within Vermeer's oeuvre.

A lost work, "Where a Lord washes his hands, in a see-through Room, with figures, artful and rare," is known only through the 1696 sale catalogue, where it was the fourth most expensive of the twenty-one Vermeers listed.[52] No other Dutch genre painting has a gentleman washing his hands as its theme. We know, however, pictures by Ter Borch and Eglon van der Neer in which the central figure is a lady washing her hands in water poured from a costly pitcher into a basin (see page 146, fig. 1). They provide some impression of what the Vermeer must have looked like.

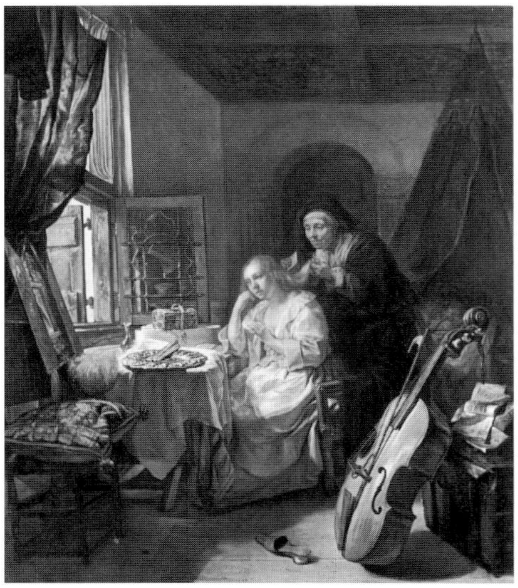

fig. 13. Gabriël Metsu, *A Lady at Her Toilet Combed by an Old Servant*, oil on panel, Norton Simon Art Collection, Pasadena

Useful Pursuits: Winding Lace, Pouring Milk, and Studying

Vermeer had an unmistakable predilection for the depiction of actions that tend to the frivolous. That is what distinguishes his young *Lacemaker* who diligently performs useful work (cat. 17). I traced the theme of a single *Lacemaker* back to Pieter Codde's picture of c. 1635 (fig. 15). In Vermeer's day the subject was quite common. Yet Vermeer drastically changed Codde's formula by minimizing space and fully zooming in upon the girl's absorption in her quiet activity. His low viewpoint brings her busy hands right to her head and eyes. To the left a "sewing cushion" lies on a table. Lacemaking and sewing were both considered most befitting a young lady. Vermeer added a small, thick book, tied up with ribbons. Among the few books that appear in other pictures of ladies engaged in lacemaking or sewing are a Bible, a patternbook, and a songbook.[53] Once again Vermeer depicted a most natural, self-evident situation, which nonetheless leaves the viewer quite some scope for his own reading.

The Milkmaid also does useful work (cat. 5). She is not a *juffer*, but of lower status even than the "drunken sleeping maid" and the housemaids in their gray "uniforms", who are on a familiar footing with their mistresses in the letter-writing scenes (cats. 18, 19, and page 58, fig. 14). The milkmaid wears a coarse, broadly stitched yellow jacket made of cheap chamois-leather.[54] She belongs only in the kitchen and represents Vermeer's sole excursion into the depiction of "the common folk."[55]

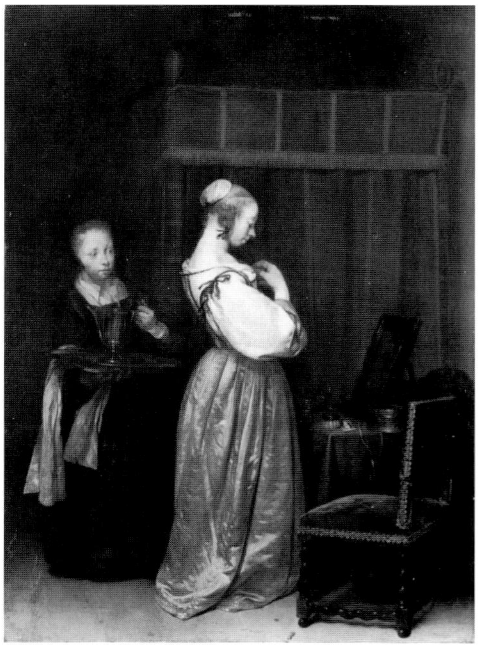

fig. 14. Gerard ter Borch, *A Girl at Her Toilet with a Young Servant Bringing Water*, oil on panel, The Metropolitan Museum of Art, New York, Gift of J. Pierpont Morgan, 1917

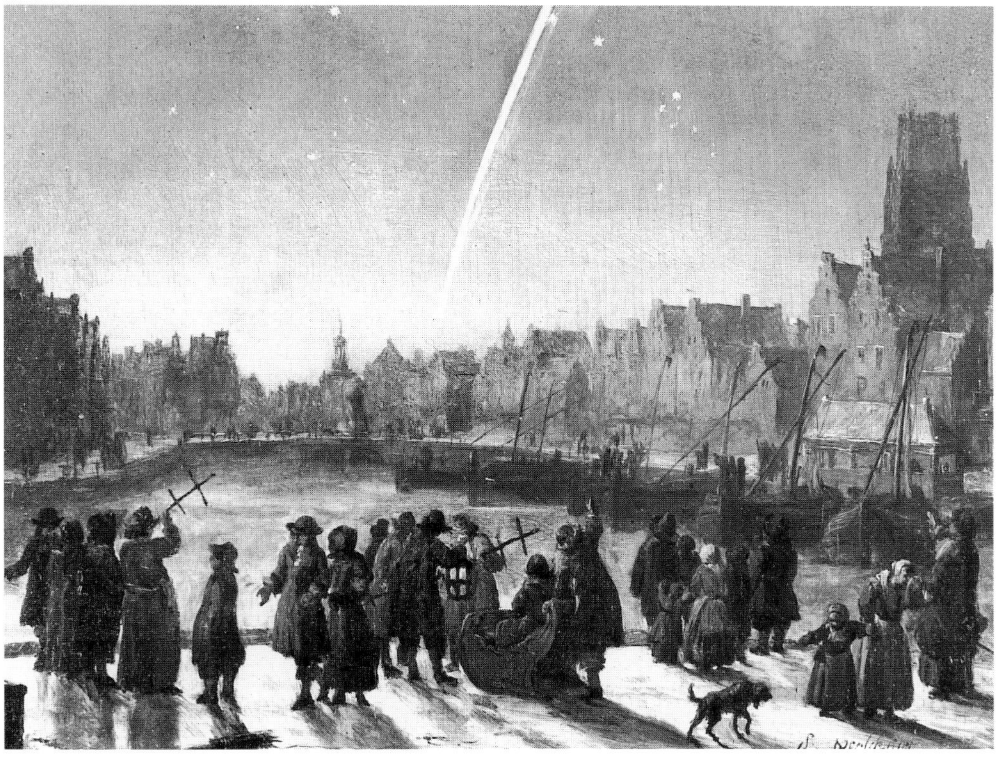

fig. 16. Lieve Verschuier, *The Comet of December 1680 as Seen in Rotterdam*, oil on panel, Historisch Museum, Rotterdam

Useful work, but on a much more sophisticated level, is carried out by the scholars who are known as *The Astronomer* and *The Geographer* (page 52, fig. 6, and cat. 16).[56] They are two variations on the same theme and the only two paintings in his oeuvre of a solitary man. The theme of the scholar in his study, surrounded by books and instruments, can be traced back to depictions of the Latin church father Saint Jerome (such as that by Jan van Eyck, Detroit Institute of Arts). It was a favorite motif with Gerrit Dou (1613–1675) and his school.[57] Vermeer pursued a more "natural" effect than his predecessors, as evident in the accuracy with which he rendered actual globes and instruments. In addition, both scholars wear the type of dressing gown then fashionable among dignified gentlemen, when they had their portraits made.

In our time, the "contemporary" aspect of the two gentlemen has elicited associations with two great scholars of Vermeer's generation, Anthony van Leeuwenhoek and Spinoza. It is, I believe, permissible to propose that Vermeer's young scholars are modern in a broader sense than De Lairesse attached to the word. They belong to the new breed of natural scientists that also appears in a painting by Lieve Verschuier (c. 1630–1686) (fig. 16). In that work such modern scholars, equipped with Jacob-staffs, study the appearance of a comet in December 1680. Dignified gentlemen keep them company. A common woman who "weeps and cries out" with averted eyes contrasts sharply with their composed behavior. She and her clergymen still interpreted that comet of 1680 as a sign of "severe plagues, punishments and bloody wars to come."[58]

It has to be added that the new scientists themselves were not at all anti-religious. Van Leeuwenhoek, for instance, saw the micro-organisms he discovered as a mark of the "providence, perfection and order of the Lord Maker of the Universe."[59]

A Woman Holding a Balance

Vermeer does not make it clear if his *Woman Holding a Balance* is usefully engaged or not (cat. 10). Nor can we determine if he intended the piece as an allegory, like his much larger *Art of Painting* and *Allegory of Faith* (page 68, fig. 2, cat. 20), or as a depiction of just an "episode." It might be an entirely successful synthesis of the two. The damsel stands at a table with a carpet pushed over to the left, enabling her to use the polished wooden edge as a working surface. It is the same situation as in the *Woman with a Pearl Necklace*, where the lady's toiletries appear at the table's edge (cat. 12). On the table of the *Woman*

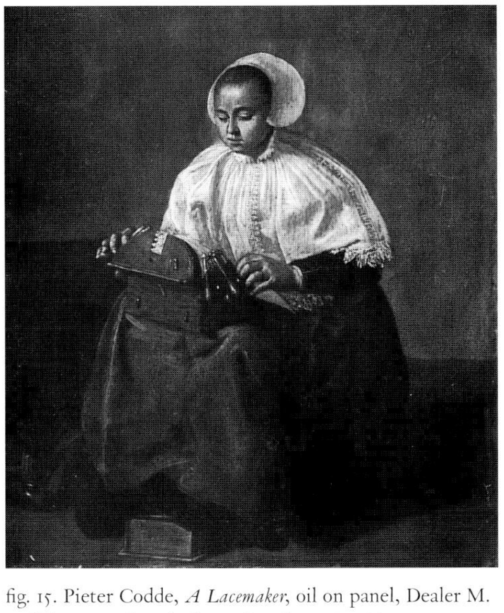

fig. 15. Pieter Codde, *A Lacemaker*, oil on panel, Dealer M. Wolff, Amsterdam, before 1983 [photo: RKD]

Holding a Balance are a gold chain and strings of pearls, with gold and silver coins in front. The box behind these may well be a case for the scales and, possibly, the weights.

A figure counting or weighing coins was a traditional motif, but in Dutch art such figures were depicted as elderly.[60] An excessive concern for riches was thought to be a characteristic of the aged. Thus *Avarice* was represented as an old man or woman absorbed in treasures, often equipped with a small balance for weighing coins (for example, see Rembrandt's painting of this theme, in Berlin). We observed that Vermeer avoided depicting old people. The classicist Caesar van Everdingen (c. 1617–1678) had done likewise in his *Allegory of Winter*, where he substituted the aged physique, usual for personifying this season, with a blooming young woman.[61] In similar fashion Metsu was the first Dutchman to make a young female *Goldweigher* the subject of a genre painting (fig. 17).[62]

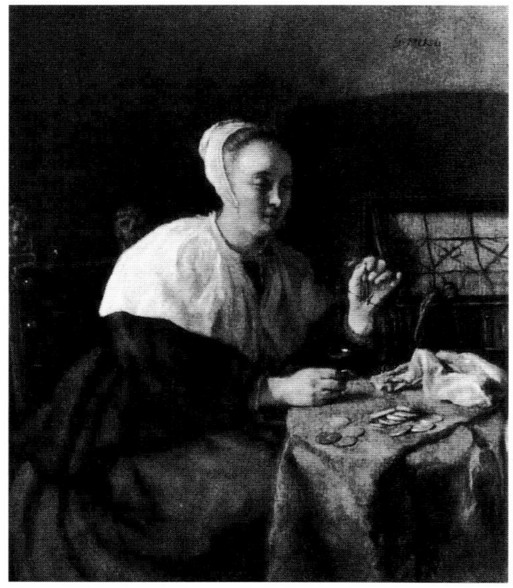

fig. 17. Gabriël Metsu, *The Goldweigher*, oil on panel, private collection

A "Second Bible"

However, Vermeer's weigher seems completely detached from her treasures. She is caught in an instant of intense concentration as the pans of the scales come to rest. Even more compellingly than in the two London paintings of a lady at the virginal (cats. 21, 22), the painting on the wall behind the weigher attracts attention. Above her head Christ floats in full majesty at the Last Judgment. Referring to this stern picture-within-the-picture, Herbert Rudolph started a trend in 1938 by interpreting Vermeer's *Woman Holding a Balance* as an example of reprehensible mundane vanity.[63] Ever since, iconologists have explained ever more Dutch "realistic" paintings as containing allusions to sinful worldly vanity.

It was forgotten that Hollanders of the seventeenth century viewed the world around them as the creation of God and, even, as a "second Bible," in which God's presence revealed itself as much as in the scriptures. Only recently has the idea emerged that this might help explain why the artists of the time depicted the world in such loving detail and so faithfully.[64]

The notion that "realistic" Dutch art, including the perfect depiction of perfect balance, would primarily consist of moralizing admonishment, becomes arbitrary. Against this widely disseminated opinion, I may submit my own conviction. It seems evident to me that Vermeer saw the beauty and wealth of earthly reality as transcendent and that he aimed to proclaim this even in the smallest detail of his paintings.

Dead at an early age, by 1675, he remained a man of the seventeenth century. He belonged to a different world than the younger De Lairesse, who lived until 1711. The latter fully adhered to the rationalism that won the day in the last quarter of the century. De Lairesse and his "classicist" companions formulated "rules" with which they sincerely believed nature could and should be "improved" upon in art. This differed fundamentally from Vermeer's complete devotion to this same nature.

Vermeer borrowed his themes from his predecessors and contemporaries. He, like no other, succeeded in touching the core of these themes. While doing so he managed to depict the truth he saw, through his own eyes, with unrivalled perfection.

A more elaborate version of this essay will be published later.

The able help of my assistant Yvonne Stuveborg proved indispensable to the research for this essay. Ideas and findings originated in part with students in my most inspiring seminar of 1994 at the University of Utrecht: Marleen Blokhuis, Jeanet Conrad, Linda Kuiper, Hetty van Lanschot, Marijke Lucas, Mien Niermeyer, and Yvonne Stuveborg. I thank Mary Yakush for her expert and patient editing of this text.

1. See Gombrich 1970, 13–14 n. 1, who quoted this "motto" of Warburg, adding: "The question of its origin is still open." It probably was Warburg's own variation of the German expression: "Der Teufel steckt im Detail" [The devil is in the detail]. I thank Professor Gombrich, London, and Sabine Rieger, Amsterdam, for this clarification.
2. "Want het Antiek gaat in alle tyden door; en het Modern verandert t'elkens van Mode..." Modern painting "is niet vry...," and can: "Niet meer als het tegenwoordige verbeelden...op een wys die nimmer stand houd, maar gestadig veranderd en vervreemd word." De Lairesse 1707, 1: 167, 172, 175.
3. De Lairesse 1740, 2: 28. This passage was never noticed. The earlier editions of the *Schilderboek* state "Van der Neer" instead of "Van der Meer," that is, Eglon van der Neer, a painter of similar refined conversation pieces. The text deals with the depiction of a figure in a niche or painted frame. Metsu and Mieris painted these; as far as I know Van der Neer and Vermeer did not. De Lairesse was concerned with a convincing suggestion of depth in such a niche. Possibly the editor (or typesetter) of the 1740 edition had a notion of Vermeer's extraordinary effects of depth. It should be noted that in the eighteenth century the *Lacemaker* (cat. 17) was copied within such a niche, which probably was an addition of the copyist (see Blankert 1988, 191, under "copies").
4. That "de Modeschilderyen van tyd tot tyd veranderen" [makes it] onwedersprekelijk" [that] "hunne waardigheid allengskens vermindert en vergaat." De Lairesse 1707, 1: 195.
5. See cat. 10, *Woman Holding a Balance.* Peter Sutton accepted the notion of the pregnancy of the women in both paintings, in Philadelphia 1984A, 343, cat. 118.
6. Copy in Philadelphia Museum of Art. See Blankert 1988, 192, ill. 123. Described as Vermeer's original in Hofstede de Groot 1907–1928, 1: 593, no. 26, and Plietzsch 1911, 62, 119.
7. And someone wearing such clothes today would be considered crazy. De Lairesse 1707, 1: 195: "hoe belagchelyk en ongerymd de dracht onzer voorouderen zich in onze oogen vertoont." Their paintings, "hoewel fraay geschilderd [are] met kleine eerbiedigheid van ons aangezien."
8. List of "huidendaegse schilders ... Van der Meer. Jonkertjes en casteeltjes. Delft." Published by Bredius 1890–1895, 12: 163, and linked to our Vermeer, yet it was never mentioned in the literature on the artist until Blankert 1988, 156, 205. The passage may have escaped notice because Sysmus gave Vermeer's Christian name at the end wrongly: "hiet Otto" (called Otto). He repeatedly erred in his first names. The "casteeltjes" (small castles) seem to indicate that Sysmus or his informant had a notion of the *View of Delft*. The word "kasteel" was also used for a citadel attached to a city (see Woordenboek, 7: col. 1757, sub 5). The gates and wall on the picture may have made this impression.
9. See Bredius 1890–1895, 8: 5 (Van der Laemen), 8 (Metsu), 9 (Ter Borch), 13 (Jansen); 302 (Netscher), 303 ("Mutsert" = Van Musscher); 12: 167 (Van der Neer).
10. On these words Woordenboek, 7: cols. 395–402, 480–492. Originally *jonkers* referred to young nobles, yet in Vermeer's time *jonkers* and *juffers* were also in use for young upper-class burghers. See also De Pauw-De Veen 1969, 171–172.
11. De Bie 1661, 159: "het seer aerdich uytbeelden" of "vrijagien, balletten, andere ghenuchtelijcke tijdt-verdrijven van malle Jonckers ende Joufvrouwen ... die seer aenghenaem en lieffelijk geschildert staen." The poem is on: "mallen en rallen,... schransen en veel ander sotterny," including "loncken en proncken," "droncken suypen, tuysen, swemmen in veel quaet, leven boven staet."
12. On Van der Laemen, Legrand 1963, 82–84.
13. See De Jongh 1967, 6–7: a print after Dirck Hals depicting merry young people. In the caption they are called "Lichtvaerdich en bedurven" (rash and daring), engaged in "ydelheyt onkuys" (unchaste vanity) and "vuyle Smoock inslurven" (inhaling filthy smoke). De Jongh in Amsterdam 1976, 55–57 (on smoking); 109–111 (on backgammon); 272–275 (on banquets and other luxuries).
14. My dates of works by Ter Borch follow Gudlaugsson 1959.
15. Versions in Berlin and Amsterdam. See Gudlaugsson 1959, 1: 96. Recently Kettering argued that Ter Borch's contemporaries: "could have interpreted *The Parental Admonition* as a courtship narrative in domestic surroundings" (Kettering 1993, 107, 116).
16. Already noticed by De Mirimonde 1961, 32, and Brown 1984, 134.
17. See Woordenboek, 7: cols. 495–503.
18. "D'een laat zich blindelings door zyn begeerte vangen,/ En blijft aan 't Jufferschap en zulk gezelschap hangen;/En schildert vorders al zyn leevens dagen niet/ Dan Jufferschap; het is al Juffers wat men ziet." Poem by W. V. Groot, printed in De Lairesse 1740, 1: 165.
19. In *A Woman Asleep* Vermeer depicted a dog that he later painted over (page 20, fig. 6).
20. "Te tuysen en te ruysen/Schoon dat Godt den Heer mishaegt," De Bie 1661, 159.
21. See Slive 1968, 457, ill. For sleeping women by Metsu, Ter Borch, and Dou, see Gudlaugsson 1968A, 25.
22. Robinson 1974, ill. 119. Hofstede de Groot 1907-1928, 1: 272, no. 65. Compare also Metsu's *Two Men and a Sleeping Woman* in the National Gallery in London, which Gudlaugsson 1968A, 25, dated to the late 1650s.
23. De Bie 1661, 159. The church and civil authorities both took offense at people dressing above their station (see Van Deursen 1978–1980, 3: 51).
24. The correspondence between the two paintings was noticed by Gudlaugsson 1959, 2: 170, who believed that Ter Borch was influenced by Vermeer. He dated the painting c. 1660, which is also about the time the Vermeer originated. It seems improbable that Ter Borch would coarsen

Vermeer's example. Ter Borch himself had introduced the motif around 1648, in an even more primitive and emphatic form (Gudlaugsson 1959, 1: ill. 68, 2: 89, cat. 68, private collection).

25. Observed by Klessman in Brunswick 1978, cat. 39; see also Naumann 1981, 1: 61 and 64. In addition to fig. 9, both authors convincingly cite its presumed pendant, Van Mieris' *The Oyster Meal*, as another model for Vermeer (Naumann 1981, 2: cat. 36).

26. Franits convincingly relates the motif to poems describing a suitor who is jealous of the dog of his sweetheart (Franits 1993, 55–56). The *caressing*, however, remains Van Mieris' invention.

27. An illustration is missing here, as obtaining a photograph of a specific moment even from important films appears impossible. Caressing the dog: the beginning of Buster Keaton's *Seven Chances* and of Billy Wilder's *Irma la Douce*. The stroking of her cat: in the hospital scene in Mario Monicelli's *Viaggio con Anita*. In the episode concerning "moon sickness" in *Kaos* by the Taviani brothers, the roles are reversed, with a girl approaching a man by touching a cat in his lap. It seems unlikely that these filmmakers copied the motif from each other and still more improbable that one of them borrowed it from Van Mieris. Comparable in literature is Chekhov's *The Lady with the Dog*, in which a gentleman succeeds in establishing his first contact with an unknown lady by signaling to her dog.

28. The figure was "read" by W. J. Müller of Kiel and published as his discovery by Klessman in Brunswick 1978, 166.

29. Woordenboek, 9: col. 1082.

30. Naumann 1981, 1: 24, no. 22, mentions previous authors who noticed the relationship between Van Mieris' *Duet* and Vermeer. Even earlier, in 1926, Hofstede de Groot observed on Van Mieris' *Duet:* "Schönes Bild, dem Delfter Vermeer verwandt" [Beautiful picture, related to Vermeer of Delft] (Hofstede de Groot 1907–1928; 10: 48, no. 185).

31. See Hecht in Amsterdam 1989, cat. 12.

32. De Mirimonde 1961, 42.

33. Moreno 1982.

34. The idea of the *clavis interpretandi* was already presented by Thoré-Bürger 1866, 460, later elaborated by Keyszelitz 1956. G. J. M. Weber recently maintained that paintings within paintings that do not display a direct connection to the main subject may well be intended as an indirect commentary, comparable to the practice in rhetorics (Weber 1994, esp. 307).

35. All early descriptions of Vermeers referred to in this essay are printed in full, with English translations, in Blankert 1988.

36. Tentatively suggested by De Mirimonde 1961, 39, 40, and notes 23, 24. Presented as new facts by De Jongh 1967, 49–50; see also De Jongh 1993, 25.

37. The motif of the spectator of the painting as possible participant in the scene was first recognized by Brown 1984, 137. The idea was subsequently developed by Sluijter 1988, 156–159 and Sluijter 1991, 54, 59–60, including (63 n. 58) a comparable interpretation of cats. 21 and 22.

38. See Frankfurt 1993, 144, cats. 8, 35, with references.

39. See Mayer-Meintschel 1978–1979, ills. 1, 3, 4; Wheelock 1981, ill. 29; Blankert 1988, 173 (with ill.).

40. Letter by Van Gogh of c. 23 July 1888: "Do you know Vermeer, who, amongst other things, painted a very beautiful, pregnant Dutch lady?" Hale 1913, 282 related this to the *Woman in Blue Reading a Letter.* Van Gogh may have seen this painting on his 1885 visit of the then newly opened Rijksmuseum. But in his letters of that year concerning that visit he writes in detail about other paintings, but nothing about the Vermeer (compare De Vries 1993).

41. The early descriptions reprinted in Blankert 1988, cat. 14.

42. Hale 1913, 156–157, identified the cushion as the one also depicted in the *Lacemaker* (cat. 17).

43. This observation earlier in Franits 1993, 48.

44. Observed by De Mirimonde 1961, 41, 52 n. 28, with reference to an emblem of 1608 by Vaenius, which compares love to sailing. See in greater detail (without reference to De Mirimonde), De Jongh 1967, 49–55; also Frankfurt 1993, 204–205.

45. Gudlaugsson 1968B, 661: "Die Stille des Innenraumes atmet einen Frieden, den der Mensch in seinem Innern nicht kennt."

46. On that work Gudlaugsson 1959, 2: cat. 144.

47. On such books with model love letters, see De Jongh in Brussels 1971, 178–179, and Frankfurt 1993, 144–146.

48. Even iconologists have felt uncertain in suggesting a connection between the picture's main scene and the conspicuous *Finding of Moses* on the back wall. Vermeer "suppressed" a clear clue here, comparable to his removal of *Cupid* from his earlier *Girl Reading a Letter at an Open Window*.

49. This dating for the Metsu proposed by Gudlaugsson 1968A, 24, 40.

50. On this picture Gudlaugsson 1959, 2: cat. 80.
51. Bloch 1963, 21: "What is [the woman] really doing?". Descargues 1966, 129: "l'invraisemblance du geste de la femme ..."; Slatkes 1981, 50: "Her movements ... are never clearly explained" and the objects suggest no "unified action." Also Blankert 1988, 109.
52. "Daer een Seigneur zyn handen wast, in een doorsiende Kamer, met beelden, konstig en raer." The painting fetched 95 guilders. Only the *View of Delft* (f 200), *The Milkmaid* (f 175) and *Woman Holding a Balance* (f 155) went for more.
53. See Blankert 1995.
54. The fabric identified by S. Honig of the Openluchtmuseum, Arnhem, orally to Y. Stuveborg.
55. Presumably inspired by Dou's and Van Mieris' most successful depictions of kitchen servants. Compare especially Naumann 1981, 2: cat. 7.
56. In the oldest references of 1720 and 1729, both are called "Astrologisten," which meant astrologers as well as astronomists, their activities not yet being strictly differentiated (see Woordenboek 1, suppl. 1956, col. 1910).
57. Compare Martin 1913, ills. 23, 62, 64, 65, 67, 69, 148–150.
58. This information from Meyerman 1976.
59. Rooseboom 1968, 21. See also Bots 1972, 1–15, on the new scientists' "fyso-theological" ideas.
60. On scales, their weights, the boxes in which they were kept and their being depicted in use by old people, see Huiskamp 1994, 29, ills. 2, 78–83 and color pls. 49, 50, 55. Compare Blankert 1988, ill. 91.
61. Rijksmuseum, Amsterdam, c. 1645; see Blankert 1991B.
62. This picture: Hofstede de Groot 1907–1928, 1: 271, no. 55, dated by Gudlaugsson 1968A, 26, 40: "probably before 1660."
63. Rudolph 1938, 409, 431.
64. Suggestions on nature as a "second Bible" as a source of inspiration for seventeenth-century Dutch artists were formulated independently from each other by: Blankert 1991A, 24, Brenninkmeyer-De Rooij 1992, 38, and Bakker 1993, 108. Compare the much earlier remarks by De Jongh in Brussels 1971, 150.

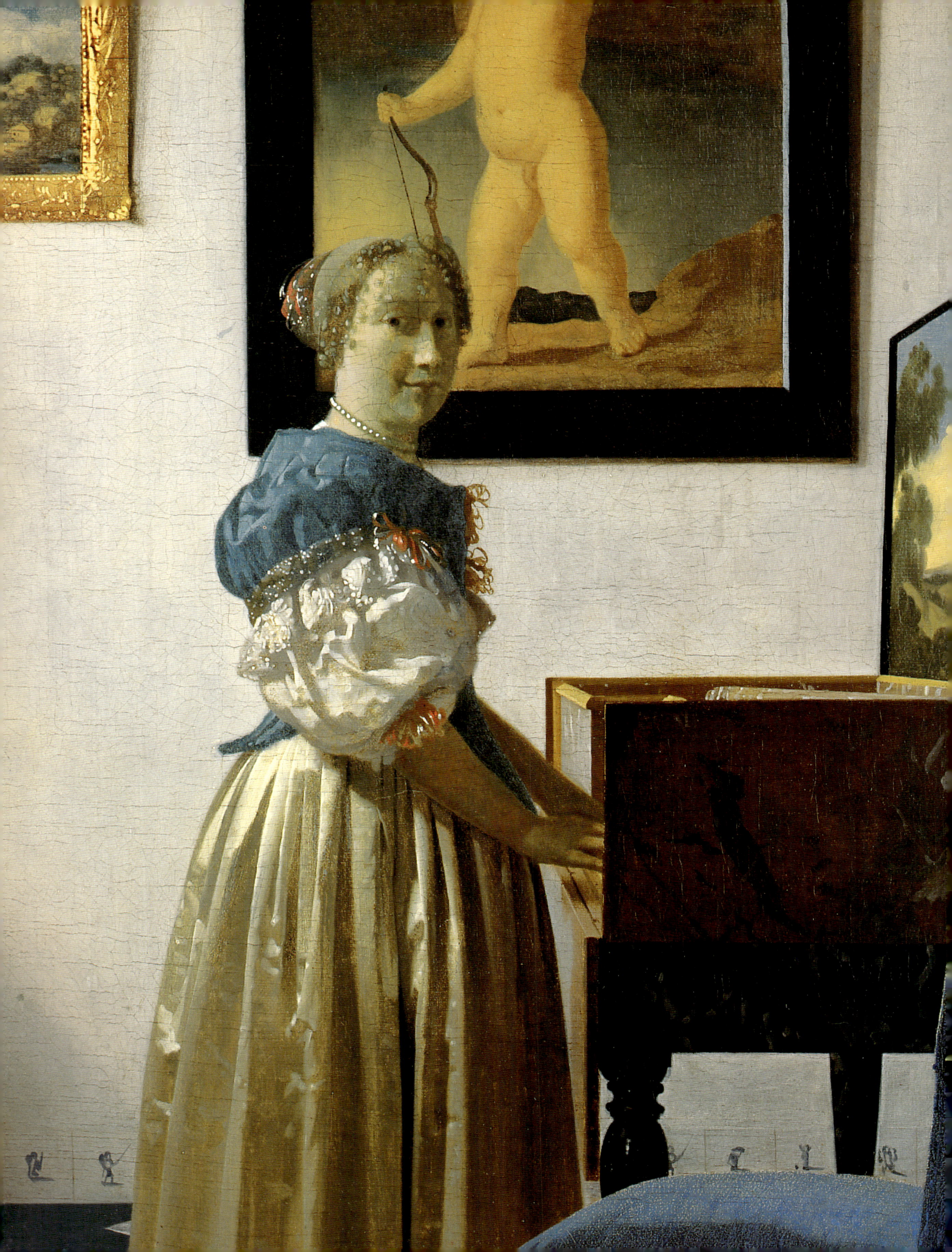

"Un celebre Peijntre nommé Verme[e]r"

BEN BROOS

ON 24 FEBRUARY 1676 VERMEER'S WIDOW, Catharina Bolnes, assigned to her mother, Maria Thins, "a piece of painting [by] her Late husband in which was depicted the Art of Painting" (page 68, fig. 2).[1] Bolnes' intention was to keep the work out of the hands of her creditors. Nonetheless, a year later the executor of Vermeer's estate auctioned off this personal manifesto of the painter. It has proved impossible to find out what happened to the masterpiece until it resurfaced in Austria in the nineteenth century. In 1813 Johann Rudolph, Count Czernin, bought the painting for a nominal sum from a saddlemaker in Vienna, unaware that he was acquiring the most famous work by the great Delft master. Count Czernin assumed that he had become the owner of a Pieter de Hooch, whose work was more marketable at the time. In the fall of 1860, the Berlin museum director Gustav Waagen recognized the *Art of Painting* as an authentic Vermeer.[2]

The history of the *Art of Painting* mirrors Vermeer's own reputation: after enjoying a brief period as a minor celebrity in the seventeenth century, he languished in obscurity in the eighteenth, and was rediscovered in the nineteenth. In the twentieth century Vermeer acquired the exalted status of a star. Nevertheless, it is superficial to label the painter a prototype of the "misunderstood genius." His work has consistently been appreciated, although the evidence for that appreciation needs to be assembled bit by bit.

I. Vermeer in Delft

VERMEER'S CLIENTS

The identification of Pieter Claesz van Ruijven (1624–1674) as the principal patron for Vermeer was the most important result of John Michael Montias' recent research, as will be explained below (see page 53). This Van Ruijven was a burgher who rarely held office but who had become very rich through inheritance and investments. His presumed near-monopoly of Vermeer's paintings has been greeted with suspicion. Although Montias may have created the impression that Van Ruijven was just about Vermeer's sole buyer,[3] the reality is that Vermeer would undoubtedly have had other clients and, moreover, was a respected burgher and even a widely esteemed painter.[4]

After Vermeer's death, the master baker Hendrick van Buyten (1632–1701) accepted two pictures from the painter's widow as security for a debt of more than six hundred guilders. This demonstrates not only that Vermeer had encountered financial difficulties toward the end of his life, but also that his paintings commanded steep prices. The first picture was described in a deed as "two personages of which the one sits and writes a letter," so that it may reasonably be assumed that this was the *Lady Writing a Letter with Her Maid* (cat. 19). The second was "a personage playing on a zither," presumably *The Guitar Player* in The Iveagh Bequest, London (page 32, fig. 1).[5] After the baker's death in 1701, the former work was encountered "in the vestibule" as "a large painting by Vermeer." In an adjacent room hung another "two little pieces by Vermeer," which cannot be identified. Before 1701 *The Guitar Player* must have been traded with, or sold to, the Van Ruijven heirs, since it was auctioned in 1696 as part of their collection.[6] Van Buyten must have appreciated Vermeer's skill, considering the fact that he owned at least four of his works.

The earliest mention of a painting by Vermeer concerns a youthful work along the lines of *Christ in the House of Mary and Martha* (cat. 2). A 1657 inventory of the Amsterdam

Detail, cat. 21

art dealer Johannes de Renialme mentioned "A Grave visitation by van der Meer."[7] Its value was assessed at twenty guilders, which is not unreasonable for a work by a beginner. De Renialme maintained close contacts in Delft, where he bought paintings regularly. In 1761 another—also lost—history painting from the beginning of Vermeer's career was called "Jupiter, Venus and Mercury, by J. ver Meer."[8] It was being auctioned from the estate of the Delft patrician Gerard van Berckel (c. 1620–1686), "Commissioner of the Finances of Holland." His art collection was inherited by his son Willem van Berckel (1679–1759), a one-time burgomaster of the city of Delft.[9] This mythological scene, presumably in the possession of the distinguished Delft family for a long time, may be considered evidence of an interest in Vermeer's work in the upper echelons of Delft society.[10]

In addition to De Renialme and Gerard van Berckel, a third incidental buyer of Vermeer's paintings can be identified. This was Nicolaes van Assendelft (1630–1692), a Delft regent who over the course of his lifetime assembled a remarkable collection that included numerous major masters of the Golden Age. In the 1711 inventory of his widow's property "A damsel playing on the Clavichord by Vermeer" was appraised at forty guilders (fig. 1).[11] This was most likely the *Lady Standing at the Virginal* (cat. 21). Of course we can't prove that he bought the painting directly from the artist, but this is not out of the question either.

Therefore, not only a baker but also a few Delft luminaries and, above all, one man of independent means – Van Ruijven – bought works by Vermeer. Perhaps Vermeer liked having a limited circle of buyers. On the one hand he did not want to work for the mass market, but neither did he seek out the munificent favor of one exclusive, powerful patron.

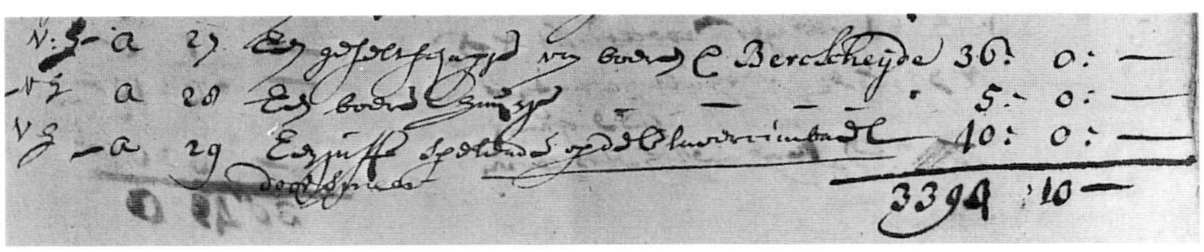

fig. 1. Nicolaes van Assendelft inventory, 1711, Gemeentearchief, Delft, ONA 3003–11, deed 375, fol. 181

DE MONCONYS

Vermeer's talent did not remain unobserved in prominent circles. The secretary of Stadholder Frederik Hendrik, Constantijn Huygens (1596–1687), and his Hague friends must have been aware of the miraculously gifted artist in the nearby city of Delft. Only that would explain how it occurred to a French connoisseur and learned diplomat, Balthasar de Monconys (1611–1665), to visit Vermeer. On 3 August 1663 he had been in Delft briefly and admired the city and the grave of William the Silent (Willem de Zwijger) in the New Church (Nieuwe Kerk). Surprisingly, he returned eight days later with but a single purpose, to meet Vermeer. He wrote on 11 August 1663, "In Delft I saw the Painter Verme[e]r."[12]

De Monconys noted in his journal that Vermeer had been unable to show him a single painting. The Frenchman did, however, see a painting in the home of a baker, but thought the price, six hundred *livres*, unjustified, as it featured only one figure, perhaps a *juffertje* (see page 32).[13] Unfortunately, De Monconys made no mention of the style and quality of such works—it appears that he judged them exclusively on the basis of the number of hours invested in them.[14]

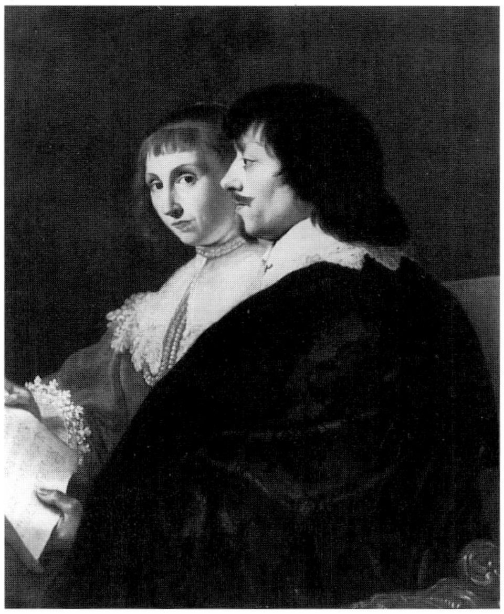

fig. 2. Jacob van Campen, *Portrait of Constantijn Huygens and Suzanna van Baerle*, c. 1635, oil on canvas, Mauritshuis, The Hague

Strangely, De Monconys' journal has never been exhaustively analyzed, even though it does serve to place Vermeer clearly in the context of his times.[15] The price of six hundred *livres* that the baker – presumably Van Buyten – thought reasonable for his painting corresponds to the six hundred *livres* that Gerrit Dou (1613–1675) asked from De Monconys two days later for a *Woman in a Window*, clearly also a painting with only one figure. Back then a Vermeer had the same market value as an authentic work by Dou, whom King Charles II of England had invited to become his court painter in 1660. De Monconys fell upon one amazement after another. Frans van Mieris the Elder (1635–1681) wanted no fewer than twelve hundred *livres* for a more elaborate figure piece of a sick lady being visited by a quack doctor. The same day, according to De Monconys, the painter Pieter van Slingelandt (1640–1691) demanded all of four hundred *livres* for a tiny work. That was too much, the Frenchman thought.[16]

One may well ask why De Monconys went to this Delft baker and not to the home of Van Ruijven, who, according to Montias, had already acquired several Vermeers by 1663.[17] After his somewhat disappointing negotiations with Van Mieris and Van Slingelandt, De Monconys visited, in Leiden, "a Mr. Beyau [Johan de Bye], who has a great quantity of the paintings of *Dau*."[18] For whatever reason, Van Ruijven was not prepared to receive De Monconys in his home on the Oude Delft, and little is known about his collection, as we will see.

CONSTANTIJN HUYGENS

De Monconys' visit to Holland in August 1663 has definite significance because of his exploration, albeit somewhat superficial, of the art market. His travel account is also important for an additional, scarcely noticed, reason. Before the Frenchman visited Vermeer in Delft, he went to pay his respects to the Huygens family in The Hague, where he admired the art collection in their house on Het Plein, which he described in detail.[19] In June 1663 De Monconys had attended the proceedings of the Royal Society in London together with Constantijn Huygens the Elder (fig. 2).[20] One can imagine how amazed Huygens must have been to hear that the Frenchman had been in Delft, without visiting Vermeer. We know that De Monconys rectified this oversight on 11 August. Having rounded out his visit to Delft, De Monconys dropped by to see the Huygens family two days later, at six a.m., to say his farewells. Father Huygens ("M. de Zulcon" [Lord of Zuylichem]) had to leave for Zeeland, so that he was unable to accompany De Monconys on his intended visit to the Leiden painters, as the Frenchman had apparently hoped he would do.[21] One gains the strong impression that it was thanks to his contacts in The Hague that the French diplomat had been able to take note of the most famous Dutch artists of that era, such as Van Mieris and Dou in Leiden, and Johannes Vermeer in Delft.

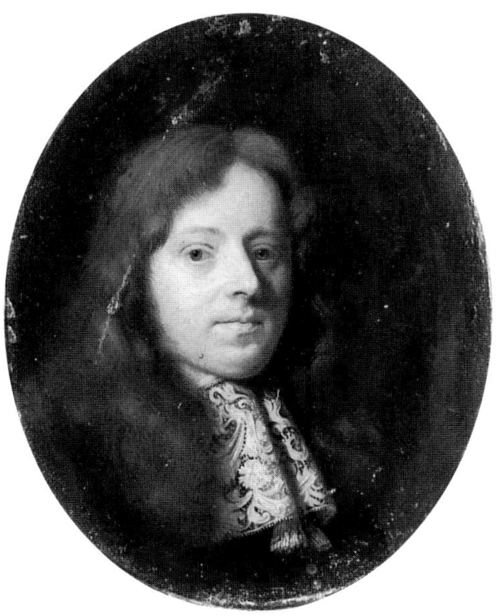

fig. 3. Caspar Netscher, *Portrait of Pieter Teding van Berckhout*, oil on copper, Teding van Berkhout Foundation, Amersfoort

Constantijn Huygens must therefore have performed a minor but vital rôle in the theater of Vermeer's life.[22] Huygens was, of course, one of the greatest authorities of his age where art was concerned. He maintained lively contacts with the Flemish painters Rubens (1577–1640) and Van Dyck (1599–1641), and his visit to the shared workshop of Jan Lievens (1607–1674) and Rembrandt (1606–1669) in Leiden is legendary.[23] Why should Huygens himself have had no contact with Vermeer, when he urged others to visit the artist's studio? One document gives reason to believe that he did, in fact, visit the artist. Pieter Teding van Berckhout (1643–1713) (fig. 3), a member of the Hague regents' class,

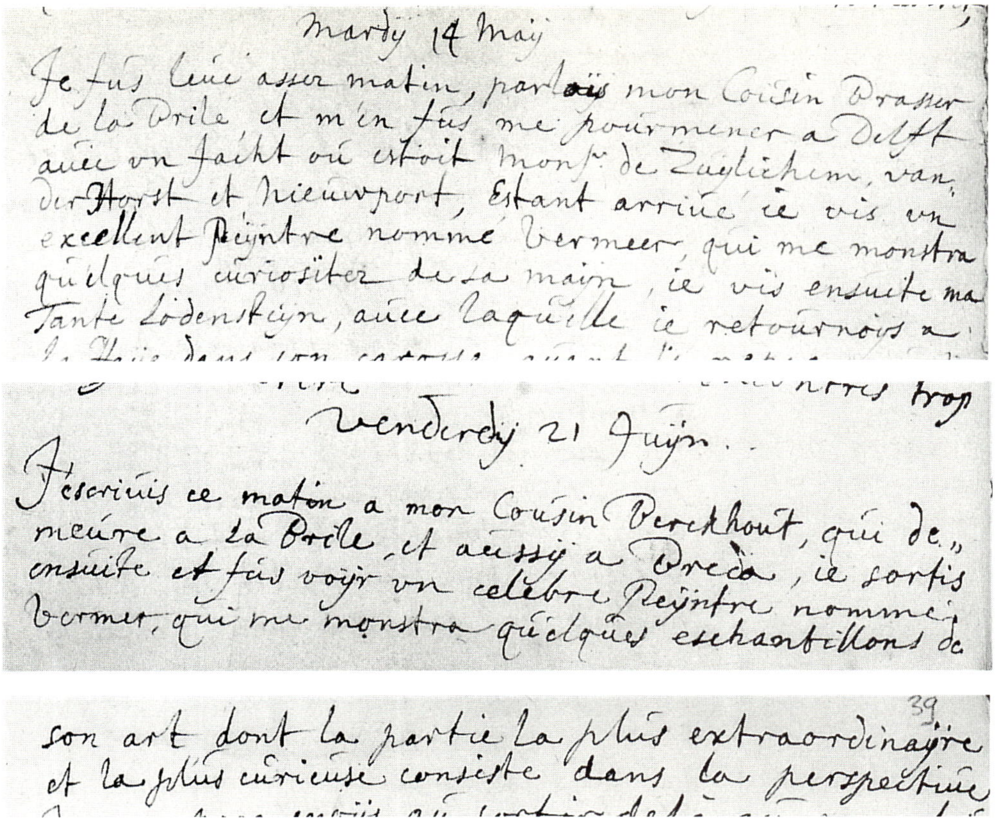
mardy 14 Maij
Je fus leué asses matin, parlois mon Cousin Brasser
de la Brile, et m'en fus me pourmener a Delft
auec vn facht ou estoit Monsr. de Zuylichem, van
der Horst et Nieuwport, Estant arriué ie vis vn
excellent Peijntre nommé Vermeer, qui me monstra
quelques curiositez de sa main, ie vis ensuite ma
Tante Lodenstein, auec laquelle ie retournois a

trop
Vendredy 21 Juijn.
J'escriuis ce matin a mon Cousin Berckhout, qui de,,
meure a la Brile, et aussy a Breda, ie sortis
ensuite et fus voijr vn celebre Peijntre nommé
Vermer, qui me monstra quelques eschantillons de

39
son art dont la partie la plus extraordinaire
et la plus curieuse consiste dans la perspective

fig. 4. Fragments of the diary of Pieter Teding van Berckhout, Koninklijke Bibliotheek, The Hague

whose sister eventually married Constantijn's son Lodewijk,[24] kept a diary. In it he recounted that he went to visit the famous painter Vermeer in Delft on 14 May 1669.[25] He had arrived there that day by towing barge and presumably disembarked at the Rotterdam or Schiedam Gate (cat. 7) "where were Monsieurs de Zuylichem [Huygens], van der Horst and Nieuwport." That is, he joined the company of Constantijn Huygens and his friends, member of parliament Ewout van der Horst (c. 1631–before 1672), and ambassador Willem Nieupoort (1607–1678).[26]

"Having arrived, I saw an excellent painter named Vermeer" (estant arrivé ie [je] vis un excellent Peijntre nommé Vermeer), wrote Van Berckhout, who was also shown several "curiosities," according to his account (fig. 4).[27] Although it does not say explicitly that all four men visited Vermeer, we may assume that Huygens and his friends did not linger at the city gate. On 21 June an apparently enthusiastic Van Berckhout repeated his visit: "I went to see a celebrated painter named Vermeer" ([Je] fus voijr un celebre Peijntre nommé Verme[e]r.) During this second studio visit he was again shown curious and exceptional works, which he described as "perspectives."[28] At the very least he must have seen the *Art of Painting*, the cherished showpiece of the Vermeer family.

That Pieter Teding van Berckhout twice visited Vermeer and twice praised him somewhat contradicts romantic notions about Vermeer's social isolation. No wonder Montias was somewhat perplexed by Van Berckhout's comments: "But it would not have occurred to me that he would be called 'célèbre'."[29] What is most interesting about this visit is that Vermeer's studio (like those of Dou and Van Mieris) was evidently considered a place of interest. Van Berckhout was an active member in The Hague society and of the most prominent Delft circles, where, judging from all appearances, Vermeer was much admired.[30]

It is hardly surprising that Van Berckhout was also a close acquaintance of Dirck van Bleyswijck,[31] whose *Beschryvinge der Stadt Delft* (Description of the City of Delft) had first appeared in 1667. In this work Van Bleyswijck published the famous poem by Arnold Bon containing a passage concerning the death of Carel Fabritius as the result of the explosion of the Delft powder magazine in 1654 (see page 51). Bon concluded enthusiastically: "luckily there arose from his fire VERMEER."[32]

VERMEER'S VIRGINALS

Constantijn Huygens must have known and admired Vermeer's work. Some additional examples will help complete the picture. In 1660 Johan (or Jean) Larson (c. 1620–1664), a London sculptor who had worked for the English and Dutch courts, and become a member of the Hague guild, was on business in Delft.[33] As a portrait specialist, he was probably intrigued by what the "celebre Vermeer" could manage in that area. In any case, he bought some kind of portrait from Vermeer. In 1664 his estate included "A character head [*tronie*] by Vermeer," a reference perhaps to the *Girl with a Pearl Earring* (cat. 15) or to *The Girl with the Red Hat* (cat. 14).[34] Larson was yet another good acquaintance of the Huygens family. In 1655 Constantijn senior had composed a poem on a portrait bust that the Englishman had made for him.[35] One wonders if Larson, too, might have visited Vermeer at the recommendation of Huygens.

A last circumstance again concerns the involvement of the Huygens family in the marketing of Vermeer's art. It appears that Constantijn junior, or senior, gave Diego Duarte (1610–1691) of Antwerp one of Vermeer's late works, possibly the *Lady Seated at the Virginal* (cat. 22), or at least advised him to buy the work.[36] This was the first Vermeer to leave Dutch hands. The younger Huygens regularly visited Duarte and admired his collection of paintings, while Duarte likewise periodically visited Holland. De Monconys also visited Duarte in Antwerp and no doubt passed on his greetings to The Hague.[37]

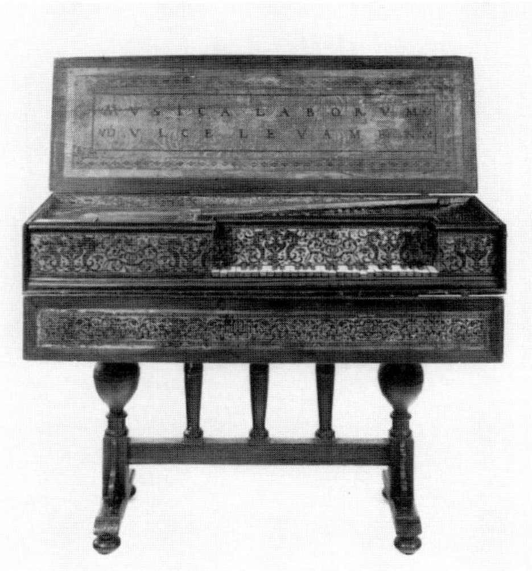

fig. 5. Virginal built by Johannes Ruckers, 1640, Gemeentemuseum, The Hague

It is particularly intriguing to note that experts believe that the virginals in Vermeer's paintings are so accurately portrayed that he must have observed them directly. The proportions and inscription MVSICA LETITIAE CO[ME]S MEDICINA DOLOR[UM], on the lid of the instrument in one painting (cat. 8), have been connected with the Antwerp Ruckers workshop.[38] Only a few of these instruments are still known, like the 1640 virginal that was built by Johannes Ruckers (1578–1642) (fig. 5). We learn from the correspondence of Constantijn Huygens senior that he ordered such a virginal in 1648, with the knowledgeable Duarte acting as middleman. The maker of this particular instrument was Jean Couchet (1615–1655), a nephew of Johannes Ruckers, who had worked in Ruckers' shop for sixteen years. Couchet had built only four such virginals to date. They were rare instruments that might be expected to go for about three hundred guilders, Duarte wrote to Huygens,[39] approximately half the cost of a painting by Dou, Van Mieris, or Vermeer. Is it not possible that Vermeer saw the "Ruckers" in the Huygens residence?[40] His preference for scenes with music-making ladies corresponds intriguingly with the well-known musical gifts of the Huygens family.

II. Vermeer in Amsterdam

"MASTERLIKE"

Vermeer was a man obsessed with detail, who might even have edited dedications to himself. That was, in any case, how Albert Blankert interpreted the subtle changes that Arnold Bon's poem underwent in Van Bleyswijck's 1667 *Beschryvinge der Stadt Delft*. In the first version of the poem lamenting the premature death of Carel Fabritius, Bon refers to Vermeer: "who, masterlike trod his path." The second version reads "who, masterlike, was able to emulate him."[41] Blankert's somewhat hesitantly expressed opinion, that it was Vermeer

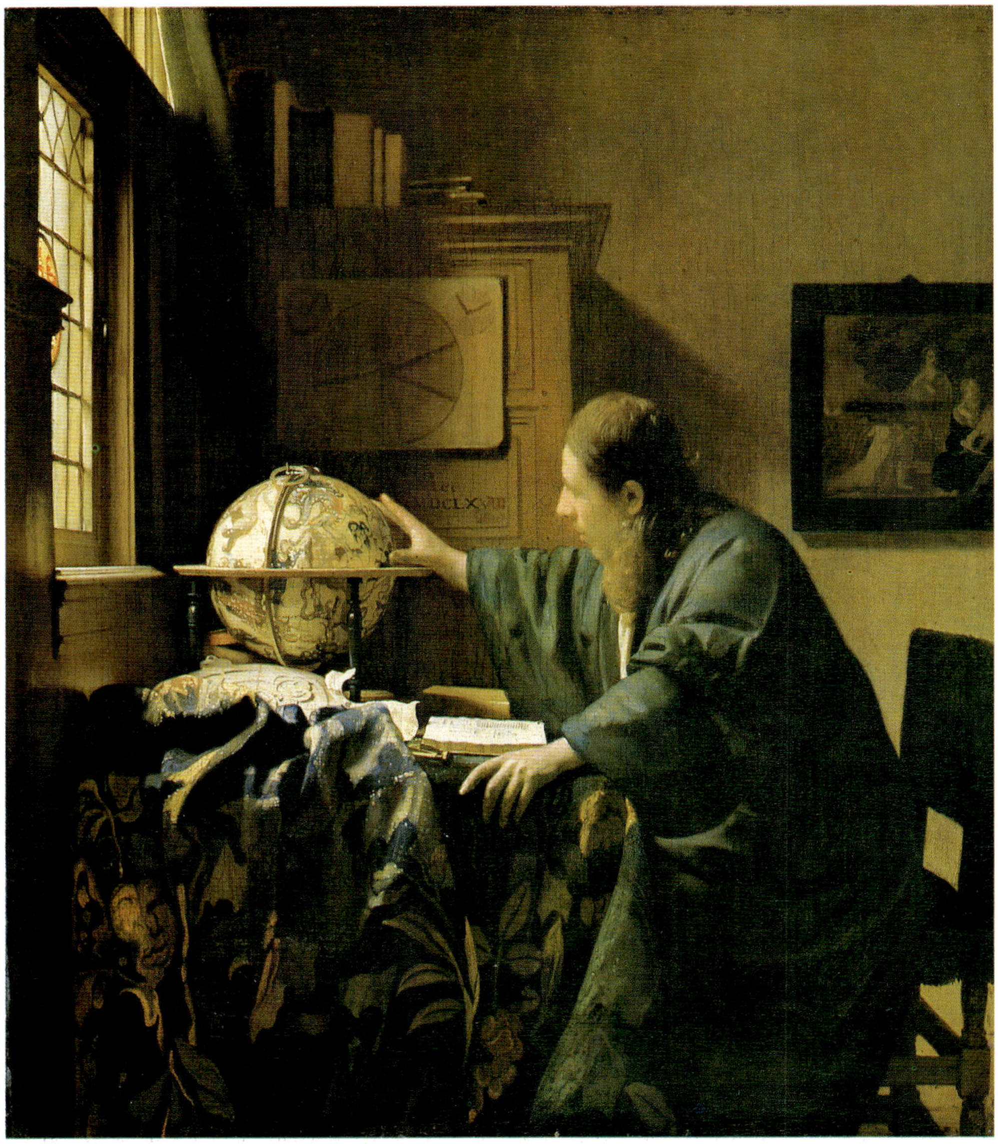

fig. 6. Johannes Vermeer, *The Astronomer*, 1668, oil on canvas, Musée du Louvre, Paris

himself who prevailed upon Bon to make this adjustment, is wholly credible.[42] The artist was hardly modest in his concepts. After all, the *Art of Painting* expressed Vermeer's high ideals about his trade and calling. At the very least he must have been familiar with stories about artists competing with each other. As far as he must have been concerned, Vermeer versus Fabritius could be added to the list of Apelles versus Protogenes, Raphael versus Michelangelo, Dürer versus Lucas van Leyden, and Rembrandt versus Rubens.[43]

While Vermeer may have polished his "masterlike" reputation a little in this way, his name did not figure prominently in the main lexicon of Dutch seventeenth-century art, Arnold Houbraken's *Groote Schouburgh*, published in Amsterdam in 1718–1721. Houbraken (1660–1719), who assembled his information from a variety of sources – personal experience, including his acquaintance with artists, their works, and their pupils; but also secondary sources, including city histories – depended heavily for his discussion of Delft artists on Van Bleyswijck's *Beschryvinge der Stadt Delft*. It was in that publication that he found the list of artists currently active in Delft in 1667[44] – including Vermeer – and it was there that he derived his long discussion of the life and death of Carel Fabritius.[45] Curiously, Houbraken edited Arnold Bon's commemorative poem about Fabritius, eliminating the last stanza citing Vermeer, though the reason remains unknown.

The deletion of these lines appears to have been fatal to Vermeer's reputation. Throughout the remainder of the eighteenth century, no biography of Vermeer was published – a fact that occasioned the amazement of Henry Havard in 1883.[46] The first scholar to attempt to placate this somewhat romanticized outrage was Albert Blankert, in 1975.[47]

Houbraken's text was widely acknowledged in the eighteenth and nineteenth century as authoritative, hence the omission was maintained. That Vermeer's biography was a closed book to Houbraken's epigones Jacob Campo Weyerman (1677–1747) and Jan van Gool (1685–1763) has nothing to do with deliberate underestimation, as people have assumed.[48]

Considering that two-thirds of Vermeer's works were in one private collection in Delft until 1696, Houbraken's oversight is hardly remarkable. The painter-writer passed the major part of his life in Dordrecht, apparently having few contacts with the then somewhat somnolent Delft.[49] By the time he moved to Amsterdam around 1709, the small oeuvre of Vermeer had been dispersed among a number of exquisite collections within the old Amsterdam canal encirclement. For a long time only a few works could be seen outside Amsterdam.

In Rotterdam, for instance, *The Astronomer* (fig. 6) and *The Geographer* (cat. 16) came under the gavel five years before the publication of the first volume of Houbraken's lexicon. They were part of the collection of the magistrate Adriaen Paets (1657–1712), the Maecenas of the painter Adriaen van der Werff (1659–1722). Houbraken, Weyerman, and Van Gool were awestruck by the vast sums that were paid for Van der Werff's paintings at the 1713 Paets auction, but they overlooked the Vermeers.[50] A year before the appearance of the third volume of Houbraken's canonical work, both of Vermeer's pictures were sold in Amsterdam as "extra choice" (*extra puyk*) items that were part of the collection of Hendrick Sorgh (1666–1720), a dealer in paintings who lived on the Keizersgracht.[51]

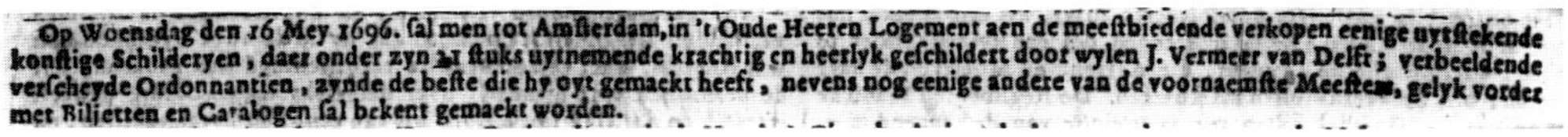
Op Woensdag den 16 Mey 1696. ſal men tot Amſterdam, in 't Oude Heeren Logement aen de meeſtbiedende verkopen eenige uytſtekende konſtige Schilderyen, daer onder zyn 21 ſtuks uytnemende krachtig en heerlyk geſchildert door wylen J. Vermeer van Delft; verbeeldende verſcheyde Ordonnantien, zynde de beſte die hy oyt gemaeckt heeft, nevens nog eenige andere van de voornaemſte Meeſters, gelyk vorder met Biljetten en Catalogen ſal bekent gemaeckt worden.

fig. 7. Advertisement in *Amsterdamsche Courant*, 19 April 1696

THE VAN RUIJVEN/DISSIUS COLLECTION

Houbraken somehow also neglected to mention a major event that occurred in Amsterdam, where the Dissius collection from Delft came under the gavel on 16 May 1696. It was the biggest group of Vermeer paintings to have ever been assembled. The *Amsterdamsche Courant* printed an announcement that on that day, in the Old Men's Lodging House (Oude Heeren Logement), would be sold "several outstandingly artful paintings, including 21 works most powerfully and splendidly painted by the late J. Vermeer of Delft; showing various Compositions, being the best he has ever made" (fig. 7).[52]

Because of the size of this collection, the Delft printer Jacob Dissius (1653–1695) was long believed to have been the patron of Vermeer.[53] Until recently authors still wrote: "His most important customer was Jacob Dissius."[54] In 1977 Wheelock had opened this matter for discussion: "curiously, no evidence of their [Vermeer and Dissius] relationship exists."[55] In fact, the Delft archives reveal that Dissius was only twenty-two years old when Vermeer passed on. He therefore could hardly have been one of Vermeer's patrons.[56]

Montias established that not Dissius but his father-in-law Pieter Claesz van Ruijven (1624–1674), son of a wealthy Delft brewer, probably had claim to the esteemed title of "Maecenas" of Vermeer. The complicated body of evidence has only come to light slowly and laboriously. In 1885 Abraham Bredius published the appearance of twenty paintings by Vermeer in a 1683 inventory of Dissius' effects, without being able to identify these works. That is why he wrote despairingly, "What a treasure! And where has all this gone?"[57] A century later, after research in the Delft archives, Montias argued that this treasure—probably two-thirds of the known oeuvre of Vermeer—had been in the possession of Pieter Claesz van Ruijven. Van Ruijven was virtually the same age as Vermeer, and died in almost the same year as the painter. He first gave Vermeer financial support in 1657.[58] Paintings produced between 1657 and 1660 were named by Montias as the property of Van Ruijven, who had described these in 1665 "in a certain book...marked with the letter A," an appendix to his will.[59] Had it survived, this document concerning Van Ruijven's collection could have given us closer insight into the scale on which Van Ruijven collected Vermeers.

Van Ruijven's widow, Maria de Knuijt, enjoyed usufruct of the estate, which, after her death in 1681, came into the hands of her daughter, Magdalena van Ruijven. Magdalena died a year later, and the 1683 document, which Bredius later published, was drawn up. Finally, by way of her father-in-law, Abraham Dissius, the paintings came into the possession of her husband, Jacob Dissius, in 1694.[60] At first, Abraham and Jacob had drawn lots for the estate of Magdalena! In 1696, a year after his death, Jacob's portion of the inheritance was sold at public auction in Amsterdam. It had in the meantime been enriched, to a total of twenty-one paintings by Johannes Vermeer, the "masterlike" painter of Delft.

AMSTERDAM AMATEURS

One buyer at the Dissius auction is well known. This was the Mennonite merchant Isaac Rooleeuw (1650–1710), who managed to acquire two excellent works. The first lot of the auction was immediately hammered down to him for 155 guilders: "A Damsel who weighs gold...painted with extraordinary art and power" (cat. 10). He also became the lucky owner of number two in the catalogue: "A Maid who pours Milk, outstandingly good" (cat. 5). Rooleeuw was even prepared to pay 175 guilders. He then let paintings by Vermeer pass by, even though they were described as: "uncommonly handsome," "very good," "artful and rare," "powerful and good" and "very handsome."[61] The most important painting, the *View of Delft* (cat. 7), went for 200 guilders to a yet unidentified art lover.

Rooleeuw did not enjoy his two Vermeers for long: in 1701 he went bankrupt. After the assessor Jan Zómer had completed the inventory of the collection, the paintings were bound together in pairs and sealed with the Amsterdam city seal before being sold to the highest bidder.[62] Zómer noted, in his elegant handwriting: "A gold Weigher, by Van der N[M]eer of Delft" and "A Milk Pourer by the same" (fig. 8).[63] After the mention of Duarte's *A Lady Seated at the Virginal*, these are the oldest written references made outside Delft to identifiable works by Vermeer.

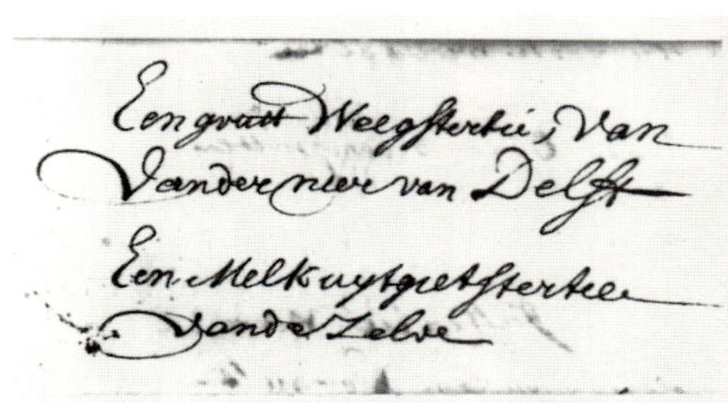

fig. 8. Isaac Rooleeuw inventory, 11 March 1701, DBK 402, fol. 171v, Gemeentearchief, Amsterdam

Another Amsterdam art lover subsequently took possession of one of Van Rooleeuw's two Vermeers. He was a merchant named Paulo van Uchelen (c. 1641–1702), the most renowned bibliophile of his time, and a collector of prints and atlases. After his death the partition of his estate between his heirs was drawn up, including "A gold weigher by van der Meer," assessed at a value of 150 guilders (fig. 9).[64] Paulo van Uchelen junior (1673–1754) inherited the painting. A condition of the testament stipulated that the paintings could not be sold within twenty-five years of the death of his father. Paulo was never prepared to part with the work at all. After his daughter Anna Geertruida van Uchelen (1705–1766) was divorced, she went to live with her father in the house "Zurich" on the Keizersgracht. Only in 1767, after her death, did the *Woman Holding a Balance* again come up for public auction (see cat. 10). The painting had hung in the house "Zurich" for more

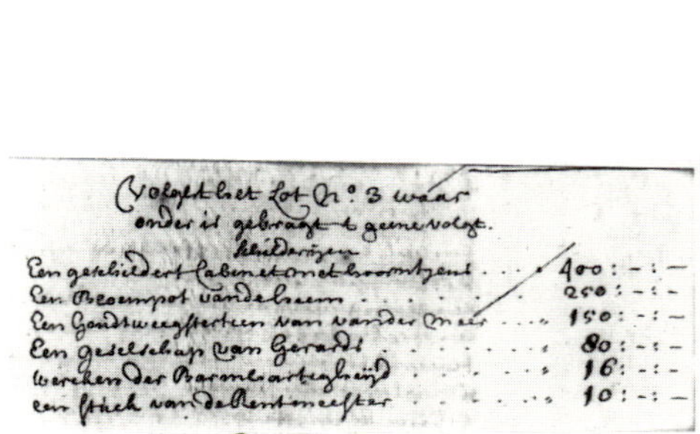

fig. 9. Paulo van Uchelen inventory, 15 August 1703. NA no. 6455, deed 170, fol. 1490, Gemeentearchief, Amsterdam

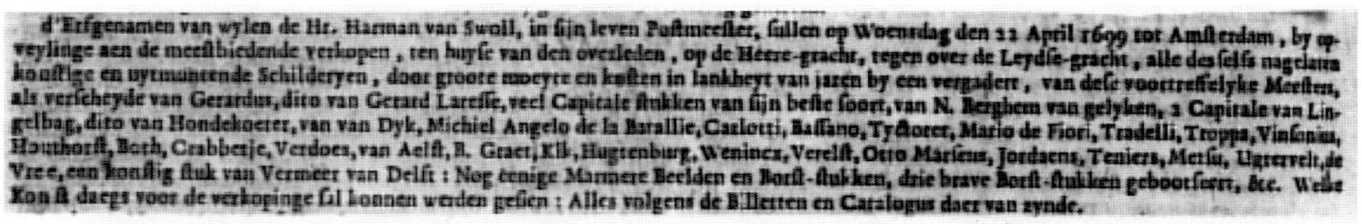
d'Erfgenamen van wylen de Hr. Harman van Swoll, in ſijn leven Poſtmeeſter, ſullen op Woensdag den 22 April 1699 tot Amſterdam, by opveylinge aen de meeſtbiedende verkopen, ten huyſe van den overleden, op de Heere-gracht, tegen over de Leydſe-gracht, alle desſelfs nagelaten konſtige en uytmuntende Schilderyen, door groote moeyte en koſten in lankheyt van jaren by een vergadert, van deſe voortreffelyke Meeſters, als verſcheyde van Gerardus, dito van Gerard Lareſſe, veel Capitale ſtukken van ſijn beſte ſoort, van N. Berghem van gelyken, 2 Capitale van Lingelbag, dito van Hondekoeter, van van Dyk, Michiel Angelo de la Batallie, Carlotti, Baſſano, Tyſtoret, Mario de Fiori, Tradelli, Troppa, Vinſonius, Houthorſt, Both, Crabbetje, Verdoes, van Aelſt, B. Graet, Klb, Hugtenburg, Weninex, Verelſt, Otto Marſeus, Jordaens, Teniers, Metſu, Ugtervelt, de Vree, een konſtig ſtuk van Vermeer van Delft: Nog eenige Marmere Beelden en Borſt-ſtukken, drie brave Borſt-ſtukken gebootſeert, &c. Welke Konſt daegs voor de verkopinge ſal konnen werden geſien: Alles volgens de Billetten en Catalogus daer van zynde.

fig. 10. Advertisement in *Amsterdamsche Courant*, 24 February 1699

than sixty years, so that Houbraken, Weyerman, and Van Gool had ample opportunity to study it.

The second painting that Rooleeuw had bought at the Dissius auction moved into the hands of another collector on the Keizersgracht, the merchant Jacob van Hoek (1671–1718). It was effectively described at his auction in 1719 as "The famous Milkmaid, by Vermeer of Delft, artful."[65] That Houbraken had never heard of this "famous" painting is to his discredit. In his time, the name of "Vermeer of Delft" or "The Delft Vermeer" was certainly fixed in the minds of art lovers in Amsterdam and its environs.

The Amsterdam city surgeon Jan Sysmus was the first person to mention Vermeer after the earlier 1657 citation in the De Renialme collection (page 47). Between 1669 and 1678 Sysmus compiled a list of the artists known to him, with concise indications of their specialties. He referred to Vermeer, painter of architectural pieces and fops (*Jonkertjes*) (see page 32), as "Van der Meer [of] Delft."[66] In short, he was known for his figure paintings (which De Monconys saw) and "perspectieven" (perspectives), which Teding van Berckhout described.

But Amsterdam certainly had collectors who could have informed Houbraken about the "masterlike" Vermeer. The Amsterdam postmaster of the Hamburg mail service, Herman van Swoll (1632–1698), had acquired the *Allegory of Faith* (cat. 20), possibly direct from a (Delft?) commissioner or from his heirs. In 1699 Van Swoll's descendants sold his fine collection, which "had been assembled with great difficulty and effort over the passing of time," out of the house of mourning on the Herengracht. The allegory merited special mention and was noted as well in an announcement in the *Amsterdamsche Courant:* "an artful piece by Vermeer of Delft" (fig. 10).[67]

Although it seems to have gone unnoticed every now and then, the name of Vermeer appeared in this newspaper in announcements of auctions in Amsterdam. On 27 February 1708, for instance, it documented the auction of the estate of Pieter Tjammens, who had lived in Groningen, on the Ossenmarkt. The advertisement included mention of a collection of "Curious Paintings by important Masters" such as "J. van der Meer" that had been kept far away from the capital.[68] On 12 May 1708 a sale was held in the Oudezijds Heerenlogement of "outstandingly artful Paintings by these great Masters, such [as]... J. Vermeer."[69] It is likely, in this instance, that the works that passed under the gavel had earlier been in the Dissius collection.

THE HAGUE

All the references summarized here indicate that the quality of Vermeer paintings appearing at auction was instantly recognized. Because the name and fame of their creator had been slowly forgotten, the paintings were more than once misattributed to the renowned Frans van Mieris the Elder, Pieter de Hooch, or Gabriël Metsu. This was in fact an honor rather than a sign of neglect.

A Lady at the Virginal with a Gentleman (The Music Lesson) (cat. 8) was acquired as a Van

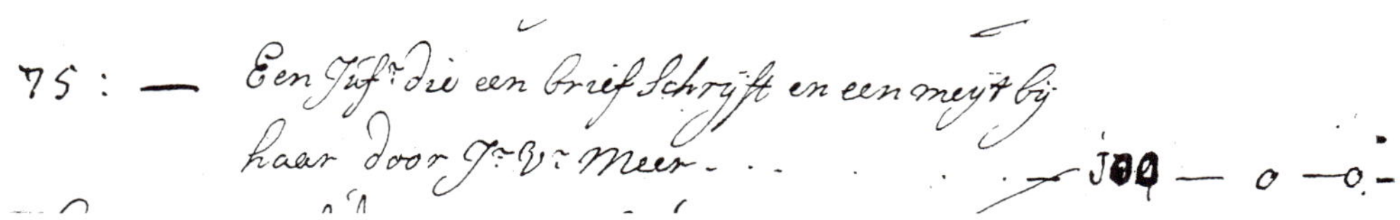

fig. 11. Estate of Franco van Bleyswijck, d. 4 October 1734, Hoge Raad van Adel, The Hague

Mieris by King George III, who in 1762 bought the collection of his consul in Venice, Joseph Smith. Smith in turn had procured the work for a song in 1741 from Angela Carriera, the widow of the painter Gianantonio Pellegrini (1675–1741). We now also know how she came across the painting. In 1696 it had been auctioned for eighty guilders out of the Dissius collection as "A Young Lady playing on the Clavichord in a Room, with a listening Gentleman."[70] On 31 May 1718 the Venetian artist had become a member of the painters' guild of The Hague, where he executed the decorations of the so-called Gouden Zaal (Golden Room) of the Mauritshuis. He also carried out commissions in Amsterdam, which is where he could have bought *The Music Lesson*. He no doubt had it in his baggage in 1719 when he traveled via London and Paris to Venice, where his wife Angela usually resided (see cat. 8).

One Vermeer was probably accessible in The Hague for a substantial period of time during the eighteenth century. It hung in a house on the Korte Vijverberg 3, a short distance from the Mauritshuis. This was the *Lady Writing a Letter with Her Maid*, also known as "the Vermeer of Lord Beit" (cat. 19). This painting had a remarkable history. After the death of Vermeer, the baker Van Buyten had accepted it from Vermeer's widow as security against a debt.[71] At some unknown time it was sold (by Van Buyten himself?) to the regent Josua van Belle, burgomaster of Rotterdam. Long after his death it continued to hang in his home on the Hoogstraat, flanked by expensive Italian works. Between 1730 and 1734 it was in the Delft collection of the magistrate Franco van Bleyswijck, a descendant of the previously mentioned city historian (see cat. 19).

Van Bleyswijck's work found a new, illustrious owner in the person of the Hague burgomaster Hendrick van Slingelandt (1702–1759). He was assigned the work at the partition of an inheritance in 1734, on which occasion it was described as "A Damsel who writes a letter and a maid next to her by J. v. Meer" (fig. 11). At first the value of the work was estimated at seventy-five guilders, but later it was raised to one hundred guilders.[72] In 1750 Gerard Hoet compiled a description of the exquisite collection on the Korte Vijverberg.[73] It turns out that for Hoet, "J. v.d. Meer van Delft" was not a forgotten painter at all. His fellow townsmen Weyerman and Van Gool, the latter of whom knew the burgomaster well,[74] remained unaware of the remarkable qualities of this masterpiece by Johannes Vermeer. Altogether unintentionally, they contributed to the eclipsed fame of the "masterlike" painter from Delft.

III. *Vermeer Abroad*

IN THE MANNER OF REMBRANDT, DE HOOCH, AND METSU

Outside Holland, works by Johannes Vermeer of Delft drew appreciation under wrong names. In 1742 the Elector of Saxony, August III, acquired the *Girl Reading a Letter at an Open Window* (page 73, fig. 11) as a Rembrandt. The attribution of the painting changed in

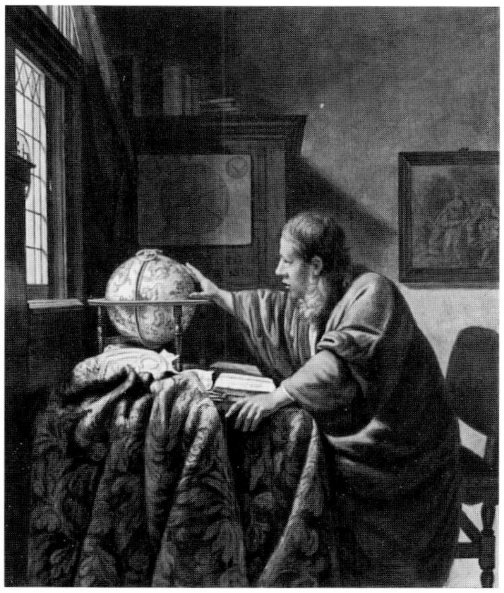

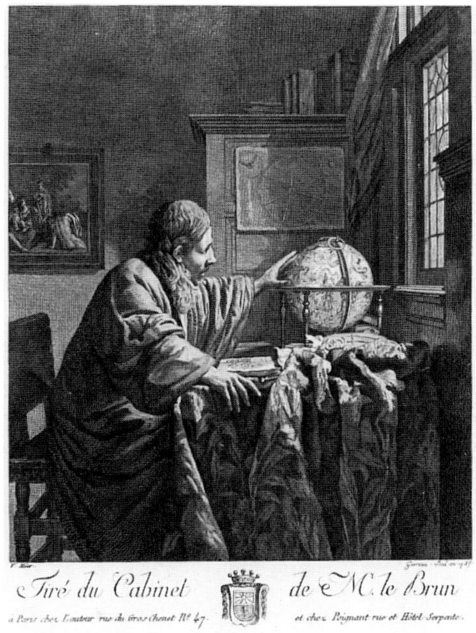

LEFT: fig. 12. Abraham Delfos, '*The Astronomer' after Vermeer*, 1794, watercolor, Rijksmuseum, Amsterdam

RIGHT: fig. 13. Louis Garreau, '*The Astronomer' after Vermeer*, engraving, from page 49 of Lebrun 1792

the course of years. In a 1747 inventory it was described as in the "Maniera di Rembran[d]t" (manner of Rembrandt) and in 1801 the name of Rembrandt's pupil Govaert Flinck was mentioned. From 1826 to 1860 it was attributed to Pieter de Hooch. Only in 1862 was Vermeer's signature published.[75]

King George III thought he was buying a painting by the universally admired Frans van Mieris when he acquired Vermeer's *Music Lesson* in 1762. Sir Oliver Millar described it as "the most important picture that George III, albeit unwittingly, added to his collection."[76] In 1784 an art dealer, Joseph Paillet (1748–1814), tried to warm Louis XVI of France to the purchase of Vermeer's *Astronomer*. His sales pitch, that paintings by the Delft master were rare, seems to have been ill-conceived. After all, the work was neither a De Hooch, nor a Metsu, leave alone a Rembrandt. The hoped-for transaction fell through.

Vermeer's *Astronomer* returned to the Netherlands and, together with *The Geographer* (cat. 16), found its way to several renowned collections in Amsterdam. In that city paintings by Vermeer had long been treasured collectors' objects. Jan Danser Nijman, merchant on the Keizersgracht, became the new owner of both paintings. In 1794 he asked Abraham Delfos (1731–1820) to render *The Astronomer* in watercolor (fig. 12), which indicates his appreciation.[77] Danser Nijman had already acquired *The Lacemaker* (cat. 17) in 1778, and he also managed to get hold of *A Lady Standing at the Virginal* (cat. 21).[78] At the 1797 sale of his collection, *The Astronomer* and *The Geographer* were together for the last time. A prominent collector, Jan Gildemeester (1744–1799), acquired *The Astronomer* for 270 guilders, while the print publisher Christiaan Josi (1768–1828) bought the "pendant" for half that amount, 133 guilders.[79]

Josi was a connoisseur who, starting in 1800, had chronicled events in the art market. His notes were published in 1821, and although rarely consulted, contain a number of acute observations concerning Vermeer. He praised the simplicity of his subjects and the truth of his expression. Reading the catalogue of the 1696 sale, Josi thought the prices paid for works by Vermeer to be on the low side, in view of their quality.[80] Josi knew *The Milkmaid* (which was with Creejans van Winter), *The Astronomer* (a self-portrait, thought Josi) and *The Geographer*, and he commented that the connoisseurs of his time knew how to appreciate the works of Vermeer. These individuals were, of course, all those collectors of Amsterdam who had owned one or more paintings by the master: Pieter (later his daughter Creejans) van Winter, Jan Gildemeester, Pieter van Lennep, Jan Danser Nijman, Hendrik Muilman, but also the dealers, such as Aarnoud de Lange, Pieter Fouquet and Jan Wubbels.[81]

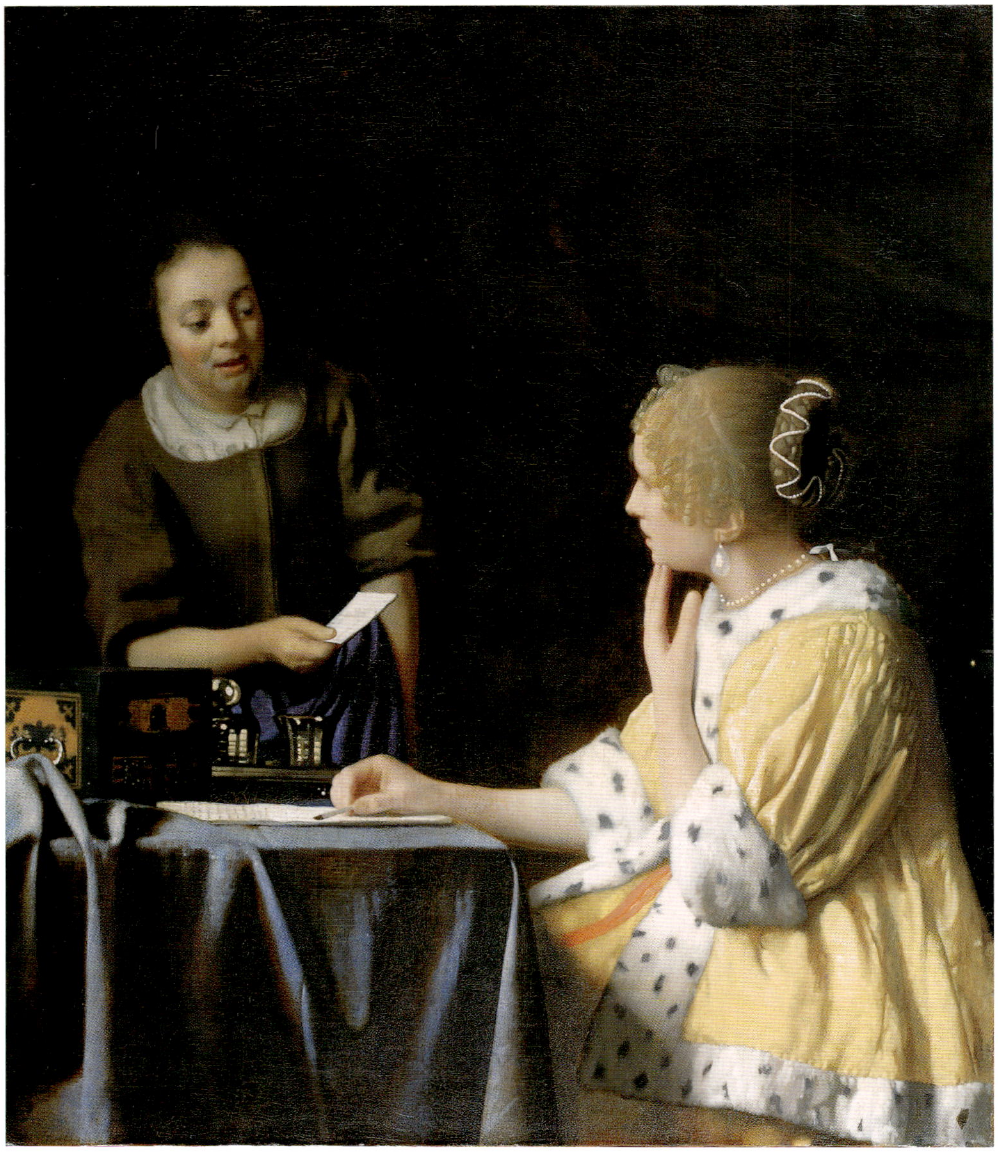

fig. 14. Johannes Vermeer, *Mistress and Maid*, c. 1667, oil on canvas, © The Frick Collection, New York

VERMEER IN TRANSIT

In 1784 the French engraver Louis Garreau, temporarily in Amsterdam, made a print after *The Astronomer*, which was at the time the showpiece of the collection of the widow Fizeaux.[82] The engraving appeared only in 1792, in a supplement to the illustrated catalogue of masterpieces published by the art dealer Jean Baptiste Pierre Lebrun (1748–1813), entitled: "Gallery of Flemish, Dutch, and German painters" (fig. 13).[83] There Lebrun made his oft-quoted comment concerning historians' neglect of Vermeer, who was appreciated in Holland but nowhere else. As mentioned, the dealer Paillet and his Dutch colleague Jean Fouquet (1729–1800) offered *The Astronomer* to the French king, with no success.[84] Lebrun attributed to Vermeer a preference for effects of sunlight and deceptive realism. "He is a very great painter, in the fashion of Metsu."[85]

After the French Revolution various Vermeers drifted away from the Amsterdam collections. How exactly this transpired is unclear. When *Mistress and Maid* (fig. 14) appeared at auction in Paris in 1802, the catalogue announced: "Here, for the first time, we have occasion to mention this able painter in our catalogues and to offer amateurs one of his striking works."[86] The concept of a good unknown artist of the Golden Age was beginning to sink in.

In 1811 a group of paintings passed under the gavel in Paris, "Coming from Journeys as much in Italy as in Flanders, in Holland, in Switzerland and in Geneva," according to the title page of the catalogue. Paillet bought *A Woman Asleep* (page 20, fig. 6),[87] which had been lost since 1737, when it was sold at an Amsterdam auction.[88] Lebrun wrote the catalogue description: "This master observer of the most pithy effects of nature has been able to render them with great success."[89]

Interest in the Delft master continued to gain momentum. In the catalogue that John Smith published in 1833 of "the Most Eminent Dutch" and other painters, Vermeer crops up as a pupil or follower of Metsu, as well as of De Hooch. "This painter is so little known, by reason of the scarcity of his works, that it is quite inexplicable how he attained the excellence many of them exhibit."[90] Like Lebrun, Smith was a well-informed art dealer. He observed that, in addition to works resembling Metsus and De Hoochs, Vermeer had also made paintings of other subjects: "for his talents were equally adapted to landscape painting, and views in towns." Smith announced: "One of his best performances in this branch, representing a view of the town of Delft, at sunset, is now in the Hague Museum." He referred to "this superb painting" as a remarkable acquisition by King William I.[91]

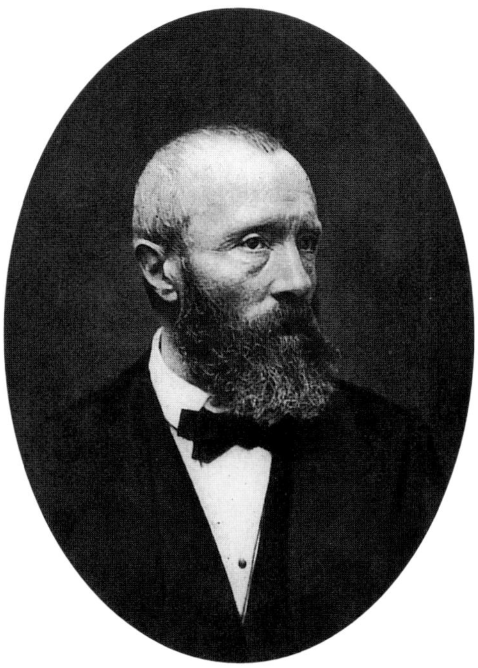

fig. 15. Photograph of Thoré-Bürger from the sale catalogue of the Thoré-Bürger collection, 1892

VERMEER REDISCOVERED

The *View of Delft* was the touchstone in Thoré-Bürger's much-celebrated "rediscovery" of Vermeer. William Bürger, pseudonym for Étienne-Joseph-Théophile Thoré (1807–1869) (fig. 15), brought Vermeer to international attention in 1866 in the *Gazette des Beaux-Arts*.[92] His invention of the sobriquet "sphinx of Delft," which is still whispered with a little *frisson*, only disguised his lack of relevant information. In spite of his inability to distinguish the hand of the Delft Vermeer from that of a Haarlem landscape painter of almost the same name, Thoré-Bürger overshadowed other efforts to rehabilitate the artist.

It was King William I who insisted on having the *View of Delft* placed in "his" Mauritshuis. His principal motivation may have been the realization that this scene depicted the Orange city of Delft, where William of Orange, the "father of the fatherland," had been murdered and buried. Thoré-Bürger must have known John Smith's 1833 description of seeing the painting in the Mauritshuis in 1842: "At the museum of The Hague, a superb and most unusual landscape arrests all visitors...."[93]

Thus it was King William I (with his advisors) and John Smith, not Thoré-Bürger, who were the true rediscoverers of Vermeer. Van Eijnden and Van der Willigen wrote in their *Geschiedenis der vaderlandsche schilderkunst*, 1816: "It goes without saying that the Works of the so-called Delft Van der Meer deserve a place in the most prestigious art collections." In addition to *The Milkmaid* and the *The Little Street* (both then with Creejans van Winter in Amsterdam) they also mentioned "A portrayal of the city of Delft ... which, being marvelously [and] artfully rendered, is greatly praised."[94]

After Josi, Van Eijnden and Van der Willigen, and Smith, compilers of lexicons and catalogues also began to mention Vermeer's name. In 1842 Immerzeel mentioned the *View of Delft* together with a painting by Egbert van der Poel that for some time enjoyed fame because it depicted the stairs in the Delft Prinsenhof where William of Orange had been murdered.[95] In 1850 Nagler knew of four paintings by the master, in 1860 Kramm claimed to know of six, and in 1862 Waagen came up with six actual titles for works.[96] Thoré-Bürger, meanwhile, did research in the collections in Berlin, Brunswick, Brussels, Dresden, Vienna, and, naturally, The Hague. He not only urged his wealthy friends to buy a Vermeer, but also advised newcomers to the art market, such as Casimir Périer, Isaac Pereire, Baron

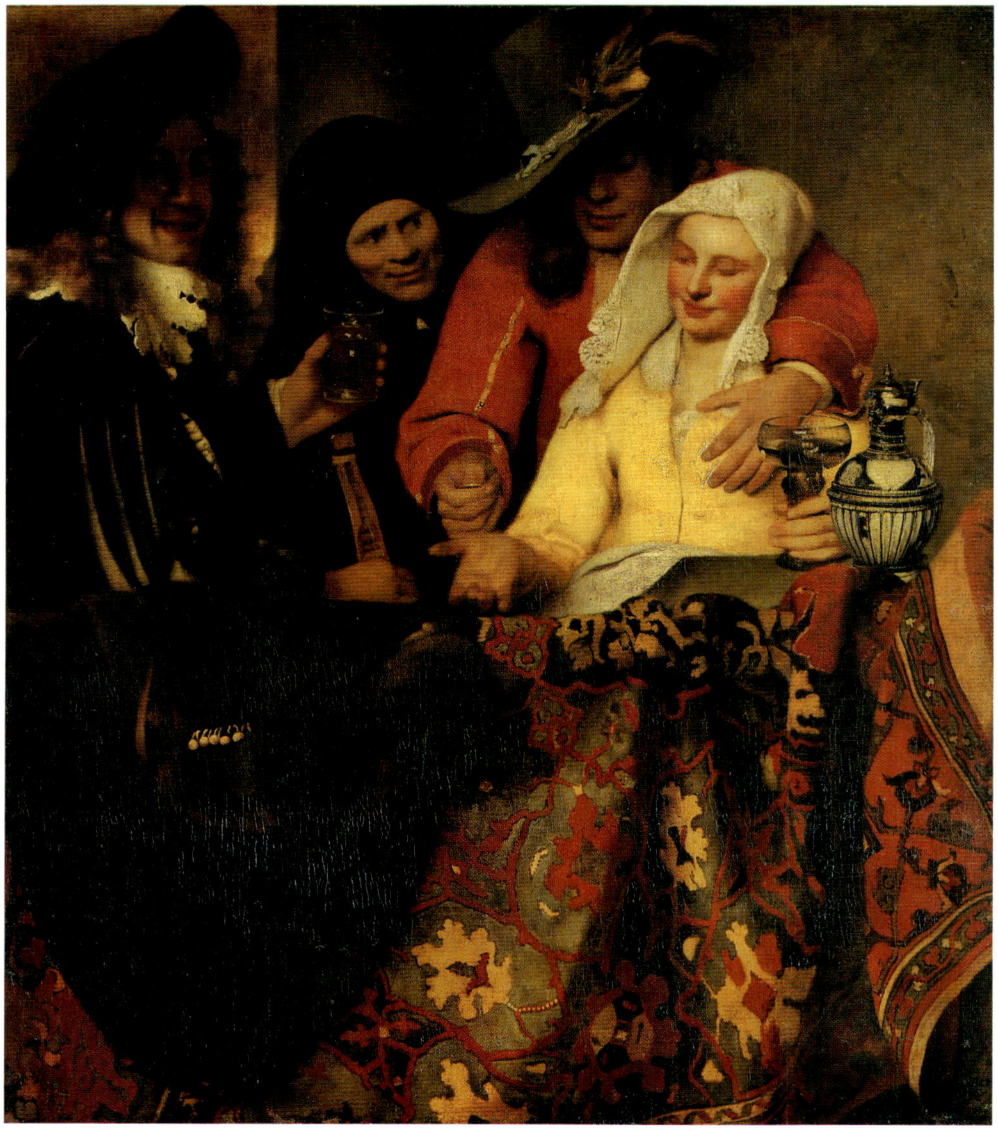

fig. 16. Johannes Vermeer, *The Procuress*, 1656, oil on canvas, Staatliche Kunstsammlungen Dresden, Gemäldegalerie Alte Meister

Cremer, Léopold Double, James de Rothschild, and Barthold Suermondt (cats. 10, 12, 16) to do the same.

In 1860, Charles Blanc published an informative report identifying Thoré-Bürger as the person who was responsible for the rehabilitation of the Delft painter.[97] Blanc listed among Thoré-Bürger's triumphs the identification of two Vermeers in German collections: *The Girl with the Wineglass* ("La Coquette") in Brunswick (cat. 6), which, back in 1849, had passed as a work by "Jacob van der Meer," and *The Procuress* in Dresden (fig. 16), which also had a nametag stating "Jacob van der Meer." In 1858 Thoré-Bürger ascribed both to Johannes Vermeer of Delft.[98] He admitted to having been swayed by a note from the Berlin museum director Gustav Waagen (1794–1864), who had been the first to recognize the hand of Vermeer in the *Girl Reading a Letter at an Open Window*, also in Dresden (page 73, fig. 11).[99] As previously stated, Waagen had also been the first connoisseur to recognize the *Art of Painting* as a genuine Vermeer, much to the resentment of Thoré-Bürger.

Blanc's article appeared with a title filled with questions: "Jean ver Meer or Van der Meer, of Delft, Born around 1632?–died in...." (fig. 17). He cited Lebrun (discussed above) as the earliest "connoisseur" of the work of the Delft painter. "This Van der Meer, about whom the historians have not spoken, says Lebrun, is a very great painter in the manner of Metsu; his works are rare."[100] He accompanied this quotation with a reproduction of a picture ascribed to Vermeer, the *Rustic Cottage* (Staatliche Museen, Berlin). This attribution disturbed no one at the time. After all, in addition to *The Little Street* (cat. 4) and the *View of Delft* (cat. 7) yet a third cityscape had been offered for sale at the 1696 auction: "A View of some Houses by ditto [J. vander Meer van Delft]."[101]

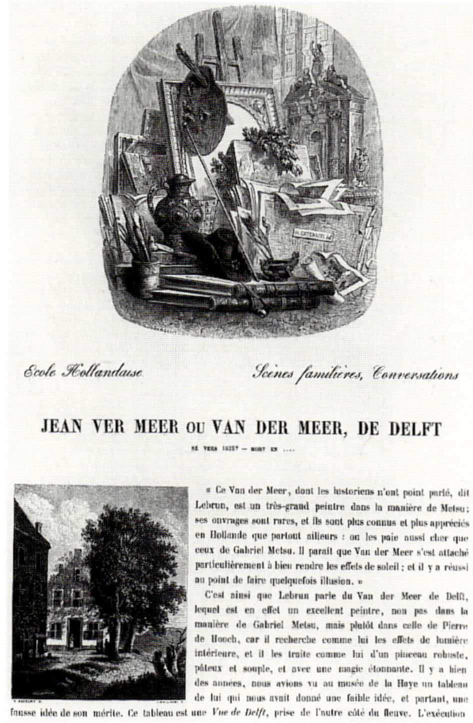

École Hollandaise — *Scènes familières, Conversations*

JEAN VER MEER OU VAN DER MEER, DE DELFT

NÉ VERS 1632? — MORT EN ....

« Ce Van der Meer, dont les historiens n'ont point parlé, dit Lebrun, est un très-grand peintre dans la manière de Metsu; ses ouvrages sont rares, et ils sont plus connus et plus appréciés en Hollande que partout ailleurs : on les paie aussi cher que ceux de Gabriel Metsu. Il paraît que Van der Meer s'est attaché particulièrement à bien rendre les effets de soleil; et il y a réussi au point de faire quelquefois illusion. »

C'est ainsi que Lebrun parle du Van der Meer de Delft, lequel est en effet un excellent peintre, non pas dans la manière de Gabriel Metsu, mais plutôt dans celle de Pierre de Hooch, car il recherche comme lui les effets de lumière intérieure, et il les traite comme lui d'un pinceau robuste, pâteux et souple, et avec une magie étonnante. Il y a bien des années, nous avions vu au musée de la Haye un tableau de lui qui nous avait donné une faible idée, et partant, une fausse idée de son mérite. Ce tableau est une *Vue de Delft*, prise de l'autre côté du fleuve. L'exécution

fig. 17. Page from *Blanc 1860–1863*

The *Rustic Cottage* was in the collection of Barthold Suermondt in Aix-la-Chapelle, who had bought it in 1856 out of a Liège collection. In 1860 Waagen himself compiled a catalogue of the Aix collection and believed he recognized the hand of Philips Koninck in this "Cottage rustique."[102] Thoré-Bürger, who had advised Suermondt on the sale, totally disagreed with Waagen and wrote in his foreword to Waagen's catalogue: "According to me, this is certainly a work–a masterpiece–by Jan van der Meer of Delft."[103] A considerable time after the Suermondt collection had been acquired by the Berlin museum, Abraham Bredius (1855–1946) published an article on this cityscape, "A pseudo-Vermeer in the Berlin Gallery." Remarkably, he ascribed the picture to the Zwolle painter and Golden Age emulator Dirk Jan van der Laan (1759–1829). Bredius was rather proud of his vision: "What heresy, is it not, to declare a Vermeer [to be] a picture of the eighteenth or nineteenth century?"[104] In 1907, Hofstede de Groot assigned dozens of paintings that soulmates of Thoré-Bürger had identified as authentic Vermeers to such diverse masters as Pieter de Hooch, Jan Steen, Jacobus Vrel, Gabriël Metsu, and Cornelis de Man.[105]

BEST SELLER

The first Vermeer in the United States was *Young Woman with a Water Pitcher* (cat. 11), which Henry G. Marquand donated in 1889 to the young Metropolitan Museum of Art in New York. It was soon followed by *The Concert* (page 17, fig. 1). Isabella Stewart Gardner (1840–1924), who knew her way around Paris, had personally acquired the work there in 1892 at the auction of Thoré-Bürger's collection.[106] This act immediately made her a formidable competitor on the international art market.[107]

Isabella's collecting rival was J. Pierpont Morgan Sr. (1837–1913). He relished comparisons to Lorenzo de' Medici, "the Magnificent." In 1907 the antique dealer G. S. Hellman showed Vermeer's *A Lady Writing* (cat. 13) to Morgan, who, unlike Isabella Stewart Gardner, had taken no notice of recent publications concerning this Delft miracle painter. "The great Dutchman's name was strange to the Morgan ear," has become a famous pronouncement. Even so, Pierpont Morgan must have recognized the absolute quality of this painting, since he thought the asking price of $100,000 justified. "'I'll take it,' snapped Morgan, and the deal was concluded."[108]

Vermeer had become a best seller. In 1928 the former director of the Mauritshuis, Abraham Bredius, sold his *Allegory of Faith* (cat. 20) to an American collector for $300,000. It had hung in the Mauritshuis, on loan, for almost twenty-five years, and in the Museum Boymans in Rotterdam for another five. Bredius had acquired it in 1899 for less than seven hundred guilders.

ETERNAL FAME

In 1935 Vermeer at last received what to many had long seemed his by right: eternal fame. The Delft painter was honored in Rotterdam with his first solo exhibition under the rubric: "Vermeer–origins and influence." The catalogue set the tone for the time: "Next to *Rembrandt* the figure of *Vermeer* rises above all other artists of the great age of the seventeenth century."[109] Jan Steen and Frans Hals were hereby relegated to Vermeer's shadow.

The author of the catalogue text, Dirk Hannema, no doubt wished to erect a kind of monument to the Delft painter but, regrettably, his optimism knew no bounds. He claimed to have assembled the largest number of Vermeers in human memory, but six of the fifteen

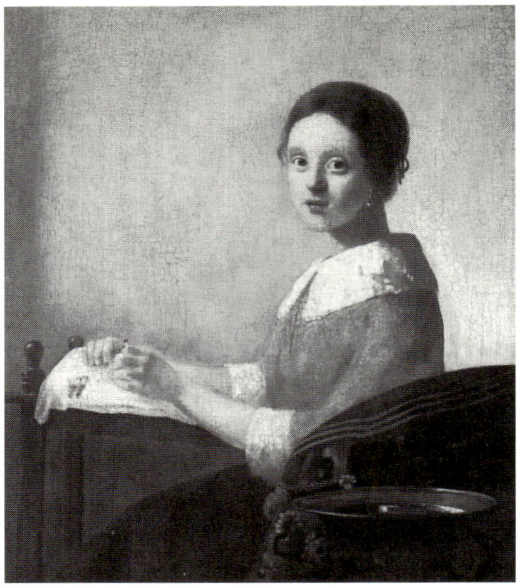

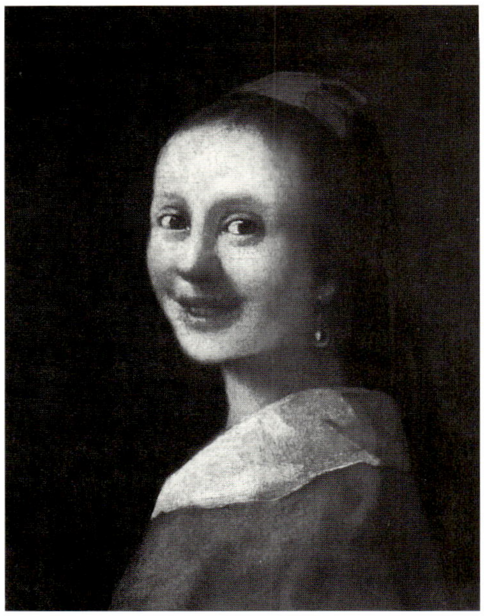

FAR LEFT: fig. 18. Anonymous twentieth-century artist, *A Lacemaker*, oil on canvas, National Gallery of Art, Washington, Special Collection

LEFT: fig. 19. Anonymous twentieth-century artist, *A Laughing Girl*, oil on canvas, National Gallery of Art, Washington, Special Collection

works exhibited were not by the hand of the master.[110] The catalogue that A. B. de Vries published four years later is a good reflection of the distorted image of Vermeer created by the Rotterdam exhibition.[111]

De Vries' book described and illustrated two works now in storage at the National Gallery of Art in Washington: a *Lacemaker* and a *Laughing Girl* (figs. 18, 19).[112] In 1937 the American collector Andrew Mellon, who bought them with the assurances of the preeminent authorities of the day, Wilhelm von Bode, director of the museum in Berlin ("convincing"), and Willem Martin, director of the Mauritshuis ("whose authorship admits to no doubt whatsoever"), bequeathed these paintings to the nation.[113]

It astonishes us today that these works were not at once recognized as imitations based on paintings in The Hague (cat. 15) and Paris (cat. 17). It was almost inevitable in this unstable context that someone like Han van Meegeren dared paint his *Supper at Emmaus* (Museum Boymans-van Beuningen, Rotterdam) (fig. 20). With the benefit of hindsight, it is incomprehensible that Bredius and Hannema pronounced this painting to be genuine. In 1938 the Museum Boymans bought the painting for more than 500,000 guilders, clearly the price of a true Vermeer. Regrettably this deliberate forgery was unmasked too late, as "An early Vermeer of 1937."[114]

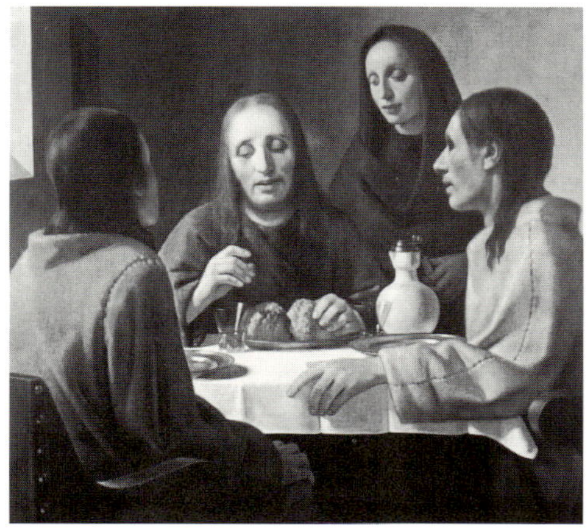

fig. 20. Han van Meegeren, *Supper at Emmaus*, c. 1937, oil on canvas, Museum Boymans-van Beuningen, Rotterdam

Fortunately Vermeer was to remain the prey of hagiographers and forgers for only a short while. The Van Meegeren affair had an unexpected cleansing effect. Though it did violence to the reputation of connoisseurship, it did cure a lot of people of their illusions. The post-Van Meegeren period saw the publication of monographs by Pieter T. A. Swillens, Sir Lawrence Gowing, Vitale Bloch, and Ludwig Goldscheider, but it was above all Albert Blankert's sober study of 1975 that acted as a kind of medicinal purge.[115] In addition to a critical catalogue, the book contained an important chapter on "Vermeer and his public." For the first time it drew attention to the group of collectors and connoisseurs of the late seventeenth, eighteenth, and early nineteenth centuries who viewed Vermeer not as a "sphinx" but as a first-class painter.[116] This elite group appeared to be much larger than everyone assumed. More important, however, is the recent rediscovery of a number of prominent connoisseurs in high circles, who described Vermeer in his lifetime as a "celebre Peijntre."

I owe several refinements in the nuances of this essay and some new data to Albert Blankert and Jaap van der Veen, to whom I am most grateful. I am also indebted to my assistant Carola Vermeeren, whose visits to the Amsterdam and Hague archives resulted in a number of new findings.

1. Gemeentearchief, The Hague (notary J. Vosch, no. 3561, fol. 28): "een stuck schilderie geschildert bij...haeren man Zal[iger] waer wert uijtgebeeld de Schilderconst...." See Bredius 1885, 220; Blankert 1992, 189 (wrongly as 24 January 1676) and Montias 1993, 383–384, doc. 363.
2. Waagen 1862, 2: 110; Blankert 1992, 189.
3. Montias 1993, 268–276 (revised Dutch edition of Montias 1989).
4. See especially Van der Veen 1992, 100, and Van der Waals 1992, 184.
5. Montias 1993, 381–383, doc. 361: "Twee personagien waeraff d'eene een brieff sit en schrijft ende d'ander mede een personagie spelende op een cyter."
6. Montias 1993, 402–403; doc. 442; Hoet 1752–1770, 1: 34, no. 4.
7. "Een Graft besoeckende van der Meer," Gemeentearchief, Amsterdam (NA 1915, notary F. Uyttenbogaert, 27 June 1657, 676); Bredius 1915–1922, 1: 233. This document was not mentioned in the Vermeer literature until Montias 1980, 47–48, no. 11.
8. Sale catalogue, Amsterdam, 24 March 1761, 3, no. 56: "Jupiter, Venus en Mercurius, door J. ver Meer." (Lugt no. 1150); see Montias 1991, 46, 49, ill. 3 and Blankert 1992, 203, no. 38a.
9. "Commies van de Finantien van Holland." On the two Van Berckels, see Wijsenbeek-Olthuis 1987, 268–269; the biographical information came from the archives of the Centraal Bureau voor Genealogie (The Hague).
10. This document was undervalued in Montias 1989, 140 n. 31, and Montias 1993, 304–305 n. 31.
11. "Een juff[e]r spelend op de Clavecimbael door Vermeer," Gemeentearchief, Delft, ONA 3003–11, deed 375, 18r; see also Wijsenbeek-Olthuis 1987, 266 and 392 n. 16.
12. "A Delphes ie [je] vis le Peintre Vermer."; De Monconys 1677, 2: 142–145. On the various editions of the diary, see De Marsy 1880, 13; for more on De Monconys and Vermeer, Bredius 1880–1881, 412–413; Neurdenburg 1951, 35–38.
13. Since Bredius 1885, 219–220, this baker has been assumed to be the baker Van Buyten.
14. De Marsy 1880, 30.
15. Thoré-Bürger was the first to quote from De Monconys' journal (Thoré-Bürger 1866, 323). De Marsy 1880 gave a survey of the journal, focusing on art matters.
16. De Marsy 1880, 31–32.
17. Montias 1987, 69.
18. "Un M. Beyau, qui a grande quantité de tableaux de *Dau*.": De Marsy 1880, 32; E. J. Sluijter does mention De Monconys' visit to Leiden, but not the one paid to De Bye (Leiden 1988, 35–36); however, see Martin 1911, 71 and 158–160.
19. De Monconys 1677, 2: 145 and 150; Amsterdam 1982, 36, 59–60, which mentions De Monconys' visit but not the one to Vermeer; "M. de Zulcon" (see De Marsy 1880, 29 n. 6) is mistakenly identified as Constantijn Huygens Jr.
20. Meinsma 1896, 227.
21. De Monconys 1677, 2: 150; De Marsy 1880, 31, omitted this second visit to Huygens from his text (Huygens Jr. lived with his father on the square called "Het Plein" until 1668, see Amsterdam 1982, 15, 65).
22. The Huygens family features only marginally in Blankert 1992, 124, 155 and 216.
23. Heesakkers 1987, 84–86; for a summary of Huygens' rôle as art advisor, see Nieuwenhuis-van Berkum 1987, 116–118.
24. Lodewijk Huygens (1631–1699) married Jacomina Teding van Berckhout in 1674 (see Van Gelder 1956A, 50, and Schutte 1974, 29–30). Pieter van Berckhout was married to a daughter of Maria Paets (Schmidt 1986, 71): later on the Paets family may have owned Vermeer's *The Astronomer* (fig. 6).
25. Manuscript in Koninklijke Bibliotheek, The Hague, inv. no. 129 D 16, vol. 1; see Schmidt 1986, 211 n. 41, Montias 1991, 48, and Montias 1993, 377–378, doc. 325*bis. Like De Monconys, Teding van Berckhout also visited the studio of Dou in Leiden (Rotterdam 1991, 219 n. 2).
26. Teding van Berckhout's French reads: "ou estoit Monsr de Zuylichem, van der Horst et Nieuwport." A. Leerintveld identified these travel companions (letter of 9 January 1995); on Van der Horst, see NNBW, 1: cols. 1157–1158; on Nieupoort, see Schutte 1976, 97–99.
27. Montias 1993, 377, doc. 325*bis.
28. On the interpretation of "perspectives," see the essays by Blankert and Wadum in this catalogue.
29. Montias 1991, 48.
30. Teding van Berckhout even moved to Delft in 1670 and served on the city council there, see: Schmidt 1986, 70–77.
31. Schutte 1974, 26: in 1707, at an advanced age, Pieter married for a second time, to Maria van Bleyswijck.
32. "Gelukkig rees' er uyt zyn vier VERMEER.": Van Bleyswijck 1667, 854 (see also Blankert 1992, 154 and 211).
33. Montias 1989, 182 n. 49; on Larson, see Neurdenburg 1948, 116, 232 and 234.
34. "Een tronie van Vermeer": Bredius 1915–1922, 1: 325, 328 (Blankert 1992, 203, no. 32b).
35. Leerintveld 1990, 181.
36. Duarte's name was already connected to Vermeer's "clavecingel" by Blankert 1975, 92, and Blankert 1978, 61; on Duarte and Huygens see also Mauritshuis 1993A, 294–296.
37. Bredius 1880–1881, 404.
38. The Hague 1994, 44–45, and 338–339.
39. Huygens 1911–1917, 4: 465, no. 4772 (see also 477, no. 4812, 486, no. 4843, 488, no. 4849, 489, no. 4851, 510–511, no. 4910).
40. According to Wijsenbeek-Olthuis 1987, 272, there used to be a rare example of a "Ruckers" in Delft (but it was in the collection of Diederik Durven (1676–1740), see Van Rhede van de Kloot 1891, 84–85). On Huygens and music, see The Hague 1994, 79 n. 10. For literature on Vermeer's virginals, see especially Blankert 1978, 77 n. 64.
41. "Die meesterlyck betrad zyn pade" and "die 't meesterlyck hem na kost klaren.": Blankert 1975, 90–91, and Blankert 1992, 154.

42. Blankert 1975, 118 n. 1a.
43. Amsterdam 1985, 4–5; on 'aemulatio' and 'imitato' see also De Jongh 1969, 56–60.
44. Houbraken 1718–1721, 1: 236.
45. Houbraken 1718–1721, 3: 337–338: Houbraken was not familiar with Fabritius' perspectives named by Van Bleyswijck, but he did mention that he was a good portrait painter.
46. Havard 1883A, 391–392, mentioned Houbraken 1718–1721, Weyerman 1729–1769, and Van Gool 1750–1751 with disdain.
47. Blankert 1975, 90–100.
48. De Vries 1939, 3; Blankert 1975, 92, first asked the question: "Was Vermeer dus inderdaad in de 18e eeuw 'volledig miskend'?"
49. Blankert 1975, 92.
50. See on the Paets sale Houbraken 1718–1721, 3: 400; Weyerman 1729–1769, 2: 409–410, 3: 57, and Van Gool 1750–1751, 1: 238, 260.
51. Sale Amsterdam, 28 March 1720 (Hoet 1752–1770, 1: 242, nos. 3–4).
52. "Eenige uytstekende konstige schilderyen, daer onder zyn 21 stuks uytnemende krachtig and heerlyk geschildert door wylen J. Vermeer van Delft; verbeeldende verscheyde Ordonnantien, zynde de beste die hy oyt gemaekt heeft"; Dudok van Heel 1975, 159, no. 41. This text does not occur in Montias 1989, 363, doc. 438, or Montias 1993, 401, doc. 438, but was reproduced for the first time by Blankert 1992, 64.
53. Blankert 1975, 9; see especially Neurdenburg 1942, 72–73, and Neurdenburg 1951, 37–38.
54. For example Blankert 1978, 61; Aillaud 1986, 156; Blankert 1992, 155.
55. Wheelock 1977B, 439.
56. Gemeentearchief, Delft, DTB 57, fol. 35 (23 November 1653); see Montias 1987, 71 n. 25, and The Hague 1990, 459.
57. "Welk een schat! En waar is dat alles gebleven?": Bredius 1885, 222 (Bredius mistakenly counted only nineteen); see also Montias 1993, 399–400, doc. 417.
58. Montias 1987, 69–71; Montias 1989, 248.
59. Montias 1993, 365: "in een seeker bouck ... geteikent met de letter A...."
60. Montias 1989, 251–255.
61. Hoet 1752–1770, 1: 34, nos. 1–2: "Een Juffrouw die goud weegt ... extraordinaer konstig en kragtig geschildert" and "Een Meyd die Melk uytgiet, uytnemende goet." Also "ongemeen fraai," "heel goet," "konstig en raer," "kragtig en goet," and "zeer fraei."
62. Dudok van Heel 1975, 162, no. 67; not with Blankert 1975, 149–150, no. 15.
63. Gemeentearchief, Amsterdam (DBK no. 402, fol. 171v/173r, 11 March 1701): "Een gout Weegstertie, van Van der Neer van Delft" and "Een Melkuytgietstertie van de zelve."
64. Gemeentearchief, Amsterdam (notary H. de Wilde, NA 6455, deed 170.1490, 15 August 1703): "Een gout Weegstertien, van vander Meer."
65. "Het vermaerde Melkmeysje, door Vermeer van Delft, konstig." (Sale Amsterdam, 12 April 1719, no. 20); Blankert 1992, 175.
66. Blankert 1992, 211–212; Bredius 1890–1895, 12: 163. Curiously, Sysmus gave the Christian name as "Otto"; Jaap van der Veen believes that Sysmus must have been the same as a "Johannes Sismus, medicinae doctor tot Haerlem," of Rotterdam origins (letter 20 January 1995).
67. Dudok van Heel 1975, 160, no. 53: "door groote moeyte en kosten in lankheyt van jaren by een [was] vergadert" and "een konstig stuk van Vermeer van Delft"
68. Dudok van Heel 1975, 168, no. 110: "curieuse Schilderyen van voorname Meesters."
69. Dudok van Heel 1975, 169, no. 116; "uytmuntende konstige Schilderyen van dese groote Meesters, als ... J. Vermeer." A Haarlem auction of 1718 may have included work by the Haarlem Vermeer (Dudok van Heel 1977A, 113, no. 185).
70. Hoet 1752–1770, 1: 34, no. 6: "Een speelende Juffrouw op de Clavecimbael in een Kamer, met een toeluisterend Monsieur."
71. Montias 1993, 381–383, doc. 361.
72. Manuscript, Family Archives Hoge Raad Van Adel, The Hague, Family Archives Van Slingelandt, inv. no. 106, partition 6 September 1761, portfolio 24, "List of the paintings that hang in the front room" (Lijst van de schilderije[n] die in de voorkamer hangen): "Een juf.r die een brief schrijft en een meijt bij haar door J. v. Meer." On the collection of Van Slingelandt, see Hofstede de Groot 1892A, 229–237.
73. Hoet 1752–1770, 2: 407–408.
74. Jaap van der Veen pointed out to me that Vermeer curiously does not appear in Hoet's list of painters Van Gool forgot to mention in his "Nieuwe schouburg" (see De Vries 1990, 262–265).
75. Hofstede de Groot 1907–1928, 1: 602, no. 34; Mayer-Meintschel 1978–1979, 91, 94 and Blankert 1992, 173–174, no. 6. Blanc illustrated the painting as Pieter de Hooch (Blanc 1860–1863, 2: 7).
76. London 1971, 126.
77. Jan Danser Nijman remains a hazy figure. His mother, Maria Danser, widow of Pieter Nijman, died in 1784 (Amsterdam, Gemeentearchief, DTB 1050, Oude Kerk, 162).
78. Jan Danser Nijman and Nyman were believed to be two different collectors by Blankert 1992, 227 and 229.
79. Sale catalogue, Amsterdam, 16 August 1797, 109–113, nos. 167–168 (Lugt no. 5640); Josi 1821, xix.
80. Josi 1821, xix; in a note he warned against confusion with the Utrecht "vander Meer," whom he believed to be the son of the Delft painter. His text was "rediscovered" by Sulzberger 1948, 37.
81. See also the index in Blankert 1992; close attention to the history of collecting Vermeers was first paid by Blankert 1975, working in collaboration with Willem van de Watering.
82. On Garreau, see Thieme/Becker, 13: 215; according to the caption the painting was in "le cabinet de Fisau" and not in the Lebrun collection, as has sometimes been believed (Havard 1888, 38, no. 39, and Hofstede de Groot 1907–1928, 1: 590, no. 6).
83. "Galerie des peintres flamands, hollandais et allemands" (Lebrun 1792).
84. Foucart 1987, 100–104.
85. Lebrun 1792, 49: "C'est un très-grand peintre, dans la manière de Metsu."
86. Sale catalogue, Paris, 25 January 1802, 64, no. 106: "Voici la première fois que nous avons occasion de citer

dans nos catalogues cet habile peintre, et d'offrir aux amateurs un de ses ouvrages marquans" (Lugt no. 6352).

87. "Provenant de voyages faits tant en Italie, qu'en Flandres, en Hollande, en Suisse, et à Genève." This unpublished record of Vermeer's *A Woman Asleep* in the 1811 auction catalogue was communicated to me by Quentin Buvelot; see Sale catalogue, Paris, 15 April 1811, 54, no. 150 (60 francs to Paillet) (Lugt no. 7970).

88. Sale Amsterdam, 19 December 1737, no. 47 (Blankert 1992, 172, no. 4).

89. Sale catalogue, Paris, 15 April 1811, title page and 54, no. 150: "Ce maître observateur des effets les plus piquans de la nature, a su les rendre avec un grand succès."

90. Smith 1829–1842, 4: 242.

91. Smith 1829–1842, 4: 110.

92. Thoré-Bürger 1866.

93. Thoré-Bürger 1866, 298: "Au musée de La Haye, un paysage superbe et très-singulier arrête tous les visiteurs ...."

94. Van Eijnden/Van der Willigen 1816–1840, 1: 167: "Wij behoeven niet te zeggen, dat de Werken van den zoogenaamden Delftschen Van der Meer in de aanzienlijkste kunstverzamelingen mogen geplaatst worden ..." and "Eene afbeelding van de stad Delft ... die, als verwonderlijk kunstig behandeld, zeer geprezen wordt."

95. Amsterdam, Rijksmuseum, inv. no. A 117 (Rijksmuseum 1976, 448, nr. A 117 and ill.). See Immerzeel 1842–1843, 180; Moes 1909, 195; Niemeijer 1969, 135–139.

96. Nagler 1835–1852, 20: 117; Kramm 1857–1864, 4: 1727; Waagen 1862, 2: 109–110.

97. Blanc 1860–1863, 2: 2.

98. Thoré-Bürger 1858–1860, 2: 75–77.

99. Waagen 1858, 35–36; see also Mayer-Meintschel 1978–1979, 91–99.

100. Blanc 1860 –1863, 2: 1: "Jean ver Meer ou Van der Meer, de Delft, Né vers 1632?–mort en ..." and "Ce Van der Meer, dont les historiens n'ont pas parlé, dit Lebrun, est un très grand peintre dans la manière de Metsu; ses ouvrages sont rares".

101. Hoet 1752–1770, 1: 35, no. 33: "Een Gesicht van eenige Huysen van dito [J. vander Meer van Delft]."

102. Thoré-Bürger/Waagen 1860, 152–153, no. 55; see also 34–35 for earlier attributions to Meindert Hobbema and Jacob van Ruisdael.

103. Thoré-Bürger/Waagen 1860, 34–35; "Pour moi, c'est incontestablement une oeuvre–un chef-d'oeuvre–de Jan van der Meer de Delft..." (see also Thoré-Bürger 1866, 568–569).

104. Bredius 1882, 70: "Ein pseudo-Vermeer in der berliner Galerie" and "Welche Ketzerei, nicht wahr, einen Vermeer für ein Bild aus dem 18. oder 19. Jahrhundert erklären zu wollen?"

105. Hofstede de Groot 1907–1928, 1: 612–613.

106. Blankert 1992, 187-188, no. 17 and ill. 17.

107. Simpson 1988, 72.

108. Allen 1965, 160.

109. Rotterdam 1935, 9: "Naast *Rembrandt* verheft zich de figuur van *Vermeer* boven alle andere kunstenaars van het groote tijdperk der zeventiende eeuw."

110. Rotterdam 1935, 35–39, nos. 79a, 80, 87, 88, 89, 89a; ills. 60, 61, 68, 69, 70 and 71.

111. De Vries 1939, 77–95, nos. 1–43.

112. De Vries 1939, 85, no. 19, ill. 45 and 89–90, no. 31 and ill. 55.

113. Bode 1926, 251: "überzeugend"; Martin 1927–1928, 6–7: "deren Autorschaft keinerlei Zweifel unterliegt." It appears that there was a kind of Vermeer factory in operation at that time.

114. Van den Brandhof 1979, 101–108: "Een vroege Vermeer uit 1937."

115. Swillens 1950; Gowing 1952; Bloch 1954; Goldscheider 1958; Blankert 1975. Swillens 1950, 63–66, nos. A-M, pointed to numerous wrong attributions, in which he included the early Vermeers in Edinburgh and The Hague (cats. 2, 3).

116. Blankert 1975, 90–110; see also the review by Gerson 1977, 288–290.

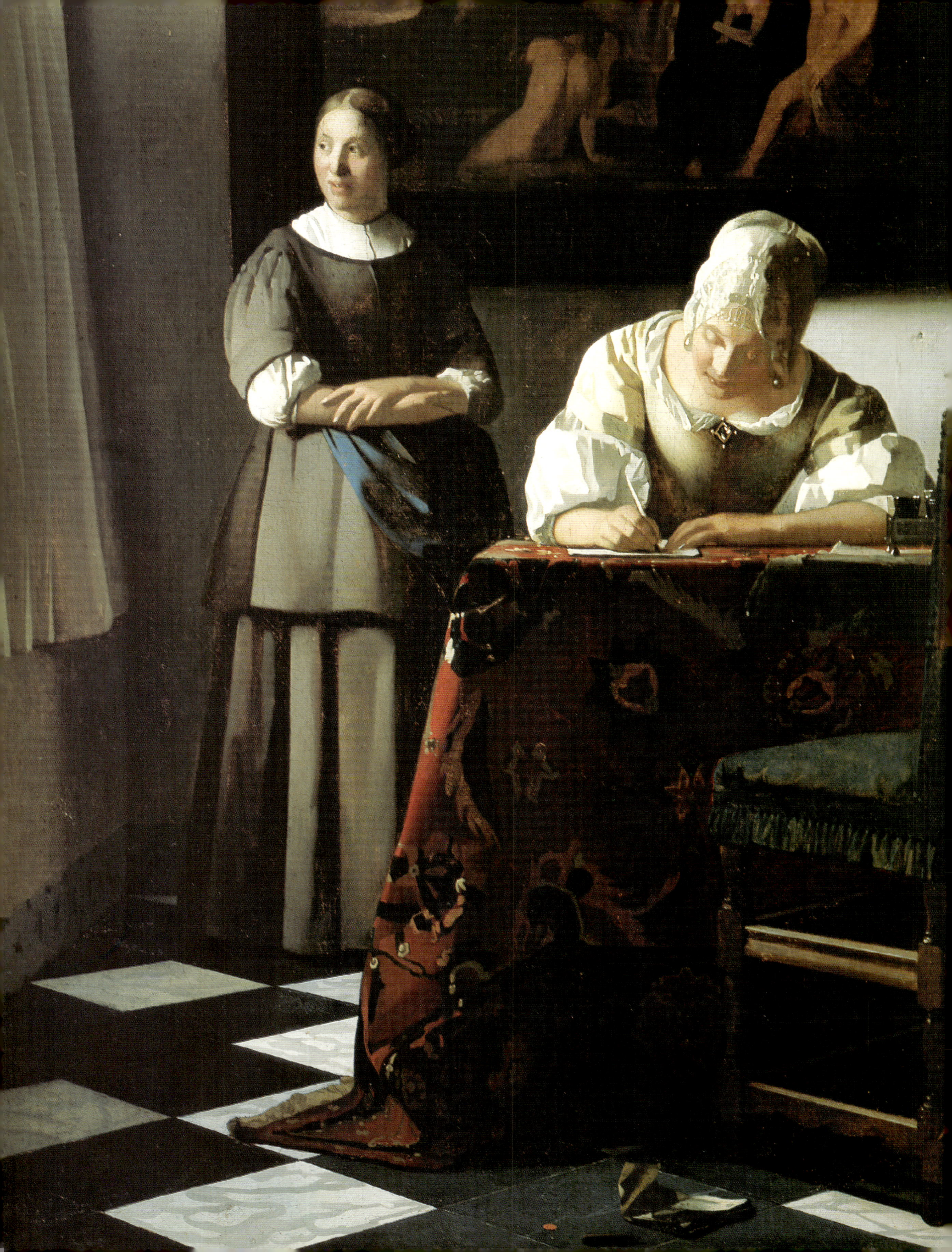

Vermeer in Perspective

JØRGEN WADUM

"KNOWLEDGE BECOMES THE PAINTER," Samuel van Hoogstraeten wrote in his 1678 *Inleyding tot de hooge schoole der schilderkonst* (Introduction to the School of Painting).[1] Clio, muse of History, is depicted at the beginning of the chapter on the image and poetic inventions (*Poetische verdichtselen*). More than ten years earlier, Vermeer had used Clio in his *Art of Painting*, in which he demonstrated not only his learning as a painter and inventor of allegories, but also, as we will see, his knowledge of perspectival theory.

In this large painting a heavy curtain appears to be held aside by an invisible hand: the viewer is invited to enter the painter's studio. The artist is seated, with his back toward us, and on his easel, on a grounded canvas, is an unfinished half-figure of Clio, sketched in white. The size of the canvas would not allow for a larger figure, nor for the trumpet of Fame, usually held by Clio.

The artist has started to paint at the top of the canvas. He seems to have finished the flesh colors and has begun to lay in the leaves of the laurel wreath. It looks like the painter—as pictured by Vermeer—is following tradition by finishing one area before setting up a new palette for the next area.[2] A similar technique can be seen in *Saint Luke Painting the Virgin and Jesus* (fig. 1) by Maerten van Heemskerck (1498–1574). In that work Saint Luke, patron saint of painters, is applying the flesh color of the Child, while the hair and flesh colors of the Virgin are already finished. The rest of the composition is still only a rough sketch.

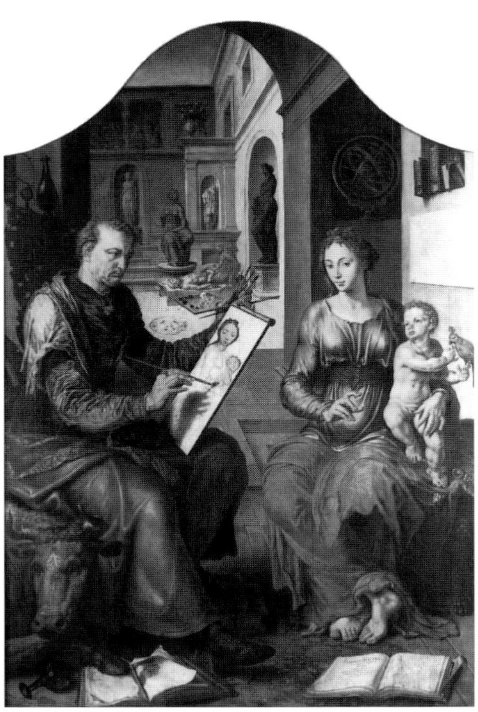

fig. 1. Maerten van Heemskerck, *Saint Luke Painting the Virgin and Jesus*, c. 1550, oil on panel, Musée des Beaux-Arts, Rennes

The general similarities between the two paintings by Van Heemskerck and Vermeer seem to acknowledge sixteenth- and seventeenth-century traditions in painting methods. Saint Luke applies the paint to a panel with a white ground, as was customary in the sixteenth century. The painter in Vermeer's *Art of Painting* (fig. 2) used a colored ground, just as Vermeer did in the majority of his works. Examination shows, however, that Vermeer himself worked areas up 'side-by-side' rather than 'piece-by-piece.' Instead of documenting his particular painting methods, Vermeer's *Art of Painting* was probably intended to emphasize contemporary accomplishments and to pay tribute to his predecessors, and hence to artistic tradition.

The Use of Central Perspective

A closed, bound book stands on end on the table in the middle ground of the *Art of Painting*, and an open book in folio appears at the right edge of the table, next to the painter's elbow. The inventory of Vermeer's estate, made in February 1676, lists a number of books in folio in a back room, and twenty-five other books of various kinds.[3] It is conceivable that some of these were guides to perspective drawing, like the one by Hans Vredeman de Vries (1526/1527–1606) or the books published by Samuel Marolois (c. 1572–c. 1627), Hendrick Hondius (1573–1649), and François Desargues (1593–1662).[4]

Vermeer was familiar with the principles of perspective described in these manuals, as can be seen in his paintings. Remarkably, thirteen paintings still contain physical evidence of Vermeer's system, by which he inserted a pin, with a string attached to it, into the grounded canvas at the vanishing point.[5] With this string he could reach any area of his canvas to create correct orthogonals, the straight lines that meet in the central vanishing point (fig. 3). The vanishing point of the central perspective in the *Art of Painting* is still visible in the paint layer just under the end of the lower map-rod, below Clio's right hand.[6]

Detail, cat. 19

To transfer the orthogonal line described by the string, Vermeer would have applied

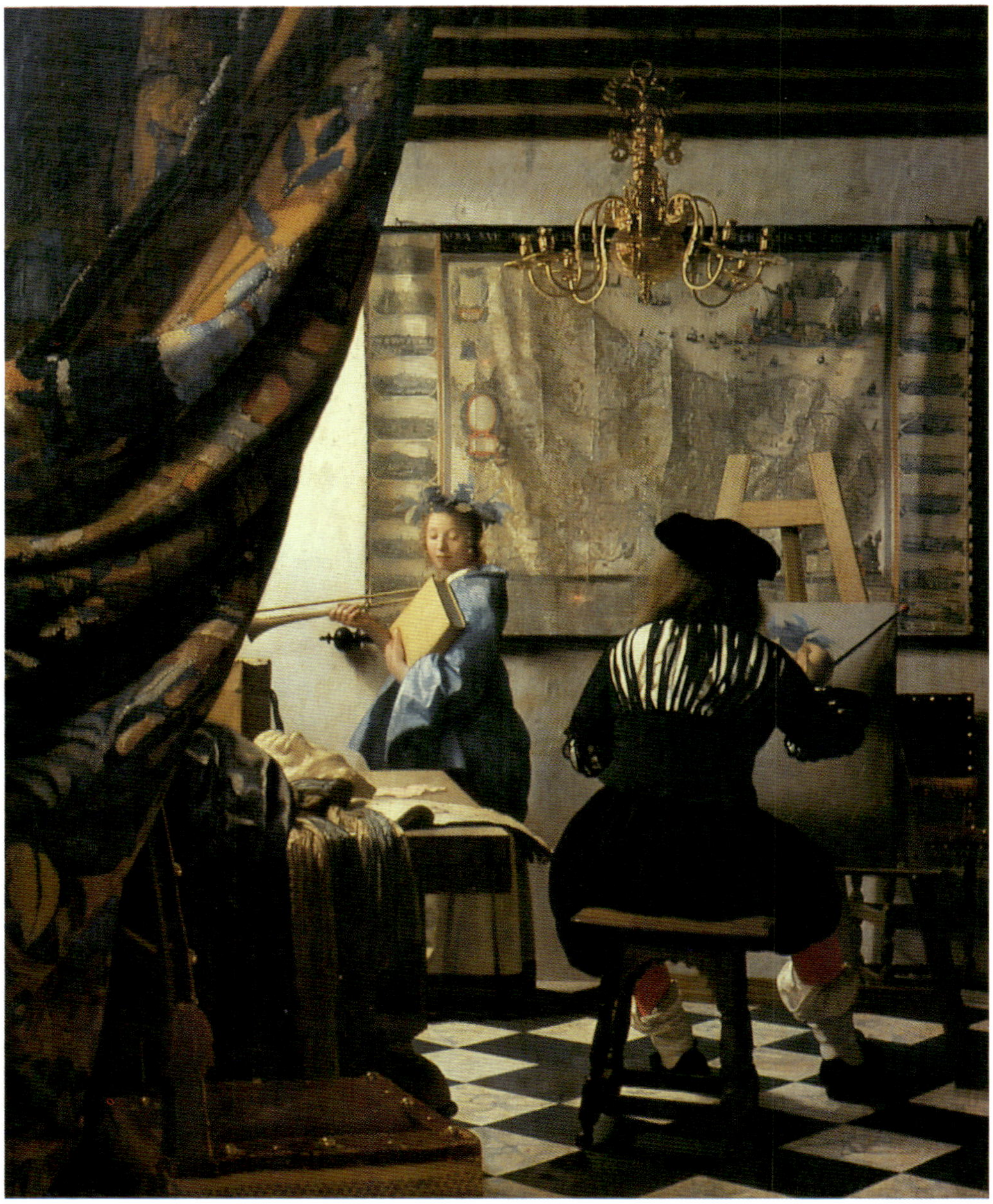

fig. 2. Johannes Vermeer, *Art of Painting*, c. 1666-1667, canvas, Kunsthistorisches Museum, Vienna

chalk to it. While holding it taut between the pin in the vanishing point and the fingers of one hand, his free hand would have drawn the string up a little and let it snap back onto the surface, leaving a line of chalk. This could then have been traced with a pencil or brush. Such a simple method of using a chalk line to make straight lines was probably used by Vermeer's Delft colleagues Leonard Bramer (1596–1674) and Carel Fabritius (1622–1654) to compose wall paintings, and is still used today by painters of *trompe l'oeil* interiors.[7]

Little or no trace of Vermeer's method – except the pinhole – remains. This is visible to the naked eye on Vermeer's *Allegory of Faith* (cat. 20). Since almost all of Vermeer's grounds contain lead white, the loss of ground where the pin was inserted usually appears on the x-radiograph as a dark spot (fig. 4).[8] This method of placing a pin through the canvas was not unique to Vermeer, but was in fact widely practiced among architecture painters of his time. It was used not only by Gerard Houckgeest (c. 1600–1661) and Emanuel de Witte (c. 1617–1692), but also by Vermeer's slightly older colleague Pieter de Hooch (1629–1684), a painter of interiors. Similarly, pictures by the genre painters Gerrit Dou (1613–1675), Gabriël Metsu (1629–1667), and others, also have irregularities in the paint surface where a pin was placed at the vanishing point.

Like most of his contemporary painters, Vermeer created the spatial illusion directly on the canvas. The Haarlem painter Pieter Saenredam (1597–1665) practiced another method. On the basis of a preparatory sketch, observed first-hand, Saenredam con-

LEFT: fig. 3. *The construction of receding lines*, from Bosse 1684, no. 28, Koninklijke Bibliotheek, The Hague. *X-Z* is the horizon, *C* the central vanishing point. Note the loose ends of the string used for the construction.

RIGHT: fig. 4. X-radiograph detail of cat. 5, showing the pinprick by which Vermeer constructed the painting's perspective

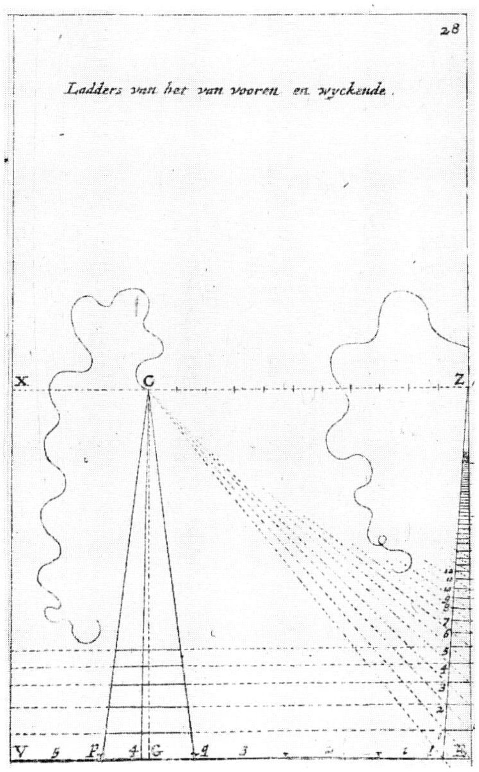

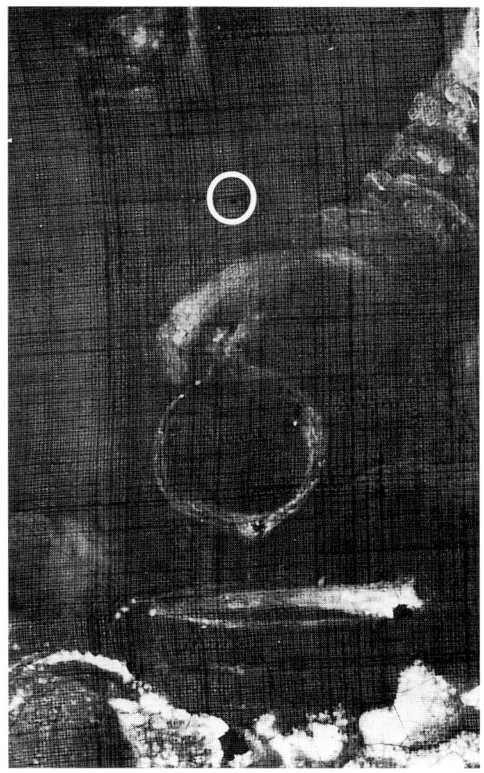

structed his perspective on a sheet of paper, later, in his studio. After having reached the final composition he would apply charcoal on the back of the paper and transfer the drawing with a sharp tool onto the surface of a prepared panel. After this the painting process could start.[9] Saenredam always used a panel support, while Vermeer apparently preferred to work on canvas.

Vermeer's Methods

In the beginning of his career Vermeer had difficulty in rendering floor tiles. The distance points, positioned at an equal distance on either side of the vanishing point on the horizon, provided the basis for the diagonals. These lines form the pattern of the floor tiles. When the horizon of his painting was relatively high and the distance points were close to the vanishing point, Vermeer apparently was vexed by the distortion of the tiles at the foreground corners. Examples of this occur in his earlier paintings such as *The Glass of Wine* (page 36, fig. 7; c. 1658–1660) and *The Girl with the Wineglass* (c. 1659–1660, cat. 6). The last example in Vermeer's oeuvre that shows a certain distortion of the floor tiles owing to the short interval between the distance points is *The Music Lesson* (c. 1662–1664, cat. 8). Here the view point, the center of projection,[10] is situated about 77 centimeters from the painted surface, the so-called picture plane. Viewed from this distance, the distortion is not noteworthy.

As Vermeer's career progressed, he solved this problem by moving the distance points farther away from the scene, thereby eliminating the distortion. This is important, particularly as he moved his vanishing point toward the edge of the painting at the same time. In *Officer and Laughing Girl* (c. 1658), the viewing angle[11] is about 53° (fig. 5a) and in

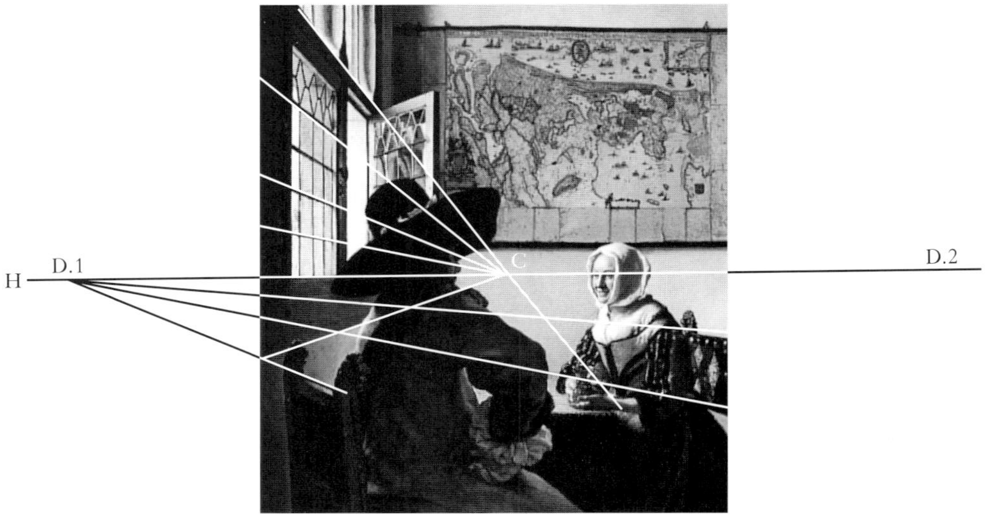

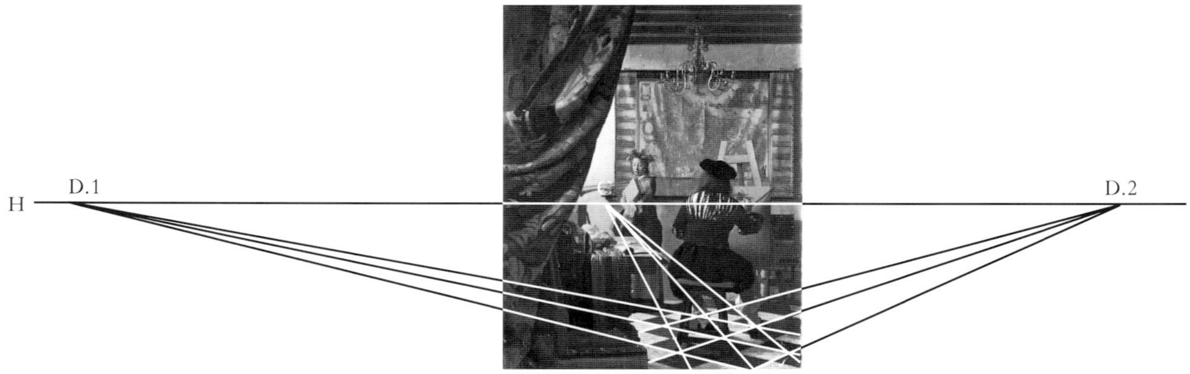

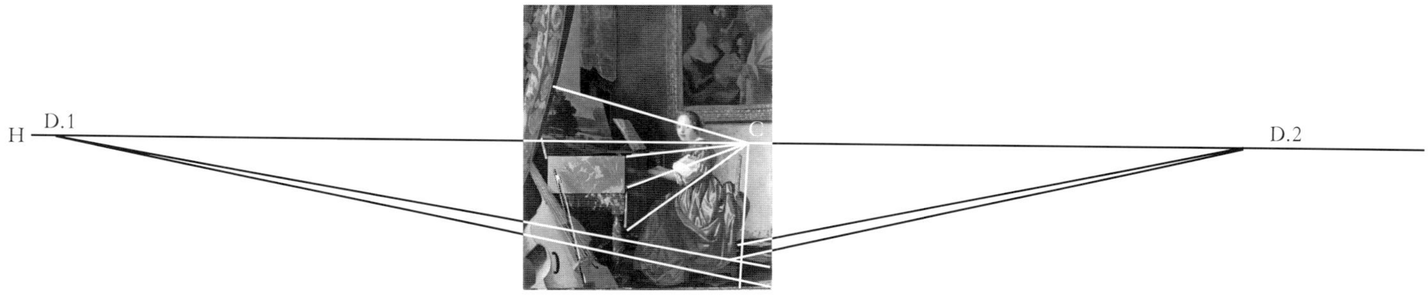

the *Art of Painting* (c. 1666–1667) the viewing angle has come down to around 30° (fig. 5b). In *The Love Letter* (c. 1669–1670, cat. 18) the angle declines to about 28°, and in the last painting executed by his hand, *A Lady Seated at the Virginal* (c. 1675, cat. 22), Vermeer reduces the viewing angle to only 22° (fig. 5c). It is interesting to note that Vermeer painted only diagonally placed floor tiles in his interiors, while De Hooch used diagonally placed as well as parallel tiles—sometimes even both within one painting—at random intervals.

Although Vermeer seems to have consistently used a string attached to a pin placed in the central vanishing point, the placement of the distance points poses a problem. At first one might expect that Vermeer determined the position of the diagonals on the edge of his canvas with the aid of a so-called "height wall" (*hoogte muur*), as some Dutch landscape painters did.[12] This would imply doing calculations or constructing of auxiliary lines in order to make space recede toward the back wall. Since no trace of marks on the edges or elsewhere on his paintings has so far surfaced, it seems highly unlikely that Vermeer used such methods.

Painters would want to create perfect central perspective without having to struggle

TOP: fig. 5a. Perspective diagram of Vermeer's *Officer and Laughing Girl*. This is the earliest painting where the vanishing point has been detected in the paint layer. Owing to the short interval between the central vanishing point and the distance points, the viewing angle is about 53°.

CENTER: fig. 5b. Perspective diagram of Vermeer's *Art of Painting*. The viewing angle has decreased to approximately 30° as the interval has lengthened between the central vanishing point and distance points.

BOTTOM: fig. 5c. Perspective diagram of *A Lady Seated at the Virginal*. In this painting, probably the last one executed by Vermeer, the viewing angle is only 22°.

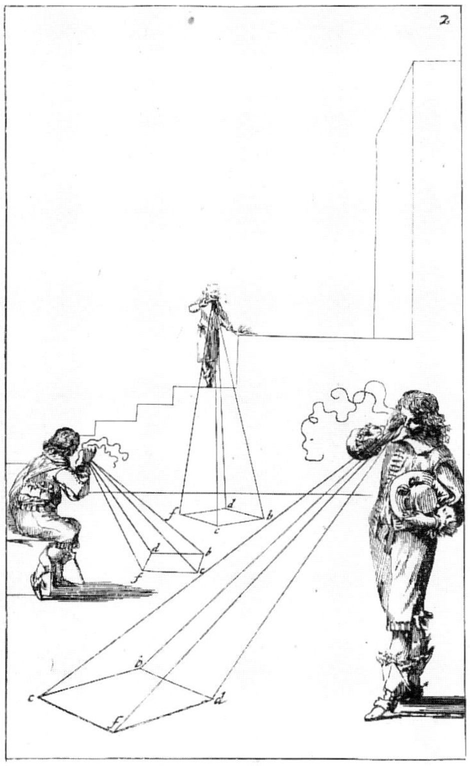

fig. 6. *The visual rays of sight*, from Bosse 1684, no. 2, Koninklijke Bibliotheek, The Hague

with complicated theories. One simple way was to use the already mentioned chalk line to determine the orthogonals, a method that Vermeer could apply to the diagonals as well. It can be assumed that Vermeer placed his canvas–usually small–against a board or a wall, with a nail on either side of the painting. These nails would be placed at the same level as the horizon in the picture. With strings attached to the nails Vermeer could again apply the chalk line for the diagonals in his constructions. The use of this simple method can be deduced from various manuals on perspective that Vermeer could have known. One such manual shows strings, held taut to one eye, attached to a square lying on the ground (fig. 6).

Strings were also used in connection with drawing tables. In contrast to what we expect, it appears that constructors of perspective in the seventeenth century used drawing tables almost as sophisticated as the ones in use today (fig. 8). With strings attached to movable devices placed at the upper corners of the drawing table, the draftsman could create any desired diagonals or orthogonals on paper. The horizon could be plotted using a sliding ruler at a fixed 90° angle to the horizontal bottom edge of the table. A horizon would be chosen at the desired level on this ruler, and by sliding the ruler across the paper a line could be drawn.[13]

Just how painters exercised the perspective can be seen in a charming sketch drawn on the wall behind the painter depicted at his easel by Barent Fabritius (1624–1673) (fig. 7).[14] In red chalk, among cartoons, the draftsman has made a spatial study with a distinct vanishing point in the middle. The orthogonals and also some of the diagonals have been drawn in.

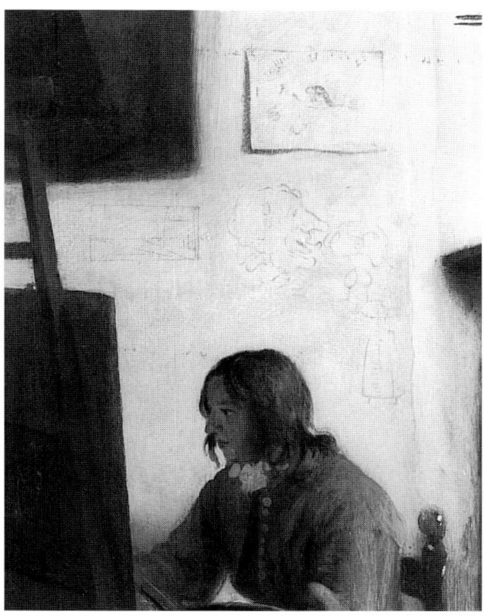

fig. 7. Detail, Barent Fabritius, *Young Painter in His Studio*, c. 1655, oil on canvas, Musée du Louvre, Paris

Construction

In 1669 Pieter Teding van Berckhout, a prominent citizen of The Hague, visited Vermeer's studio and described the paintings that he saw as extraordinary and curious "*perspectives*."[15]

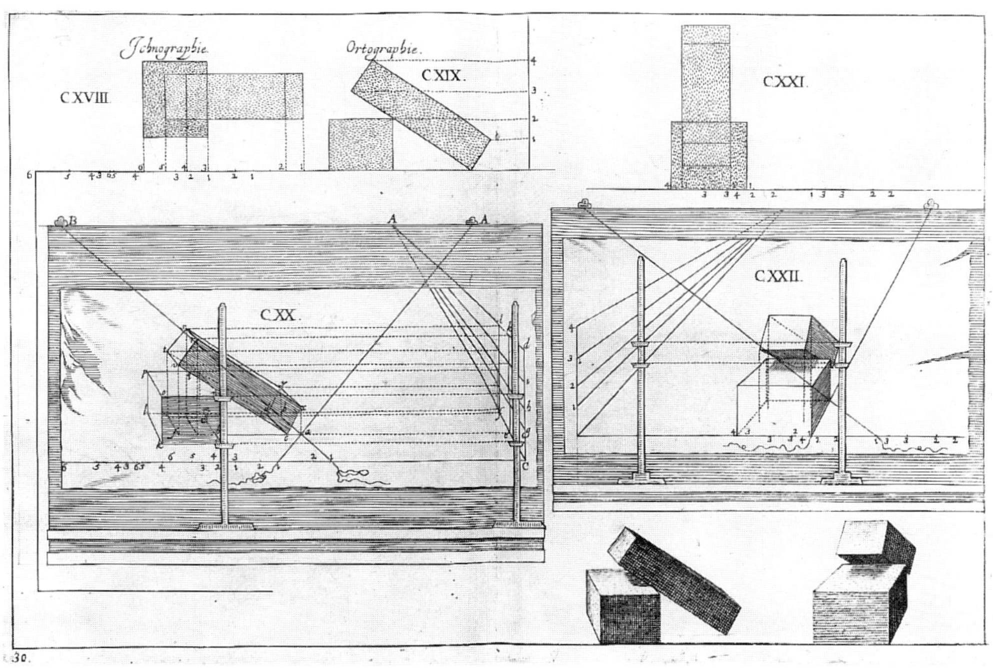

fig. 8. Hendrick Hondius, *Drawing table*, from Marolois 1628, no. 30, Koninklijke Bibliotheek, The Hague

Teding van Berckhout might have referred to Vermeer's interior scenes, which were very carefully constructed. This leads us to the conclusion that Vermeer should be considered first and foremost as a practical and skilled master in creating his interiors just the way he wanted them. Numerous authors have argued that the artist reproduced the scenes he saw in front of him, either by careful copying, using drawing frames, or by means of a camera obscura.[16] That Vermeer traced an image with this device is unlikely; however, a number of paintings are believed to have been created with the camera obscura as a compositional aid.[17] The way Vermeer occasionally applied the final paint layer or highlights in a pointillistic manner may have been influenced by the vision one gets by looking through a camera obscura (but see page 25).

Vermeer was completely aware of the spatial illusion he wanted to create, which he accomplished by combining his skill in constructing space with his talent for composition, color, technique, and iconography. Without the use of a camera obscura as a drawing aid he created images that looked "photographic," which deceive the spectators into *believing* that the scenes are real. With this illusionism Vermeer attained the highest level of artistic ambition to which a seventeenth-century painter could aspire.[18]

Since Vermeer created his compositions very carefully, one must ask if the figures and the many accessories in the paintings were also constructed. Close study of the foreshortened furniture has revealed that it has been just as carefully built up as the overall perspective. Once again, the chalk lines attached to the distance points formed by the nail in the wall next to the picture would have served as the base for the receding lines of the chairs and tables in Vermeer's interiors (fig. 9).

The horizon in Vermeer's earlier paintings in general (cat. 2 and page 20, fig. 6) is observed to be relatively higher than in the later ones. Although high horizons also occur in later works, the position of the horizon in combination with the viewpoint of the spectator is significant.[19] In the majority of Vermeer's works the viewpoint is indeed below the eye level of the depicted figures. It has been argued that when using a camera obscura placed on a table, the artist's vantage point would naturally be low.[20] However, Vermeer may have deliberately sought this effect, in order to keep the spectator at a distance. As

fig. 9. Perspective diagram of cat. 8. The distance points of the construction of the chair are marked *D.ch.1* and *D.2*. Both points are carefully placed at an equal distance to the left of the distance points (*d.1* and *d.2*) of the overall composition.

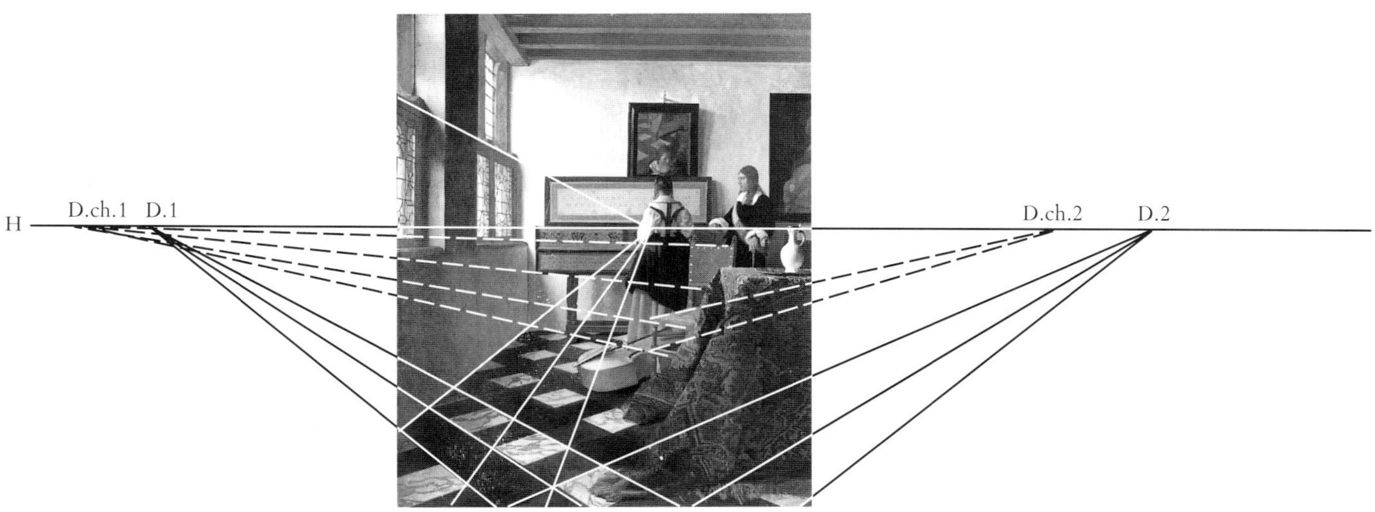

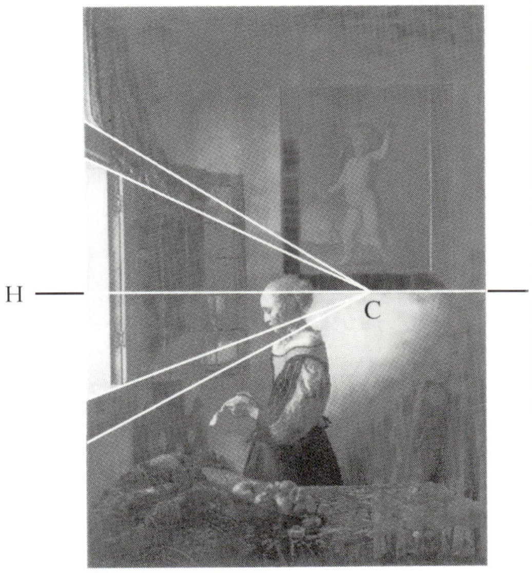

TOP: fig. 10. Reconstruction of fig. 11

RIGHT: fig. 11. Johannes Vermeer, *Girl Reading a Letter at an Open Window*, c. 1657, oil on canvas, Staatliche Kunstsammlungen Dresden, Gemäldegalerie Alte Meister

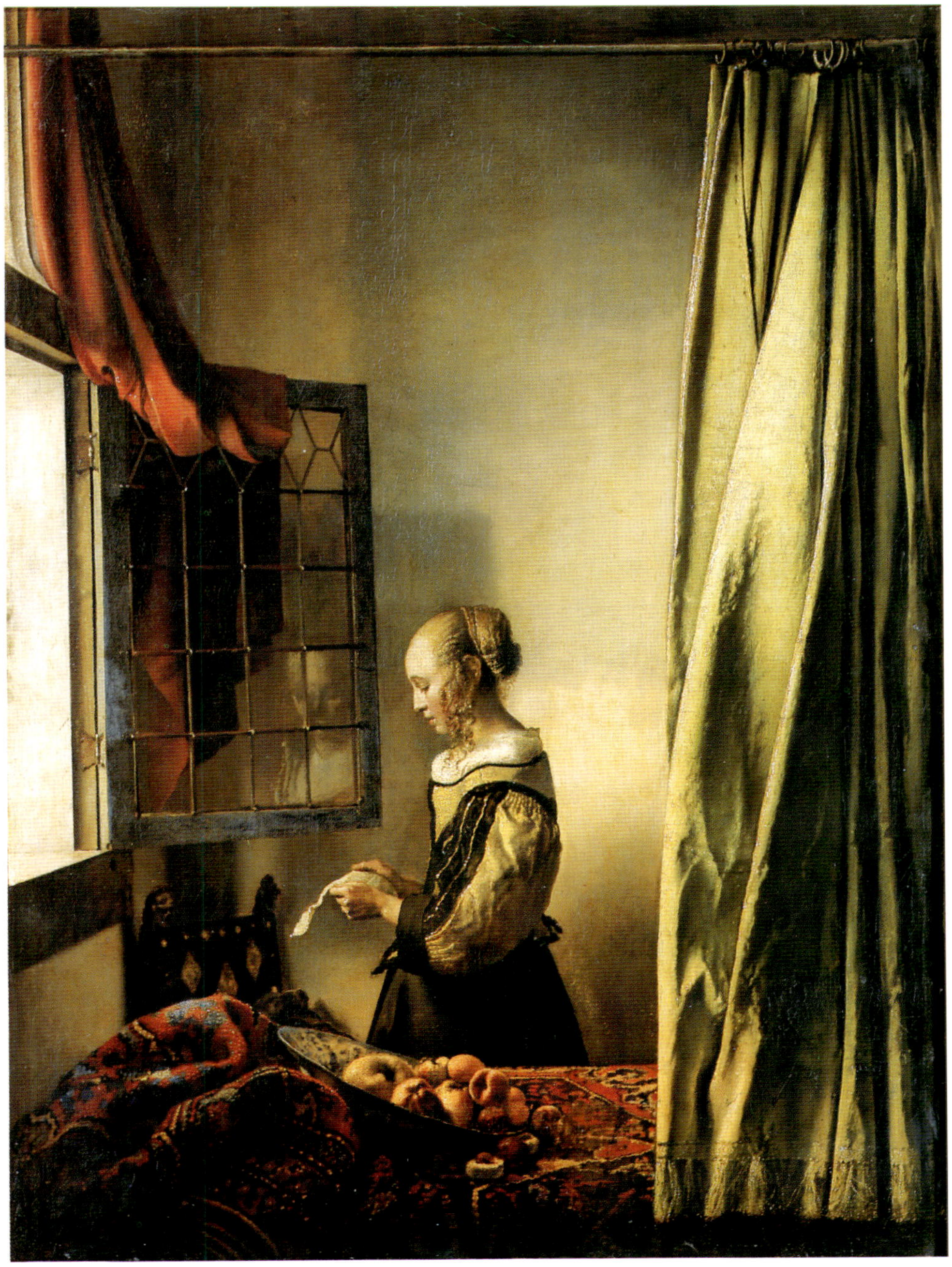

we almost always have a frog's eye view, from below, the figures automatically increase in stature, even in a small painting such as *The Milkmaid* (cat. 5).

Vermeer also deliberately places the vanishing point behind a *répoussoir* or other barrier between the viewer and the scene. This seems to have been a hallmark throughout his oeuvre as seen in paintings from the *Procuress* (page 60, fig. 16) and *Girl Reading a Letter at an Open Window* (fig. 11) to the *Art of Painting* (fig. 2) and *The Love Letter* (cat. 18).

In the early *Girl Reading a Letter at an Open Window* the horizon is placed in such a way that it divides the painting in half. The vanishing point is placed between the girl's neck and the green curtain to the right. The reason for the position of the vanishing point behind the reading girl seems irrational, as it does not lead the eye of the spectator into the composition. At an early stage in the development of this picture, however, a painting of Cupid hung just above the vanishing point on the back wall.[21] To stress the amorous content of the letter, the orthogonals to the vanishing point would lead the eye of the spectator via the Cupid to the girl and back, which would be logical (fig. 10). But Vermeer has obscured the meaning by overpainting the Cupid, and leaves us only with a very naturalistic and sensual reflection of the girl in the leaded glass window. Despite the changes that Vermeer made to the composition, he did not alter the perspective design.

Acquiring Expertise

Where or with whom Vermeer trained in the use of perspective is entirely unknown. In the introduction of his book on perspective, Desargues writes that a painter who wants to know more about the *Meet-konst* (art of measurement) should consult the *Landmeeter* (cartographer) in order to make use of his expertise.[22] According to Desargues this would lead to a better understanding of *Doorzicht-kunde* (perspective). He further suggests that the painter should look around him at other crafts and take advantage of the knowledge of, for instance, carpenters, bricklayers, and cabinetmakers.[23]

A painter like Saenredam acquired his first instruction in the rules of perspective from the local *landmeeter* (cartographer) Pieter Wils, when he was already established as an artist.[24] In Haarlem this profession was included in the painter's guild of Saint Luke, and also in Vermeer's home town of Delft one could receive education in this *métier.* At the age of thirty-six Anthony van Leeuwenhoek, who may have known Vermeer, obtained his diploma in cartography in Delft–that is, when Vermeer had already made a number of 'perspectives.'[25] The knowledge of perspective was essential to the succesful creation of a correct spatial illusion, which was so popular with Delft painters after 1650. The importance of good training was stressed by Van Hoogstraeten, who explained that without this learning, "so many ignorant painters are shipwrecked."[26]

It was only after some years of practice that Vermeer became an expert in the use of perspective. In his early work, such as *Christ in the House of Mary and Martha* (cat. 2), the interior does not have a correct and carefully constructed perspective. Nor do his following paintings, including *A Woman Asleep* (page 20, fig. 6), which is an ambitious attempt to create a literal "Through-view" (*Doorzicht*). Around 1658 Vermeer's interest changed into creating space in a carefully constructed way. This resulted in the *Officer and Laughing Girl* (page 35, fig. 6), the first painting where Vermeer employed a string attached to a pin. Throughout the rest of his career he continued to use this method.

Vermeer's Studio

In order to visualize Vermeer's studio we have to look at written sources and his paintings other than the *Art of Painting*, from which little can be deduced. There the painter steadies his right hand, resting it on a maulstick held in his left hand. No other painting materials or accessories other than the maulstick, and the brush are present.

In addition to the already mentioned books the inventory of Vermeer's studio also included two Spanish chairs, a stick with an ivory knob, two easels, and three palettes. Three bundles of various prints were found, probably on the reading desk also described in the inventory. In another small room Vermeer kept five or six books, and in the attic, the inventory reads, he had a stone table and a muller to grind his pigments.

Alas, no pigments, pots, or bottles of oils are listed. Nor are water basins, in which to keep the paint from drying out, varnish bottles, or containers for turpentine. The inventoried wooden box with drawers may have contained some of his painting materials. Such boxes not only appear in many artists' self portraits, holding small pots with various liquids, brushes, and pigments, but also in depictions of painters' studios (fig. 12).

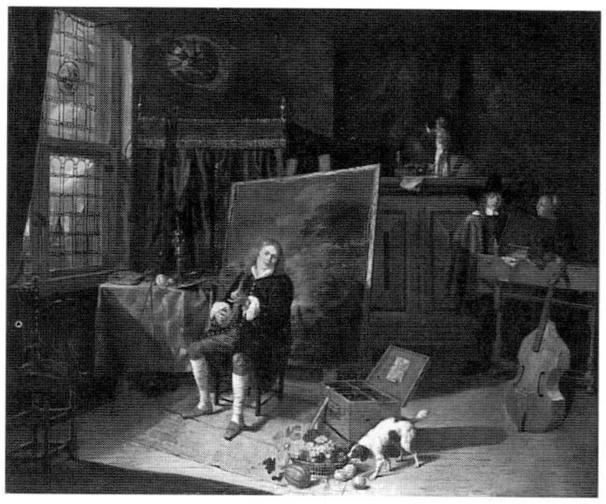

fig. 12. Gonzales Coques, *Painter in His Studio*, oil on canvas, Staatliches Museum Schwerin

Classical sculpture and casts were common in studio interiors from the seventeenth century, but none is mentioned in the inventory. However, in the *Art of Painting* a cast of fig. 13. Johannes Vermeer, *Portrait of a Young Woman*, c. 1666–1667, oil on canvas, The Metropolitan Museum of Art, New York, Gift of Mr. and Mrs. Charles Wrightsman, in memory of Theodore Rousseau, Jr., 1979

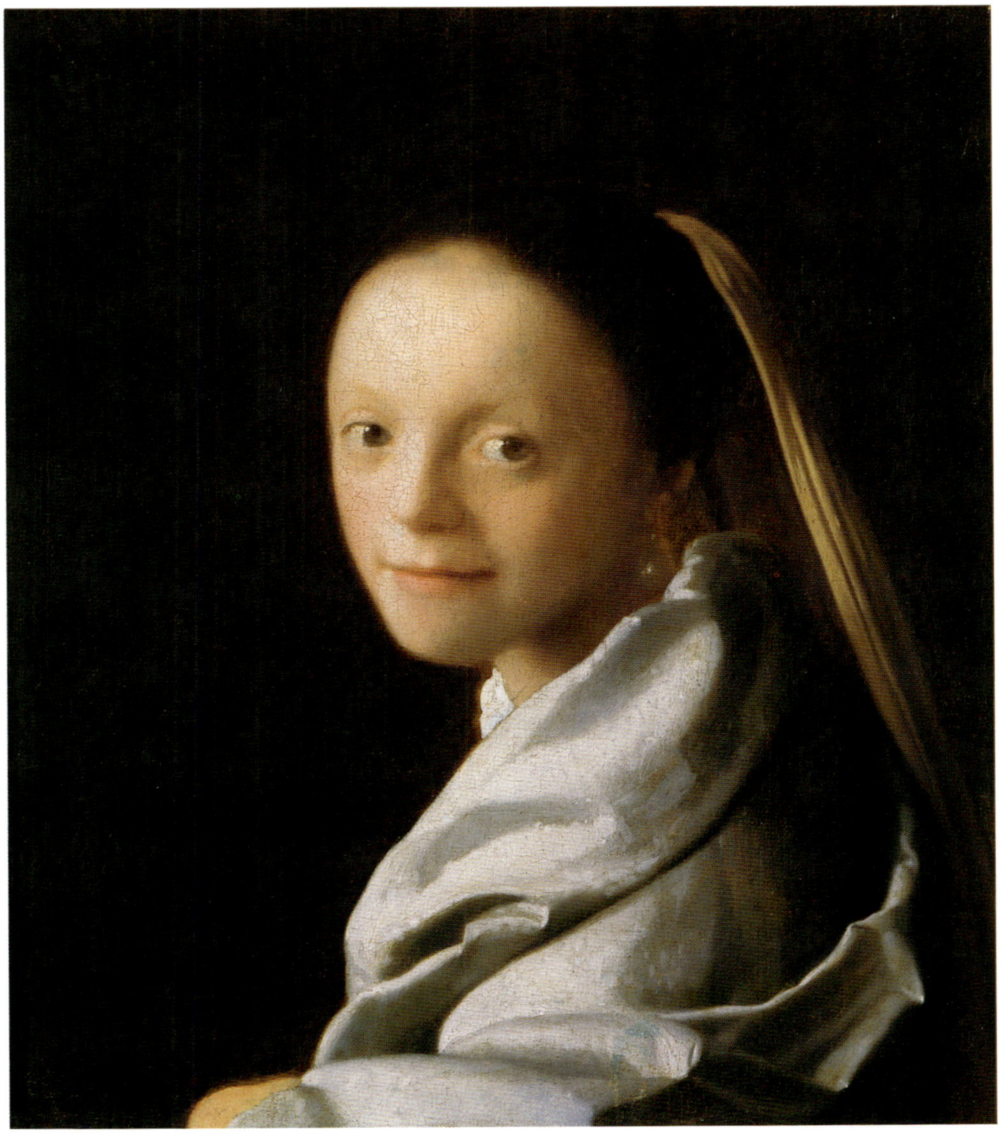

a male face lies face-up on the table. Vermeer's maulstick is also missing in the inventory, but maybe he used the stick with an ivory knob for this purpose.

The eighteenth-century Dutch artists' biographer Arnold Houbraken (1660–1719) noted that the painter Aert de Gelder (1645–1727) had different jackets, curtains, and fabrics such as silk and satin, in his studio, which he used to clothe his model from head to foot in the way that suited his interest.[27] Vermeer's inventory includes many of the items and jackets depicted in his paintings, such as the fur-trimmed, yellow satin jacket found in six paintings. Whether Vermeer had a lay figure we do not know. However, looking at the *Portrait of a Young Woman* (fig. 13) and the anatomy of her left hand, which does not seem to fit with the foreshortening of her shoulder and arm, and the drapery over her shoulder, one gets the impression that a lay figure may have been used.[28]

The fact that Vermeer's inventory includes no frames for stretching canvas, common in many seventeenth-century studios, is very interesting. Contemporary depictions of artists' studios show them at work on canvases both strung in larger frames, often identified as the Dutch method, and tacked onto strainers (fig. 14). The paint layer does not extend over the tacking edges in any of Vermeer's paintings so far examined,[29] indicating that Vermeer preferred his canvas stretched onto its strainer before starting painting. This is corroborated by reading his inventory, in which are noted ten canvases as well as six panels standing ready to be painted.

A fine craquelure pattern running parallel to the edges of Vermeer's paintings reveals information on the size of the original strainers that he used: they were between two-and-a-half and three-and-a-half centimeters wide. The larger strainers, such as those used for the *View of Delft* (cat. 7) and the *Art of Painting*, had central crossbars and corner braces similar to those seen in an allegorical painting by Ferdinand van Kessel (1648–1696) (figs. 15a and b).

When Vermeer started to work on a painting, we can assume that he went up to his attic in order to prepare his pigments, which, as suggested by recent analysis, were mixed with linseed oil,[30] on the stone table. Back in his studio he would be able to work on one of his two easels, the size and construction of which we can surmise from his *Art of Painting*. Vermeer probably used one of the palettes mentioned in the inventory for the lighter colors and another for the darker. We do not learn anything from the inventory about his stock of brushes, but his brushstrokes reveal that he used a number of larger square-tipped and smaller round-tipped brushes. Many brush hairs became embedded in the paint, particularly in scumbles: fine brown hairs in the half-tones in the face of the *Girl with a Pearl Earring* (cat. 15) and in the gray-brown scumble rendering the reflection of the town in the water in the *View of Delft*. In this painting also thick white hairs were found in the white underpainting of the sky.[31] The latter are presumably hog's hair and the former could be squirrel or otter hair.[32]

The Purchase of Materials[33]

For the purchase of his materials, such as (prepared) canvases and panels and current kinds of paint, Vermeer could turn to an artists' supplier. One or more of these could

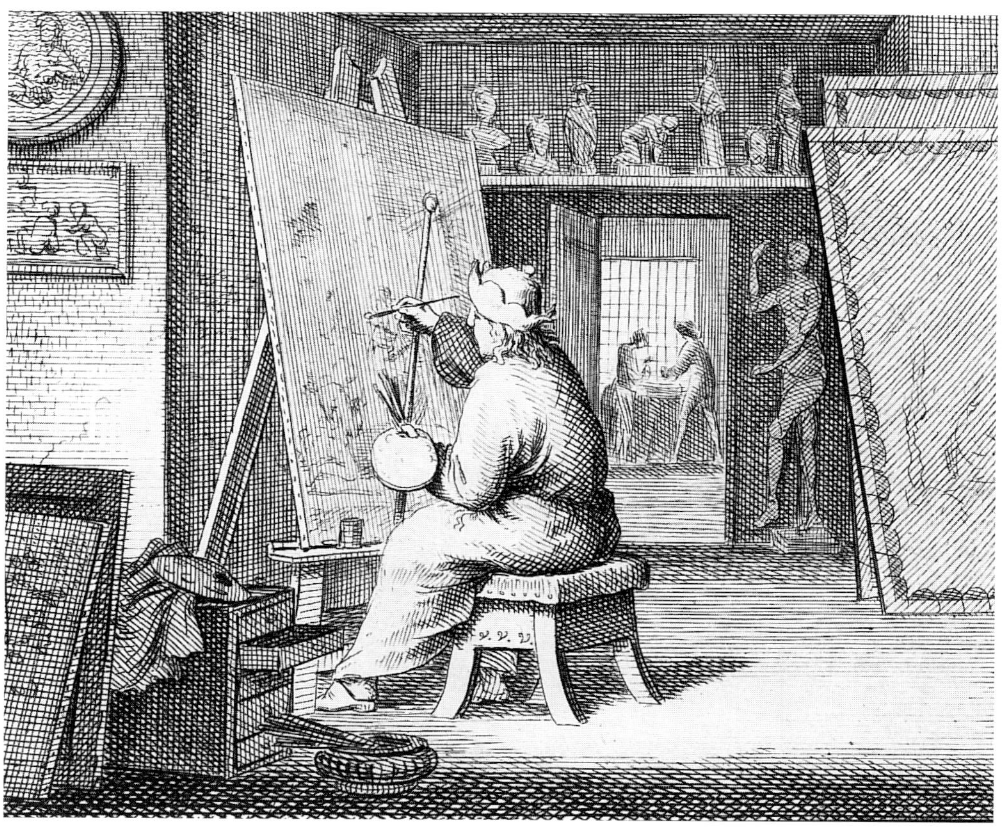

fig. 14. Vincent van der Vinne, *Painter in His Studio*, engraving, Rijksprentenkabinet, Amsterdam

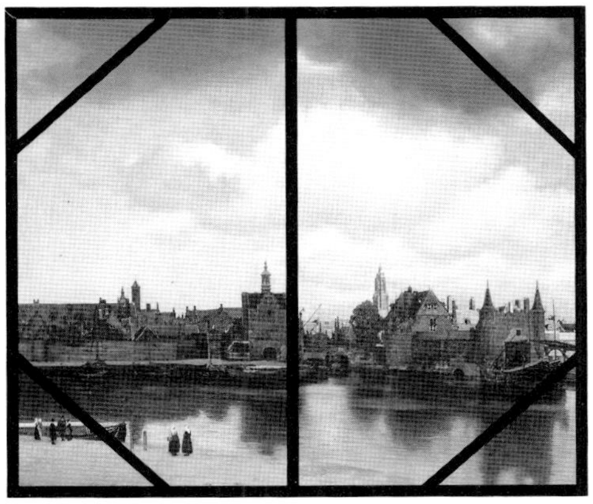

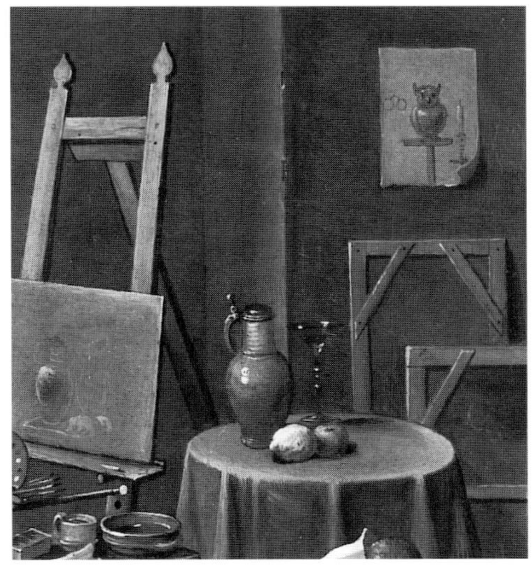

LEFT: fig. 15a. Craquelure in the paint layer of the *View of Delft* indicates an original strainer as depicted in fig. 15b.

RIGHT: fig. 15b. Detail, Ferdinand van Kessel, *A Monkey Painters' Studio*, oil on copper, Courtesy R. Valls, London. The two canvases are stretched on strainers similar to the ones originally used for Vermeer's larger paintings.

probably be found in Delft, and certainly in nearby Rotterdam.[34] In the seventeenth century, Van Hoogstraeten and others advised artists not to bother trying to make pigments, which could be bought easily in various places.[35] The precious natural ultramarine that Vermeer used even in the underpainting of a number of pictures is, however, not encountered in surviving inventories of seventeenth-century artists' suppliers. For small quantities of pigments such as this, one could turn to the apothecary, the forerunner of the artists' supplier.

The inventory of the Delft apothecary D. de Cock,[36] where Vermeer had a debt for medicines,[37] lists substances that could be used for the preparation of paint and varnish. Possibly Vermeer acquired these substances from De Cock, since the massicot or lead tin yellow, listed in his inventory, was employed in many paintings, most evidently in the texture and light of the yellow satin jackets (cat. 13). Gold leaf, obtainable in small booklets, was only once applied by Vermeer, to the studs of the chair in *A Woman Asleep*. All these materials, as well as lead white, Venetian turpentine, and linseed oil, were mentioned in De Cock's inventory.

Already in the sixteenth century Delft apothecaries appear to have acquired a measure of renown for their skill in preparing pigments. The learned French physician M. de l'Obel (1538–1616) first learned from the Delft apothecary M. D. Cluyt (active in the second half of the sixteenth century) how one could make a serviceable red lacquer for the painter.[38] Not just apothecaries but also specialists involved in the production of Delft earthenware were adept in the manufacture of pigments.[39]

Vermeer's preference for the relatively expensive blue pigments such as natural ultramarine might be related to the fact that his market consisted of a small group of amateurs and connoisseurs who regularly bought work without directly commissioning it. A large proportion of the surviving works points to a single purchaser (see pages 22 and 53). The rarity of Vermeer's work has been connected with his technique: up until now it was presumed that he was a slow painter. However, brushstrokes applied wet-in-wet indicate that some parts at least were rapidly executed, although it appears that the artist may have worked on a painting at intervals. He developed a composition very carefully, sometimes changing or deleting elements, such as the above-mentioned painting of a Cupid in *Girl Reading a Letter at an Open Window*.

A true understanding of Vermeer's painting cannot be achieved without technical data. The most fascinating is that instead of using a camera obscura, he established perspectively correct paintings, simply with the aid of a pin and strings. As previously stated, this method was also used in Vermeer's *Art of Painting*, in which the pinhole has given us a direct connection with Vermeer's own studio. In his paintings Vermeer deceives us into believing that the depicted scenes are real—according to Van Hoogstraeten this was the highest level of artistic ambition the seventeenth-century painter could aim for, a level that Vermeer surely achieved.[40]

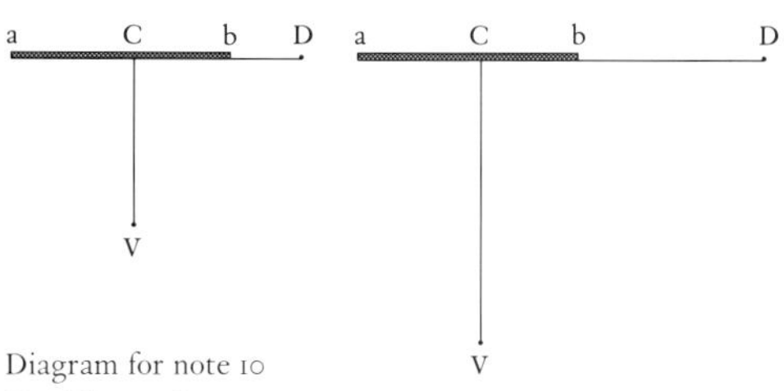

Diagram for note 10
V = View point.
C = Central vanishing point.
D = Distance point.
Distance C - D = C - V.

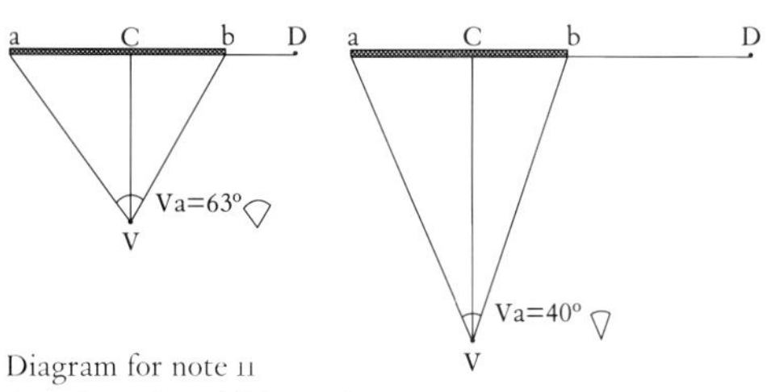

Diagram for note 11
C = Central vanishing point.
D = Distance point.
V = View point.
Va= Viewing angle.

I am indebted to Nicola Costaras and Koos Levy-van Halm for their assistance and information.

1. Van Hoogstraeten 1678, 88: "Geleertheit versiert de Schilders."
2. See Van de Wetering 1993 and Van de Wetering 1995.
3. Montias 1989, 339–344, doc. 364.
4. Vredeman de Vries 1604; Marolois 1628; Hondius 1647 and Bosse/Desargues 1664.
5. *Officer and Laughing Girl*, *The Milkmaid*, *The Glass of Wine*, *The Music Lesson*, *The Astronomer*, *The Geographer*, *Art of Painting*, *The Love Letter*, *Woman Holding a Balance*, *Lady Writing a Letter with her Maid*, *Allegory of Faith*, *A Lady Standing at the Virginal*, and *A Lady Seated at the Virginal*.
6. Hultén was the first to actually record and illustrate a discernible vanishing point in one of Vermeer's paintings (Hultén 1949, 90–98).
7. On these wall paintings, see Montias 1982, 188, 192; on Bramer, see Delft 1994.
8. Where the lead-white absorbent paint is missing, the x-rays will pass easily to the film and blacken it. In two instances there are light spots at the relevant points on the x-radiograph due to a surplus of lead white from an overlying layer that has filled the loss in the ground (in *Officer and Laughing Girl* and *Woman Holding a Balance*).
9. See Ruurs 1987, 49–50, and Jeroen Giltaij in Rotterdam 1991, 16 (a summary in Schwartz 1989, 78–82 and ill. 86).
10. The view point (V), or center of projection, is placed on the horizon at a distance from the picture plane (the canvas) equal to the distance between the central vanishing point (C) and the distance point (D). If the distance between the central vanishing point (C) and the distance point (D) is enlarged, the view point (V) also moves farther away from the picture plane.
11. In the view point (V) the viewing angle (Va) can be measured. The viewing angle is established by drawing two lines from the view point to the two vertical edges of the painting. As the distance between the painting and the view point is equal to the interval between the central vanishing point (C) and the distance point (D), it becomes clear that as the distance points move farther away from the picture, the view point (V) and the viewing angle (Va) also become smaller.
12. Ruurs 1983, 191.
13. Marolois 1628, chapters CXII-CLVII, engravings by H. Hondius.
14. See Foucart 1994, 69–70.
15. Montias 1991, 48: "extraordinaijre...curieuse...perspective" (Montias 1993, 377, doc. 325*bis).
16. For a survey of the previously published literature on this subject see Wadum 1995.
17. Wheelock 1995.
18. Van Hoogstraeten 1678, 275.
19. Arasse 1994.
20. Seymour 1964, 328.
21. Mayer-Meintschel 1978–1979, 95–96 and ill.; see also Wheelock 1987, 410–411 and ill.
22. Bosse/Desargues 1664, 9: "Turn to the surveyors, for they can teach you the rudiments of geometry and mathematics and instruct you further, nothing more, but also nothing less than that" (in translation).
23. In Bosse/Desargues 1664, 17, the following passage is found: "A large crowd of workers in various kinds of art who use three-dimensional form, such as carpenters, masons, joiners, and those who apply geometry in their work, had fully mastered it [geometry] and used it effortlessly" (in translation).
24. Ruurs 1987, 87.
25. Wijbenga 1986, 206.
26. Van Hoogstraeten 1678, 273:"zoo veel waenwijze Schilders schipbreuk lijden."
27. Houbraken 1718–1721, 3: 207.
28. One gets the same impression with Rembrandt's etched self-portrait from 1639, which shows the same pose as the *Portrait of a Woman* (see Berlin 1991, 2: 200–202, no. 13 and ill.).
29. Original tacking edges, folded over the edge of the strainer and fixed with wooden pegs or nails, are present on seventeen of the canvases examined so far.
30. See Kühn 1968; this was also confirmed by recent scientific analysis at the National Gallery of Art, Washington, and the Central Research Laboratory, Amsterdam.
31. Wadum 1994, 13–15.
32. Several theoreticians mentioned the use of these and other brushes, see Welther 1991.
33. We are indebted to Koos Levy-van Halm for this and the following important information.
34. Henny 1994.
35. Van Hoogstraeten 1678, 222.
36. Gemeentearchief, Delft, records of Notary N. Vrijenbergh, no. 2061.
37. Montias 1989, 318, doc. 297.
38. Bosman-Jelgersma 1979, 62.
39. Wijbenga 1986, 188–189.
40. Van Hoogstraeten 1678, 275.

1591
Birth of Vermeer's father, Reynier Jansz, the son of Jan Reijersz, a tailor whose family had moved from Flanders to Delft by 1597.

1615
19 July, marriage of Reynier Jansz, a weaver (*kaffawercker*), and Digna Baltens, in Amsterdam.

1620
15 March, baptism of Geertruijt, the couple's first child, in Delft.

c. 1627–1630
Reynier Jansz, who since 1625 has called himself Vos, rents an inn on the Voldersgracht, in Delft, called The Flying Fox (De Vliegende Vos).

1631
13 October, Reynier Jansz Vos joins the Guild of Saint Luke as "Master Art Dealer" (Mr. Constvercoper).

1632
31 October, Johannes Vermeer is baptized as "Joannis" in the New Church (Niewe Kerk), in Delft.

1640
6 September, Reynier signs himself Vermeer in a deposition.

1641
23 April, Reynier Jansz Vos buys the house and adjoining inn called "Mechelen" on the Grote Markt, in Delft.

1652
12 October, Reynier Jansz Vos is buried in Delft.

1653
5 April, Johannes Vermeer registers his intentions to marry Catharina Bolnes (born 1631), youngest daughter of Maria Thins (born c. 1593) and Reynier Bolnes (died 1674; he and Maria Thins had separated in 1641). Two witnesses, the painter Leonard Bramer (1596–1674) and a Captain Bartolomeus Melling, state that on the previous evening Maria Thins had refused to sign a formal statement consenting to the marriage, but had declared that she "would suffer the [marriage] banns be published and would tolerate it."

20 April, Johannes Vermeer and Catharina Bolnes marry in Schipluiden, a village an hour's walk south of Delft.

22 April, Vermeer and the painter Gerard ter Borch (1617–1681) jointly sign a document in Delft.

29 December, Vermeer is registered in the Guild of Saint Luke as a master painter.

1654

10 January, Vermeer serves as witness to a notarized obligation of debt and is described as "master painter."

1655

14 December, Vermeer and his wife Catharina declare themselves secondary sureties and co-principals for a debt incurred by the now deceased Reynier Jansz Vos. The document is signed "Johannes Reijnijersz Vermeer," with "Vosch" crossed out.

Vermeer signs and dates *Saint Praxedis.*

1656

24 July, Vermeer pays the remaining portion of his master's fee in the Guild of Saint Luke, in Delft.

Vermeer signs and dates *The Procuress.*

1657

18 June, Maria Thins' first testament is drafted, leaving her jewels to Vermeer's daughter, her namesake, and the sum of three hundred guilders to Vermeer and Catharina.

30 November, Vermeer borrows two hundred guilders from Pieter Claesz van Ruijven (1624–1674), a wealthy burgher.

1660

27 December, "a child of Johannes Vermeer [living] on the Oude Langedijck" is buried in the Old Church (Oude Kerk), in Delft. This is the earliest evidence that Vermeer and his family were residing in Maria Thins' home in the Papists' corner of the city.

1662

Johannes Vermeer is elected headman of the Guild of Saint Luke, for a term of two years.

1663

August 11, a French diplomat, Balthasar de Monconys (1611–1655), visits Vermeer.

1663 or 1664

Vermeer's first son, Johannes, is born.

1664

Johannes Vermeer is mentioned in a list of Delft militia men.

1667

Vermeer is praised as the artistic successor to Carel Fabritius (1622–1654) in a poem by Arnold Bon published in Dirck van Bleyswijck's *Description of the City of Delft* (*Beschryvinge der Stadt Delft*).

10 July, an infant son of Vermeer and Catharina is buried in the New Church, in Delft.

1668

Vermeer signs and dates *The Astronomer.*

1669

14 May, Pieter Teding van Berckhout (1643–1713), a prominent citizen of The Hague, visits Vermeer's studio in Delft.

21 June, Van Berckhout returns to Delft and again visits Vermeer.

16 July, a child of Vermeer is buried in the family grave in the Old Church, in Delft.

1670

13 February, Digna Baltens, Vermeer's mother, is buried in the New Church, in Delft.

2 May, Vermeer's sister Geertruijt is buried in the New Church, in Delft; Vermeer inherits 148 guilders and the family house known as "Mechelen."

Vermeer is again elected headman of the Guild of Saint Luke, in Delft, for two years.

1672

Vermeer leases out "Mechelen."

23 May, Vermeer and the Delft painter Johannes Jordaens (1616–1680) are called as art experts to The Hague to examine twelve paintings that have been described as outstanding Italian works. They testify before a notary in The Hague that the works are "great pieces of rubbish and bad paintings."

1673

27 June, a child of Vermeer is buried in the family grave in the Old Church.

21 July, Vermeer sells two bonds totaling eight hundred guilders, one of which, worth 500 guilders, is in the name of Magdalena Pieters (1655–1682), daughter of Pieter Claesz van Ruijven, from whom Vermeer had borrowed money in 1657.

1674

Reynier Bolnes, Vermeer's father-in-law, dies. Vermeer travels to Gouda to settle the estate.

1675

20 July, Vermeer borrows 1,000 guilders in Amsterdam.

16 December, Vermeer, age forty-three, is buried in the Old Church, in Delft. He is survived by his wife Catharina and eleven children, ten of them minors.

1676

27 January, Catharina Bolnes sells two of her late husband's paintings to the baker Hendrick van Buyten (1632–1701) to settle a debt of 617 guilders 6 stuivers.

10 February, the art dealer Jan Coelenbier, acting for Jannetje Stevens, one of Vermeer's creditors, buys twenty-six paintings from Catharina for five hundred guilders and transports them to Haarlem.

24 February, Catharina attempts to settle a debt with her mother by transferring to her the *Art of Painting.*

29 February, an inventory of the movable goods of Vermeer's estate is compiled.

24 and 30 April, Catharina petitions the high court of Holland and Zeeland to issue letters of cession to her creditors because of the disastrous conditions resulting from the war with France and her husband's death. Her request is granted.

30 September, the Lords Aldermen of Delft appoint Anthony van Leeuwenhoek (1632–1723), inventor of the microscope, executor of Vermeer's estate.

1677

2 and 5 February, Anthony van Leeuwenhoek appears before the Lords Aldermen of Delft to settle Vermeer's debt with Jannetje Stevens, who then transfers back to Vermeer's estate the twenty-six paintings in the possession of Jan Coelenbier. A public sale of Vermeer's paintings is planned.

12 March, in a notarized deed, Maria Thins formally notifies Anthony van Leeuwenhoek that the *Art of Painting* was transferred to her on 24 February 1676 by Catharina Bolnes, and that the painting should therefore not be included in the planned sale of paintings from Vermeer's estate in the Guild Hall of Saint Luke.

13 March, Anthony van Leeuwenhoek denies the legality of the transfer and states that should Maria Thins "pretend to have any rights thereto, she would have to enter a claim as a preferred creditor."

15 March, the sale of paintings from Vermeer's estate, including the *Art of Painting*, takes place in the Guild Hall of Saint Luke.

1680

27 December, Maria Thins is buried; her daughter Catharina Bolnes inherits her possessions.

1687

30 December, Catharina Bolnes is given the Last Sacraments and is buried three days later.

This text is based primarily upon documents published in Montias 1989.

Note to the Reader

Titles and dates published here are those proposed by the authors.

Dimensions are in centimeters, followed by inches within parentheses, with height preceding width. Measurements were taken from painted edge to painted edge.

The entries were jointly written by Arthur K. Wheelock, Jr., who provided the art historical interpretation, and Ben Broos, who discussed the provenance and compiled the chronological summaries of the provenance, literature, and exhibition history. Nicola Costaras wrote most of the technical descriptions.

In the exhibitions, collection catalogues, and literature sections of the entries, and in the endnotes: Abbreviations are explained in the bibliography and listing of collection and exhibitions catalogues, beginning on page 210; numbers in parentheses following "Lugt no." refer to sale catalogues listed in Frits Lugt, *Répertoire des catalogues de ventes publiques*, 3 vols., The Hague, 1938–1964; vol. 4, Paris, 1987.

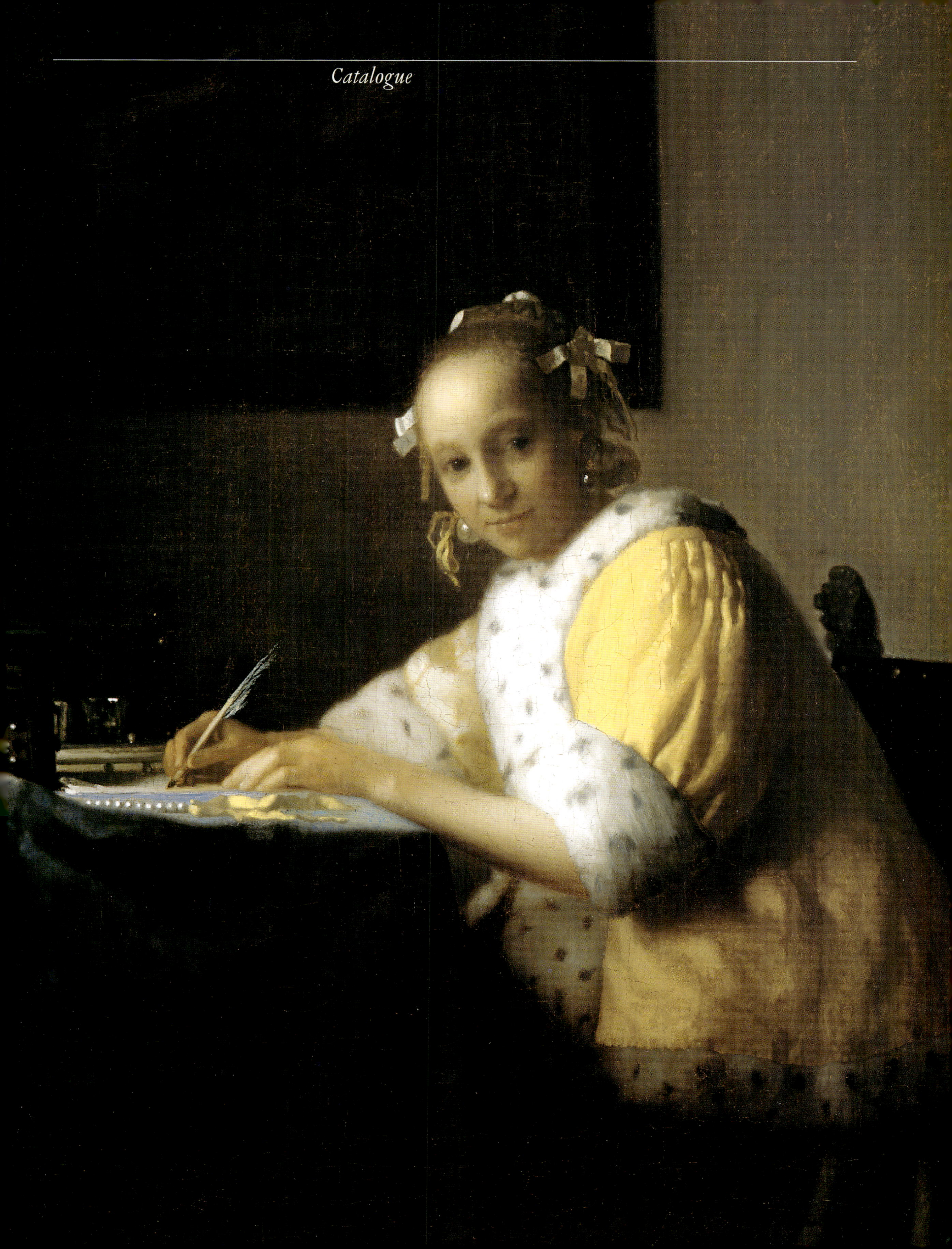

1

Saint Praxedis

1655

inscribed lower left: *Meer 1655;* lower right: *Meer N R[..]o[.]o*

oil on canvas, 101.6 x 82.6 (40 x 32½)

The Barbara Piasecka Johnson Collection Foundation

PROVENANCE

Erna and Jacob Reder, New York, 1943–1969; [Spencer Samuels & Co, New York, 1969–1987]; to the present owner in 1987

EXHIBITIONS

New York 1969, 44–45, no. 39 and ill. 22; New York 1984, no. 14; Warsaw 1990, II, 272–277, no. 48 and ill.; Cracow 1991, 8–28, and several ills.

TECHNICAL DESCRIPTION

The plain-weave canvas support has a regular weft of 10 threads per centimeter. The painting has been relined.

The light brown ground consists primarily of lead white, iron oxides, and calcium. A darker brown imprimatura layer exists under the sky, which is painted with natural ultramarine. The gown, lips, and blood are painted in red lakes over lead white. The pigments in the yellow paint on the rim of the urn are lead white and yellow ocher. Many different textural effects have been created with the use of glazing, scumbling, impasto, and dry brushstrokes.

The painting is in excellent condition, with only a few small losses along the right side and bottom.

Until recently it had been difficult to comprehend fully the implications of Vermeer's conversion to Catholicism after his marriage to Catharina Bolnes in 1653. The discovery of *Saint Praxedis* some years ago, however, has raised our appreciation of the seriousness of Vermeer's commitment to his new faith and its implications for his art.

Saint Praxedis was first publicly shown in 1969 in an exhibition on Florentine painting at the Metropolitan Museum of Art,[1] where it was attributed to a Florentine artist, Felice Ficherelli (1605–c. 1669).[2] The signature and date "Meer 1655" inscribed on the painting were noted in the catalogue.[3] Yet the subject matter was then so unexpected for Vermeer that only one reviewer of the exhibition seriously considered the possibility that the Delft artist might have executed a copy of a well-known composition by the Florentine painter.[4] Other scholars demurred, and the painting remained outside the accepted canon of Vermeer's paintings for another fifteen years.[5]

The painting was not published as a Vermeer until 1986.[6] In the meantime the model for the painting had been found in a private collection in Ferrara (fig. 1). A second signature was also discovered along the lower right edge of the painting, which could be deciphered as: "[Ver]Meer N[aar] R[ip]o[s]o" or "Vermeer After Riposo." Riposo was the Italian nickname of Ficherelli.[7]

In 1987 the painting was acquired by Mrs. Barbara "Basia" Piasecka Johnson. Mrs. Johnson, widow of J. Seward Johnson (1895–1983), has in recent years assembled an outstanding collection of modern and old master paintings, many of which have religious subjects.[8]

Saint Praxedis (or Prassede), a Roman Christian from the second century A.D., was revered for having cared for the bodies of those martyred for their faith.[9] She and her sister, Saint Pudentiana, who may be seen walking near the martyrium in the right background, both followed their father Pudens, a disciple of Saint Paul, in devotion to the Christian faith during a time of intense persecution. This striking painting depicts the kneeling saint collecting the blood of a decapitated martyr. As she squeezes the blood from a sponge into an elegant ewer, her mood is one of reverence and quiet contemplation.

Although some scholars still question the attribution to Vermeer and speculate that it was painted by Jan van der Meer of Utrecht,[10] the arguments for the attribution to the Delft master are many. To begin with, the signatures and date are integral to the paint surface. The paint and ground layers have been analyzed, and have been shown to be entirely consistent with those used by seventeenth-century Dutch artists, including Vermeer.[11] Even the manner of laying on the paint is similar. In the lighter areas of the gown, for example, Vermeer painted a thin layer of madder lake over a lead white base to suggest the softly luminous

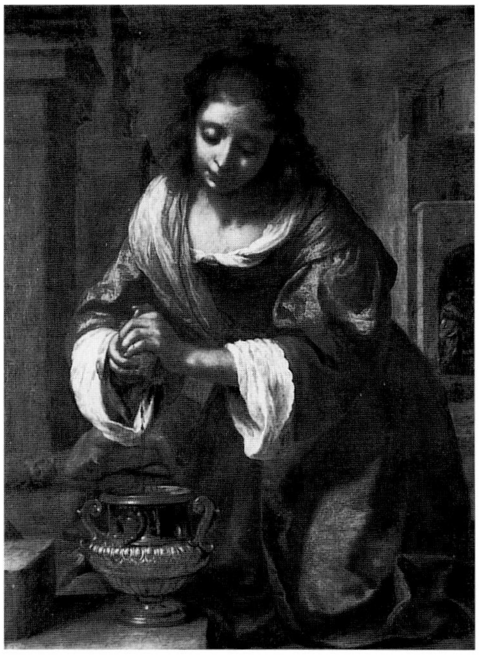

fig. 1. Felice Ficherelli, *Saint Praxedis*, c. 1645, oil on canvas, Collection Fergnani, Ferrara

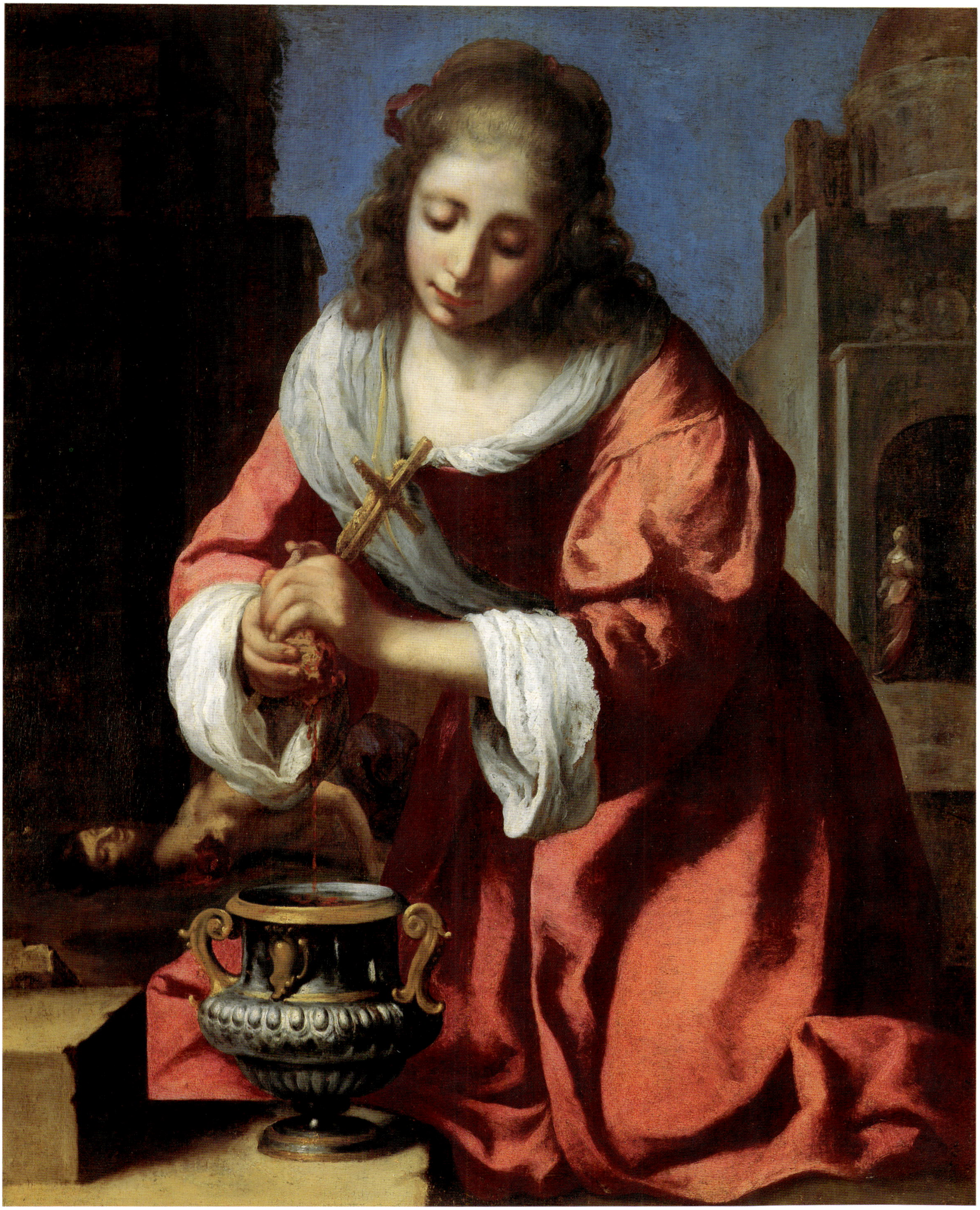

material. He used a similar technique in Mary's blouse in *Christ in the House of Mary and Martha* and in the red blouse of the nymph seated next to Diana in *Diana and Her Companions* (cats. 2, 3). Indeed, the handling of the folds on the right arms of Saint Praxedis and the nymph is quite similar. The more flickering character of Saint Praxedis' left sleeve resembles in technique and style the sleeve of the nymph kneeling before Diana. One other point of comparison between *Saint Praxedis* and the Mauritshuis painting is the technique used to paint the deep blue sky. Vermeer, perhaps following the lead of Ficherelli, executed both skies in an unusual manner for a Dutch artist – natural ultramarine laid over a dark *imprimatura* layer.

Subtle modifications in the modeling of the figure, moreover, are consistent with painting techniques seen in other of Vermeer's early works. The most personal and sensitively rendered area of the painting is the saint's face. Vermeer subtly altered Ficherelli's work by elongating the head and painting broader planes of light and dark across the forehead. He softened the edges of these planes and painted the facial features with numerous small brushstrokes. As a result, the image evokes a quiet, pensive mood appropriate to the saint's actions. The physiognomy of Saint Praxedis, and her reflective attitude with downcast eyes, resembles that of other female figures in Vermeer's paintings. The most striking comparison is in *A Woman Asleep*, c. 1657 (page 20, fig. 6). An almost mirror image of Saint Praxedis, this woman has the same long, straight nose and wide bridge between the eyebrows.

The most significant difference between Ficherelli's and Vermeer's paintings, however, is not stylistic but iconographic, and, as does his innovative handling of the story of Christ in the house of Mary and Martha, speaks to Vermeer's strong commitment to the Catholic faith. Vermeer's *Saint Praxedis* holds a crucifix as she squeezes the sponge. The crucifix in this context symbolically suggests the co-mingling of Christ's blood with that of the martyred Christian. Its presence thus accentuates the sacramental character of Saint Praxedis' actions and affirms the Catholic doctrine of the Communion of Saints.[12]

The reasons why Vermeer painted this profoundly Catholic painting are not known. They may have been personal, although it is also possible that the painting was commissioned by a Jesuit patron, perhaps one of Maria Thins' circle in Delft. The ideal of dedication to one's faith, so exemplified by the legends attached to the saints' lives, paralleled closely the concept of sanctity propagated at that time by the Jesuits. Saint Praxedis was also celebrated because she, as well as other early saints, reinforced the primacy of the Catholic faith. One can also imagine that the saint's merciful care of the dead and maimed would have struck a poignant chord in Delft in 1655, shortly after a devastating gunpowder explosion of 12 October 1654 took the lives of hundreds of citizens. Whether the image came about as a personal reflection or a commission, it may have served as a spiritual balm in a time of profound need for healing and comfort.

The close relationship between *Saint Praxedis* and its Florentine prototype demonstrates the international flavor of Vermeer's early history paintings (something only implicitly evident in *Christ in the House of Mary and Martha*). While it is not known where Vermeer saw Ficherelli's painting, whether in the Netherlands, Flanders, or Italy, the last possibility should not be excluded. Indeed, it seems probable that Vermeer was not present in Delft during the early 1650s since no documents locate him there before April 1653. One could imagine that Leonard Bramer (1596–1674), with whom Vermeer had both personal and professional connections, would have recommended a study trip to Italy similar to the one he himself had taken.

Ficherelli's painting could have been in the Netherlands, but, if so, probably not in Delft. Although Vermeer's father was a picture-dealer and his mother-in-law inherited a substantial art collection, the number of Italian works in Delft collections was quite limited. Montias' scrupulous examination of Delft archival records only turned up five paintings attributed to Italian masters from around mid-century. Montias speculates that at least three of these works, and perhaps all five, were copies. Nevertheless, the very presence in Delft of copies after Italian paintings indicates the existence of a market for such works.[13]

More Italian paintings were to be found in Utrecht and Amsterdam than in Delft. Given the probability that Vermeer visited, and perhaps studied in, both of these centers, it is possible that he encountered Ficherelli's painting somewhere other than in his native town. The Amsterdam art dealer Johannes de Renialme, for example, who listed a now-lost "Grave Visitation" by Vermeer in his 1657 inventory, owned ten Italian pictures.[14] Since De Renialme was registered as an art dealer in the Delft guild, and was closely acquainted with Willem de Langue, the Vermeer family notary, the probability is great that Vermeer knew these paintings, and similar ones, in Delft. In any event, Vermeer was certainly familiar with Italian art, for otherwise he would not have been summoned to The Hague in 1672 as an expert in Italian paintings.[15] Furthermore, as seen in the discussions of *The Milkmaid* (cat. 5) and *Allegory of Faith* (cat. 20), he was familiar with, and adapted motifs from, other Italian seventeenth-century paintings.

1. New York 1969, 44–45, no. 39. and ill. 22.
2. For Ficherelli's life, see Baldinucci 1681–1728, 6:219–225; and Cracow 1991, 7. Ficherelli was born in San Gimignano in 1605. As a young boy he went to Florence where he began his training in the studio of Jacopo Chimenti, called Jacopo da Empoli (1554–1640). For a time he lived in the palace of Alberto de' Bardi, who worked closely with Cardinal Carlo de' Medici, another influential patron of the arts. The artist received many commissions for the churches of Florence and the surrounding area, including Sant'Egidio and the Certosa. Despite his quiet, modest nature, which earned him the nickname, "il Riposo," his favorite subjects were scenes of dramatic action, even violence, particularly martyrdoms and famous murders of the past. He died c. 1669 in Florence and was buried in the church of Santa Maria sopr'Arno.
3. Vermeer's signature in the lower left was noted in the catalogue (New York 1969, 44–45) after it had been examined by Ted Rousseau and members of the conservation department at the Metropolitan Museum of Art (information courtesy of Mr. Spencer Samuels).
4. Kitson 1969, 410. This consideration was followed by Hannema 1974–1975, 22; and Hannema 1978, 95 and ill. 6.
5. Blankert 1975, 112 n. 5, deemed the calligraphy of the signature to be "irregular" and the execution of the painting as a whole to be "coarse"; Blankert 1978, 75 n. 13, later called the painting "no more than a copy after the Florentine painter Felice Ficherelli." Wright 1976, 7 and fig. 3, included the painting in the introduction to his book, although not in the catalogue, as "attributed to Vermeer."
6. Samuels bought the painting in 1969 from Mrs. Erna Reder, who, with her husband Jacob had owned the painting since 1943. Its earlier provenance is not known. See Richard 1987, 18, and Wheelock 1986. Vermeer's *Saint Praxedis* and Ficherelli's *Saint Praxedis* were subsequently the subject of a focus exhibition; see Cracow 1991.
7. Egbert Haverkamp-Begemann first deciphered the second signature. Wheelock 1986, 74–75 and ill. 4.
8. See, in particular, Warsaw 1990.
9. The earliest depiction of Saint Praxedis is probably a mosaic in the Saint Zenone chapel in the Basilica di Santa Prassede in Rome, in which she lies buried. See Henze 1962, 256; on the theme see Réau 1955–1959, 3:1119.
10. Weber 1993, 300–301, has argued that the painting by Ficherelli never left Italy and that the artist who copied it was not Johannes Vermeer of Delft, but Johan van der Meer from Utrecht (c. 1630–1688), who is known to have been in Rome in the mid-1650s, and who reportedly painted in the manner of Guido Reni. In fact, however, nothing is known about the location of Ficherelli's painting at this time. The stylistic and thematic connections of *Saint Praxedis* to Vermeer of Delft's paintings, moreover, are far more compelling than to those of Van der Meer from Utrecht. Indeed, at one time or another, all of Vermeer's early history paintings have been attributed to the latter artist (see cats. 2, 3), whose mediocre talents would seem to preclude his involvements with any of these works.
11. The most extensive analytical report, dated 27 June 1972, was prepared by Dr. Hermann Kühn from the Doerner Institut, Munich. Although he indicated that technical examination could not confirm the attribution to Vermeer, he did write that: "Sowohl das Verteilungsmuster der Spurenelemente im Bleiweiss als auch der Fullstoff Kreide in der Grundierung sprechen mit grosser Wahrscheinlichkeit dafür, daß das untersuchte Bild in den Niederlanden entstanden ist..."; curatorial files, National Gallery of Art.
12. This belief unites the faithful on earth, the saints in heaven, and those souls in purgatory in the active union of shared sacramental grace known as the Mystical Body of Christ. I would like to thank Karen N. Sinderson, a graduate student at the University of Maryland, for drawing my attention to the significance of this union of a martyr's blood with that of Christ.
13. Montias 1982, 249–250. For further discussion of Italian paintings in the Netherlands, see Lugt 1936.
14. Montias 1982, 250 n. hh. Montias 1989, 141. De Renialme also owned a copy of an "Interment" by Titian made by the Utrecht artist Cornelis van Poelenburgh (c. 1586–1667).
15. Montias 1989, 333–334, doc. 341. Vermeer and the other expert, the Delft painter Johannes Jordaens, concluded that the paintings in question were "not outstanding Italian paintings, but, on the contrary, great pieces of rubbish and bad paintings...."

LITERATURE

Kitson 1969, 410; Burlington Magazine 1969, unpaginated and pl. 33; Hannema 1974–1975, 22 and ill. 30; Blankert 1975, 112 n. 5; Wright 1976, 7 and ill. 3; Blankert 1978, 75 n. 13; Hannema 1978, 95 and ill. 6; Aillaud 1986, 163 n. 5; Wheelock 1986, 71–89, ills. 1, 3–4, 7–13, 15–16 and 19–20; Plechl 1987; Richard 1987, 18 and ill.; Wheelock 1988, 8, 13, 50–51 and pl. 2; Montias 1989, 140–143, 146 and ill. 17; Blankert 1992, 163 n. 5; Chong 1992, 21, 89 n. 23; Liedtke 1992, 96, 104–105 nn. 37–38 and ill. 3; Mauritshuis 1993A, 314 n. 41; Montias 1993, 162–163 and ill. 17; Weber 1993, 301 and ill. 7; Wheelock 1995, 7, 20–27, 29, 34, 36, 113, 163, 169, and ill. 8

2

Christ in the House of Mary and Martha

c. 1655
inscribed lower left, on the bench: *IVMeer* (IVM in ligature)
oil on canvas, 160 x 142 (63 x 56)

National Galleries of Scotland, Edinburgh

PROVENANCE
(?) John Hugh Smyth Pigott, Brockley Hall, 1829; Abbot Family, Bristol, c. 1880; Furniture and antique dealer, Bristol, sold in 1884 to a private party for £10 and bought back for £13; Arthur Leslie Colley, London (purchased for £140, along with two paintings, by Raeburn); [Forbes & Paterson, London, 1901, sold to Coats]; William Allan Coats, Skelmorlie Castle, Dalskairth (Dumfries and Galloway, Scotland), 1901–1926; Thomas H. Coats and J. A. Coats, 1926–1927; to the present owner in 1927 (donation of the Coats heirs)

EXHIBITIONS
London 1929A, 147, no. 310; Amsterdam 1935, 26-27, no. 162 and ill. 162; Rotterdam 1935, 34, no. 79 and ill. 59; Utrecht 1952, 57-58, no. 92 and ill. 71; Edinburgh 1992, 150-151, no. 71 and ill.

TECHNICAL DESCRIPTION
The support is a fine, plain-weave linen with a thread count of 12 x 17 per cm^2. A vertical seam is in line with Christ's elbow. The canvas has been paste-lined and the original tacking edges have been removed. The double ground consists of a layer of white chalk bound with a protein medium followed by a red earth layer.[1]

In the background and in the shadowed flesh tones of Christ and Martha the red ground is only partially covered by very thin brown glazes. What appears to have been a glaze on Christ's violet tunic is preserved only in the texture of the brushwork. The highlights on all the drapery are painted with impasto; on Christ's blue robe, which was painted with indigo, smalt, and lead white, the brushstrokes are about 1 cm wide and indicate a square-tipped brush. Numerous wet-in-wet touches include the details of Martha's waistband, the modeling of the headclothes, and the decoration on the carpet. The speed of execution and the fluidity of the paint is also signified by the splashy, broken edges of many of the forms, such as the upper edge of the table and Mary's profile.

There are several alterations: Christ's profile and ear; the fingers of His left hand; and the edge of Martha's right sleeve. The edges of some of the forms encroach significantly on adjacent areas such as the upper edge of Christ's robe overlapping His tunic. Mary's left hand appears to have been painted over Christ's blue robe.

This painting, when encountered for the first time, comes as a shock. *Christ in the House of Mary and Martha* is so large, and so different in appearance from the images generally associated with Vermeer, that the viewer's expectations must be adjusted to a different set of criteria. Not only is the scene drawn from the New Testament instead of from daily life, but the figures are life size, or even larger, and placed within a vaguely defined, ocher interior, rather than a light-filled room. The paint, applied fluidly and in broad planes of color, is unusual for Vermeer, particularly the purple of the tunic worn by Christ and the orange-yellow found in both Martha's bodice and the tablecovering.

Of course, to react in surprise at the appearance of *Christ in the House of Mary and Martha* is to react with a hindsight gained from knowledge of Vermeer's mature style. However, one must be careful about interpolating too much about Vermeer's artistic approach in the mid 1650s from this one work. It seems probable that *Christ in the House of Mary and Martha* was a commissioned piece, since the scale and subject matter make it quite improbable that the painting would have been sold on the open market. Thus, the composition and/or iconography may have been influenced by the desires of a patron, whether an individual or a church body. It is, of course, entirely possible that a body of genre scenes and landscapes, or other history paintings in a different style, may have existed among Vermeer's now-lost juvenilia.

Given such qualifications, the style and iconography of this work demonstrate not only important artistic and theological currents with which Vermeer contended at the beginning of his career, but also his artistic prowess.[2] While the general stylistic characteristics of this work, which probably dates c. 1655, are comparable to those seen in history paintings executed in other Dutch artistic centers around mid-century, Vermeer's execution has virtually nothing to do with Delft artistic traditions from the late 1640s and early 1650s.[3] This painting thus suggests that Vermeer not only received his training but also continued to seek his artistic inspiration outside Delft, even after he had joined the Saint Luke's Guild at the end of 1653.

The style of *Christ in the House of Mary and Martha* relates to works found in Utrecht, particularly paintings by Abraham Bloemaert (1564–1651), a distant relative of Vermeer's mother-in-law's family,[4] and Hendrick ter Brugghen (1588–1629). Ter Brugghen's paintings from the late 1620s, among them his *Saint Sebastian* in Oberlin (fig. 1), depict comparably large-scale figures tightly framed in a triangular arrangement within the foreground of his composition. The mood in both the Oberlin and Edinburgh paintings is remarkably quiet, even pensive. Faces are

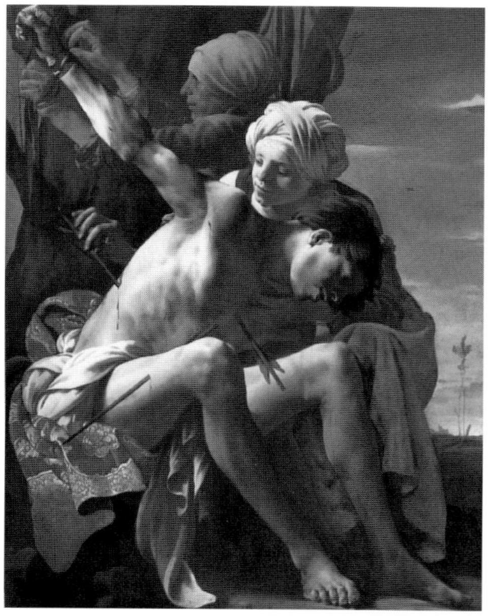

fig. 1. Hendrick ter Brugghen, *Saint Sebastian*, 1625, oil on canvas, Allen Memorial Art Museum, Oberlin College, Ohio, R. T. Miller, Jr. Fund, 1953

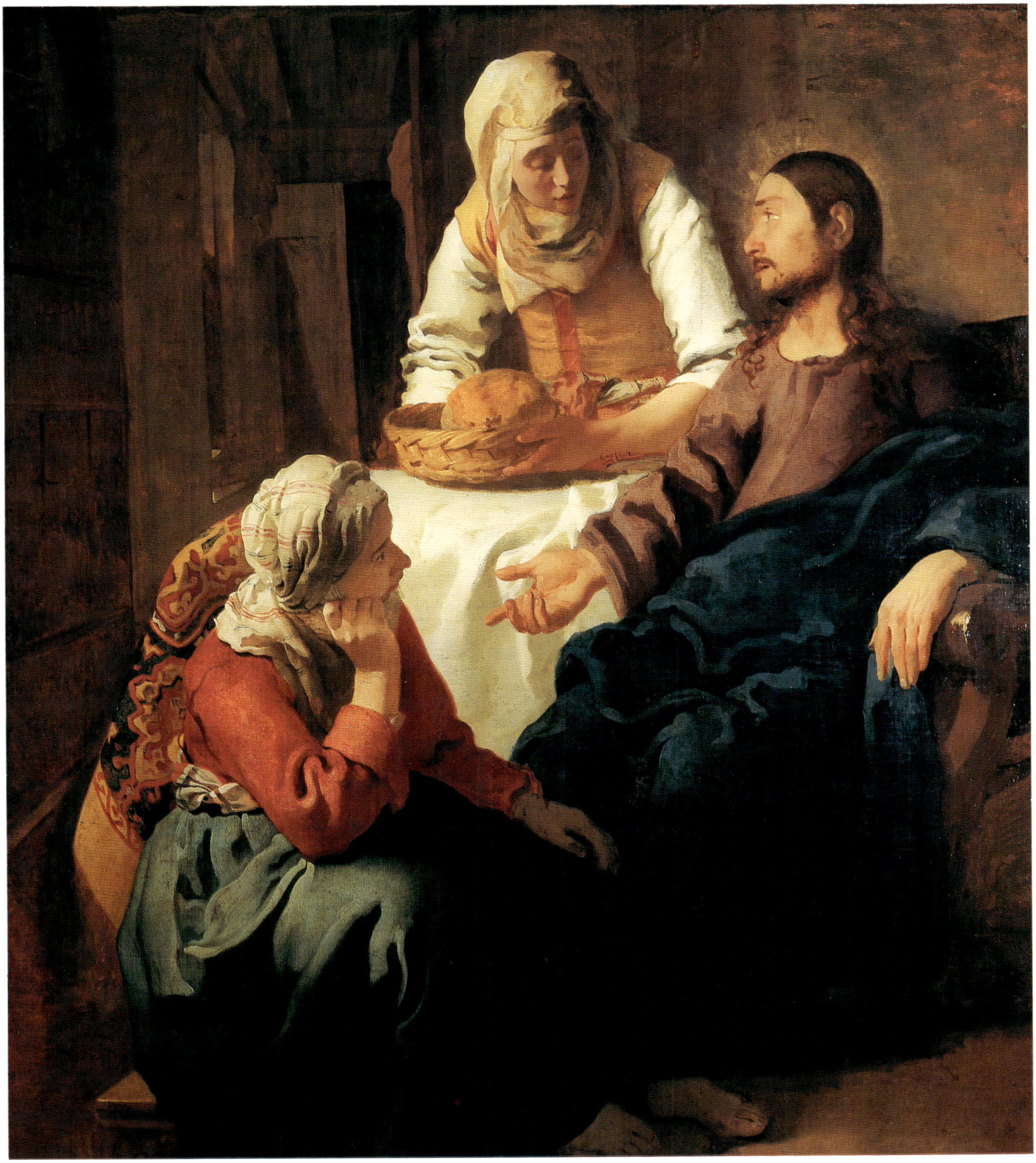

generalized and broadly modeled, with shadows falling across the features. The women's heads are similarly covered, and broad, relatively flat planes of color in the draperies are suddenly interrupted by quick rhythms of folds.

Neither Bloemaert nor Ter Brugghen, however, ever depicted the theme of *Christ in the House of Mary and Martha*, which suggests that other prototypes may exist for this work. The story of Christ in the House of Mary and Martha, represented by Pieter Aertsen (1509–1575) and Joachim Beuckelaer (c. 1530–1573) in the mid-sixteenth century, continued to interest seventeenth-century Dutch, Italian, and Flemish painters. As Ludwig Goldscheider noted, Vermeer was familiar with the pictorial tradition for this subject and adopted the pose of Christ from a type widely found in Italian and Flemish painting.[5] While no exact prototype has been identified, interesting connections exist between this work and a large canvas (fig. 2) in Valenciennes, which was executed about 1645 by the Flemish artist Erasmus II Quellinus (1607–1678).[6] Similarities between these two works include the pose and Italianate features of Christ, the vaguely defined doorway behind the figures, and the relatively free and fluid brushwork highlighting the ridges of the drapery folds, which is quite unlike Dutch stylistic traditions.

Although the precise pictorial source for *Christ in the House of Mary and Martha* is not known, he could have been inspired by a painting encountered while traveling outside Delft. Quellinus' painting, for example, was in Antwerp,[7] which Vermeer could well have visited. While no documents confirm a study trip, it is also true that no documents locate him in Delft prior to April 1653. The Dutch could travel freely after the Treaty of Münster in 1648, and the flourishing art market in the Flemish city may well have been of interest to Vermeer, who had inherited his father's art dealing business in 1652. Another Delft art dealer, Abraham de Coge, had extensive contacts in Antwerp during these very years.[8]

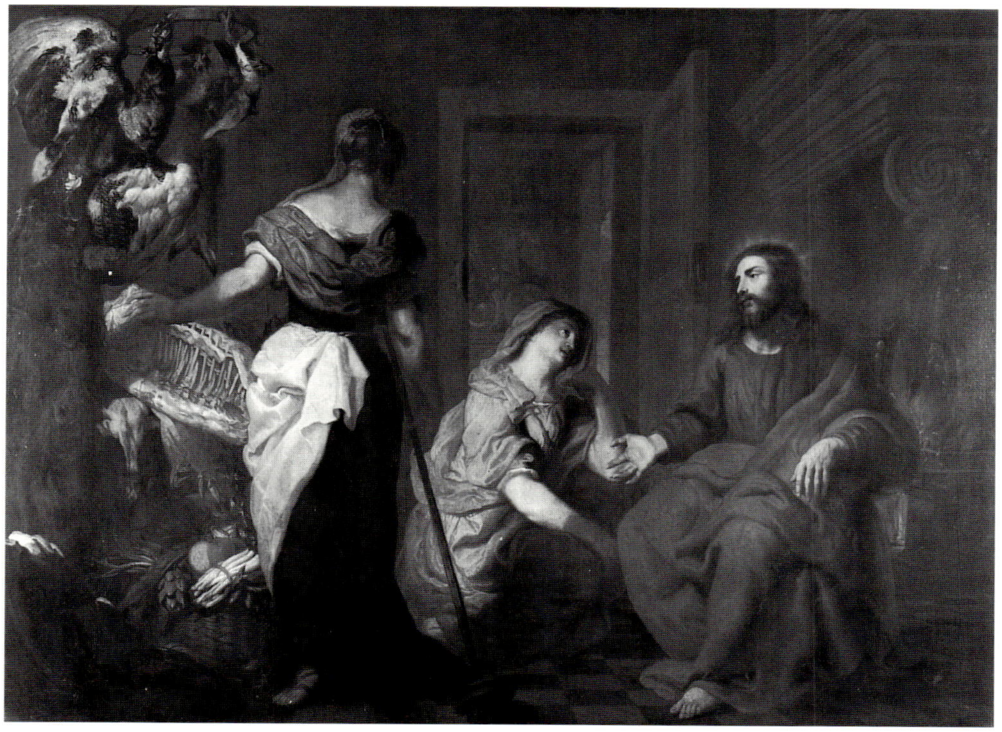

fig. 2. Erasmus Quellinus II, *Christ in the House of Mary and Martha*, c. 1645, oil on canvas, Musée des Beaux-Arts, Valenciennes, Photographie Giraudon

Frequently overlooked in discussions that place *Christ in the House of Mary and Martha* stylistically within the framework of mid-seventeenth-century Dutch history painting is the young Vermeer's remarkably sophisticated theological interpretation of the story from the Gospel of Saint Luke 10: 38–42. Christ, traveling with His disciples, had reached a village where He was welcomed in the home of Martha and her sister Mary. While Martha busied herself providing food and service, Mary sat at the feet of Jesus and listened to him speak. Dismayed with Mary's lack of assistance, Martha protested to Christ, asking that He tell Mary to help. His response was gentle but firm: "Martha, Martha, you are anxious and troubled about many things; one thing is needful. Mary has chosen the better part, which shall not be taken from her."

While Quellinus' and Vermeer's interpretations of the subject are superfically similar, they have different theological implictions. Quellinus, who portrays Martha with her back to the viewer, holding a broom, and adjacent to an abundant still life, clearly juxtaposes her concern for Christ's physical well-being with Mary's pensive demeanor as she raptly gazes at Christ. Although Quellinus places the protagonists in the foreground instead of deep within his pictorial space, his basic approach is comparable to that seen in representations of the scene by Aertsen and Beuckelaer, where a contrast is established between the *vita activa*, represented by Martha, and the *vita contemplativa*, represented by Mary. The message conveyed

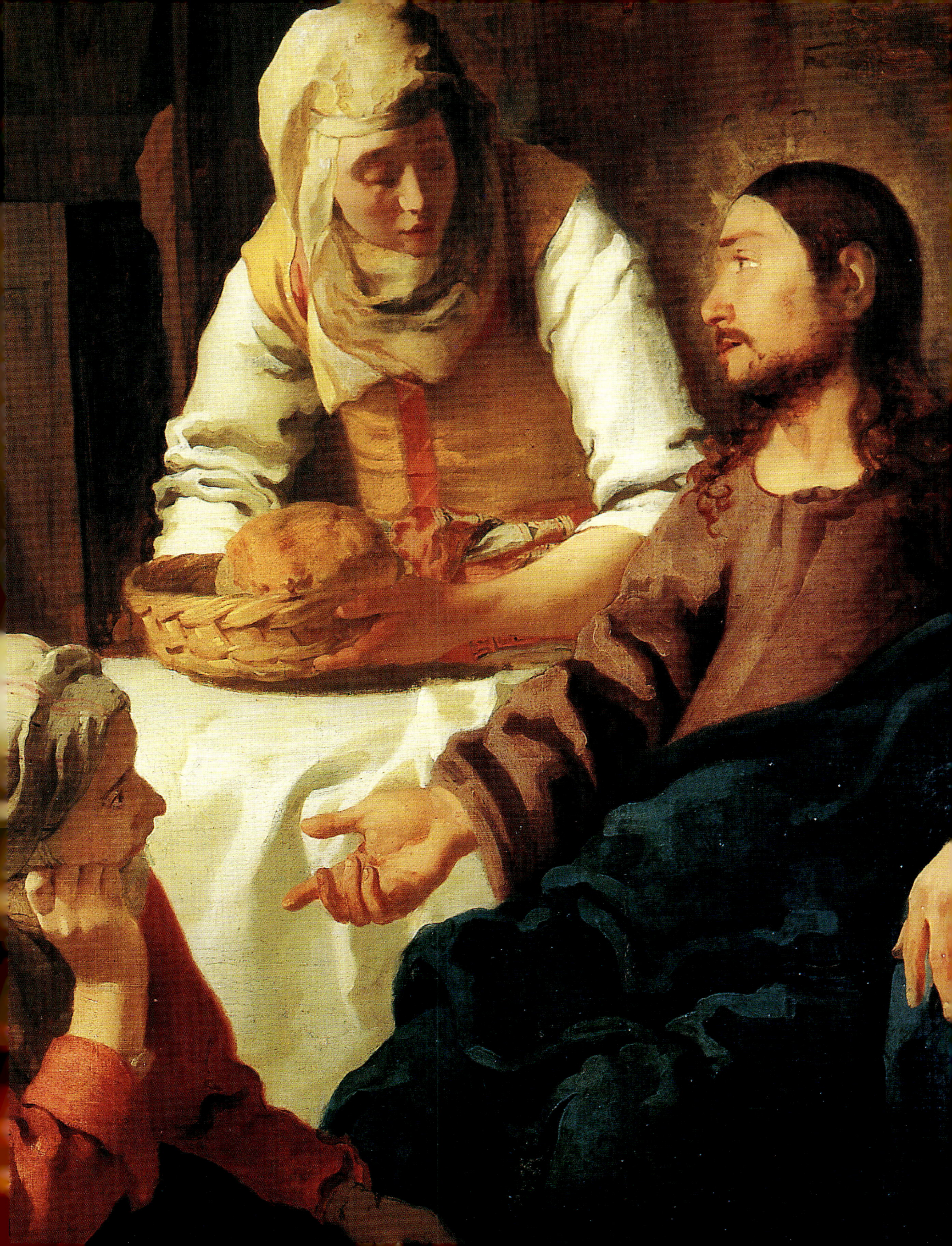

is that the *vita contemplativa* is to be preferred to the *vita activa*, for the former focuses on eternal life rather than the temporal world.

In this painting Vermeer has thus touched upon one of the most fundamental theological disputes between Protestants and Catholics: the proper path to salvation.[9] While Catholics believe that salvation is earned by joining faith with good works, Protestants view salvation, or grace, as a gift given directly by God. Indeed, the Catholic interpretation of this biblical story is that the active and the contemplative are both essential components of a Christian life.[10] Caring for others was, in fact, one of the Acts of Mercy indicated by Christ as necessary for admittance into the kingdom of heaven. The sixteenth-century humanist Erasmus interpreted Christ's mild rebuke to Martha as an appeal to restraint, a warning against paying excess attention to physical requirements when only "one thing was needed."[11]

Vermeer departs from the traditional representation of this biblical episode by knitting together the three protagonists rather than by separating Martha compositionally from Mary and Christ. Far from being preoccupied with a variety of accoutrements associated with worldly needs, Vermeer's Martha serves but one thing, a basket of bread. The eucharistic implication of her offering, which Vermeer has placed at the very center of the composition, further dignifies her role within the story.

The circumstances surrounding this painting's discovery at the end of the nineteenth century are fascinating for the history of Vermeer connoisseurship. *Christ in the House of Mary and Martha* first surfaced around 1880, but its appearance caused little excitement until 1901, when cleaning undertaken by Forbes & Paterson, the London dealers who owned the painting, revealed the signature "IVMeer."[12] In that very year Abraham Bredius, at the time director of the Mauritshuis, and Willem Martin, the recently appointed deputy director, visited the London dealer to examine the painting. The work particularly interested them because the *Diana and Her Companions* in their museum was also signed "IVMeer." The attribution of *Diana and Her Companions* had been a matter of dispute.[13] Some believed it to have been executed by the Johannes Vermeer (or Van der Meer) from Delft, but others, including Bredius, believed that the artist had been Johan van der Meer from Utrecht, whom Houbraken described as having visited Rome where he purportedly worked in an Italianate style.[14]

Bredius, who kept a notebook of his observations in London, found similarities in the colors of the two paintings and recognized that the works had been executed by the same artist (see page 100, fig. 4). For him, however, the fact that the two history paintings appeared to have been painted "under Italian influence" made their attribution to the "Utrecht Vermeer" all the more plausible.[15] Martin, on the other hand, concluded that both paintings had been executed by the Delft Vermeer, noting that the colors in these works were similar to those in Vermeer's *The Procuress*, 1656, in Dresden (page 60, fig. 16).[16] A few years later he expressed his excitement at this discovery by exclaiming: "that it was truly a Vermeer: the thirty-second, therefore!"[17] In subsequent years only P. T. A. Swillens has disputed this assessment, reverting in 1950 to Bredius' attribution to the "Utrecht Vermeer."[18]

The interest of Bredius and Martin in the painting was primarily academic, for they made no effort to acquire this work. In April of 1901 the canvas became the property of the Scottish sewing-thread manufacturer William Allan Coats (1853–1926). In a letter dated 2 October 1903, Coats recalled what he knew about the provenance of the painting: "My large Vermeer of Delft was sold to an old lady by a dealer in 1884 for £10 and resold for £13 – Colley bought it from a dealer who bought it from its owner, a Bristol man called Abbot."[19] Earlier in the nineteenth century, it had probably been in the collection of John Hugh Smyth Pigott in Brockley Hall, where, in 1829, "The Saviour with Martha and Mary" hung under the name of Raphael.[20] From the 1890s on, Coats had collected old masters, which William Paterson catalogued in 1904.[21] Upon his death, his sons, Thomas H. and Major J. A. Coats, sold the collection, but in 1927 they donated the Vermeer to the National Gallery of Scotland in Edinburgh in memory of their father.[22] According to a commentary of the time, it was the most handsome Vermeer in all of England, and was estimated to be worth £60,000.[23]

1. Kühn 1968, 177.
2. Liedtke 1992, 93–96, argues that *Christ in the House of Mary and Martha* is a more sophisticated composition than *Diana and Her Companions* and, hence, should be dated later than the Mauritshuis painting.
3. The one possible exception being the Caravaggisti paintings by Christiaen van Couwenbergh (1604–1667). Van Couwenbergh, who was profoundly influenced by the Utrecht painter Gerard van Honthorst (1590–1656), painted for the Prince of Orange as well as at the Huis ten Bosch. He left Delft in 1654 and moved to Cologne. See cat. 8, n. 4.
4. Montias 1991, 43, notes that Bloemaert was the uncle-in-law of Jan (Geensz) Thins, the cousin of Maria Thins "who had bought the house in Delft where Vermeer spent his mature years and died."
5. Goldscheider 1967, 125, cat. 1, refers to a number of Italian prototypes and illustrates, in reverse, the figure of Christ from Giovanni Biliverti's *Christ and the Samaritan Woman* (Kunsthistorisches Museum, Vienna), executed in Florence in the 1640s. As noted by Wheelock 1981, 66, fig. 60, Leonard Bramer depicted the figure of Christ in an identical pose in his drawing *Disciple Washing the Feet of*

Christ, Rijksmuseum, Amsterdam.
6. The attribution of the still life in this painting is uncertain. Although Quellinus did paint still lives, he may have collaborated here with the still life specialist Adriaen van Utrecht (1599–1652/1653).
7. De Bruyn 1988, 143, cat. 66, believes that the painting was in the Sint-Michielsabdij in Antwerp.
8. Montias 1982, 210–211.
9. For the following interpretation I am much indebted to Kathleen Crowe, who discussed this issue of salvation in her 1994 masters thesis at the University of Maryland, "All the Differences in Jan Vermeer's *Christ in the House of Mary and Martha*."
10. See, in particular, Buijs 1989, 93–128. Karen Sinderson, a student at the University of Maryland, has also pointed out in a 1994 seminar report on this painting that this view is consistent with the position given the story within the Gospel of Saint Luke. Christ's visit to the house of Martha and Mary follows the account of the Good Samaritan's example of mercy, with Christ's admonition to "go and do likewise," and precedes Christ's teaching the disciples the Lord's Prayer.
11. Buijs 1989, 104–105.
12. Edinburgh 1992, 150 n. 3, no. 71; Norman Forbes Robertson discovered the signature, as was recalled in *The Morning Post*, 14 January 1927, 9. See also MacColl 1901, 17–18, who discussed the signature of the Edinburgh painting in detail.
13. For a further discussion of the attribution issues surrounding this work, see cat. 3.
14. Houbraken 1718–1721, 3: 291–292. Johan van der Meer from Utrecht (c. 1630–1688) was reportedly in Rome in the mid-1650s and painted in the manner of Guido Reni.
15. Travel notes made by Bredius (London, March 1901; Mauritshuis documentation archives); first published by Marjolein de Boer in Mauritshuis 1993A, 310–311, ills. 2a–b: "Gezien bij Forbes + Robertson – Delftsche (?) Vermeer gem[erkt] 'IVMeer': en ook wel onder ital[iaanse] invloed."
16. Notebook Willem Martin 1889–1901, 126 (RKD): "Zelfde kleuren keeren op 'Diana' in Den Haag terug. Oordeel: zelfde hand als Diana, doch ook wel Dresden". ["The same colors return in the "Diana" in The Hague. Conclusion: the same hand as Diana but also Dresden"]. The attribution of *The Procuress*, signed and dated JVMeer 1656, to Vermeer of Delft had been made by Thoré-Bürger 1858–1860, 2:77. It had previously been attributed to "Vermeer of Utrecht." See Gemäldegalerie Dresden 1982, 331, no. 1335.
17. Martin 1904, 4: "dat het werkelijk een Vermeer was: de twee-en-dertigste dus!"
18. Swillens 1950, 161–164.
19. Edinburgh 1992, 150 and nn. 7–8: Arthur Lesley Colley; nothing else is known about Abbot.
20. According to a letter from Maria Mendes Maurao (Museum Art Gallery, Bristol) to the National Gallery of Scotland (19 May 1976); the "Raphael" painting was mentioned in Rutter 1829, 27.
21. In his residence Skelmorlie Castle in Scotland, Coats cherished paintings by artists such as Caesar van Everdingen, Frans Hals, Salomon Koninck and Pieter Saenredam, as well as an enigmatic *Portrait of Vermeer and His Wife*. See: Coats 1904, ill. 38.
22. On Coats and Paterson, see Edinburgh 1992, 161–162.
23. Bodmer 1927, 67.

COLLECTION CATALOGUES

National Gallery Scotland 1929, 277; National Gallery Scotland 1936, 315–316, ill.; National Gallery Scotland 1957, 285–286, no. 1670; National Gallery Scotland 1978, 110–111, no. 1670.

LITERATURE

Bredius 1901, unpaginated; MacColl 1901, 5, 14–18; Athenaeum 1901, 409; Coats 1904, ill. 37; Martin 1904, 1–3 and ill.; Holmes 1904–1905, 330 and ill; Hofstede de Groot 1907–1928, 1: 587, no. 1; Plietzsch 1911, 12–13, 119, no. 36 and ill. 1; Borenius 1923, 37–38 and ill. B; Morning Post 1927a, 9; Morning Post 1927b, 9; Bodmer 1927, 66–67 and ill.; Th. 1936, 157–159 and ill. 1; Hale 1937, 163–167 and pl. 38; De Vries 1939, 33–34, 77–78, no. 2, ills. 5–6 and 28; Swillens 1950, 161–164, no. B and pl. 34; Gowing 1952, 79–84, no. 1 and ills. 1–3; Goldscheider 1967, 18, 125, no. 1 and pls. 1–4; Blankert 1975, 14–17, 21–23, 50, 113 n. 16, 138, no. 1 and pl. 1; Wheelock 1977A, 268 and ill. 64; Blankert 1978, 13–17, 34, 76 n. 24, 155, no. 1 and pl. 1; Slatkes 1981, 14–17 and ills.; Wheelock 1981, 15, 64–67, and pls. 1–2; Aillaud 1986, 40, 51, 72, 74–77, 79, 98, 164 n. 16, 171, no. 1, and pl. 2; Wheelock 1988, 48–49 and pl. 1; Montias 1989, 99, 105, 107, 132, 139, 142, 146 and ill. 14; Nash 1991, 44–45, 46, 53, and ill. Blankert 1992, 40, 52, 71–72, 76–77, 98, 164 n. 16, 170, no. 1 and pl. 2; Wheelock 1995, 21, 26, 27, 163, 169, and ill. A1.

3

Diana and Her Companions

c. 1655–1656

inscribed on rock at lower left, between dog and thistle: *JVMeer* (VM in ligature [barely legible])

oil on canvas, 97.8 x 104.6 (38½ x 41³⁄₁₆)

Royal Cabinet of Paintings Mauritshuis, The Hague

PROVENANCE

[Dirksen, The Hague, before 1866, to Goldsmid for *f* 175]; Neville Davison Goldsmid, The Hague, 1866–1875; Eliza Garey, widow of Goldsmid, The Hague/Paris 1875–1876; Goldsmid sale, Paris, 4 May 1876, no. 68 (purchased by Victor de Stuers for the State for *ffr* 10,000 as by Nicolaes Maes); to the present owner in 1876

EXHIBITIONS

London 1929A, 148, no. 313; Amsterdam 1945, 22, no. 133; Delft 1950, 11, no. 26; Milan 1951, 99, no. 187 and ill. 130; Zurich 1953, 72, no. 170 and ill. 27; Milan 1954, 69, no. 170 and ill. 43; Rome 1954, 69, no. 170 and ill. 43; New York 1954, no. 6 and ill.; The Hague 1966, no. 1 and ill.; Paris 1966, no. 1 and ill.; Tokyo 1968, no. 69 and ill.; Washington 1980, 41, 210-211, no. 54 and ills.; Tokyo 1984, 108-109, no. 39 and ill.

TECHNICAL DESCRIPTION

The support is a plain-weave linen with a thread count of 14.3 x 10 per cm^2. The tacking edges have been largely removed. Cusping is present on three sides, but not on the right edge, which has been cut down. The support has a glue/paste lining. An off-white ground, which includes chalk lead white, umber, and a little charcoal black, extends to the edges of the original canvas on all sides.[1] Over the whole painting, except possibly in the sky, extends a thin, transparent reddish brown layer, which is employed in most halftones and shadows.

The composition was first outlined with dark brown brushwork, some of which is visible as pentimenti in the skirt and foot of the woman washing Diana's foot. All the shadows were first blocked in with a dark paint that is especially evident in the flesh tones of Diana and her seated companions. Smalt is present in all the pale flesh tones, mixtures containing white, and the foliage. Vermeer used the handle of the brush to scratch hairs on the dog's ear.

The paint surface is abraded. Vertical lines of paint loss are evident to the left of center. Weave emphasis and squashed cupping have resulted from the lining process.

In the gathering dusk Diana has joined four of her companions near the edge of a wood. Clothed in a loose-fitting yellow dress bound with a sash made from animal skin, Diana sits on a rock in a dark landscape while an attendant tenderly sponges her foot. The nymphs – one sitting with her back to the viewer, another clasping her left foot in her hand, and a third standing to the rear – are shown with heads bowed and eyes averted, each seemingly absorbed in thought. The mood is somber, detached, and reverent. Diana, her face in shadow, stares ahead, as though she, too, is preoccupied with her thoughts and oblivious to the presence of the others.

This painting has no visual precedent, and no obvious literary source.[2] The scene depicts neither the abrupt intrusion of Actaeon nor the shocking discovery of Callisto's pregnancy, themes that abound in mannerist painting at the beginning of the seventeenth century.[3] Vermeer does not depict Diana's rash temper or the harsh judgments that followed these indiscretions. Neither bow and arrow nor dead game signifies Diana's prowess as a huntress, and her gentle dog is unlike the quick hounds that normally accompany her. Her only attribute is the crescent moon upon her forehead, symbolic of her aspect as goddess of the night.

A rich tradition of allegorical portraits had developed by the mid-seventeenth century in which women posed as Diana, the virgin huntress who personified chastity. Among the most imposing of these is the large-scale *Diana and Her Nymphs*, painted in Amsterdam around 1650 by Jacob van Loo (c. 1615–1670) (fig. 1). Here the woman posed as Diana sits in a woodland glade accompanied by a number of

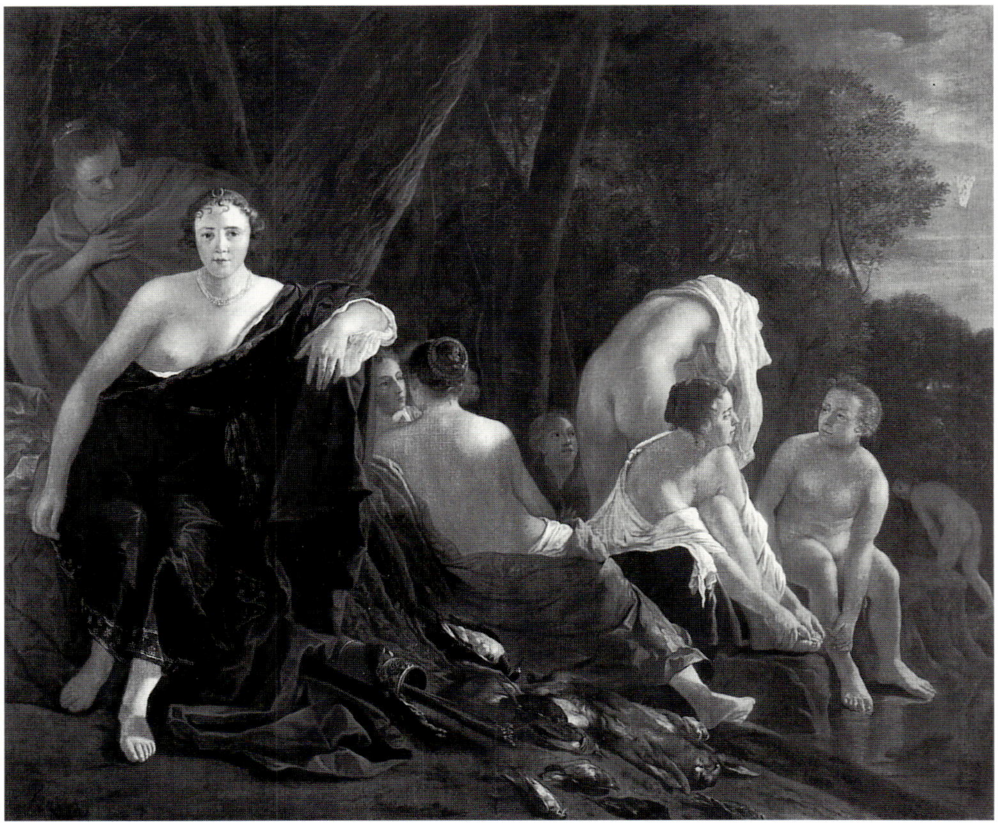

fig. 1. Jacob van Loo, *Diana and Her Nymphs*, c. 1650, oil on canvas, Herzog Anton Ulrich-Museum, Brunswick

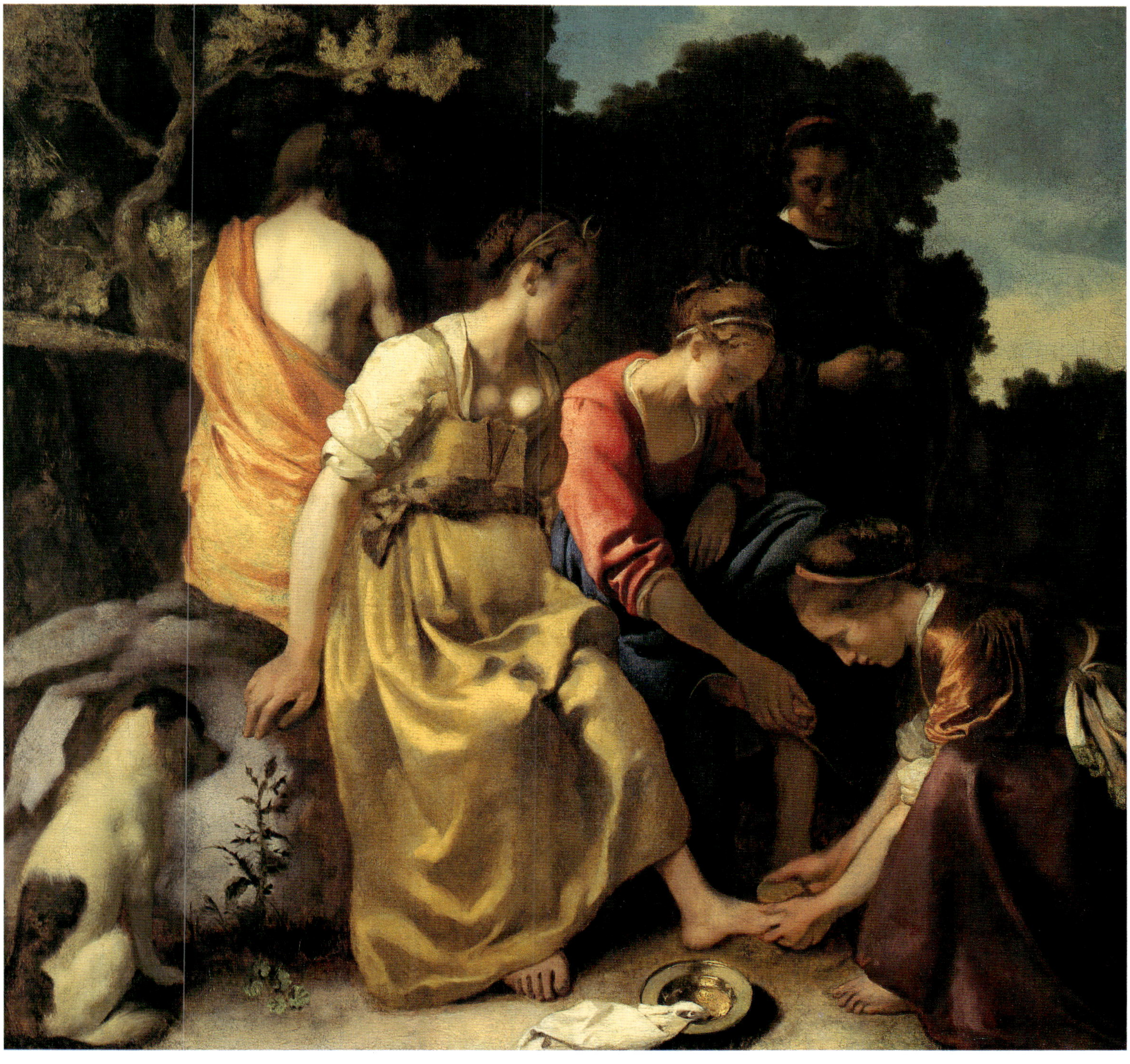

female companions. The differences in mood between the two works, however, are striking. Vermeer's Diana is most assuredly not a portrait, and no discourse occurs between her and her contemplative companions.

Although Diana is modestly dressed and has at her feet a brass basin and a white cloth, these indications of chastity and purity are tempered by an overwhelming sense of solemnity more associated with Christian than with mythological traditions. Numerous thematic relationships were seen to exist between mythological and biblical stories in the seventeenth century, and Vermeer may well have sought to fuse them in this work.[4] In Christian tradition, for example, the ritual of foot-washing is not only associated with purification, but also with humility and approaching death. Indeed, the dignity with which Diana's companion performs her service recalls Mary Magdalene washing Christ's feet with her tears[5] and Christ kneeling before his disciples to wash their feet at the Last Supper.[6] The thistle prominently placed in the foreground is another Christian reference, alluding to earthly sorrow.[7] Finally, the thorn, symbol of Christ's grief and tribulation, is implicitly present in the nymph holding her foot, whose pose is reminiscent of the antique statue Spinario, known through small bronzes (fig. 2), and the "Nymph alla Spina."[8]

As is clear from *Saint Praxedis* (cat. 1), derived from one identifiable prototype, Vermeer was adept at emulating another artist's technique. This technique, once learned, became part of his own repertoire. In *Diana and Her Companions*, for example, he used the same Italian technique for painting the sky – blue paint over a dark underlayer. Also reminiscent of Italian painting, Venetian rather than Florentine, is the broad handling of forms, the large, classically conceived figure, the rich, warm colors, and the idealized landscape. Diana's blocky form, however, recalls Rembrandt's figures, which the artist must have seen in Amsterdam. Indeed, Diana's somber mood and her pose, as well as that of her kneeling attendant, are so similar in concept and feeling to Rembrandt's (1606–1669) *Bathsheba* of 1654 (fig. 3) that it seems highly probable that Vermeer knew this work firsthand. As did Rembrandt, Vermeer modeled his figure with thick impastos and brushstrokes that follow the contours of folds rather than lie across them. He also allowed imprimatura layers to remain as active design elements in the final composition. Finally, Vermeer cast the faces in shadow to enhance the expressive potential of his scene, a device that Rembrandt also exploited.

Vermeer may well have learned about Rembrandt's philosophy and technique of painting from one of his former pupils, Carel Fabritius (1622–1654). Although nothing is known about his contacts with Vermeer, Fabritius' presence in Delft is documented from 1650 to his death in October 1654. To judge from *The Sentry*, 1654 (page 19, fig. 5), Fabritius also brought to his paintings an emotional character not far removed from the quiet pensiveness that pervades *Diana and Her Companions*.[9]

As goddess of the night, Diana is closely associated with death, particularly when accompanied by thistle and geranium, both symbols of earthly sorrow,[10] and the act of foot-washing, an age-old reference to death. Perhaps the memory of the tragic gunpowder house explosion that ripped through Delft on 12 October 1654 and killed Fabritius, among others, underlies Vermeer's conception. The quiet, reflective countenances of Diana and her attendants are those of individuals who singularly must come to terms with a shared grief.

The associations between this painting and the Rembrandt school are hardly new,

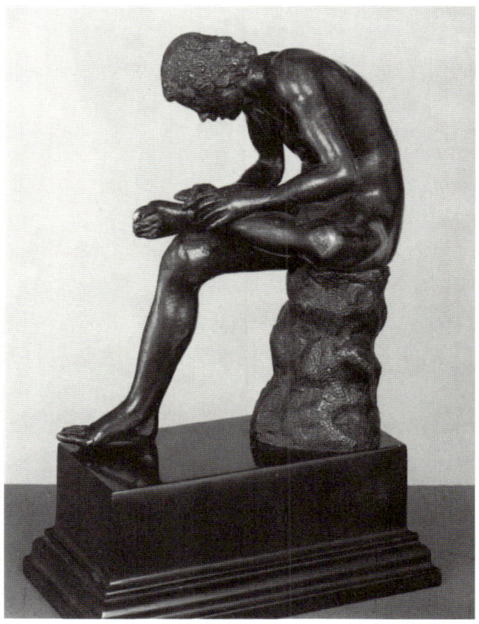

fig. 2. North Italian artist, *The Spinario*, first quarter of the sixteenth century (after the antique), bronze, National Gallery of Art, Washington, Samuel H. Kress Collection

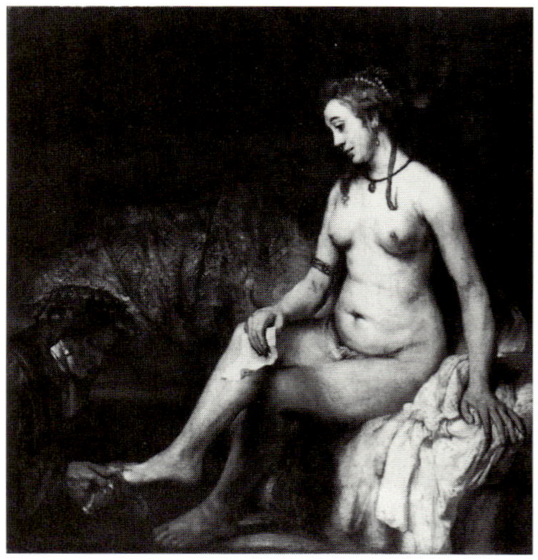

fig. 3. Rembrandt, *Bathsheba*, 1654, oil on canvas, Musée du Louvre, Paris

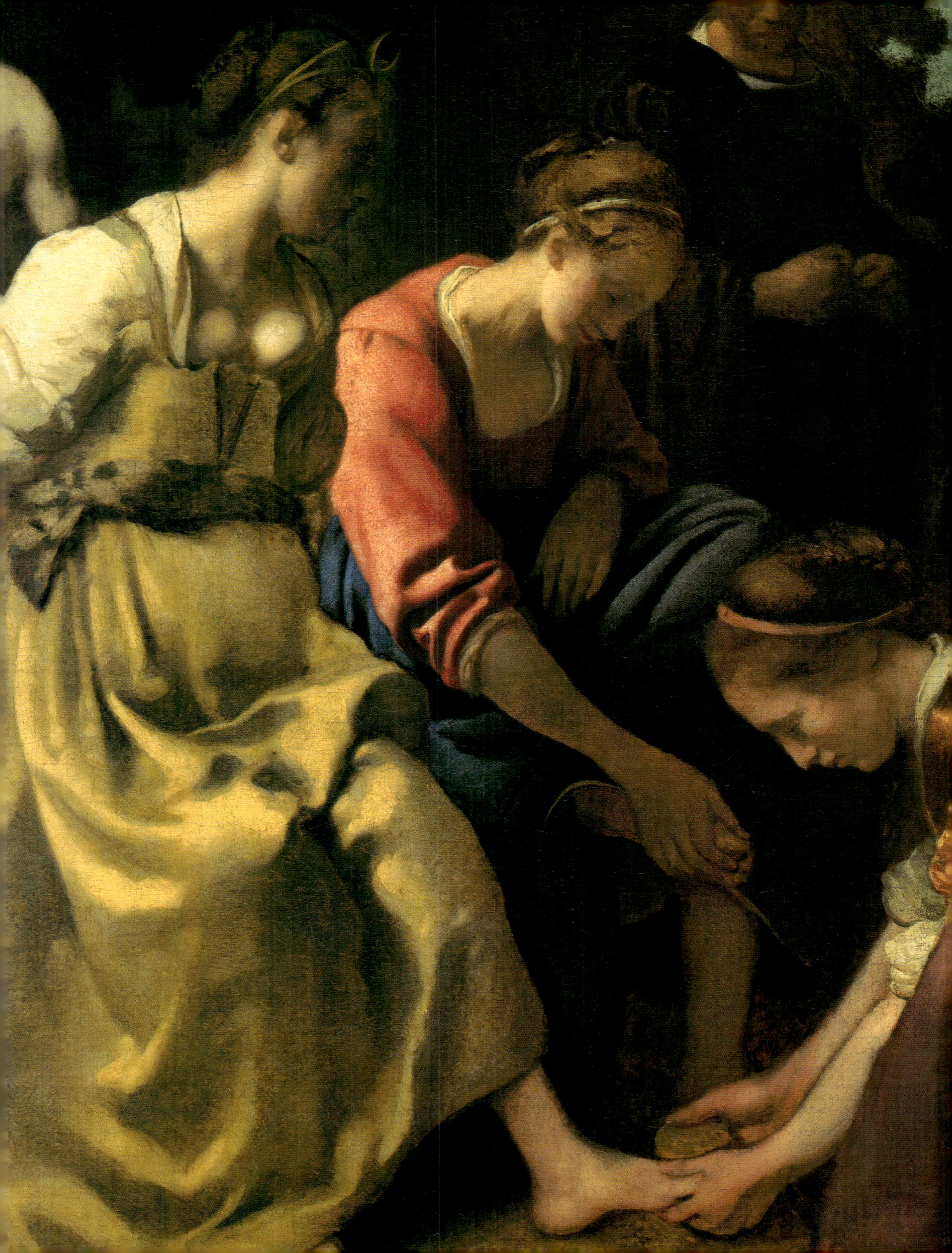

for when *Diana and Her Companions* appeared at an auction in Paris on 4 May 1876 it was attributed to Rembrandt's pupil Nicolaes Maes (1634–1693). Carel Vosmaer even declared it one of Maes' masterpieces.[11] The painting, previously acquired from the Hague art dealer Dirksen, had been part of the collection of a London engineer and entrepreneur, Neville Davison Goldsmid (1814–1875), who lived in The Hague. Goldsmid was an enthusiastic collector of paintings, drawings, and prints, receiving advice from the Hague School painter Jan Weissenbruch (1822–1880) and his brother, the lithographer Frederik Hendrik Weissenbruch (1828–1887).[12]

The Mauritshuis' director, J. K. J. de Jonge, who knew that the Goldsmid Collection would be auctioned, set his hopes on the acquisition of three paintings. Victor de Stuers, Advisor for the Arts at the Ministry of Internal Affairs and renowned advocate for the preservation of Dutch cultural patrimony, traveled to Paris to do the bidding. De Stuers not only purchased the three paintings recommended by De Jonge, but nine others, including the "Nicolaes Maes." De Jonge was not pleased with these additional purchases, particularly the Maes, writing: "however attractive the colors of this painting by N. Maes, it has lost many of its original qualities, even in the contours of the figures. It was therefore far too expensive, at 10,000 francs, to have been bought."[13] In his 1879 museum guide, De Jonge complained further: "a Nicolaes Maes, *Diana and Her Companions*, would have been an important painting had it not suffered so [much]."[14]

The attribution to Nicolaes Maes was short-lived. After an examination of the Maes monogram in 1885, the attribution was changed to "Ver Meer van Delft."[15] The difference in style between this work and the *View of Delft* (cat. 7), which hung in the same room, however, was so pronounced that for a number of years it was questioned whether the same artist could have created both works. In 1892 Abraham Bredius, at the time director of the Mauritshuis, and his Deputy Director, Cornelis Hofstede de Groot, undertook further examination of the monogram. After applying mineral spirits to the signature, the restorer, Z. L. van den Berg, determined that a false Maes monogram "N.M." had been made from the remnants of a signature that read: "J V Meer."[16]

This discovery, however, did not convince Bredius about the attribution of the painting to the Delft master. According to him, the picture "clearly showed the traces of having been painted under Italian influence."[17] Consequently, he concluded that the present painting had to be a work by Jan Vermeer of Utrecht (or Johan van der Meer) (c. 1630–1688), a genre and portrait painter who had worked in Italy in the 1650s.[18] In the Mauritshuis catalogue of 1898, *Diana and Her Companions* was still attributed to the Utrecht Vermeer, although the catalogue text indicated the uncertainty of the attribution and the fact that the painting had previously been given to "Maes and by some to the Delft Vermeer."[19] Uncertainty about the attribution still existed in 1900, for one author wrote in that year: "but I see that several [scholars] hold out for Van der Meer de Delft."[20]

The opinion of Bredius as a scholar was decisive for the appreciation of the painting. In 1901 his judgment took an abrupt turn. In March of that year Bredius and the young Willem Martin, the Mauritshuis' deputy director, together visited the art dealer Forbes & Paterson in London. There they encountered for the first time the large *Christ in the House of Mary and Martha* (cat. 2), which was clearly signed *IVMeer.* Bredius wrote: "exactly as the M[aurits]huis Diana. Very colorful & *exactly the same colors without any doubt* by the same hand but without *any pointillé;* and also under Ital[ian] influence – could both still be by [the] *Utr[echt]* Vermeer?" (fig. 4)[21] His fellow traveler Martin noted that the same colors reappear in the *Diana and Her Companions* and *The Procuress* (page 60, fig. 16) in Dresden.[22] In the end, the coloristic relationship to *The Procuress*, dated 1656, proved to be the decisive element in convincing both scholars that the paintings in The Hague, Edinburgh, and Dresden were all by the Delft Vermeer.[23]

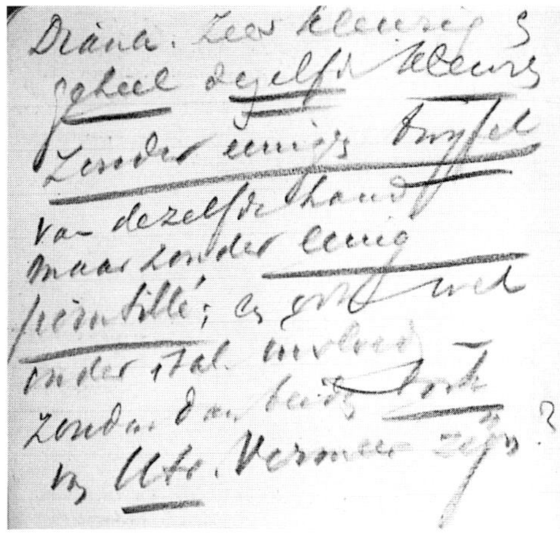

fig. 4. Notes from Abraham Bredius, March 1901, Mauritshuis documentation archives

1. Kühn 1968, 177.
2. Ovid/Miller 1966, 1, 93, does mention that prior to discovering Callisto's pregnancy, Diana first washed her feet before disrobing with her nymphs to bathe. It is, however, difficult to relate the mood of this painting to that episode.
3. For an excellent analysis of mythological scenes in Dutch art, see Sluiter 1986, 167–198.
4. Sluiter 1986, 170, 189, discusses Christological interpretations of the Diana myths of Actaeon and Callisto.
5. Luke 7: 36–50.
6. John 13: 1–16.
7. Its meaning stems from the curse God levied against Adam for his disobedience: "cursed is the ground for thy sake; in sorrow shalt thou eat of it all the days of thy life;

thorns also and thistles shall it bring forth to thee..." Genesis 3: 17–18.
8. "Nymph alla Spina," presently in the Uffizi, was also well-known through drawings and statuettes. See Bober 1986, 97–98. This statue, although earlier than the Spinario, is so named because of its visual association with the latter. I would like to thank Lynn Russell for drawing my attention to this visual source.
9. A curious similarity in the two paintings is the identical position of the dog seated alertly in the lower left.
10. The geranium was often included in images of the Passion of Christ, as it was considered a medicine for sadness. See Levi D'Ancona 1977, 154. I thank Aneta Georgievska-Shine and Quint Gregory for drawing my attention to this plant's significance.
11. Vosmaer 1868, 232.
12. Van Westrheene 1868, 89–94, esp. 90–91; M. de Boer in Mauritshuis 1993A, 206–308. The Goldsmid Collection numbered about 150 seventeenth-century Dutch paintings, primarily ones by minor masters. One year after Goldsmid's death in 1875 his widow, Eliza Garey, had the collection auctioned in Paris.
13. Mauritshuis 1993A, 208 and 314 n. 7: "de overigens door kleur aangename schilderij van N. Maes [heeft] veel van hare oorspronkelijkeid zelfs in de lijnen der figuren verloren. Zij wordt dan ook geacht te duur, voor 10.000 francs, te zijn aangekocht."
14. Mauritshuis 1879, 25, no. 406: "un Nicolaes Maes, Diane et ses compagnes, qui serait un tableau important s'il n'avait tant souffert."
15. Mauritshuis 1885, 16, no. 71a (see also Mauritshuis 1993A, 314 n. 14).
16. A facsimile of the signature is reproduced in Mauritshuis 1895, 448. See also De Vries 1954, 40, and Ainsworth 1982, 26.
17. Mauritshuis 1993A, 310 and 314 n. 20: "duidelijk de sporen [vertoonde] van onder Italiaansche invloed geschilderd te zijn."
18. Mauritshuis 1893, 36, no. 194.
19. Mauritshuis 1898, 85, no. 406: "Maes en door sommigen aan den Delftschen Vermeer toegeschreven."
20. Geffroy 1900, 120: "mais je vois que plusieurs d'entre eux tiennent pour Van der Meer de Delft." See also Vanzype 1925, 46.
21. These notations were first published by Marjolein de Boer in Mauritshuis 1993A, 310–311, ills. 2A–B, 314 nn. 24–25.
22. Willem Martin's notebook of 1889–1901, 126 (preserved in the R. K. D. in The Hague).
23. Martin 1904, 2–4; Mauritshuis 1935, 373.

COLLECTION CATALOGUES

Mauritshuis 1877, 9, no. 71a; Mauritshuis 1895, 448–449, no. 406 (194), with ill. of the signature; Mauritshuis 1993A, 306-314, no. 37 and ill. (with extensive literature)

LITERATURE

Vosmaer 1868, 232; Van Westrheene 1868, 90–91; Geffroy 1900, 120 and ill.; Martin 1904, 4; Hofstede de Groot 1907–1928, 1: 588–589, no. 3; Hofstede de Groot 1907–1930, 1: no. 3 and ill.; Plietzsch 1911, 12–14, 116, no. 19 and ill. 2; Borenius 1923, 37–38; Vanzype 1925, 46 and pl. 18; Hale 1937, 49, 72–73, 75, 113, 171–172, 208 and fig. 40; De Vries 1939, 29, 32–33, 77, no. 1 and ill. 27; De Vries 1948, 95 and 100; Swillens 1950, 63–64, 157-161, 165, no. A and ill. 33; Gowing 1952, 24, 79, 93–97, no. 4; De Vries 1954, 40–42 and ill.; Van Gelder 1956, 245–247; Goldscheider 1967, 14, 18, 26, 125, no. 2 and ills. 5–7; Blankert 1975, 14–17, 20, 22–23, 112–113 nn. 7, 8, 13, 138–139, no. 2 and pl. 2; Wheelock 1977A, 268–269 and ill. 65; Blankert 1978, 13–17, 75–76 nn. 15, 16, 21, 155, no. 2 and pl. 2; Slatkes 1981, 18–19 and ill.; Wheelock 1981, 15, 68–69, and pl. 3; Aillaud 1986, 40, 72–74, 76, 77, 79, 164 nn.7–8, 171–172, no. 2, and pl. 1; Wheelock 1986, 75–77, 82-85, 89 and ill. 6; Wheelock 1988, 13, 52–53 and pl. 3; Montias 1989, 105–106, 139–140, 143, 145–146, 150, 201 and ill. 16; Nash 1991, 44, 46, 47, 53, 88; Blankert 1992, 40, 76–77, 164 nn. 7–8, 171, no. 2 and pl. 1; Wheelock 1995, 21, 25, 26, 27, 28–37, 55, 163, 164, 170, and ill. 13

4

The Little Street

c. 1657–1658

inscribed below window at left: *i VMeer* (VM in ligature)

oil on canvas, 53.5 x 43.5 (21 1/16 x 17 1/8)

Rijksmuseum, Amsterdam

PROVENANCE

(?) Pieter Claesz van Ruijven, Delft, before 1674; (?) Maria de Knuijt, Widow Van Ruijven, Delft, 1674–1681; (?) Magdalena van Ruijven and Jacob Dissius, Delft, 1681–1682; Jacob Dissius (with his father, Abraham Dissius, 1685–1694), Delft, 1682–1695; Dissius sale, Amsterdam, 16 May 1696, no. 32 (*f* 72.10) or no. 33 (*f* 48); Gerrit Willem van Oosten de Bruyn, Haarlem, before 1797; Widow van Oosten de Bruyn, Haarlem, 1797–1799; Van Oosten de Bruyn sale, Haarlem, 8 April 1800, no. 7 (*f* 1,040 to Van Winter); Pieter van Winter, Amsterdam, 1800–1807; Lucretia van Winter (Six-van Winter after 1822), Amsterdam, 1807–1845; Jonkheer Hendrik Six van Hillegom, Amsterdam, 1845–1847; Jonkheer Jan Pieter Six van Hillegom and Jonkheer Pieter Six van Vromade, Amsterdam, 1847–1899/1905; Jonkheer Willem Six van Wimmenum, Amsterdam, 1905–1919; Jonkheer Jan Six, Amsterdam/'s Graveland, 1919–1921; Six sale, Amsterdam, 12 April 1921 (bought in); to the present owner in 1921 (gift of Sir Henry Deterding, bought from Six for *f* 625,000)

EXHIBITIONS

Amsterdam 1872, 22, no. 143; Amsterdam 1900, 17, no. 71; London 1929A, 149–150, no. 316 and pl. 80; Amsterdam 1935, 28, no. 165 and ill. 165; Rotterdam 1935, 36, no. 83 and ill. 64; Paris 1950, no. 98; London 1952, 1: no. 529, 2: ill. 13; New York 1954, ill. 7; Rome 1956, 246, no. 31 and pl. 28

TECHNICAL DESCRIPTION

The support is a fine, plain-weave linen, with a thread count of 14 x 14 per cm^2. The original tacking edges are present and marks from the original strainer bars are 3.5 cm. from the edge on all sides. Of the two lining canvases one is probably attached with glue/paste, the other with wax resin.

The gray ground visible along the silhouette of the right house and in parts of the brick façade contains umber, a little chalk, and lead white.[1] Coarse particles of lead white protrude through the thin paint layers of the façade and in the brown shadows. Along the left edge of the painting secondary cusping is evident.

The sky was underpainted with lead white, over which the chimneys on the v-shaped roof line were painted. Azurite was used in the underpainting of the three upper windows, including sills and surrounds, of the right house, followed by a creamy yellow layer. The sequence of paint layers is reversed in the ground-floor windows of this house. The foliage was painted with an azurite and lead tin-yellow mixture, three different shades of an ultramarine and lead white mixture, and pure ultramarine.

The Little Street is an intimate work, both in scale and subject matter. Within its small compass it conveys much about the character of Vermeer's Delft – its quiet streets, its picturesque buildings, and the sense of community shared by its citizens. Vermeer's view across a cobblestone street depicts portions of two sixteenth-century dwellings joined by a wall with doors that lead through passageways to inner courtyards. The red brick façades, wooden doorways and shutters, and small leaded-glass windows of these dwellings provide a visually varied setting for the figures – a woman absorbed in the task of handwork in the doorway of her home, a maidservant busying herself in an adjacent passageway, and children engrossed by their game as they kneel at street's edge.

The painting, however, is less about Delft, or even a small fragment of a streetscape in Delft, than about the poetic beauty of everyday life. The buildings have no distinguishing architectural features, wall plaques, or signs, and no church spire rises in the background to help locate them. In the flat light of this cloudy day, the scene is timeless. The women and children, quietly situated within their architectural niches, remain separate and anonymous. Together, however, they impart an ideal of domestic virtue. Not only were industriousness with needlework and diligence with house cleaning highly esteemed values for women in Dutch society, so also was the proper care of children. The vines growing on the building at the left, which since Antiquity have symbolized love, fidelity, and marriage, may also allude to domestic virtue.[2]

One of the unanswered questions about Vermeer's career is how and why this artist changed from history paintings to scenes of daily life, whether single figures within interiors or views along a city street.[3] Whether the impetus came from other artists or from the wishes of a patron, the transformation was radical and complete. Not only does *The Little Street* derive its basis from careful observation of reality rather than a literary or visual source, it is relatively small in scale and is executed with a delicacy of touch nowhere to be found in Vermeer's early history paintings.

While the contrast in handling between *The Little Street* and, for example, *Diana and Her Companions* (cat. 3) is striking, in fact, a number of Dutch artists, ranging from Hendrick Goltzius (1558–1617) to Gerbrandt van den Eeckhout (1621–1674), used markedly different techniques for different types of subject matter. Van den Eeckhout painted religious subjects in a Rembrandtesque manner, with loose brushwork and pronounced chiaroscuro contrasts, while his portraits exhibit a clearer, crisper style similar to that of Bartholomeus van der Helst (1613–1670). The pronounced differences in style between the early genre scenes and later portraits of Nicolaes Maes (1634–1693) prompted some earlier historians to speculate that there must have been two different artists by that name.[4] An interesting parallel, of course, exists with Vermeer, since all of his early history paintings have at one time or another been attributed to Johan van der Meer from Utrecht.

Less surprising than the different technique that accompanied the new type of subject matter is Vermeer's extraordinary mastery of it. With remarkable economy, he suggested not only the physical presence of the buildings, but something of their aged character as well. Rather than contouring each and every brick, Vermeer conveyed the weathered appearance of the buildings' façades by subtly modulating the colors of the bricks and mortar. He indicated repairs made to settling cracks, and missing roof tiles above the passageway doors, as well

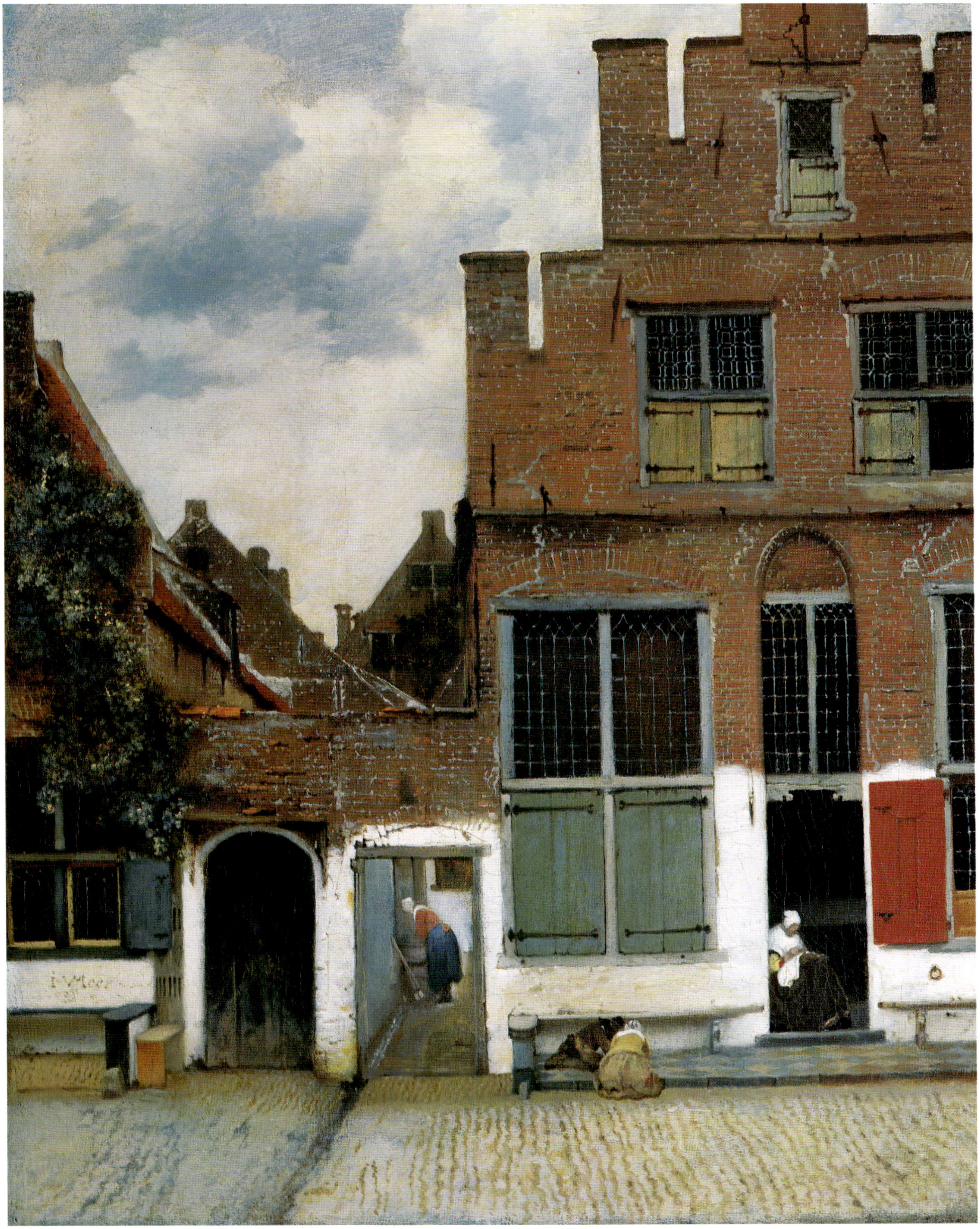

as the worn appearance of the closed door on the left. Finally, he effectively used the whitewashed walls at ground level as an important compositional device. This band of white not only separates the textural intricacies of cobblestone and brick, it draws the eye to the figural elements in the composition.

Vermeer's compositional sensitivity is also remarkable for an artist presumably entering into this genre for the first time. Although the dwellings facing the street are parallel to the picture plane, Vermeer places his buildings off-center, allowing each to extend beyond the picture frame. This compositional decision confirms that Vermeer's true subject is the ambience of the street scene, rather than the depiction of individual buildings. To help establish the three-dimensionality of the buildings, Vermeer extended the pronounced orthogonal of the drainage trench, visible among the worn cobblestones in the immediate foreground, past the façades and into the open passageway. This orthogonal directs the viewer's eye to the maidservant leaning over a barrel, an element that emphasizes the thematic significance of domestic life in the painting. Infrared reflectography has revealed that to provide this visual access to the inner courtyard Vermeer eliminated a figure seated in the doorway (fig. 1).

Whether or not Vermeer turned to this type of subject through the inspiration of Pieter de Hooch, similarities in approach and technique indicate that the artists knew each other's paintings (page 21, fig. 9). One interesting facet of De Hooch's working method is that he imaginatively combined architectural elements from disparate sources into one seemingly realistic architectural space.[5] Although each of De Hooch's imaginative recreations appears convincing, his manipulations of reality have been discovered because different arrangements of identifiable architectural elements exist in a number of his courtyard scenes. Since *The Little Street* appears so convincing, and since no other comparable paintings exist that might raise questions about Vermeer's adherence to reality, no one has ever doubted that Vermeer depicted an actual site. Nevertheless, as with De Hooch, Vermeer has here adjusted architectural elements for compositional purposes. For example, the doorway in which the woman sits with her handwork should be aligned with the center of the building and equidistant from the double set of flanking windows. It is not, probably because Vermeer wanted to place the red shutter to the right of the door flat against the wall to establish a sense of closure for the right side of the composition.

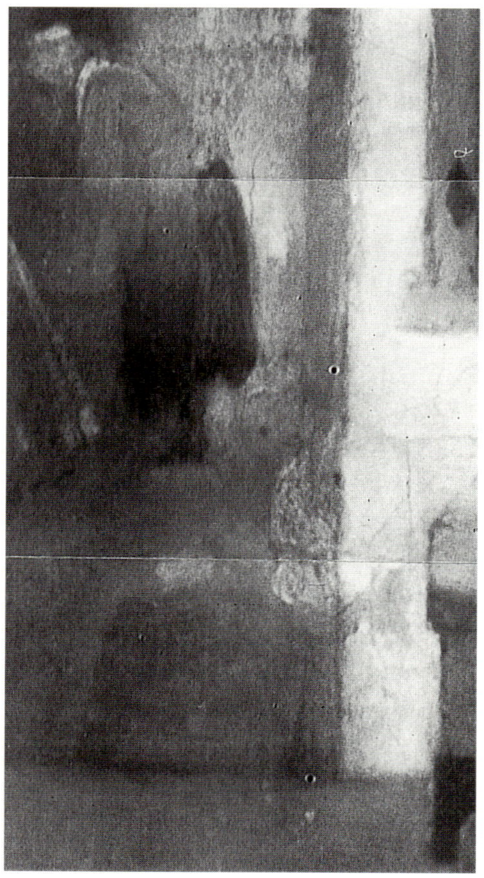

fig. 1. Detail of infrared reflectogram, *The Little Street*

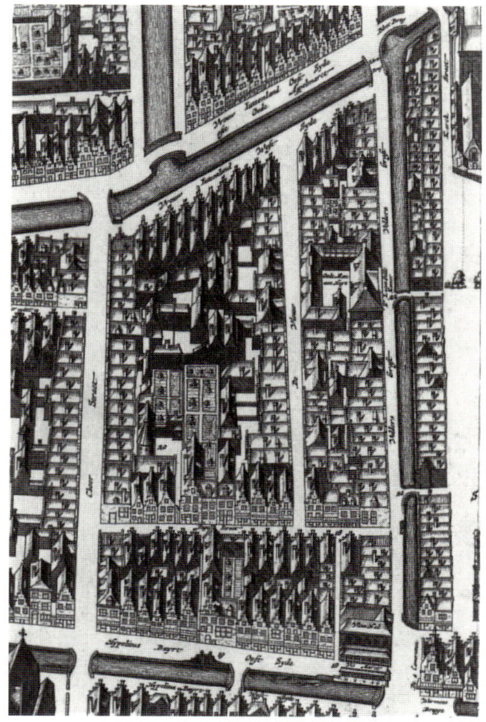

2. Detail, *Large Figurative Map of Delft*, Amsterdam, 1675–1678, National Gallery of Art Library, Washington

Vermeer almost certainly made even greater adjustments. As De Hooch frequently did, Vermeer probably joined two buildings that were, in reality, separate. The possibility that his streetscape is actually a composite, drawn from two different locations, may help identify at least part of the site depicted in *The Little Street*. A longstanding hypothesis is that Vermeer painted this work from the second floor of his house, "Mechelen," which overlooked a narrow canal and street named the Voldersgracht (fig. 2).[6] Across the street were the Old Man's and Old Woman's Almshouse, at least until 1661 when the chapel became the site of the Saint Luke's Guild. The theory, however, has been disputed for a number of reasons, most significantly because no building comparable to the large dwelling on the right of Vermeer's painting existed at that location.[7] Eighteenth-century representations of the Saint Luke's Guildhall,

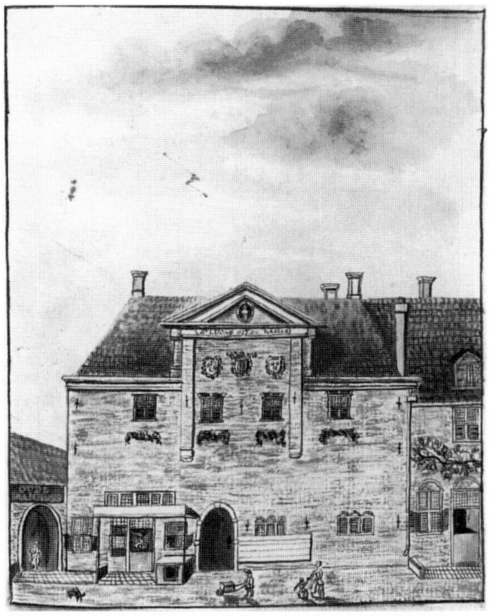

fig. 3. *Guildhall of Saint Luke, Delft*, 18th century, drawing, National Gallery of Art Library, Washington

built in the 1660s, however, do show the Old Man's House to the left, which has a slanted roofline and an adjacent wall with an arched door that are virtually identical to those in Vermeer's painting (fig. 3).[8] Thus it may well be that Vermeer did depict a building from his window, but combined it with another structure to create this extraordinary image.

Vermeer's free adaptation of reality in *The Little Street* is consistent with his broader artistic approach, which anticipates ideas espoused by Samuel van Hoogstraeten two decades later in his treatise on the art of painting.[9] Through convincing light and texture, suggestive cropping, and subtle perspective, Vermeer here mirrored reality while bringing to it an added dimension, a sense of intimacy and permanence reflective of domestic virtue.

The appeal of this intimate scene has been longstanding. At the end of the eighteenth century, for example, *The Little Street* was in the collection of Gerrit Willem van Oosten de Bruyn (1727–1797),[10] who also owned Frans Hals' well-known *Portrait of Willem van Heythuysen* (Alte Pinakothek, Munich).[11] At the auction of his splendid art collection (upon the death of his widow, Maria Croon, in 1799) the Hals portrait raised only *f* 51, whereas *The Little Street* was hammered down at *f* 1,040.[12] The pictorial qualities of this canvas drew recognition in 1800. It was praised as being "marvelously naturally and handsomely painted."[13] The new owner was Pieter van Winter (1745–1807), an Amsterdam merchant in indigo, and a literary figure of repute.[14]

After his death in 1807, his daughter, Lucretia Johanna ("Creejans") van Winter (1785–1845), inherited his collection, including the Vermeer. With her marriage in 1822 to Jonkheer Hendrik Six (1790–1847), two collections with numerous masterpieces of the Golden Age were joined on the Herengracht 509–511. Six was the owner of Rembrandt's famous *Portrait of Jan Six* (Six Foundation, Amsterdam).[15] In 1823 the inveterate traveler Sir John Murray visited the Six Collection in Amsterdam. Murray described *The Little Street*, giving his opinion that: "The whole is touched with that truth and spirit which belong only to this master."[16] From Murray, this was a remarkably open-minded comment.

After the death of Hendrik and Creejans in 1845 and 1847, their two sons, Jan Pieter Six van Hillegom (1824–1899) and Pieter Hendrik Six van Vromade (1827–1905), continued to live for years as bachelors in the parental home. After Jan Pieter eventually wed in 1860, the house on the Herengracht was set up as a museum, becoming an attraction in the capital city "where an oaken spiral staircase carried half of Europe to the 'Six Gallery'."[17] Jan Pieter's son Jan Six (1857–1926) (fig. 4), a classicist and art historian, governed the collection after 1899. Gradually works in the collection had to be sold (see cat. 5). When his brother Willem Six van Wimmenum passed on in 1919, he left Jan, amongst other art, *The Little Street*, and also some real-estate, but insufficient funds to pay the succession taxes.[18]

The inevitable came to pass. On 12 April 1921, Jan Six put *The Little Street*, "The pearl of the Six Collection," up for auction.[19] Vermeer's painting was bought in when it was discovered that there was no bona fide buyer.[20] A disappointed Jan Six then sent the painting to the Louvre in Paris for more than a week in the hope of attracting buyers there but to no avail, though it did attract international attention.

The "salvation" of the painting came when Sir Henry W. A. Deterding (1866–1939), who was to celebrate his twenty-fifth anniversary as Director of the Royal Petroleum Company in 1921, acquired *The Little Street* as a gift for the Dutch nation, for "only" *f* 625,000.[21] The philanthropist

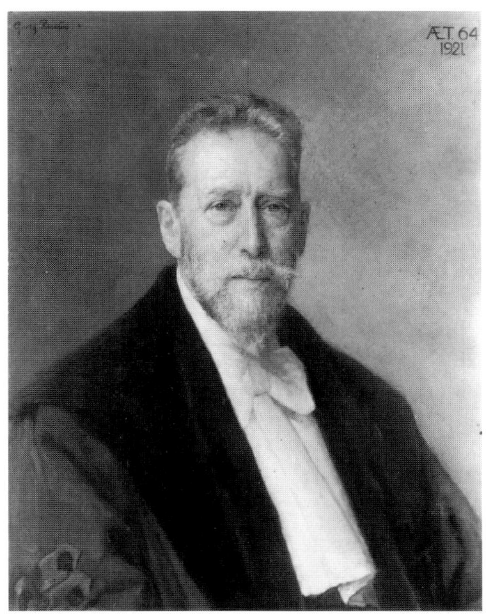

fig. 4. Georg Rueter, *Portrait of Jan Six*, canvas, Six Collection, Amsterdam

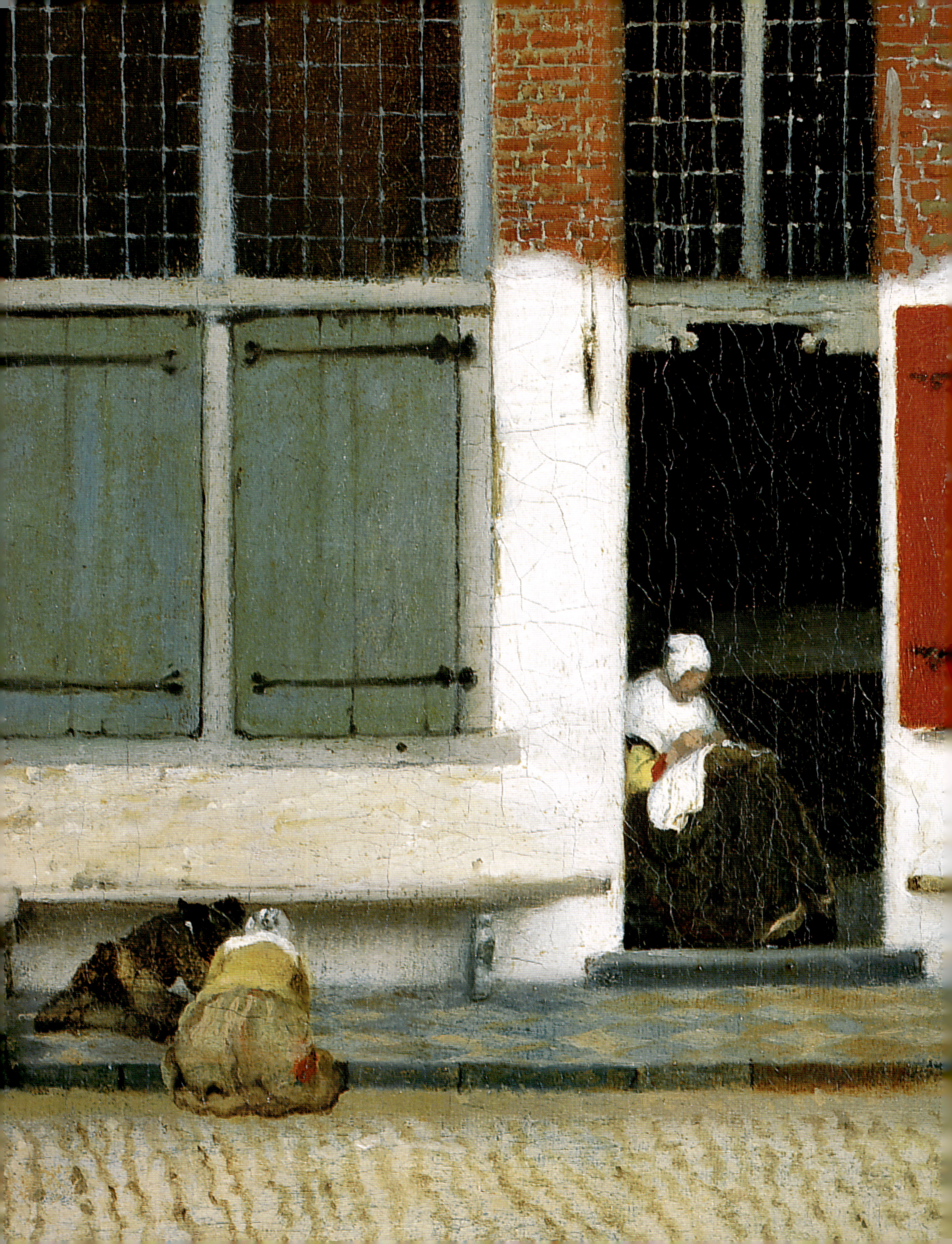

wanted the picture displayed in the Rijksmuseum, but he threatened to take it back at once if any attempt were made to decorate him in gratitude.[22] Fortunately for the museum, he never received a decoration for his noble gift.

1. Kühn 1968, 183.
2. For a discussion of the ideals of domestic virtue in Dutch life, as well as its literary framework, see Franits 1993, particularly 75–82. As Franits notes, the third verse of Psalm 128 refers to the vine metaphorically to describe domestic life: "Thy wife shall be as a fruitful vine by the sides of thine house."
3. Vermeer apparently painted more than one view of a city street. In the Dissius sale of 1696, no. 32 in the catalogue was described as "A view of a house standing in Delft," and no. 33 as "A view of some houses." See Montias 1989, 364, doc. 439.
4. See Rosenberg 1966, 186.
5. See National Gallery Washington 1995, 139–140.
6. Swillens 1950, 94.
7. Van Peer 1959, 243–244; Wheelock 1995, 192 n. 1.
8. For a history of the construction of this building, and another watercolor representation of the site, see F. ten Hengel in Delft, 1981, 1: 57, 2: fig. 42.
9. Van Hoogstraeten 1678. For a discussion of Van Hoogstraeten's ideas, see Wheelock 1995, 14–16.
10. NNBW, 6: col. 228: Mr. Van Oosten de Bruyn was a rich Haarlem burgomaster.
11. Inv. no. 14101; Washington 1989, 178–180, no. 17 and ill.
12. The inventory of the estate of Van Oosten de Bruyn was published by Bredius 1921, 60–62 (Haarlem, Notary Scholting, inv. no. 1547, record 84, unpaginated).
13. Sale catalogue, Haarlem, 8 April 1800, no. 7: "wonder natuurlyk and fraai geschildert" (Lugt no. 6054).
14. NNBW, 4: col. 1468; Elias 1903–1905/1963, 2: 1040–1041; Wijnman et al. 1974, 393 and 405.
15. Gerson 1969, 211, 570–571, no. 276 and ill.
16. Murray 1819–1823, 155.
17. Van Lennep 1959, 140: "waar een eikenhouten wenteltrap half Europa naar de 'Galerie Six' heeft gevoerd"; see also The Hague 1990, 154.
18. Six 1918, 33: "het juweel dat mijn broeder toebehoort" (the jewel belonging to my brother): he had hoped to sell it to the Dutch Government for one million guilders, see: Heijbroek 1992, 226–227.
19. Sale catalogue, Amsterdam, 12 April 1921, without no.: "La perle de la collection Six" (Lugt no. 81985).
20. Batavus (M. D. Henkel) 1921, 345.
21. For a long time the amount was known only to Deterding and the Six family; further documentation concerning *The Little Street* resides with the Six family (see Heijbroek 1992, 231 n. 4).
22. Van Kleffens 1980, 172; Heijbroek 1992, 230.

COLLECTION CATALOGUES
Rijksmuseum 1976, 571–572, no. A 2860 and ill. (with extensive literature)

LITERATURE
Hoet 1752–1770, 1: 35, no. 32; Van Eijnden/Van der Willigen 1816–1840, 1: 166; Murray 1819–1823, 155; Thoré-Bürger 1858–1860, 2: 68, 69; Thoré-Bürger 1866, 298, 303, 310, 463, 467 and 568, no. 49; Fromentin 1876/1976, 304; Havard 1888, 39, no. 50, and ill.; De Vries 1900, 504–506 and ill.; Hofstede de Groot 1907–1928, 1: 606–607, no. 47; Hofstede de Groot 1907–1930, pl. 32; Plietzsch 1911, 114, no. 4, pl. 8; Six 1918, 33; Johansen 1920, 189 and 195–197; Batavus 1921, 345; Bredius 1921, 59–60; Dacier 1921, 275–278 and ill.; Martin 1921, 107–108; Bouricius 1925, 272–273; Hale 1937, 179–181, pl. 8; De Vries 1939, 38–39, 80, no. 8 and ill. 34; Blum 1946, 183, no. 49 and ills. 1–2; Swillens 1950, 93–96, 130, 133, 176, 61, no. 26 and pl. 26; Gowing 1952, 109, no. 7, 111–112, 129 n. 96, and pls. 14–15; Goldscheider 1958, 27 n. 35, 138–139, no. 7 and ills. 18–20; Van Peer 1959, 243–244; Broer 1969, 49 and ill. 8; Blankert 1975, 55–59, 63, 96, 98 and 115–116 n. 45, 143–144, no. 9 and ill.; Wheelock 1977A, 277–278 and ill. 80; Blankert 1978, 7, 36–40, 43, 64, 65, 77 n. 56, 158, no. 9, pls. 9 and 9a-b; Slatkes 1981, 36–39 and ill.; Wheelock 1981, 9, 80, and pl. 9; Heijbroek 1983, 164; Aillaud 1986, 102, 104, 105, 108, 158, 159, 167 n. 51; 177–178, no. 9, and pl. 9; Wheelock 1988, 62–63 and ill. 8; Montias 1989, 149, 197, 199–200 and n. 88, 248, 255 and ill. 24; The Hague 1990, 65–66; Nash 1991, 6, 12, 13, 26, 29; Blankert 1992, 48, 104, 108, 156–160, 166 n. 50, 177–178, no. 9, 217, 223, and ills. 9, 39 and 114; Heijbroek 1992, 225–231 and ill. 1; Lindenburg 1992, 680–690 and ill.; Wheelock 1995, 48–53, 64, 77, 165, 172, 192 n. 1, and ill. 29

5

The Milkmaid

c. 1658–1660

oil on canvas, 45.4 x 40.6 (17 7/8 x 16)

Rijksmuseum, Amsterdam

Exhibited Mauritshuis only

PROVENANCE

(?) Pieter Claesz van Ruijven, Delft, before 1674; (?) Maria de Knuijt, Widow Van Ruijven, Delft, 1674–1681; (?) Magdalena van Ruijven and Jacob Dissius, Delft, 1681–1682; Jacob Dissius (with his father Abraham Dissius, 1685–1694), Delft, 1682–1695; Dissius sale, Amsterdam, 16 May 1696, no. 2 (*f* 175); Isaac Rooleeuw, Amsterdam, 1696–1701; Rooleeuw sale, Amsterdam, 20 April 1701, no. 7 (*f* 320); Jacob van Hoek, Amsterdam, 1701–1719; Van Hoek sale, Amsterdam, 12 April 1719, no. 20 (*f* 126); Pieter Leendert de Neufville, Amsterdam, before 1759; Leendert Pieter de Neufville, Amsterdam, 1759–1765; De Neufville sale, Amsterdam, 19 June 1765, no. 65 (*f* 560 to Yver); Dulong sale, Amsterdam, 18 April 1768, no. 10 (*f* 925 to Van Diemen); Jan Jacob de Bruyn, Amsterdam, 1781; De Bruyn sale, Amsterdam, 12 September 1798, no. 32 (*f* 1550 to J. Spaan); Hendrik Muilman sale, Amsterdam, 12 April 1813, no. 96 (*f* 2125 to J. de Vries for Van Winter); Lucretia van Winter (Six-van Winter after 1822), Amsterdam, 1813–1845; Jonkheer Hendrik Six van Hillegom, Amsterdam, 1845–1847; Jonkheer Jan Pieter Six van Hillegom and Jonkheer Pieter Six van Vromade, Amsterdam, 1847–1899/1905; to the present owner in 1908 (for *f* 550,000 along with 38 other works, from the Six van Vromade heirs with the support of the Rembrandt Society)

EXHIBITIONS

Amsterdam 1872, 21, no. 142; Amsterdam 1900, 17, no. 70; Paris 1921, 10, no. 105; London 1929a, 144, no. 302, and pl. 77; Amsterdam 1935, 27, no. 163, and ill.; Rotterdam 1935, 35, no. 81, and ill. 62; New York 1939, 194–195, no. 398 and pl. 71; Detroit 1939, 19, and ill. 52; Detroit 1941, 19, and ill. 62; Zürich 1953, 72, no. 171, and ill. 28; The Hague 1966, no. 2 and ill.; Paris 1966, no. 2, and ill.

TECHNICAL DESCRIPTION

The closed, plain-weave linen still has its original tacking edges. The thread count is 14 x 14.5 per cm^2. The canvas was relined with wax/resin in 1950 over an existing paste lining.

The ground is a pale brown/gray, containing chalk, lead white, and umber.[1] Apart from a strip above the milkmaid's head along the upper edge of the painting, there is a dark underpainting in the background. Infrared reflectography shows broad black undermodeling in the shadows of the blue apron. A pinhole with which Vermeer marked the vanishing point of the composition is visible in the paint layer above the right hand of the maid.

A red lake glaze is used as an underpaint in the flesh color of the maid's right hand. It is followed by an ocher layer in the shadows, and a white layer followed by a pink layer in the highlights. Several areas were painted wet-in-wet: the glazing bars, the maid's white cap and the details of her yellow bodice. The still life is richly textured with a combination of glazing, scumbling and thick impasto. The bright blue edge to the maid's skirt is created by the luminosity of the underlying white layer.

As she stands pouring milk into an earthenware bowl in the corner of a simple, unadorned room, the kitchen maid conveys a physical and moral presence unequaled by any other figure in Dutch art. Her forcefulness stems from the steadfastness of her gaze as she measures the flow of milk, and the care with which she guides the earthenware pitcher with her strong arms and hands. The light striking her from the window not only accents her white cap and densely painted forehead, but also emphasizes the deep and broad folds of her rolled-up sleeves. Finally, her stature is enhanced by the wholesomeness of her endeavor: the providing of life-sustaining food, as indicated by the varied loaves of bread displayed in the basket and on the table before her.

By the late 1650s, when Vermeer created this image, he had already executed some three or four genre paintings, none of which, unfortunately, could be included in this exhibition (page 60, fig. 16; page 20, fig. 6; page 73, fig. 11; page 35, fig. 6). In these earlier representations, Vermeer explored ways in which he could create an atmosphere or mood in his work by carefully relating his figures to the architectural space they inhabited. In part he achieved this effect through his control of light and in part through his mastery of perspective. In *A Woman Asleep*, c. 1657 (page 20, fig. 6), for example, Vermeer reinforced the sense of melancholy indicated by the woman's pose by placing her in a dark, rather claustrophobic corner of a room, closed in by the table and the door. There seems for her no access to the light-filled and ordered room beyond. Technical analysis confirms that Vermeer sought the suggestiveness of mood in this work rather than the specifics of a narrative. The artist eliminated compositional elements – a dog in the foreground and a man in the back room – that would have defined the framework for the woman's state of being.[2]

Although *The Milkmaid* is entirely different in mood – heroic rather than melancholic – Vermeer has likewise carefully related his figure to the space she inhabits. Her rugged, rough-hewn character seems at home in this simple room with its broken pane of glass and pitted, bare walls. Aside from the pail and marketing basket hanging on the wall, little here distracts from the focus of her concerns. To reinforce this sense, Vermeer once again effectively manipulated his perspective and lighting. The orthogonals of the window, for example, recede to a point at the crux of the milkmaid's right arm, a juncture that visually reinforces the importance of her action, the pouring of milk. Moreover, the low horizon line on which this vanishing point falls enhances the maid's physical presence. In *A Woman Asleep*, where the horizon line is above the figure's head, the viewer looks down upon the woman, whereas in this painting the viewer looks up to the milkmaid.[3]

Light defines the mood as much as the perspective does. As it floods the room, it falls directly on the maid, modeling the massive bulk of her form. Vermeer emphasized her physical presence by creating striking, light-dark contrasts between the figure and the rear wall. To bring the milkmaid's right hand forward, the artist juxtaposed it with a shadowed portion of the wall. Vermeer painted the wall more brightly on the right side of the composition, forming a light backdrop for the shaded portion of the woman's body. To emphasize the figure's strong silhouette Vermeer painted a white contour line along the woman's arm and shoulder.

As with *A Woman Asleep*, Vermeer made certain modifications to his composition to create the mood he wanted to establish. X-radiography (fig. 1) indicates that he

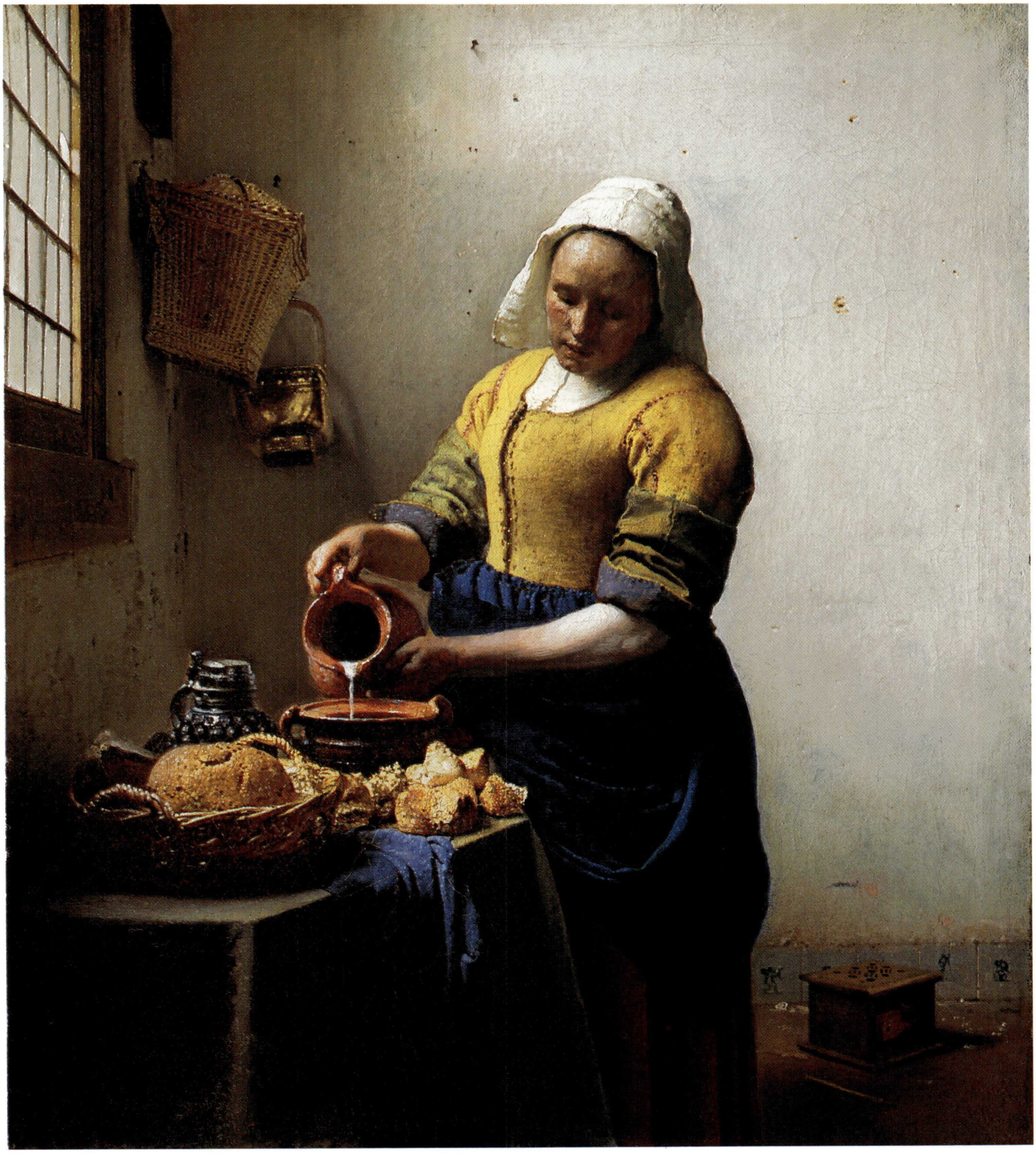

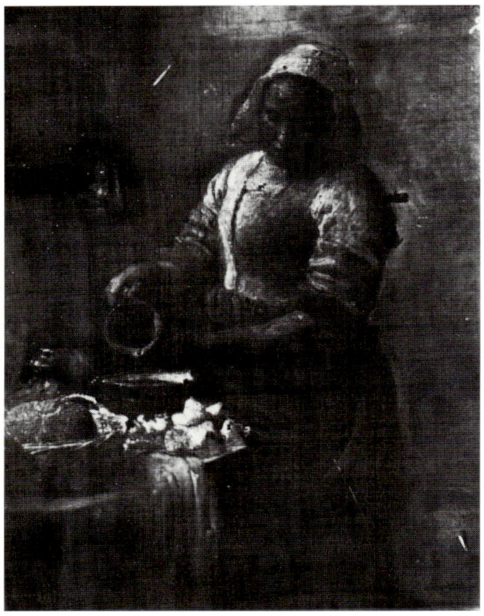

fig. 1. Detail of x-radiograph, *The Milkmaid*

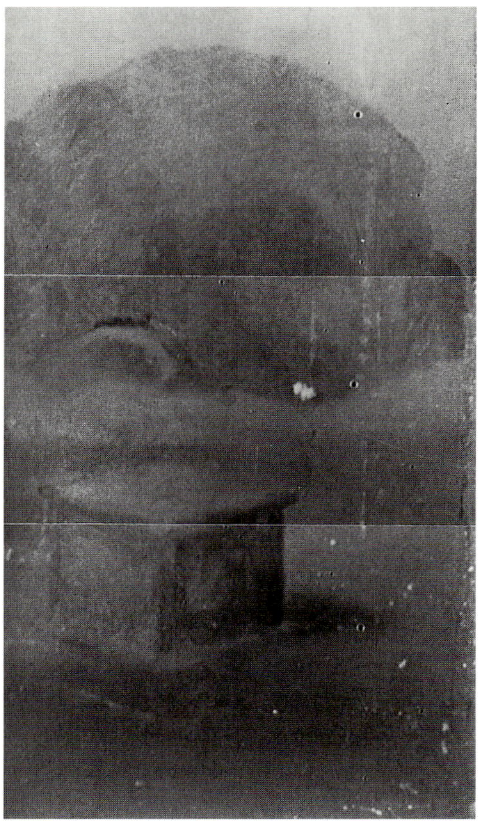

fig. 2. Detail of infrared reflectogram, *The Milkmaid*

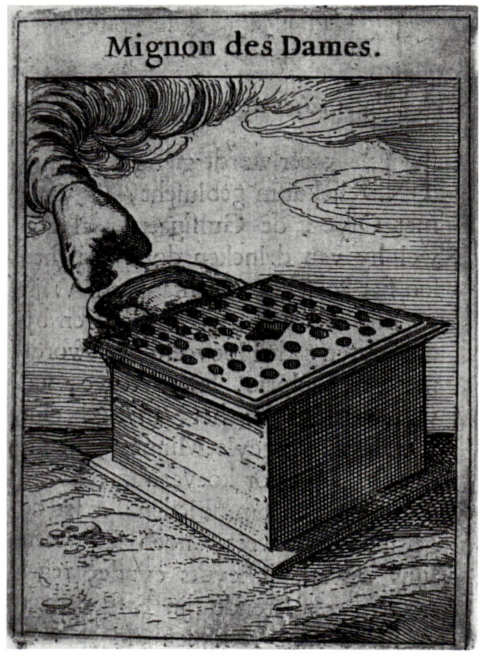

fig. 3. Roemer Visscher, "Mignon des Dames," *Sinnepoppen*, Amsterdam, 1614, National Gallery of Art Library, Washington

eliminated a wall hanging, possibly a map, behind the milkmaid, a compositional element that would have seriously compromised the impression of the stark, unadorned interior setting he ultimately chose to create. An infrared reflectogram (fig. 2), moreover, reveals that Vermeer originally had filled the right corner of the composition with a basket of clothes instead of the floor, footwarmer, and tiles bordering the lower edge of the wall. Not only does this compositional change allow for a greater feeling of space, the scale of the footwarmer relates to that of the wicker basket and copper pail hanging on the wall.

This adjustment almost certainly had iconographic implications as well. The basket of clothes would have taken away from the concentrated focus on the maid's role as a provider of sustenance by indicating another of her household responsibilities. The footwarmer had emblematic associations with a lover's desire for constancy and caring, ideas reinforced by the cupid images on the tiles directly behind it (fig. 3).[4] Rather than being associated with romantic love, however, these elements here relate to the maid's human warmth and evident devotion to her task as she assiduously provides for the nourishment of others.

The role of a maid in Dutch society is, surprisingly, not a subject frequently discussed in contemporary treatises on domestic life. Jacob Cats (1577–1660), for example, who wrote extensively about women as they passed through the various stages of their lives, focused primarily on the role of the woman in relation to family life.[5] Nevertheless, the ideal of womanhood he espoused – virtuous life, modesty, and constancy – certainly can be understood as underlying Vermeer's image. In this respect Vermeer was not different from other artists. The dignity of his milkmaid relates to contemporary images of virtuous women, particularly those by Nicolaes Maes (1634–1693) (page 176, fig. 1).[6] A singular focus on a maid, however, is rare in Dutch painting; indeed, a milkmaid, alone and at work in the kitchen, is not a subject otherwise found in Dutch art.

Despite its broad connection to other Dutch genre paintings, Vermeer's figure has an iconic character that is unprecedented in Dutch art. Jørgen Wadum has proposed an explanation: that Vermeer based the maid's pose on an image from Italian art, a painting of Queen Artemesia by Domenico Fiasella (1589–1669) (fig. 4).[7] Beyond the striking similarities in pose, each figure projects enormous moral authority.[8]

Vermeer's approach, drawing upon history painting as a foundation for scenes of daily life, parallels the classical ideals of Dutch seventeenth-century art theory, particularly those expressed by Samuel van Hoogstraeten.[9] While Vermeer used his mastery of light, perspective, and painting

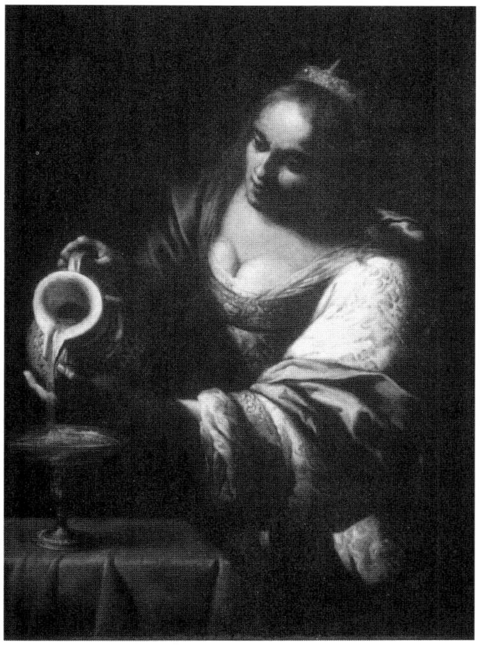

fig. 4. Domenico Fiasella, *Queen Artemesia*, c. 1645, oil on canvas, private collection

technique to suggest the immediacy and presence of reality itself, the regal source for this image of a Dutch maid elevated the scene into one of lasting significance. The milkmaid transcends the specifics of time and place, however real and tangible she may appear. There is something timeless in her presence, as though the milk she carefully measures will never cease to flow.

This small painting has been renowned throughout its history. The title given to the painting in 1719 already speaks volumes: "The famous Milkmaid, by Vermeer of Delft, artful."[10] Apparently this simple interior, and the name "Vermeer of Delft" or "The Delft Vermeer" were well-known among connoisseurs of Amsterdam and its environs.

When Jacob van Hoek (1671–1718), an Amsterdam merchant-collector on the Keizersgracht, died in 1719, the painting was part of his estate. He had presumably bought it in person at the 1701 Rooleeuw auction. Isaac Rooleeuw (c. 1650–1710) had been a Mennonite merchant, who in turn had bought this "famous Milk Maid" for 175 guilders along with *Woman Holding a Balance* (cat. 10) at the Dissius sale in 1696.[11] Rooleeuw's two acquisitions demonstrate that he had an eye for Vermeer's particular style. His paintings were sold by foreclosure after his bankruptcy, with the art broker Jan Pietersz Zómer drawing up the inventory. He described the present painting as "A milk pourer by the same [Van der Meer]" (page 54, fig. 8).[12]

The Amsterdam merchant Pieter Leendert de Neufville (c. 1706–1759), the first known owner of *The Milkmaid* after Jacob van Hoek, was another such amateur. His collection somehow survived a 1735 bankruptcy and was inherited by Leendert Pieter de Neufville (1729–after 1774), who turned out to be even less fortunate in business than his father. In 1765 Leendert Pieter went bankrupt and thus his father's collection, enriched with serious acquisitions of his own, fell under the gavel. Two years earlier Leendert, already under suspicion of fraud, had attempted to exempt the best paintings from public sale.[13] A broker, Pieter Yver, bought the present painting for 560 guilders. The picture was praised as "being powerful in light and brown [chiaroscuro], and having a strong effect."[14]

The work moved by way of the Dulong Collection to the wealthy Amsterdam broker, banker, and collector Jan Jacob de Bruyn (1720–1792).[15] In 1781 the English painter and critic Sir Joshua Reynolds visited De Bruyn. Reynolds praised the striking quality of *The Milkmaid:* "A woman pouring milk from one vessel to another; by D. Vandermeer."[16] When the De Bruyn Collection was auctioned six years after his death, the picture was called "This outstanding and handsome Scene [...] one of the most beautiful by this inimitable Master," and sold for the very high price of 1,550 guilders.[17]

The art dealer who acquired the painting in 1798, J. Spaan, was probably acting for the rich Amsterdam banker Hendrik Muilman (1743–1812).[18] Following his death in 1813, Muilman's impressive cabinet of paintings (he also owned Vermeer's *Lacemaker* [cat. 17]) was sold in his house on the Herengracht 476, where he had died.[19] The art broker Jeronimo de Vries, representing the most important Dutch woman collector of the time, Jonkvrouwe Lucretia Johanna van Winter (1785–1845), paid no less than 2,125 guilders for *The Milkmaid.*

"Creejans" van Winter had in 1807 already fallen heir to half of the renowned art collection of Pieter van Winter, including *The Little Street* (cat. 4), which she brought into her marriage with Jonkheer Hendrik Six van Hillegom.[20] Sir John Murray saw the two top works by the Delft painter at Herengracht 509–511 while journeying through Holland. About *The Milkmaid* he had mixed feelings: "the figure is clumsy, but there is great nature and beauty in the execution."[21]

Next to the State collection in the Trippenhuis, the Six Collection was one of the most important attractions of the Dutch capital during the second half of the nineteenth century.[22] Professor Jan Six (1857–1926), grandson of Hendrik and Creejans, later recalled that the paintings were enjoyed by hundreds of thousands over more than six decades "thanks to the noble altruism of the owner."[23] At the time he wrote this, *The Milkmaid* had just been sold to the Dutch State, in the face of considerable public opposition. After Hendrik and Creejans' son Jonkheer Pieter Hendrik Six van Vromade (1827–1905) died in the summer of 1905, there was an agreement in principle that the thirty-nine paintings in his estate

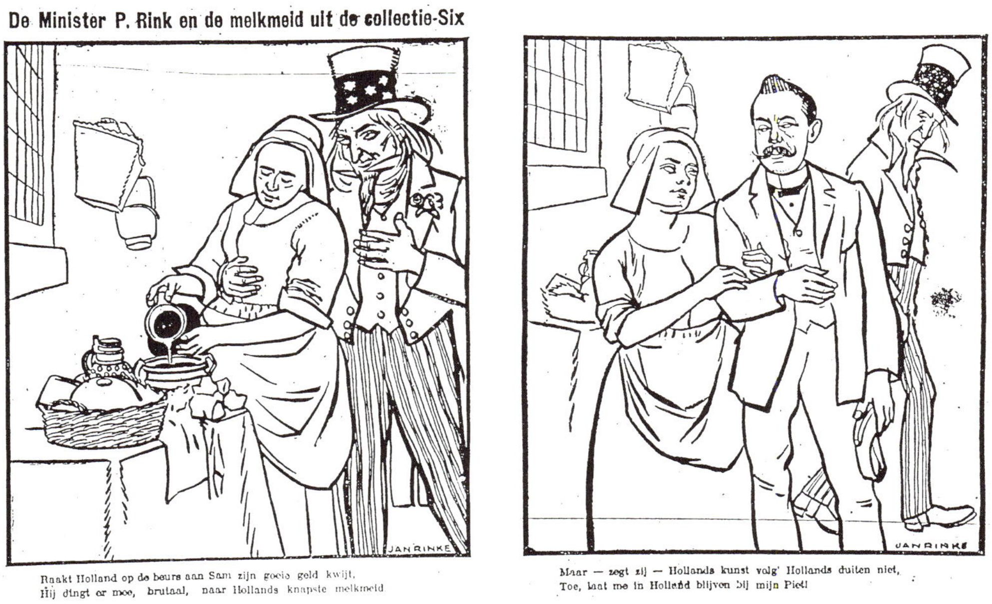

fig. 5. Jan Rinke, "The Minister P. Rink and the Milk Maid from the Six Collection," cartoons from *Het Vaderland*, 9 November 1907

would be acquired by the Rembrandt Society.[24] "Rembrandt" could muster only 200,000 guilders, so that the State was expected to supply the remaining 550,000 guilders.

The business came to public attention in a spectacular way as the result of a brochure by Frits Lugt, a twenty-three-year-old art historian in the employ of the Mensing auction house. The title of this pamphlet was "Is the acquisition by the State of a part of the Six Collection to be recommended?"[25] Lugt's answer was a resounding "no!" He believed that quite a few works in the collection were not worthy of a place in the Rijksmuseum. He considered the "main act, around which everything evolves, namely the 'Milk Maid' by VERMEER" of lesser importance than, and certainly not equal in fame to, Rembrandt's *Nightwatch* or Potter's *Bull*.[26]

The Director of the Mauritshuis, Abraham Bredius, who was advising the government in this matter, reacted fiercely to Lugt's brochure, charging partisanship. Bredius was convinced that J. Pierpont Morgan wanted the painting. After all kinds of squabbling in the press, the issue was finally resolved in parliament. The leader of the opposition was the socialist Troelstra, an advocate of the acquisition of modern art; he faced off against Victor de Stuers, who argued for the preservation of the national patrimony. The parliamentary majority sided with the latter, and *The Milkmaid* was purchased. Cartoons showed "Holland's best-looking milkmaid" turning down her American suitor, "Uncle Sam" (fig. 5).[27] On 13 January 1908 thirty-nine paintings from the Six Collection were hung in one of the easterly cabinets of the Rijksmuseum.[28]

1. Kühn 1968, 185.
2. Wheelock 1981, 74, fig. 68.
3. The table does not appear to be rectangular in shape, which suggests that Vermeer altered its shape for compositional reasons. While the front edge is parallel to the picture plane, its angled right side draws the eye directly toward the milkmaid.
4. Visscher 1614, 178, emblem 56. The emblem's motto "Mignon des Dames" can best be translated as "favorite of the ladies." For a discussion of this issue, see Wheelock 1995, 71.
5. See, in particular, Cats 1625 (in Jacob Cats *Alle de Wercken*, Amsterdam, 1712, 235–424). Cats, in discussing the role of the mistress of the house (*Alle de Wercken*, 309–310), writes that "De keucken is voor al haer eygen heerschappy" (The kitchen is above all her own domain). Her responsibility is also to supervise the maids and to ensure that their chores are equitably distributed.
6. While Gerard ter Borch and Pieter de Hooch also represented scenes of domestic virtue at about this time, none situated a single figure within a defined interior space as effectively as did Maes. See, in particular, Ter Borch's *A Mother Fine-Combing the Hair of Her Child*, c. 1655, Mauritshuis, The Hague (inv. no. 744), and *A Boy and His Dog*, c. 1655, Alte Pinakothek, Munich (inv. no. 589). Although De Hooch never focused on one individual demonstrating domestic virtue, he did paint a number of multi-figure compositions reflecting this theme about 1657. See Sutton 1980, cats. 17, 18.
7. Kindly communicated by Jørgen Wadum.
8. Artemisia was the wife of Mausolus, who died in 353 B.C. She erected a great monument to his memory, the Mausoleum at Halicarnassus. The scene depicted is Artemisia pouring liquid into a vessel containing her husband's ashes, which she then drank, making herself a living tomb. Artemisia came to symbolize a widow's devotion to the memory of her husband.
9. For a discussion of the artistic ideals espoused by Van Hoogstraeten 1678, see Wheelock 1995, 14–16.
10. Hoet 1752–1770, 1:221, no. 20: "Het vermaerde Melkmeysje, door Vermeer van Delft, konstig."
11. On Van Hoek, see Dudok van Heel 1977, 114, no. 189; on Rooleeuw, Broos 1984, 33 n. 17.
12. Dudok van Heel 1975, 162, no. 67: "Een melkuytgietstertje van dezelve (Van der Meer)."
13. On both De Neufvilles, see The Hague 1990, 339–341, 344 nn. 3–8.
14. Sale catalogue, Amsterdam, 19 June 1765, 10, no. 65: "zynde krachtig van licht en bruin, en sterk werkende" (Lugt no. 1470).
15. Wijnman et al. 1974, 425.
16. Reynolds 1781, 84: "The cabinet of mr. Le Brun"; see also Goldscheider 1958, 139, no. 9.
17. Sale catalogue, Amsterdam, 12 September 1798, 13–14, no. 32: "Dit uitmuntend en fraai Tafreel" … "een der schoonste van deezen onnavolgbaaren Meester" (Lugt no. 5804).
18. Mauritshuis 1993A, 50–51.
19. Sale catalogue, Amsterdam, 12 April 1813, 30–31, no. 96 (Lugt no. 8345); on Muilman, see Elias 1903–1905/1963, 1: 958–959, Heerkens Thijssen 1948, 7–9, and De la Fontaine Verwey 1976, 567–568.
20. Van Riemsdijk 1900, 442.
21. Murray 1819–1823, 155.
22. Van Eeghen 1958, 226.
23. Six 1908, 2: "door de hooghartige onbaatzuchtigheid van den eigenaar."

24. Heijbroek 1983, 190 n. 37; the extensive exchange of letters concerning a possible acquisition extends from 1899 to 1908 (Rijksmuseum archives, Amsterdam).
25. "Is de aankoop door het rijk van een deel der Six-collectie aan te bevelen?" Lugt 1907; see also Duparc 1975, 160–162; Heijbroek 1983, 164–170; and Buijsen 1990, 64–68.
26. Lugt 1907, 11: "hoofdnummer, waarom alles draait, nl. het 'Melkmeisje' van VERMEER."
27. The whole affair was summarized by Heijbroek 1983 (from the minutes of the Rembrandt Society) and Buijsen 1990 (from numerous newspaper accounts) (see n. 25 above); Steenhoff 1908 and Martin 1908 supplied contemporary commentary.
28. Heijbroek 1983, 170.

COLLECTION CATALOGUES

Rijksmuseum 1976, 572, no. A 2344, and ill. (with extensive literature)

LITERATURE

Hoet 1752–1770, 1: 34, no. 2; 62, no. 7, and 221, no. 20; Reynolds 1781, 84; Murray 1819–1823, 155; Josi 1821, s.v.; Thoré-Bürger 1858–1860, 1: 68, 69, 75, 76, 82, and 86; Waagen 1863–1864, 26–27; Thoré-Bürger 1866, 298, 303, 306, 322–323, 328, 459, 467, and 553–554, no. 25; Havard 1873, 55–56, 125, no. 142; Havard 1883a, 394, and ill. p. 393; Havard 1888, 10, 37, no. 28, and 17, ill.; Hofstede de Groot 1907–1928, 1: 594–595, no. 17; Hofstede de Groot 1907–1930, pl. 10; Lugt 1907, 11–14, and 21–22; Six 1908, 1–5; Steenhoff 1908, 206–211, and ill.; Plietzsch 1911, 36–37, 113, no. 3, and ill. 7; Johansen 1920, 192; Swillens 1929, 143, and ill. 12; Hale 1937, 70, 98, no. 2, 102, 113, 175–177, 180, 200, and pl. 6; De Vries 1939, 39–40, 81, no. 10, ills. 9–10 and 36; Blum 1946, 169, no. 25, 197, no. 11, and ill.; Swillens 1950, 74, no. D 3, 56–57, no. 18, 85, 135, 140, and pls. 18, 52 a-b; Gowing 1952, 109–112, no. 8, and ills. 16–17; Van Gelder 1958, 13 a-b, and ill.; Goldscheider 1958, 139, no. 9, and ills. 22–25; Blankert 1975, 48, 50, 52, 59, 94, 96, 98, 141–143, no. 7, and pl. 7; Couprie 1975, 2; Dudok van Heel 1975, 162, no. 67; Wheelock 1977A, 282, and ill. 89; Blankert 1978, 32, 35, 40, 63–65, 157–158, no. 7, and pl. 7; Slatkes 1981, 33–34, and ill.; Wheelock 1981, 39, 66, 86–89, 90, 96, 116, and pls. 12–13; Heijbroek 1983, 164 and 169; Brown 1984, 149, and ill.; Aillaud 1986, 48, 64, 98–101, 102, 108, 157, 158–159, 169 n. 92, 174–176, no. 7, and pl. 8; Wheelock 1988, 37, 66–67, and pl. 10; Montias 1989, 161, 196, 199–200, 250, 255, and ill. 28; The Hague 1990, 65–68, and ill. 8; Nash 1991, 26, 28–29, 94–96, and ill.; Blankert 1992, 48–49, 66, 94, 100–101, 108, 156–160, 168 n. 93, 174–176, no. 7, 217, 223, ill. 111, and pl. 8; Wheelock 1995, 18, 50, 61, 62–71, 77, 139, 165, 173, and ill. 42

6

The Girl with the Wineglass

c. 1659–1660
inscribed lower right window pane: *IVMeer* (VM in ligature)
oil on canvas, 77.5 x 66.7 (30½ x 26¼)

Herzog Anton Ulrich-Museum, Brunswick

PROVENANCE

(?) Pieter Claesz van Ruijven, Delft, before 1674; (?) Maria de Knuijt, Widow Van Ruijven, Delft, 1674–1681; (?) Magdalena van Ruijven and Jacob Dissius, Delft, 1681–1682; Jacob Dissius (with his father Abraham Dissius, 1685–1694), Delft, 1682–1695; Dissius sale, Amsterdam, 16 May 1696, no. 9 (*f* 73); Duke Anton Ulrich, Brunswick, before 1710; to the present owner in 1714 (1807–1815 in the Louvre, Paris)

EXHIBITIONS

Berlin 1929, "Nachtrag," no. 103a and ill.; Schaffhausen 1949, 76, no. 188 and ill.; Brunswick 1978, 164–168, no. 39 and ill.

TECHNICAL DESCRIPTION

The fine, plain-weave linen with a thread count of 14 x 15 per cm^2 retains its original tacking edges; on both left and right sides are selvedges. The support has been glue/paste lined.

The double ground consists of a white layer, containing chalk, lead white, and umber,[1] followed by a reddish brown layer. The ground was left uncovered along several outlines of the figures and the wine jug. It extends a few millimeters over the tacking edges.

Parts of the window, red dress, chair, and many of the highlights were painted wet-in-wet, with impasto in the highlights, the fruit, and the red skirt of the figure in the window. Ultramarine is used extensively: in the window, the background, the tablecloth, and in the underpaint of the shadows of the girl's red dress. The position of the heads of the standing man and the girl, and the bows in her hair, have been slightly altered. Some parts of the painting appear unfinished, such as the wall between the male figures, and the arm and the cuff of the girl. There is degraded medium in the ultramarine mixtures and the pigment appears discolored.

Within this well-ordered interior a scene of seduction unfolds. While a melancholic young man in the background of this spacious room rests his head on his hand, a young woman, elegant in her red satin dress, delicately holds a glass of white wine handed to her by an attentive gentleman. As the young woman smiles out at the viewer, she appears to accept not only the wineglass but also the attentions of her solicitous suitor. Indeed, her wide grin has led many to believe that she is already somewhat intoxicated, having willingly yielded to his urgings.[2]

Vermeer's painting belongs to a genre of domestic scenes prevalent in mid-seventeenth century Holland in which the mores of contemporary life, particularly those pertaining to love and courtship, were depicted and commented upon. Many of these scenes focus on the foibles of human relationships and man's inability to restrain his sensual appetite. For example, Gerard ter Borch (1617–1681), in one of his paintings of the mid-1650s, features a forlorn young woman drinking by herself while her male companion sleeps off the narcotic effects of tobacco.[3] In 1658 Pieter de Hooch (1629–1684) depicted a more elaborate scenario involving wine and tobacco in his *Woman Drinking with Soldiers* (fig. 1). Within De Hooch's light-filled room a male figure holding a clay pipe sits before an open window, while another young man pours wine into a glass held by a seated woman. An older woman behind the couple, who appears to play the role of procuress, suggests that the wine will eventually lead to a sexual encounter.[4] De Hooch provides a commentary on the scene through a painting of Christ and the Adulteress (John 8:1–11) hanging on the rear wall of the room. While the Biblical moral "He that is without sin among you, let him first cast a stone" does not condone the sensual pleasures being enjoyed by the protagonists, it does warn the viewer about responding self-righteously to the actions of others.

Such paintings certainly inspired Vermeer when he came to paint *The Girl with the Wineglass*, and a somewhat earlier scene of seduction, *The Glass of Wine*, c. 1658–1660 (page 36, fig. 7). The concentration of the action in a corner of a spacious room is a compositional schema borrowed directly from De Hooch. In *The Girl with the Wineglass*, however, Vermeer brings the figures closer to the picture plane than does De Hooch so that they, rather than the architectural structure of the room, become the dominant elements in the composition. Vermeer eliminates accessories that De Hooch uses to create a context for the figures' interactions, and, with this simplification, weaves together the compositional elements more intricately than does his colleague.

One aspect of the image that Vermeer does not eliminate, however, is moralizing commentary. Whereas De Hooch introduces his commentary through a picture-within-

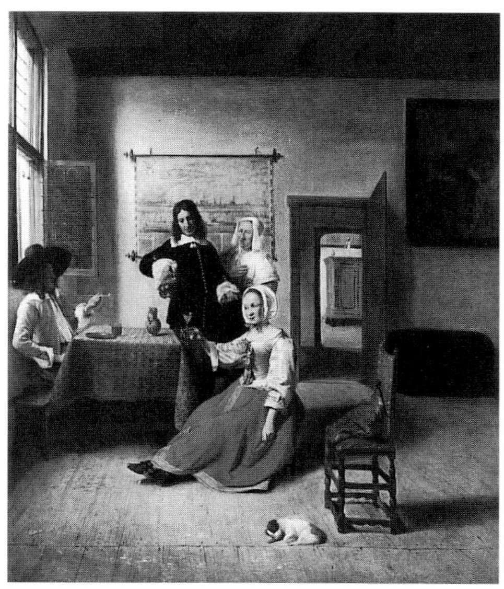

fig. 1. Pieter de Hooch, *Woman Drinking with Soldiers*, 1658, oil on canvas, Musée du Louvre, Paris

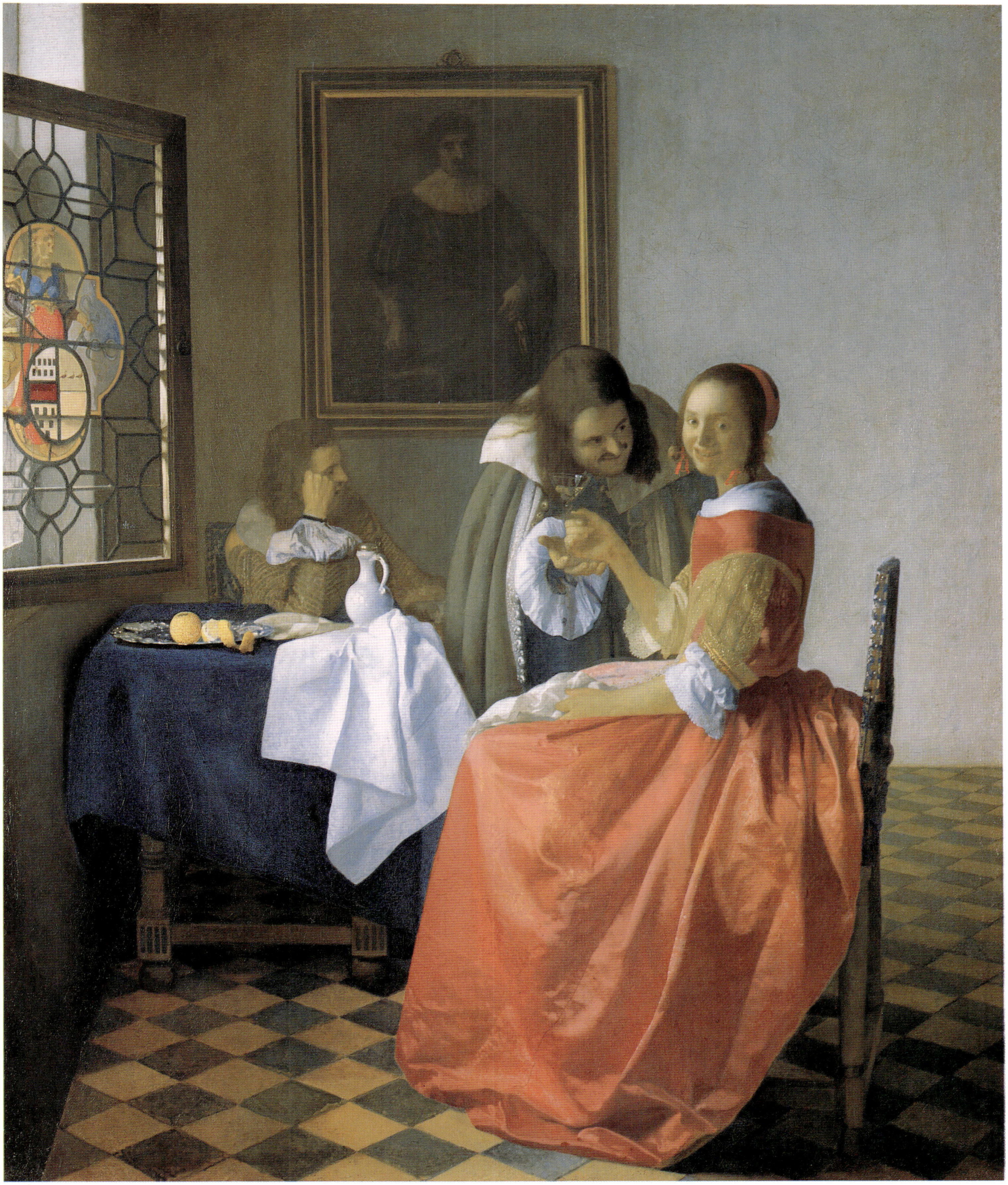

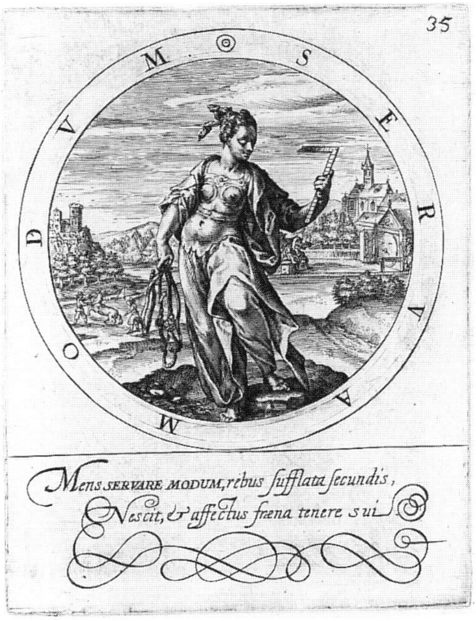

fig. 2. Gabriel Rollenhagen, "Serva Modum," *Selectorum Emblematum Centuria Secunda*, Arnhem, 1613, The Folger Library, Washington

the-picture, Vermeer subtly incorporates his in the leaded glass window. As Rüdiger Klessman has stressed, the colored glass panes in the window contain the allegorical figure of Temperance holding a bridle,[5] which resembles closely an emblematic image from Gabriel Rollenhagen's *Selectorum Emblematum* of 1613 (fig. 2). The emblem's epigram "Serva Modum" (Observe moderation) is elaborated upon in the accompanying text, which freely translated reads: "The heart knows not how to observe moderation and to apply reins to feelings when struck with desire."[6]

The emblematic imagery, and the staid portrait decorating the rear wall, provide a fascinating counterpoint to the protagonists' evident lack of restraint. Much as with the sleeping figure in Ter Borch's genre scene, the man resting his head on his hand behind the table has succumbed to the narcotic effects of tobacco: the bowl of his clay pipe is just evident above the rolled sheet of paper on the table. Meanwhile, the relationship of the couple in the foreground is characterized by unrestrained sensual attraction, enhanced by the consumption of wine.

Judging from Vermeer's careful placement of the upright ancestral portrait between the two male figures, each devoted in his own way to sensual pleasure, the focus of the artist's concern seems to be the lack of male restraint in contemporary life.[7] Indeed, although it has been generally assumed that the male suitor is responsible for plying the young woman with drink, the nature of the seduction is more complex than at first appears. As in Frans van Mieris' (1635–1681) *The Oyster Meal*, 1661 (Mauritshuis, The Hague) (fig. 3), a painting often compared with this work, body language discloses much about relationships between figures. While the woman in Van Mieris' painting lounges seductively in her chair, the maiden in Vermeer's painting sits erectly, her pose suggesting self-control. Rather than exchanging glances with her suitor as in Van Mieris' painting, Vermeer's woman turns toward the viewer, effectively separating herself psychologically from him. Indeed, as in paintings by Nicolaes Maes (1634–1693) (fig. 4) where the mistress shares a private communication with the viewer, so here the woman's smile is a knowing one, indicating not only that she is aware of what is transpiring but also that she is in control. Although her suitor is entirely unaware of the fact, he rather than she is the one being seduced.[8] In this context it is fascinating, as is discussed below, that Thoré-Bürger christened the painting "La coquette" in the nineteenth century.

This scenario, where the male fawns over a beautiful woman with ruby mouth and ivory skin, resplendent in fine satins, only to be rejected and betrayed, is one that was fashionable among seventeenth-century poets, who based their ideas of unrequited love on the sonnets of Petrarch.[9]

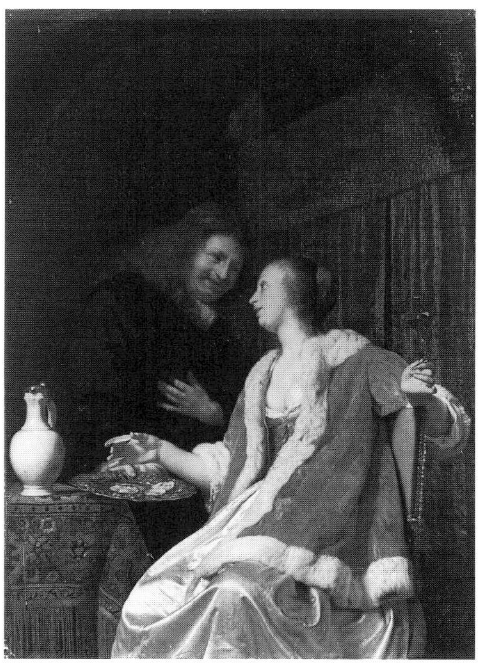

fig. 3. Frans van Mieris, *The Oyster Meal*, 1661, oil on panel, Mauritshuis, The Hague

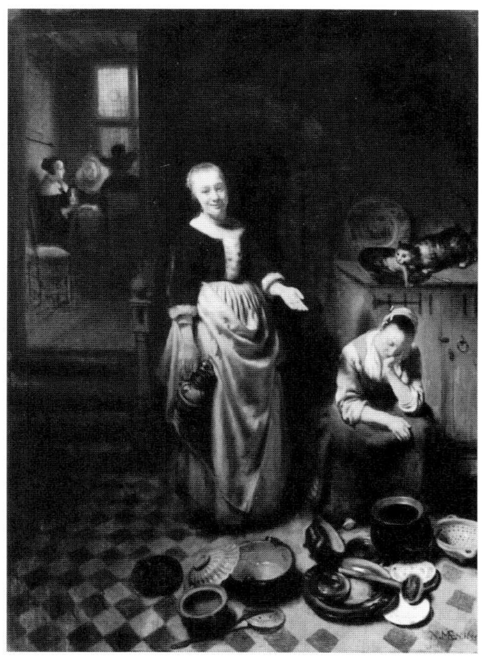

fig. 4. Nicolaes Maes, *The Idle Servant*, 1655, oil on panel, Reproduced by courtesy of the Trustees, The National Gallery, London

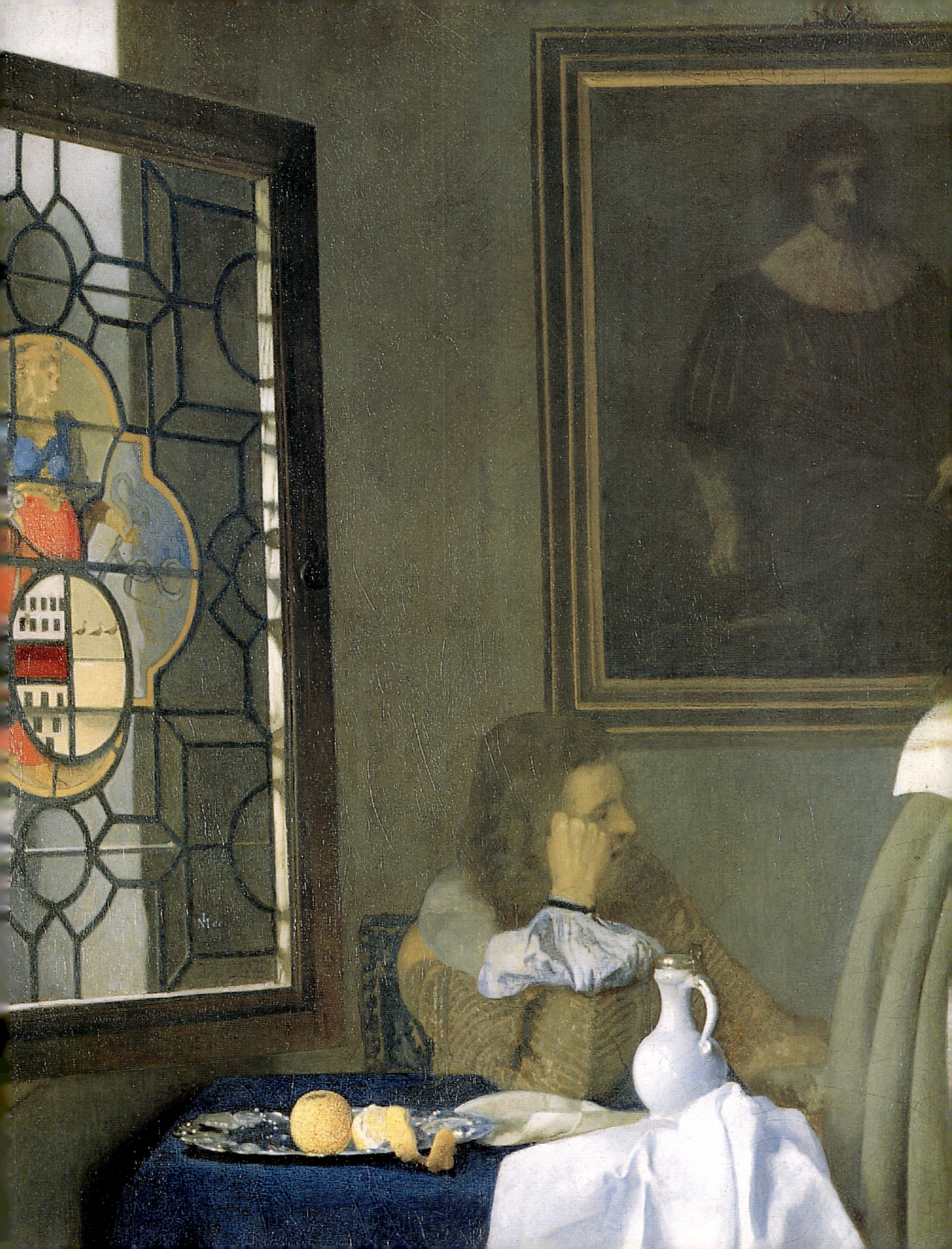

However, whereas this fourteenth-century lyricist idealized love for being pure and unattainable, Dutch seventeenth-century poets and artists transformed Petrarch's almost Neo-Platonic ideas into earthly reality. Human foibles rather than the earthly boundaries of the human heart are the factors that preclude attainment of perfect union. The artist who most fully embraced this Dutch vision of Petrarchan ideas of love was Gerard ter Borch,[10] and it may well have been his paintings that inspired Vermeer's conception for this work.[11]

Beyond general relationships to his contemporaries, comparisons between this work and Vermeer's other genre scenes of the late 1650s demonstrate the artist's ability to adapt his painting technique to the character of his subject. In *The Milkmaid*, for example, Vermeer stressed strength and vitality, defining the working-class figure and the still life before her with bold and direct brushwork. In the more sophisticated and upper-class scene of *The Girl with the Wineglass*, Vermeer blended his strokes to depict the soft sheen of satin and the smooth glint of a silver tray. This ability to adapt his painting techniques to relate to the character of his subject is one of the most remarkable aspects of Vermeer's mastery as an artist.

The first description of *The Girl with the Wineglass* appeared in the catalogue of the spectacular Dissius sale in Amsterdam in 1696. It was described as "a merry company in a Room, powerful and good by ditto," and sold for 73 guilders.[12] We can assume that the painting was bought by an agent of Anton Ulrich, Duke of Brunswick (1633–1714) (fig. 5), whose collection was his life's work. Ulrich's pleasure mansion, Salzdahlum, was called an "art treasury."[13] Its rooms were arranged thematically. Dutch kitchen pieces hung in the room of the duchess, for instance, whereas the "cabinet" of the duke housed the most important paintings, including the Italian ones. In 1710 the first catalogue of the collection of paintings appeared, written by the painter Tobias Querfurt (c. 1670–1730), who had likely bought the painting for Anton Ulrich. Vermeer's *Girl with the Wineglass* is called, again, "A merry company, admirably painted, especially the clothes."[14] Considering the wording he used, Querfurt must have cited the catalogue for the 1696 sale in Amsterdam.

The title of the picture changed over the ensuing years. A hand-written inventory of 1744 called it "a young gentleman with his loved one."[15] An expanded text appeared in 1776 in a *Verzeichnis der herzoglichen Bilder-Galerie zu Salzthalen* by the "Galerieinspektor" Christian Eberlein. He mentioned the laughing girl and wrote: "Behind her stands a male person, who holds on to her glass with her, and looks at her affectionately."[16] The sitting man behind the table occurs in neither text, so that it has been assumed that he had been painted over.[17] This train of thought is understandable but probably unfounded, as this figure is mentioned in 1836, when he was pointed out by Pape in a new collection catalogue: "In the background sits a man with his arms resting on a table, who appears to be sleeping."[18] In this catalogue, however, the artist is identified as "Jacob van der Meer," a mistake that led Thoré-Bürger to ask whether the artist was the painter Jacob Vermeer, born in Schoonhoven and active in Utrecht.[19] Further complicating Thoré-Bürger's efforts to reconstruct Vermeer's oeuvre was the discovery in Brunswick of a *Dune Landscape* signed "JVMeer" that seemed in no way related to the interior scene. Thoré-Bürger did not realize that yet another artist of a similar name existed, Jan van der Meer [Vermeer] of Haarlem (1628–1691), a landscape painter. His confusion led to a succession of misconceptions that have contributed to the aura of mystery surrounding Vermeer.[20]

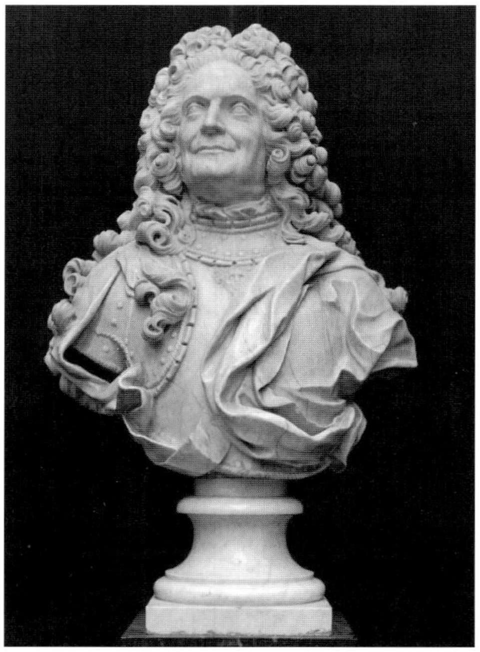

fig. 5. Balthasar Permoser, *Portrait of Duke Herzog Anton Ulrich of Braunschweig*, c. 1704, alabaster, Herzog Anton Ulrich-Museum, Brunswick

Thoré-Bürger felt a genuine admiration for the painting that he had called "La coquette." In 1868 he published a list of his favorite figure pieces by Vermeer, that is, excluding the cityscapes and landscapes. He named *The Procuress* (page 60, fig. 16) the most important, *Art of Painting* (page 68, fig 2) the most interesting, and *The Milkmaid* the most admirable, but he chose *The Girl with the Wineglass* as the most attractive painting on account of its composition, the elegance of its rendering, and the refinement in the facial features.[21]

Even so, "La coquette" has not always been positively judged. "This painting can hardly be called one of Vermeer's best, though it has admirable bits. The girl's head...shows unfortunately by no means the best rendering," thought Philip Hale in 1937.[22] Soon after De Vries was to share his misgivings: "The work has suffered a lot. The expression of the woman, which at present looks rather unpleasant, is due to restoration."[23] Indeed, the subsequent restoration of 1989 removed old, disfiguring repaint.

The painting had previously left Brunswick only once, when Napoleon ordered the art treasures from Salzdahlum to be transported to Paris; there Vermeer's genre piece hung among paintings belonging to the Stadtholder William V that had been looted from The Hague.[24] Eight years later the ducal collection, like that of the Stadtholder, was returned to its place of origin. On 8 November 1815 a major portion of Anton Ulrich's paintings made its triumphal entry into Brunswick.[25]

After the ducal collection had become state property in 1924, Vermeer's painting once more attracted the attention of the international press. That was during the Depression, in 1930, when the management of the Herzog Anton Ulrich-Museum considered selling the painting. Duveen Brothers had offered £150,000.[26] However, it was decided not to set a precedent that might threaten all German art treasures.[27] As the result, *The Girl with the Wineglass* is still the only Vermeer that has resided so long within a single collection.

1. Kühn 1968, 187.
2. Brunswick 1978, 165–168, no. 39; Blankert 1992, 180.
3. Philadelphia 1984A, cat. 11, pl. 70.
4. For a discussion of this painting, see Philadelphia 1984A, 217–218, cat. 52.
5. Klessman in Brunswick 1978, 167–168. This figure of Temperance is seen in conjunction with a coat of arms. Neurdenburg 1942, 69 n. 2., identified the heraldic emblem as being that of Jannetje Vogel (d. 1624), the first wife of Vermeer's neighbor, Moses J. Nederveen. While it seems probable that Vermeer would have based the image of the window upon a specific prototype, it should be noted that the colors of the figure are different in the Berlin painting, where it also appears. It would thus seem that Vermeer took certain liberties in the accuracy of his representation. Whether or not the family commissioned either of these works or had anything to do with Vermeer's choice of subject matter is unknown.
6. Rollenhagen 1613. "Mens SERVARE MODUM, rebus sufflata secundis, Nescit, et affectus fraena tenere sui."
7. To judge from the costume, the portrait must date from the mid-1630s. See, for example, Frans Hals' portrait of Lucas de Clercq from c. 1635 (Frans Halsmuseum, Haarlem), ill. in Slive 1970–1974, 2: pl. 169.
8. The woman's striking red satin dress adds to her seductive character.
9. Kettering 1993, 101–104, has stressed that poets and playwrights from P. C. Hooft to Jan Harmens Krul developed this literary genre from the writings of Petrarch.
10. See, for example, *The Suitor's Visit*, c. 1658, National Gallery of Art, Washington, as discussed in National Gallery Washington 1995, 27–28.
11. Although Ter Borch and Vermeer are documented as having met in 1653, no future contact is known. Nevertheless, it does appear that both artists sold paintings through the same Amsterdam dealer, Johannes de Renialme, until his death in 1657. See Montias 1989, 139, and Kettering 1993, 104.
12. Hoet 1752–1770, 1: 34, no. 9: "Een vrolyk gezelschap in een Kamer, kragtig and goet van dito."
13. Fink 1954, 24: "Schatzkammer der Kunst."
14. Herzog Anton Ulrich-Museum 1710, unpaginated: "Eine lustige Gesellschaft admirable gemalet, sonderlich die Kleidung."
15. Manuscript 1744 (archive Herzog Anton Ulrich-Museum, Brunswick): "ein junger Herr mit seiner Geliebten" (see also Herzog Anton Ulrich-Museum 1983, 208).
16. Herzog Anton Ulrich-Museum 1776, 127–128, no. 30: "Hinter ihr steht eine Mannsperson, welcher ihr Glas mit anfaßt, und sie zärtlich ansieht."
17. Blankert 1978, 159, no. 11 and Blankert 1992, 179, no. 11.
18. Herzog Anton Ulrich-Museum 1836/1849, 52–53, no. 142 (quoted from the third edition; the first edition appeared in 1836): "Hinterwärts sitßt ein Mann, mit dem Arme auf den Tisch gelehnt; der zu schlafen scheint."
19. Thoré-Bürger 1858–1860, 2: 73; see also Thoré-Bürger 1866, 304–308; the title "eine Kokette" was taken over in the 1867 Brunswick catalogue (see Herzog Anton Ulrich-Museum 1882, 331–332).
20. Thoré-Bürger 1866, 307. Cornelis Hofstede de Groot's catalogue raisonné of Vermeer's oeuvre was the first modern attempt to solve this issue (Hofstede de Groot 1907–1928, 1: 587–614, esp. 612–613).
21. Thoré-Bürger 1868, 262.
22. Hale 1937, 192.
23. De Vries 1939, 82, no. 13: "Het stuk heeft zeer geleden. De uitdrukking der vrouw, die thans eerder onaangenaam aandoet, is te wijten aan restauratie."
24. Fink 1954, 90–94.
25. Fink 1954, 100–106.
26. Hale 1937, 192; according to Winkler 1931a, 489, Duveen offered 2.7 million deutschmarks.
27. Winkler 1931a, 488–489; Winkler 1931b, 74–76; Jesse 1931, 32–33; see also Fink 1954, 126.

COLLECTION CATALOGUES

Herzog Anton Ulrich-Museum 1710, unpaginated; Herzog Anton Ulrich-Museum 1776, 127–128, no. 30; Herzog Anton Ulrich-Museum 1836/1849, 52–53, no. 142; Herzog Anton Ulrich-Museum 1870, no. 1; Herzog Anton Ulrich-Museum 1882, 331–332; Herzog Anton Ulrich-Museum 1983, 208–210, no. 316 (with extensive literature)

LITERATURE

Hoet 1750–1772, 1: 34, no. 9; Thoré-Bürger 1858–1860, 2: 72–76 and 80; Thoré-Bürger 1859, 34; Blanc 1860–1863, 1: s.v., 2; Kramm 1857–1864, 6: 1727; Waagen 1862, 2: 110; Thoré-Bürger 1866, 316, 460 and 547, no. 6; Thoré-Bürger 1868, 262–263; Havard 1888, 35, no. 6; Hofstede de Groot 1907–1928, 1: 603–604, no. 38; Plietzsch 1911, 115, no. 10; Jesse 1931, 33–35; Winkler 1931a, 489; Winkler 1931b, 74–76 and 369; Hale 1937, 99, 135, 190–192 and pl. 47; De Vries 1939, 82, no. 13 and ill. 39; Blum 1946, 161, no. 6; Van Thienen 1949, 20 and ill.; Swillens 1950, 55, no. 14, 67, 73, 78, 82, 84, 85, 87, 89 and pl. 14; Gowing 1952, 130, no. 14 and ills. 33–36; Fink 1954, 43, 93, 126 and ill. 16; Goldscheider 1958, 39, 140–141, no. 15 and ills. 41–42; Van Regteren Altena 1960, 177; Bedaux 1975, 35 and 38, ill. 23; Blankert 1975, 59–60, 62, 93–94, 116 n. 48, 145–146, no. 11 and pl. 11; Van Straaten 1977, 56–57 and ill.; Wheelock 1977a, 281 and ill. 87; Blankert 1978, 41, 62, 63, 77 n. 59, 159, no. 11 and pl. 11; Slatkes 1981, 48–49 and ill.; Wheelock 1981, 92 and pl. 15; Aillaud 1986, 108, 111, 112, 157, 167 n. 53, 179–180, no. 11, and pl. 12; Wheelock 1988, 70–71, pl. 12; Montias 1989, 190, 265 and ill. 41; Nash 1991, 24–25, no. 9, 36 and ills.; Blankert 1992, 109, 112, 114, 156, 166 n. 52, 179–181, no. 11 and pl. 12; Wheelock 1995, 59, 89, 174, and ill. AII

7

View of Delft

c. 1660–1661

inscribed lower left, on the boat: *IVM* in ligature

oil on canvas, 96.5 x 115.7 (38 x 45 9/16)

Royal Cabinet of Paintings Mauritshuis, The Hague

PROVENANCE

(?) Pieter Claesz van Ruijven, Delft, before 1674; (?) Maria de Knuijt, Widow Van Ruijven, Delft, 1674–1681; (?) Magdalena van Ruijven and Jacob Dissius, Delft, 1681–1682; Jacob Dissius (with his father Abraham Dissius, 1685–1694), Delft, 1682–1695; Dissius sale, Amsterdam, 16 May 1696, no. 31 (*f* 200); Willem Philip Kops, Haarlem, Bloemendaal, before 1805; Cornelia Kops-de Wolf, Bloemendaal, 1805–1820; Anna Johanna Teding van Berkhout-Kops, Haarlem, 1820–1822; Stinstra et al. sale, Amsterdam, 22 May 1822, no. 112 (*f* 2,900, to J. de Vries); Royal Cabinet of Paintings Mauritshuis, The Hague, 1822

EXHIBITIONS

Paris 1921, 10, no. 104; London 1929A, 144, no. 304; Amsterdam 1945, no. 132; Delft 1950, 11, no. 25; The Hague 1966, no. 3 and ill.; Paris 1966, no. 3 and ill; Paris 1986, 350–357, no. 53, ill. (with extensive literature)

TECHNICAL DESCRIPTION

The support is a fine, plain-weave linen with a thread count of 14 x 13 per cm² and selvedges on both left and right sides. Strainer bar marks have resulted from a vertical cross bar and corner braces. The canvas has been lined.

The buff-brown ground, bound with oil and some protein, contains chalk, lead white, ocher, a little umber, and a little black.[1]

The composition was built up in light and dark passages. The sky, foreground, and light parts of the water were laid in with lead white, while the town and its reflection were left in reserve. Some parts of the townscape are underpainted with black. A rough surface texture was created in many places, particularly in the stone façades, and in the roofs, by underpainting with lead white containing exceptionally coarse pigment particles mixed with sand. The fine yellow ocher paint of the step gable at left contains transparent rounded particles of sand.

Vermeer depicts Delft from the south, as seen across a harbor that linked waterways to Rotterdam, Schiedam, and Delfshaven. Although dark clouds looming overhead shade the foreground and the far shore, including the city walls, the Schiedam Gate with its clock tower and the Rotterdam Gate with its twin towers, the city beyond is bathed in strong sunlight. The orange tile roofs of buildings lining Delft's canals sparkle in the light, as does the imposing tower of the Nieuwe Kerk rising to the right of center.

In many ways Vermeer's *View of Delft* belongs to a tradition of topographical painting whose origins can be traced to the city profiles bordering large wall maps of the Netherlands. These views, as well as those of artists who subsequently painted city profiles as independent works of art, invariably situated the cities at the far side of a body of water. Examples include Esaias van de Velde's (c. 1590/1591–1630) *View of Zierikzee*, 1618 (Staatliche Museen zu Berlin), and Hendrick Vroom's (c. 1566–1640) two topographical views of Delft in 1615 (fig. 1).[2] Vroom, in fact, emphasized the city's architectural character rather than its commercial and civic activities. He consciously chose a site where the distinctive towers of the two major churches in Delft, the Oude Kerk and the Nieuwe Kerk, dominate the city profile. The few figures he depicts serenely go about their daily affairs in the foreground landscape, far removed from city life.

Vermeer, however, so transformed this topographic tradition when he painted *View of Delft* that connections to it are more superficial than substantive. One fundamental difference, already noted in the 1822 Stinstra sale catalogue, is the bold and expressive manner of Vermeer's execution. No other artist has conveyed to such an extent the physical presence of the city lying before him, whether it be the rough stone of a bridge, the brick and mortar of walls, or the rippling of roof tiles. No topographical artist ever relegated the foreground of his cityscape to shadow, as did Vermeer, not only to suggest the expansiveness of the receding sky, but to draw the viewer into the sunlit interior of the city. Finally, no topographic artist ever moved beyond descriptive realism to create a mood that conveys something of the history and character of a given city.

The forcefulness of Vermeer's conception and the surety of his brushwork, now more evident since the removal of vestiges of old, discolored varnish during the 1994 restoration,[3] is all the more remarkable

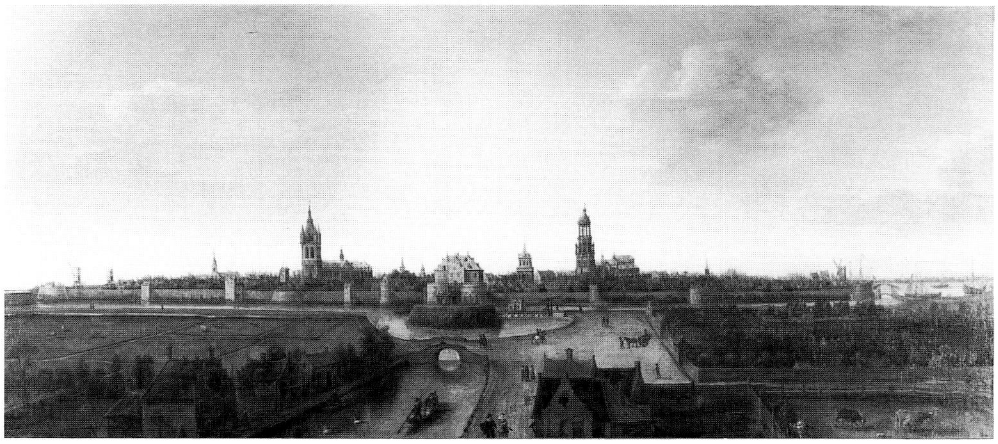

fig. 1. Hendrick Vroom, *View of Delft*, 1615, oil on canvas, Stedelijk Museum Het Prinsenhof, Gemeente Musea Delft

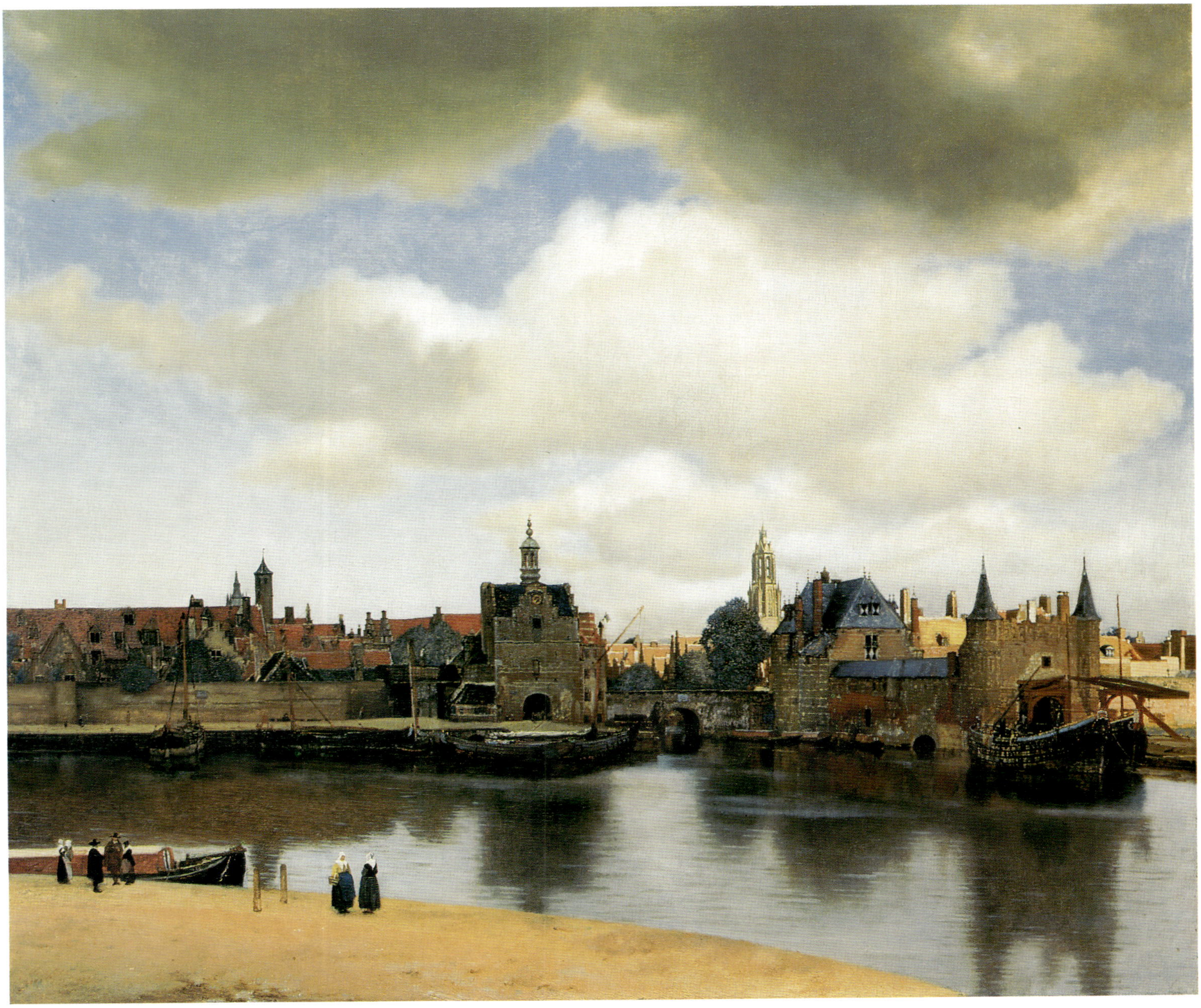

because *View of Delft* is an anomaly within Vermeer's oeuvre. Other than *The Little Street* (cat. 4), Vermeer seemed to have little interest in depicting life outside the confines of the home.[4] Indeed, most views through the windows in his interiors are implied rather than explicitly recorded. Just why Vermeer came to paint this cityscape is not known; neither a commission for the work nor a description of the painting from the artist's lifetime has survived.

Vermeer used a wide range of techniques to create the varied textures in his cityscape.[5] He suggested the rough, broken quality of the red roof tiles at the left by overlaying a thin reddish-brown layer with numerous small dabs of red, brown, and blue paint. Vermeer enhanced the texture of these tile roofs by first applying an underlayer of sand mixed with large lumps of white lead.

This texture is quite different from those found in the sunlit roofs, where Vermeer minimized individual nuances of the tile. Here he emphasized the physical presence of the tiles by using a thick layer of salmon-colored paint. Vermeer's use of impasto is even more striking in the tower of the Nieuwe Kerk where he seems almost to have sculpted the sunlit portions of the tower with a heavy application of lumpy lead-tin yellow.

Perhaps the most distinctive effects Vermeer created in *View of Delft* are the diffused highlights enlivening the surface of the boat in the lower right. Painted in a variety of ochers, grays, and whites, these highlights are quite large and have a comparatively regular circular shape. Vermeer layered the paint in this area in a complex manner, occasionally applying opaque highlights wet-in-wet on the diffused highlights.

Although Vermeer introduced small dabs or globules of paint to enhance textural effects almost from the beginning of his career, the diffused highlights on the boat function differently. He employs them here not to accent textural effects, but to indicate flickering reflections from the water onto the boat. The character of these highlights, which compares closely to those seen in unfocused images of a camera obscura, has indicated to many that Vermeer executed this painting with the use of this optical device.[6]

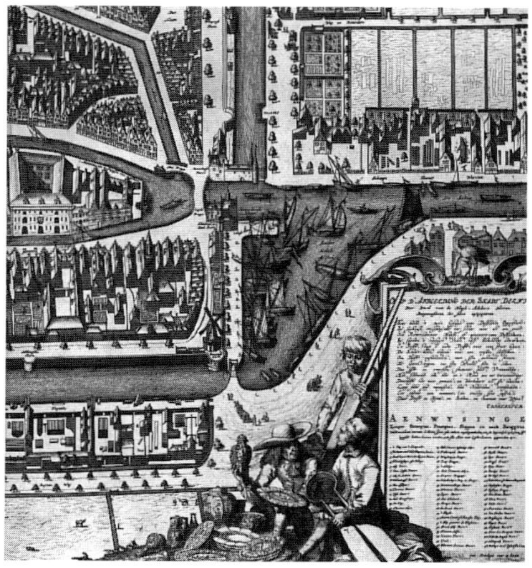

fig. 2. Detail, *Large Figurative Map of Delft*, Amsterdam, 1675–1678, National Gallery of Art Library, Washington

Although no documentary evidence indicates that Vermeer actually worked with a camera obscura, it is worth noting that a house where he could have set one up, which would have provided a view similar to that seen in his painting, was situated across the harbor from the Schiedam and Rotterdam gates (fig. 2).[7]

To suggest that Vermeer achieved his pictorial effects in the *View of Delft* because of a camera obscura, however, misconstrues the work's essence as much as does characterizing it as a topographical painting. While Vermeer apparently derived a number of optical effects from a camera obscura, he generally transformed and exploited them. For example, diffused highlights comparable to those on the boat would occur in an unfocused image of a camera obscura, but only if the boat were in bright sunlight, not if it were in shadow as it is in the painting.

The artist, moreover, adapted whatever topographical information the camera ob-

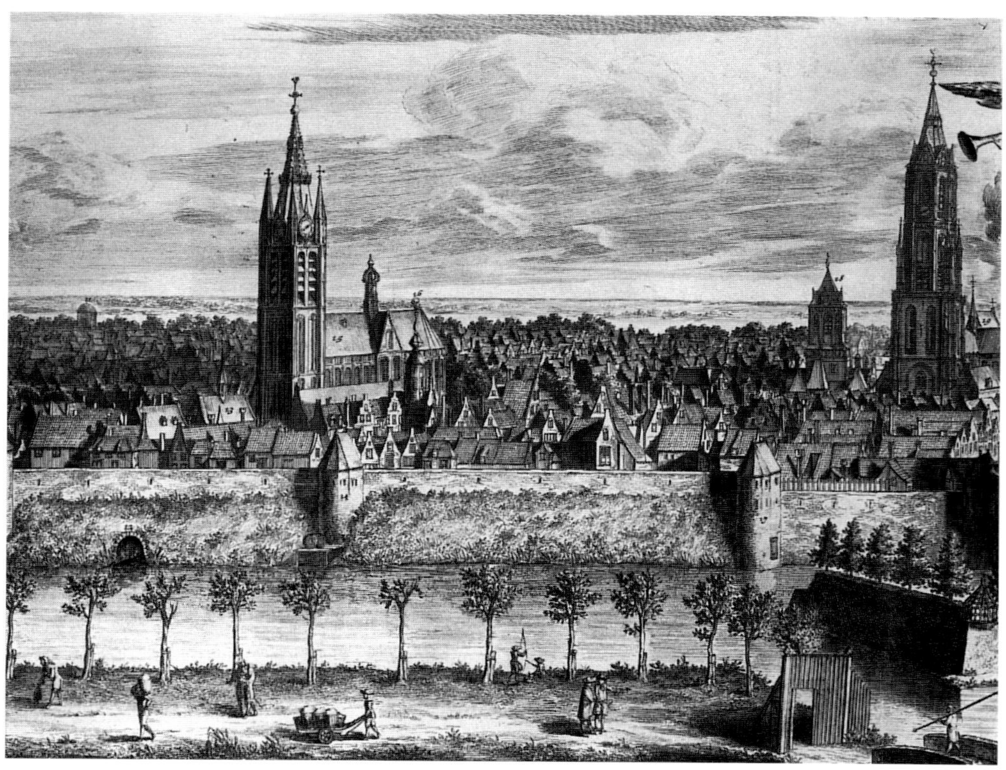

fig. 3. Detail, *Large Figurative Map of Delft*, Amsterdam, 1675–1678, city seen from the west, National Gallery of Art Library, Washington

scura provided for his pictorial purposes. Although virtually all of the buildings in the painting can be identified from contemporary maps and late seventeenth- and early eighteenth-century representations of this view, Vermeer has subtly adjusted their relationships to emphasize the parallel orientation of the buildings. Comparing the site with a section of the large *Figurative Map of Delft* from the mid-1670s (fig. 3) reveals clearly that the topography is more irregular than Vermeer suggested.

A topographical drawing of the site (fig. 4) by the eighteenth-century artist Abraham Rademaker (1675–1735) further demonstrates that Vermeer sought to reinforce the strong friezelike character of the city profile. In Rademaker's drawing the city profile appears quite jagged and uneven; buildings are taller, narrower, and set more closely together than in the *View of Delft*. To emphasize the horizontals of the cityscape, Vermeer apparently straightened the bowed arch of the bridge, perhaps elongating it in the process.[8] Most views of the city from the south place the two gates somewhat closer together than he did.[9] Finally, as is evident in both the map and Rademaker's drawing, the twin towers of the Rotterdam Gate project far out into the water.[10] Vermeer flattened the angle of the gate by altering the perspective. The building is virtually at right angles to the picture plane and, to be consistent with the rest of the composition, Vermeer should have drawn the focal point of the perspective so that it would fall at the vanishing point, slightly left of center. He constructed his perspective, however, so that the orthogonals along the side walls of the gate join far to the left of the painting.

Rademaker achieved the three-dimensional projection of the Rotterdam Gate in part through strong light and shadow contrasts on the towers.[11] X-radiography and infrared reflectography (fig. 5) indicate that Vermeer initially also painted the twin towers of the Rotterdam Gate in bright sunlight.[12] By casting this area of the painting in shadow, he eliminated the pronounced light and shadow contrasts, flattening the forms, conveying their weathered, aged character. To further emphasize the contrast between the dark foreground buildings and the bright sky beyond, Vermeer heightened a number of the contours of the buildings with a white line, a technique he previously used in both *The Little Street* and *The Milkmaid* (cats. 4, 5).[13]

A further important change in the composition, visible in x-radiograph and infrared reflectography, was the adjustment of the reflection of the twin towers of the Rotterdam Gate. The original reflections denoted the architectural forms of the building on the far shore quite precisely. In his final design, however, Vermeer extended them downward so that they intersect with the bottom edge of the picture. The effect of the combined reflection of the Rotterdam Gate towers and the Schiedam Gate in the center (both of which reach the foreground shore) is to bind the city profile and foreground elements in a subtle yet essential manner. The reflections, which function almost as shadows, give added weight and solemnity to the mass of buildings along the far shore. Moreover, beyond anchoring these structures in the foreground, the exaggerated reflections of

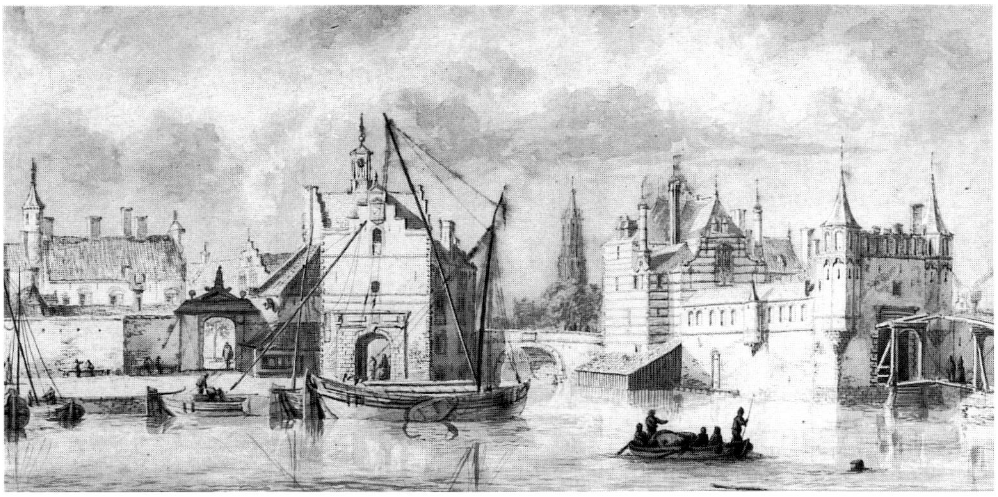

fig. 4. Abraham Rademaker, *View of Delft with Schiedam and Rotterdam Gates*, n.d., drawing, pen, brown ink, and wash, Stedelijk Museum Het Prinsenhof, Gemeente Musea Delft

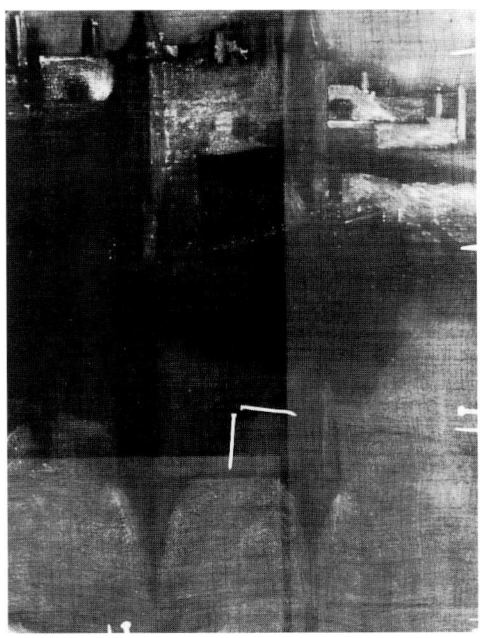

fig. 5. *View of Delft*, detail of x-radiograph

specific portions of the city profile create accents that establish a secondary visual pattern of horizontals, verticals, and diagonals across the scene.

The subtle adjustments Vermeer made in conceiving his image served to elevate his view beyond the merely topographic. Although *View of Delft* has an almost tangible reality, it also is an iconic image. The physical presence, serenity, and beauty of Delft, are there to be admired but only from a distance. The city cannot be approached from the viewpoint Vermeer chose. From across the water the dark, weathered walls and city gates serve as reminders of Delft's ancient foundations. The light that floods the interior of the city acts symbolically as well as naturally. It creates a positive accent, suggesting the city's life and vitality.

The strongest accent of light, however, is on the Nieuwe Kerk, which is in many ways the symbolic center of the city. Not only is it situated at one end of the great marketplace, the focus of civic life in Delft, it is the site of the tomb of William the Silent. The Nieuwe Kerk thus served as a constant reminder of the intimate connections that existed between Delft and the House of Orange, an emphasis made all the more emphatic in Vermeer's painting because the tower of the other great church, the Oude Kerk, is largely obscured.[14] Whether or not Vermeer consciously sought to glorify the connections between Delft and the House of Orange in *View of Delft*, it certainly had that impact on King William I over 160 years later when he decreed that the painting should hang in "His Majesty's Cabinet."[15]

The story of how the *View of Delft*, the most famous painting in the Mauritshuis, came to The Hague in 1822 is remarkable, for it was not a work that the director at the time was anxious to purchase. The possibility for acquiring the *View of Delft* suddenly presented itself when the painting was included in the sale of the Stinstra collection in May 1822. Until now, nothing was known of the history and location of the *View of Delft* between the time of the Dissius sale in Amsterdam in 1696, where it is first mentioned,[16] and the 1822 Stinstra sale in Amsterdam.[17] By the early nineteenth century, however, the painting appears to have achieved a great fame. In 1814 a painted copy was exhibited in Amsterdam with the inscription: "A Cityscape, being a copy after a famous Painting by the Delft Van der Meer."[18] Two years later the writers Roeland van Eijnden and Adriaan van der Willigen described the *View of Delft* as being "greatly praised as astonishingly well done... though we do not know where it is presently located."[19]

When van Eijnden and van der Willigen wrote these words, the painting was in the possession of the Kops family of Haarlem.[20] Until now it has understandably been assumed that it belonged to the "Cabinet of the late Gentleman S. J. Stinstra of Harlingen," which was auctioned in 1822 in Amsterdam. The qualification on the title page of the catalogue, that the offerings were "largely constituted" of works from the Stinstra Cabinet, appears to have been unjustly neglected.[21] No more than half of the collection that was sold in 1822 came from the estate of Gooitjen Stinstra (1763–1821). The initials "S. J." are those of Simon Johannes Stinstra (1673–1743), the predeceased patriarch of the family, which is to say that the catalogue actually appeared under a kind of pseudonym. Gooitjen's testamentary inventory, which mentions ninety-three paintings, does not include the *View of Delft*.[22]

A seemingly irrelevant rumor once making the rounds concerning the provenance of the *View of Delft* now turns out, upon closer examination, to have been of great importance after all. Around 1835 the art dealers C. J. Nieuwenhuys and John Smith claimed that the Kop[p]s family had been the previous owners of the work.[23] These worthies were referring to a very rich Baptist merchant of Haarlem named Willem Philip Kops (1755–1805), who became especially well known for his collection of old master drawings.[24] During his summers he occupied the country estate "Wildhoef" in Bloemendaal, where the *View of Delft* was kept, unbeknownst to Van Eijnden and Van der Willigen. Kops died in 1805, but his spouse lived until 1820, at which time her daughter, Anna Johanna Kops, presumably inherited the *View of Delft*.[25]

Anna Johanna was married to Jan Pieter Teding van Berkhout (1785–1825), deputy to the Provincial Council of Northern Holland.[26] That this man was also a descendent of Pieter Teding van Berckhout, who twice visited Vermeer in 1669 (see page 50), is only a coincidence. On 15 April 1821 the art dealer Jeronimo de Vries wrote to the aforementioned Van der Willigen that he had visited Teding van Berkhout to negotiate the sale of a number of paintings. In addition to several less important works, he was especially interested in two masterpieces: Vermeer's *View of Delft* and Meindert Hobbema's *Ruins of Brederode Castle* (National Gallery, London).[27]

"In my view they are well suited to the Rijksmuseum, providing people remain reasonable," De Vries opined optimistically.[28] Six months later an impatient De Vries again wrote to Van der Willigen: "Where is now Hobbema; where the van der Meer?"[29] At the initiative of Jeronimo de Vries, the two masterpieces by Vermeer

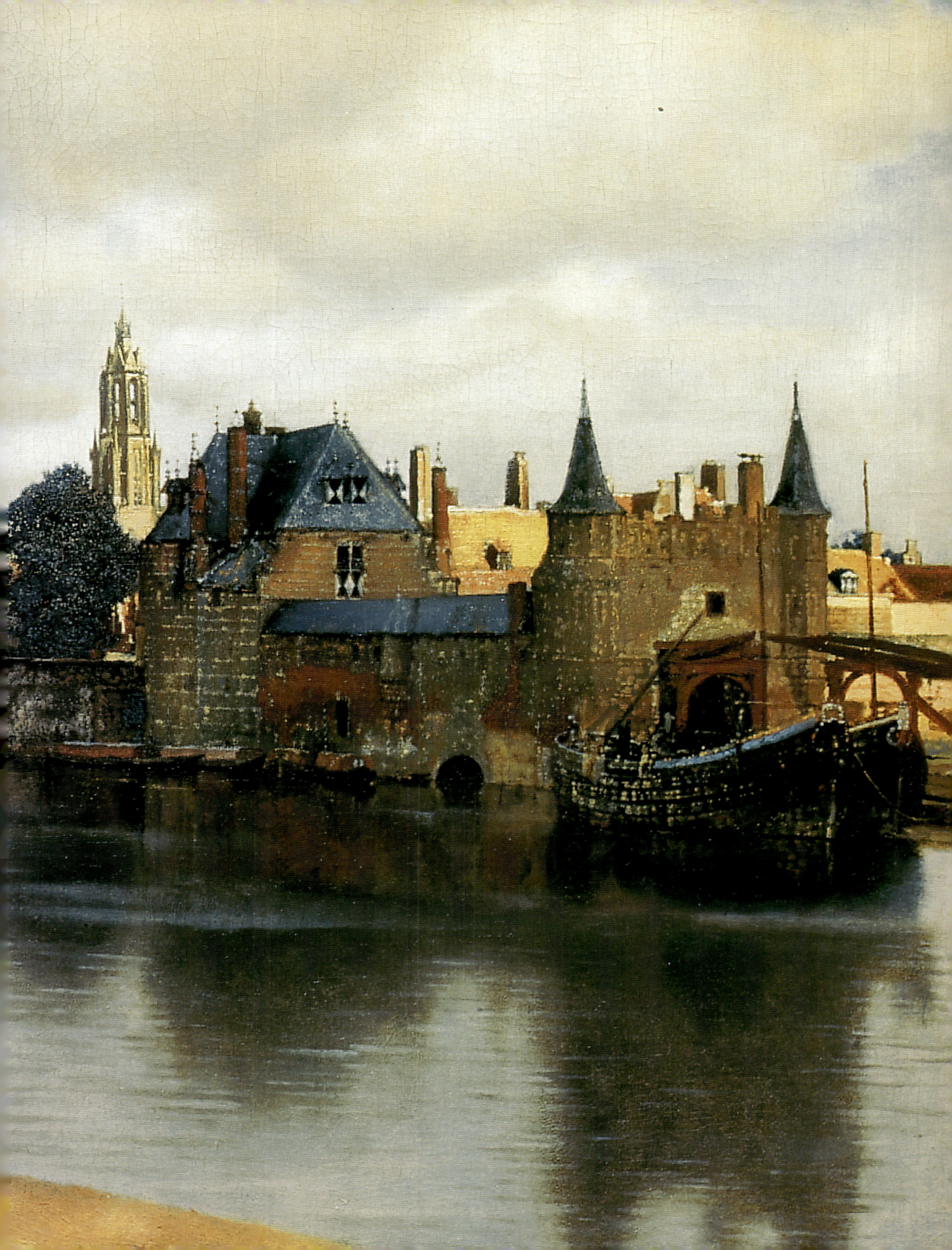

and Hobbema were included in the 1822 sale of what was known to the outside world simply as the S. J. Stinstra Collection.

The writer of the sale catalogue described the *View of Delft* as being "the most outstanding and renowned painting by this Master."[30] Less enthusiastic in his appraisal, however, was the director of the Mauritshuis, Jonkheer Johan Steengracht van Oostkapelle when he considered the painting for a possible acquisition. He merely found the painting "unusual." In the end he felt that it was not particularly suited for the newly established cabinet of paintings, perhaps because the picture was too large.[31]

The director of the Rijksmuseum in Amsterdam, Cornelis Apostool, on the other hand, was enthusiastic about the painting and wrote to the Dutch Minister to urge its acquisition.[32] The minister, in turn, made an appeal to King William I for a financial contribution, which was immediately granted.[33] With adequate funds in hand, the state succeeded in acquiring the painting for 2,900 guilders. Much to the surprise of Steengracht and to the disappointment of Apostool, however, the king decreed that the painting should be placed in "His Majesty's Cabinet" in The Hague rather than in the Rijksmuseum.[34]

The personal intervention of the king in the acquisition and placing of this picture – in fact running counter to the advice of the director of the museum – is a striking occurrence.[35] The most probable explanation is that the subject matter held personal associations for the king. The apse of the Nieuwe Kerk had been the final resting place of members of the House of Orange since William the Silent was entombed there.[36]

Although the associations with the House of Orange may have been a determining factor in the King's decision to help the State acquire *View of Delft*, it seems probable that he, as well as Apostool, was swayed by the bravura of Vermeer's painting technique, which was described in the catalogue as being the "boldest, most powerful, and masterful that one could imagine."[37]

1. Analysis Karin Groen 1994, Mauritshuis documentation archives.
2. Vroom donated these paintings to the city of Delft in 1634.
3. On the restoration, see Wadum 1994, 30–41 and ills.
4. In fact, two street scenes by Vermeer are listed in the Dissius sale of 1696. See Montias 1989, 364, doc. 439, no. 32–33.
5. Wheelock 1982.
6. One other optical phenomenon in this painting that relates to an image in a camera obscura is the saturation of light and color. Color accents and contrasts of light and dark are intensified and apparently exaggerated through the use of a camera obscura, thus giving an added intensity to the image. This phenomenon has the subsidiary property of minimizing effects of atmospheric perspective.
7. Recent scientific projections of his viewpoint undertaken by Mr. W. F. Weve of the Delft Polytechnic have reinforced that hypothesis. See Wheelock 1982, 19 n. 13, 32, fig. 23.
8. One may compare, for example, the bridge in Vermeer's painting to a drawing by Josua de Grave, 1695, showing the bridge from the inside of the city. See Wheelock 1982, 24, fig. 16.
9. Some artists, however, wanted to show more buildings within their frames and thus compressed the scene. All topographical views of this scene vary slightly, however, and no single view can be relied upon for its accuracy.
10. The extent to which they project can clearly be seen in two drawings by Josua de Grave in which the gate is seen from a location to the far right of Vermeer's painting. See Wheelock 1982, 19, figs. 11, 11a.
11. Rademaker, like many other artists who depicted this area, emphasized the horizontal bands on the side of the Rotterdam Gate that were made by alternating levels of brick and light-colored natural stone, whereas Vermeer merely suggested their presence with a series of shifting light-colored dots of paint.
12. The examination of the *View of Delft* with infrared reflectography was kindly undertaken by J. R. J. van Asperen de Boer in collaboration with the author.
13. This line can be seen above many of the roofs, most clearly above the Schiedam Gate.
14. The distant spires on the top of the tower of the Oude Kerk are visible just above the red roof to the left of center.
15. See note 34.
16. Hoet 1752–1770, 1: 35, no. 31: "De Stad Delft in perspectief, te sien van de Zuyd-zy, door J. vander Meer van Delft." The painting sold for 200 Dutch guilders, the highest price in the sale.
17. The painting was known to at least three eighteenth-century artists, Hendrik Numan (1744–1820), Reinier Vinkeles (1741–1816), and Wybrand Hendricks (1744–1831). They all made watercolor copies. Blankert 1992, 179, no. 10, gave an incomplete list of the copies; see also Hofstede de Groot 1907–1928, 1: 607, no. 48.
18. This copy, made by P. E. H. Praetorius (1791–1876), was described in Amsterdam 1814, 13, no. 116: "Een Stadsgezicht, zijnde een kopij naar een beroemd Schilderij van den Delftschen Van der Meer".
19. Van Eijnden/Van der Willigen 1816–1840, 1: 166–167: "... als verwonderlijk kunstig behandeld, zeer geprezen wordt. ... doch ... [wij] weten niet, waar het tegenwoordig geplaatst is."
20. This conclusion is based on research undertaken by Ben Broos, Daan de Clercq, Yme Kuiper, and Carola Vermeeren, which will be published in a forthcoming issue of *Oud Holland*.
21. Sale catalogue, Amsterdam, 22 May 1822, title page: "merendeels uitmakende het kabinet van wijlen den heer S. J. Stinstra, van Harlingen." (Lugt no. 10255)
22. Rijksarchief Friesland (NA inv. no. 49014); Daan de Clercq compiled the Stinstra family tree (letter of 21 March 1995, Mauritshuis documentation archives).
23. Nieuwenhuys 1834, 143; Smith 1829–1842, 6: 132; Quentin Buvelot drew my attention to the importance of the passage in Smith, which still met with disbelief in National Gallery London 1991, 1: 180.
24. Post 1992, 65–66; the sale of his collection took place in Amsterdam on 14 March 1808.
25. The marriage of her sister Margaretha (1788–1825) brought Vermeer's *Love Letter* to the Van Lennep family (cat. 18).
26. *Nederlands patriciaat* 40 (1954), 226; Schutte 1974, 57, no. 35.
27. National Gallery London 1991, 1: 179–180; 2: ill. 159.
28. Van der Willigen archives (RKD, The Hague), 15 April 1821: "My dunkt, zy zyn voor het Ryksmuseum, mits men redelyk zy, wel geschikt."
29. Van der Willigen archives (RKD, The Hague), 8 August 1821: "Waar blyft nu Hobbema, waar de van der Meer?"
30. Sale catalogue, Amsterdam, 22 May 1822, 30, no. 112: "Dit kapitaalste en meestberoemde Schilderij van dezen Meester."
31. Mauritshuis documentation archives, inv. no. 1822–186; Algemeen Rijksarchief, The Hague, 2.04.01–4133, no. 1108 (27 April 1822): "Er zyn nog op deeze verkoping Een schilderij van Hobbema en Een door den Delftschen Van der Meer welke byzonder zijn, dog na mijn oordeel, minder geschikt voor het Cabinet" (There are also [available] at this sale a painting by Hobbema and one by the Delft Van der Meer that are unusual but, in my opinion, less suited for the Cabinet).
32. Algemeen Rijksarchief, The Hague, 2.04.01–4133, no. 1171 (2 May 1822): "een zeldzaam voorkomend stuk van den zoogenaamden Delfschen van der Meer ... mede een zeer beroemd meester onder die der Hollandsche School, dit stuk is ten uiterste natuurlijk en belangrijk" (a rarely encountered piece by the so-called Delft van der Meer ... who is also a very famous master among this Dutch School, this work being exceedingly natural and important).

33. The king made the amount of *f* 6,550 available to buy the *View of Delft*, as well as paintings by Adriaen van de Velde and Jacob Jordaens.
34. On 5 June the Minister communicated the surprising news to Steengracht: "His Majesty has ordained that of the acquired paintings, that by *van der Meer* is to be placed in the local [The Hague] cabinet." Mauritshuis documentation archives, inv. no. 1822–189 (5 June 1822): "Zijne Maj[esteit] heeft gelast, dat van de aangekochte schilderijen, dat van *van der Meer* op het Cabinet alhier zal worden geplaatst." On 11 June a disappointed Apostool informed Steengracht that the painting was to be sent to "His Majesty's Cabinet." Mauritshuis documentation archives, inv. no. 1822–190 (11 June 1822): "Z[ijne] M[ajesteits] Cabinet."
35. In Mauritshuis 1826–1830, 2: 37, no. 49, Steengracht van Oostcapelle lauded the work: "This painting was rendered with admirable truth and force" (Ce tableau est peint avec une vérité et une force admirable). But Steengracht was able to glean little information about the Delft painter in the literature known to him: he did not know Vermeer's first name, nor the dates of his birth and death. Steengracht included the first reproduction of the cityscape in the catalogue.
36. It was almost certainly for comparable historic reasons that in 1764 Stadholder William v, the father of King William I, had acquired a painting of the tomb of William of Orange in Delft, 1651, by Gerard Houckgeest (c. 1600–1661); Mauritshuis 1987, 218–224, no. 58, ill. In 1767 William v bought still another Delft church interior by Houckgeest (The Hague, Mauritshuis, inv. no. 57; Mauritshuis 1987, 220, ill. 2).
37. Sale catalogue, 22 May Amsterdam 1822, 30, no. 112: "De schildering is van de stoutste, kragtigste en meesterlijkste, die men zich kan voorstellen; alles is door de zon aangenaam verlicht; de toon van lucht en water, de aard van het metselwerk en de beelden maken een voortreffelijk geheel, en is dit Schilderij volstrekt eenig in zijn soort" (The execution is the boldest, most powerful and masterful that one could imagine; everything is pleasantly bathed in sunlight; the tone of air and water, the nature of the masonry and figures make for an excellent whole, and this Painting is altogether one of a kind).

COLLECTION CATALOGUES

Mauritshuis 1826–1830, 2: 37, no. 49, and ill.; Mauritshuis 1874, 73–74, no. 72; Mauritshuis 1895, 446–447, no. 92, ill.; Mauritshuis 1985, 312–313, no. 97, ill., 456, no. 92, ill.; Mauritshuis 1987, 382–389, no. 65, ill. (with extensive literature)

LITERATURE

Hoet 1752–1770, 1: 35, no. 31; Van Eijnden/Van der Willigen 1816–1840, 1: 166–167; Murray 1819–1823, 50; Thoré-Bürger 1858–1860, 1: 272–273; Thoré-Bürger 1859, 31, 34, 36; Thoré-Bürger 1866, 298–299, ill., 302, 330, 462, 464–465, 467, 568, no. 48; Bredius 1885, 222; Havard 1888, 34, 39, no. 49; Bredius 1903, unpaginated; Hofstede de Groot 1907–1928, 1: 607, no. 48; Plietzsch 1911, 40–43, 116, no. 18, ill. 9; Dacier 1921, 276; Huyghe 1936, 14, ills. 26–27; Hale 1937, 7, 11, 13, 51, 168–170, 172, 180, 213, 215 and pl. 3; De Vries 1939, 5, 9, 11, 27, 38–39, 80–81, no. 9 and ill. 35; Blum 1946, 83, 183, no. 48; Swillens 1950, 61–62, 90–93, 130, 133, 144, pls. 27, 69a–b and 70; Gowing 1952, 38, 71–72 nn. 26–27, 112, 128–130, no. 13, and pl. 30–32; Malraux 1952, 98–104, ill.; Goldscheider 1958, 20, 127, no. 10, ills. 26–29; De Wilde 1959, 32a–b, ill.; De Vries 1967, 55; Blankert 1975, 49, 58–59, 63, 98, 100–102, 144–145, no. 10, and pl. 10; Rijksmuseum 1976, 19; Wheelock 1977A, 283, 291–297, 300 and ill. 92; Blankert 1978, 40, 43, 66–67, 69, 158–159, no. 10 and pls. 10, 10a–b; Slatkes 1981, 12, 33, 37–38, 40–43, 55 and ills.; Wheelock 1981, 20, 32–33, 38–39, 44, 46, 47, 86, 94–97, 102, and pls. 16–17; Wheelock 1982, 9–35, ills. 6–9, 13–14, 20; Aillaud 1986, 10, 64, 101, 104, 106–107, 108, 159–161, 170 n. 97, 178–179, no. 10, and pl. 10; Wheelock 1988, 18, 30, 36–37, 42, 44, 66, 72–75, no. 13, ill. 32 and pls. 13–14; Montias 1989, 187, 197, 200 n. 89, 250, 255, 261, 265, ill. 34; Nash 1991, 6–10, 11–12, 26, 29, 38; Chong 1992; Blankert 1992, 10, 48, 66, 98, 104, 108, 116, 159–161, 169 n. 99, 178–179, no. 10, 212, 217–218, 222–223, pl. 10, ills. 7–8 and 115; Wheelock 1995, 1, 2, 5, 18, 61, 72–83, 126, 139, 154, 159, 174, and ill. 51

8

A Lady at the Virginal with a Gentleman (The Music Lesson)

c. 1662–1664

inscribed lower picture frame at right: *IVMeer* (IVM in ligature)

oil on canvas, 74 x 64.5 (29 1/8 x 25 3/8)

Lent by Her Majesty Queen Elizabeth II

PROVENANCE

(?) Pieter Claesz van Ruijven, Delft, before 1674; (?) Maria de Knuijt, Widow Van Ruijven, Delft, 1674–1681; (?) Magdelena van Ruijven and Jacob Dissius, Delft, 1681–1682; Jacob Dissius (with his father, Abraham Dissius, 1685–1694), Delft, 1682–1695; Dissius sale, Amsterdam, 16 May 1696, no. 6 (*f*80); Gianantonio Pellegrini, Amsterdam/The Hague, 1718, Venice, 1741; Angela Carriera, widow Pellegrini, Venice, 1741–1742; Joseph Smith, Venice and Mogliano, 1742–1762; King George III, Windsor Castle, 1762 (acquired by Richard Dalton with the Smith Collection for £20,000); Royal Collection, Windsor Castle and Buckingham Palace, since 1762

EXHIBITIONS

London 1876, no. 211; London 1895, 92–93, no. 127; London 1929A, 144, no. 305 and pl. 78; London 1929B, 89, no. 107 and ill.; London 1946, 108, no. 305; The Hague 1948, 30, no. 10 and ill.; London 1952, 1: no. 515, 2: ill. 45; London 1971, 19 and 74, no. 10; Philadelphia 1984A, 344–345, no. 119 and ill. 109

TECHNICAL DESCRIPTION

The plain-weave linen support has a thread count of 15 x 14 per cm^2. The original tacking edges have been removed. Cusping occurs on all sides, more pronounced along top and bottom edges. The canvas has been lined.

The light brownish gray ground contains lead white, chalk, and a little umber, with aggregates of lead white particles.[1]

The paint is thinly and smoothly applied although some texture is present, as on the nearest edge of the bass viol, which stands out due to curling impasto. The bottom half of the painting has a strong blue cast. The dark tiles in the foreground are blue while those further back in the composition are dark gray and contain no blue pigment. The shadow of the carpet on the table in the right foreground is dominated by a bright blue, which may be discolored. A pinhole with which Vermeer marked the vanishing point of the composition is visible in the paint layer.

Vermeer's images are so restrained that loud, discordant voices or abrupt sounds seem alien. The delicate strains of a virginal, however, are a different matter, for its measured rhythms are comparable to those underlying Vermeer's balanced and harmonious compositions.

The expansive space of this elegantly appointed interior seems to reverberate with the music being played at the virginal. Contrasting patterns of shapes and colors create major and minor accents that parallel the structure of the music: bold diagonals of black and white tiles against intricate red, blue, and yellow designs on the table covering; stark black rectangular picture frames in opposition to the elegant decorative frieze of seahorses lining the front panel of the virginal. As with music, the composition has a focus, in this instance the vanishing point of the perspective system that falls with great insistence on the woman's left sleeve.

The metaphorical relationships between Vermeer's composition and musical forms are many, but one is particularly fascinating: the building of rectangular shapes around the woman to give visual emphasis to her importance, a structural technique akin to the repetition of motifs in music developing toward a thematic climax. Then, as though returning to an earlier theme, but in a minor key, Vermeer reconsiders the woman through a mirror, revealing aspects of her that would otherwise never be known.

The virginal the woman plays was undoubtedly constructed by the famed Antwerp instrument maker Andreas Ruckers (1579–1654). Although the instrument seems not to have survived, its finely wrought craftsmanship is characteristic of Ruckers' creations (see page 51, fig. 5).[2] A virginal such as this would have been found only in a wealthy household, where a young woman might take on a private tutor to instruct her in this most refined of domestic arts. As is evident from the popular title given this work, *The Music Lesson*, many have believed that the elegant gentleman in this painting is the woman's tutor. Visual and iconographic evidence, however, suggests that Vermeer's concerns were directed to ideals of love rather than to musical instruction.

Since no documents record that Vermeer possessed a virginal, the instrument probably belonged to a family the artist knew (see page 51).[3] Nevertheless, other objects in the room – the chair, the bass viol, and the wine pitcher – are identical to those in other Vermeer paintings, and were probably owned by the artist. The painting partially seen on the back wall, representing the story of Cimon and Pero (*Roman Charity*), is almost certainly one that had been inherited by Vermeer's mother-in-law, Maria Thins.[4] Thus, it seems that Vermeer brought together objects from various sources to create his setting.

Vermeer quite consciously announces his own presence by including a portion of his easel in the mirror's reflection, and, indeed, his compositional control is evident throughout this work. For example, light convincingly floods the deep recesses of the room, yet its effects are not naturalistic. While Vermeer has depicted one strong shadow falling diagonally at the base of the far window, a similarly angled shadow would have occurred at the window's top as well. Not only did he eliminate the upper shadow, allowing the upper wall to be bathed in light, but he painted this shadow at a different angle than the one falling from the bottom of the window. In each instance Vermeer angled the shadow so that it would intersect a significant point on the virginal – the upper shadow with the corner of the lid, and the lower shadow with the juncture of the legs and the floor – thus subtly linking

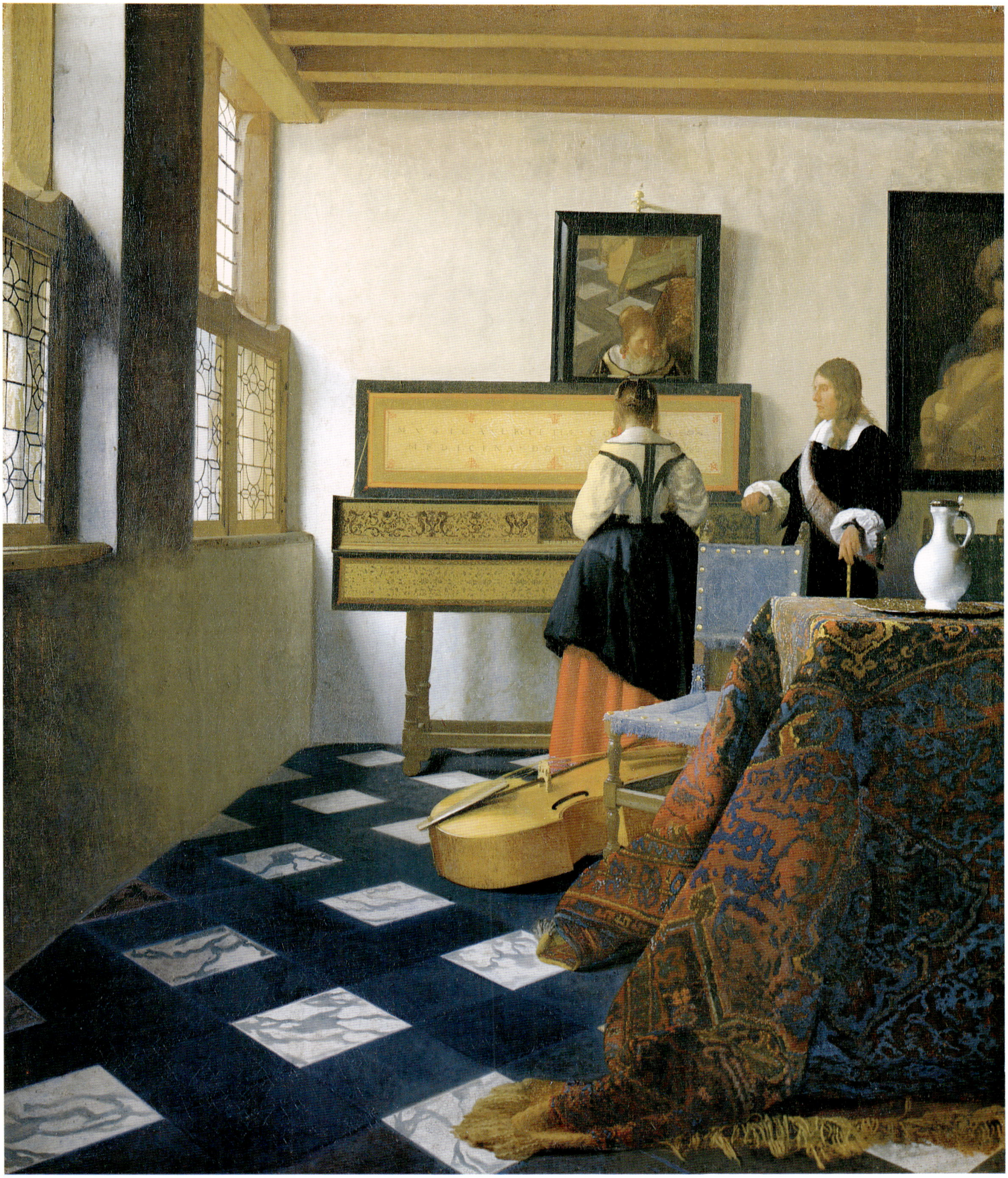

the instrument to the surrounding space.

One means by which Vermeer emphasizes the light-filled character of the back of the room is to allow less light through the windows in the front of the room. Nevertheless, while the foreground floor tiles are appropriately shaded, the white ceramic pitcher on the table is not. Its brightly illuminated form is optically illogical, indicating that Vermeer sought to accent it for compositional and thematic reasons.

Vermeer also carefully integrated the figural group within the deeply recessive space of the room through his placement of furniture. While the sharply angled perspective of the wall and foreground table lead the eye quickly to the woman at the virginal, Vermeer slowed the progression of the perspective on the right by placing the blue chair between the table and the vanishing point. The chair also links the couple in the background, shielding and protecting their private communion.

Another element that physically separates the viewer from the couple is the bass viol lying on the floor, which Vermeer added at a late stage in the execution of the painting: infrared reflectography has shown that he painted it over the tiles and the woman's red dress. Vermeer almost certainly included the bass viol for iconographic as well as compositional reasons. The relationship of this instrument, lying adjacent to the virginal, is similar to the unattended lute lying near a lute player in Jacob Cats' well-known emblem, "Qvid Non Sentit Amor" (fig. 1)[5]; the accompanying text explains that the resonances of the lute being played echo onto the other just as two hearts separated can exist in total harmony. These sentiments seem to capture perfectly the sense of harmony felt in the unbroken gaze of the gentleman as he listens intently to the woman's music.

A similar emblematic relationship can be established between this painting and P. C. Hooft's emblem "Sy blinckt, en doet al blincken" (It shines and makes everything shine) (fig. 2).[6] Like Vermeer's painting, Hooft's emblematic image consists of two vignettes, Cupid holding a mirror reflecting the sun, and a gentleman raptly observing a woman playing a musical instrument, which Hooft elucidates as follows: just as a mirror reflects the sunlight it receives, so does love reflect its source in the beloved.

Harmony of love, however, is only one element of music's metaphorical role. As explicitly indicated in the text on the lid of the virginal (MVSICA LETITIAE CO[ME]S MEDICINA DOLOR[VM]), music is the companion of joy, balm for sorrow. Indeed, the lyrics that often accompanied music written for the virginal extolled love, both human and spiritual, and the solace that could be gained from that love. Another thematic concern is suggested by the painting of *Roman Charity*.[7] The succor and nourish-

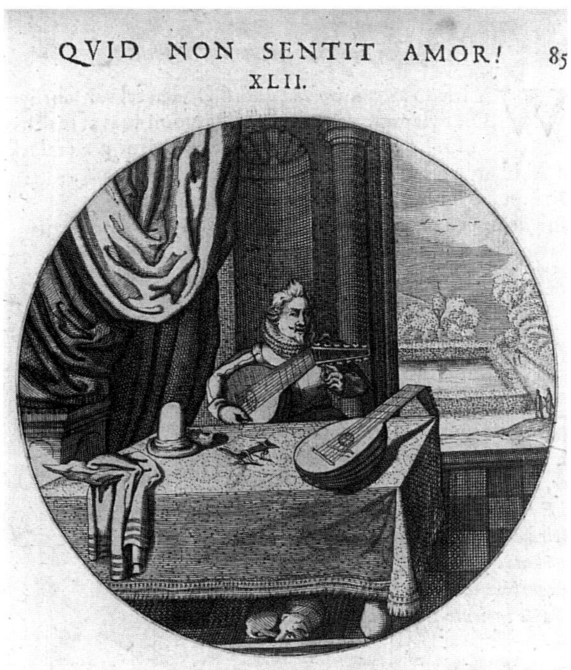

fig. 1. Jacob Cats, 'Qvid Non Sentit Amor,' *Proteus, ofte, Minne-beelden verandert in sinne-beelden*, Rotterdam, 1627, National Gallery of Art Library, Washington

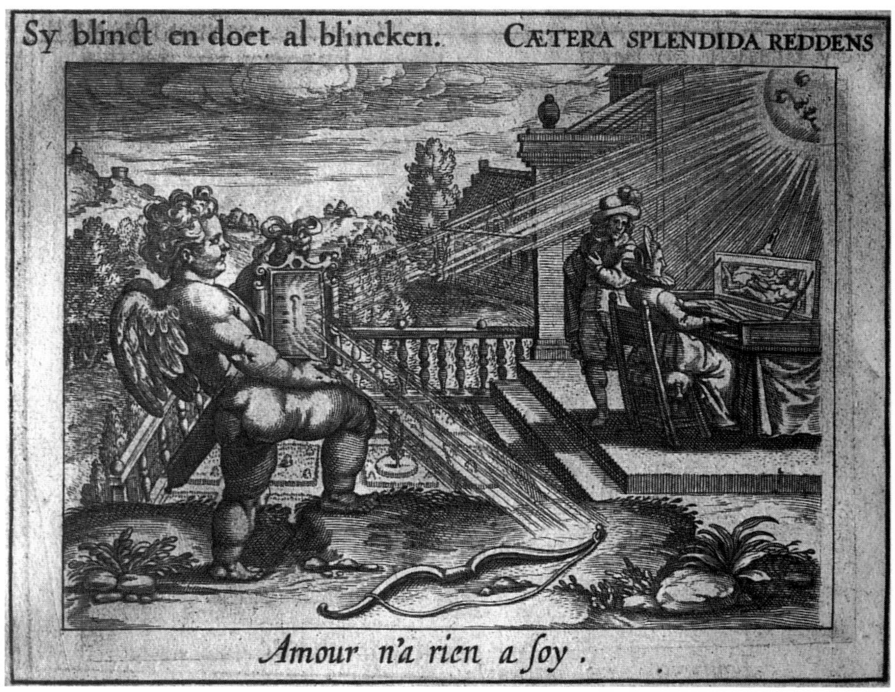

fig. 2. P. C. Hooft, 'Sy blinckt, en doet al blincken,' *Emblemata Amatoria*, 1611, in *Werken*, Amsterdam, 1671, National Gallery of Art Library, Washington

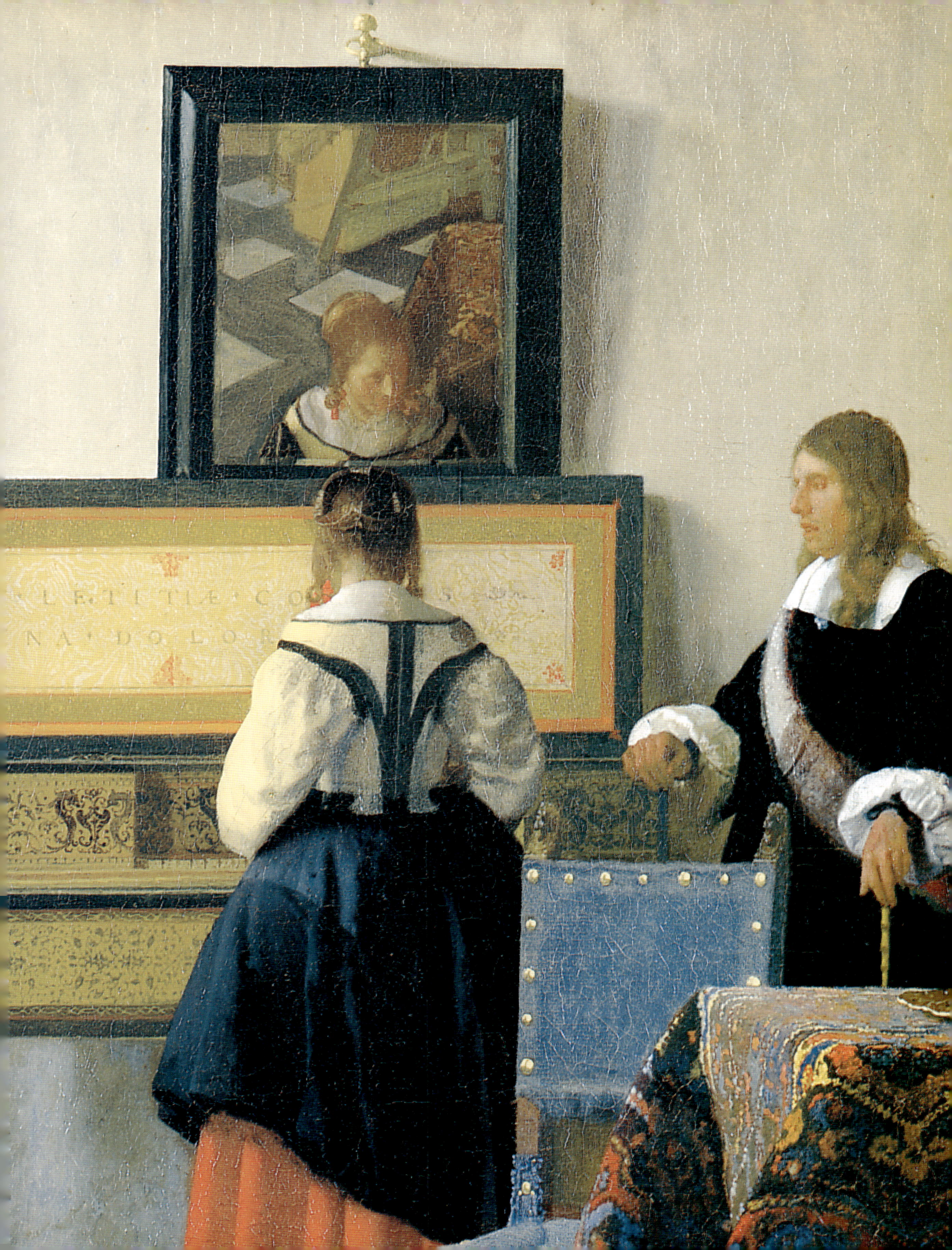
LETITIÆ CO
NA DOLOR

ment Pero gave to her imprisoned father, Cimon, served as an exemplum for human behavior. It also came to symbolize the ideal of Christian charity, with the daughter's love for her father being perceived in spiritual terms, for such love ennobles and allows the spirit to ascend closer to God.[8] The sunlit white ceramic wine pitcher may also have served a similar symbolic function. While its elegant form echoes the curve of the gentleman's arm, and thus helps link foreground and background, the placement of this vessel just below Cimon and Pero alludes to its function as a container providing sensual nourishment.[9] It thus reinforces the central theme of solace and comfort provided by love, whether sensual or spiritual.

Despite its great reknown, *The Music Lesson* was not always attributed to Vermeer. One of the most distinguished and knowledgeable collectors of the eighteenth century, for example, Joseph Smith (1675–1770), the British Consul in Venice, interpreted the signature "IVMeer" as that of Frans van Mieris. We see this in an inventory of the paintings that he sold to King George III of England in 1762, where he called the work: "Frans van Mieris ... A Woman playing on a Spinnet in presence of a Man seems to be her father."[10]

How Smith came to possess this painting has gradually been revealed. Until recently all that was known of the earliest provenance of the picture was that it must have been the same work mentioned at the Dissius sale of 1696 (see page 56): "A playing Lady on the Clavichord in a Room, with a listening Gentleman by the same [J. vander Meer van Delft]."[11]

More than two decades later the Italian painter Gianantonio Pellegrini (1675–1741) was residing in the Low Countries, where his un-Dutch room decors were greatly appreciated. The States General of Holland commissioned him to do nine allegorical depictions for the so-called "Gouden Zaal" (Golden Room) of the Mauritshuis, where they remain to this day.[12] In 1719 he traveled via London and Paris to Venice, where his wife Angela usually resided.[13] He no doubt brought with him the Vermeer picture that he had bought in 1718 in Amsterdam (where he also carried out commissions) or The Hague.

His collection of works by northerners such as Rubens (1577–1640) and Frans Post (c. 1612–1680) must have caused a stir in his native city. His taste, in any case, appealed to the British consul Smith, who was an enthusiastic patron of Pellegrini's sister-in-law Rosalba Carriera.[14] Pecuniary distress forced Angela Pellegrini-Carriera to dispose of her husband's collection after his death in 1741. An inventory of his paintings was drawn up in 1740, and describes "[A Painting] with a Lady at the Spinet." Although the name of the artist is not mentioned, it was undoubtedly the painting now in the English Royal Collections.[15]

In the early eighteenth century Joseph Smith had settled as a merchant in Venice. His house became a cultural meeting place for the Italian "beau monde" and the local English mission. He financed scholarly editions and traded in, as well as collected, books, minor arts, and paintings. On 6 July 1757 the young architect Robert Adam (1728–1792) visited Smith, and saw "as pretty a collection of pictures as I have ever seen...not large pictures but small ones of great masters and very finely preserved."[16] In 1762 Smith drew up a list of his paintings of the northern schools, which he sold to King George III. Only a copy of this list, dating from 1815, has survived. In this "Catalogue of the Flemish & Dutch Schools all in Fine Preservation, in new gilt carved Frames, in Elegant Taste," the painting by "Frans van Mieris" occurs with specification of its dimensions: two feet and five inches by two feet and one-and-a-half inch. This was without a doubt the present painting.[17]

In 1819 Pyne described it in his *History of the Royal Residences:* "Painted by Mieris, perhaps William, the youngest son of the distinguished Francis Mieris, as the colouring is cold, and the style not equal to the works ascribed to the father."[18] Other commentaries of the time also struck a somewhat negative note. Anna Jameson, in her *Handbook to the Public Galleries of Art*, judged the work harshly: "Tasteless, the figures being too far back."[19] In 1868 the frame of the painting had a small sign with the name of Eglon van der Neer, but a contemporary inventory first makes cautious mention of "Jan van der Meer" or "Jan Fermeer."[20] It was not until the exhibition in the Royal Academy in London in 1876 (and in the Guildhall in 1895) that the attribution was changed to Johannes Vermeer.[21] As Sir Oliver Millar in his 1971 catalogue of "The Queen's Gallery" admitted: "Almost by accident, therefore, George III bought one of the finest Dutch pictures in the royal collection."[22]

1. Kühn 1968, 190.
2. For a summary listing of comparable instruments by Andreas Ruckers the Elder see Royal Collection 1982, 144. See also The Hague 1994, 333–334.
3. Whether Vermeer initiated the idea to paint this subject or whether the owner of the virginal commissioned it is not known. It is possible that the owner of the virginal is the gentleman represented in the painting. Unfortunately nothing certain is known about the painting's provenance prior to its appearance in the Dissius sale of 1696. See below.
4. Montias 1989, 122. The picture is described as "A painting of one who sucks the breast." Montias believes that virtually all of the paintings in this collection stem from the Utrecht school. Nevertheless, compositionally the painting most closely resembles Christiaen van Couwenbergh's (1604–1667) *Roman Charity*, 1634, in the Hermitage, St. Petersburg (Maier-Preusker 1991, ill. 38).
5. Cats 1627, 254–259, emblem 43.
6. Hooft 1611, 32–33, emblem 11. In Hooft 1671, 132.
7. The story is taken from Valerius Maximus, *Factorum et Dictorum Memorabilium*, book 9, chapter 4.

8. For the allegorical interpretations of this story in seventeenth-century thought, see Alain Tapié in Caen 1986, 42–44.
9. That the wine pitcher is to be understood symbolically rather than as part of a narrative is further evident through the absence of wine glasses.
10. Blunt 1957, 21, no. 91; Vivian 1962, 332 n. 33; Royal Collection 1982, 143. See on the acquisition of the Smith Collection by King George III, London 1993, passim.
11. Hoet 1752–1770, 1: 34, no. 6: "Een speelende Juffrouw op de Clavecimbael in een Kamer, met een toeluisterend Monsieur door den zelven [=J vander Meer van Delft]"; according to Blankert 1975, 150, no. 16 and Blankert 1992, 186, no. 16, this may well be *A Lady Seated at the Virginal* (but see cat. 22).
12. Inv. no. 834a; Mauritshuis 1993B, 110–112, no. 834a and ill.; Aikema 1993, 225–228 and ills. 9–15.
13. Thieme/Becker, 26: 360; see also Aikema 1993, 216.
14. Vivian 1962, 331, 333 n. 35.
15. Vivian 1962, 332: "Altro [Un Quadro] con Donna alla Spinetta."
16. Fleming 1959, 171.
17. Blunt 1957, 21, no. 91; manuscript in the Lord Chamberlain's Office, London.
18. Pyne 1819, 1: 137–138; Blunt 1957, 14; concerning its later whereabouts in the Royal Collection, see Nicolson 1946, 14; Royal Collection 1982, 143.
19. Jameson 1842, 1: 249; London 1971, 19 n. 26.
20. Royal Collection 1982, 144; Waagen 1854, 2: 433, knew the painting as a work by Eglon van der Neer.
21. London 1876, no. 211 (see also H. W. 1877, 616); London 1895, 92–93, no. 127
22 London 1971, 19.

COLLECTION CATALOGUES
Royal Collection 1906, unpaginated, s.v.; Royal Collection 1982, 143–145, no. 230 and pl. 202 (with literature)

LITERATURE
Hoet 1752–1770, 1: 34, no. 6; Pyne 1819, 1: 137–138; Jameson 1842, 1: 249, no. 84; Waagen 1854, 2: 433; Thoré-Bürger 1866, 549, no. 10; H.W. 1877, 616; Hofstede de Groot 1907–1928, 1: 599, no. 28; Hofstede de Groot 1907–1930, pl. 17; Plietzsch 1911, 61, 63, 68, 120, no. 38 and ill. 21; Graves 1913–1915, 4: 1474; Duveen 1935, 226; Hale 1937, 152–154 and pl. 2; De Vries 1939, 83–84, no. 16 and ill. 42; Nicolson 1946, 3–24 and ills.; Van Thienen 1949, 17, 22, no. 9 and ill. 14; Swillens 1950, 51, no. 3, 67, 70, 74, 79, 84–85, 87, 89, 117, 140 and ill. 3; Gowing 1952, 37–40, 52, 55, 119–127, no. 12 and ills. 24–29; Blunt 1957, 14 and 21, no. 91 and n. 24; Goldscheider 1958, 140, no. 13 and ills. 35–38; De Mirimonde 1961, 47; Vivian 1962, 331–333 n. 33; Haskell 1963, 307; Gerson 1967, col. 742; Fink 1971, 500 and 502–504; Blankert 1975, 64, 66, 71, 87, 93 and 116 n. 53, 150–151, no. 16 and pl. 16; Gerson 1977, 288; Millar 1977, 126 and ill. 13; Blankert 1978, 44, 45, 49, 56, 62, 77 n. 64, 162, no. 16 and pls. 16–16a; Slatkes 1981, 62–65 and ill.; Wheelock 1981, 100–103, 116, 120, 122, and pls. 19–20; Aillaud 1986, 118–120, 126, 167–168 n. 58, 185, no. 16, and pl. 16; Wheelock 1988, 78–79 and pl. 16; Montias 1989, 122, 192, 193, 195, 201, 266 and ill. 48; Lloyd 1991, 143, 152–155, no. 53 and ill.; Nash 1991, 16, 24, 29, 35, 74, ills. page 17 and 74; Blankert 1992, 122, 126, 156, 167 n. 57, 186–187, no. 16, 223, ill. 49 and pl. 16; London 1993, 46 and ill. 36; The Hague 1994, 44–45, 62 nn. 35–36, 334 and ill. 12; Wheelock 1995, 5, 18, 84–95, 107, 113–116, 119, 131, 136, 159, 165, 175, and ill. 60

9

Woman in Blue Reading a Letter

c. 1663–1664

oil on canvas, 46.6 x 39.1 (18 11/32 x 15 13/32)

Rijksmuseum, Amsterdam

PROVENANCE

(?) Pieter van der Lip sale, Amsterdam, 14 June 1712, no. 22; Mozes de Chaves, Amsterdam, 1759; Sale, Amsterdam, 30 November 1772, no. 23 (*f* 40 to Fouquet); P. Lyonet sale, Amsterdam, 11 April 1791, no. 181 (*f* 43 to Fouquet); Sale, Amsterdam, 14 August 1793, no. 73 (*f* 70); Herman ten Kate, Amsterdam, 1793(?)–1800; Ten Kate sale, Amsterdam, 10 June 1801, no. 118 (*f* 110 to Taijs?); Sale [Lespinasse de Langeac], Paris, 16 January 1809, no. 85 (Frf 200); Lapeyrière sale, Paris, 19 April 1825, no. 127 (Frf 2,060 to Berthaud); [John Smith, London, after 1833–1839, sold for £70 to Van der Hoop]; Adriaan van der Hoop, Amsterdam, 1839–1854; Academy of Fine Arts, Amsterdam, 1854–1885; to the present owner in 1885 (on loan from the city of Amsterdam)

EXHIBITIONS

London 1929A, 141, no. 298 and ill.; Amsterdam 1935, 30, no. 168; Rotterdam 1935, 37, no. 86 and ill. 67

TECHNICAL DESCRIPTION

The support is a fine, plain-weave linen with a thread count of 14.3 x 14.4 per cm.[2] The support has been wax-resin lined and the original tacking edges have been removed.

The dark gray ground contains chalk, umber, and lead white.[1] The paint layers extend to the edge of the trimmed canvas on all sides. Some areas, such as the chair and the woman's yellow skirt, have ocher underpainting.

The surface is pitted, primarily in the white mixtures, but also in the blue parts of the background and jacket. Some blanching is evident in the blue tablecloth. The paint surface is slightly abraded, particularly in the raised edges of the paint.

The compositional refinements in Vermeer's paintings are so exquisite that it is difficult to understand how he achieved them. His mastery of perspective does not account for the sensitive arrangement of his figures or for the subtle proportions he established between pictorial elements. Perhaps he worked with a compass and ruler, as did Pieter Saenredam (1597–1665), or perhaps he developed a mathematical system for determining the relationships of compositional elements. Whatever the system, it succeeded because of the artist's unique sensitivity to structure as a vehicle for his artistic aims.

In no other painting did Vermeer create such an intricate counterpoint between the structural framework of the setting and the emotional content of the scene. A mere description of the subject – a young woman dressed in a blue jacket reading a letter in the privacy of her home – in no way prepares the viewer for the poignancy of this image, for while the woman betrays no outward emotion, the intensity of her feelings is conveyed by the context Vermeer creates for her.

Vermeer situates the woman in the exact center of his composition, her form almost fully visible between the table and chair in the immediate foreground. These structural elements, as well as the chair against the wall behind the table, appear to lock her in space. Likewise, the woman's hands are held fast visually by the horizontal of the black bar behind them. While Vermeer uses this geometric framework to restrict any sense of physical movement, he alludes to her emotional intensity through the meandering ocher patterns of the map behind her.

Vermeer's design sensitivity, however, is not limited to the placement of objects in his composition, but also extends to the patterns of shapes between objects. The asymmetrical balance of the three broadly rectangular areas of white wall is crucial to establishing the sense of quiet permanence. Vermeer's awareness of their compositional importance is evident from the x-radiograph (fig. 1), where it is clear that he extended the map several centimeters to the left. This adjustment reduced the width of the wall to the left of the map so that it would be equal to the width of the wall to the right of the woman. The x-radiograph also reveals that Vermeer altered the shape of the woman's jacket. In the original conception it flared out, just as in *Woman Holding a Balance* (cat. 10). Infrared reflectography also reveals that the jacket originally had a fur trim (fig. 2). The changes gave the woman a more statuesque profile and at the same time strengthened the rectangular shapes of the white wall on either side of the woman.

Vermeer was equally sensitive to the optical effects of light and color. The blue tonalities of the woman's jacket, the chair, and the table coverings are calming, restful

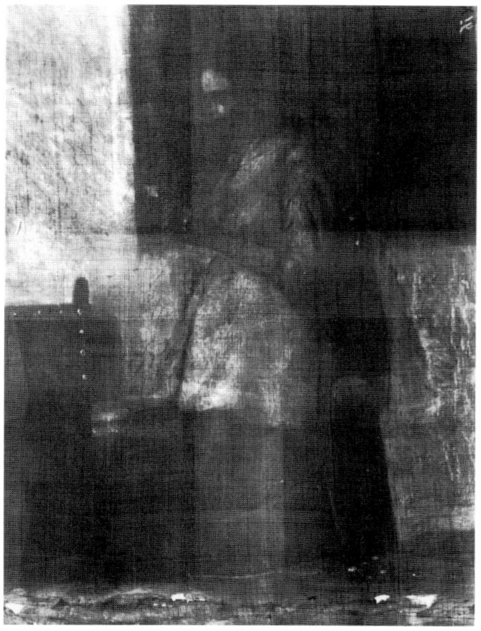

fig. 1. Detail of x-radiograph, *Woman in Blue Reading a Letter*

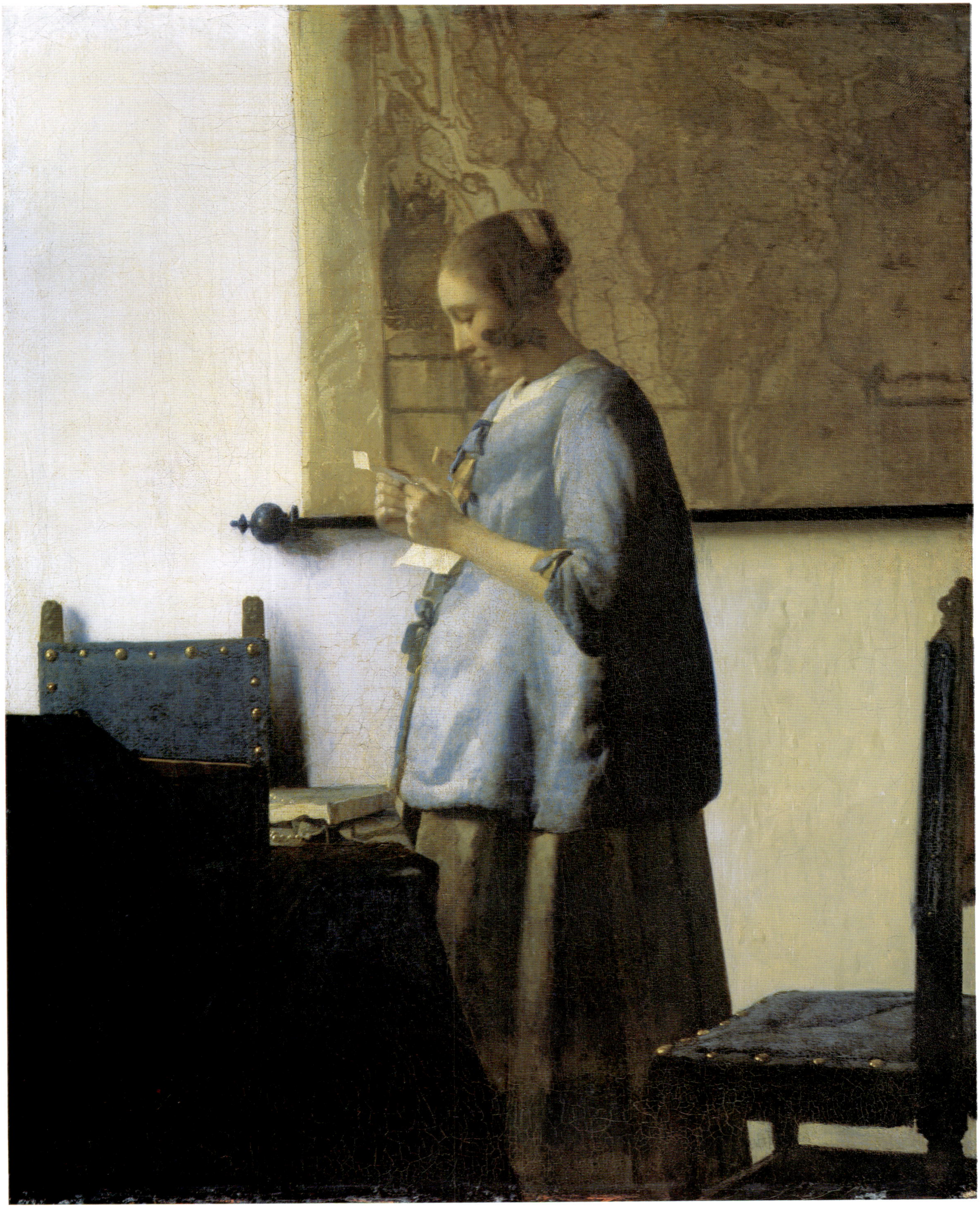

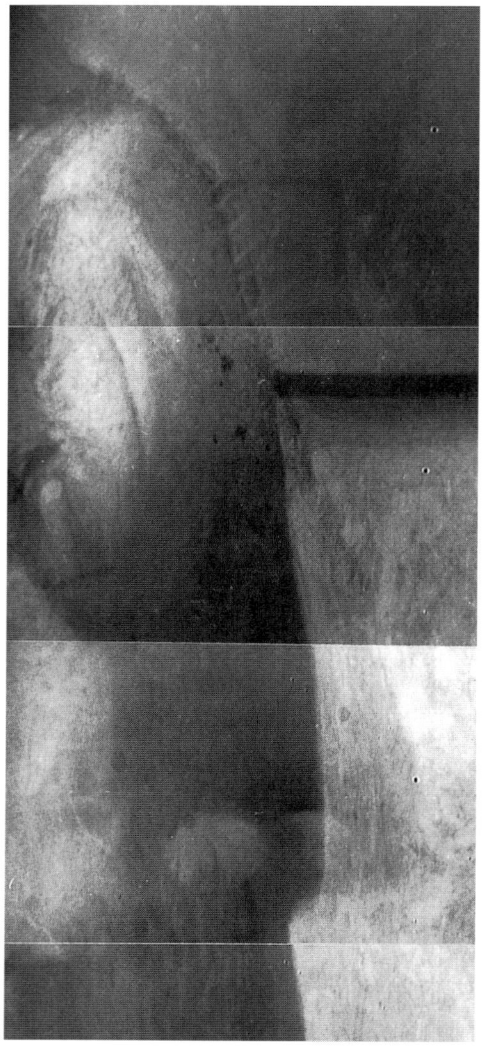

fig. 2. Detail of infrared reflectogram, *Woman in Blue Reading a Letter*

colors, as are the ochers of the dress and map. Light comes from two sources, creating both primary and softly diffused secondary shadows on the wall next to the chair behind the table. With his awareness of light's optical qualities, Vermeer gives the shadows a bluish cast. He infuses light into the woman's form by diffusing the contour at the back of her jacket. He also manipulates the flow of light quite arbitrarily for compositional reasons. For example, while the chair and the map cast shadows, the woman, who appears to stand quite close to the wall, does not. Vermeer thus separates her from the temporal framework of the room, and in the process, enhances the sense of permanence that so pervades the scene.

This use of color, light, and perspective to reinforce the emotional impact of a scene is characteristic of his work throughout his career. In *Officer and Laughing Girl* from the late 1650s (page 35, fig. 6), for example, Vermeer intensified the relationship between the two figures through the vivid red and yellow of their clothing, the dramatic foreshortening of the window, and the sparkling effects of light flickering off the woman's striped sleeves and the map. Indeed, it is interesting to compare the map in these two paintings, for they are one and the same: a map of Holland and West Friesland designed by Balthasar Florisz van Berckenrode in 1620 and published by Willem Jansz Blaeu a few years later.[2] In his earlier painting Vermeer used colors to differentiate land and water and clearly articulated topographical features, but in *Woman in Blue Reading a Letter* the map is larger in scale, monochromatic, and has a less defined topographical character. While certain of these differences are related to his own stylistic evolution, the willingness to modify shape, size, and color of objects for compositional reasons is a constant phenomenon in his oeuvre.

The reflective mood of this work, of course, is related to the subject: the reading of a letter. In Dutch art depictions of women reading letters almost always have love associations, and artists found various means to portray both the air of expectation at the arrival of a letter and the subsequent reaction to the written word. Often, as with Gerard ter Borch's (1617–1681) portrayal of a young peasant girl reflecting on the contents of a letter (fig. 3), the emotional consequences are evident in the figure's posture and expression. Vermeer's *Girl Reading a Letter at an Open Window*, c. 1657 (page 73, fig. 11), focuses on the woman's response to the letter by painting her reflection in the leaded glass window. Although the self-contained character of Vermeer's woman in *Woman in Blue Reading a Letter* provides no hint about the letter's content, the bend of the woman's neck, the parted lips, and the drawn-up arms infuse her with a sense of expectancy.

Although Vermeer provides little context for the letter, it appears to have come unexpectedly, since she has interrupted her toilet to stop and read it. Her pearls lie unattended on the table, with another sheet of the letter partially covering them.[3] Significant, undoubtedly, is the map, which may allude to an absent loved one, as does perhaps the empty chair in the foreground. The woman's shape is also suggestive. It is decidedly matronly, perhaps as a result of fashion, but more likely, because she is pregnant. Vermeer, however, remains entirely circumspect about the circumstances of the woman's life, allowing each

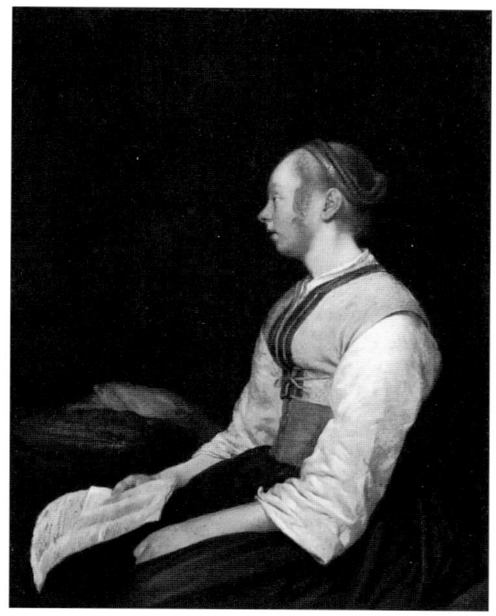

fig. 3. Gerard ter Borch, *Peasant Girl Reflecting on a Letter*, c. 1650, oil on panel, Rijksmuseum, Amsterdam

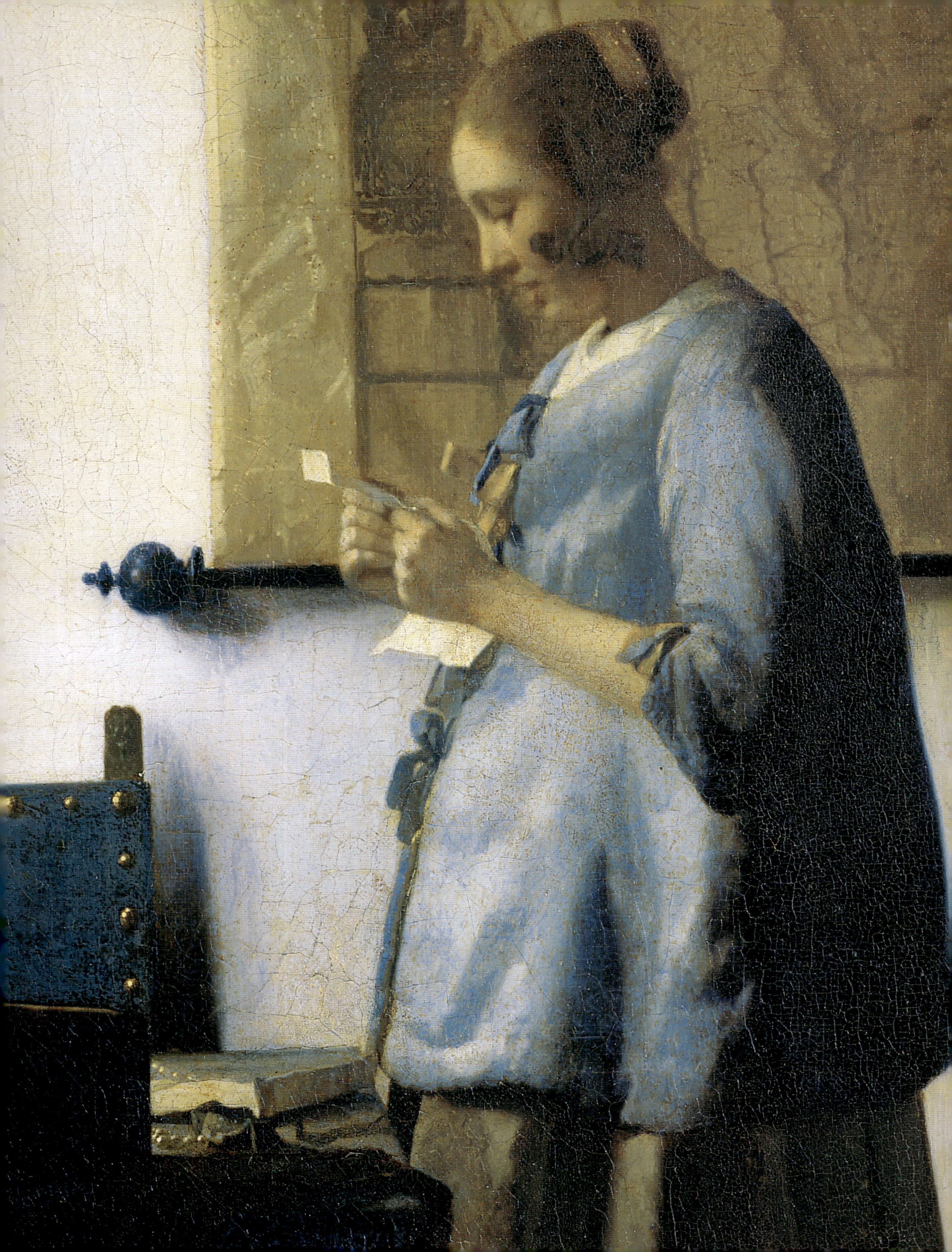

viewer to ponder the image anew in his or her own way.

This painting was extravagantly praised in eighteenth-century sale catalogues: in 1772 as "very handsome, meticulously and naturally rendered"; in 1791, "its graceful light and dark bestows a beautiful [sense of] well-being"; and in 1793 as "extraordinarily handsome, meticulously and masterfully painted."[4] In every instance connoisseurs knew this unsigned work to be a creation of Vermeer (or Van der Meer), whom they did not know by his surname, Johannes, but as "the Delft [painter]" (de Delfts[ch]e). Vermeer had already acquired that sobriquet in collectors' circles of the early eighteenth century.

Herman ten Kate (1731–1800), the last Dutch collector to own the painting in the eighteenth century,[5] was a wealthy Amsterdam cloth merchant and member of parliament, who modeled himself after his great-uncle, the famous art and book collector Lambert ten Kate (1659–1727).[6] After Herman ten Kate's ownership, the *Woman in Blue Reading a Letter* came into the hands of the English dealer John Smith by way of two French collections (in 1809 and 1825).[7] In 1839 Smith traded it, as well as *The Hermit* by Gerrit Dou (1613–1675) and *The Holy Family* by Garofalo (1481–1559) (both in Amsterdam, Rijksmuseum),[8] for a painting by Carel Dujardin (c. 1622–1678).

Adriaan van der Hoop (1778–1854) (fig. 4) of Amsterdam became the new owner. He had been a partner of the famous banking house Hope & Co. since 1811, after the directors of this firm (the heirs of its founder John Hope) had fled Holland during the French occupation. Van der Hoop made his fortune quickly, becoming a millionaire by about 1840.[9] In September of 1839 he "made a trade in London with J. Smith & Sons, having bought from him... a good painting by the Delft van der Meer, representing a reading woman dressed in blue."[10]

The Van der Hoop Collection was the most enviable Dutch collection of its time.[11] Van der Hoop did a lot of his buying in the second quarter of the nineteenth century. Because he had no direct heirs, he bequeathed his 225 paintings to the city of Amsterdam in 1847. About a year later the French critic Thoré-Bürger visited Van der Hoop, and recalled him as "a very likeable man and very simple in his habits despite his immense fortune."[12] When Van der Hoop died, the city of Amsterdam was not able to accept his bequest until the collectors Carel Joseph Fodor and Jacob de Vos pledged to pay the succession taxes, which amounted to fifty thousand guilders; otherwise the City Council of Amsterdam would not have agreed to accept Van der Hoop's three most important works: *Woman in Blue Reading a Letter*, by Vermeer, the *Jewish Bride*, by Rembrandt (1606–1669), and *The Mill at Wijk bij Duurstede*, by Jacob van Ruisdael (1628/1629–1682).[13]

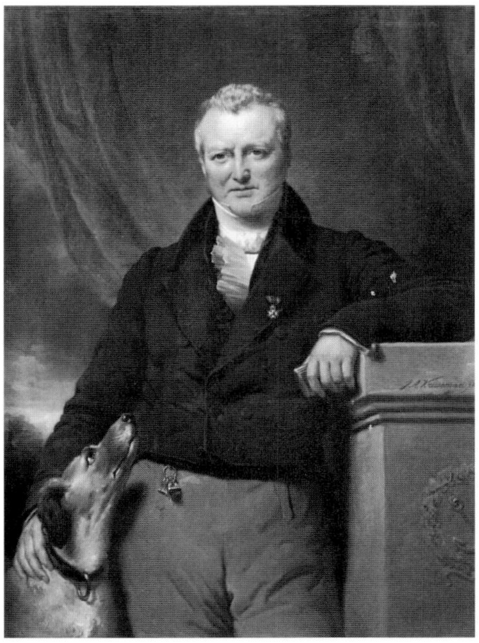

fig. 4. Jan Adam Kruseman, *Portrait of Adriaan van der Hoop*, 1835, canvas, Rijksmuseum, Amsterdam

The Van der Hoop Collection was subsequently housed in the Old Men's Home, which was also the location of the Academy of Fine Arts.[14] Thoré-Bürger described the *Woman in Blue Reading a Letter* in 1860, exclaiming: "Encore le sphinx!" Thoré-Bürger described only six signed works by the Delft master at the time, so that he apparently had some difficulty accepting this single unsigned work. But he was won over by the incidence of light and by the color ("this pale light, these tender blues"), sighing in resignation: "This devil of an artist must no doubt have had several styles."[15] In 1860 Thoré-Bürger pleaded in vain for the gathering together of the Mauritshuis and Museum Van der Hoop collections in one "Dutch Louvre."[16] After Van der Hoop's widow died in 1880, it was decided to move the collection to the newly constructed Rijksmuseum. In 1885 a wing of the building was cleared for the collection.[17] The *Woman in Blue Reading a Letter* was the first Vermeer painting in the Rijksmuseum, which today owns four (see cats. 4, 5, 18).

1. Kühn 1968, 192.
2. See Welu 1975, 532–533. In *Officer and Laughing Girl* the land mass is blue, a color traditionally used to designate water areas. Whether Vermeer consciously chose to paint the area this unusual color, or whether he originally painted it green, and the color has changed over time, is not known. The only extant example of the map, in the Westfries Museum, Hoorn, is monochromatic.
3. I owe this observation to Aneta Georgievska-Shine.
4. Sale catalogue, Amsterdam, 30 November 1772, 8, no. 23: "Zeer fraai, uitvoerig en natuurlyk behandeld" (Lugt no. 2082); Sale catalogue, Amsterdam, 11 April 1791, no. 181: "het bevallig ligt en donker geeft een schoone welstand" (Lugt no. 4706); Sale catalogue, Amsterdam, 14 August 1793, 19, no. 73: "ongemeen fraai, uitvoerig en meesterlyk gepenceeld" (Lugt no. 5100).
5. Many collections moved via Paris to England during the French Revolution. See The Hague 1990, 425 (with references).
6. Familieblad 1976, 95–99, and 315 (on Lambert ten Kate as collector, see Van Gelder 1970, 139–186).
7. Sale catalogue, Paris, 16 January 1809, no. 85 (Lugt no. 7502); Sale catalogue, Paris, 19 April 1825, no. 127 (Lugt no. 10869); in 1833 Smith was not yet aware of this painting (Smith 1829–1842, 4: 110 and 242).

8. See Knoef 1948, 63.
9. On the various generations of this family as collectors, see: Niemeijer 1981, 168; The Hague 1990, 420–422, 423 nn. 10–17.
10. "Lijst van de schilderijen van Adriaan van der Hoop te Amsterdam" (List of the paintings of Adriaan van der Hoop in Amsterdam), Rijksmuseum Archives, Amsterdam (inv. no. 388, 24): "te Londen met J. Smith & Sons eene ruil gedaan, hebbende van hem gekocht...een goed schildery van den Delftschen van der Meer, voorstellende eene lezende vrouw, in het blaauw gekleed."
11. Knoef 1948, 51; Rijksmuseum 1976, 31.
12. Thoré-Bürger 1858–1860, 1: 1: "un homme très-aimable et très-simple de moeurs, malgré son immense fortune."
13. Rijksmuseum 1976, 472, no. c216 and ill. (Rembrandt); 487, no. c211 and ill. (Van Ruisdael).
14. Museum Van der Hoop 1855, 10, no. 171 and Museum Van der Hoop 1872, iii-v, 50, no. 129.
15. Thoré-Bürger 1858–1860, 2: 67–68: "Encore le sphinx!"; "cette lumière pâle, ces bleus tendres"; and "Ce diable d'artiste a eu sans doute des manières diverses."
16. Thoré-Bürger 1858–1860, 2: 3: "Louvre de la Hollande."
17. Rijksmuseum 1976, 30–31: in addition to the Vermeer, Rembrandt, and Van Ruisdael, the collection also contained outstanding works by Hals, Hobbema, De Hooch, Potter, Rubens, Saenredam, Steen and many others; see also Fromentin 1876/1976, 302–303.

COLLECTION CATALOGUES

Museum Van der Hoop 1855, 10, no. 71; Museum Van der Hoop 1872, 50, no. 129; Rijksmuseum 1887, 179, no. 1536; Rijksmuseum 1976, 31 and 572, no. c251 and ill. (with extensive literature)

LITERATURE

Josi 1821, unpaginated, s.v.; Thoré-Bürger 1858–1860, 2: 67–69; Waagen 1863–1864, 3: 27; Thoré-Bürger 1866, 327, 459 and 558, no. 32; Havard 1888, 38, no. 35; Martin 1904, 4; Hofstede de Groot 1907–1928, 1: 600, no. 31; Hofstede de Groot 1907–1930, pl. 20; Plietzsch 1911, 43–47, 113, no. 1 and ill. 10; Johansen 1920, 191 and 198; De Vries 1939, 46–47, 87, no. 25 and ill. 1 and 14; Knoef 1948, 51–52 and 63; Hale 1937, 81, 84, 142, 174–175, 196, and pl. 5; De Vries 1948, 42 and 95, no. 21; Swillens 1950, 54–55, no. 11, 67, 78, 83–84, 88, 140, 144, 175 and pl. 11; Gerson 1952, 40 and ill. 113; Gowing 1952, 136, no. 21, and pls. C, 48–49; De Vries 1965, 39 a-b and ill.; Rosenberg 1966, 116, 119, 121 and ill. frontispiece; Goldscheider 1967, 14, 129, no. 17 and ills. 44–47; Blankert 1975, 62, 63, 71, 82, 94, 109, 147–148, no. 14 and pl. 14; Welu 1975, 532–533, 541 and ill. 3; Welu 1977, 40–41 and ill. 52; Blankert 1978, 42–43, 49, 54, 63, 77 n. 48, 160–161, no. 14, and pl. 14; Slatkes 1981, 27, 55, 58–59, and ill.; Wheelock 1981, 33, 104–105, 110, 134, and pl. 21; Alpers 1983, 122, 192, 203–206 and ills. 147, 224; Wheelock 1984, 396–398 and ill. 10–12; Aillaud 1986, 49, 112, 114–115, 157, 182–183, no. 14, ills. 87b, 117, and pl. 14; Wheelock 1988, 27, ill. 27, 80–81 and pl. 17; Montias 1989, 162, 190, 192, 259 n. 51, 266 and ill. 29; Blankert 1992, 51, 114–116, 126, 140, 157, 182–184, no. 14, 218, 223 ills. 90, 118 and pl. 14; Wheelock 1995, xii, 6, 7–19, 21, 58, 102, 103, 106, 107, 110, 142, 157, 165, 176, and ill. 1

10

Woman Holding a Balance

c. 1664

oil on canvas, 40.3 x 35.6 (15 7/8 x 14)

National Gallery of Art, Washington, Widener Collection

PROVENANCE

(?) Pieter Claesz van Ruijven, Delft, before 1674; (?) Maria de Knuijt, Widow Van Ruijven, Delft, 1674–1681; (?) Magdalena van Ruijven and Jacob Dissius, Delft, 1681–1682; Jacob Dissius (with his father Abraham, 1685–1694), Delft, 1682–1695; Dissius sale, Amsterdam, 16 May 1696, no. 1 (*f* 155); Isaac Rooleeuw, Amsterdam, 1696–1701; Paulo van Uchelen, Amsterdam, 1701–1702 (estimated at *f* 150); Paulo van Uchelen the Younger, Amsterdam, 1703–1754; Anna Gertruijda van Uchelen, Amsterdam, 1754–1766; Van Uchelen sale, Amsterdam, 18 March 1767, no. 6 (*f* 170 to Kok); Nieuhoff sale, Amsterdam, 14 April 1777, no. 116 (*f* 235 to Van de Boogaerd); Trochel et al. sale, Amsterdam, 11 May 1801, no. 48 (*f* 60 to Van der Schley); King Maximilian I Jozef, Nymphenburg, before 1825; King of Bavaria sale, Munich, 5 December 1826, no. 101 (DM 800 to Caraman); Victor-Louis-Charles de Riquet, Duke of Caraman, Vienna and Paris, 1826–1830; Caraman sale, Paris, 10 May 1830, no. 68 (Ff 2410); Casimir Périer, Paris, 1830–1832; Heirs Périer, Paris, 1832–1848; Périer sale, London, 5 May 1848, no. 7 (£ 141.15.– to Lord Hertford); Auguste Casimir Victor Laurent Périer, Paris, 1848–1876; Jean Paul Pierre Casimir Périer, Paris, 1876–1907; Countess De Ségur-Périer, Paris, 1907–1911; [P. & D. Colnaghi & Co., London, and M. Knoedler & Co., New York, 1911]; Peter A. B. Widener, Lynnewood Hall, Elkins Park, Philadelphia, 1911–1915; Joseph E. Widener, Lynnewood Hall, Elkins Park, Philadelphia, 1915–1942; National Gallery of Art, Washington, 1942 (Widener bequest)

EXHIBITIONS

New York 1912, 53, no. 49; Detroit 1925, no. 33 and ill.; Chicago 1933, 13, no. 80 and ill.; Philadelphia 1984A, 342–343, no. 118 and pl. 108.

TECHNICAL DESCRIPTION

The support is a fine, plain-weave linen with a thread count of 20 x 16 per cm². The original tacking edges are present. The canvas has been glue lined.

The ground is a warm buff color containing chalk, lead white, black and an earth pigment.[1]

The layer structure of the paint is varied, creating different effects and textures, from thick impasto to thin glazes and scumbles. The edges of forms are rarely hard, but overlap only slightly or do not quite touch, allowing the ground to show through. Almost all areas were painted wet-in-wet. In selected areas of the painting, especially in the blue jacket, a dark, reddish-brown undermodeling is visible, particularly in the shaded folds. A gray-green underpaint is found in many shadowed areas. The vanishing point of the composition is visible as a small, white spot on the x-radiograph, to the left of the hand holding the balance. The balance was enlarged, as can be seen in the infrared reflectogram.

The ground and paint are in a good state of preservation.

Contemporary scholars generally divide Vermeer's oeuvre into categories – history paintings, scenes of daily life, tronies, cityscapes, and allegories – each relating to distinctive stylistic and iconographic traditions. Such an approach, however, denies the consistent philosophical framework underlying Vermeer's work. Whether depicting a mythological goddess, a woman in the privacy of her home, or an allegory of painting, Vermeer examined through his art the fundamental moral and spiritual truths of the human experience.

The artificiality of imposing separate categories upon Vermeer's oeuvre becomes particularly evident when considering *Woman Holding a Balance*, a painting stylistically similar to three other works from the mid-1660s: *Woman in Blue Reading a Letter* (cat. 9), *Woman with a Pearl Necklace* (cat. 12), and *Young Woman with a Water Pitcher* (cat. 11). Although each painting depicts a standing woman preoccupied with her thoughts in a domestic setting, the latter three are generally characterized as genre scenes, while *Woman Holding a Balance* has been allegorically interpreted. Indeed, some argue that *The Last Judgment* scene behind the woman provides a theological context for the scales she holds: to judge is to weigh.[2]

In fact, the difference between *Woman Holding a Balance* and these three paintings is merely one of degree. In each work Vermeer infuses a specific image of domesticity with broad implications about emotions and ideals central to human existence–the expectancy of love, the radiance of spiritual purity, and the importance of moderation. Just as the balance provides a thematic focus for broader philosophical concerns, so the letter, water pitcher, and pearl necklace serve similar functions.

While generally accepted as an allegory, *Woman Holding a Balance* has been interpreted in many ways over the years. Most early authors assumed that the pans of the woman's balance contained precious objects, generally identified as gold or pearls. Consequently, the painting was described until recently as either the *Goldweigher* or the *Girl Weighing Pearls*. In addition, some contemporary authors speculate that the woman is pregnant while others conclude that her costume reflects a style of dress current in the early to mid-1660s.[3] Others interpret the painting theologically, viewing the woman as a secularized image of the Virgin Mary, who, standing before the Last Judgment, assumes the role of intercessor and compassionate mother.[4] One scholar argues that the image of a pregnant Virgin Mary contemplating balanced scales would have been understood by a Catholic viewer as an anticipation of Christ's life, his sacrifice, and the eventual foundation of the Church.[5]

While such an array of interpretations calls for caution, microscopic examination has resolved at least one dispute: the woman is not weighing gold. Vermeer did not paint the highlights in the scale pans with lead-tin yellow, the pigment he uses elsewhere in this painting to represent gold. Although the pale, creamy color of these accents is similar to that of pearls, he applies the paint here differently. Vermeer represents pearls in the mid 1660s with two layers of paint – a thin grayish one beneath a white highlight – a technique that permits him to depict both their specular highlights and their translucence. In the band of pearls draped over the box, for example, the size of the pearl (the thin, diffused layer) remains relatively constant while the highlights on the pearls (the thick, top layer) vary considerably in size according to the amount of light hitting them. Vermeer paints the highlights

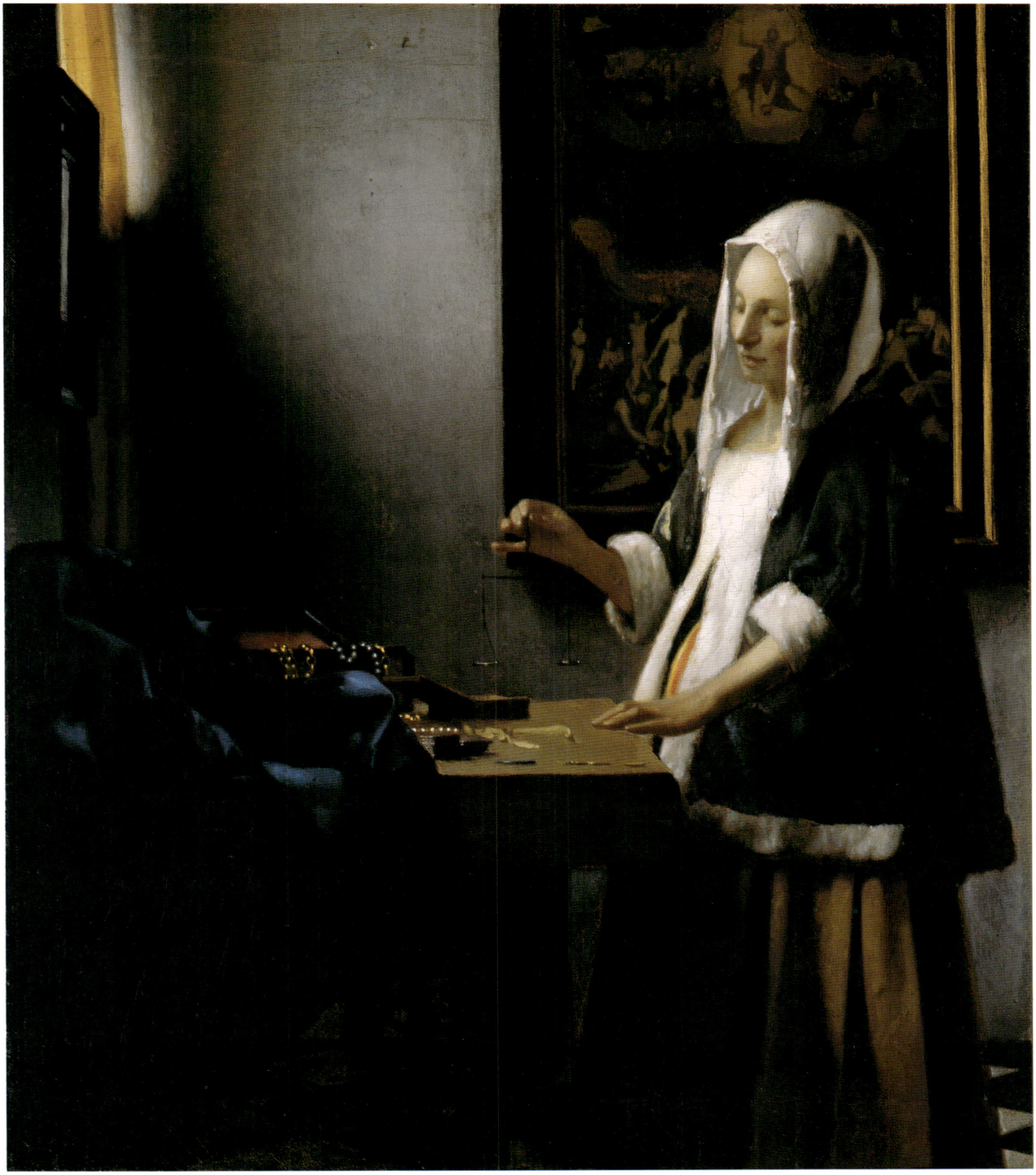

on the scales with only one layer, thereby indicating diffused reflections of light from the window. Further reinforcing the conclusion that the scales are empty are the bound strands of pearls on the jewelry boxes and table. No single pearl lies separately, waiting to be weighed or measured against another.

Although the scales of the balance are empty, the jewelry boxes, strands of pearls, and gold chain on the table belong to, and are valued within, the temporal world. They represent, in a sense, temptations of a material splendor.[6] Nevertheless, pearls take on many symbolic meanings, ranging from the purity of the Virgin Mary to the vices of pride and arrogance. As the woman concentrates on the balance in her hand, she exudes inner peace and serenity, as opposed to the psychological tension that would suggest a conflict between her action and the implications of the *Last Judgment*. While Christ's judgments are eternal and the woman's are temporal, her pensive gaze toward the balance suggests that her act of judgment, although different in consequence, is as conscientiously considered.

The essential message appears to be that one should conduct one's life with temperance and balanced judgment. Indeed this message, with or without its explicit religious context, appears in paintings from all phases of Vermeer's career and must, therefore, represent one of his fundamental beliefs. The balance, an emblem of Justice, and eventually of the final judgment, denotes the woman's responsibility to weigh and balance her own actions.[7] Correspondingly, the mirror on the wall directly opposite the woman represents self-knowledge.[8] As Otto van Veen (1556–1629) wrote in an emblem book Vermeer knew, "a perfect glasse doth represent the face, Iust as it is in deed, not flattring it at all."[9] In her search for self-knowledge and in her commitment to maintenance of equilibrium in her life, she seems to be aware, although not in fear, of the final judgment that awaits her. Vermeer's painting thus expresses the essential tranquility of one who understands the implications of the Last Judgment and who searches to moderate her life in order to warrant salvation.

The character of the scene conforms closely to Saint Ignatius of Loyola's recommendations for meditation in his *Spiritual Exercises*, a devotional service with which Vermeer was undoubtedly familiar through his contacts with the Jesuits. As Cunnar has emphasized, before meditating Saint Ignatius urged the meditator first to examine his conscience and weigh his sins as though he were at Judgment Day standing before his Judge. Ignatius then urged that he "weigh" his choices and choose a path of life that will allow him to be judged favorably in a "balanced" manner.[10]

> I must rather be like the equalized scales of a balance ready to follow the course which I feel is more for the glory and praise of God, our Lord, and the salvation of my soul.[11]

This painting exemplifies Vermeer's exquisite sense of harmony from the early to mid-1660s. The woman holds the scale gently in her right hand, extending her small finger to give a horizontal accent to the gesture. Her left arm, gracefully poised on the edge of the table, closes the space around the balance and echoes the gentle arc of sunlight sweeping down from the window. Vermeer suspends the scales, perfectly balanced but not symmetrical, against the wall in a small niche of space reserved for them. Indeed, the bottom edge of the picture frame before the woman is higher than it is behind her, thus allowing sufficient space for the balance. Throughout, the interplay of verticals and horizontals, of mass against void, and of light against dark, creates a subtly balanced but never static composition.

The 1994 restoration of the painting, moreover, provided new insight into Vermeer's extraordinary sensitivity to light and color, particularly in the subtle modeling of the blue robe on the table. Most startling is the discovery of extensive overpaint covering the black frame of *The Last Judgment*. The gold trim now revealed creates an accent in the upper right that visually links with the yellow curtain and the yellow and red accents on the woman's costume, thereby restoring Vermeer's original, and more dynamic, compositional intent.

Vermeer's achievement has often been compared to Pieter de Hooch's (1629–1684) *A Woman Weighing Gold*, c. 1664 (fig. 1), a painting so similar in concept that it is difficult to imagine that the two images were painted independently even though De Hooch was at that time living in Amsterdam.[12] While De Hooch's painting lacks Vermeer's compositional refinement, theological implication, and subtlety of mood,[13]

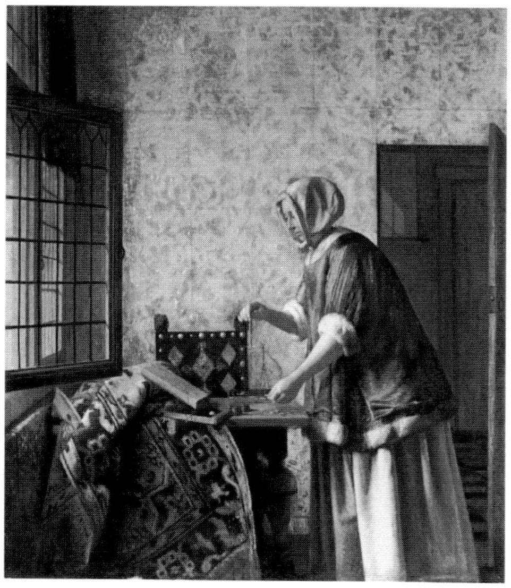

fig. 1. Pieter de Hooch, *A Woman Weighing Gold*, c. 1664, oil on canvas, Staatliche Museen zu Berlin, Gemäldegalerie

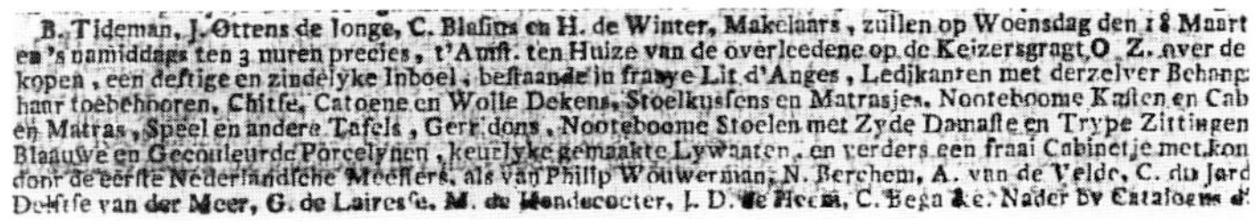

B. Tideman, J. Ottens de Jonge, C. Blasius en H. de Winter, Makelaars, zullen op Woensdag den 18 Maart
en 's namiddags ten 3 uuren precies, t'Amst. ten Huize van de overleedene op de Keizersgragt, O. Z. over de
kopen, een deftige en zindelyke Inboel, bestaande in fraaye Lit d'Anges, Ledikanten met derzelver Behang
haar toebehooren, Chitse, Catoene en Wolle Dekens, Stoelkussens en Matrasjes, Nooteboome Kasten en Cab
en Matras, Speel en andere Tafels, Gerridons, Nooteboome Stoelen met Zyde Damaste en Trype Zittingen
Blaauwe en Gecouleurde Porcelynen, keurlyke gemaakte Lywaaten, en verders een fraai Cabinetje met kon
door de eerste Nederlandsche Meesters, als van Philip Wouwerman, N. Berchem, A. van de Velde, C. du Jard
Delfse van der Meer, G. de Lairesse, M. de Hondecoeter, J. D. de Heem, C. Bega &c. Nader by Catalogus d

fig. 3. Advertisement from *Amsterdamsche Courant*, 1767

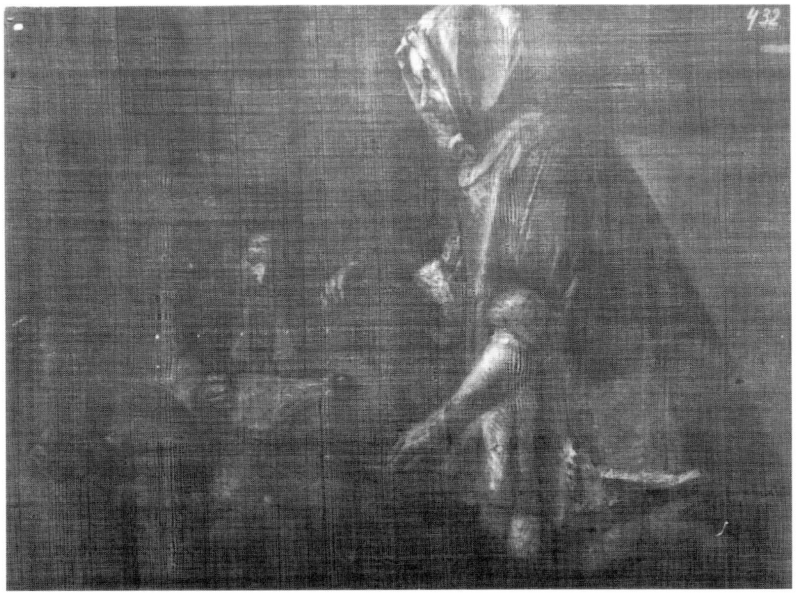

fig. 2. Detail of x-radiograph, Pieter de Hooch, *A Woman Weighing Gold*

Vermeer probably based his composition on De Hooch's. X-radiography indicates that De Hooch originally included the figure of a man seated at the far side of the table (fig. 2). It seems unlikely that De Hooch would have introduced the figure of the man, and then removed it, had he derived his composition from *Woman Holding a Balance*, as has been generally assumed. De Hooch had probably painted out the second figure before Vermeer saw the painting. This evidence suggests that Vermeer remained indebted to De Hooch after the latter artist had moved to Amsterdam.[14]

Vermeer's painting has a distinguished provenance traceable in a virtually unbroken line to the seventeenth century. Enthusiastic descriptions of the work in sale catalogues and critics' assessments attest to its extraordinary appeal to each generation. The first and perhaps most fascinating reference is in the Dissius sale catalogue published in Amsterdam in 1696. The first painting listed in a sale that included twenty-one paintings by Vermeer, it is described as: "A young lady weighing gold, in a box by J. van der Meer of Delft, extraordinarily artful and vigorously painted."[15] We know nothing more of the box in which it was kept, but it may have been a protective device designed to keep light and dust away from its delicate surface. Whether Vermeer conceived the composition to be seen within the box and whether the box was itself painted are questions that cannot be answered.[16]

The buyer at the Dissius sale was Isaac Rooleeuw (c. 1650–1710), who was also the owner of *The Milkmaid* (cat. 5).[17] Isaac Rooleeuw, a Mennonite merchant, was an artist and a pupil of Arnoud ten Himpel (1634–1686).[18] Rooleeuw went bankrupt five years after the Dissius sale, and his paintings were sold by foreclosure. After an inventory was taken by the appraiser Jan Zómer, the paintings were tied back-to-back and sealed with the city coat-of-arms. One of the works was described as "A gold weigher, by Van der Neer of Delft" (page 54, fig. 8).[19]

One of the two Rooleeuw Vermeers was acquired by the Amsterdam amateur and merchant Paulo van Uchelen (c. 1641–1702), the most renowned bibliophile of his time and a collector of prints and atlases. After his death, an estate division was drawn up on August 1703 on behalf of his sons Pieter and Paulo and his son-in-law. "A gold weigher by Van der Neer" (page 54, fig. 9) went to his namesake Paulo (1673–1754).[20]

In 1767 the painting passed under the gavel for a second time in Amsterdam in what has up to now been known as an anonymous sale. However, the name of the deceased owner could be retrieved from an advertisement (dated 28 February 1767) in the *Amsterdamsche Courant* (fig. 3).[21] She was Anna Gertruida van Uchelen (1705–1766), Paolo's daughter. After divorcing, she had joined her father in the house "Zurich" on the Keizersgracht (no. 173). She died without issue or heirs, so that in 1767 her property had to be sold off to the highest bidder.[22] For more than sixty years, three generations of Amsterdam Van Uchelens had treasured the Vermeer picture. The sale catalogue called it "powerfully detailed and Sunnily painted on Canvas."[23]

Ten years later the scene was described as "very lushly and thickly painted, and also in the best period, of this master."[24] The owner at the time was "the art-loving Mister NICOLAAS NIEUHOFF" (1733–1776), also an Amsterdam merchant.[25] *The Woman Holding a Balance* remained in Holland until 1801. At that time the owner was a certain P. P., and the sale catalogue commended the work for showing "everything corresponding to the truth, and attractively painted."[26] The painting surfaced twenty-five years later in the collection of the deceased king of Bavaria, Maximilian I (1756–1825), who had resided at Nymphenburg castle near Munich since 1799. In the sale catalogue the attribution had been changed to Gabriël Metsu, apparently confirmed by a monogram reading "G M." The reliability of this signature was not absolutely accepted, as the catalogue reported in fairness: "van der Meer according to others."[27]

The buyer at this auction, the Duke of Caraman (1762–1839), thought the latter ascription more likely. He had been the French ambassador in Vienna since 1816. The day he was elevated to the dukedom on 11 May 1830, he put his paintings up for sale in Paris.[28] Rembrandt's *Saul and David* (Mauritshuis, The Hague), which only later became famous, raised only 250 French francs,[29] while the Metsu/Vermeer turned out to be worth ten times that (2410 francs). One could read in the catalogue that the improved attribution to the Delft painter was owing to the connoisseurship of the Duke of Caraman. The text closed with a remarkable recommendation: "The productions of Vander Meer of Delft are so rare that we cannot exempt ourselves from pointing him out and commending him to amateurs."[30] The revaluation of Vermeer was, so to speak, in the air (see page 57).

Casimir Pierre Périer (1777–1832) became the new owner of the painting. Périer was a famous minister of the July Monarchy, who supported the Belgians in their struggle against the Dutch.[31] After his death his various private possessions were auctioned in two stages: 1838 for paintings and curios, and 1848 for the (primarily) Dutch paintings. Lord Hertford bought the Vermeer.[32] The Périer family was apparently attached to the painting, since the minister's son, Auguste Casimir Périer (1811–1876), bought the painting back from Hertford. This is apparent from a communication from Thoré-Bürger, who saw the painting in 1866 in the home of its owner: "how much pleasure it gave us to see it with M. Casimir Perier."[33]

This last communication must have put Hofstede de Groot on the trail of the masterpiece, which had not been exhibited in public since the Périer sale. The enquiries he made in 1910 established that it was still in the possession of the family. The grandson of the ex-Minister, Jean Paul Casimir Périer (1842–1907), gained prominence as President of France for six months in 1894.[34] In December of 1910, Hofstede de Groot published a reproduction of the painting in *The Burlington Magazine:* "I ...succeeded the summer of the present year in identifying the picture in the collection of the Comtesse de Sègur, sister of the late President Casimir Périer."[35] The Dutch press reported that the newly discovered painting had in the meantime been offered for sale at the dealers P. and D. Colnaghi in London, adding: "The work will probably soon leave for America."[36]

In 1911 the American collector Peter A. B. Widener (1834–1915) did in fact buy the *Woman Holding a Balance* by Vermeer. He stipulated in his testament that his son and heir, Joseph E. Widener (1872–1943), was to bequeath his imposing art collection to a museum.[37] Since 1942 the painting has been one of the prized possessions of the National Gallery of Art.

1. Personal communication from Melanie Gifford, who examined the painting in 1994.
2. For a review of the diverse interpretations in the earlier literature on this painting see National Gallery Washington 1995, 375–376 n. 5.
3. The theory that the woman is pregnant was first proffered in Carstensen/Putscher 1971. The authors concluded that the woman, following an old folk tradition, was weighing pearls to help her divine the sex of the unborn child. Since then, many authors have accepted as fact her pregnant state, including Walsh 1973, 79, and Grimme 1974, 54, who, as a consequence of the supposed pregnancy, attempted to identify the model as Vermeer's wife, Catharina Bolnes, mother of his fourteen children. Salomon 1983 suggested that a pregnant woman holding scales would have been interpreted as a Catholic response to the religious controversy about the moment a Christian soul obtains grace and salvation, a theory accepted by Sutton in Philadelphia 1984A, 342–343. In my opinion it seems unlikely that the woman is pregnant. As seen in numerous paintings by Vermeer's contemporaries, Dutch fashions in the mid-seventeenth century seem to have encouraged a bulky silhouette. The short jacket the girl wears, called a *pet en lair*, covered a bodice and a thickly padded skirt. The impression created, that of a forward-thrusting stomach, was evidently a desirable one (see also Aillaud 1986, 181).
4. Jones 1989; Cunnar 1990.
5. For an argument that Vermeer represented here "the divine truth of revealed religion," see Gaskell 1984. To support his argument Gaskell refers to one of the personifications of Truth described by Cesare Ripa in the 1644 Dutch edition of the *Iconologia*.
6. Rudolph 1938, 409, proposed that the woman was a personification of *Vanitas*. Actually since Christian iconography treats the pearl, the most precious jewel, as a symbol of salvation, it would be unusual for it to have strong *vanitas* connotations. See Ferguson 1959, 23.
7. Ripa 1644, 144, 432. Ripa describes how the balance is one of the attributes of equality, *Vgvalita* or *Gelijckheyt* ("Door de Weeghschaele wort verstaen de oprachte en waerachtige recht vaerdigheyt, die een ygelijck geeft, dat hem toebehoort"), and of Justice, *Giustitia* or *Gerechtigheyt*.
8. The mirror is frequently considered the attribute of *Prudentia* and *Truth*. For a discussion of the various connotations of the mirror in emblematic literature of the mid-seventeenth century, see The Hague 1974, 98.
9. Van Veen 1608, 182. The full verse is:

Fortune is loues looking-glass
Eu'n as a perfect glasse doth represent the face,
Just as it is in deed, not flattring it at all.
So fortune telleth by aduancement or by fall,
Th'euent that shall succeed, in loues luick-tryed case.

For further discussions of Vermeer's use of *Amorum emblemata* see De Jongh 1967, 49–50.
10. Cunnar 1990, 501–536. Although Cunnar overinter-

prets the painting in many respects, he presents a fascinating range of theological issues current in the seventeenth century.

11 Mottola 1964, 85.

12. Oil on canvas, 61 x 53 cm. See Staatliche Museen Berlin 1978, 212. The comparison of this painting with Vermeer's *Woman Holding a Balance* is not new. For comparisons with slightly different emphases see Bode 1919, 86–89, and Rudolph 1938, 405–412.

13. De Hooch's woman weighs her gold before a wall richly decorated with a gilded-leather wallcovering and a half-open door leading into a second room. Neither of these elements reinforces the basic thematic gesture of a woman with a balance as strongly as does the painting of the *Last Judgment*.

14. I would like to thank Jan Kelch for providing me with the x-radiograph. For another probable instance of Vermeer deriving a compositional idea from De Hooch in the 1660s, see cat. 18.

15. Blankert 1975, 136, doc. 62: "Een Juffrouw die goud weegt, in een kasje van J. vander Meer van Delft, extraordinaer konstig en kragtig geschildert" (Hoet 1752–1770, 1: 34, no. 1). It sold for 155 guilders, the third highest price in the sale.

16. In the 1683 inventory of goods accruing to Jacob Dissius after the death of his wife, Magdalena van Ruijven, three of Vermeer's paintings are listed as being in boxes (*kasies*). See Montias 1989, 359, doc. 417. Presumably one of these was *Woman Holding a Balance.*

17. Dudok van Heel 1975, 162, no. 67; not in Blankert 1975, 149–150, no. 15.

18. Broos 1985, 33 n. 17; he lived in the house "De Rotgans" (Nieuwendijk 35) that had been bought by his father, Isaac Jacobsz Rooleeuw (see Wijnman 1959, 61 and 69; and Wijnman et al. 1974, 262).

19. Gemeentearchief, Amsterdam (DBK., no. 402, fol. 171/3, 11 March 1701; see also DBK., no. 144, fols. 105v and 135v).

20. "Een Goudtweegstertien van vander Meer." Gemeentearchief, Amsterdam (Notary H. de Wilde, no. 6454, second sheet; no. 6455, deed 170, fol. 1490); see also Dudok van Heel 1975, 162, no. 67. On Van Uchelen, see De la Fontaine Verwey 1970, 103–106 and Van der Veen 1992, 329–330.

21. *Amsterdamsche Courant*, 28 February 1767, no. 26, second sheet: not previously published.

22. Gemeentearchief, Amsterdam (DTB, no. 189, 11; DTB, no. 719, 325; DTB, no. 1105, fol. 25v: with thanks to Bas Dudok van Heel and Carola Vermeeren).

23. Sale catalogue, Amsterdam, 18 March 1767, 5, no. 6: "kragtig uytvoerig en Zonagtig op Doek geschildert." The buyer was a certain Kok, who is mentioned elsewhere in this catalogue (copy RKD) as a painter and broker.

24. Sale catalogue, Amsterdam, 14 April 1777, 62, no. 116: "zeer malsch en vet in de verf geschilderd, en wel in den besten tyd, van dezen meester " (Lugt no. 2673).

25. Gemeentearchief, Amsterdam (DTB 610, 57; DTB 1060, fol. 21): "den kunstlievenden Heer NICOLAAS NIEUHOFF." The introduction to the sale catalogue has nothing more to say about the deceased collector.

26. "alles overeenkomstig, de waarheid, en bevallig gepenceeld." This was the auction of the collection of the physician G.H. Trochel, where paintings by various contributors were sold; see sale catalogue, Amsterdam, 11 May 1801, 12, no. 48 (Lugt no. 6261).

27. Sale catalogue, Munich, 5 December 1826, 25, no. 101: "nach andern van der Meer" (Lugt no. 11305).

28. BNF, 7: cols. 1099–1100.

29. Mauritshuis 1993A, 283, 289 n. 16.

30. Sale catalogue, Paris, 10 May 1830, 35, no. 68: "Les productions de Vander Meer de Delft sont si rares, que nous ne pouvons nous dispenser de signaler celle-ci...aux amateurs" (Lugt no. 12364). See also Von Frimmel 1912–1913, 49.

31. Larousse 1865–1890, 12:609–610; since Blankert 1975, 150, no. 15 we also encounter the incorrect spelling "Pereir."

32. Sale catalogue, Paris, 18 April 1838 (Lugt no. 15028); Sale catalogue, Paris, 5 May 1848, 4, no. 7 (Lugt no. 19009).

33. Thoré-Bürger 1866, 555–556: "Payé 141 livres 15 shillings (sans doute par M. Casimir Perier fils)" and "que nous avons eu tant de plaisir à voir chez M. Casimir Perier."

34. DBF, 3: 885.

35. Hofstede de Groot 1910–1911, 134.

36. *Delftsche Courant*, 6 December 1910 (Mauritshuis Clippings Book, 59).

37. Comstock 1946, 129–135; Widener 1948, 7–9.

COLLECTION CATALOGUES

Widener 1913–1916, 1: no. 47 and ill.; Widener 1923, unpaginated, ill.; Widener 1931, 50 and ill.; Widener 1948, 65, no. 693 and ill.; National Gallery Washington 1975, 362–363, and ill.; National Gallery Washington 1985, 421 and ill.; National Gallery Washington 1995, 371–377 (with extensive literature)

LITERATURE

Hoet 1752–1770, 1: 34, no. 1; 62, no. 6; Thoré-Bürger 1866, 555–556, no. 27; Havard 1888, 37, no. 30; Hofstede de Groot 1907–1928, 1: 586–587, no. 10; Hofstede de Groot 1910–1911, 133–134 and ill.; Bode 1911, 1–2 and ill.; Plietzsch 1911, 49–50, 98, 119, no. 35 and 132–133; Von Frimmel 1912, 48–49; Lloyd 1925, 124, 128 and ill.; Hale 1937, 140–142, 222 and pl. 27; Rudolph 1938, 407–412, 433 and ill. 2; De Vries 1939, 46, 58, 76, 86–87, no. 23 and ill. 48; Blum 1946, 30, 42, 60, 135, 171–172, no. 27; Van Gelder 1948, 36; Boström 1949, 21–24; Swillens 1950, 57–58, no. 20, 72, 78, 82, 84, 86, 88, 105, 118 and pl. 20; Gowing 1952, 44, 53, 135–136, no. 20 and ills. 44–46; Constable 1964, 117 n. 2; Goldscheider 1967, 14, 27, 130, no. 21 and ills. 51–52; Gerson 1967, col. 744; Carstensen/Putscher 1971, 1–6 and ill.; Blankert 1975, 62–64, 73, 82, 102, 149–150, no. 15 and pl. 15; Alpers 1976, 25, 35 and ill. 12; Harbison 1976, 83, 86–87 and ill. 8; Wheelock 1977B, 439, 441; Blankert 1978, 22, 42–44, 49, 54, 67, 161–162, no. 15 and pls. 15–15a; Seth 1980, 24, 26 and 34; Sutton 1980, 45, 68 n. 37 and ill.; Naumann 1981, 1: 65 n. 4 and 68; Slatkes 1981, 53, 55–56 and ill., 126, 130; Wheelock 1981, 41–42, 106–109 and ill.; Alpers 1983, xxi; Salomon 1983, 216–221 and ills. 1–2; Gaskell 1984, 557–559 and ill.; Aillaud 1986, 48, 49, 51, 64, 112, 114–117, 183–185, no. 14, and pl. 14; Reutersward 1988, 56–57 and ill. 2; Wheelock 1988, 40 and 82–83 and ill. 18; Nash 1991, 26, 28, 39, 98–101, and ill; Blankert 1992, 49–52, 66, 114–118, 126–128, 140, 160, 184–185, no. 15, 223 and pl. 15; Wheelock 1995, 96–103, 105, 111, 122, 124, 176, 195 n. 1, 196 nn. 10, 13, and ill. 70

11

Young Woman with a Water Pitcher

c. 1664–1665

oil on canvas, 45.7 x 40.6 (18 x 16)

Lent by The Metropolitan Museum of Art, New York, Marquand Collection, Gift of Henry G. Marquand, 1889

PROVENANCE

Robert Vernon, London, 1801(?)–1849; Vernon sale, London, 21 April 1877, no. 97 (£404.5 to M. Colnaghi); Lord Powerscourt, Castle Powerscourt, near Dublin, 1878–1887(?); [Agnew, London]; [Bourgeois Frères, Paris]; [Pillet, Paris, 1887, for $800 to Marquand]; Henry G. Marquand, New York, 1887–1888; on loan to The Metropolitan Museum of Art, New York, 1888; to the present owner in 1889

EXHIBITIONS

London 1838, 9, no. 29; London 1878, 50, no. 267; New York 1909, 138, no. 137; Amsterdam 1935, 29, no. 167, and ill. 85; Rotterdam 1935, 37, no. 85 and ill. 66: The Hague 1966, no. 4 and ill.; Paris 1966, no. 5 and ill.

TECHNICAL DESCRIPTION

The support is a plain-weave linen with a thread count of 14 x 14 per cm^2. The canvas has been lined and the original tacking edges have been removed.

The ground is pale gray and contains lead white, chalk, and umber.[1]

In the brightly lit areas of the wall is a thin gray layer, slightly paler than the ground, containing some ultramarine. Yellow ocher was added to this layer in the shadows and half-shadows. The left, shaded side of the basin has a red underpaint that extends under the adjacent part of her skirt. It is visible as a red outline describing the top edge.

The composition has been altered. There once was a chair with lion's head finials in the lower left foreground and the map on the back wall was placed further to the left in line with the left edge of the woman's headgear.

The red velvet lining of the jewelry box lid has faded, though the color is still intense where it has been shaded by the frame. Abrasion along all edges and in thin-glazed shadows, as well as scattered flake losses, are present.

Much as a poet who searches for the essence of reality, Vermeer created his images by distilling his visual impressions of the physical world. In a Neo-platonic fashion, the artist found that beneath the accidents of nature there exists a realm infused with harmony and order. His genius rests in giving visual form to that realm, and in revealing moments of human existence.

Vermeer sought, and found, that inner harmony in everyday life, primarily in the confines of a private chamber. Within the world of his interiors, individual objects – chairs, tables, walls, maps, or window frames – become vehicles for creating a sense of nature's underlying order. His carefully chosen objects are never randomly placed; their positions, proportions, colors, and textures work in concert with his figures. Light plays across the image, further binding these elements together. The various means by which Vermeer constructs his images reflect the extraordinary awareness he had for formal compositional relationships; less understood, however, is how these same concerns enhance the mood and thematic focus of his paintings.

The poetry of Vermeer's vision is nowhere better seen than in *Young Woman with a Water Pitcher.* As though transfixed in a moment of time, a young woman stares absently toward the window, resting her right hand on the frame and holding a water pitcher in the other. While her embracing pose welcomes the cool light filtering through the leaded panes of the open window, her expression imparts a sense of repose and inner peace. Vermeer reinforces this mood through the quiet, restrained framework of geometric shapes surrounding her.

The serenity of this work is so all-encompassing that it is hard to identify any recognizable narrative. Unlike the understandable, physical activity in *Woman Washing Her Hands* (fig. 1) by Eglon van der Neer (1634–1703), the central presence of the water pitcher in Vermeer's painting is not easily explained. If the woman prepares her morning toilet, why is there an open jewelry box with pearls, but no mirror, comb, or powderbrush, objects generally associated with such an activity? Why has Vermeer depicted her with a wide, white linen collar covering her shoulders, an accessory probably related to the toilet but not otherwise found in his paintings?[2] Finally, does the wall map of *The Seventeen Provinces* that Vermeer included so prominently behind the woman relate to a narrative, particularly since he depicts only the portion representing the southern provinces?[3]

Such questions, while appropriate to ask when considering some of Vermeer's works and most genre paintings by his contemporaries, seem irrelevant in the presence of a painting such as this. While Vermeer conceived *Young Woman with a Water Pitcher* within an accepted iconographic framework, he differed from other artists in that

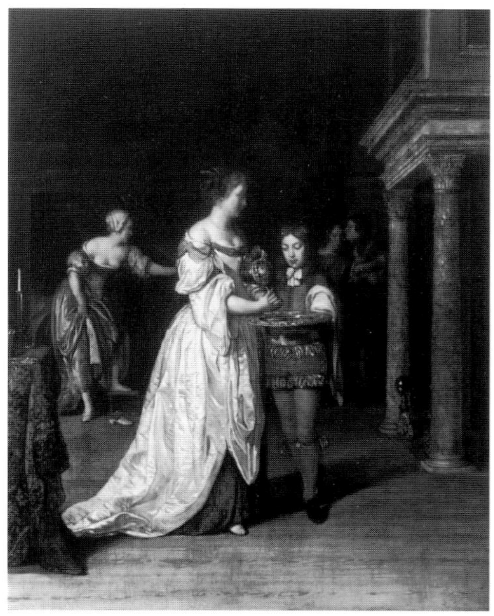

fig. 1. Eglon van der Neer, *Woman Washing Her Hands*, 1675, oil on panel, Mauritshuis, The Hague

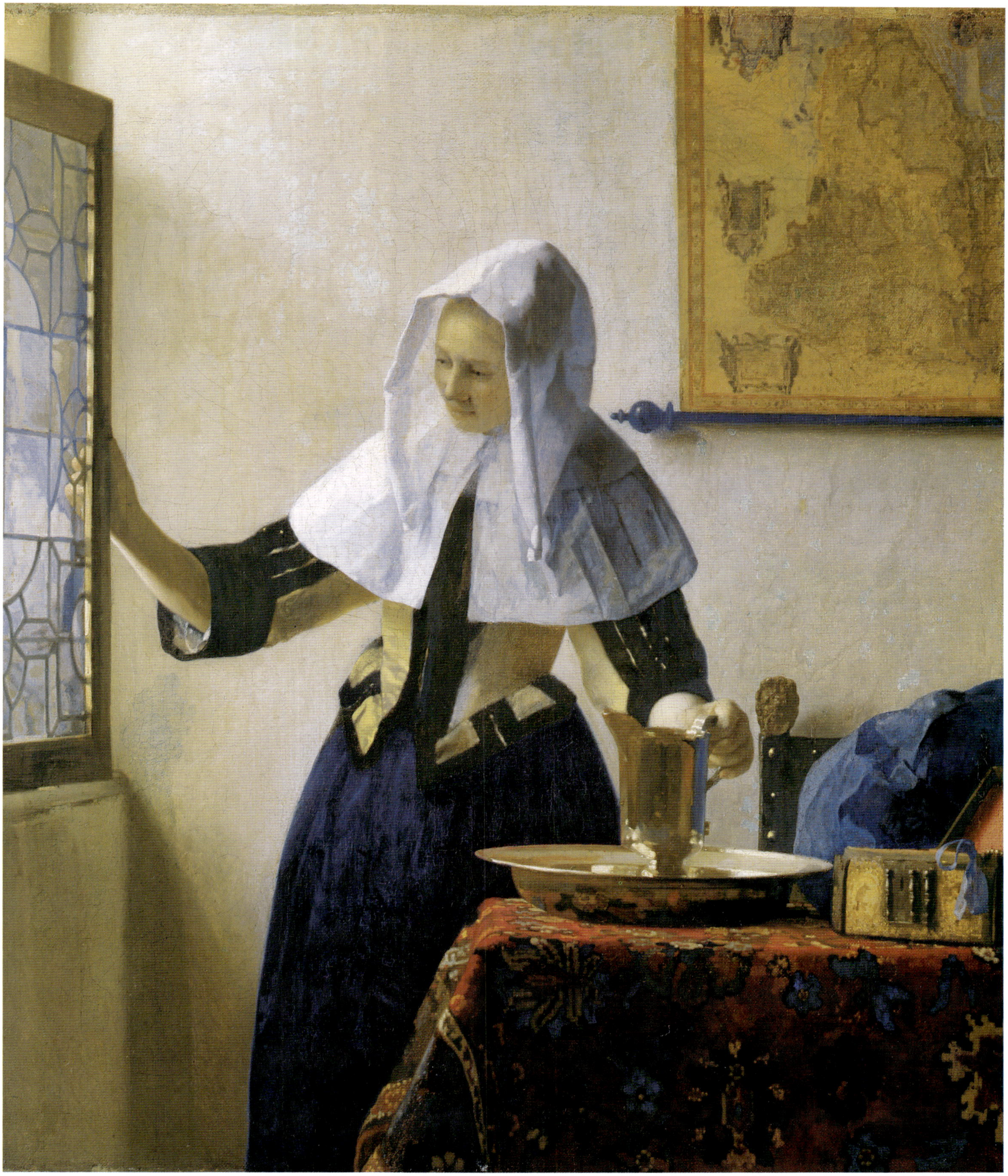

he avoided narrative as a means for communicating meaning. For example, Van der Neer used the motif of hand-washing both for its narrative potential and for its symbolic meaning. In Dutch emblematic traditions, cleansing symbolizes purity and innocence, as De Jongh has noted.[4] The gesture of hand-washing in Van der Neer's painting thus symbolically differentiates one woman's moral character from that of another who emerges from the bed in the background. While the ideals of cleanliness and purity are also at the core of Vermeer's image, the artist expresses them in an entirely different way. As the woman stands poised between the window and the water pitcher, her actions seem suspended in time. Hers is a lasting, rather than fleeting, moment, one given further significance by Vermeer's pristine harmonies of light, color, and shape.

Vermeer's subtle compositional adjustments reveal the care with which he conceived his image. One of these adjustments, clearly visible with the naked eye, is a chair with lion-head finials that once occupied the left foreground. An infrared reflectogram demonstrates that Vermeer also altered the position of the wall map that originally hung directly behind the woman (fig. 2). In both instances Vermeer blocked in these initial compositional ideas with gray paints.

With these changes, Vermeer created a dynamic tension within the painting. The energy encompassed by the woman's body and gaze is now skillfully counterbalanced by the concentration of objects on the right. Moreover, by removing the chair and changing the position of the map, Vermeer preserved the purity of the white wall between the woman and the window, thus allowing light to flow directly onto her, uninterrupted by any visual interference.

As the entering light follows the graceful arc of the woman's arm, it reveals the smooth planes of the white linen cowl draped gracefully around her head, and the sheen of her yellow jacket. The light, however, does not merely illuminate the woman, it infuses her with an inner radiance. Vermeer captures this radiance most vividly along the contour of the woman's blue skirt, an edge he has subtly diffused to suggest the interaction of light and form. The artist further captures this quality in the softly modulated half-tones of her lowered face.

From the nuances of ocher and blue in the leaded glass of the window that make up the woman's reflection, to the glistening highlights on the pitcher and basin, Vermeer's sensitivity to the interaction of light and color is remarkable. To help create the reflective surface of the basin Vermeer painted its form over a reddish tone applied over the ground. This selective ground layer, visible along the upper left rim of the basin, also extends under the woman's blue skirt, where it warms that otherwise cool color. As is often the case with Vermeer, this blue passage consists of small particles of natural ultramarine mixed with bone black. High concentrations of natural ultramarine exist only along the ridges of the folds. Indeed, Vermeer's restraint with bright pigments includes his exclusive use of lead-tin yellow for the highlights of the woman's jacket, allowing a more subtle underlayer of ocher to define the shaded yellows of the costume.

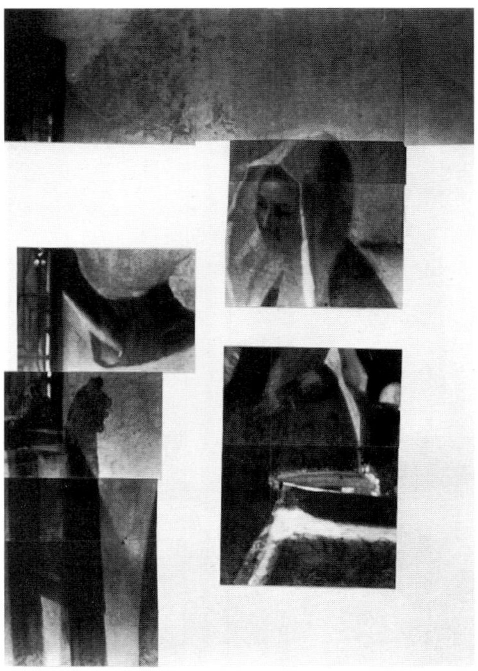

fig. 2. Infrared reflectogram, *Young Woman with a Water Pitcher*

Remarkably, the *Young Woman with a Water Pitcher* was long taken for a work by Gabriël Metsu (1629–1667). Under that name the picture was shown in the 1838 exhibition in the British Institution in London.[5] Robert Vernon (1774–1849), one of the most remarkable British collectors of the nineteenth century, owned it at the time. Since 1820 he had collected paintings, primarily contemporary masters, of which he gave a part to the British nation in 1847.[6] In 1877, long after his death, a remnant of the Vernon Collection, comprising historical portraits and old masters, was auctioned in London where this interior scene with a woman at an open window was exhibited and sold under the name "Metzu."[7] An anonymous commentator on the auction noted: "those acquainted with the works of Van der Meer at once recognized the master's hand."[8]

The dealer Martin Colnaghi bought the "Metzu" in 1877 and sold it to Lord Powerscourt, who became convinced of Vermeer's authorship. He parted with his acquisition for the 1878 exposition in the Royal Academy, where it was shown as "Jan van der Meer, of Delft."[9] Mervyn Wingfield (1836–1904), seventh Viscount Powerscourt (fig. 3), was transformed into a precocious Vermeer admirer. In 1864 he had become a board member of the National Gallery of Ireland, for which he made acquisitions during his continental

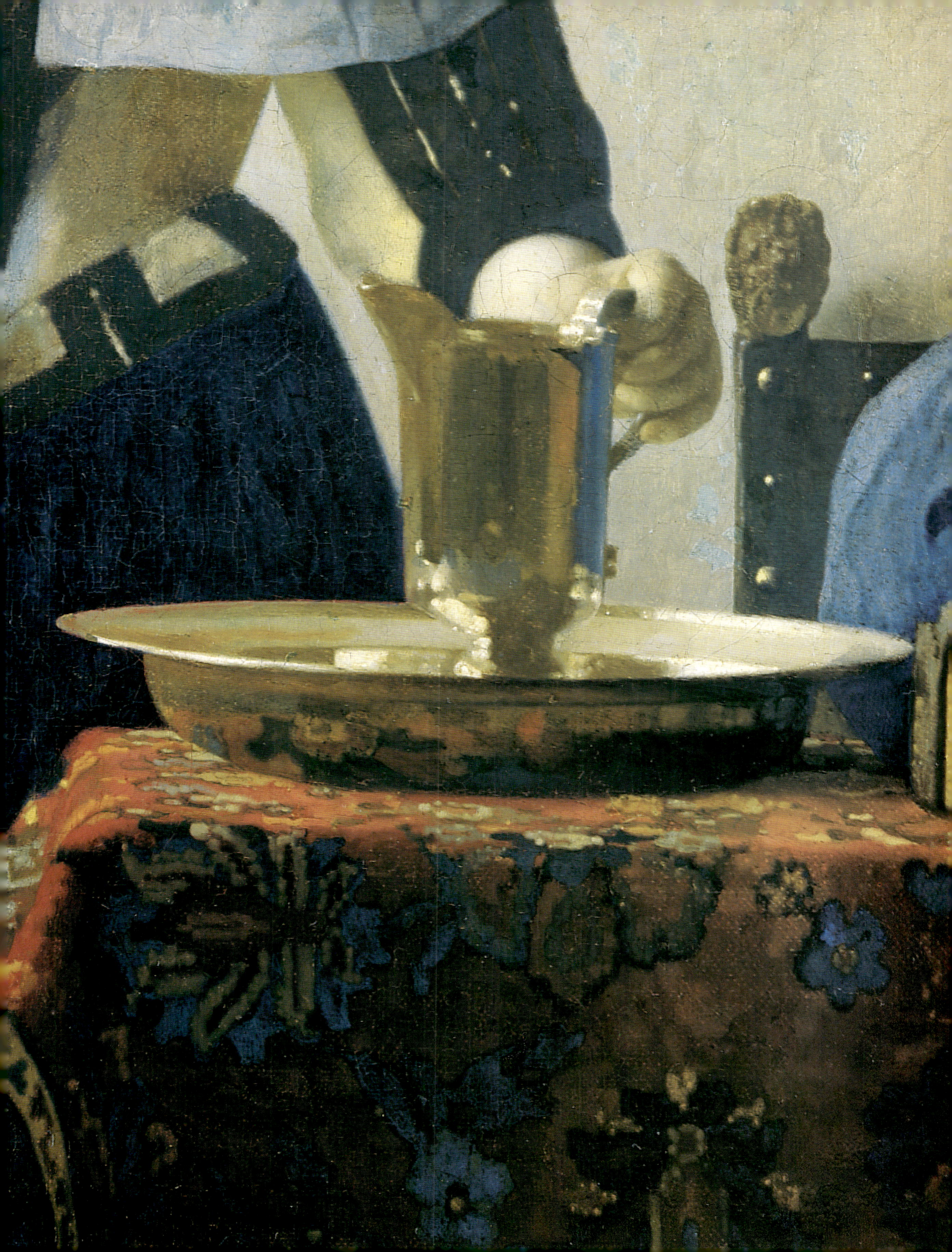

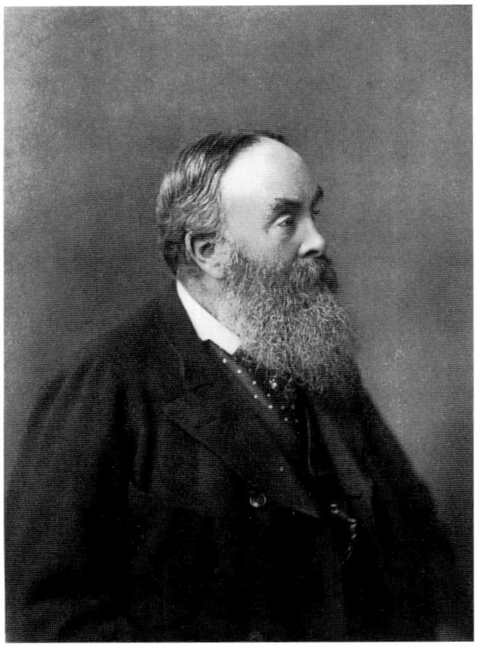

fig. 3. Portrait of Mervyn Wingfield, Lord Powerscourt, 7th Viscount, from *Powerscourt 1903*

art tours.[10] His son, the eighth Viscount of Powerscourt (1880–1947), distinctly remembered his father's preference for the rare Delft painter. In 1881 he had already given a lecture in Dublin in which he sounded the praise of Vermeer, paying special attention to the *View of Delft*, which he had seen in The Hague (cat. 7).[11] He further lauded the "beautifull effects in his works, especially his way of depicting the effect of light through bluish window-glass, which seems to be the principal aim in many of his pictures, and which I do not remember to have seen so succesfully rendered by any other painter."[12]

In 1887, the *Young Woman with a Water Pitcher* was bought by Henry G. Marquand (1819–1902) (fig. 4), who was a successful banker in his native city of New York. After retiring, he dedicated himself to the public welfare and to charity and became one of the moving forces behind the new Metropolitan Museum of Art, becoming its treasurer in 1882. His own home also resembled a museum, as "He bought like an Italian Prince of the Renaissance."[13]

In 1888 Marquand lent his Vermeer to an exhibition of his collection at the Metropolitan Museum of Art. The spontaneous enthusiasm of the public was so great that Marquand decided to donate all thirty-five of the paintings exhibited at that time to the museum.[14] His magnaminity earned him great praise as a benefactor. A Dutch commentator wrote: "Honor be to the liberal and patriotic donor; may his noble deed evoke the emulation of all right-thinking men!"[15] Finally, in 1889 he was elected the second President of the Metropolitan.

In 1909 Vermeer became the revelation of the Hudson-Fulton Commemorative Exhibition in the Metropolitan Museum of Art. With J. Pierpont Morgan's *A Lady Writing* (cat. 13), the *Young Woman with a Water Pitcher* was one of the gems of the exhibition.[16] For example, a certain William Howe Downes opined in the *Boston Evening Transcript* of 18 September 1909: "The rare and incomparable artist Vermeer...might be called the revelation and the bright, particular star of this grand collection." According to him, the *Young Woman with a Water Pitcher* was "one of the immortal productions of the art of Holland, a gem of purest ray serene."[17]

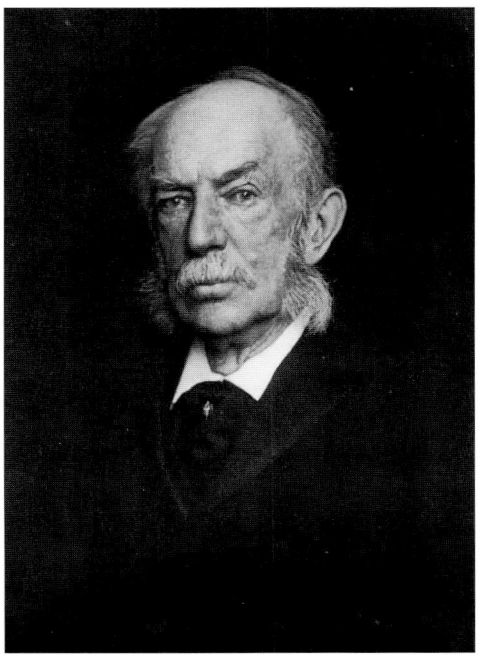

fig. 4. Henry G. Marquand, photograph

1. Kühn 1968, 186.
2. The one possible exception is the original shape of the collar seen in the *Officer and Laughing Girl* in The Frick Collection (page 35, fig. 6). See Wheelock 1995, fig. 40.
3. Welu 1975, 534–535, has identified the map as one published by Huyck Allart (active c. 1650–1675). South in this map is oriented to the left. A version of the map, dated 1671, is located in the University Library, Leiden (Bodel Nijenhuis Collection, No. P I N 69). Welu noted that Allart acquired the plates from an early seventeenth-century source and reprinted the map with added decorative elements.
4. De Jongh in Amsterdam 1976, 195, cat. 48. The emblem De Jongh cites, and illustrates, is found in B[artholomeus] H[ulsius], *Emblematia sacra, dat is, eenighe geestelicke sinnebeelden*, no location, 1631, 100–104. The tradition relating to cleansing and purity, of course, goes back to the Bible. A pitcher and basin, similar to those in Vermeer's painting, are represented in Jan Lievens' *Pilate Washing His Hands* (Stedelijk Museum De Lakenhal, Leiden). For an illustration of Lievens' painting, see Sumowski 1983, 3: 1180.
5. London 1838, 9, no. 29: "A female at a window. Metzu"; Graves 1913–1915, 2: 773 (1838, no. 29).
6. DNB, 58: 281–282; in 1876 his collection was housed in the National Gallery in London and later in the Tate Gallery; according to Hamlyn 1993, 193, Vernon inherited most of the old masters in his collection from his father, a London stable keeper, who died in 1801.
7. Sale catalogue, London, 21 April 1877, 12, no. 97 (Lugt no. 37364).
8. H. W. 1877, 616.
9. London 1878, 50, no. 267.
10. Burke's 1963, 1985.
11. Hale 1937, 109–110 (letters from the eighth Viscount Powerscourt to Hale, dated 18 January and 24 February 1936).
12. Hale 1937, 109.
13. DAB, 12: 292–293.
14. Loffelt 1889, 61 (quoting from a letter from Marquand to the museum), and Tomkins 1970, 74. Valentiner 1910, 11, mistakenly believed that Marquand had bought the painting as a De Hooch, an opinion still believed by Walter Liedtke in The Hague 1990, 17.
15. Loffelt 1889, 62: "Eere den onbekrompen en vaderlandslievenden schenker, wiens edele daad den naijver van alle weldenkenden moge opwekken!"
16. New York 1909, 137 no. 136, and 138, no. 137.
17. Clipping in the Mauritshuis documentation archives.

COLLECTION CATALOGUES

Metropolitan Museum 1895, 95, no. 297; Metropolitan Museum 1920, 311; Metropolitan Museum 1980, 1: 191, 3: 446 and ill.

BIBLIOGRAPHY

H.W. 1877, 616; Havard 1888, 39, no. 56; Loffelt 1889, 62; Bode 1895, 18; Roberts 1897, 1: 268–269; Hofstede de Groot 1907–1928, 1: 271 and 595–596, no. 19; Hofstede de Groot 1907–1930, ill. 11; Cortissoz 1909, 166; Stephenson 1909, 168, 172 and ill.; Cox 1909–1910, 246; Breck 1910, 41–42 and ill.; Friedländer 1910, 98; Valentiner 1910, 11; Plietzsch 1911, 50–51, 118, no. 27 and ill. 12; Graves 1913–1915, 2: 773, 4: 1474; Lloyd 1925, 124–125 and ill.; Hale 1937, 107–111 and ill. 1; De Vries 1939, 40, 81–82, no. 11 and ill. 37; Swillens 1950, 56, no. 16, 72, 83–88, 118, 144 and pl. 16; Gowing 1952, 130–131, nr. 15 and ill.; Constable 1964, 105; Gerson 1967, col. 742; Goldscheider 1967, 141, no. 16 and ill. 43; Tomkins 1970, 74; Blankert 1975, 60, 62, 109, 146–147, no. 12 and pl. 12; Welu 1975, 534 and ill. 5; Blankert 1978, 41, 73, 159–160, no. 12 and pl. 12; Slatkes 1981, 50–51 and ill.; Wheelock 1981, 44, 48, 114–116, and pls. 26–27; Aillaud 1986, 50, 108–109, 112, 180–181, no. 12, and pl. 11; Wheelock 1988, 42 and 88–91, and pls. 21–22; Montias 1989, 190, 266 and ill. 42; The Hague 1990, 17 and ill. 1, 37, 39 and 43; Nash 1991, 26, 28, 31, 96–98, and ill.; Blankert 1992, 52, 109, 114, 181, no. 12, 223, ill. 38 and pl. 11; Hamlyn 1993, 193 and ill. on cover; Wheelock 1995, 104–111, 159, 178, and ill. 75

12

Woman with a Pearl Necklace

c. 1664

inscribed on the tabletop: *IVMeer* (IVM in ligature)

oil on canvas, 51.2 x 45.1 (20 5/32 x 17 3/4)

Staatliche Museen zu Berlin, Gemäldegalerie

PROVENANCE

(?) Pieter Claesz van Ruijven, Delft, before 1674; (?) Maria de Knuijt, Widow Van Ruijven, Delft, 1674–1681; (?) Magdelena van Ruijven and Jacob Dissius, 1681–1682; Jacob Dissius (with his father Abraham Dissius, 1685–1694), Delft, 1682–1695; Dissius sale, Amsterdam, 16 May 1696, no. 36 (*f* 30); Johannes Caudri, Amsterdam, before 1809; Caudri sale, Amsterdam, 6 September 1809, no. 42 (*f* 55 to Ths. Spaan); D. Teengs sale, Amsterdam, 24 April 1811, no. 73 (*f* 36 to Gruijter); Sale, Amsterdam, 26 March 1856, no. 93 (*f* 111 to Philip); Henri Grevedon, Paris, before 1860; Thoré-Bürger, Paris, c. 1860–1868; Bürger et al. sale, Brussels, 22 April 1868, no. 49 (Bf 3,500 to Sedelmeyer for Suermondt); Barthold Suermondt, Aachen, 1868–1874; acquired as part of Suermondt collection in 1874

EXHIBITIONS

Paris 1866 (not in cat.); Paris 1914, 52, no. 24, and ill.; Amsterdam 1950, 56, no. 112, and ill. 107

TECHNICAL DESCRIPTION

The support is a fine, plain-weave, linen with a thread count of 21.6 x 15 per cm². The original tacking edges are still present. The top tacking edge is wider than the others and appears to have been folded double. Marks from the original strainer bars are evident along the top and right edges. The support has been lined and placed on a stretcher larger than the original strainer.

Over an off-white ground, black underpainting indicates the shadow on the woman's back. An ocher layer on top of the ground may cover the entire painting. It is not covered by other paint layers in parts of the figure and in the stained glass window. The woman's yellow jacket is underpainted with white, followed by lead tin yellow in the light parts and two layers of a black and yellow ocher mixture in the shadows. In the flesh colors are various mixtures of white, ocher, and black, well blended into one another. The pearl necklace was painted wet-in-wet in white over a gray/ocher layer.

A young woman stands transfixed, gazing into a mirror and holding the ribbons of her pearl necklace tautly in her hands. Elegantly dressed in an ermine-trimmed yellow satin jacket, her hair decorated with an orange-red star-shaped bow, she seems to be giving the finishing touches to her toilet, for before her on the table, partially hidden behind a dark cloth, are a basin and a powder brush. Light floods into the room through the leaded-glass windows. The scene is a familiar one, yet it transcends the common occurences of daily life. All movement has stopped, as though the young woman has just seen herself in the mirror for the first time.

This focus on a solitary woman standing in the corner of a room resembles three other of Vermeer's paintings from the mid-1660s, *Woman in Blue Reading a Letter*, *Woman Holding a Balance*, and *Young Woman with a Water Pitcher* (cats. 9, 10, 11). Nevertheless, Vermeer has infused the taut, sparse composition of *Woman with a Pearl Necklace* with a different level of emotional energy. The blank expanse of the white wall and the yellows of the curtain and woman's jacket provide an intensity of color not seen in the other paintings, where blues and ochers predominate. The most important difference lies in the forcefulness of the woman's gaze. Instead of being quietly reflective, she is actively engaged. Indeed, as the woman stares across the room at the mirror, her gaze activates the entire void of space in the center of the composition.

While representations of women at their toilet became a favorite subject for a number of Dutch artists during the 1650s and 1660s, in particular Gerard ter Borch (1617–1681) and Gabriël Metsu (1629–1667), the closest prototype for Vermeer's composition is a small panel painting by Frans van Mieris (1635–1681), *Young Woman before a Mirror* (fig. 1). Although apparently similar in general concept, the differences in the thematic content of these two works are striking. In Van Mieris' painting the darkness of the setting and the woman's languid pose, low decolletage, and wistful gaze are replete with sensuality, whereas Vermeer's woman appears modest and self-contained. She stands alone, caught in a pose that betrays no movement, while Van Mieris' woman is accompanied by an expectant black servant girl who, with upturned eyes, holds the jewelry box up to her.

The folded letter on the table in Van Mieris' painting reaffirms that the subject is related to love. The mirror would thus seem to relate metaphorically to love's transience, a common theme in Dutch emblematic traditions.[1] Metaphorical associations with mirrors, however, are numerous and frequently contradictory, ranging from the sense of sight to indications of pride and vanity. Indeed, in Vermeer's painting the woman's act of gazing into the mirror while adorning herself with a pearl neck-

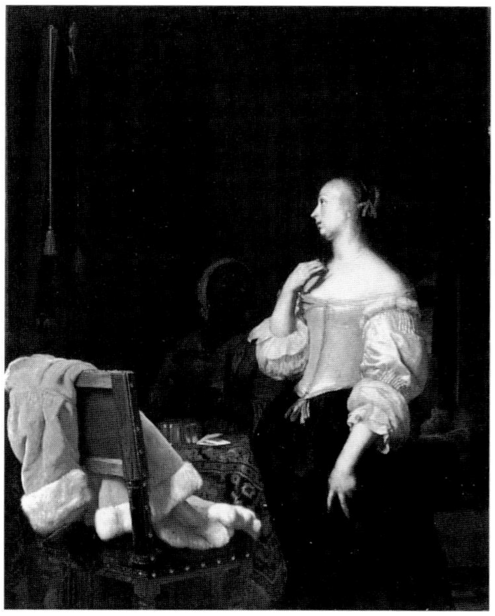

fig. 1. Frans van Mieris, *Young Woman before a Mirror*, c. 1662, oil on panel, Staatliche Museen zu Berlin, Gemäldegalerie

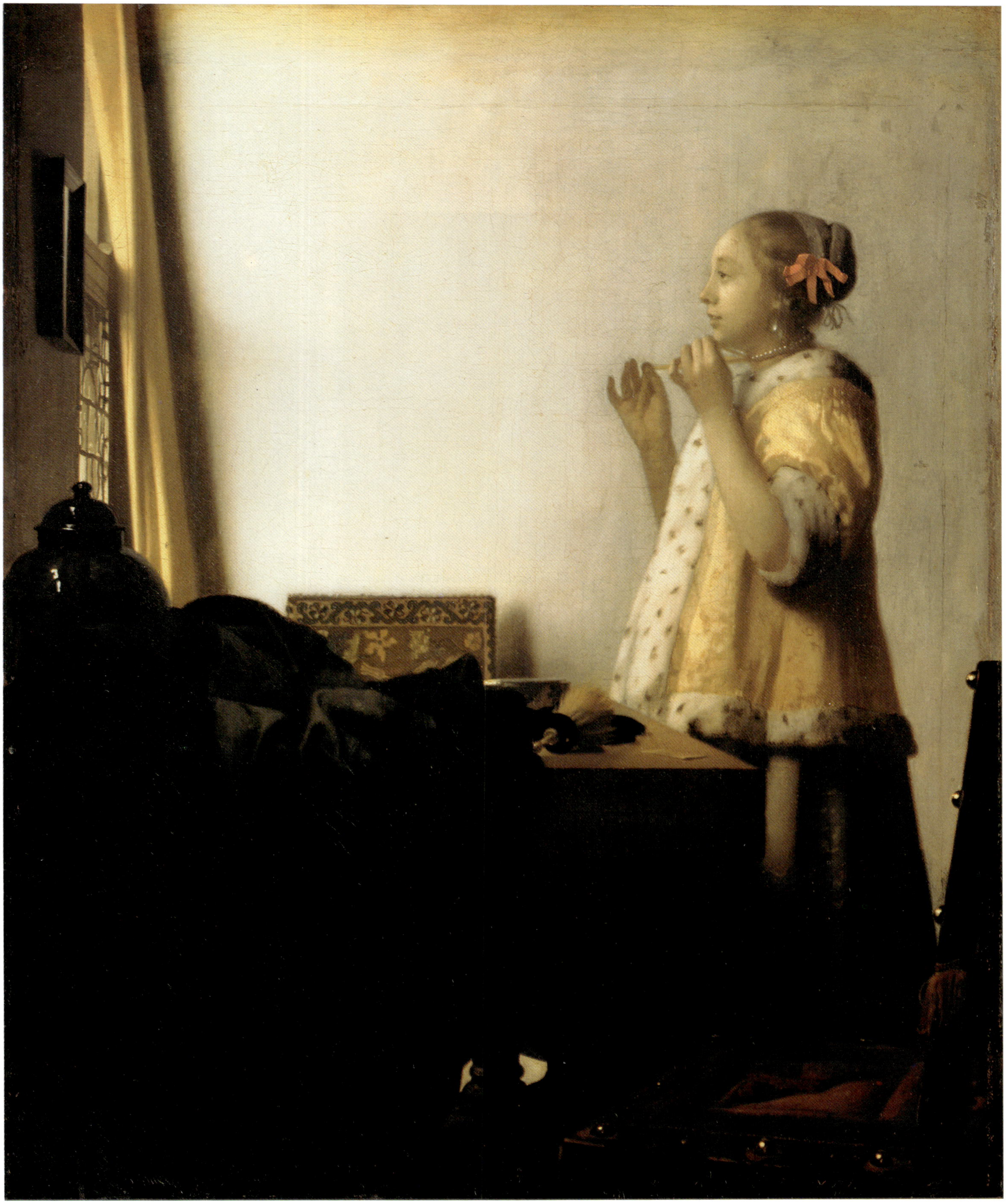

lace has been interpreted by scholars as a vanitas theme.[2] Yet, no other compositional elements reinforce such a negative message.[3] More in keeping with this serene image are those positive metaphorical associations traditionally connected with the mirror: self-knowledge and truth. According to Cesare Ripa in his *Iconologia*, a mirror is one of the attributes of Prudence, for with it she achieves self-knowledge. It is also an attribute of Truth. Just as a mirror accurately reflects reality, so does man achieve understanding when he comprehends the true character of the physical world.[4] Otto van Veen related the elements of truth and love to a mirror's reflection in his emblem "Cleer and pure."[5]

The woman's relationship to the mirror, however, cannot be separated iconographically from the pearls, which, like mirror reflections, had numerous metaphorical associations, both positive and negative.[6] As highly prized, worldly possessions they were linked symbolically with human vanity; even guileful "Vrouw Wereld" ["Lady World"] was said to be bedecked with pearls.[7] The white, flawless luster of the pearl, however, was equally associated with faith, purity, and virginity.[8]

One of the most remarkable aspects of Vermeer's genius is the elusiveness of his meaning, especially in the genre paintings, which are so carefully conceived. Vermeer avoided making overtly didactic statements. Rather than use explicit gestures or objects with unambiguous iconographic meaning, he conveyed meaning through mood. The calm serenity of the woman as she stands in bright daylight, poised almost as a priest holding the Host during the Eucharist, dismisses any possibility that Vermeer had conceived this image in a negative light. The gesture, mirror, and pearls together form a positive sense of wholeness, truthfulness, and purity.

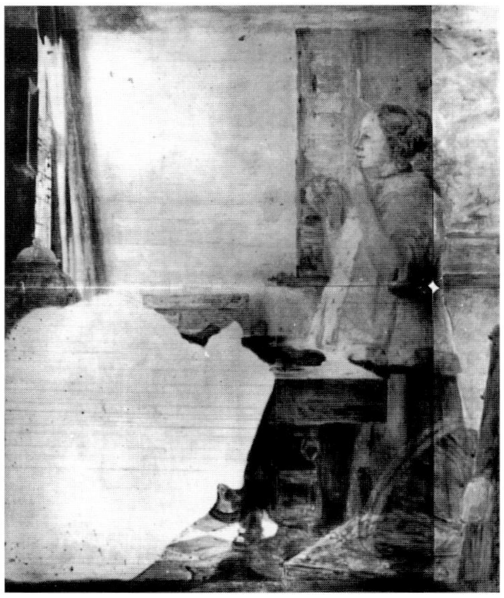

fig. 2. Neutron autoradiograph, *Woman with a Pearl Necklace*

Technical examination of the painting reveals significant pentimenti, indicating many careful refinements to the composition. Neutron autoradiography shows that Vermeer originally included a musical instrument, probably a lute, on the chair in the foreground (fig. 2). An even more startling discovery, however, is that Vermeer originally planned to include a wall map, similar to that in *The Art of Painting* (page 68, fig. 2), behind the woman on the rear wall. Finally, this examination technique revealed that the dark cloth on the table covered less of the tile floor under the table.

The change in the shape of the cloth eliminated much of the light area beneath the table, leaving only the shape of one table leg to orient the viewer. As a result of this alteration the viewer's attention is focused more exclusively on the light-filled space above. While the elimination of the map and lute also simplifies the composition, it may also be related to thematic reasons. The map, representing the physical world, and the musical instrument, referring to sensual love, would have given a context for interpreting the mirror and the pearls negatively rather than positively. Indeed, the sensual, earthy connotations are similar to those associated with images of "Vrouw Wereld".[9] By removing the map and lute he transformed the character of the image into a poetic one evoking the ideals of a life lived with purity and truth.

Although *Woman with a Pearl Necklace* has elicited great admiration throughout its history, none was more enamored of it than Thoré-Bürger, who described the painting as "delicious," after he acquired it around 1860.[10] Later, he proudly recalled that while the work was in his possession it had drawn the admiration of Ludwig Knaus (1829–1910), a celebrated painter of genre scenes, who looked to Holland's Golden Age for his inspiration. Knaus, who was well acquainted with the industrialist and collector Barthold Suermondt (1818–1887), whom he joined in visits to art dealers and museums,[11] probably convinced his friend to buy this painting when Thoré-Bürger sold it in 1868. The picture became

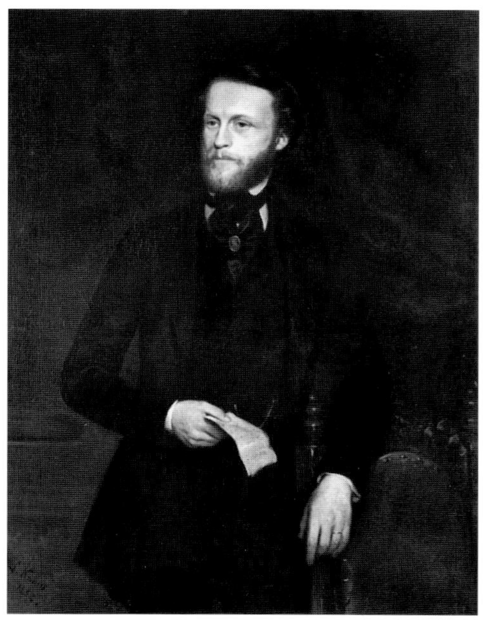

fig. 3. Ludwig Knaus, *Portrait of Barthold Suermondt*, oil on canvas, Suermondt Ludwig Museum, Aachen

the sensation of the Suermondt Gallery, which was particularly popular with artists from all over Germany.

The son of a Utrecht mint master, Suermondt had amassed a fortune in Belgium before settling in Aachen, where he assembled an extensive art collection. His friend and connoisseur Carel Vosmaer had this to say of Suermondt's aggressive manner of collecting: "His fortune allowed him to indulge his passion, and once he wanted something, he never let go."[12] The Berlin museum director Gustav Waagen wrote a catalogue for the "Galerie Suermondt" that appeared in 1860 with a foreword by Thoré-Bürger.[13] In 1874 this collection – the largest private one of the time – was sold to the royal museum in Berlin.

The early history of the painting can be traced back to Amsterdam in the seventeenth and early nineteenth centuries. There it had first been auctioned in 1696 as part of the Jacob Dissius collection (see page 53). The winning bid on "A Grooming ditto [young lady], very handsome by ditto [J vander Meer van Delft]" was only thirty guilders.[14]

In 1809 a description of the picture read: "In a furnished Room stands a graceful young Lady at a table...who seems to be Grooming herself...this charming scene is one of the most naturally and meticulously painted [works] by this famous master."[15] The collection in question had been "assembled with skill over many years" by the Amsterdam collector Johannes Caudri (1725–1809), "In his lifetime [the] Oldest Paymaster of the former East-Indies Company." He died without issue, so that his collection went to public auction.[16]

After being described in laudatory terms in sale catalogues of 1811 and 1856, the painting appeared in France, where thanks to Thoré-Bürger, interest in the "forgotten" painter from Delft had been revived. Thoré himself acquired the *Woman with a Pearl Necklace* out of the collection of the lithographer Henri Grevedon (1776–1860).[17] Thoré presumably bought the painting at Grevedon's death in 1860, and, as mentioned above, sold it in Brussels in 1868.[18] Later, when Suermondt sold it, it became one of the proud possessions of the Staatliche Museen.

1. Van Veen 1608, 126–127. In an emblem entitled "Out of sight out of mynde" Cupid gazes at his own reflection in a mirror. The accompanying text provides the moral: "The glasse doth shew the face whyle thereon one doth look, /But gon, it doth another in lyke manner shew, / Once beeing turn'd away forgotten is the view, / So absence hath bin cause the louer loue forsook."
2. Walsh 1973, unpaginated, and Slatkes 1981, 53, associated the painting with the theme of vanitas. Kelch 1988, identified the mirror as an attribute of "Superbia" [Pride], and associated the woman with this vice. I would like to thank Jan Kelch for providing me with a typescript of his lecture.
3. This opinion was also expressed by De Jongh 1975/1976, 84.
4. Ripa 1644, 622 ("Prudenza. Wijsheyt... "Het spiegelen bediet de kennisse zijns selven, konnende niemand zijne eygene saecken rechten, soo hy zijne eygene gebreken niet kent."); 590 (Verita. Waerheyt... En de Spiegel bediet, dat de Waerheyt, als nu, in haere Volkomentheyt is, als wanneer, gelijck geseyt is, het verstand sich vast maeckte mette verstandelijcke dingen: gelijck de Spiegel goed is, wanneer zy de waerachtige gestaltenisse van de saecke vertoont, die aldaer uytblinckt...).
5. Van Veen 1608, 6. "Euen as the perfect glasse doth rightly shew the face, / The louer must appear right as hee is in deed, / For in the law of loue hath loyaltie decreed, / That falshood with true loue must haue no byding place."
6. For an excellent discussion of the multiple associations given to the pearl in Dutch literary and pictorial traditions, see De Jongh 1975/1976.
7. De Jongh 1975/1976, 82. Both G. A. Bredero and Joost van den Vondel described "Vrouw Wereld" as wearing pearls.
8. De Jongh 1975/1976, 88, has noted that the great Dutch poet and playwright Joost van den Vondel used the pearl as a token of the guileful "Dame World," a symbol of faith, and then of chastity.
9. For a discussion of Jan Miense Molenaer's *Vrouw Wereld*, see Eddy de Jongh in Amsterdam 1976, 176–179, cat. 43.
10. Thoré-Bürger 1869, 171: "Cette jeune fille en caraco citron, sur le fond de lambris pâle, d'un ton gris-perle, est délicieuse."
11. Thieme/Becker, 20: 570–574.
12. Vosmaer 1887, 97–98: "Zijn vermogen vergunde hem aan zijn hartstocht te voldoen en hij liet niet los als hij iets hebben wilde." See also Amsterdam 1989, 61–62.
13. Thoré-Bürger/Waagen 1860.
14. Hoet 1752–1770, 1: 36, no. 36: "Een Paleerende dito [Juffrouw], seer fraey van dito [J vander Meer van Delft].
15. Sale catalogue, Amsterdam, 6 September 1809, 14, no. 42: "In een gemeubileerde Kamer staat eene bevallige jonge Dame voor een tafel...en schijnt zich te Paleeren... dit bevallig tafreel is een der natuurlijkste en alleruitvoerigst gepenceelden van deze beroemde Meester" (Lugt no. 7632).
16. Sale catalogue, Amsterdam, 6 September 1809, title page: "in vele jaren met kunde bijeen verzameld" and "In leeven Oudste Soldy-Boekhouder der voormalige Oost-Indische Compagnie." The dates have been taken from an undated manuscript (Centraal Bureau voor Genealogie, The Hague).
17. Thoré-Bürger 1866, 559, no. 33. Thieme/Becker, 15: 15; Henri Grevedon (not Grévedon or Crevedon) literally grew up in the Louvre, where his father lived in an official residence.
18. Sale catalogue, Brussels, 22 April 1868, 25–26, no. 49 (Lugt no. 30452) (bought by Sedelmeyer for BF3500, according to the Le Roy index cards, RKD, The Hague, no. 157).

COLLECTION CATALOGUES

Staatliche Museen Berlin 1883, 271, no. 912 B; Staatliche Museen Berlin 1891, 167, no. 912 B; Staatliche Museen Berlin 1921, 279, no. 912 B; Staatliche Museen Berlin 1975, 453–454, no. 912 B and ill.; Staatliche Museen Berlin 1986, 78, 347, no. 881 and ill.

LITERATURE

Hoet 1752–1770, 1: 36, no. 36; Thoré-Bürger 1866, 326–328, 459, 463, 558–559, no. 33 and ill.; Thoré-Bürger 1869, 171; Lemcke 1878, 19; Havard 1888, 38, no. 36; Hofstede de Groot 1907–1928, 1: 596, no. 20; Plietzsch 1911, 47, 89, 114, no. 5 and ill. 11; Eisler 1916, 263–264 and ill. 28; Hale 1937, 76, 81, 84–86, 106, 114, 142, 175, 187–189, 196 and pl. 9; De Vries 1939, 46, 87, no. 24 and ill. 49; Blum 1946, 175, no. 33; Van Thienen 1949, 22, no. 21 and ill. 21; Swillens 1950, 56, no. 17, 72, 78, 81, 84–85, 87–88, 118, 176 and pl. 17; Gowing 1952, 68 n. 5, 77 n. 4, 134, no. 19 and ill. 43; Goldscheider 1958, 141, no. 19 and ills. 48–49; Gerson 1967, cols. 743–744; Klessmann 1971, 50; Blankert 1975, 36, 62–63, 71, 82, 147, no. 13 and pl. 13; Blankert 1978, 25, 42–43, 49, 54, 77 n. 48, 160, no. 13 and pl. 13; Slatkes 1981, 52–53, 55, 60, 74 and ill.; Wheelock 1981, 25, 110, 124, 134, and pl. 24; Aillaud 1986, 46, 49, 57, 112–114, 181, no. 13, and pl. 13; Wheelock 1988, 84–85, 104 and ill. 19; Montias 1989, 184, 191, 256 and ill. 43; Nash 1991, 25, 29, 101–103 and ill.; Blankert 1992, 46, 51, 58, 85, 114, 116, 126, 140, 163, 181–182, no. 13, pl. 13 and ill. 89; Wheelock 1995, 102, 105, 177, and ill. A17

13

A Lady Writing

c. 1665

inscribed on the bottom of the frame of the still life: *IVMeer* (IVM in ligature)

oil on canvas, 45 x 39.9 (17¾ x 15¾)

National Gallery of Art, Washington, Gift of Harry Waldron Havemeyer and Horace Havemeyer, Jr., in memory of their father, Horace Havemeyer

PROVENANCE

(?) Pieter Claesz van Ruijven, Delft, before 1674; (?) Maria de Knuijt, Widow Van Ruijven, Delft, 1674–1681; (?) Magdalena van Ruijven and Jacob Dissius, Delft, 1681–1682; Jacob Dissius (with his father Abraham Dissius, 1685–1694), Delft, 1682–1695; Dissius sale, Amsterdam, 16 May 1696, no. 35 (*f*63); J. van Buren, The Hague; Van Buren sale, The Hague, 7 November 1808, no 22; Cornelis Jan Luchtmans, Rotterdam, 1808–1816; Luchtmans sale, Rotterdam, 20 April 1816, no. 90 (*f*70); F. Kamermans, Rotterdam, by 1819; Kamermans sale, Rotterdam, 3 October 1825, no. 70 (*f*305 to Lelie); Reydon sale, Amsterdam, 5 April 1827, no. 26 (to De Robiano); François-Xavier, Count De Robiano, Brussels, 1827–1837; De Robiano sale, Brussels, 1 May 1837, no. 436 (BF 400 to Héris); Ludovic, Count De Robiano, Brussels, 1837–1887; Heirs De Robiano, 1888–1906; [J. & A. LeRoy, Brussels, 1907]; J. Pierpont Morgan, New York, 1907–1913 (bought for £100,000 from G.S. Hellman); J. Pierpont Morgan, Jr. (between 1935–1939, on consignment with M. Knoedler and Co., New York), New York, 1913–1940; Sir Harry Oakes, Nassau, Bahamas, 1940–1943; Lady Eunice Oakes, Nassau, Bahamas, 1943–1946; [M. Knoedler and Co., New York, 1946]; Horace Havemeyer, New York, 1946–1956; by inheritance to Harry Waldron Havemeyer and Horace Havemeyer, Jr., New York, 1956–1962; National Gallery of Art, Washington, 1962 (gift of Harry Waldron Havemeyer and Horace Havemeyer, Jr. in memory of their father, transferred in 1966)

EXHIBITIONS

Brussels 1873, 76, no. 264; New York 1909, 137, no. 136; Rotterdam 1935, 37, no. 86a; New York 1939, 195, no. 399, pl. 72; New York 1941, 18–19, no. 17; New York 1942, 89 and 159, no. 68, ill.; New York 1946, no. 15, ill.; Paris 1976, no catalogue; Leningrad 1976; Tokyo 1987, no. 86; Saint Petersburg 1989, 34, no. 14; The Hague 1990, 456–462, no. 67, ill. (with extensive literature); Frankfurt 1993, 314–316, no. 85

TECHNICAL DESCRIPTION

The support is a fine, plain-weave linen with a thread count of 12 x 14 per cm². Remnants of the original tacking edges survive, and the canvas has been glue-lined.

The ground appears to be a single layer of a warm, light ocher color, containing chalk, (plant?) black, red, and yellow iron oxide (perhaps burnt sienna and yellow ocher), and lead white.[1]

The brushwork of the final paint layers is very thin, except in the lighter tones. Thicker paint has been used only in the form of rounded dots for the highlights. Two preparations of lead-tin yellow were used in the yellow jacket: one coarsely ground, and the other more finely ground and paler, used for the highlights on the shoulder pleats. X-radiography and infrared reflectography indicate that Vermeer made an alteration to the angle of the quill and to some of the fingers holding it.

In a dimly lit interior, a young woman looks up from her letter and stares out at the viewer. Holding the sheet of paper with one hand and a quill pen with the other, it appears that she has just been interrupted, yet neither her pose nor her expression indicates a recent disturbance.

At once direct and yet suggestive, this painting represents a subject frequently found in Dutch painting, and one that occurs in two other works by Vermeer, including *Mistress and Maid*, c. 1667–1668 (page 58, fig. 14), and *Lady Writing a Letter with Her Maid* (cat. 19). Within the thematic traditions of Dutch art, the subject of a woman writing a letter almost always relates to love, an association conveyed in many ways. Gerard ter Borch (1617–1681), for example, placed his letter-writer before a bed, an allusion to the letter's romantic content (fig. 1). Vermeer, in his two other depictions of letter-writers, included a maid, who either delivers the letter or awaits a reply. The narrative content of *A Lady Writing*, however, is negligible. The only indication that its theme has a romantic connotation is the dark and barely distinguishable painting hanging on the back wall. It appears to be a still life with musical instruments, including a bass-viola.[2] As musical instruments often carry implications of love, it may be understood that the letter she writes is directed to an absent lover.[3]

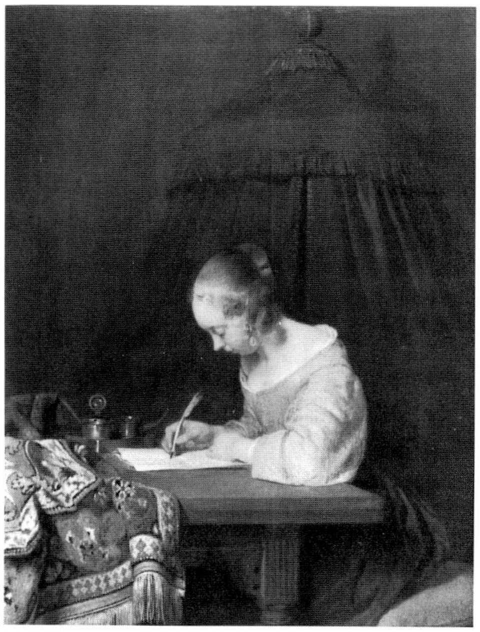

fig. 1. Gerard ter Borch, *Letter-writer*, c. 1655, oil on panel, Mauritshuis, The Hague

Vermeer organized his compositional elements so as to enhance the tranquility of the scene. The woman rests her arms gently on the writing table and turns easily toward the viewer, her chair angled toward the picture plane. Other than the chair and a fold in the blue drapery that parallels the woman's arm, few diagonals exist. Vermeer provided a horizontal and vertical framework for the woman's form by means of the foreground table and the painting on the rear wall. Not only does the dark form of the painting provide a chiaroscuro contrast for the woman's head, its size, which extends two-thirds of the way across the background wall, relates proportionally to the width of the composition. Other proportional relationships further indicate the care with which Vermeer conceived his composition. The width of the wall to the right of the picture, for example, is equal to the height of the table, which is half the distance between the bottom of the picture on the back wall and the base of the painting.

Although *A Lady Writing* is not dated, its composition and technique, as well as the woman's costume and hairstyle, relate to other of Vermeer's paintings from the mid-1660s. The woman's elegant yellow jacket, for example, is found in *Woman with a Lute*, c. 1664 (page 26, fig. 13), *Woman with a Pearl Necklace*, c. 1664 (cat. 12), and *Mistress and Maid* in the Frick Collection. The ink wells and the decorated casket on the table are similar to those in the Frick

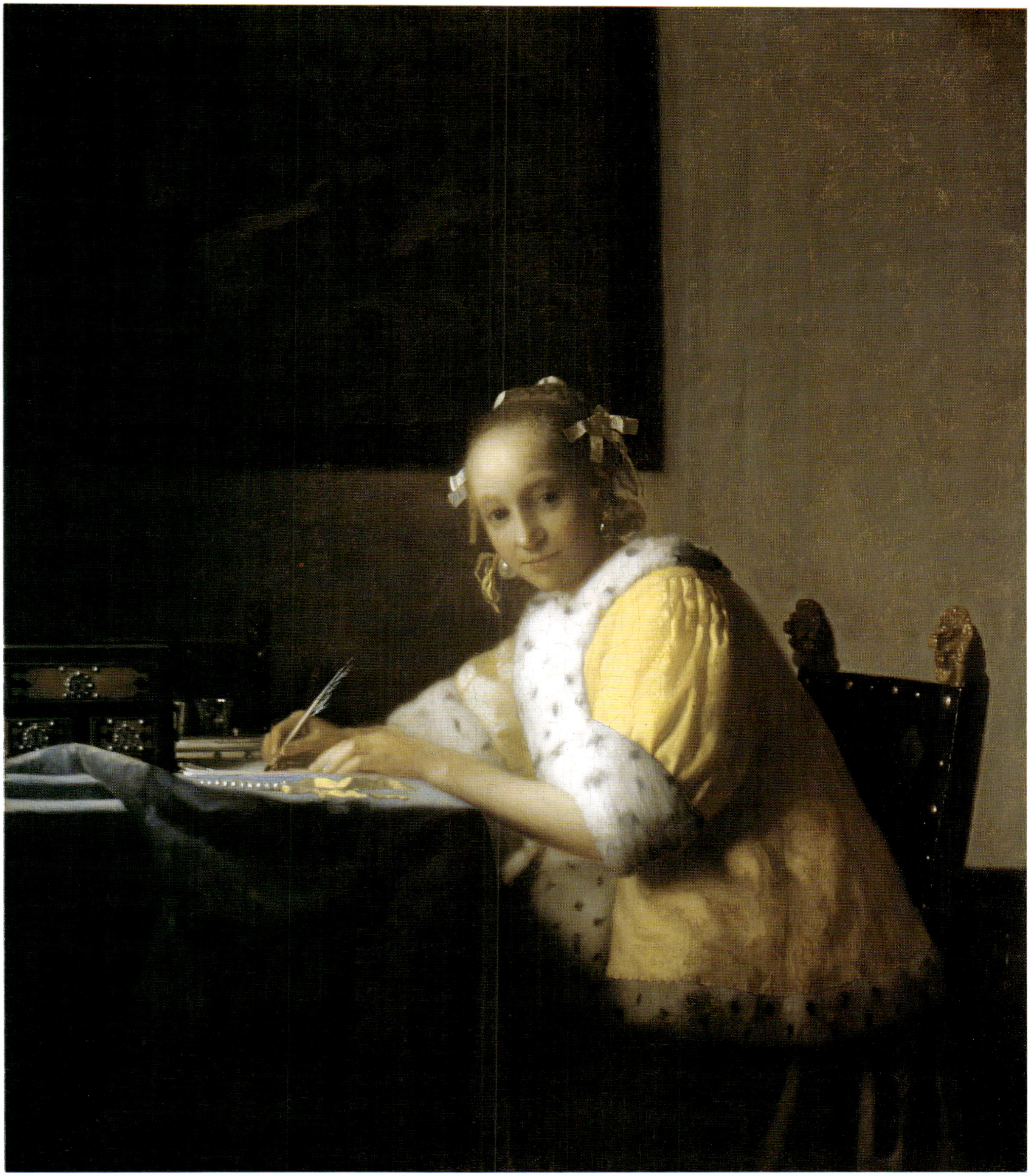

painting. The hairstyle, with a braided chignon and the ribbons tied in bows formed like stars, was popular in the third quarter of the seventeenth century, particularly after the early 1660s.[4]

Vermeer's other depictions of single figures in interiors during the 1660s portray women engaged in some activity, whether it be reading a letter, holding a water jug, or playing a musical instrument. None of these women seems remotely aware of the presence of a viewer peering into their private worlds. *A Lady Writing* differs profoundly in that the woman not only looks directly at the viewer, but has also interrupted her activity, the writing of a letter.

Just why Vermeer chose to break from the successful compositional formula he had already established is not known. One would expect the artist, like Ter Borch before him, to depict the woman concentrating upon the letter she was writing. Perhaps Vermeer felt that such a composition would have conformed too closely to established iconographic traditions.
By depicting the woman looking out at the viewer Vermeer introduced an added component to the letter writing theme: the arrival of an unseen visitor to this quiet and ordered private chamber. The woman's calm demeanor as she looks up and pauses in the midst of her letter, however, does not indicate surprise or agitation. On the contrary, the only acknowledgment of the viewer's presence is the hint of a smile crossing her face. Indeed, even with his innovative adaptation of the letter-writing theme, which lends itself to a narrative encounter, Vermeer subordinated all physical action to focus upon the woman's reflective state of being.

One other possible explanation for the woman's striking pose is that this may be a portrait. By means of the letter-writing theme he achieved a convincing sense of naturalism that formal portraits often lacked. Although no documentary evidence confirms that Vermeer painted portraits, certain compositional characteristics in this work seem to reinforce this hypothesis. Vermeer has posed the woman in the foreground of the painting, thereby enhancing her physical and psychological presence. Her distinctive features – a large forehead and long, narrow nose – are portrait-like characteristics that resemble those of *Portrait of a Young Woman* (page 75, fig. 13), and are not as idealized as those of women in his other genre scenes of the same period. Finally, her form is modeled with delicate brushstrokes that articulate her features. The subtle modulations in the colors of her flesh are particularly evident since the recent restoratation of the painting.

The problem of identifying the sitter, however, seems insurmountable. The most likely possibility is that she is his wife, Catharina Bolnes, who, having been born in 1631, would have been in her early-to-mid thirties when Vermeer painted this work. While it is difficult to judge the age of models in paintings, such an age does seem appropriate for this figure. Little else, however, confirms this hypothesis. Although the yellow satin jacket with white ermine trim is almost certainly the same jacket mentioned in the inventory of household effects made after Vermeer's death,[5] it is worn by a different model in *Mistress and Maid.*

The earliest certain reference to *A Lady Writing* is the 1696 Dissius sale in Amsterdam, where the painting was described as "a writing young lady, very good, by the same [J. vander Meer]."[6] It is not known who bought the painting at the sale. More than a hundred years later *A Lady Writing* was part of the collection of J. van Buren, who was Bailiff of Noordwijkerhout, an area between between Leiden and Haarlem. In 1808 his substantial collection of books, miniatures, prints, drawings and paintings was auctioned in The Hague. The catalogue lavished praise on Vermeer's painting: "A fetching young woman dressed in yellow satin [trimmed] with fur...exceedingly lovely, meticulously and masterfully painted by the Delft van der Meer...very rare."[7]

The painting was bought by (or for) Cornelis Jan Luchtmans (1777–1860), a physician in Rotterdam, where, in 1816, he sold a number of his paintings.[8] The Vermeer was presumably bought by F. Kamermans, an aged Rotterdam shipbuilder. In 1819 the painting was seen at Kamerman's home by Sir John Murray during his journey through Holland, who described it as being "remarkable for its softness."[9]

One of the owners after Kamermans was François-Xavier, Count De Robiano (1778–1836), who in 1816 became chamberlain to King William I in Brussels. In 1830, shortly after he acquired this Vermeer painting, he sided with the Belgian patriots and fell out of royal favor.[10] When the collection of the Belgian count was auctioned in 1837, his eldest son, Ludovic, bought back the painting. After his death in 1887, the painting passed to his sister (d. 1900) and her husband, Gustave, Baron de Senzeille, who kept the painting until his death in 1906.[11]

The work disappeared from public view, but in 1907 it turned up in New York, where it was soon acquired by J. Pierpont Morgan, Sr. (1837–1913) (fig. 2).[12] Morgan's acquisition of the painting has provided posterity with a fascinating anecdote about his collecting acumen. The antique dealer G. S. Hellman, who brought the canvas to the collector's attention, noticed to his amazement that Morgan had never heard

Vermeer's name. While Morgan gazed at the picture, Hellman informed him about the painter, his place in the history of art, and the amounts that were then paid for one of his paintings. Morgan then asked the price. "One hundred thousand dollars," said the dealer and the deal was concluded.[13] After Morgan acquired the painting he generously lent it to the Metropolitan Museum of Art, where it was on view until his death in 1913.[14]

After Morgan's death the canvas came into the possession of his son, who once more put it on the market. The painting was eventually sold in 1940 to Sir Harry Oakes (1874–1943) in Nassau in the Bahamas, who, however, died shortly thereafter.[15] In 1946 his widow, Lady Eunice Oakes, sold the painting to Horace Havemeyer (1886–1956), son of renowned collectors Louisine and Horace Havemeyer.[16] In 1962 his two sons, Horace, Jr. and Waldron donated the painting to the National Gallery of Art. It was one of the last authentic paintings by Vermeer to move from private ownership into the public domain.[17]

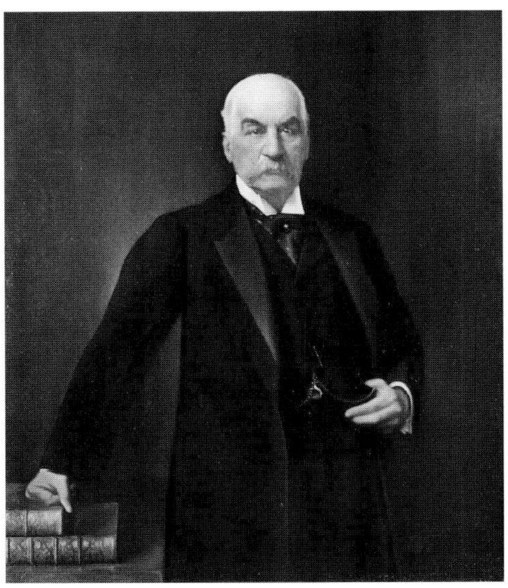

fig. 2. Carlos Baca-Flor, *Portrait of J. Pierpont Morgan*, c. 1914, oil on canvas, The Metropolitan Museum of Art, New York

1. Robert L. Feller, Carnegie Mellon University, Pittsburgh, identified the elements in the ground. His report dated 26 June 1974 is available in the scientific research department, National Gallery of Art.
2. Boström 1951, suggests that the painting may have been by Cornelis van der Meulen (1642–1692). The evidence, however, is not sufficient to sustain an attribution. A painting depicting "a bass viol with a skull" is listed in the inventory of Vermeer's possessions after his death in 1676. See Montias 1989, 340, doc. 364.
3. This thematic association was first suggested by De Mirimonde 1961, 40. For emblematic literature relating musical instruments to love see De Jongh 1967, 50–51.
4. This information was kindly supplied by A. M. Louise E. Mulder-Erketens, keeper of textiles, Rijksmuseum, Amsterdam,
5. Montias 1989, 339, doc. 364: "a yellow satin mantle with white fur trimming."
6. Montias 1993, 402, doc. 439: "Een Schryvende Juffrouw heel goed van denzelven [J. vander Meer]."
7. Sale catalogue, The Hague, 7 November 1808, 264, no. 22 (Lugt no. 7474), first mentioned in Blankert 1988, 210: "Een bevallig vrouwtje in 't geel satyn met bond gekleed .... uitmuntend fraai, uitvoerig en meesterlyk gepenseeld door de Delfsche van der Meer...zeer raar."
8. Sale catalogue, Rotterdam, 20 April 1816, 26, no. 90 (Lugt no. 8868).
9. Murray 1819–1823, 29.
10. Concerning De Robiano, see The Hague 1990, 458–459, 461 nn. 3, 10. During his employment in the Netherlands he had frequented auctions and bought Dutch paintings of the Golden Age. At the Reydon sale, for instance, he bid successfully on a second Vermeer, which later turned out to be a Jacob Vrel. See sale catalogue, Amsterdam, 5 April 1827, 6, no. 27 (Lugt no. 11405); The Hague 1990, 461 n. 11.
11. The Hague 1990, 458, 461 nn. 4–7: the reconstruction of this nineteenth-century history was largely the work of Marjolein de Boer.
12. For Morgan as collector, see Rigby 1944, 282–285.
13. Allen 1949, 199; Canfield 1974, 107.
14. Shortly thereafter, Cornelis Hofstede de Groot saw the Vermeer in the Metropolitan Museum of Art and noted: "Is het schilderij dat zoolang zoek is geweest. Het is het vrouwtje, dat den beschouwer aankijkt" ([It] is the painting that has been lost for so long. It is the little woman who looks out at the observer); The Hague 1990, 458–459, 461 nn. 8–9.
15. He was apparently murdered by the Mafia because he would not tolerate a casino on the island. See Highsmith 1976, 853; De Marigny 1990; The Hague 1990, 460, 462 nn. 31–33.
16. Constable 1964, 76–79.
17. *The Lady Writing a Letter with Her Maid* (cat. 19), which was stolen in 1986 and only recently recovered, is now the property of the National Gallery of Ireland.

COLLECTION CATALOGUES

National Gallery Washington 1975, 362–363, and ill.; National Gallery Washington 1985, 421, and ill.; National Gallery Washington 1995, 377–382 (with extensive literature)

LITERATURE

Hoet 1752–1770, 1: 36, no. 35; Murray 1819–1823, 29; Thoré-Bürger 1866, 564, no. 40; Havard 1888, 38, no. 43; Hofstede de Groot 1907–1928, 1: 603, no. 36; Plietzsch 1911, 118, no. 31 (36); Hale 1937, 101, no. 35, 226; De Vries 1939, 46–47, 88, no. 26 and ill. 50; Blum 1946, 179, no. 40; Swillens 1950, 53, no. 8, 67, 78, 82, 87, 89, 108, 155 and pl. 8; Goldscheider 1958, 141–142, no. 20 and ill. 50; Blankert 1975, 11, 36, 82–84, 109, 153–154, no. 20 and pl. 20; Blankert 1978, 10, 25, 54, 73, 164, no. 20 and pls. 20–20a; Slatkes 1981, 70–71 and ill.; Wheelock 1981, 124–127 and ills. 31–32; Brown 1984, 139–140 and ill.; Aillaud 1986, 11, 46, 52, 85, 132, 189–190, no. 20, and pl. 22; Wheelock 1988, 22, 96–97, no. 25 and ill.; Montias 1989, 191–192, 196, 256, 266 and ill. 44; Nash 1991, 19; Blankert 1992, 11, 46, 52, p. 189–190, no. 20 and pl. 22; Wheelock 1995, 145, 179, and ill. A22

14

The Girl with the Red Hat

c. 1665
inscribed upper left-center: *IVM* in ligature
oil on panel, 22.8 x 18 (9 x 7 1/16)

National Gallery of Art, Washington, Andrew W. Mellon Collection

PROVENANCE

(?) Pieter Claesz van Ruijven, Delft before 1674; (?) Maria de Knuijt, Widow Van Ruijven, Delft 1674–1681; (?) Magdalena van Ruijven and Jacob Dissius, Delft, 1681–1682; (?) Jacob Dissius (with his father Abraham Dissius 1685–1694), Delft, 1682–1695; (?) Dissius sale, Amsterdam, 16 May 1696, possibly no. 38 (*f* 36) or 39 (*f* 17) or no. 40 (*f* 17); LaFontaine sale, Paris, 10 December 1822, no. 28 (Ffr 200); Louis Marie, Baron Atthalin, Colmar, 1823–1856; Gaston, Baron Laurent-Atthalin, Limay (Seine et Oise), 1856–1911; Baroness Laurent-Atthalin, Paris, 1911–1925; [Knoedler Galleries, London and New York, 1925]; Andrew Mellon, Washington, 1925–1932; The A. W. Mellon Educational and Charitable Trust, Pittsburgh, 1932–1937; National Gallery of Art, Washington, 1937

EXHIBITIONS

New York 1925, no. 1; New York 1928, no. 12

TECHNICAL DESCRIPTION

The support is probably oak, with a vertical grain. A slightly larger cradle 24.3 x 19.2 (9 9/16 x 7 9/16) and wooden collar protect the edges of the panel. X-radiography shows, over the white chalk ground, a portrait of a man with a large hat. *The Girl with the Red Hat* was painted directly over this earlier image (see below). The painting is in remarkably good condition, with only slight abrasion to the thin glazes of the face and a few scattered minor losses.

The Girl with the Red Hat, widely admired for both its intimacy and its immediacy, is small even by Vermeer's standards. The girl appears large in scale, however, because of her close proximity to the picture plane. As she turns and rests her arm on the back of a chair, she communicates directly with the viewer, her mouth half opened, her eyes lit with expectancy.

The artist's use of color is exquisite, in both its compositional and psychological aspects. Setting the figure against the muted tones of a tapestry backdrop,[1] Vermeer concentrates his major color accents, red and blue, in two distinct areas, the hat and the robe. The intensely warm flame-red bordering the girl's broad, feathered hat dominates, advances, and psychologically activates the image. It heightens the immediacy of the girl's gaze, an effect Vermeer accentuates by subtly casting its orange-red reflection across her face. The blue of the robe is cool and recessive, counter-balancing the red.

Vermeer's sensitivity to the effects of reflected light is seen in the deep purple hue of the underside of the hat, and in the greenish glaze that shades the girl's face. As in *Woman Holding a Balance* (cat. 10), Vermeer adds an inner warmth by painting the blue robe over a reddish-brown ground. He then accents folds with yellow highlights. Finally, Vermeer animates materials by depicting light reflecting from the hat, the blue robe, and the lion-head finials. At the center of the composition, the vivid white of the girl's cravat cradles her face and focuses attention on her expression.

Vermeer's technique in *The Girl with the Red Hat* generally parallels that in his other paintings from the mid-to-late 1660s, particularly *A Lady Writing* (cat. 13). In both examples Vermeer lays thin, semi-transparent glazes over thin paint layers. The rich, feathered effect of the girl's hat, for example, is the result of a succession of semi-transparent strokes of light red and orange over an opaque layer of deeper orange-red paint. Similarly, many of the diffused yellow, white, and light blue highlights on the girl's blue robe are thin, allowing the underlying blue to show through.[2]

Vermeer's technique for painting the light reflections on the lion-head finials is parallel to that in the pearls of *A Lady Writing*, where opaque white highlights are applied over a thinly painted white underlayer. Their smooth transition into the underlying paint suggests that Vermeer may have painted them wet-in-wet. In *The Girl with the Red Hat* Vermeer extensively used the underlying layer to help model the form.

The surety of Vermeer's modeling is particularly evident in the white cravat, which he achieves by stroking away parts of the thick impasto with a blunt tool. To lend animation and vitality to the figure, Vermeer paints colored highlights in the mouth and left eye. He accents the shaded lower lip with a small pink highlight, and enlivens the pupil of her left eye with a light green highlight. He used this technique in the keys of the musical instrument lying on the table in *The Concert* (page 17, fig. 1), and in the colored yarn of *The Lacemaker* (cat. 17).

Despite similarities in approach between this painting and other works from the mid-to-late 1660s, *The Girl with the Red Hat* is undeniably different. With the possible exception of *Young Girl with a Flute* (cat. 23), Vermeer painted no other works on panel.[3] It would be quite understandable, however, for Vermeer to paint such a small bust, or *tronie*, on panel. Indeed, documents confirm that Vermeer painted *tronien*.[4] The descriptions of these *tronien* – in "Turkish fashion" in the inventory of his

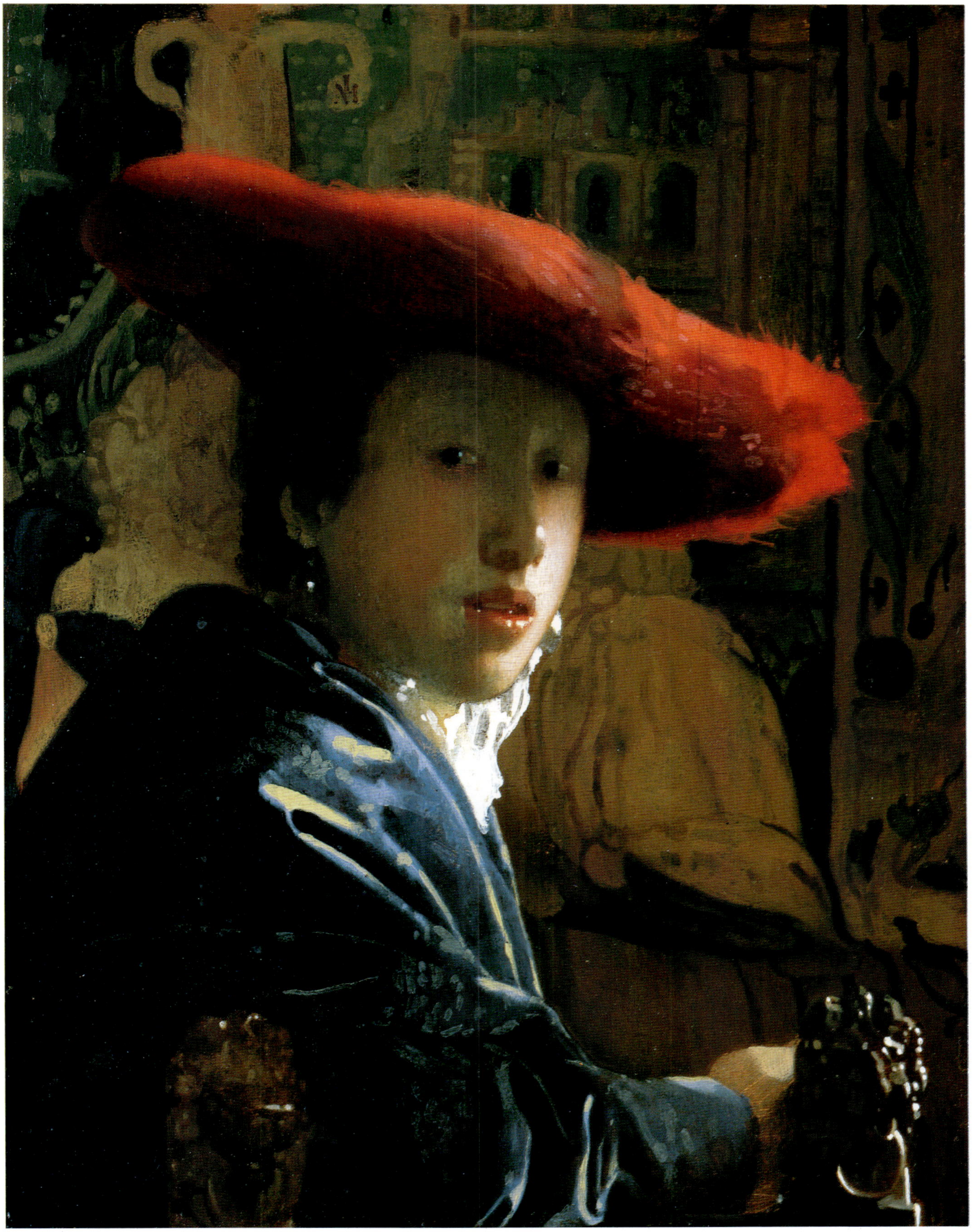

effects, and in "antique dress" in the Dissius sale – could also apply to the exotic costume worn by this young girl.[5]

Another major difference is the remarkable spontaneity and informality of *The Girl with the Red Hat*. Even *Girl with a Pearl Earring* (cat. 15) seems studied and cerebral in comparison. To a certain degree the fluid execution seems related to Vermeer's use of a camera obscura. The idea that Vermeer might have used this device while painting *The Girl with the Red Hat* was convincingly argued by Charles Seymour, who demonstrated the affinities between Vermeer's fluid, painterly treatment of the lion-head finial and the unfocused appearances of an image seen in a camera obscura (figs. 1, 2).[6] Seymour further argued that Vermeer exploited this effect both to animate his surface and to distinguish different depths of field.[7]

Seymour, along with others, assumed that Vermeer faithfully recorded models, rooms, and furnishings he saw before him.[8] To the contrary, however, Vermeer's compositions are the products of intense control and refinement. Figures and their environments are subtly interlocked through perspective, proportion, and color. The paintings themselves are evidence that Vermeer's approach must have been the same whether he observed his subject directly or through a camera obscura. Thus, it is most unlikely that he traced its image directly on the panel.[9]

For example, even though Vermeer painted the diffused, specular highlights on the finials in emulation of effects seen in a camera obscura, he creatively embellished other parts of his composition where he seems to have used a similar technique. The diffuse yellow highlights on the girl's blue robes, for example, would not be seen with a camera obscura; rather, unfocused areas of cloth illuminated by intense light would have appeared blurred.

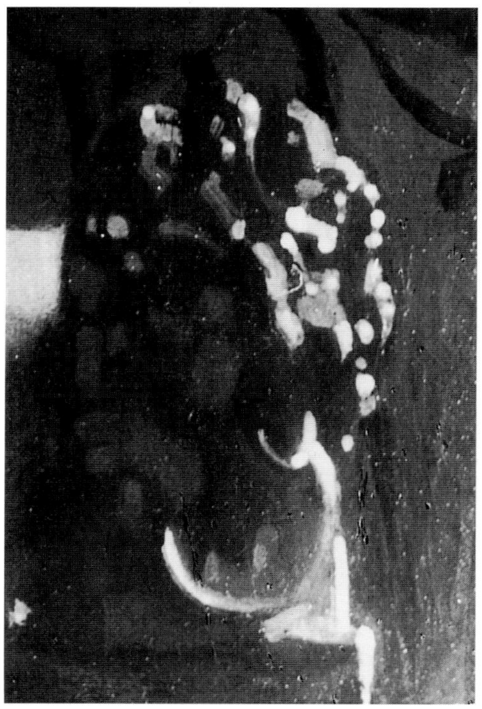

fig. 1. Detail, lion head finial, of *The Girl with the Red Hat*

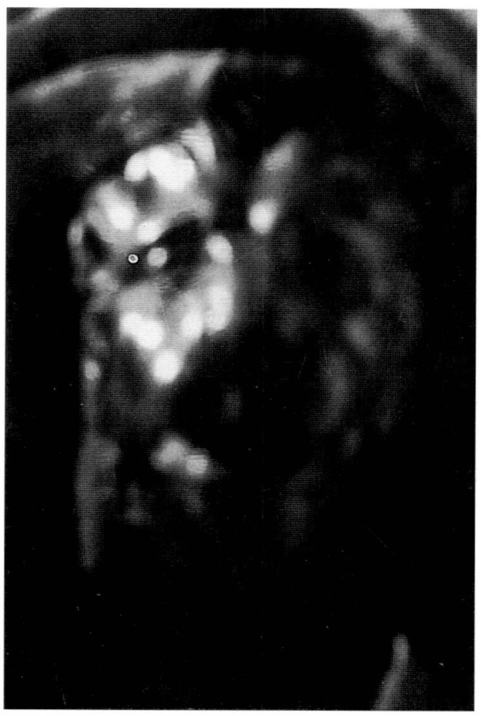

fig. 2. Photograph of lion head finial seen through camera obscura

The most remarkable adjustment Vermeer made in this painting occurs with the lion-head finials. The left finial is much larger than the right one and is angled to the right. The top of the chair, if extended to the left finial, would intersect it above the bottom of the ring that loops through the lion's mouth. The finials, moreover, face the viewer, whereas if they belonged to the girl's chair, they should face her.[10] While some scholars have argued that the position of the finials creates reason to doubt the attribution of the painting, these modifications of reality are consistent with those found in Vermeer's other paintings.[11] The finials, as they are painted, effectively define the foreground plane of the composition, while, by being slightly out of alignment, they allow sufficient space for the girl's arm to rest on the chair's back.

The unusual support may relate to Vermeer's experimental use of the camera obscura. Vermeer's attempt to exploit optical phenomena visible in a camera obscura – intense colors, accentuated contrasts of light and dark, and circles of confusion – suggests that the artist sought to recreate the impression of such an image. He may have decided to paint on a hard, smooth surface to achieve the sheen of an image seen in a camera obscura, traditionally projected onto a ground glass or tautly stretched oiled paper.

The panel Vermeer chose had already been used. An underlying image of a bust-length portrait of a man, upside-down relative to the girl's position, is visible in an x-radiograph (fig. 3). His wide-brimmed hat, and the great flourish of strokes to the right of his face – representing his long, curly hair – are visible with infrared reflectography (fig. 4).[12] The style in which the face is painted is very different from Vermeer's. The face is modeled with a number of rapid, unblended strokes.

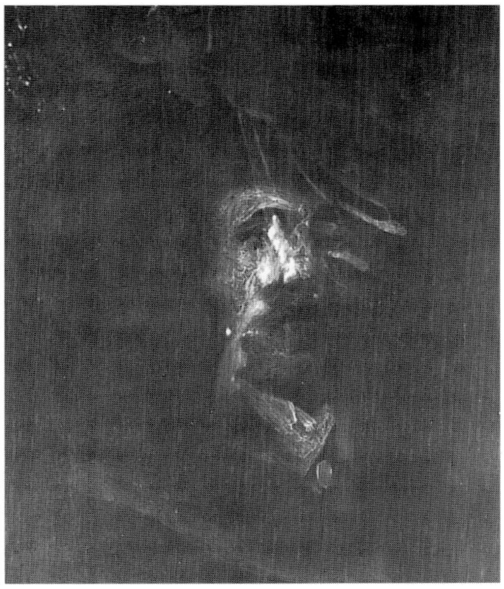

fig. 3. *The Girl with the Red Hat*, x-radiograph

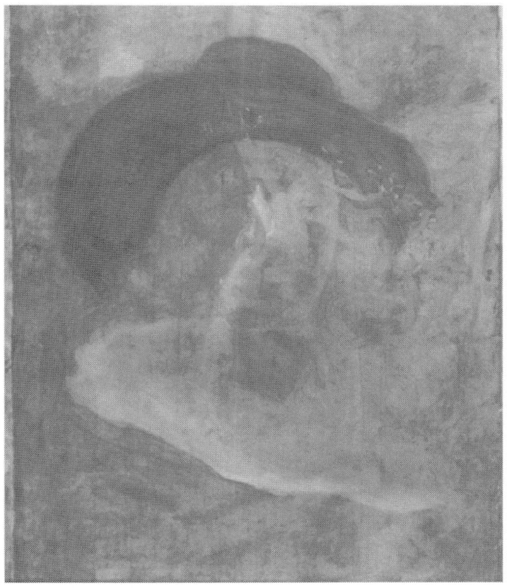

fig. 4. *The Girl with the Red Hat*, infrared reflectogram

Although one cannot attribute a painting solely on the basis of an x-radiograph, the brushstrokes and impasto of the underlying head are similar in style to those found in figure studies by Carel Fabritius (1622–1654) from the late 1640s, such as the *Man with a Helmet* (fig. 5).[13] At his death Vermeer owned two *tronien* by Fabritius.[14] Vermeer could have owned other works by Fabritius, under whom he may have studied.

When Thoré-Bürger made notes in 1866 on a number of Vermeer paintings unknown to him, "To be researched, to be verified, to be studied,"[15] he only knew *The Girl with the Red Hat* from an 1822 sale catalogue. He inaccurately transcribed the text,

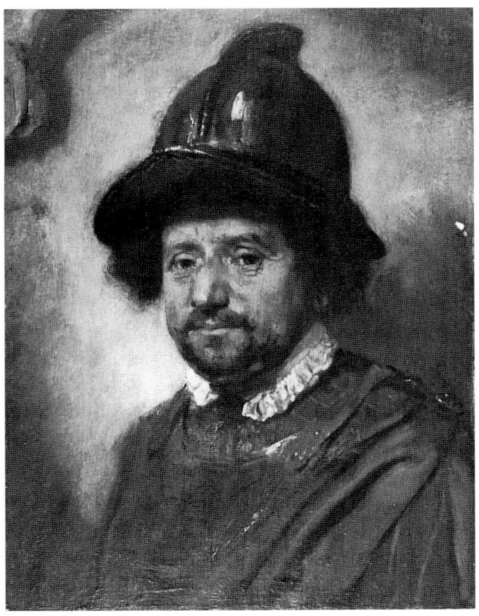

fig. 5. Carel Fabritius, *Man with a Helmet*, c. 1648–1649, oil on panel, Groninger Museum, Groningen

"Young woman portrayed in a little more than bust length" as "Young man portrayed in a little more than bust length." He failed to quote the justifiably laudatory words dedicated to the depiction: "There is in this charming painting everything by which one knows the true painter; the execution is flowing, the color strong, the effect well felt."[16]

Between 10 and 12 December 1822 the Parisian art dealer La Fontaine sold his stock, consisting primarily of paintings of the Dutch and Flemish schools.[17] Despite warm praise, his Vermeer fetched only 200 Francs. Baron Atthalin bought the painting a year after the sale: a clipping with the relevant text from the auction catalogue is still glued to the back of the panel.[18] Louis Marie, Baron Atthalin (1784–1856), a French general and landscape painter, treasured the charming head of a girl hanging in the study of his "hôtel" in Colmar. Baron Gaston Laurent-Atthalin (1848–1911), an adopted son of Louis Marie's sister, inherited the panel which, after his death, came into the possession of his widow. In her Paris apartment Pierre Lavallée, curator at the École Nationale des Beaux-Arts, encountered the painting, which he published in 1925. An unknown Vermeer suddenly became world news.[19]

The periodical *The Connoisseur* at once made itself clear. "It would make a most desirable addition to the [London] National Gallery, where Vermeer is hardly as strongly represented as he might be."[20] Virtually all the press notices and articles in art periodicals spoke enthusiastically of the quality of the rendering.[21] The dealer Knoedler & Co. sold the painting in November 1925 for $290,000 to Andrew W. Mellon (1855–1937),[22] banker and Secretary of the Treasury under three American presidents, who conceived and endowed the National Gallery of Art.

Mellon (fig. 6), like his friend Henry Clay Frick (1849–1919), was a collector of old masters. Frick had already bought his first Vermeer, *Girl Interrupted at Her Music* (page 24, fig. 10), in 1901.[23] Mellon's main criteria for acquiring a painting were that it had to be in good condition and not too dark.[24] He loved "the very human faces of the Dutch Masters."[25] At first Mellon collected for his own pleasure but in 1927 he decided to found a national museum that would have his collection as its core. In 1937, four years after his death, the

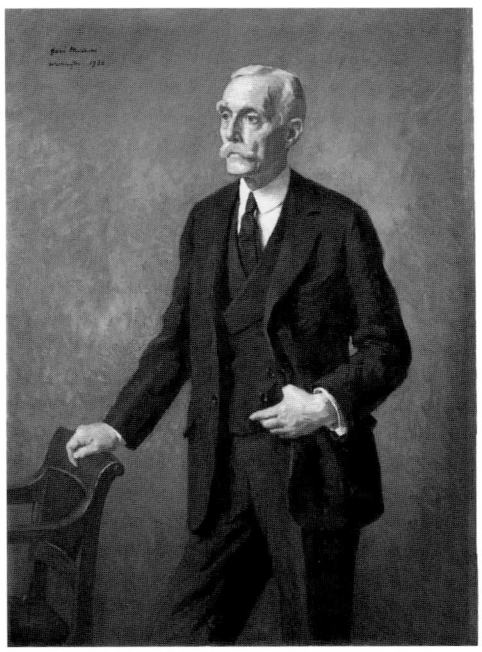

fig. 6. Gari Melchers, *Andrew W. Mellon*, 1930, canvas, National Gallery of Art, Washington, Gift of Donald D. Shepard

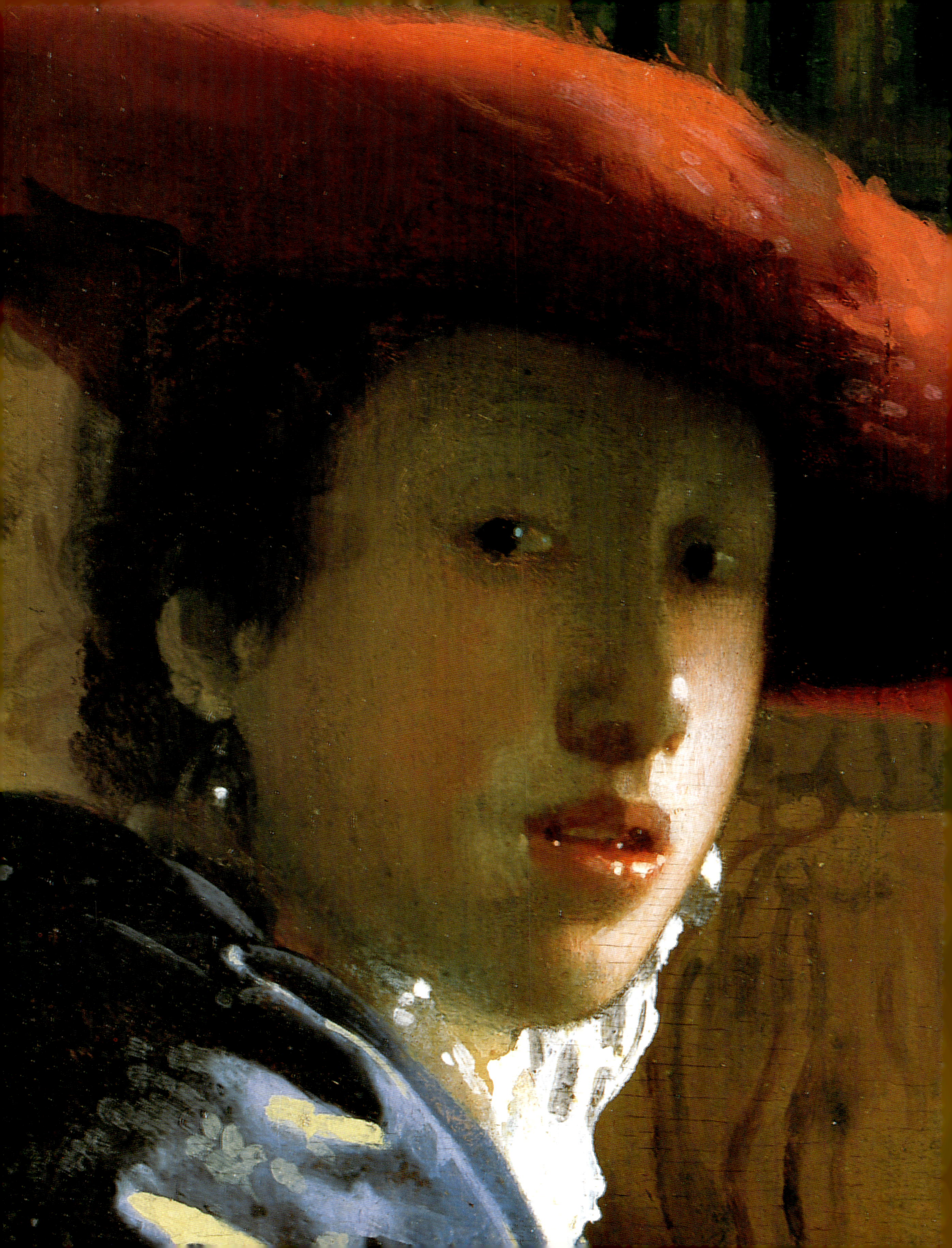

National Gallery of Art opened.[26] *The Girl with the Red Hat*, which he had kept atop the piano in his sumptuous apartment on Massachusetts Avenue in Washington, was the first Vermeer in the new museum.

1. Although only a portion of the tapestry in *The Girl with the Red Hat* is visible, it appears that two rather large-scale figures are depicted behind the girl. The patterned vertical strip on the right is probably the outer border. A. M. Louise E. Muler-Erkelens, Keeper of Textiles, Rijksmuseum, Amsterdam, relates this format to late sixteenth-century tapestries of the southern Netherlands. She also notes that other tapestries in Vermeer's paintings belong to the same period (letter, National Gallery of Art, curatorial files).
2. Under microscopic examination, small pits, or craters, are visible in the yellow paint of these highlights, suggesting that Vermeer may have used an emulsion medium in his paint. Similar pitting occurs in the opaque yellow highlights of *Woman Holding a Balance* (cat. 10) and *A Lady Writing* (cat. 13), although in those two paintings the pits are smaller and less extensive.
3. A number of scholars cite the unusual panel support as one reason for doubting the attribution of these two paintings. The attribution of *The Girl with the Red Hat* to Vermeer has been doubted by Van Thienen 1949, 23. The painting was rejected by Swillens 1950, 65; Blankert 1975, 167; Blankert 1978, 172; Brentjens 1985, 54–58; and Aillaud 1986, 200–201.
4. The term *tronie* (*tronij*, *tronye*, *tronike*) derived from the old French, *trogne*, meaning a character head, in contradistinction to a portrait head. On *tronie* see De Pauw-de Veen 1969, 190–199; Bruyn 1983, 209–210; Paris 1986, 290 n. 21; Ford 1990; and Stuckenbrock 1993, 36–37.
5. Montias 1989, 340, doc. 364; 364, doc. 439. The exotic style of the red hat is quite remarkable, and no exact prototypes are known. A similar hat, however, is worn by Saskia in Rembrandt's portrait from the mid-1630s in the Gemäldegalerie, Cassel (Br. 101). See also the engravings of bust-length men and women Michael Sweerts published in 1656, ill. in Bolton 1985, 96.
6. See Seymour 1964. For another point of view, see page 72 in the present catalogue.
7. Vermeer may also have recognized that the peculiarly soft quality of these unfocused highlights would beautifully express the luminosity of pearls. Thus even in paintings like the *Woman Holding a Balance*, whose genesis probably has little to do with the camera obscura, these optical effects are apparent.
8. This misconception lies at the basis of the interpretation of Vermeer's use of the camera obscura advanced by Fink 1971.
9. As suggested by Seymour 1964.
10. The first art historian to note this discrepancy was Wilenski 1929, 284–285. He hypothesized that the peculiar arrangement of the finials arose as a result of Vermeer's use of a mirror. His reconstruction of Vermeer's painting procedure, however, is untenable.
11. See, for example, the shift in the position of the lower edge of the frame of the Last Judgment in *Woman Holding a Balance*.
12. The infrared reflectogram of *The Girl with the Red Hat* shows only a partial view of the underlying image because of the different transparencies of pigments to infrared radiation. The natural ultramarine of the girl's cloak, for example, is transparent in the near infrared range, whereas the green of the tapestry is not.
13. Groninger Museum, panel, 38.5 x 31 cm.
14. Montias 1989, 339, doc. 364.
15. Thoré-Bürger 1866, 567, no. 47: "A rechercher, à vérifier, à étudier."
16. Sale catalogue, Paris, 10 December 1822, 12, no. 28: "Jeune femme représentée un peu plus qu'en buste" became "Jeune homme représenté un peu plus que'en buste." Also, "Il y a dans ce joli tableau tout ce qui fait connaître le véritable peintre; l'exécution est coulante, la couleur forte, l'effet bien senti" (Lugt no. 10352).
17. Sale catalogue, Paris, 10 December 1822, unpaginated: "Avertissement."
18. New York 1925, unpaginated; the date 1823 is taken from a letter, 8 July 1952 from C. R. Henschel (Knoedler & Co.) to John Walker, then chief curator (National Gallery of Art, curatorial files).
19. Lavallée 1925, 323–324 and ill.; biographical data was taken from DBF, 3: cols. 1430–1431 and IBF, 3: 1283; see also a letter from Baron Laurent-Atthalin, 9 April 1974 (National Gallery of Art, curatorial files).
20. Grundy 1925, 119.
21. See the literature for the year 1925.
22. Hale 1937, 133; the Louvre had wanted to buy the painting as well (according to the letter mentioned in n. 18).
23. Inv. no. 01.1.125; Blankert 1992, 204, no. B2 and ill.
24. Mellon 1949, v.
25. Gregory 1993, 144.
26. Mellon 1949, vi and xiii; see also Finley 1973.

COLLECTION CATALOGUES

Mellon 1949, 94, no. 53, and ill.; National Gallery Washington 1975, 362–363, and ill.; National Gallery Washington 1985, 420 and ill.; National Gallery Washington 1995, 382–387 (with extensive literature)

LITERATURE

Thoré-Bürger 1866, 567, no. 47; Hofstede de Groot 1907–1928, 1: 606, no. 46a; Hale 1913, 359; Barker 1925, 223 and ill. 226–227; Borenius 1925, 125–126; Constable 1925, 269; Grundy 1925, 118–119; Flint 1925, 3; L.G.S. 1925, 1; Lavallée 1925, 323–324 and ill.; Waldmann 1926, 174 and 186–187; Hofstede de Groot 1907–1930, 3: 4–5, 11 and ill. 49; Alexandre 1933, 164; Hale 1937, 132–133, no. 22 and ill.; De Vries 1939, 48, 89, no. 29 and ill. 53; Van Thienen 1949, 23, no. 25; Swillens 1950, 65, no. G; Gowing 1952, 21, 138, 145–147, no. 27, 148, and ill. 57; Reiss 1952, 182; Goldscheider 1958, 143, no. 25 and ill. 60; Gerson 1967, col. 740; Blankert 1975, 108–110, 120 n. 27, 167–168, no. B 3 and ill.; Brown 1977, 57; Van Straaten 1977, 36–37, ill. 43; Wheelock 1977A, 292, 298 and ill. 99; Blankert 1978, 73–74, 79 n. 109, 172, no. B3 and ill.; Glueck 1978, 55–56; Wheelock 1978, 242–256, ills. 1, 7, 13, 17; Slatkes 1981, 96–97 and ill.; Wheelock 1981, 39, 130 and pl. 34; Brentjens 1985, 54–58 and ill.; Aillaud 1986, 200–201, cat. b3, and ill.; Wheelock 1988, 37, 45, 100–101, 114, 126 and ill.; Montias 1989, 265–266; Blankert 1992, 205–206, no. B 3 and ill. 126; Gregory 1993, 144 and ill.; Wheelock 1995, 18, 119, 120–127, 134, 154, 159, 180, and ill. 84

15

Girl with a Pearl Earring

c. 1665–1666

inscribed top left corner: *IVMeer* (IVM in ligature)

oil on canvas, 44.5 x 39 (17 ½ x 15 ⅜)

Royal Cabinet of Paintings Mauritshuis, The Hague

PROVENANCE

(?) Pieter Claesz van Ruijven, Delft, before 1674; (?) Maria de Knuijt, Widow Van Ruijven, Delft, 1674–1681; (?) Magdalena van Ruijven and Jacob Dissius, Delft, 1681–1682; (?) Jacob Dissius (with his father, Abraham Dissius, 1685–1694), Delft, 1682–1695; (?) Dissius sale, Amsterdam, 16 May 1696, no. 38 (*f* 36) or no. 39 (*f* 17) or no. 40 (*f* 17); Braams sale, The Hague, 1881 (day and month unknown), for *f* 2.30 to Des Tombe; A. A. des Tombe, The Hague, 1881–1902 (on temporary loan to the Mauritshuis in 1881); Royal Cabinet of Paintings Mauritshuis, The Hague, 1902 (bequest of Des Tombe)

EXHIBITIONS

The Hague 1890, 57, no. 117; Paris 1921, 10, no. 106; Rome 1928, 100, no. 125 and ill.; London 1929a, 145, no. 306; The Hague 1945, no. 134; Antwerp 1946, no. 91 and ill.; Delft 1950, 11, no. 27; Washington 1982, 120–121, no. 38 and ill.; Paris 1986, 358–362, no. 54 and ill.

TECHNICAL DESCRIPTION

The fine, plain-weave linen support, which has been lined, has a thread count of 14.7 x 14.3 per cm². Only fragments of the original tacking edges survive.

The composition was laid in with light and dark areas. The ground is a thick, yellowish-white layer containing lead white, chalk, and possibly umber.[1]

The dark background and the deeper shadows of the girl's face, turban, and bodice were established with a mixture of black and earth pigments, and further modeled with a paler, ocher color. The shadow of her nose was underpainted with red lake while the highlights on her nose, right cheek, and forehead have a thick, cream-colored underpaint. The turban was painted with varying shades of an ultramarine and lead-white mixture, wet-in-wet, over which a blue glaze was applied, except in the highlights. A thin, off-white scumble of paint over the brown shadow of the girl's neck defines the pearl, and is painted more opaquely at the bottom where the pearl reflects the white collar. Small hairs from Vermeer's brush are found in the half-tones of the flesh areas.

As this young girl stares out at the viewer with liquid eyes and parted mouth, she radiates purity, captivating all that gaze upon her. Her soft, smooth skin is as unblemished as the surface of her large, teardrop-shaped pearl earring. Like a vision emanating from the darkness, she belongs to no specific time or place. Her exotic turban, wrapping her head in crystalline blue, is surmounted by a striking yellow fabric that falls dramatically behind her shoulder, lending an air of mystery to the image.

Dating this remarkable image has proven difficult, not only because the costume has no parallel with contemporary Dutch fashions, but also because the painting is so different in concept from Vermeer's interior genre scenes of the late 1650s and early 1660s. An effort to date the painting to the 1670s through an identification of the model as Maria, the oldest of Vermeer's children, is unconvincing.[2] In none of his paintings from the 1670s does Vermeer achieve the softly diffused flesh tones evident here, created by layering a thin flesh-colored glaze over a transparent undermodeling.

Vermeer developed this technique for rendering flesh tones during the mid-1660s in paintings such as *Woman Holding a Balance* and *Young Woman with a Water Pitcher* (cats. 10, 11). In both works, moreover, Vermeer effectively suggested the shaded portions of the woman's headdress by painting a thin glaze over a selectively applied dark imprimatura layer. Vermeer exploited these techniques in *Girl with a Pearl Earring*, using them in an even bolder and more expressive manner. The soft contour of the girl's face creates a warmth that permeates the image. To enliven her face Vermeer placed light accents in her eyes, and, as was recently discovered in the 1994 restoration of the painting, accentuated the extremities of her mouth with small dots of pink paint.[3] The free and strikingly bold application of blue glazes in the turban contributes further to the sense of immediacy.

The expressive character of Vermeer's paint application is surprising given the care with which he designed his works. It also separates his style from that of a number of his contemporaries, including Frans van Mieris (1635–1681), who painted comparable subjects (fig. 1), but in a meticulous manner that has its roots in an entirely different tradition. Vermeer's broad manner of painting, which allows him to generalize forms and to suggest the subtle nuances of light falling across surfaces, is a fundamental aspect of his classicism, the origins of which are to be found in his early history paintings.

Girl with a Pearl Earring exhibits another aspect of the classicism that pervades Vermeer's work, from *Diana and Her Companions*, *View of Delft*, to *Young Woman with a Water Pitcher* – timelessness. Set against a dark, undefined background, and dressed in an exotic costume, this striking young

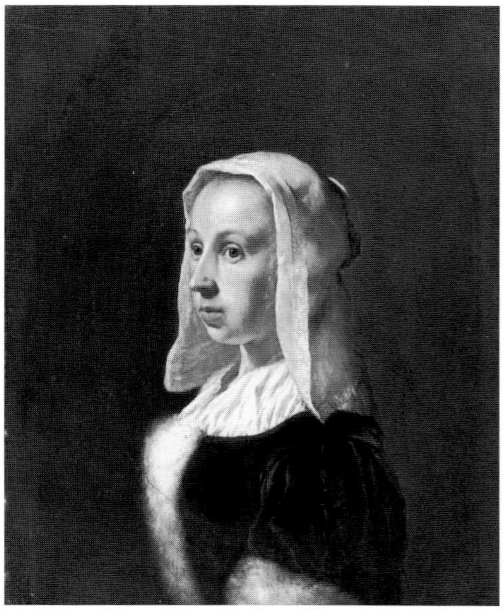

fig. 1. Frans van Mieris, *Portrait of the Artist's Wife, Cunera van der Cock*, c. 1657–1660, oil on panel, Reproduced by courtesy of the Trustees, The National Gallery, London

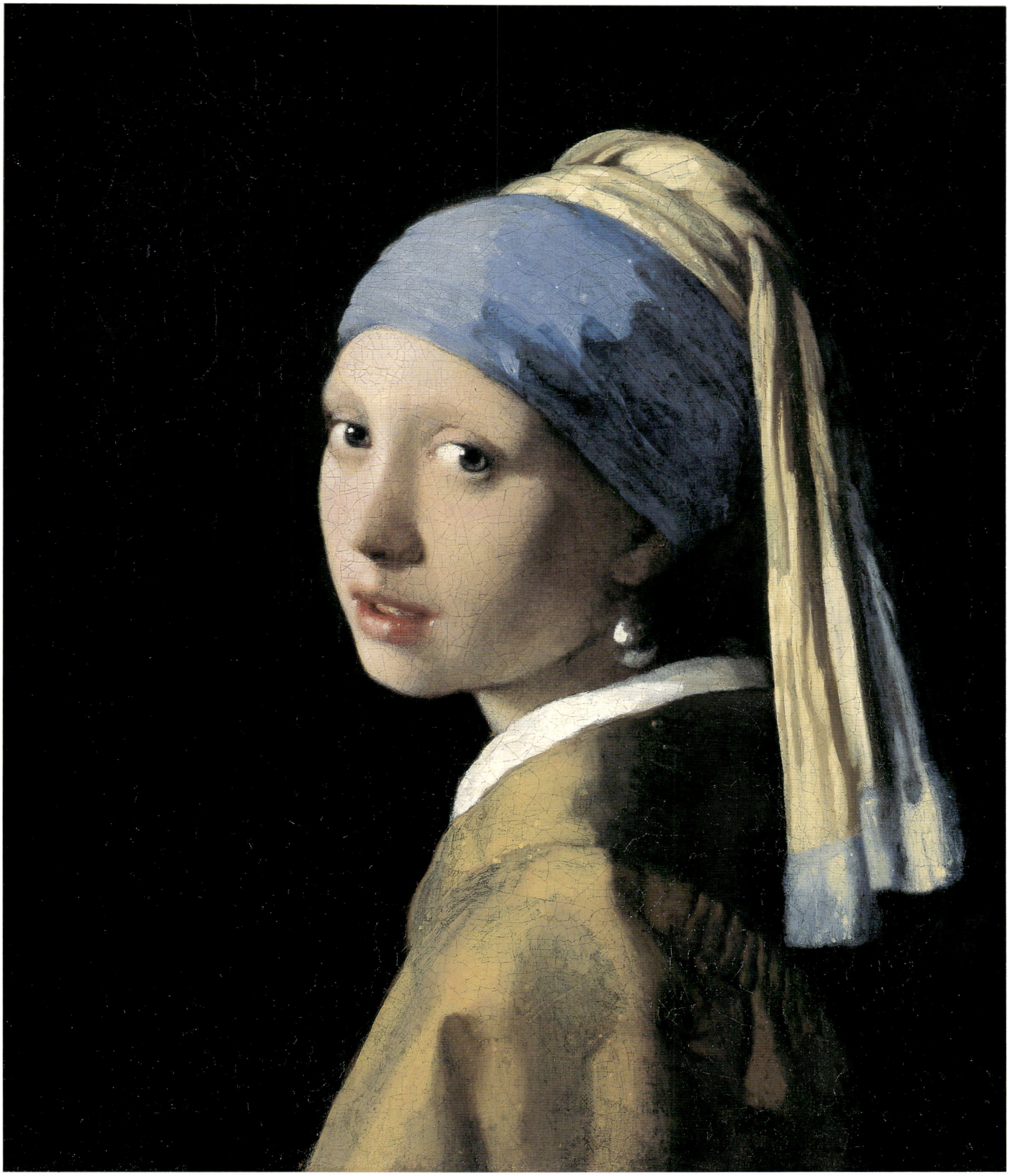

woman cannot be placed in any specific context. She holds no attributes that might, for example, identify her as an allegorical figure, perhaps a muse or a sybil.[4] Almost certainly, however, it is this very absence of a historic or iconographic framework that conveys such immediacy to all who view her.

While this work shares fundamental relationships with Vermeer's other paintings, it is, nevertheless, different in many respects. It is the first to focus on a single figure against a dark background. The scale of the head is larger and the image is closer to the picture plane than in any of his genre scenes. While it is entirely possible that Vermeer arrived at this compositional solution on his own, stylistic connections with the paintings of Michael Sweerts (1624–1664) are so striking that the possibility of contact between these two artists should be raised, particularly as Sweerts was living in Amsterdam in 1660–1661.[5] Sweerts, who had been an assistant at the Accademia di San Luca in Rome, and who had established an "academy for drawings from life" in Brussels after his return to his native city in about 1656, shared with Vermeer the ideal of investing scenes of daily life with classical dignity.[6] During his Amsterdam sojourn Sweerts painted a number of busts of youths with similarly pure profiles set against dark, undefined backgrounds (fig. 2). They all stare out of the picture plane with wet, lucid eyes, and at least one wears an exotic turban.[7] Despite the absence of documented contact between the two artists, Vermeer could have seen Sweerts' paintings in Amsterdam, where he had contacts throughout much of his life.[8]

It is remarkable that nothing is known about the early history of *Girl with a Pearl Earring*, although, as with *The Girl with the Red Hat* (cat. 14), it has been associated with references to *tronies* in Vermeer's inventory: "2 *Tronies* painted in Turkish fashion."[9] The first certain reference to the work did not occur until 1881, when the collector Arnoldus Andries des Tombe (1818–1902) bought it in The Hague for next to nothing. According to a newspaper notice, Victor de Stuers (1843–1916) recognized the work as a Delft Vermeer. It was offered by a Hague auction house and Des Tombe came to an understanding with De Stuers that they would not bid against each other.[10] That is how the latter managed to buy the work for two guilders, with a thirty cent premium.[11] Des Tombe sent the badly neglected canvas to Antwerp, where the painter Van der Haeghen restored it.

Des Tombe's collection in The Hague was accessible to the general public. Des Tombe, who was of distinguished ancestry, was married to *jonkvrouwe* Carolina Hester de Witte van Citters. Abraham Bredius – who occasionally advised Des Tombe – was the first to sing the praises of the girl's head: "VERMEER slays them all; the head of a girl, which would almost have one forget that one is looking at a canvas, and that unique glow of light, takes sole hold of your attention."[12] In 1890 Des Tombe lent the picture to an exhibition at Pulchri, the artists' society in The Hague, and in 1900 it was for some time on view in the Mauritshuis, together with the *Allegory of Faith* (cat. 20).[13] Des Tombe died on 16 December 1902. He bequeathed twelve paintings, including *Girl with a Pearl Earring*, to the Mauritshuis.[14] The media recalled how the work had been acquired for only a couple of guilders, reporting that its current value had been assessed at more than forty thousand guilders.[15] The public quickly took the "Dutch Mona Lisa" to its bosom. In 1908 Jan Veth articulated a widespread sentiment: "More than with any other VERMEER one could say that it looks as if it were blended from the dust of crushed pearls."[16]

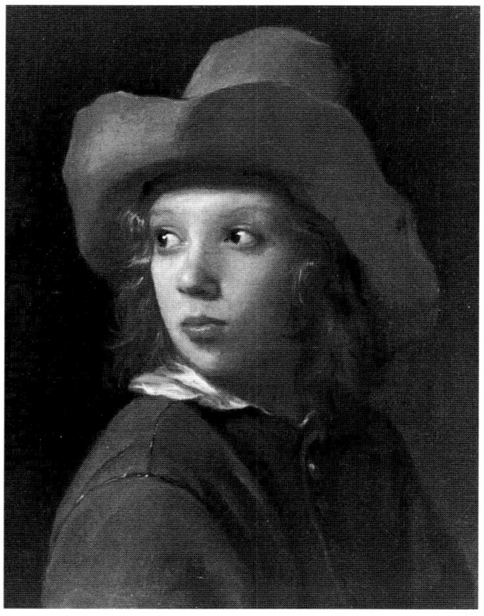

fig. 2. Michael Sweerts, *Portrait of a Boy*, c. 1659, oil on canvas, Wadsworth Atheneum, Hartford, The Ella Gallup Sumner and Mary Catlin Sumner Collection Fund

1. Kühn 1968, 191.
2. Malraux 1952, 114. Maria's exact date of birth is not known, although it was probably in 1655 or 1656. She is mentioned in a document dated 18 June 18 1657. See Montias 1989, 311, doc. 268.
3. Wadum 1994, 23 and ill. 49.
4. Slatkes 1981, 69, first raised this possibility: "The unusually direct contact between sitter and spectator, and the slightly parted position of the lips, presents a sense of immediacy so great as to imply strongly some specific act or identity – such as a sybil uttering her prophecy or some biblical personage."
5. The stylistic associations between Vermeer's and Sweerts' paintings have long been noted. See, for example, The Hague 1966, no. 28, where Sweerts' *Sense of Hearing* from Stuttgart was included in the exhibition because of its association with Vermeer.
6. See, for example, his *Interior of an Inn*, c. 1660, Munich, Alte Pinakothek, inv. no. 854, as discussed in Washington 1988, 124, 125, cat. 29, and ill.
7. Thyssen-Bornemisza 1989, 226–228, no. 49. Sweerts' painting is titled: *Boy in a turban holding a nosegay.*
8. As Meredith Hale has kindly suggested, Sweerts' depiction of *A Painter's Studio* (Rijksmuseum, Amsterdam, inv. no. A 1957) may be one of the visual sources for Vermeer's *Art of Painting* (page 68, fig. 2).
9. Montias 1993, 386, doc. 364: "2 Tronijen geschildert op sijn Turx"; less probable is the association with "Een Tronie in Antique Klederen, ongemeen kunstig" [A *Tronie*

in Antique Dress, exceptionally artful] in the Dissius sale of 16 May 1696; see Blankert 1975, 152, no. 18 and 165, no. 37.
10. *Het Vaderland*, 3 March 1903 (Mauritshuis clippings book, 41).
11. *Nieuwe Courant*, 2 March 1903 (Mauritshuis clippings book, 41); 1882 is always given (wrongly) as the year in which the Braams (usually adduced as Braam) sale took place; this on the authority of Mauritshuis 1914, 407, no. 670.
12. Bredius 1885, 222: "VERMEER doodt ze allen; het meisjeskopje, dat men haast vergeet een doek voor zich te hebben, en dat éénige licht uitstralende, behoudt geheel alleen uwe aandacht."
13. The Hague 1890, 57, no. 117; Geffroy 1900, 118 claimed to have seen both Vermeers in the Mauritshuis.
14. Mauritshuis documentation archives (1903–1930; old inventory book).
15. *Frankfurter Zeitung*, 23 March 1903 (Mauritshuis clippings book, 40).
16. Veth 1908, 10: "Meer nog dan in één anderen VERMEER zou men kunnen zeggen, dat het uit stof van gestampte paarlen saamgesmolten lijkt."

COLLECTION CATALOGUES

Mauritshuis 1987, 390–394, no. 66 and ill. (with extensive literature)

LITERATURE

Bredius 1885, 222; Lafenestre 1898, 106; Geffroy 1900, 118–119 and ill.; Martin 1904, 4; Hofstede de Groot 1907–1928, 1: 606, no. 44; Veth 1908, 10; Plietzsch 1911, 117, no. 21 and pl. 16; Hale 1937, 173–174 and pl. 4; De Vries 1939, 42, 84, no. 17; Swillens 1950, 62, no. 28, 105–108 and pl. 28; Gowing 1952, 137–139, no. 22, ill. 39 and pl. 49; Bloch 1963, 34, no. 49 and ill. 3; Goldscheider 1967, 27, 130, no. 23 and pls. 54–55; Blankert 1975, 66–68, 88, 152, no. 18 and ill.; Van Straaten 1977, 73, no. 93a and ill.; Blankert 1978, 46, 59, 163, no. 18 and pls. 18–18a; Slatkes 1981, 68–69 and ill.; Wheelock 1981, 118, 132, and pl. 28; Brentjens 1985, 55–56 and ill. 3; Aillaud 1986, 122, 142, 146, 186, no. 18, and pl. 18; Wheelock 1988, 92–93 and ill.; Montias 1989, 182–183, 196, 221, 266 and ill. 40; Nash 1991, 19, 31, 33 and ill. 34; Blankert 1992, 122, 148, 188, no. 18 and pl. 18; Wadum 1994, 18–29 and ills.; Wheelock 1995, 103, 123, 124, 178, and ill.

A20

16

The Geographer

c. 1668–1669

inscribed on cupboard: *Meer*, and above map: *I. Ver Meer MDCLXVIIII*

(neither inscription original)

oil on canvas, 52 x 45.5 (20 1/2 x 17 15/16)

Städelsches Kunstinstitut, Frankfurt am Main

PROVENANCE

Sale (Paets et al?), Rotterdam, 27 April 1713, no. 10 or 11 (*f* 300, with *The Astronomer*); Hendrik Sorgh, Amsterdam, 1713 (?)–1720; Sorgh sale, Amsterdam, 28 March 1720, no. 3 or 4 (*f* 160, with *The Astronomer*); Govert Looten, Amsterdam, before 1727; Looten sale, Amsterdam, 31 March 1729, no. 6 (*f* 104, with *The Astronomer*); Jacob Crammer Simonsz, Amsterdam, before 1778; Crammer Simonsz sale, Amsterdam, 25 November 1778, no. 19 (with *The Astronomer*); Jean Etiènne Fizeaux, Amsterdam, 1778–1780; Widow Fizeaux, Amsterdam, 1780–1785(?); [Pieter Fouquet, Amsterdam, and Alexandre Joseph Paillet, Paris, 1784–1785]; Jan Danser Nijman, Amsterdam, before 1794(?); Danser Nijman sale, Amsterdam, 16 August 1797, no. 168 (*f* 133 to Josi); Arnoud de Lange, Amsterdam, 1797(?)–1803; De Lange sale, Amsterdam, 12 December 1803, no. 55 (*f* 360 to Coclers); (?) Johann Goll van Franckenstein, Jr., Velzen/Amsterdam, before 1821; Pieter Hendrick Goll van Franckenstein, Amsterdam, before 1832; Goll van Franckenstein sale, Amsterdam, 1 July 1833, no. 47 (*f* 195 to Nieuwenhuys); Alexandre Dumont, Cambrai, before 1860; Isaac Pereire, Paris, 1866 (via Thoré-Bürger from Dumont); Pereire sale, Paris, 6 March 1872, no. 132; Max Kann, Paris, 1872(?); [Sedelmeyer, Paris, c. 1875]; Prince Demidoff, San Donato, near Florence, before 1877–1880; Demidoff sale, San Donato, 15 March 1880, no. 1124; A. J. Bosch sale, Vienna, 28 April 1885, no. 32 (ÖS 8000 to Kohlbacher); to the present owner in 1907

EXHIBITIONS

Paris 1866, 35, no. 106; Paris 1874, 60, no. 332; Paris 1898, 104, no. 87 and ill.; Paris 1914, 54, no. 25 and ill.; Rotterdam 1935, 38, no. 87 and ill. 68

TECHNICAL DESCRIPTION

The support is a closed, plain-weave linen with a thread count of 14 x 11 per cm^2; the original tacking edges of which are still present. The canvas was lined, resulting in weave emphasis.

A gray ground containing chalk, umber, and lead white extends to the tacking edges.[1] The paint was applied wet-in-wet in places. Many different textural effects have been created with the use of glazing, scumbling, impasto, and dry brushstrokes. The vanishing point of the composition is visible in the paint layer on the wall between the chair and the cupboard. Some abrasion, particularly in the shadows in the map, has resulted from past cleaning.

The seventeenth century was a time of discovery, when the charting of new and unexplored worlds was a dream realized not only by adventurers and traders but also by geographers and astronomers. Although charts and maps had guided explorers for centuries, new information about land masses and coastlines, as well as improved surveying techniques, helped make the Netherlands the center for map making. The Amsterdam publishing firms Hondius, Blaeu, and Visscher, among others, dominated the industry, and their maps appear in numerous depictions of middle-class interiors, including those by Vermeer (see cats. 9, 11).[2] Among those who collected elaborately decorated atlases and wall maps, ranging from world views to city vistas, were philosophers, scholars, and "amateurs," who found great intellectual satisfaction in pondering the physical character of the earth and the underlying laws of nature.[3]

Vermeer's geographer is, above all else, someone excited by intellectual inquiry. Surrounded by maps, charts, books and a globe, he stares searchingly toward the window as he rests one hand on a book and holds dividers with the other. Although Vermeer reveals neither the questions the geographer asks nor the answers he seeks, his active stance indicates an alert, penetrating mind. His scholarly mode of dress, blue robe with red trim and long hair pulled behind his ears, further confirm the seriousness of his endeavor.

The energy in this painting is markedly different from Vermeer's quiet, contemplative images of women in interiors. It is conveyed most notably through the figure's pose, the massing of objects on the left side of the composition, and the sequence of diagonal shadows on the wall to the right.[4] To reinforce this effect, Vermeer subtly adjusted the composition. The vague shape of the geographer's forehead can be seen to the left of the figure, an indication that the artist originally portrayed his head at a different angle, presumably looking down at the chart lying on the table.[5] Vermeer also altered the position of the dividers: they originally pointed downward rather than across the geographer's body. Finally, Vermeer eliminated a sheet of paper that once lay on the small stool at the right, probably to darken the right foreground corner of the composition.

Another means by which Vermeer conveyed the geographer's active nature was through the crisp, angular folds of his blue robe. Vermeer used these remarkably abstract folds only to describe the sunlit blue robe: the broad, rolling folds of the floral table covering in the foreground are closer to the carefully modulated folds of the yellow jacket in *A Lady Writing* (cat. 13), painted a few years earlier. Thus, in *The Geographer* Vermeer seems to have selectively introduced this technique of modeling drapery, which becomes an important characteristic of his late style (see cat. 19), to enhance the dynamic character of his image.

Vermeer not only captured the scholar's energy, he surrounded him with accurately rendered cartographic objects appropriate for a geographer's study. The decorative sea chart on the rear wall, showing "all the Sea coasts of Europe," is by Willem Jansz Blaeu,[6] while the terrestrial globe was published in Amsterdam in 1618 by Jodocus Hondius.[7] As James Welu notes, Vermeer treats the globe, in its four-legged stand, as a scientific object by turning its decorative cartouches to the side to reveal the Indian Ocean – *Orientalis Oceanus*.[8] Other instruments include the dividers, used to mark distances, a square

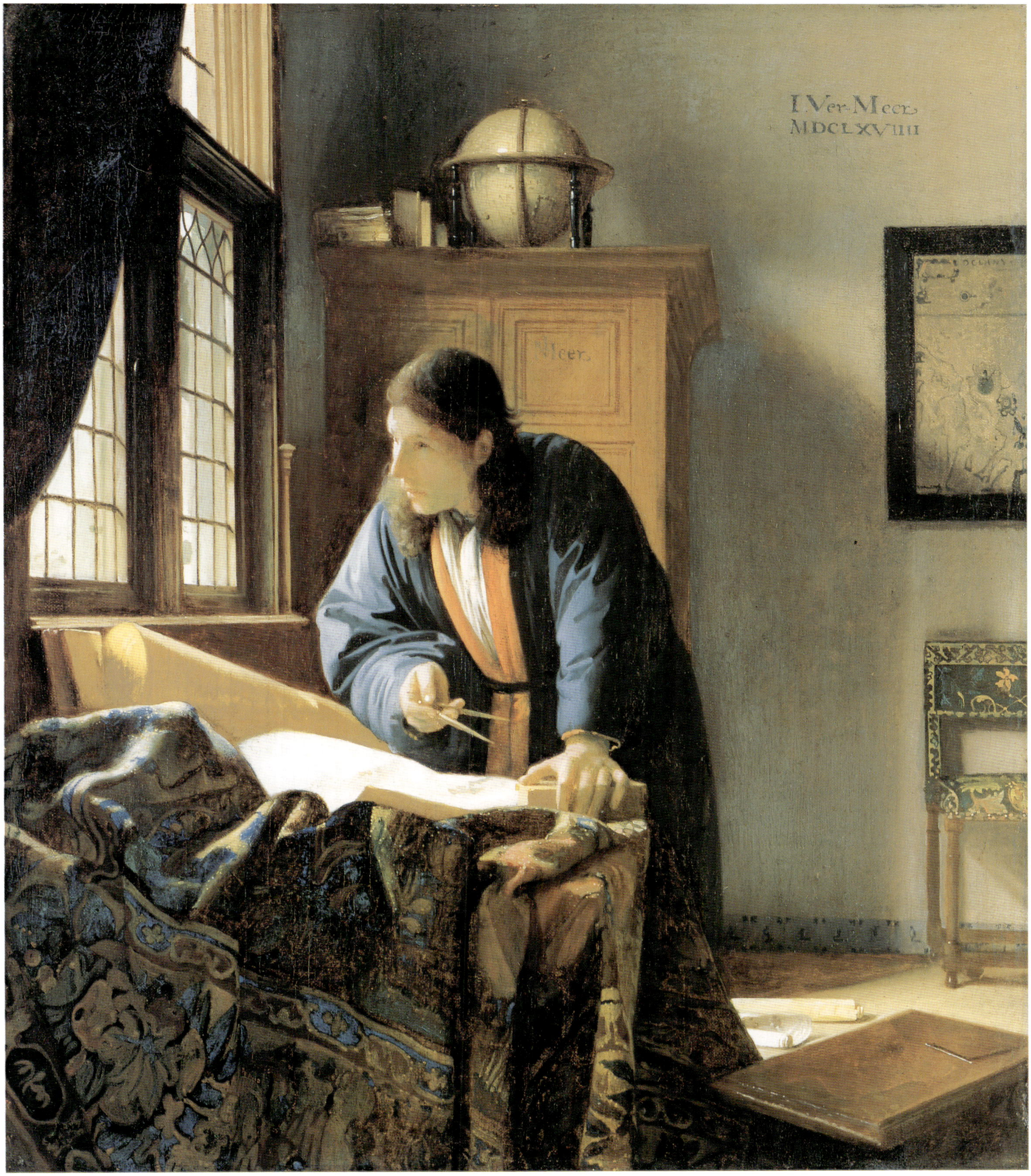
I Ver-Meer
MDCLXVIIII
Meer

lying on the stool in the foreground, and a cross-staff, used to measure the angle of the elevation of the sun and stars, hanging from the center post of the window. Among the various rolled charts in the room, the large one on the table is of particular interest. Welu proposes that, given its translucence, it is on vellum, and from a few faint lines, that it is a nautical chart.[9]

Vermeer must have been guided in his depiction by a scholar familiar with geography and navigation, as a comparably sophisticated awareness of cartographic instruments and books informs the pendant to this painting, *The Astronomer*, signed and dated 1668 (page 52, fig. 6).[10] Since the same young man modeled as both the geographer and the astronomer, it is possible that he was the source of Vermeer's scientific information.

This individual was most probably Anthony van Leeuwenhoek (1632–1723), the famed Delft microscopist, who in 1676 was named trustee for Vermeer's estate (see page 16).[11] Although no documents link Vermeer and Van Leeuwenhoek during their lifetimes, it seems hardly possible that they did not know each other. Both were born in Delft in the same year, both families were involved in the textile business, and each was fascinated with science and optics.[12] Indeed, as one author wrote only six years after Van Leeuwenhoek's death, aside from his interest in microscopy, he was so skilled in "navigation, astronomy, mathematics, philosophy, and natural science...that one can certainly place him with the most distinguished masters in the art."[13] In 1668–1669 Van Leeuwenhoek would have been about thirty-six years old, the approximate age of the sitter in *The Geographer*. Moreover, as far as one can judge from an image of the scientist made in 1686 by the Delft artist Jan Verkolje (1650–1693) (fig. 1), Van Leeuwenhoek's broad face and straight, angular nose resemble those of the sitter in the painting.[14]

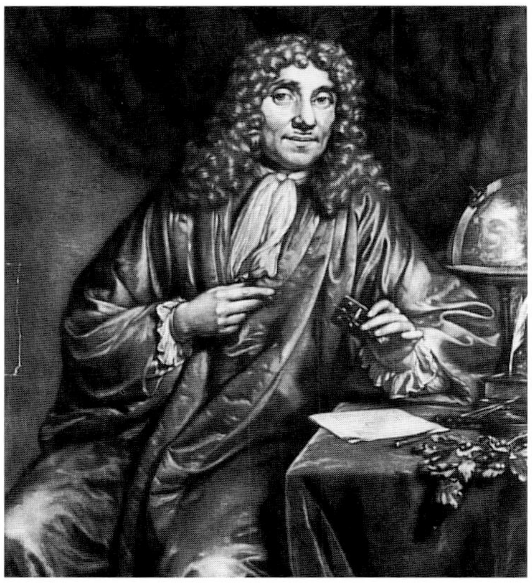

fig. 1. Jan Verkolje, *Portrait of Anthony van Leeuwenhoek*, 1686, mezzotint, Rijksmuseum, Amsterdam

The sudden appearance in the late 1660s of paintings depicting an astronomer and a geographer involved in scientific inquiry is surprising given Vermeer's predominant thematic concern, women in a domestic setting. Nothing we know about Vermeer's life accounts for this new interest. Van Leeuwenhoek's life, however, does offer one explanation for Vermeer's interest in these subjects: in 1668 and 1669 he must have been actively involved in scientific studies since on 4 February 1669 he passed his examination for surveyor.

Even if Van Leeuwenhoek inspired, or commissioned, Vermeer to paint *The Astronomer* and *The Geographer*, these paintings represent far more than mere portraits of scholars in their studies. Vermeer has conveyed in these works the excitement of scholarly inquiry and discovery. It seems likely, moreover, that the pendant relationship is more complex than the mere depiction of related scientific disciplines. Studies of the heavens and the earth represent two realms of human thought that have quite different theological implications, the former concerned with the realm of the spirit and the latter with God's plan for man's passage through life.[15] The charts and cartographic instruments in these paintings, thus, may have allegorical meaning as well as scientific application. While the astronomer, reaching for a celestial globe, allegorically searches for spiritual guidance, the geographer looks forward into the light, dividers in hand, with assurance that he has been given the tools to chart the proper course of his life.[16]

While it seems probable because of the specific subject matter that *The Geographer* and *The Astronomer* were commissioned works, we have no information about their whereabouts in the seventeenth century. Neither work appears in the Dissius sale of 1696. The two were paired during most of the eighteenth century.[17] They were considered to be pendants even though the measurements do not altogether correspond and the compositions are not necessarily interdependent. In 1713 they were auctioned as pendants in Rotterdam for the considerable sum of three hundred guilders, as "A work depicting a Mathematical Artist, by vander Meer" and "A ditto by the same."[18] This "Mathematical Artist" must be the Frankfurt painting, where the man holds a compass in his hand. J. G. van Gelder believed that this anonymous sale was the tail end of the Paets' sale of the previous day, 26 April 1713.[19] Adriaen Paets (1657–1712) was Receiver of the Admiralty and an influential city council member of Rotterdam. He was the Maecenas of the young painter Adriaen van der Werff (1659–1722) and, it follows, a lover of highly refined painting (*fijnschilderkunst*). The sale of the Paets' collection was a major event that was announced even in the *Amsterdamsche Courant*.[20]

The paintings then, or shortly thereafter, moved on to Amsterdam, where they were auctioned in 1720 out of the collection of the art broker Hendrick Sorgh (1666–1720) who was the grandson of the painter of the same name (1611–1670).

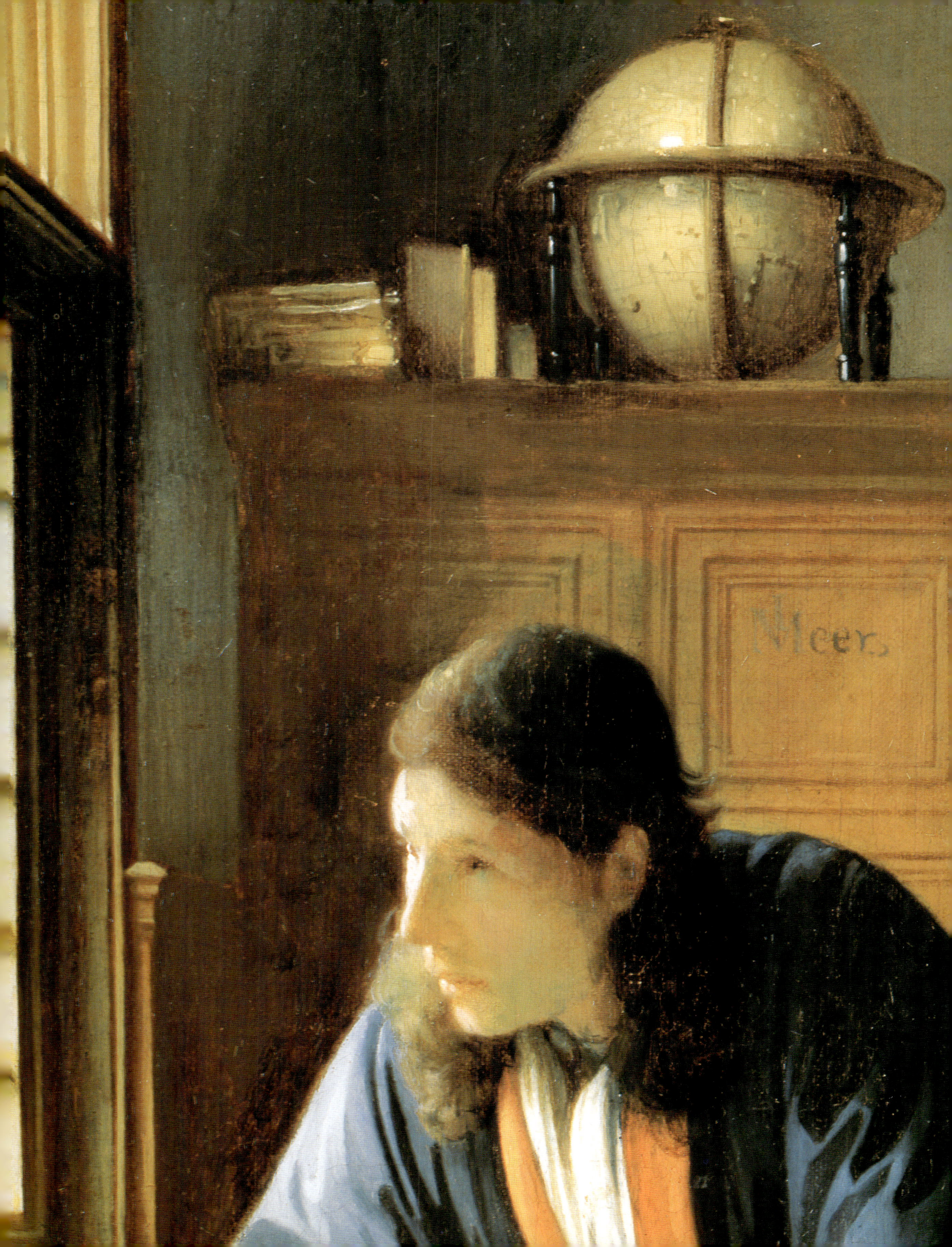
Meer

Sorgh lived in Amsterdam all his life as a bachelor.[21] At the sale of his property the two paintings went for 160 guilders, as "An Astrologer" and "A repeat." The laudatory commentary on the two depictions read "extra choice" and "no less."[22]

A neighbor of Sorgh obtained the two Vermeers. Govert Looten (1668–1727), who, like Sorgh, lived on the Keizersgracht, became the next owner. He was a grandson of the Amsterdam merchant Marten Looten, who had been portrayed by Rembrandt (Los Angeles County Museum of Art).[23] Unlike that portrait, the two Vermeers were sold out of Looten's estate in Amsterdam a year and a half after his death. The price had come down to 105 guilders for the two pictures, though the commendation was no less warm: "sublimely and artfully painted."[24]

Fifty years later these two paintings, which had always been called "Astrologers," were instead believed to be a pair of philosophers. They hung on the Prinsengracht at that time, in the home of Jacob Crammer Simonsz (1725–1778).[25] Crammer Simonsz was an amateur who had two other Vermeers in his possession, *The Lacemaker* (cat. 17) and a now unknown genre piece of a lady pouring wine.[26] After the death of Crammer Simonsz, *The Astronomer* and *The Geographer* appeared in the collection of the Huguenot banker Jean Etiènne Fizeaux (1707–1780),[27] who lived on the Kloveniersburgwal. At his death he left a bankrupt estate and a notable art cabinet specializing in works by the *fijnschilders*. His widow governed the cabinet, which was known to only a few art lovers, until 1797, when the collection came under the gavel.

It appears that the Widow Fizeaux had earlier attempted to sell several works, including the two Vermeers, to Louis XVI of France. To this end, she employed the services of the painter and art buyer Pieter Fouquet, Jr. (1729–1800), who regularly acted for foreign clients.[28] As has recently become clear, Fouquet in turn involved the French dealer Alexandre Joseph Paillet (1748–1814).[29] Paillet undertook numerous foreign journeys between 1777 and 1786 to buy works of art for the French king. In 1785 he described a number of paintings that he had taken into consignment in Holland the year before, including Vermeer's *Geographer* ("an architect") and *Astronomer* ("an astronomer studying a terrestrial sphere"). He added: "No one here knows of any work by this master. They are so very rare...."[30] Perhaps he would have done better to omit this comment, because the transaction fell through, so that the two paintings were returned to Amsterdam. Fouquet was able to find a buyer there.

In 1794 Abraham Delfos (1731–1820) made a watercolor of *The Astronomer* (page 57, fig. 12). Together with *The Geographer* it was then presumably in the collection of Jan Danser Nijman, a true Vermeer lover.[31] He had bought *The Lacemaker* in 1778, which he may have sold to Jan Wubbels, and also found an opportunity to acquire *A Lady Standing at the Virginal* (cat. 21).[32] It was at the 1797 sale of his collection that *The Astronomer* and *The Geographer* were first separated. The connoisseur and print publisher Christiaan Josi (1768–1828) purchased *The Geographer* for 133 guilders, while the famous collector Jan Gildemeester (1744–1799) bought the "pendant" for twice this amount.[33] Josi sold his painting, conjecturing years later: "I believe they are both in England."[34]

The Astronomer was indeed in the English art trade for a time, but *The Geographer* remained in Dutch possession, specifically, in two famous Amsterdam collections. In 1803 the work was auctioned

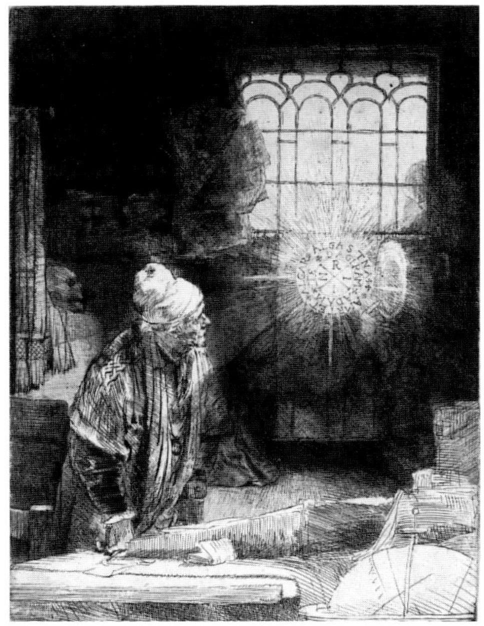

fig. 2. Rembrandt, *Faust*, c. 1652, etching and drypoint, National Gallery of Art, Washington, Gift of R. Horace Gallatin

out of the collection of the art broker and collector Arnoud de Lange (1740–1803), who had also laid claim to Cornelis Ploos van Amstel's collection of Rembrandt etchings. When De Lange died, Josi was the executor of his testament.[35] Pieter Hendrik Goll van Franckenstein (1787–1832) became the next owner of *The Geographer*. He represented the third generation of a dynasty of rich merchants, originally from Frankfurt am Main, who were among the most renowned Dutch art collectors of the eighteenth and nineteenth centuries.[36]

After Goll van Franckenstein's death, *The Geographer* also went abroad. Lambert Jan Nieuwenhuys (1777–1862) bought the Vermeer for 195 guilders at the Goll van Franckenstein sale and, via his firm in Brussels, the work ended up with Alexandre Dumont in Cambrai.[37] Paul Mantz "discovered" it there in 1860 and announced proudly that Thoré-Bürger did not yet know the work.[38] Not much later Thoré-Burger was able to buy it from Dumont for his friend Isaac Pereire (1806–1880), a French banker and member of parliament.[39] Thoré-Burger alerted the latter to the truly striking resemblance of *The Geographer* to Rembrandt's etching *Faust* (fig. 2) of about 1652.[40] By way of the dealer Sedelmeyer, the painting entered the collection of Prince Demidoff in San Donato near Florence in 1875 and was therefore briefly (after *The Music Lesson* [cat. 8], which was for some time on view in Venice) the only Vermeer south of Vienna.[41] Charles Blanc included it in his description of the Demidoff collection in 1877.[42] It made its last appearance at an auction in 1885, when it was finally purchased in Vienna for the Frankfurter Kunstverein.[43]

1. Kühn 1968, 199.
2. On the map-making industry in Amsterdam, see Van den Brink 1989.
3. For the intellectual content implicit in the decorative elements on maps, see, in particular, Bennett 1990.
4. Indeed, the combined shadows of the globe and the cupboard echo the pose of the geographer.
5. Vermeer, in fact, may have altered this figure yet again, for a vague indication of an earlier head can also be detected above the current form.
6. Welu 1975, 543–544. Welu illustrates (fig. 17) the precise map Vermeer depicted, which is in the Deutsche Staatsbibliothek, Berlin.
7. Welu 1975, 542 n. 70, indicates that the only extant terrestrial globe of this date by Hondius is in the Germanisches Nationalmuseum, Nuremberg, No. WI 296. Vermeer used the identical globe in *Allegory of Faith* (cat. 20).
8. Welu 1986, 256–264.
9. Welu 1975, 544.
10. Welu 1986.
11. For Van Leeuwenhoek see Dobell 1932.
12. Van Leeuwenhoek lived in Amsterdam from 1648 to 1654, where he worked for a Scottish cloth merchant. He returned to Delft in 1654 where he married Barbara de Mey, daughter of a *saydrapier* (dealer in serge), and worked in the textile business. Over the years he was granted a number of remunerative municipal positions. In 1660 he was appointed Chamberlain to the Sheriffs. In 1667 he also became *generaal-wijkmeester* (alderman), and, in 1679 he was named wine-gauger of Delft.
13. Boitet 1729, 765.
14. This mezzotint is based on the artist's portrait of Van Leeuwenhoek in the Rijksmuseum, Amsterdam, inv. no. A957.
15. De Jongh 1967, 67, associates the allegorical content of *The Geographer* with the sentiments expressed in emblem twenty-nine in Adriaan Spinniker's *Leerzaame Zinnebeelden*, Haarlem, 1714.
16. The allegorical implications of *The Astronomer* are more explicit since Vermeer has hung a religious scene on the back wall of the room. This work, *The Finding of Moses*, was traditionally associated with the guidance of Divine Providence. For further discussion of the allegorical implications of *The Finding of Moses*, see *Lady Writing a Letter with Her Maid* (cat. 19), where the same painting appears, but at a much larger scale.
17. Blankert 1992, 194–196, no. 24 and pl. 25.
18. Hoet 1752–1770, 2: 365, nos. 10-11: "Een stuk verbeeldende een Mathematis Konstenaar, door vander Meer" and "Een ditto door denzelven."
19. Van Gelder 1974, 168–169.
20. Dudok van Heel 1977A, 109, no. 158; See, on the Paets sale, where six Van der Werffs were hammered down for an unheard of price of 16,000 guilders, for instance, Houbraken 1718–1721, 3: 400; Weyerman 1729–1769, 2: 409–410, 3: 57; Van Gool 1750–1751, 1: 238 and 260.
21. Gemeentearchief, Amsterdam (DTB 1103, Westerkerk, 43): buried on 23 January 1720; see also Van Kretschmar 1974, col. 258; Dudok van Heel 1977A, 115, no. 199.
22. Hoet 1752–1770, 1: 242, nos. 3–4: "extra puyck" and "niet minder."
23. Bruyn 1986, 190–198, no. A 52 and ill.; on Looten's descendants, see Van Eeghen 1957, 154; see also the Looten Genealogy (Manuscript, Gemeentearchief, Amsterdam).
24. Hoet 1752–1770, 1: 333, no. 6: "heerlyk en konstig geschildert." The paintings were not mentioned in the inventory belonging to the testament of Govert Looten (Gemeentearchief, Amsterdam, NA 8098, no. 400, notary H. van Aken, 26 May 1728).
25. Gemeentearchief, Amsterdam (DTB 101, Zuiderkerk, fol. 54 and DTB 1060, 28).
26. Hofstede de Groot 1907–1928, 1: 604, no. 40a.
27. His name is generally spelled incorrectly as "Fiseau" (Blankert 1992, 194) or "Fisau" (Foucart 1987, 100), but see Mauritshuis 1993, 113.
28. The Hague 1990, 136.
29. Edwards 1986, 197.
30. Edwards 1986, 197 and 200 nn. 9–11: "un architecte," "un astronome etudiant sur le globe de la terre" and "On ne conois ici aucun ouvrage de ce peintre. Ils sont tres rarres...."
31. Jan Danser Nijman remains a somewhat shadowy figure: his mother Maria Danser, widow of Pieter Nijman, died in 1784 (Gemeentearchief, Amsterdam, DTB 1050 Oude Kerk, 162).
32. Nijman had a special predilection for Cornelis Troost, see sale catalogue, Amsterdam, 16 August 1797, title page (Lugt no. 5640), and Niemeijer 1973, 439.
33. Sale catalogue, Amsterdam, 16 August 1797, 33, no. 167.
34. Josi 1821, xix: "Je les crois tous les deux en Angleterre."
35. Laurentius 1980, 99–103: Aarnoud de Lange, Christiaan Josi and Cornelis Ploos van Amstel were close friends or related; see also Dudok van Heel 1977B.
36. Knoef 1948–1949.
37. Sale catalogue, Amsterdam, 1 July 1833, 19, no. 47 (Lugt no. 13358); Mantz 1860, 304–305; Blanc 1860–1863, 2: s.v., 3.
38. Mantz 1860, 305.
39. Thoré-Bürger 1866, 559: "C'est M. Dumont qui a bien voulu me céder, pour la galerie Pereire, cette superbe peinture"; on Pereire (not Périère, see Swillens 1950, 60), see GDEL, 7: 7978.
40. Bartsch no. 270; see Berlin 1991, 2: 258–260, no. 33, and ill.
41. Sale catalogue, Florence, 15 March 1880 (Lugt no. 39989), no. 1124.
42. Blanc 1877, 416, speaks of the Max Kam [=Kann] sale before the painting came to San Donato.
43. Städelsches Kunstinstitut 1971, 62.

COLLECTION CATALOGUES

Städelsches Kunstinstitut 1971, 62, no. 1149 and ill. 52

LITERATURE

Hoet 1752–1770, 1: 242, no. 4, 333, no. 6; 2: 365, no. 10; Josi 1821, xix; Mantz 1860, 305; Thoré-Bürger 1866, 559, no. 34, 561 and ill.; Blanc 1877, 416; Havard 1888, 7, 38, no. 37 and ill.; Hofstede de Groot 1907–1928, 1: 589–590, no. 5; Plietzsch 1911, 116, no. 5; Hale 1937, 126, 128; De Vries 1939, 93, no. 39 and ill. 62; Blum 1946, 30–32, 60, 64 and 175–176, no. 34; Sulzberger 1948, 37; Knoef 1948–1949, 286; Van Thienen 1949, 18, 23, no. 31 and ill.; Swillens 1950, 59–60, no. 23, 74, 76, 78–79, 83, 85–86, 109, 116, 133, 135, 171, 176 and pls. 23, 53a; Gowing 1952, 147–151 and pls. 59–61; Goldscheider 1967, 144–145, no. 28 and ills. 63, 65; Van Gelder 1974, 169; Blankert 1975, 83–84, 119 n. 11, 157–158, no. 24 and pl. 24; Welu 1975, 544–547 and ill. 16; Dudok van Heel 1977B1, 54; Blankert 1978, 13, 55, 63, 77 n. 48, 166–167, no. 24 and pl. 24; Laurentius 1980, 99; Slatkes 1981, 84-85 and ill.; Wheelock 1981, 13, 36, 47, 136–138, 140, and pl. 38; Dollekamp 1983–1984, 54; Foucart 1983, 280-281 and ill.; Aillaud 1986, 136, 140, 191–193, no. 24, and pl. 25; Welu 1986, 263-267 and ill. 2; Wheelock 1988, 44, 108–109 and pl. 31; Montias 1989, 189, 225 and 266; Elovsson 1991, 17-25 and ills. 1–2; Nash 1991, 26, 28–29, 36, 106–107 and ill.; Blankert 1992, 140, 142, 194–196, no. 24, pl. 25 and ill. 103; Wheelock 1995, 114, 182, and ill. A28

17
The Lacemaker
c. 1669–1670
inscribed upper right: *IVMeer* (IVM in ligature)
oil on canvas transferred to panel, 23.9 x 20.5 (9 13/32 x 8 1/2)

Musée du Louvre, Paris

PROVENANCE
(?) Pieter Claesz van Ruijven, Delft, before 1674; (?) Maria de Knuijt, Widow Van Ruijven, Delft, 1674–1681; (?) Magdalena van Ruijven and Jacob Dissius, Delft, 1681–1682; Jacob Dissius (with his father Abraham Dissius, 1685–1694), Delft, 1682–1695; Dissius sale, Amsterdam, 16 May 1696, no. 12 (*f* 28); Jacob Crammer Simonsz, Amsterdam, before 1778; Crammer Simonsz sale, Amsterdam, 25 November 1778, no. 17 (*f* 150 to Nijman); Jan Danser Nijman, Amsterdam, 1778–before 1792; Jan Wubbels sale, Amsterdam, 16 July 1792, no. 213 (*f* 210 to J. Spaan); Hendrik Muilman sale, Amsterdam, 12 April 1813, no. 97 (*f* 84 to Coclers); A. Lapeyrière sale, Paris, 14 April 1817, no. 50 (Ffr 501 to Coclers); Anne Willem Carel, Baron van Nagell van Ampsen sale, The Hague, 5 September 1851, no. 40 (*f* 260 to Lamme); Dirk Vis Blokhuyzen, Rotterdam, 1851(?)–1869; Vis Blokhuyzen sale, Paris, 1 April 1870, no. 40 (*f* 3,150 [Frf 6,000] to Gaucher); Louvre, Paris, 1870 (for Frf 7,900 from Féral)

EXHIBITIONS
Amsterdam 1935, 29, no. 166 and ill. 84; Rotterdam 1935, 36–37 and ill. 65; The Hague 1966, no. 7 and ill.; Paris 1966, no. 8 and ill.; Paris 1970, 228–229, no. 222 and ill.

TECHNICAL DESCRIPTION
The support is a slightly open, plain-weave canvas with a thread count of 12 x 12 per cm². The canvas has been glued onto an oak panel measuring 23.9 x 20.5 cm. X-radiography shows lines of tack holes and cracks from former fold lines at the left and right edges. Strainer bar marks are evident also at the sides, 2 cm from the fold lines. Along the top edge the line of cracking is 1.4 cm from the edge of the canvas and along the bottom edge 2 cm. Assuming that the strainer bars were of equal width, this would suggest that only the tacking edge has been removed from the bottom edge and the tacking edge plus 6 mm from the top edge. This would give original measurements of 24.5 x 19.3 cm, making the painting slightly narrower and taller than at present.

The thin, gray-brown ground contains chalk, lead-white, and umber.[1] The red, pink, and light blue areas were painted wet-in-wet. Brushmarks impart texture to the background paint, and impasto touches are found on the highlights. X-radiography shows a pentimento: the knee was lower so that a triangle of wall was visible under the tabletop.

The blue in the tablecloth is discolored. The flattened tacking edges along the left and right sides have been retouched.

In this, one of Vermeer's most beloved paintings, a young lacemaker bends over her work, tautly holding the bobbins and pins essential for her craft. Sitting very close to the foreground, behind a lacemaking table and a large blue sewing cushion, Vermeer's lacemaker devotes every ounce of her attention to this one activity, while the viewer peers in with equal intensity, mesmerized by her adeptness and artistic skill.[2]

The viewer's emotional engagement is unique in Vermeer's *oeuvre*. The painting's intimacy, derived from its small scale, personal subject matter, and informal composition, draws the viewer to it, challenging the barrier between image and reality. Vermeer suggests the lacemaker's total absorption in her task through her constricted pose and the bright yellow of her bodice, an active and psychologically intense color.[3] Even her hairstyle conveys something of her physical and psychological state of being, for it is likewise both tightly constrained and rhythmically flowing. Finally, the crisp accents of light that illuminate her forehead and fingers emphasize the precision and clarity of vision required by this demanding craft.

Vermeer further engages the viewer by simulating an optical experience that occurs when observing a scene closely—different depths of field. In one of his most striking passages, Vermeer softly and fluidly applies red and white strokes of paint to create the illusion of diffused, colored threads flowing from the partially opened sewing cushion. Their liquid forms spill out onto the equally suggestive floral patterns of the table covering. By recreating this optical phenomenon, where forms situated nearest the eye appear diffused and unfocused, Vermeer pulls the viewer close to the picture plane. At the same time, these diffused forms encourage the eye to pass over the foreground and to focus on the clearly defined middleground, consisting of the lacemaker herself. A soft ringlet silhouetted against the white wall marks a more distant plane beyond the field of focus. Indeed, the threads and ringlet curl serve as a visual foil to the taut threads of the bobbins, thereby setting the lacemaker's activity apart from her surroundings.

Although Vermeer remained remarkably sensitive to light and color throughout his career, he frequently altered their natural effects for compositional reasons. Nevertheless, the abstract shape and texture of the red and white threads in the foreground of this painting are without parallel, the closest equivalent being the lion-head finial in the right foreground of *The Girl with the Red Hat* (page 162, fig. 1). As with the diffused, almost fragmented finial, the optical effect of the threads certainly derives from a camera obscura image (see page 162). Indeed, the informality of this tightly framed composition, so different from the more traditional representations of lacemakers by Nicolaes Maes (1634–1693) (fig. 1) and Caspar Netscher

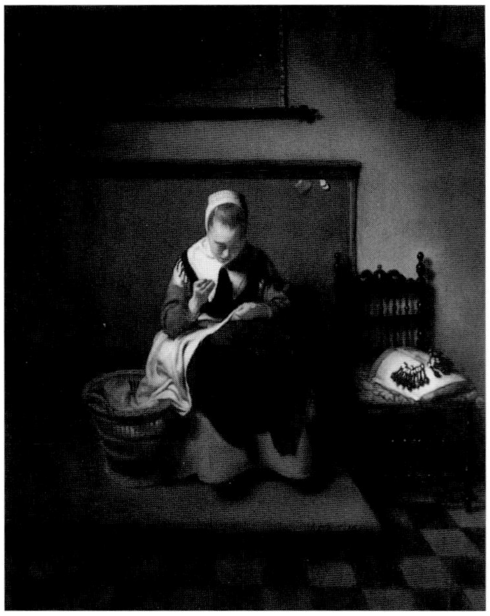

fig. 1. Nicolaes Maes, *A Woman Making Lace*, 1655, oil on panel, The Corporation of London, Mansion House, The Harold Samuel Collection

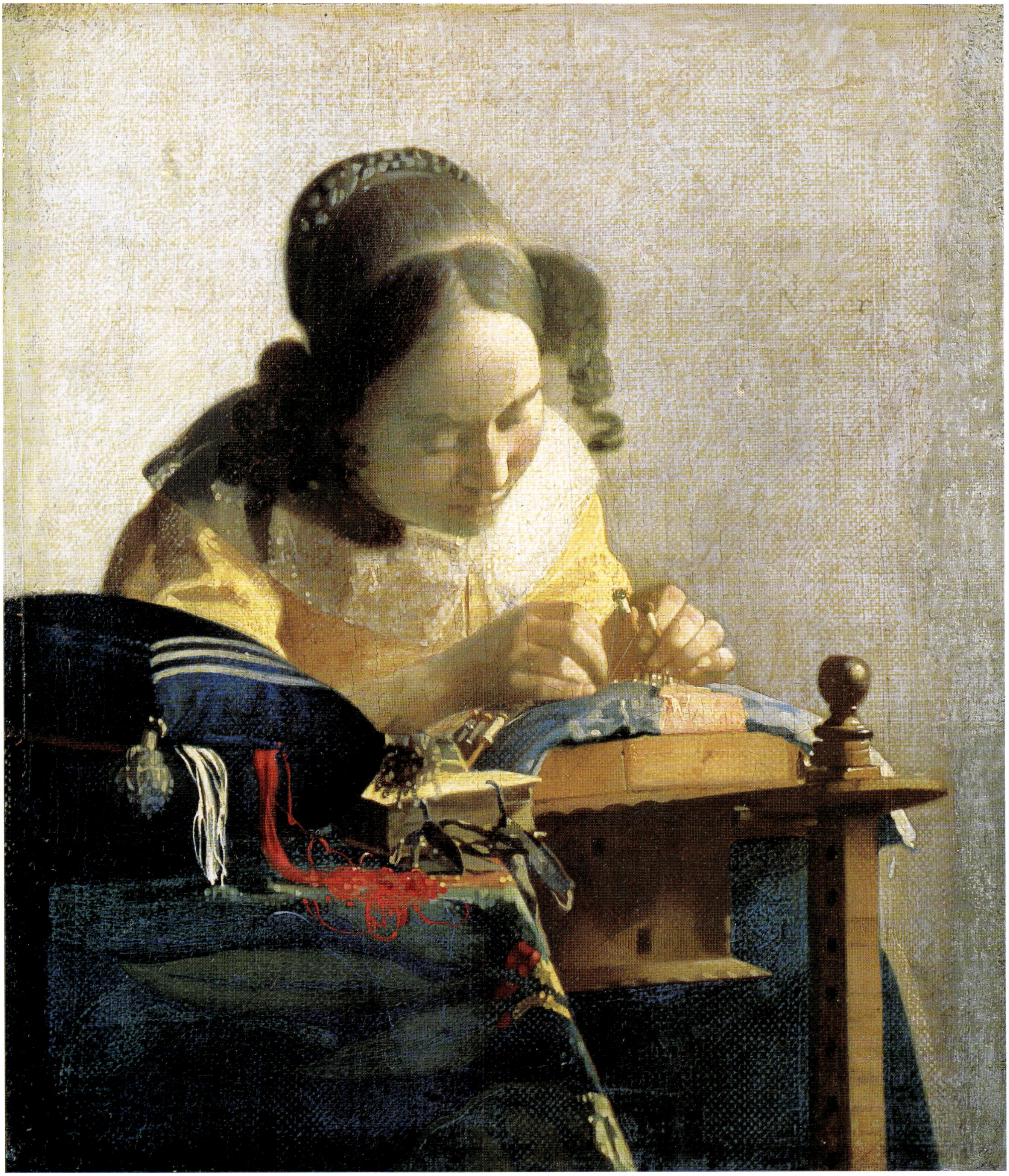

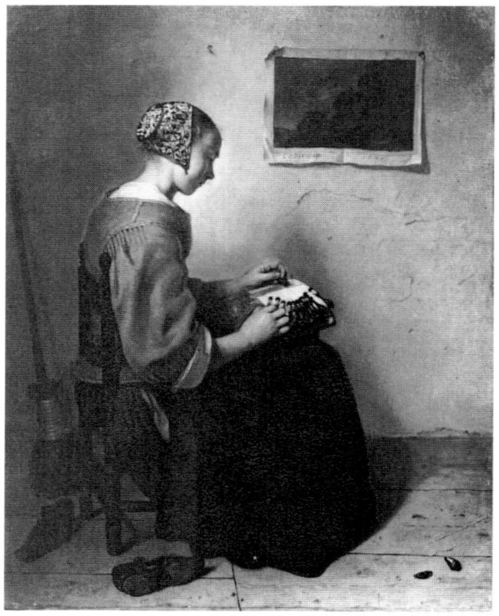

fig. 2. Caspar Netscher, *The Lacemaker*, 1664, oil on canvas, Reproduced by permission of the Trustees of the Wallace Collection, London

(1639–1684) (fig. 2), may also have been stimulated by the use of this device.

Although the small scale of the painting, the informal pose of the lacemaker, and the clearly articulated differences in depth of field support the hypothesis that the artist viewed the scene through a camera obscura, Vermeer would not have painted on top of an image projected onto the canvas by this optical device. As in *The Girl with the Red Hat*, the subtleties of his composition preclude such a possibility.

Within Dutch literary and pictorial traditions, the lacemaker's industriousness would have indicated domestic virtue, a theme Vermeer reinforced through the small book with parchment cover and dark ties on the table beside her.[4] Although the book has no identifying features, it almost certainly represents a prayer book or small Bible.[5] Nevertheless, such moralizing concerns seem secondary in this small yet dynamic image. The concerns here are far more with the craft of lacemaking, and, even more broadly, with the human capacity to create.[6]

Despite its renown, in 1869 the Museum Boymans in Rotterdam failed in its efforts to acquire *The Lacemaker*. At that time the painting was in the well-known Rotterdam collection of Dirk Vis Blokhuyzen (1799–1869), a member and secretary of the board of the Museum Boymans from its very inception. In 1869 he left his enormous collection of paintings, drawings, prints and books to the city of Rotterdam, with the understanding that his heirs were to be compensated with 50,000 guilders. The estate included a large number of prints and drawings by Dürer (1471–1528) and Rembrandt (1606–1669), paintings by Frans Hals (1581/1585–1666) and Gerard ter Borch (1617–1681), and, of course, the Vermeer. This led to heated discussion, because the city council claimed it could not raise the sum. Citizens subsequently organized fund drives but were unable to come up with enough money.[7]

When the Vis Blokhuyzen Collection was auctioned in Paris in 1870 it was acquired by the collector Eugène Féral, who sold it at a profit of almost 2,000 francs two months later to the Louvre.[8] It was the first Vermeer to enter a public collection in France.

The early history of the brilliant work can be reconstructed with only a few lacunae. First, it was at the Dissius sale of 1696 in Amsterdam: "A Damsel doing needle work, by the same [J vander Meer van Delft]."[9] The painting circulated in Amsterdam, where it eventually came into the hands of Jacob Crammer Simonsz (see cat. 16). In the 1778 catalogue of the auction of his art collection, it was called "very naturally and cheerfully painted. On Panel."[10] Thus we see that the canvas had been attached to its wooden support before 1778.

The panel was purchased by Jan Wubbels (c. 1725–1792), a modestly gifted painter of seascapes, who also collected old master paintings, dealt in art, and worked as a restorer for the famous collector John Hope (1737–1784).[11] A colleague of Wubbels, Jan Spaan (1744–1821), bought Vermeer's *Lacemaker* at the Wubbels sale for 210 guilders. He was a frame maker and restorer in the service of the Nationale Konstgallery in The Hague.[12]

Subsequently, Spaan sold the Vermeer to Hendrik Muilman (1743–1812), a banker, who frequently served as alderman and council member in Amsterdam (fig. 3). With his second marriage he became Lord of Heemstede and owner of the handsome castle there.[13] In his residence on the Amsterdam Herengracht hung a highly select collection of paintings that included Rembrandt's *Portrait of Elisabeth Bas* (Rijksmuseum, Amsterdam), and Vermeer's *Milkmaid* (cat. 5) and *The Lacemaker*. After his death, Bernard Coclers bought *The Lacemaker* for eighty-four guilders. The sale catalogue stated, "every-

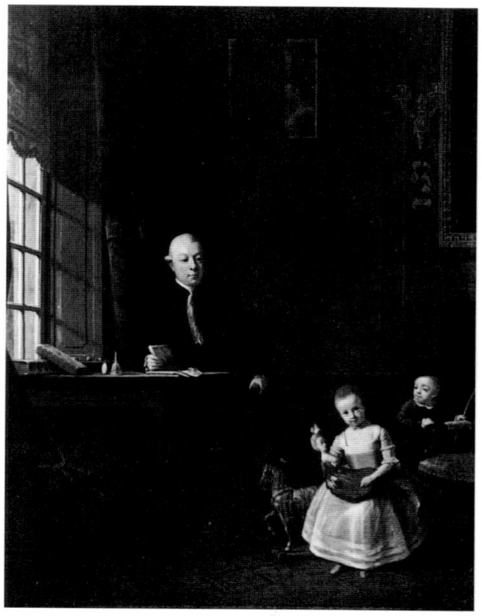

fig. 3. Hendrik Numan, *Hendrik Muilman and His Children*, 1776, oil on canvas, private collection

thing is broadly and substantially painted, and pleasing in color."[14]

Coclers (born 1770) was the son of the Welsh painter Louis Bernard Coclers, who had moved to Amsterdam in 1789.[15] Bernard also painted, but was primarily an art dealer. In 1817, he again bid successfully for the painting by Vermeer, which had in the meantime moved on to France. This time, at the Lapeyrière sale in Paris, Coclers, probably acting on behalf of Baron van Nagell, paid 501 francs for the picture.[16]

Anne Willem Carel, Baron van Nagell van Ampsen (1756–1851), Dutch ambassador to London, was dismissed during the French Revolution and withdrew to his estate in Gelderland. After the period of French domination he became Minister of Foreign Affairs, until 1824.[17] In 1851 his collection of old and modern paintings was sold in The Hague. Arie Lamme (1812–1900), the dealer who later became director of the Museum Boymans, bought it there for 260 guilders, no doubt for his friend Dirk Vis Blokhuyzen of Rotterdam.[18] At the auction of his collection in Paris, *The Lacemaker* was bought for the Louvre, which became the proud owner of this beautiful painting.

1. Kühn 1968, 195.
2. For an extensive analysis of the construction of this work table see Nash 1991, 110–113.
3. Imagine, for example, the difference in mood were the bodice a more calming color, such as blue.
4. On this subject, see, in particular, Stone-Ferrier 1985, 84–100, and Franits 1993, 72–85.
5. In this connection it is interesting to note that the woman sewing in Gabriël Metsu's *The Hunter's Gift*, c. 1658–1660, Rijksmuseum, Amsterdam, reaches for a similar small prayer book or bible when confronted by the hunter's proposition. See Philadelphia 1984, 250–251, cat. 71.
6. Interestingly, some twenty years earlier Diego de Velàzquez came to a similar compositional solution for seemingly comparable reasons in his *The Needlewoman* (National Gallery of Art, Washington).
7. Haverkorn van Rijsewijk 1909, 215–233.
8. The press censured the fact that a private citizen had become almost two thousand francs richer in less than a few months. The museum later mentioned only 1,200 francs as the purchase price (L'Art 1877, 117; Louvre 1891, 154, no. 2456).
9. Hoet 1752–1770, 1: 35, no. 12: "Een Juffertje dat speldewerkt, van den zelven [J vander Meer van Delft]."
10. Sale catalogue, Amsterdam, 25 November 1778, 7–8, no. 17: "zeer natuurlyk en sonaghtig beschilderdt. Op Paneel" (Lugt 2915).
11. Van Eijnden/Van der Willigen 1816–1840, 3: 414; see also Thieme/Becker, 36: 287.
12. Moes 1909, 22 and 29 n. 1; Bille 1961, 1: 58 n. 56: not to be confused with the painter Jan Spaan (1742–1810).
13. Elias 1903–1905/1963, 1: 958–959.
14. Wijnman 1976, 567–568; Sale catalogue, Amsterdam, 12 April 1813, 31, no. 97: "alles is breed en fiks gepenseeld, en bevallig van kleur."
15. Thieme/Becker, 7: 150–51.
16. Sale catalogue, Paris, 14 April 1817, 19–20, no. 30 (Lugt 9098).
17. NNBW, 2: cols. 977–978.
18. Sale catalogue, The Hague, 5 September 1851, 15, no. 40 (Lugt 20483); on Lamme, see: Haverkorn van Rijsewijk 1909, 234–237 and Thieme/Becker, 22: 266.

COLLECTION CATALOGUES

Louvre 1979, 145, no. M.I. 1448 and ill.

LITERATURE

Hoet 1752–1770, 1: 35, no. 12; Gault de Saint Germain 1818, 2: 184; Thoré-Bürger 1858–1860, 2: 71–72; Thoré-Bürger 1866, 300–301, 459, 562, no. 37; L'Art 1877, 117; Havard 1883B, 214, 224 and ill.; Havard 1888, 38, no. 40; Hofstede de Groot 1907–1928, 1: 592–593, no. 11; Haverkorn van Rijsewijk 1909, 229–230, 232; Plietzsch 1911, 119, no. 32 and pl. 29; Johansen 1920, 191, 197; Valentiner 1933, 310, 322 and ill.; Hale 1937, 64, 70, 76, 100, 105, 135–136, 177, 184–186 and ill. 44; De Vries 1939, 49, 90, no. 32 and ill. 56; Blum 1946, 178, no. 37 and ill.; Sulzberger 1948, 37; Van Thienen 1949, 23, no. 27 and ill. 27; Swillens 1950, 58, no. 21, 76, 84, 89, 136 and pl. 21; Gowing 1952, 144–145, no. 24 and pl. 53; Goldscheider 1967, 130, no. 22 and pl. 53; Gerson 1967, cols. 742–743; Blankert 1975, 84, 159–160, no. 26 and pl. 26; Gerson 1977, 289; Van Straaten 1977, 43, no. 54 and ill.; Wheelock 1977A; 298–299 and ill. 97; Blankert 1978, 167–168, no. 26 and pl. 26; Slatkes 1981, 94–95 and ill; Wheelock 1981, 37, 47–49, 144, and pl. 41; Aillaud 1986, 64, 140, 193–195, no. 26, and pl. 26; Wheelock 1988, 45, 114–115 and ill. 34; Montias 1989, 182, 197, 256, 266 and ill. 53; Nash 1991, 25, 31 110–112 and ill.; Blankert 1992, 66, 142, 197–198, no. 26 and pl. 26; Wheelock 1995, 18, 123, 154, 183, and ill. A29

18

The Love Letter

c. 1669–1670

inscribed above the basket: *IVMeer* (IVM in ligature)

oil on canvas, 44 x 38 (17⅜ x 15)

Rijksmuseum, Amsterdam

Exhibited Mauritshuis only

PROVENANCE

Pieter van Lennep, Amsterdam, c. 1810(?)–1850; Margaretha Catharina van Lennep (married to Jan Messchert van Vollenhoven from 1850), Amsterdam, 1850–1891; J.F. van Lennep, Amsterdam, 1892; Messchert van Vollenhoven/Van Engelenberg sale, Amsterdam, 29 March 1892, no. 14 (*f* 45,100 to J. Ankersmit of the Vereniging Rembrandt); Vereniging Rembrandt, Amsterdam, 1892–1893; Rijksmuseum, Amsterdam, 1893

EXHIBITIONS

Amsterdam 1867, 18, no. 113; The Hague 1890, 56, no. 116; Amsterdam 1892, unpaginated, no. A; Amsterdam 1935, 30, no. 169; New York 1954, no. 86 and ill.; Rome 1956, 245–246, no. 310, and pl. 27; London 1964, 44, no. 74, and ill. 5; Stockholm 1967, 26 and ill. 9; Brussels 1971, 132–133, no. 112, and ill; Amsterdam 1976, 268–271, no. 71, and ill.

TECHNICAL DESCRIPTION

The existing canvas may not be original.[1] X-radiography shows a closed plain-weave with a thread count of 16.25 x 14 per cm.[2]

The apparently double ground comprises a red layer followed by a gray layer containing chalk, umber, and a little lead white. Between the two is a thin, unpigmented layer.[2] The red layer may be related to a transfer process.

The paint surface is smooth, with few individual brushstrokes discernible. The dark gray tiles were painted first, and then the white tiles were painted before the gray tiles were dry. The chair and part of the scarf draped over it in the right foreground were underpainted with red lake. The maid's blue apron was painted with a blue-gray underpaint followed by a mixture of blue and white with a final blue glaze. The blue appears to be ultramarine, a lighter patch of which on the mistress' lap can be seen to extend under the bottom edge of the lute. Infrared reflectography indeed reveals that there was a cloth on the lady's lap under the lute. The vanishing point of the composition is visible on the x-radiograph.

The painting was cut off the stretcher during its theft in 1971. The resulting paint loss was mainly restricted to a band approximately 0.5 centimeter wide on either side of the cuts, although there are more serious losses in the top right corner and the center-right area. There is some surface abrasion.

When Pieter Teding van Berckhout, a wealthy young art lover, visited Vermeer in 1669, he remarked that he had seen "some examples of his art, the most extraordinary and most curious aspect of which consists in the perspective" (see page 50 and fig. 4). Although he did not identify any of the paintings he saw, he may have had *The Love Letter* in mind. Vermeer used perspective not only to construct a complex sequence of rooms, but also to reinforce the sense of privacy fundamental to the painting's subject: the mistress' unguarded expression as she turns from her musical instrument and looks to her maid in response to the letter she has just received.[3]

Although Vermeer allows the viewer to witness this private encounter through the doorway of a darkened anteroom, he carefully prevents any intrusion. While the perspective of the tiles draws the eye into the light-filled interior, the vanishing point actually falls on the wall of the anteroom, slightly above the finial of the chair. Thus Vermeer subtly locates the viewer in the foreground plane. He further emphasizes the sense of privacy through the partially draped curtain and the broom and shoes lying near the doorway.

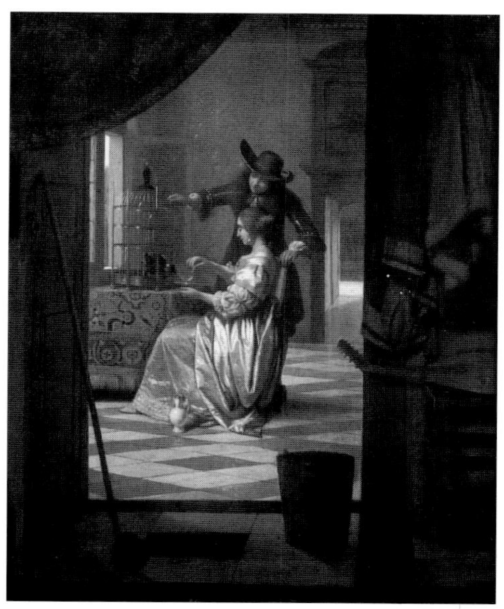

fig. 1. Pieter de Hooch, *A Couple with a Parrot*, 1668, oil on canvas, Wallraf-Richartz-Museum, Cologne

Throughout his career Vermeer devised various means to establish private spaces for his figures, but this is the only extant painting in which he used the remarkable concept of presenting the scene through a doorway.[4] Only one other early painting, *A Woman Asleep* (page 20, fig. 6), includes a doorway into an inner room. While this compositional idea may have been his own invention, it is also possible that he drew inspiration from his former colleague in Delft, Pieter de Hooch (1629–1684). De Hooch often included figures seen through doorways in his interior genre scenes, particularly after he moved to Amsterdam in the early 1660s.

A specific rather than a generic relationship may exist between Vermeer's *The Love Letter* and De Hooch's *A Couple with a Parrot* (fig. 1), in which two figures are viewed through a darkened room in the foreground. The relationship between the two works extends even beyond their compositional similarities. As Jørgen Wadum has discovered, the perspectival systems in the two paintings are practically identical, which suggests that the same principles of perspective underlie each of the works.[5]

Scholars have proposed, on the basis of costume, that De Hooch's painting dates from the 1670s, and have therefore concluded that its composition derives from *The Love Letter*.[6] However, the relationship between the works seems to be quite the opposite. Not only does De Hooch's painting bear a signature and date of 1668, its stylistic features are consistent with his other paintings from the late 1660s.[7] Although *The Love Letter* is not dated, stylistic comparisons with other of Vermeer's paintings suggest a probable date of execution around 1669–1670.[8]

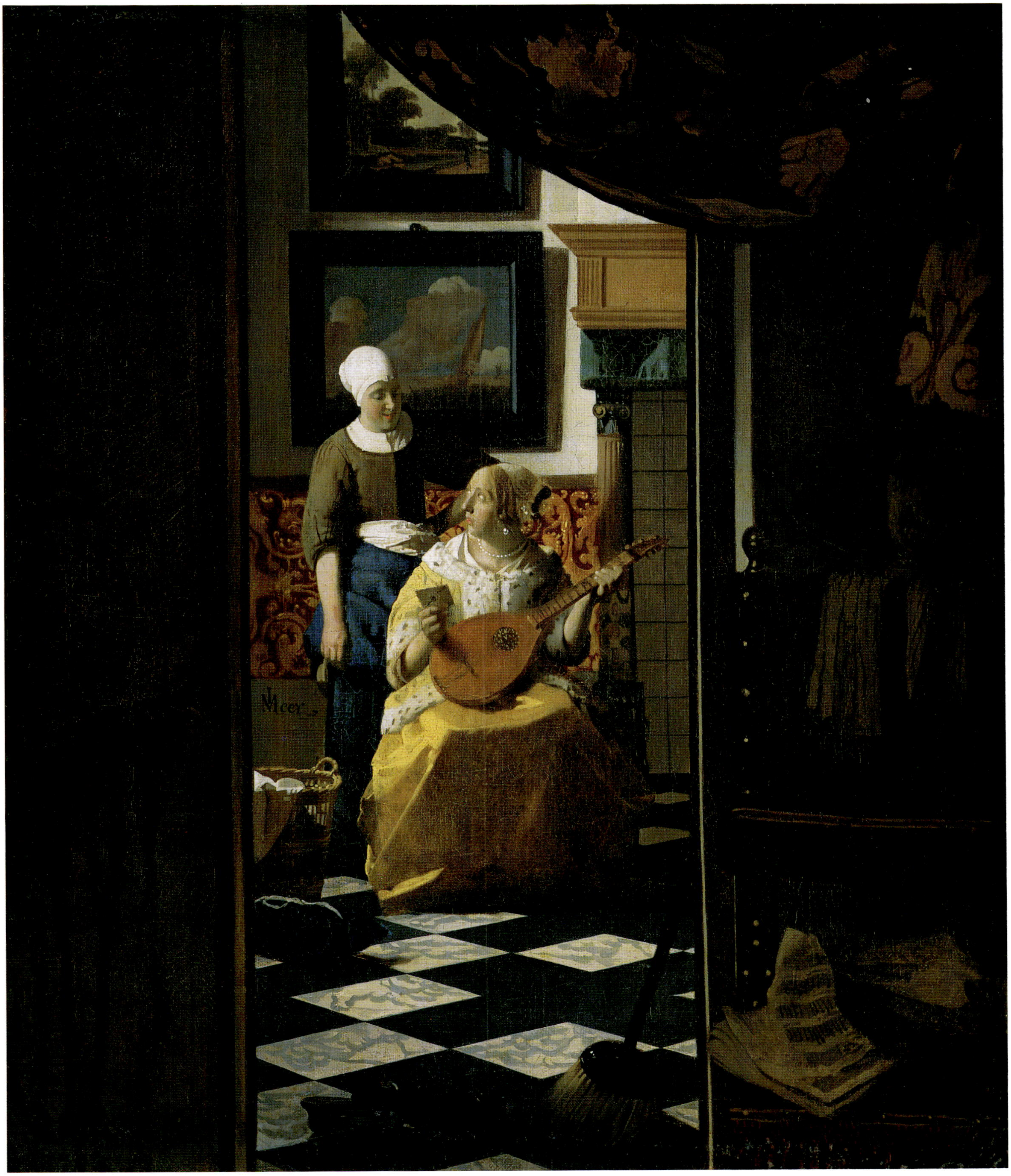

Should Vermeer have maintained contact with De Hooch during the 1660s, as seems probable, he would have continued to be inspired by De Hooch's themes, as well as his compositional constructions. During these years De Hooch favored scenes that focused upon daily events of domestic life, primarily arrivals or departures. He often includes a seated mistress and a standing maid, similar to those in Vermeer's painting.[9] However, while De Hooch portrayed the encounter of mistress and maid primarily for its narrative potential, Vermeer also exploited it for its psychological impact.

Within Dutch art, iconographic traditions for specific subjects, including love letters, seem to have been well understood and shared by painters working in different geographical centers. Most works related to this theme by Vermeer and his contemporaries depict love letters being either written or read (page 156, fig. 1). Occasionally an attendant waits for a letter to be finished or a confidant listens to its content. In *The Love Letter*, however, the mistress' expression reveals the uncertainties of love that disrupt the serenity of a seemingly ordered existence, suggested here by the crystalline light flooding into her well-appointed interior, decorated with paintings, gilded-leather wall coverings, and an elegant mantel.[10]

While De Hooch's painting may have inspired Vermeer to frame the encounter between the mistress and maid within the doorway, his portrayal of the anxiety associated with the arrival of a letter derives from his own *Mistress and Maid*, c. 1667–1668, in the Frick Collection (page 35, fig. 6). Although its large-scale figures and lack of architectural framework differentiate this painting from *The Love Letter*, the reaction of the mistress, who looks up with parted lips and worried eyes, is very

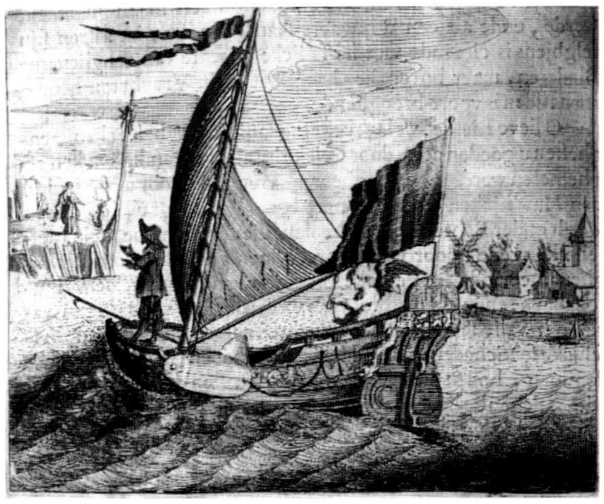

fig. 2. Jan Harmensz Krul, "Al zyt ghy vert, noyt uyt het Hert," *Eerlycke Tytkorting Bestaende in verscheyde Rymen*, Haarlem, 1634, National Gallery of Art Library, Washington

much the same. The primary thematic difference between the two is that the anxiety of the mistress in the Frick painting is left unresolved, whereas in *The Love Letter* Vermeer intimates through the maid's smiling countenance that the mistress' concerns are unfounded. Her judgment seems reinforced by the calm seascape hanging on the wall directly behind her. In Dutch emblematic traditions a calm sea represents a good omen in love (fig. 2), and one may assume that the idyllic landscape hanging directly above it would have been similarly regarded.[11]

Nevertheless, Vermeer may intend a message somewhat more complex than that of the letter. The very thought that this wealthy mistress would be troubled by a love letter is surprising. A confident and virtuous outward appearance, however, often masks inner anxieties stemming from the uncertainties of love. The mistress appears to be in such a situation, for her concerns about love have kept her from her domestic responsibilities. As she sits, playing a musical instrument, probably a cittern, a clothes hamper, a lacemaking pillow, and a broom lie unattended around her. Vermeer may well have used this complex spatial construction to reinforce metaphorically his thematic concern with the contrast of external appearance and inner feelings. While the mistress sits in a bright room with elegant decor, the viewer sees her from a dimly lit, private space, where stains discolor the wall beneath the map at the left and a wrinkled music book lies on the chair at the right.[12] Although the precise reasons for this visual contrast are not entirely clear, the juxtaposition of foreground and background elements is unsettling.[13]

The first public notice of this painting only occurred in 1892 when it was sold in Amsterdam along with other paintings from the Messchert van Vollenhoven Collection.[14] Jan Messchert van Vollenhoven (1812–1881), Burgomaster of Amsterdam from 1858–1866, had come into the possession of a handsome art collection through his marriage to Margaretha Catharina van Lennep. The auction featured mainly (but not exclusively) paintings that came from the collection of Margaretha's father, Pieter van Lennep (1780–1850), which, according to the introduction to the sale catalogue, had been formed in the early nineteenth century as a small but choice ensemble, "a true string of pearls."[15]

Pieter van Lennep was a merchant trading on the Levant. In 1810 he married Margaretha Cornelia Kops (1788–1825), herself a scion of a dynasty of art collectors.[16] The Vermeer painting possibly entered the Van Lennep Collection via Margaretha.

The daughter of Pieter van Lennep and Margaretha Kops, also called Margaretha, had married Burgomaster Van Vollenhoven in April of 1850, only a month before her father's death (fig. 3).[17] In 1892 the Messchert van Vollenhoven-Van Lennep Collection consisted of twenty-seven works, including the Vermeer and expensive pictures

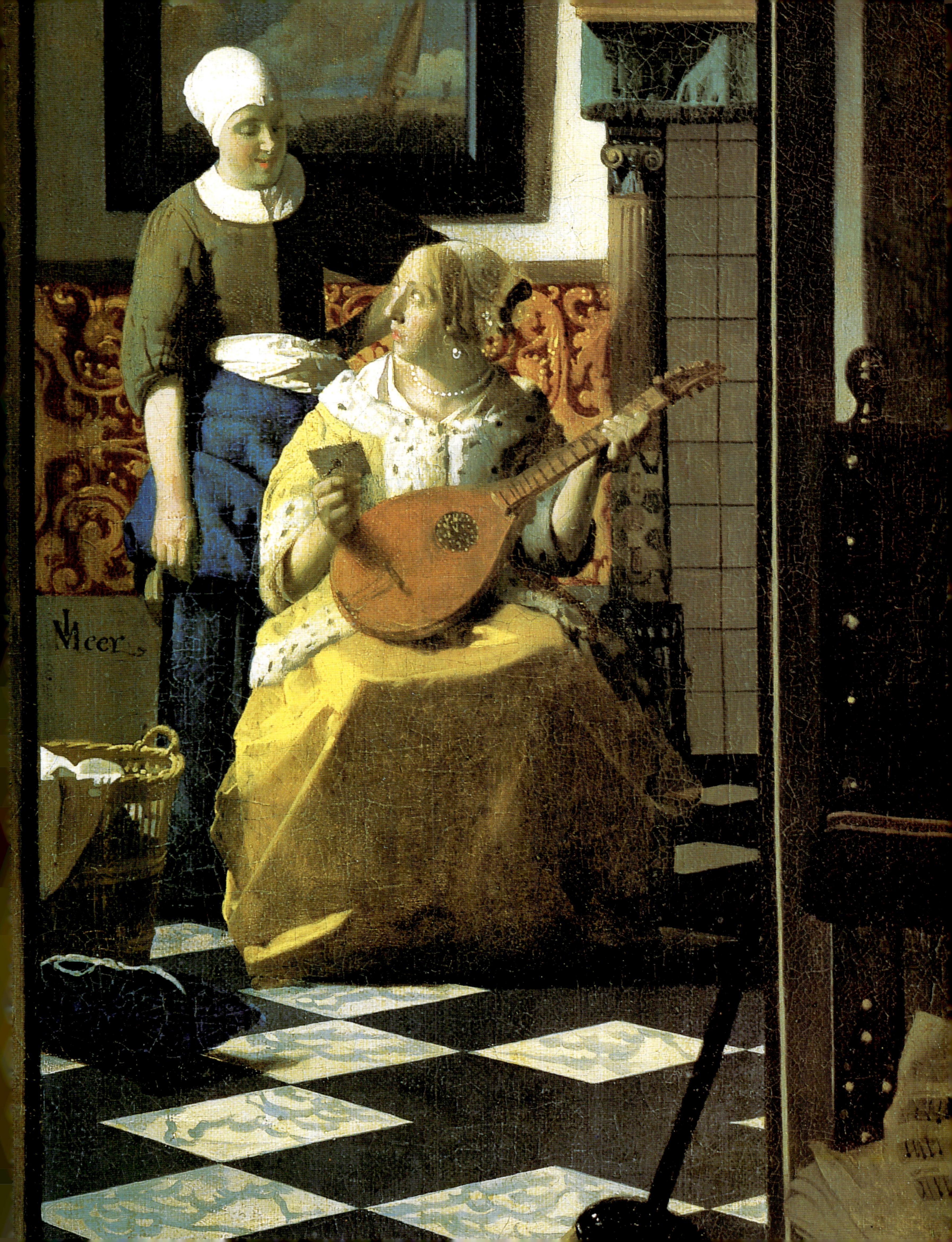

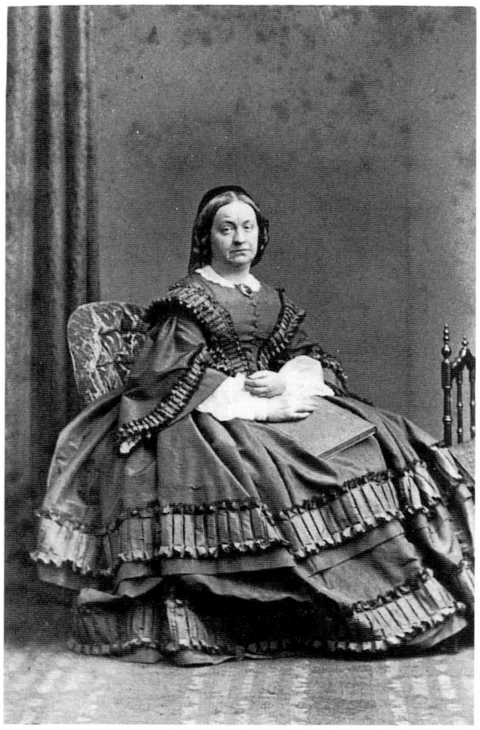

fig. 3. Margaretha van Lennep, photograph, Iconographisch Bureau, The Hague

by Jacob van Ruisdael (1628/1629–1682) and Philips Wouwerman (1619–1668).[18]

Three days before the auction of 29 March 1892, the director of the Rijksmuseum, F. D. O. Obreen, alerted the Minister of External Affairs to the opportunity to acquire the rare Vermeer. Obreen estimated that *The Love Letter* would go for *f* 35,000 to *f* 40,000. The director of the Mauritshuis, Abraham Bredius, however, had a negative reaction to the painting. He wrote to J. Ankersmit, the Chairman of the Rembrandt Society: "I only hope that we are not committing a folly; if we later get the two Vermeers with Six, this lesser work will surely be completely redundant."[19] Nevertheless, Ankersmit proposed to the minister that the society should buy Messchert van Vollenhoven's most important works, so that the state could later purchase them in installments.

The Love Letter turned out to be the absolute star of the auction (fig. 4), and was bought for *f* 41,000 (45,100 with premium) by the Rembrandt Society. Under great public attention, Ankersmit bid against several English collectors. This sale was later exposed as a show performance, because the Rembrandt Society had already bought *The Love Letter* a few days earlier, directly from one of the heirs, Jonkheer J. F. van Lennep. The society probably paid *f* 15,000, which was the starting bid at the auction.[20] A century later this action by the Rembrandt Society was labeled as the first important exploit of this national fund for the preservation of the Dutch national patrimony.[21]

The Vermeer was then displayed in the exhibition room of the artists' society "Arti et Amicitiae" as a new purchase by the Rembrandt Society, along with three other acquisitions and five paintings that Margaretha van Lennep's daughter had transferred to the City of Amsterdam at the request of her mother. Queen Emma opened the exhibition and Jan Veth made an etching of the Vermeer for the society's annual report.[22] On 31 January 1893 the board of the Rembrandt Society solemnly presented *The Love Letter* to Obreen, director of the Rijksmuseum.[23]

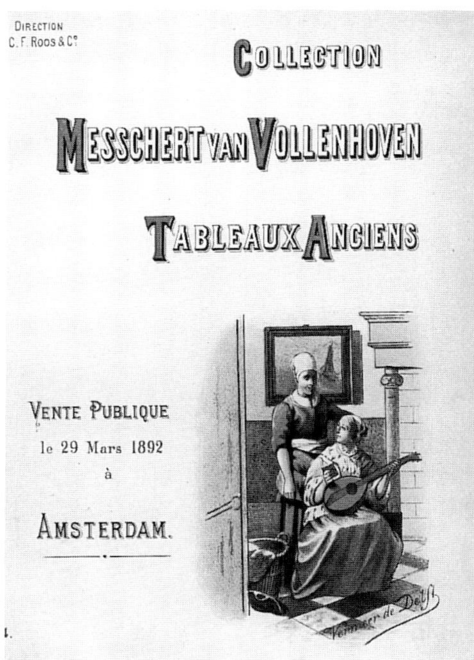

fig. 4. Frontispiece of Messchert van Vollenhoven sale catalogue, Amsterdam, 29 March 1892

1. Van Thiel 1972, 136; on the restoration of the painting see Van Thiel 1972, and Kuiper 1972.
2. Kühn 1968, 197.
3. De Jongh in Amsterdam 1976, 271 n. 6, describes the instrument as a now unknown combination of lute and cittern.
4. Vermeer may have painted one other work with a similar composition, a now lost painting listed as number 5 in the Dissius sale in 1696 "in which a gentleman is washing his hands in a see-through room with sculptures." See Montias 1989, 364, doc. 439.
5. Jørgen Wadum (personal communication) has noted the major difference: that De Hooch did not correctly place the distance points of the floor tiles on the horizon as did Vermeer, but slightly lower. He may have done so to avoid making the visual distortions of the tiles in his much more deeply receding interior space too obvious.
6. Sutton 1980, 39, 110–111, cat. 122.
7. The signature and date were recorded in the Vermeer exhibition held in Rotterdam in 1935 (Rotterdam 1935, no. 53, as signed and dated "P.d.Hooch f 1668"). I would like to thank Ekkehard Mai, curator of old master paintings at the Wallfraf-Richartz-Museum, for confirming that the signature and date " ooch f 1668" are still legible on the painting (letter, December 1994). The diamond pattern of the marble floor tiles is characteristic of De Hooch's paintings from the late 1660s and not those of the mid-1670s (see Sutton 1980, cat. 70, pl. 73; cat. 72, pl. 75; cat. 82, pl. 85). The woman's costume in the Cologne painting, moreover, is virtually identical to that worn by the woman playing the cittern in De Hooch's *Three Women and a Man with a Monkey on a Terrace*, 1669, private collection, England (see Sutton 1980, cat. 91, pl. 94).
8. See Wheelock 1981, 140–142.
9. See, for example, Sutton 1980, cats. 87, 88, plates 90, 91.
10. A segment of gilded-leather wall covering with a slightly different design is seen in *Allegory of Faith* (cat. 20).
11. The connections between this seascape and Krul's emblem, "Al zyt ghy vert, noyt uyt her Hert" (Although he goes far, never from the heart), were first made by De Jongh 1967, 52–55 and ills. 39–40.
12. A similar contrast of spaces, with comparable psychological implications is to be found in Vermeer's *A Woman Asleep* (page 20, fig. 6). See Wheelock 1995, 38–47.
13. I would like to thank Meredith Hale for her thoughtful comments about the thematic implications of the different character of the two rooms.
14. Hale 1937, 178, has suggested that *The Love Letter* appeared at the Dissius sale of 1696: "A Lady who is brought a letter by a Maid ... 70,-," but this description more closely fits the painting in the Frick Collection

(page 35, fig. 6) (See Blankert 1975, 154, cat. 21).
15. Sale catalogue, Amsterdam, 29 March 1892, unpaginated: "un vrai chapelet de perles" (Lugt no. 50649).
16. *Nederlands Patriciaat* 1954, 225–226; see also the provenance section of cat. 7.
17. In the sale catalogue the collection is described as "la Collection de feu Madame la Veuve M.C. MESSCHERT VAN VOLLENHOVEN, née VAN LENNEP"; see sale catalogue, Amsterdam, 29 March 1892, unpaginated (foreword).
18. See the transcription from C.S. Roos' annotated copy of the 1892 sale catalogue (with prices and provenances for the remaining pictures), Rijksmuseum documentation archives, Amsterdam.
19. According to an undated letter (Rembrandt Society Archives), see Van Thiel 1983, 197: "Ik hoop maar, dat wij geen malligheid doen, als we later de twee Vermeers van Six krijgen is dit mindere stuk toch geheel overbodig." See for Obreen's estimate of the price of *The Love Letter* Rijksmuseum copy book 1892–1899 (inv. no. 290, 1–2).
20. In a ministerial communication of 29 April 1892 (Rijksmuseum documentation archives, inv. no. 172, no. 55) there is mention of a donation of 15,000 guilders by Mr. [M. L.] J.F. van Lennep. Further on he is also mentioned as owner of the painting (see Hofstede de Groot 1907–1928, 1: 601; Hale 1937, 178; De Vries 1939, 91, no. 34).
21. Van Thiel 1983, 197.
22. Van Thiel 1983, 199.
23. Rijksmuseum documentation archives, inv. no. 290, 48.

COLLECTION CATALOGUES

Rijksmuseum 1976, 572, no. A 1595 and ill. (with extensive literature)

LITERATURE

Hofstede de Groot 1907–1928, 1: 600–601, no. 32; Plietzsch 1911, 74–76, 113, no. 2, 152 and ill. 28; Johansen 1920, 193; Swillens 1929, 137–138, and ill. 2; Hale 1937, 9, 106, 177–179 and pl. 8; De Vries 1939, 51, 91, no. 35 and ill. 58; Hyatt Mayor 1946, 19; De Vries 1948, 98, no. 28; Swillens 1950, 52, no. 5, 54, 71, 75, 79–80, 82, 84, 86–87, 117 and pl. 5; Gowing 1952, 56–60, 77 n. 4, 78 n. 5, 146–147 n. 121, 151 n. 125, 152, no. 30 and pl. 62–63; Goldscheider 1958, 141 and ill. 69–70; De Mirimonde 1961, 40 and ill.; De Vries 1966, 45a–b and ill.; De Jongh 1967, 50 and 55, ill. 40; Van Uitert 1968, 7 and ill.; Broos 1971, 25; Kuiper 1972, 147–167 and ill. 11–20; Van Schendel 1972, 127–128; Van Thiel 1972, 129–146 and ill. 1–10; Sipkes 1973, 10–15 and ill.; Blankert 1975, 78–84, 117 n. 63, 155–156, no. 22 and pl. 22; Blankert 1978, 53–55, 77 n. 48, 165, no. 22 and pl. 22; Slatkes 1981, 72–75, 101, 122, and ills.; Wheelock 1981, 43, 140–142, 144, 146, and pls. 39–40; Van Thiel 1983, 197–199 and ill. 2; Aillaud 1986, 128, 168 n. 69, 189–190, no. 22, and pl. 21; Wheelock 1988, 41, 110–114, ill. 32–33; Montias 1989, 149, 191–192, 194, 198, 200, 265 n. 2, 266 and ill. 46; Nash 1991, 37, 82–84, and ill.; Blankert 1992, 134, 136, 140, 142, 167, 192–193, no. 22, 223, pl. 21 and ill. 120; Wheelock 1995, 58, 162, 184, and ill. A31

19

Lady Writing a Letter with Her Maid

c. 1670

inscribed on the paper hanging over the edge of the table: *IVMeer* (IVM in ligature)

oil on canvas, 72.2 x 59.7 (28 13/32 x 23 1/2)

National Gallery of Ireland, Dublin

PROVENANCE

Catharina Bolnes, Widow Vermeer, Delft, 1676; Hendrick van Buyten, Delft, 1676–1701; Josua van Belle, Rotterdam, before 1710; Ida Catharina van der Meyden, Widow Van Belle, Rotterdam, 1710–1729; Van Belle sale, Rotterdam, 6 September 1730, no. 92 (*f* 155); Franco van Bleyswijck, Delft, 1734 (appraised at *f* 100); Catharina van der Burch, married to Hendrick van Slingelandt, The Hague, 1734–1761; Heirs Van Slingelandt, The Hague, 1761 (appraised at *f* 30); Maria Catharina van Slingelandt, The Hague, 1761–1771 or Agatha van Slingelandt, The Hague, 1761–1775; (?) Barthout van Slingelandt, Dordrecht, 1771–1798 or Willem Bentinck, The Hague, 1775–1798; Viktor von Miller zu Aichholz, Vienna, before 1881; [Charles Sedelmeyer, Paris, 1881, bought from Von Miller zu Aichholz; sold for Frf 60,000 to Secrétan]; E. Secrétan, Paris, 1881–1889; Secrétan sale, Paris, 1 June 1889, no. 140 (Frf 62,000 to Bousod, Valadon & Co); Collection Marinoni, Paris; [F. Kleinberger, Paris]; Alfred Beit, London, c. 1895–1906; Sir Otto Beit, Bt, London, 1906–1930; Sir Alfred Beit, 2nd Bt, London and (since 1952) Russborough near Dublin, 1930–1987 (stolen in 1974 and 1986); The National Gallery of Ireland (bequeathed by Beit in 1987; the painting was recovered in 1993)

EXHIBITIONS

Paris 1898, 102, no. 86; Paris 1914, 48, no. 22 and ill.; London 1929A, 148–149, no. 314; Amsterdam 1935, 28, no. 164; Rotterdam 1935, 35–36, no. 82 and ill.; London 1938, 1: 106, no. 253, 2: 62, ill. 253; Cape Town 1949, 2 and 13, no. 35; New York 1954, no. 111; The Hague 1966, no. 10 and ill.; Paris 1966, no. 11 and ill.

TECHNICAL DESCRIPTION

The support is a plain weave, linen canvas with a thread count of 14 x 14 per cm^2. The canvas has been lined and the original tacking edges have been removed. Strainer bar marks 2.6 cm from the fold edge can be seen on the top, bottom, and right edges. The lesser degree of cusping on the left side, together with the lack of strainer marks, may indicate that the canvas has been cut down on this side.

The ground, a warm buff-gray is visible on the window frame where the lead casts shadows; along a few contours in the figures, and in places along the shadowed edge of the carpet.

The carpet is very sketchy and appears almost unfinished: instead of soft transitions bright blocks of color have been placed next to each other. The lady's white sleeve was painted wet-in-wet. Incised lines were used to define the tiled floor; the trailing corner of the carpet can be seen to flow into these lines. A dent in the paint in the lady's left eye marks the vanishing point of the composition. The background paint overlaps the maid's blue apron. The edge of the lower part of the green curtain appears to have been slightly further to the left.

An essential component of Vermeer's poetic imagery is the universal that he reveals within the realm of the everyday, through his distinctive manner of painting and his careful choice of narrative moment. Vermeer avoids the anecdotal, where actions and gestures become tied to specific events or situations. To reinforce a sense of timelessness, he purifies his compositions both by eliminating incidental objects unrelated to the painting's theme, and by manipulating light, color, and perspective. All of these qualities exist in *Lady Writing a Letter with her Maid*, one of Vermeer's most glorious achievements of the early 1670s.

Vermeer's scene appears deceptively simple: two women – one writing, one standing – coexist in a spacious, elegantly austere interior. One writes and the other turns to gaze toward the window. No communication exists between them. It is a quiet scene, with no movement and no hint of unexpected interruption. Colors, with the exception of the red table covering, are muted, and shapes are self-contained. Strong horizontals and verticals, particularly the stark black picture frame on the rear wall, help establish the restrained framework so important for the subdued tenor of the painting. Within these parameters, however, Vermeer establishes a contrast in the characters of the two women that gives the painting its remarkable psychological insight.

Vermeer achieves this effect, in part, through the postures of the two women – the statuesque calm of the maid as she looks toward the light and the intent concentration of the mistress as she writes her letter. However, he also indicates their different psychological states through his painterly techniques. The self-contained gravity of the maid, visually reinforced by her central placement in the composition and the vertical of the picture frame behind her, is also denoted by the simple, regular folds of her muted, floor-length costume. Vermeer paints her in an appropriately broad manner, with blended brushstrokes. The mistress, on the other hand, leans on her left arm while writing, conveying an inner intensity and emotional energy that is heightened by the compressed space between her and the right edge of the painting. Vermeer accents the left side of her body with strong light, which he further emphasizes by silhouetting her against the shaded wall and black picture frame. The light creates sharply defined planes on her dress and blouse, angular rhythms of folds that seem to suggest the acuity of her emotional state.

Although the two women are separate and distinctive entities, Vermeer subtly integrates them through his perspective system. Orthogonals follow the receding forms of the lower and upper window frame passing across both the maid's folded arms and her illuminated forehead as they project to the vanishing point, situated at the left eye of the mistress. The viewer thus is visually drawn to the maid before the eye rests on the mistress, the primary focus of the painting.

Just as Vermeer used perspective so effectively in *The Love Letter*, so here his dynamic spatial configuration provided him with a framework for depicting a subtle drama. Indeed, the calm demeanor of the maid serves as foil to the psychological intensity of the mistress. Nevertheless, Vermeer does not provide a clear narrative context, such as might be expected from another painter, to elucidate the mistress' frame of mind. Instead, as with *The Love Letter* (cat. 18), he offers only hints and allusions.

One allusion to the mistress' concerns is found on the black and white marble floor just before her writing table: a crum-

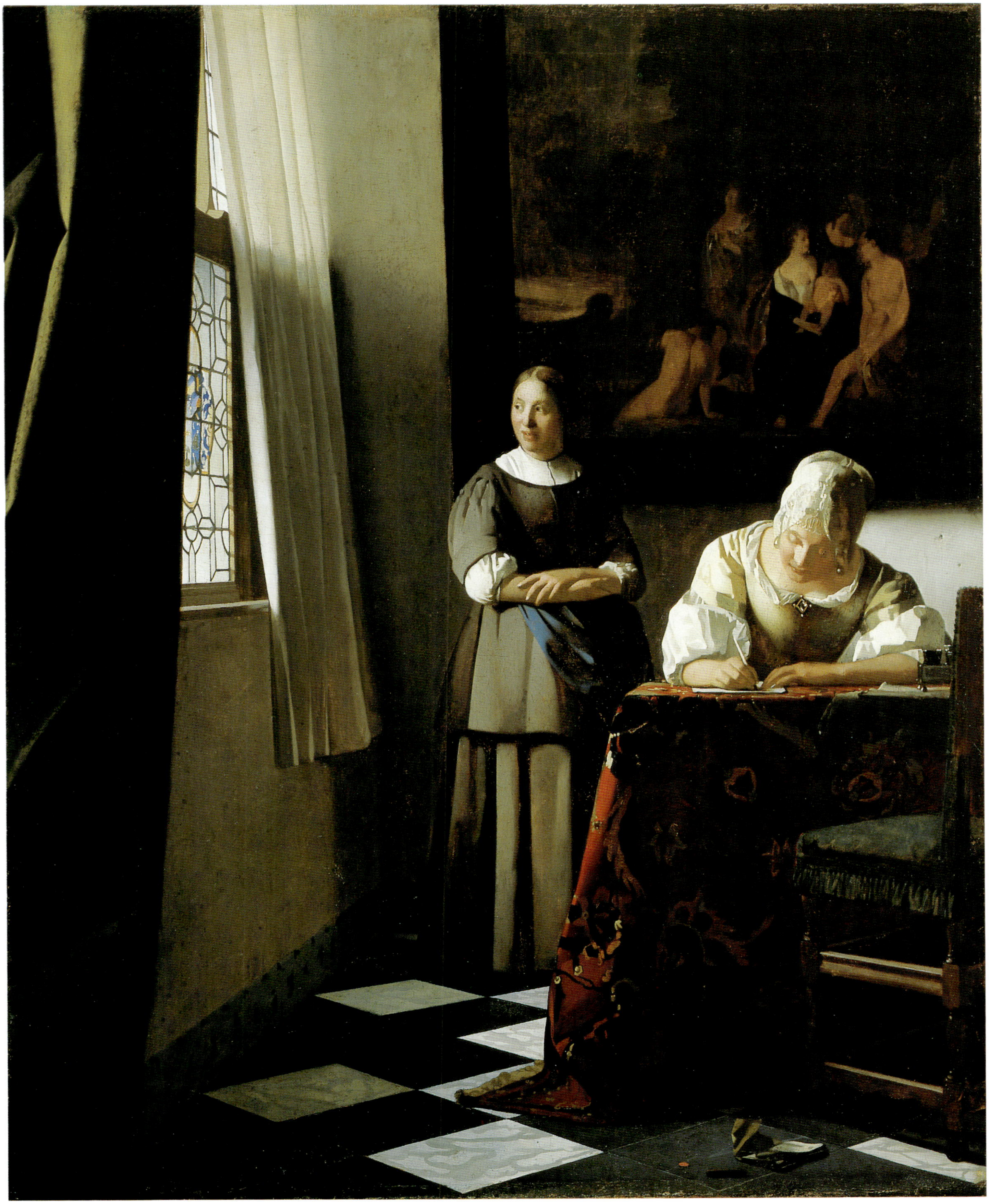

pled letter. As a red wax seal also lies on the floor, the letter must be one she has received rather than a discarded draft of the one she composes.[1] Letters were highly valued and not objects to be thrown aside, except, perhaps, in anger. As Vermeer never included extraneous compositional elements, the letter must be of great thematic consequence. Indeed, it may explain the mistress' intense concentration as she writes, presumably in response.

Another allusion is the large painting of the *Finding of Moses* on the rear wall, the same painting that appears, at a much smaller scale, in *The Astronomer* (page 52, fig. 6).[2] Biblical scenes such as this were generally understood allegorically, providing insight into human nature and God's divine plan. Among Old Testament stories the Dutch particularly revered that of Moses.[3] This episode (Exodus 2:1–10) represents the moment after the Egyptian Pharaoh's daughter and her handmaidens discovered a Hebrew baby in a basket among the bulrushes. The boy had been hidden by his mother to escape the Pharaoh's decree that all male Hebrew babies be killed. The Pharoah's daughter saved the child and named him Moses. The story was interpreted in the seventeenth century both as evidence of divine providence[4] and as an indication of God's ability to bring together opposing factions. A Dutch minister, for example, associated this story with one of Salomon's proverbs: "When a man's ways please the Lord, / he makes even his enemies to be at peace with him" (Proverbs 16:7).[5]

Letter-writing scenes are traditionally related to love rather than theology in the seventeenth century, but, as is evident in the emblematic writings of Jacob Cats, the meaning of an image could apply equally to social and religious issues and concerns of the heart.[6] Although the relationship between the *Finding of Moses*, the discarded letter, and the mistress is oblique, the conjunction may indicate a theme related to achieving reconciliation and peace of mind. Vermeer seems to suggest that reconciliation comes through one's own endeavors, carried out in concert with an abiding faith in God's divine plan. Through that combination comes also the serenity so effectively embodied in the maid.

Lady Writing a Letter with Her Maid was never sold during Vermeer's lifetime. After his death, on 27 January 1676 his widow Catharina Bolnes gave two paintings as security to a baker, Hendrick van Buyten (1632–1701), as she owed him 617 guilders and 6 *stuivers* for bread he had delivered. One of the two paintings was described in this document as "portraying two personages of which the one sits and writes a letter."[7] At his death in 1701 Van Buyten left behind three Vermeers, one a large painting, presumably this work, and "Two small works by Vermeer."[8]

The dimensions of the Dublin painting correspond more or less with those of "A sitting young Lady writing a letter, next to which a Maid stands waiting, by Vander Meer" that was sold at the 1730 Van Belle sale in Rotterdam.[9] Josua van Belle (1637–1710) was a merchant trading with Spain and had been Burgomaster of Rotterdam in 1705.[10]

On 9 October 1734 Franco van Bleyswijck, ex-member of Delft's Council of Forty, was interred in the Oude Kerk.[11] His estate was divided between two universal heirs, Hendrik and Johan Diederik van Slingelandt, who were full cousins as well as brothers-in-law. Lot A went to Hendrik (1702–1759), alderman and Burgomaster of The Hague. This made him the owner of "A Damsel who writes a letter and a maid next to her by J. v. MEER," appraised at 100 guilders.[12] In 1740 Hendrik van Slingelandt and his wife Maria Catharina van der Burch (1707–1761) drew up their testament in favor of their son and two daughters.[13]

After Hendrik died in 1759, and his wife two years later, the Hague painter Aert Schouman examined and priced the contents of the estate. He believed that "A writing Woman by J. VAN DER MEER" was worth no more than thirty guilders.[14] One of the two daughters, either Agatha or Elisabeth Maria, inherited the "writing Woman."

The subsequent history of the painting is unrecorded until 1881, when a Paris dealer bought the canvas from Viktor von Miller zu Aichholz (1845–1910), an Austrian industrialist and, later, banker, numismatist, and art collector.[15] Though we do not know why he sold the Vermeer during his lifetime, we have such information concerning the next owner, E. Secrétan, who acquired it from the Paris dealer for 60,000 francs. A director of the "Société des Metaux," he had gotten into financial difficulties. The famous Secrétan Collection had served as security for loans, and the executors of his bankruptcy decided for a public sale.[16] The Vermeer ("Le Billet doux") remained in a Paris collection (Marinoni), and then came into the hands of dealer Kleinberger, who eventually sold it to Alfred Beit.[17]

Beit had begun collecting around 1895 and the Vermeer was one of his first acquisitions.[18] Alfred Beit (1853–1906) was born in Hamburg, but left at age seventeen for South Africa, where he became fabulously rich by diamond and gold mines. He died a single man and left his fortune to his brother Otto (1865–1930), who had assisted him in the diamond trade since 1888.[19] In 1928 Otto Beit was raised to the baronetcy. He passed the title on to his son, who was named after his uncle Alfred (1903–1994). The young Alfred Beit became a member of parliament and, after World War II, went to South Africa to look after the family interests there. In 1952 he bought a Palladian country residence called Russborough, in Blessington near Dublin, where he installed his inherited collection of paintings. With the Rothschilds and the Queen of England, he was one of the last private individuals to own a Vermeer.[20]

In 1974 Russborough became the target of an attack, by members of the IRA, who stole nineteen paintings. The booty was recovered a week later. The Vermeer was only slightly damaged and could be repaired.[21] Twelve years later, on 21 May 1986, the Beit collection again fell victim to a bold robbery. This time the Dublin underworld was responsible and the take amounted to seventeen paintings, including the Vermeer. Years of secret negotiations and international detective work followed which fortunately led to the recovery of all the stolen works, including the Vermeer, on 1 September 1993.[22] Sir Alfred Beit, who died on 14 May 1994, at the age of 91, lived to see the rescue of the paintings. He had already bequeathed "his" Vermeer to the Dublin museum in 1987.[23]

1. The discovery of the wax seal was made by Andrew O'Connor when he conserved the painting in 1974. See O'Connor 1977, 275 n. 4.
2. Blankert 1975, 156, cat. 23, agrees with W. L. van de Watering on the attribution of this painting to Sir Peter Lely (1618–1680), who worked in the Netherlands as a history painter until he moved to England in the early 1640s. Lely, who trained in Haarlem in the entourage of Frans Pieter de Grebber, would have known De Grebber's son, Pieter de Grebber, who also painted this subject in a similar fashion (signed and dated, 1634, Dresden, Staatliche Kunstsammlungen, Gemäldegalerie Alte Meister; illustrated in Amsterdam 1991, 56, fig. 40.
3. Schama 1987, 104–117.
4. The connection between the finding of Moses and divine providence is made in the 1758–1760 Hertel edition of Ripa, *Iconologia*. See: Maser 1971, 162. Although this connection has not yet been found in a seventeenth-century reference, the association probably is an old one.
5. See Marloes Huiskamp in Münster 1994, 55–56. The association between the story of Moses and Proverbs was made in 1609 by an Utrecht preacher by the name of Henricus Caesarius.
6. See, for example, Cats 1627.
7. Montias 1993, 381–383, doc. 361: "d'eene vertoonende twee personagien waeraff d'eene een brieff sit en schrijft."
8. Montias 1993, 403, doc. 442: "Twee stuckjes van Vermeer." Montias assumed that the large painting must have been the letter writer that had served as security for the *f* 617 debt, and that it must therefore have been the same as the large canvas *Mistress and Maid* (page 58, fig. 14). However, the woman in that work is not writing but looks up from a letter while a servant brings her a letter. (Blankert 1992, 58 and Montias 1993, 239 and 281; compare also Montias 1987, 75 n. 54).
9. Hoet 1752–1770, 1: 359, no. 92: "Een Juffrouw zittende een Brief te Schryven daer de Meid nae staet te wagten, door Vander Meer."
10. Engelbrecht 1973, 174, no. 34, and 246–248, no. 198; Van Gelder 1974, 169; Rotterdam 1994, 36–37.
11. Van Beresteyn 1938, 49.
12. Hoge Raad van Adel, The Hague, Family Archives Van Slingelandt, portfolio 24, no. 75: "Een Juf: die een brief schrijft en een meijt bij haar door J: V: Meer... *f* 100.–.–." (see also Hofstede de Groot 1892A, 235–236).
13. Their collection was described in Hoet 1752–1770, 2: 407–408.
14. Hoge Raad van Adel, The Hague, Family Archives Van Slingelandt, portfolio 6, no. 17: "Een Schrijvent Vrouwtje door J. van der Meer op... *f* 30.–.–." (see also Hofstede de Groot 1892, 230–231, no. 17).
15. ÖBL, 6: 304–305: he was always called "Miller von Aichholz" in the Vermeer literature.
16. Garnier 1889, 145.
17. Hofstede de Groot 1907–1928, 1: 602, no. 35.
18. Bode 1904, 8–10.
19. Burke's 1963, 213; NDB, 2: 23.
20. Concerning Beit, see *The Times and The Independent*, 14 May 1994 (Mauritshuis documentation archives); on the Beit Collection, see Watson 1960, 156–163.
21. O'Connor 1977.
22. Spaans 1994, 40–44; numerous newspaper articles were written about this affair in 1993 and 1994 (Mauritshuis documentation archives).
23. National Gallery Ireland 1988, 54; for the Beit obituaries, see the items mentioned in n. 20.

COLLECTION CATALOGUES
National Gallery Ireland 1988, 3–4 and 54–55, no. 17 and ill.

LITERATURE
Hoet 1752–1770, 1: 359, no. 92, 2: 408; Blanc 1860–1863, 2: s.v., 4; Thoré-Bürger 1866, 548; Havard 1888, 36, no. 8; Hofstede de Groot 1892A, 231 n. 1 and 236; Bode 1904, 8–10; Hofstede de Groot 1907–1928, 1: 602, no. 35; Hofstede de Groot 1907–1930, unpaginated, ill. 23; Hofstede de Groot 1910–1911, 133; Plietzsch 1911, 62–63, 117, no. 24 and ill. 19; Bode 1913, 9–10, ill. 6 and 85, no. 69; Vanzype 1925, 82; Borenius 1929, 25; Hale 1937, 34, 101, no. 35, 145, 158–159, 186 and ill. 33; De Vries 1939, 85, no. 21 and ill. 13 and 47; Blum 1946, 194, no. 8, 203, no. 15 and ill.; Van Thienen 1949, 9, 18, 23, no. 32 and ill.; Swillens 1950, 31, 53–54, no. 9, 67, 72, 78, 82, 84, 87–88, 103, 116 and pls. 9, 78; Gowing 1952, 20, 44, 55, 63–64, 71 n. 17, 96, 153–154, no. 31, colorpl. D and pls. 64–67; Watson 1960, 157–158 and ill. 2; Gerson 1967, col. 743; Goldscheider 1967, 133, no. 30 and ill. 69, 70, 73; Van Gelder 1974, 169; Blankert 1975, 36, 84, 87, 161, no. 27 and pl. 27; O'Connor 1977, 272–275 and ill. 68; Blankert 1978, 25, 56, 168–169, no. 27, pls. 27 and 27a–b; Slatkes 1981, 82, 94, 100–101 and ill.; Wheelock 1981, 33, 134, 146, 150, and pl. 42; Aillaud 1986, 54, 57, 140, 195, no. 27, and pl. 27; Montias 1987, 75 n. 54; Wheelock 1988, 116–117, 120 and pl. 35; Montias 1989, 266 and ill. 41; Dumas 1991, 180–181 and ill. 35; Nash 1991, 84, 87 and ill.; Blankert 1992, 55, 58, 85, 142, 198–199, no. 27, pl. 27 and ill. 105; Spaans 1994, 43 and ill.; Wheelock 1995, 5, 6, 7, 31, 156–162, 184, and ill. 107

20

Allegory of Faith

c. 1671–1674
oil on canvas, 114.3 x 88.9 (45 x 35)

Lent by The Metropolitan Museum of Art, New York, The Friedsam Collection, Bequest of Michael Friedsam, 1931

PROVENANCE
Herman Stoffelsz van Swoll, Amsterdam, before 1698; Van Swoll sale, Amsterdam, 22 April 1699, no. 25 (*f* 400); Sale, Amsterdam, 13 July 1718, no. 8 (*f* 500); Sale, Amsterdam, 19 April 1735, no. 11 (*f* 53); David Ietswaart sale, Amsterdam, 22 April 1749, no. 152 (*f* 70 to Ravensberg); Private collection, Austria, 1824; Dmitrii Tchoukine, Moscow, 1899; [Wächtler, Berlin, 1899, to Bredius for DM 700]; Abraham Bredius, The Hague, 1899–1928; Mauritshuis, The Hague, 1899–1923 (on loan from Bredius); Museum Boymans, Rotterdam, 1923–1928 (on loan from Bredius); [F. Kleinberger, Paris, 1928]; Michael Friedsam, New York, 1928–1931 (bought for $300,000); and by bequest to the present owner, 1931

EXHIBITIONS
Delft 1952, 216–217, no. 324 and ill.

TECHNICAL DESCRIPTION
The support is a fine, plain-weave linen with a thread count of 14.5 x 12 cm^2 and has been wax/resin lined. The original tacking edges are present.

The light gray-brown ground contains chalk, lead white, and umber.[1]

Underdrawing lines, which appear to be in black chalk, are visible between the floor tiles and the line separating the ceiling from the wall.

The paint has been thinly and smoothly applied, though some impasto in the curtain and in the blue areas is apparent. Areas of the curtain were painted wet-in-wet as were some of the flesh tones. The vanishing point of the painting is visible as a small depression in the paint layer.

The seriousness of moral purpose underlying Vermeer's history paintings, cityscapes, and scenes of daily life endows them with a gravity and grandeur not found in the paintings of his contemporaries. Although little is known about the individuals and events that framed the artist's intellectual and philosophical approach to painting, Vermeer's conversion to Catholicism prior to his marriage in 1654 must have had a profound impact upon his life and art (see page 16).[2] Vermeer's Catholicism, for example, almost certainly affected his choice and interpretation of subjects in his early history paintings.[3] Only in *Allegory of Faith*, however, does he explicitly incorporate abstract theological concepts into a visual vocabulary similar to his other paintings.

The domestic interior in *Allegory of Faith* is comparable in scale and character to the one Vermeer designed for his earlier allegory, *Art of Painting* (page 68, fig. 2). Indeed, the perspectival systems for the two paintings are virtually identical. In both paintings, moreover, Vermeer depicts a multicolored tapestry that is pulled to the left to reveal the allegory.

Allegory of Faith focuses on a woman wearing an elegant white and blue satin dress trimmed in gold. As she sits on a raised platform covered by a green and yellow rug, she rests her right foot on a terrestrial globe. With her right hand at her breast, she gazes intently upward toward a glass orb hanging from a blue ribbon. An open Bible, a chalice, and an ebony crucifix lie on the table beside her, the crucifix accentuated by an elaborately designed gilt leather panel situated along the rear wall. On the black and white marble floor lie an apple and a snake crushed by a large cornerstone. The final element of the allegory is the large painting of the Crucifixion that serves as a visual backdrop for the scene.

As has long been observed, Vermeer derived most of the components of this allegory from Cesare Ripa's *Iconologia*, which he would have known from D. P. Pers' 1644 Dutch translation.[4] Ripa describes four separate allegorical figures of Faith, some sharing common characteristics and attributes, but none matching exactly the disposition of the woman in Vermeer's allegory. Vermeer's image – from the color of the woman's robes to her gesture, from the presence of the chalice to the crushed snake and apple – is, in fact, a composite of elements found in two of these descriptions of Faith.[5]

The attributes that Vermeer chose to represent underscore their importance for the meaning of the scene. As Ripa relates in one of his texts, Faith is the most important of the virtues. She is depicted as a woman dressed in white, relating symbolically to light and purity. Blue, as he mentions in another of his texts, relates to heaven. Faith's pose of hand on breast indicates that a living faith resides in her heart. The cornerstone that has crushed the snake represents Christ, while the apple is a reminder of original sin.

Ripa does not mention specifically other elements in Vermeer's allegory, among them the globe, the crucifix, the painting of the Crucifixion, and the glass orb.[6] Indeed, Vermeer used considerable artistic license to interpret Ripa's texts. For example, Vermeer interpreted quite literally Ripa's description of Faith as "having the world under her feet" by including a terrestrial globe, made by Hendrick Hondius.[7]

Other elements provide the allegory with a more Catholic, and even Jesuit, content than that suggested by Ripa. Rather than having Faith hold the chalice and rest her hand on a book, as Ripa describes, Vermeer places these attributes on the

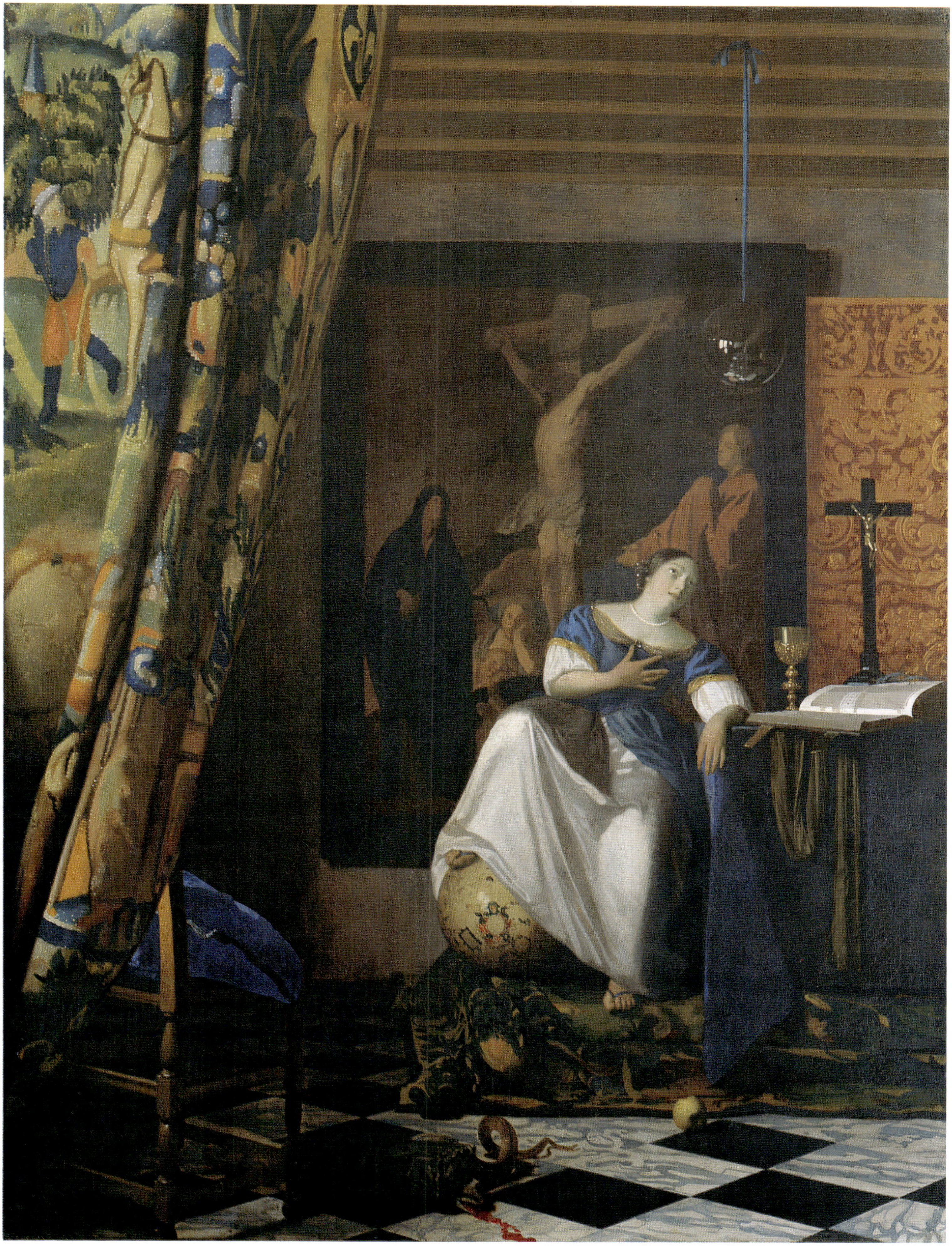

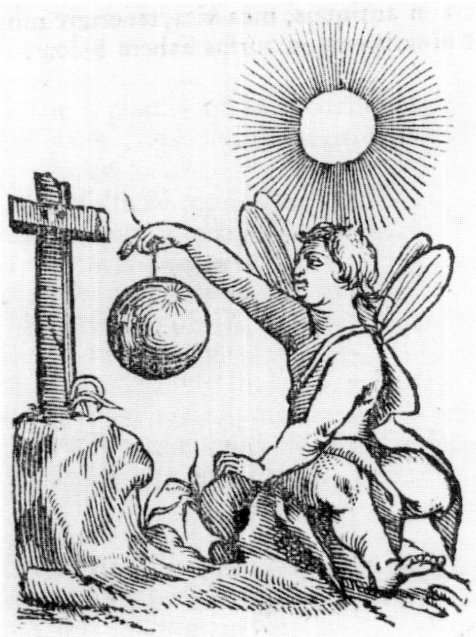

fig. 1. J. C. Jegher, after Erasmus Quellinus, "Capit Quod Non Capit," from Hesius, *Emblemata sacra de fide, spe, charitate*, Antwerp, 1636, National Gallery of Art Library, Washington

table next to the crucifix, an assemblage that gives the image a Eucharistic character not found in the text. Indeed, Vermeer gives these elements added prominence by depicting them against contrasting backgrounds – the ebony crucifix against gold and the gilded chalice primarily against black.[8] By slightly overlapping the chalice and the crucifix's gold backdrop, Vermeer may symbolically suggest the essential role of the Eucharist in bridging the physical and spiritual realms.[9]

One other significant difference exists between Ripa's texts and Vermeer's image. Although Ripa alludes to the story of Abraham and Isaac as a symbol of the triumph of Faith, Vermeer replaces this Old Testament prefiguration of the sacrifice of Christ with a painting of the *Crucifixion* itself, a change that reflects the central importance of Christ's sacrifice to the Jesuits.[10] Saint Ignatius, for example, closes the first of his Spiritual Exercises by writing: "Imagine Christ our Lord before you, hanging upon the cross. Speak with Him of how, being the creator he then became man, and how, possessing eternal life, He submitted to temporal death to die for our sins."[11]

As De Jongh has noted, the glass orb extends the Jesuit content of the allegory, for Vermeer must have adapted it from an emblem by the Jesuit author Willem Hesius (fig. 1),[12] in which a winged boy, representing the soul, lifts a sphere upon which the adjacent cross and the sun are reflected. The accompanying poem compares the capacity of the sphere to reflect the vastness of the universe with the ability of the mind to believe in God.

The circumstances surrounding the execution of this remarkable allegorical image are not known. Perhaps, as has been suggested, Vermeer executed this large-scale painting for the Jesuit Order in Delft or for a wealthy Catholic patron.[13] The Jesuits' emphasis on prayer within the privacy of one's own room may help explain Vermeer's decision to place the allegory within a domestic setting.[14] It seems unlikely, however, that he was given an iconographic program. The imaginative way in which he expanded the meaning of Ripa's emblems parallels his approach to *The Art of Painting*.[15] Moreover, a number of the objects he included in the allegory – Jacob Jordaens' (1593–1678) Crucifixion (fig. 2), the ebony crucifix, and the gilt leather panel – belonged to his own household.[16] Since Ripa mentioned none of these objects, and all were important for the meaning of the allegory, it stands to reason that Vermeer, not a patron, decided to incorporate them.

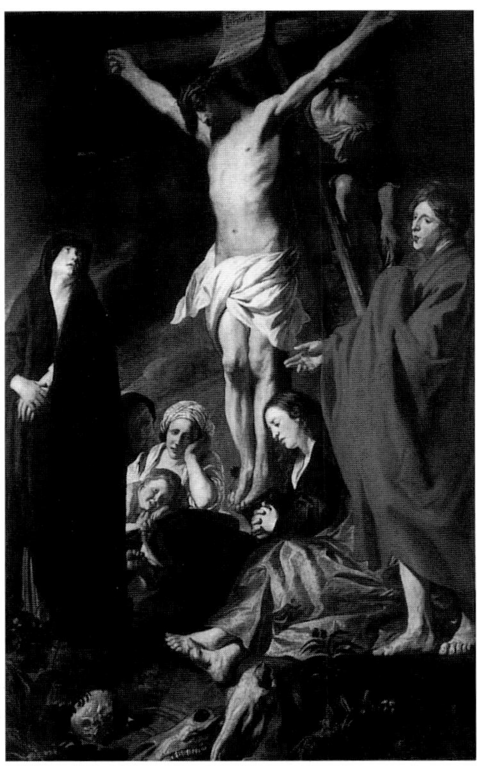

fig. 2. Jacob Jordaens, *Crucifixion*, c. 1620, oil on canvas, private collection, Hugo Maertens Photography

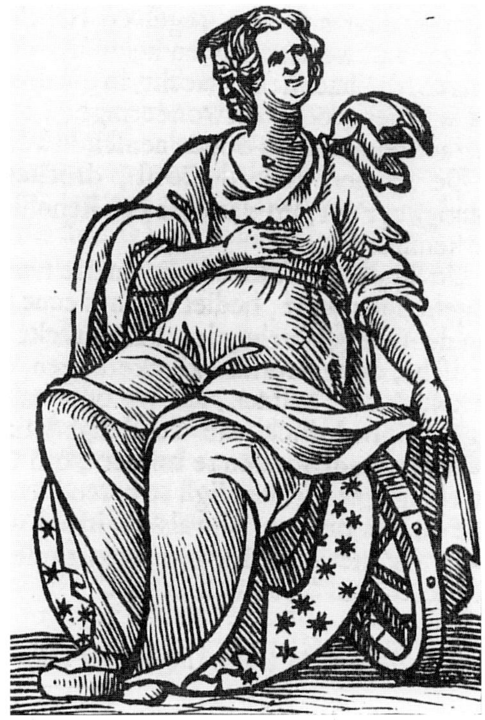

fig. 3. "Theology", from Cesare Ripa, *Iconologia*, Amsterdam, 1644, National Gallery of Art Library, Washington

While the woman's pose fulfills certain of Ripa's descriptions for Faith, Ripa does not illustrate this particular allegorical concept. Similarities in pose between Vermeer's Faith and Ripa's allegorical image of Theology (fig. 3) suggest that the artist may have turned to this related concept for a visual prototype.[17] The rough woodcut images in Ripa's *Iconologia*, however, could hardly have served as the sole stylistic basis for Vermeer's idealized female image. While the particular disposition of Faith, with one hand to the breast and eyes glancing upward, is not commonly found in Dutch art, this pose frequently appears in Italian art, particularly in the paintings of Guido Reni (1575–1642),[18] which Vermeer could have seen in Dutch collections. It should not be forgotten that during the very years that Vermeer cre-

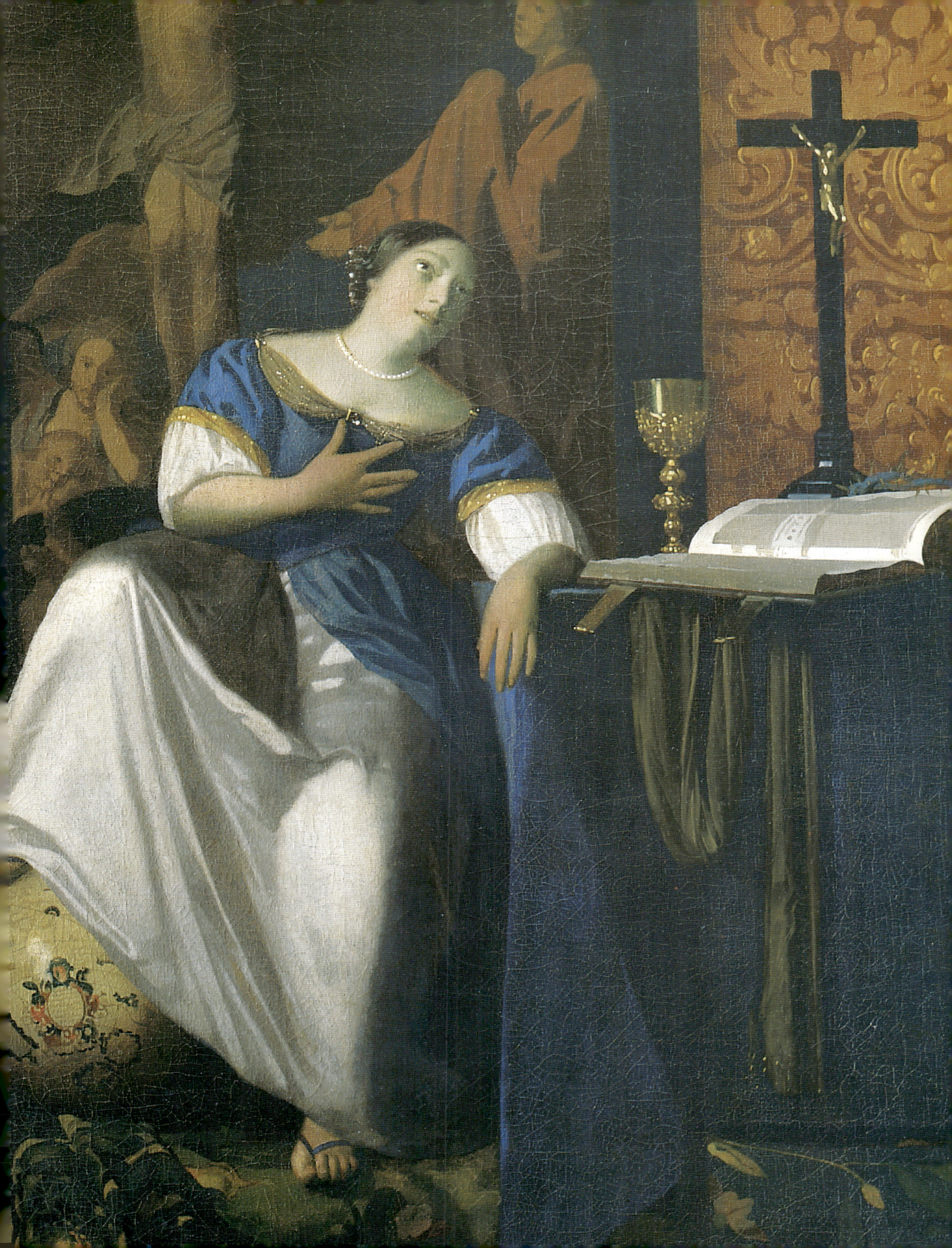

ated this allegory he was called to The Hague as an expert in Italian painting.[19]

Despite the iconographic integrity of the allegory, the painting proves a difficult one for twentieth-century viewers to accept with the same enthusiasm engendered by Vermeer's other works.[20] Indeed, this painting demands a different response from the viewer. While one can accept the fundamental reality of Vermeer's other images, and appreciate it without concern for symbolic meaning, the viewer cannot approach *Allegory of Faith* so directly. Both the woman's demeanor and the crushed snake announce that the viewer must first decipher this image to appreciate and understand it.

One may also question whether Vermeer's style of painting, which is built from a rational foundation and fundamentally grounded in creating a semblance of reality, was suited for portraying this particular allegorical concept.[21] In other paintings Vermeer expresses abstract ideas through physical objects and human situations that appear to belong to their surroundings. Although he applied this framework to his represention of the Catholic faith, the iconographic demands of this subject strained the credibility of his realistic approach. While essential for the painting's symbolic content, the ecstatic pose of the woman and the crushed snake seem incongruous within this Dutch setting. Vermeer's crisp style of the 1670s, moreover, does not easily suggest movement, or even the emotional energy implicit in the woman's pose. Thus, her gesture and upward gaze appear contrived rather than, as Ripa envisioned, expressive of her living faith. Despite these difficulties, the painting is a remarkable tour de force, which reveals much about the artist and his beliefs at this crucial stage of his career.

Whether or not the Jesuits or a rich, Catholic patron commissioned *Allegory of Faith*, its first documented owner, a Postmaster by the name of Herman Stoffelsz van Swoll (1632–1698), was a Protestant and was buried in the Noorderkerk on 23 December 1698.[22] In 1699, the year after his death, Van Swoll's collection, which included Italian paintings as well as the Vermeer, was auctioned in Amsterdam. *Allegory of Faith* was described as: "A sitting Woman with deep meanings, depicting the New Testament." The author of the sale catalogue enthusiastically added: "powerfully and glowingly painted."[23] Van Swoll was one of the few who had managed to acquire a Vermeer before the Dissius sale of 1696 (see page 55). It is not known when he started buying art. A famous collector, Gerard Reynst, was best man at his wedding in 1656, so he must have been familiar with those pursuits.[24]

In 1718 the painting "depicting the New Testament" was once more auctioned in Amsterdam, this time from an unknown collection.[25] At another anonymous auction in 1735 the recommendation read "artfully and minutely painted."[26] The Ietswaart sale of 1749 provides a variation on this praise by labelling it "as good as Eglon vander Neer."[27] David Ietswaart was a wholesale dealer in paintings. His name often appears as a bidder at art sales of the first half of the eighteenth century.[28] The high prices the painting at first commanded (*f* 400 in 1699 and *f* 500 in 1718) were not subsequently equalled (*f* 53 in 1735 and *f* 70 in 1749).

In the early nineteenth century the canvas was apparently in an Austrian collection, for it is shown hanging in the background of Ferdinand Georg Waldmüller's *Portrait of a Cartographer and His Wife*, 1824 (fig. 4).[29] Waldmüller was a Viennese painter who had learned the

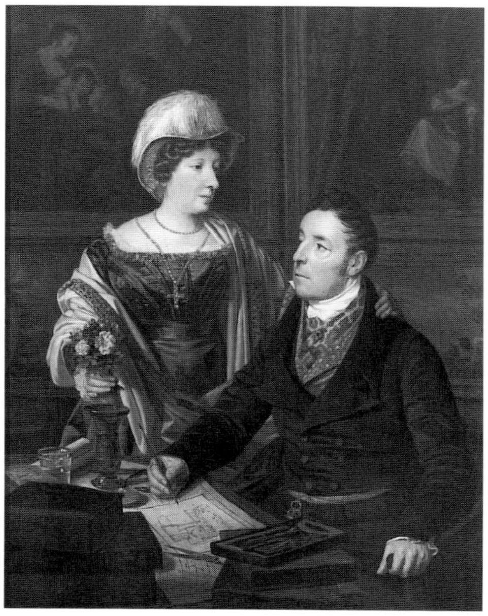

fig. 4. Ferdinand Georg Waldmüller, *Portrait of a Cartographer and His Wife*, 1824, panel, Westfälisches Landesmuseum, Münster

trade by making copies after old masters. The atlases next to the couple mainly contain maps of Vorarlberg and Tirol, which could indicate the location of Vermeer's painting at this time.[30] By the end of the century, the *Allegory of Faith* was in Moscow, in the collection of Dmitrii Tchoukine, the first and only Vermeer to ever be in Russian possession, albeit under the name of Eglon van der Neer.[31] Tchoukine consigned the work in 1899 to the dealer Wächtler in Berlin.[32]

When Abraham Bredius obtained the painting for about DM 700 Dutch newspapers waxed triumphant about the purchase:[33] "With this acquisition of the new Delft Vermeer, 'the New Testament,' as an Eglon van der Neer, Dr. Bredius has once again found a bargain with his perspicacious eye."[34] After the purchase Bredius presented it on loan to the Mauritshuis, where it stayed for twenty-four years.

Though Bredius was certainly proud of his eye, he never had much affinity with his purchase. In 1907 he called the Allegory "a large but unpleasant Vermeer."[35] In 1923 Bredius gave the painting on long-term loan to the Museum Boymans in Rotterdam, where it was to hang until 1928.[36] He then sold it by way of the dealer Kleinberger to Colonel Michael Friedsam in New York, who bequested the painting in 1931 to the Metropolitan Museum of Art.[37]

1. Kühn 1968, 200.
2. Without Catholic, and specifically Jesuit, leanings Vermeer and his wife would not have named one of their sons, Ignatius. Montias 1989, 174. Their eldest daughter, who was born by 1657, was named Maria. Her name may have been chosen to honor the Virgin Mary and/or Maria Thins, the mother of Catharina Bolnes.
3. See, in particular, his early paintings *Saint Praxedis* (cat. 1) and *Christ in the House of Mary and Martha* (cat.2).
4. Barnouw 1914, 50–54, first established the connection between this painting and Ripa 1644, 147–149.
5. Ripa 1644, 147, "Fede. Geloof," is one text used by Vermeer. The second (p. 148) is titled: "Fede Catholica. Catholijck of algemeen Geloof."
6. De Jongh 1975/1976, 75, also associates the woman's pearls with faith.
7. Welu 1975, 541–543 identifies the globe as one published in 1618. The only extant version of this globe is in the Germanisches Nationalmuseum, Nuremberg, No. WI 296. Welu also notes that the cartouche facing the viewer in Vermeer's painting honors Prince Maurits of Orange (1567–1625). Whether or not Vermeer chose to position the globe to reveal the cartouche for specific iconographic reasons is not known. Welu speculates that by doing so Vermeer may have hinted at the theme of transience. This theory is quite plausible for, by including this reminder of the temporality of earthly existence, Vermeer provides a thematic foil for the essential core of Ripa's Christian message: faith in Christ offers the promise of eternal life.
8. Meredith Hale has observed that Vermeer emphasizes the chalice by situating it against the black frame of the painting of the *Crucifixion*.
9. I owe this observation to Quint Gregory.
10. The depicted painting, versions of which are in the Terningh Foundation, Antwerp, and the Musée des Beaux-Arts, Rennes, apparently belonged to Vermeer. The 1676 inventory of his collection lists "a large painting representing Christ on the Cross." (Montias 1989, 340, doc. 364).
11. Mottola 1964, 56.
12. De Jongh 1975/1976, 73–74, fig. 3. The emblem appears in Hesius 1636, 88–90. De Jongh translates Hesius' verse as follows: "The vast universe can be shown in something small/ A small globe encompasses endless skies/ And captures what it cannot hold. Our mind is large enough/ though people think it small./ If only it believe in God, nothing can be larger than that mind/ Nothing broader than that mind; never can he who believes/ Appreciate the greatness of this mind./ The mind is larger than the largest sphere because it is human."
13. De Jongh 1975/1976, 75, believes that the commission came from the Jesuits in Delft. Montias 1989, 202 n. 94, believes that the Jesuits would have insisted on a more conventionally religious iconography, and proposes that the commission came from a wealthy patron.
14. See, for example, O'Malley 1993, 164. I would like to thank Aneta Georgievska-Shine for bringing this reference to my attention.
15. Whereas in *Allegory of the Faith* Vermeer expanded upon Ripa's allegorical concept by including a painting of the Crucifixion and the hanging orb, in *Art of Painting* Vermeer enlarged upon the meaning Ripa vested in his allegorical description of Clio through the map he depicted on the back wall and the hanging chandelier. Similar also is the use of a curtain to introduce the allegory. For a discussion of *Art of Painting*, see Wheelock 1995, 128–139.
16. They are found in the inventory of his own possessions (Montias 1989, 339–344, doc. 364). A similar gilt leather panel is seen in the background of *The Love Letter* (cat. 18).
17. "Theologia" is discussed by Ripa 1644, 175–176. Theology is described by Ripa as having two heads, one the head of an old woman looking down to the earth and the other the head of a young woman looking to the heavens. Rather than having the earth under her as does Faith, Theology sits on a blue orb decorated with stars. I would like to thank Meredith Hale for calling my attention to the similarity in poses between Theology and Vermeer's allegorical figure of Faith.
18. The pose of Vermeer's woman relates to Italian images of the Repentant Magdalene. See, for example, Reni's *The Magdalene*, 1634, Volterra, Cathedral, Capella di S. Carlo, which is illustrated in Pepper 1984, cat. 151, ill. 177. An earlier version of this composition, where Magdalene's right hand does not come to her breast (Palazzo Corsini, Rome) was engraved in 1672 (Pepper 1984, cat. 130).
19. Vermeer was called to The Hague in May 1672 (Montias 1989, 333–334, doc. 341).
20. Wheelock 1981, 148, described it as Vermeer's "one mistake."
21. Vermeer's remarkably rational approach to the depiction of the concept of Faith can be contrasted with a comparable allegory by David Teniers, where a few angels hover above a similarly posed woman. For an illustration of Teniers' painting (Hermitage, St. Petersburg), see De Jongh 1975/1976, 79, fig. 8.
22. Gemeentearchief, Amsterdam (13513 DTB 1075, fol. 28).
23. Hoet 1752–1770, 1: 48, no. 25: "Een zittende Vrouw met meer beteekenisse, verbeeldende het Nieuwe Testament" and "kragtig en gloejent geschildert."
24. Van der Veen 1992, 329; Gemeentearchief, Amsterdam (3590 DTB 475, fol. 285). Van Swoll as an early Vermeer collector went missing in Montias 1989 (he does occur in Montias 1987, 74 and n. 44, and Montias 1993, 279 and 326 n. 46).
25. Hoet 1752–1770, 1: 216, no. 8: "verbeeldende het Nieuwe Testament."
26. Hoet 1752–1770, 1: 438, no. 11: "konstig en uytvoerig geschildert."
27. Hoet 1752–1770, 2: 248, no. 152: "zo goed als Eglon vander Neer."
28. Bille 1961, 1: 201.
29. Grimschitz 1957, 286, no. 129 and ill.; first connected with the Vermeer by Plietzsch 1939, 57; see also De Vries 1948, xix, no. 29.
30. Westfälisches Landesmuseum 1975, 170.
31. This incorrect attribution was probably based on the suggestion in the catalogue of the Ietswaart sale.
32. Tchoukine is first mentioned as owner of the painting in De Vries 1948, xix, and Blankert 1975, 163. It had a false signature of Caspar Netscher on the stone in the lower center (Report Mauritshuis 1899, 56 n. 1).
33. NRC, 23 April 1899: "Een' Delftschen Vermeer als een' Eglon van der Neer voor een schuifje geld te vermeesteren is geen dagelijksch werk ..." (to take possession of a Delft Vermeer as an Eglon van der Neer for a trifle is no [regular] day's work) (Mauritshuis clippings book, 22).
34. Flugi van Aspermont 1899–1900, 34: "Met den aankoop van den nieuwen Delftschen Vermeer, 'het Nieuwe Testament' als Eglon van der Neer, heeft Dr. Bredius met zijn scherpziend oog weder eens een koopje gedaan". For a considerable time the painting had been known only from sale catalogues: Thoré-Bürger 1866, 566, no. 41: "A retrouver"; Havard 1888, 38, no. 46: "Elle a disparu depuis."
35. Duparc 1975, 161: "een *groote* maar hoogst onbehagelijke Vermeer."
36. Boymans Annual Reports 1923, 7, and 1928, 9; Boymans 1925, 38, no. 466; Boymans 1927, 97, no. 466.18.
37. On the acquisition by Friedsam, see *De Courant*, 19 October 1928 (Mauritshuis clippings book, facing 1); on Friedsam's bequest, see Burroughs 1932, 5–52.

COLLECTION CATALOGUES

Mauritshuis 1899, 38, no. 46; Mauritshuis 1903, 91, no. 625; Mauritshuis 1914, 406–407, no. 625; Boymans 1925, 38, no. 466; Boymans 1927, 97, no. 466; Metropolitan Museum of Art 1980, 1: 191; 447, ill.

LITERATURE

Hoet 1752–1770, 1: 48, no. 25, 216, no. 8, 438, no. 11; 2: 248, no. 152; Thoré-Bürger 1858–1860, 2: 86; Thoré-Bürger 1866, 566, no. 41; Havard 1888, 38, no. 46; Flugi van Aspermont 1899–1900, 34; Bode 1906, 52; Hofstede de Groot 1907–1928, 1: 587–588, no. 2; Harms Tiepen 1909, 2; Plietzsch 1911, 82–84, 117, no. 20 and ill. 32; Hale 1913, 304–307; Harms Tiepen 1913, 36; Barnouw 1914, 50–54 and ill.; Swillens 1929, 136 and ill., 139–140; Hale 1937, 75, 115–117 and pl. 13; Knipping 1939, 1: 28; De Vries 1939, 19, 51, 94, no. 40 and ill. 63; Neurdenburg 1942, 10; Blum 1946, 60, 65 and 180, no. 41; Van Peer 1946, 468–470; De Vries 1948, xviii–xix, no. 29 and ill.; Zijderveld 1949, 117 n. 1; Swillens 1950, 21, 50, 60, no. 24, 72, 81, 84–86, 96–102, 118, 135, 171, pls. 24 and 73; Gowing 1952, 153–155, no. 33 and pls. 71–73; Grimschitz 1957, 286, no. 129 and ill.; Goldscheider 1958, 133, no. 31, 134–135, no. 37 and ills. 82–84; Constable 1964, 126; Blankert 1975, 88, 111 n. 2, 162–164, no. 29 and pl. 29; Duparc 1975, 161; Westfälisches Landesmuseum 1975, 170; Welu 1975, 541 and 544; De Jongh 1975–1976, 69–75 and ills. 1–2; Blankert 1978, 10, 58–59, 75 n. 2, 77 n. 48, 169–170, no. 29 and pl. 29; Slatkes 1981, 16, 74, 78, 106–109, 130 and ills.; Wheelock 1981, 16, 44–45, 146, 150, and pl. 43; Aillaud 1986, 10, 12 45, 51, 54, 55, 64, 142, 196–197, no. 29, and pl. 31; Sutton 1986, 180–181, ill. 256; Montias 1987, 73–74; Wheelock 1988, 42–43, 118–120 and pl. 36; Montias 1989, 149, 155, 188, 191–192, 202, 215, 257, 266 and ill. 39; The Hague 1990, 52; De Boer 1991, 48, ill. 1, 49–50 nn. 7–9; Nash 1991, 19, 21, 26, 28, 30, 106, 108, and ill.; Blankert 1992, 10, 13, 46, 52, 55, 57, 67, 146, 148, 200–201, no. 29, 223, pl. 31, ills. 37 and 41; Montias 1993, 279 and 326 n. 46; Wheelock 1995, 5, 37, 185, and ill. A34

21

A Lady Standing at the Virginal

c. 1672–1673

inscribed at left, above the virginal: *IVMeer* (IVM in ligature)

oil on canvas, 51.8 x 45.2 (20 13/32 x 17 25/32)

The Trustees of the National Gallery, London

PROVENANCE

(?) Diego Duarte, Antwerp, 1682 (sold before 1691) and Dissius sale, Amsterdam, 16 May 1696, no. 37 (*f* 42.10); or (?) Nicolaes van Assendelft, Delft, before 1692, and Widow Van Assendelft, Delft, 1711; (?) Sale, Amsterdam, 11 July 1714, no. 12 (*f* 55); Danser Nijman sale, Amsterdam, 16 August 1797, no. 169 (*f* 49 to Bergh); (?) Edward Solly, Berlin/London, before 1844; Edward William Lake sale, London, 11 July 1845, no. 5 (15 guineas to Farrer); J.T. Thom sale, London, 2 May 1855, no. 22 (14½ guineas to Grey); Thoré-Bürger, Paris, before 1866–1869; Paul Lacroix, Paris, 1869–1884; Widow Lacroix, Paris, 1884–1892; Thoré-Bürger sale, Paris, 5 December 1892, no. 20 (Frf 29,000 to Bourgeois and/or Lawrie & Co); purchased by the present owner for £2,400 or Frf50,000 in 1892

EXHIBITIONS

Paris 1866, 36, no. 108; Amsterdam 1867, 39, no. 274; The Hague 1966, no. 11 and ill.; Paris 1966, no. 12 and ill.; London 1976, 92–93, no. 116 and ill.

TECHNICAL DESCRIPTION

The fine, plain-weave linen support has a thread count of 14 x 14 per cm.[2] The original tacking edges have been removed. Cusping is visible along top and bottom, and very faintly along both sides. The support has been lined. The double ground consists of a pale gray beneath a pale, warm gray/buff. The first layer contains lead white, chalk, and charcoal black; the second contains lead white, chalk, and a red-brown earth.[1]

The flesh color was painted with green earth over a pink layer; the shadows with two additional layers, a mixture containing green earth followed by a deep red shadow. The blue upholstery was underpainted with a gray-blue layer; the highlights were modeled with a blue, then a pale blue layer and the shadows with gray. The outlines of the tiles at the bottom of the wall were scratched in the wet paint. A pinhole by which Vermeer marked the vanishing point is visible in the paint layer on the sleeve of the woman's dress.

There is some abrasion in the three paintings within the painting, in the lady's right cheek and the dark blue of her tunic, and in the blue upholstery. The ultramarine pigment in the darker blues of the chair has deteriorated.

A young woman, standing in the corner of an elegantly decorated room, looks out confidently at the viewer as her hands rest lightly on the keys of a virginal. She wears a fashionable dress with a stiff satin skirt and a blue bodice edged at the shoulders in lace. Red ribbons decorate her white puffed sleeves at the elbow and shoulder, and wrap around her stylish chignon. Around her neck she wears a pearl necklace. The character of the room and its furnishings reinforce a sense of wealth and well-being. Indeed, such a virginal, with marbelized case and painted lid, would be found only in a wealthy home. The two paintings displayed behind her, a Cupid framed in black and a landscape framed in gold, likewise suggest discriminating taste.[2]

The painting's focus on a young woman engaged in a private activity resembles in many respects Vermeer's depictions of single figures from the mid-1660s, such as *Woman in Blue Reading a Letter* (cat. 9). The mood and atmosphere of *A Lady Standing at the Virginal*, however, are quite different. Crystalline light, no longer softly diffused, floods through the leaded glass windows, creating brilliant accents on the gold picture frame, sharp ridges on the folds of the woman's satin dress, and hard edges on the musical instrument. Vermeer further accents this crisp definition of form by silhouetting both the black picture frame and the black edge of the virginal's lid against the white wall.

From the mid-1660s to the early 1670s, when he executed this work, Vermeer's paintings become crisper in character, with greater atmospheric clarity. The carefully modulated tones and colors of the 1660s give way to a more direct, even bolder technique. In this painting, he defines the sharp folds of the woman's dress with quickly applied strokes of white paint. Rapid, impastoed strokes of lead-tin yellow dramatically indicate light striking the intricate gold frame. Last, and perhaps most important, Vermeer paints edges of objects with sharply defined rather than diffused contours.

In striving for greater atmospheric clarity, Vermeer's painting technique has also become simpler. His method for suggesting the soft texture of the velvet seat cover is, in fact, a simplified variant of the one he used to create the rugged appearance of the red tile roofs in *View of Delft* (page 25, fig. 12). To create this textural effect, he applied an underlayer of gray-blue paint containing lumps of lead white that protrude through the thinly applied layers of blue paint. Vermeer varied another early technique for the modeling of the woman's face and pearl necklace. He created the half-light that illuminates her by laying a thin greenish glaze over an ocher ground, much as he had done in *Girl with a Red Hat* (cat. 14). He imbued the flesh with inner warmth, as in the cheek, for example, by thinning the glaze and allowing the ground to show through. Most interesting is Vermeer's use of the green layer as the base tone for the necklace, defining its shape on either side with the thick, flesh-colored impasto of the neck. He indicated the luster of the pearls with single dots of white paint rather than with the more complex, two-layer technique that he used in his earlier *Woman Holding a Balance* (cat. 10).

The resulting mood is quite different from that of Vermeer's interior scenes of the mid-1660s, where muted light and diffused contours encourage quiet reflection. Indeed, this image asserts itself. The eye contact the young woman makes with the viewer is neither coy nor quizzical, but, rather, insistent and purposeful. Thus she draws attention to the Cupid in the painting immediately behind her.

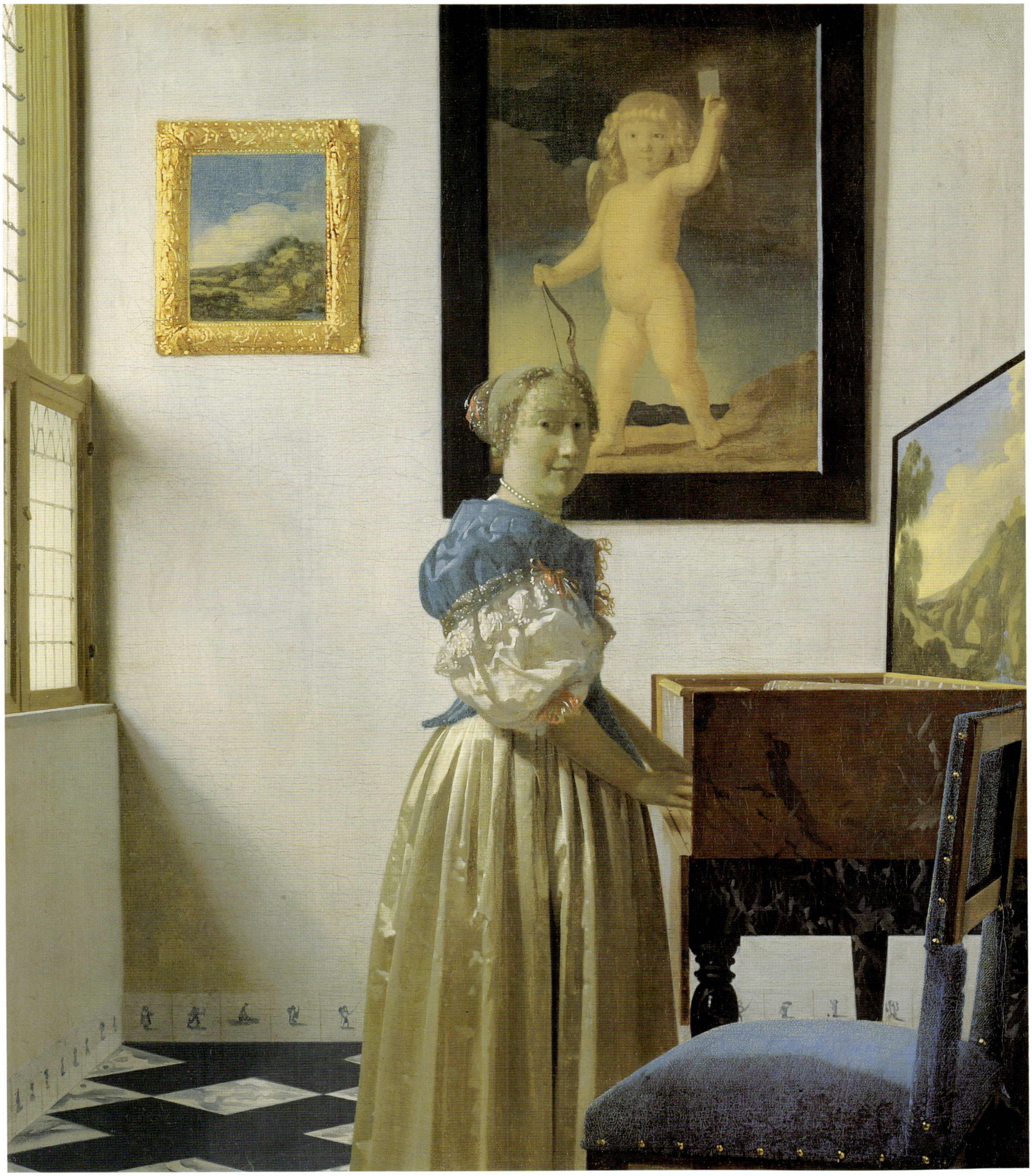

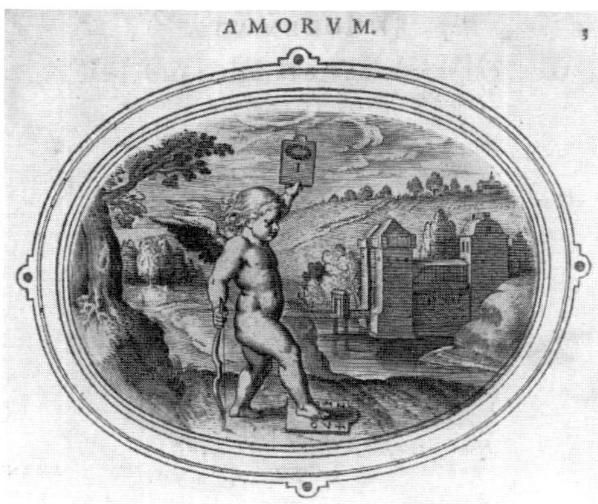

fig. 1. Otto van Veen, "Only one," *Amorum Emblemata*, Antwerp, 1608, National Gallery of Art Library, Washington

Contemporary viewers would have recognized the iconographic source for Cupid as an image from Otto van Veen's well-known emblem book *Amorum Emblemata* of 1608 (fig. 1).[3] Although Van Veen's image is more detailed – Cupid holds aloft a card containing a laurel wreath and the number "1" while stepping on another card containing multiple numbers – Vermeer clearly intended the painting to convey the same sentiment: "a louer ought to loue only one."[4]

Other elements that reinforce this thematic concern with love include the virginal, traditionally associated with pure love, and the Cupids enlivening the tiles of the baseboard.[5] The pastoral landscape decorating the virginal's cover and the landscape on the wall surely served an iconographic as well as visual function, for seventeenth-century songs and poems frequently compared female innocence and beauty to nature.[6] The invitation to contemplate and even to share pure, harmonious love comes from the woman herself, through the strength of her outward gaze. Vermeer further establishes a climate of moral certitude for this thematic emphasis on love through the clarity and harmony of his composition.

The stylistic and thematic precedents for this work derive almost exclusively from Vermeer's paintings of the mid-1660s. Nevertheless, the evolution of his style in the 1670s, toward crisply articulated forms and explicitly moralizing subject matter, relates to the approach taken by other Dutch artists of this period. For example, Cornelis de Man (1621–1706), with whom Vermeer served as Headman of the Saint Luke's Guild in 1670 and 1671, depicted didactic genre scenes of middle-class life in clearly defined interiors.[7] Beyond such general characteristics, however, comparisons of paintings by Vermeer and De Man demonstrate the extraordinary restraint of Vermeer's approach to pictorial representation. Unlike De Man, Vermeer introduces no movement or explicit gesture to inform the viewer of the painting's meaning. He relies instead on his pictorial vocabulary – light, color, texture, proportion, and perspective – to reinforce and enhance the moral authority projected by the decor and the young woman's demeanor.

The early history of this painting cannot be reconstructed with certainty. Although it may have been a part of the Duarte collection by 1682 (see cat. 22), it is also possible that the first owner of this picture was Nicolaes van Assendelft (1630–1692), a Delft alderman and member of the Council of Forty.[8] Van Assendelft assembled a remarkably handsome collection that included a portrait of himself by Johannes Verkolje (1650–1693), as well as works by Adriaen van Ostade (1610–1685), Jan Steen (c. 1625–1679) and Philips Wouwerman (1619–1668). In 1711, nearly twenty years after his death, the inventory of the estate of his widow was drawn up and these paintings were appraised along with "A damsel playing on the clavichord by Vermeer" (page 48, fig. 1).[9] Its value was estimated at forty guilders. Since Van Assendelft lived in Delft while Vermeer was alive, it is possible that he bought the picture, whether *A Lady Standing at the Virginal* or *A Lady Seated at the Virginal*, from the painter himself.

It also remains unclear which picture can be connected with a reference in a 1714 Amsterdam sale to "a Harpsichord player in a room, by Vermeer of Delft," to which was added: "artfully painted."[10] *The Lady Standing at the Virginal* probably remained in one or more collections in Amsterdam, where we can trace it to a sale of 1797: "A Lady standing at a Harpsichord; on the Wall hang paintings; very comely in brush work."[11] The exquisite collection in question was assembled by Jan Danser Nijman. He owned no less than four Vermeers, *A Lady Standing at the Virginal*, *The Astronomer* (page 52, fig. 6), *The Geographer* (cat. 16), and *The Lacemaker* (cat. 17).[12]

Like so many Dutch masterpieces, this one migrated to prosperous England during the troubled years of the French Revolution. It is supposed to have been in the possession of a very rich English lumber merchant living in Berlin, Edward Solly (1776–1844), who began collecting on a grand scale in 1811.[13] The painting appeared later at the 1845 auction of the estate of Edward William Lake, where it was bought by the art dealer Farrer. Ten years later it was again auctioned in London, from the collection of one J. T. Thom.[14] Around 1860 it became part of the collection of the French "rediscoverer" of Vermeer, Etienne-Joseph Théophile Thoré-Bürger (1803–1869).

When, in 1866, Thoré published his series of articles on Vermeer in the *Gazette des Beaux-Arts*, he included a reproduction by Valentin of *A Lady Standing at the Virginal* (fig. 2).[15] Other works, such as *A Lady Seated at the Virginal*, were also in Thore's collection at the time, which was exhibited

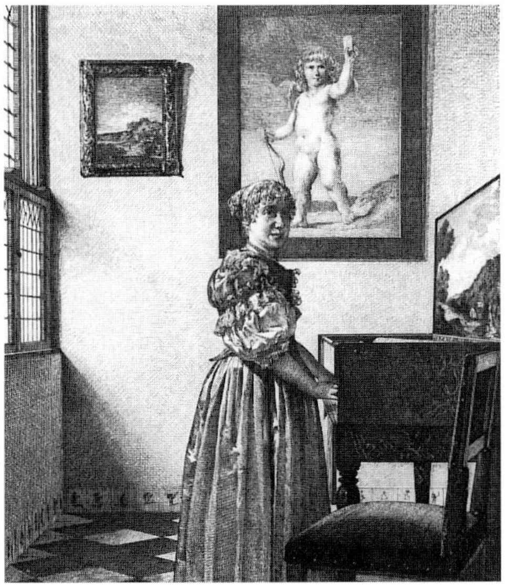

fig. 2. Henry Augustin Valentin, etching after *A Lady Standing at the Virginal*, in Thoré-Bürger 1866

in 1866.[16] Upon Thoré-Bürger's death in 1869, his collection was bequeathed to Paul Lacroix (1807–1884), a versatile publisher who carried the nickname "Le Bibliophile Jacob."[17]

In partnership with his friend Thoré-Bürger, Lacroix had founded the "Alliance des Arts" which, from 1842, published a bulletin to promote the practical knowledge of art.[18] Lacroix treasured Thore-Bürger's Vermeers, as did his widow after him until 1892. The Thoré collection then came under the gavel in Paris. The most remarkable work at this auction was Carel Fabritius' (1622–1654) *Goldfinch* (Mauritshuis, The Hague), which fetched 5,500 French francs.[19] The best of the three genuine Vermeers, *A Lady Standing at the Virginal*, raised several times that amount, namely 29,000 francs.[20] In the same month, the art dealers Bourgeois, respectively Lawrie and Co., sold the painting to the National Gallery for 50,000 francs.[21]

1. Kühn 1968, 202.
2. The artists responsible for these paintings have not been identified with any certainty. The most convincing attribution for the painting of Cupid has been to Caesar van Everdingen (first proposed by Delbanco 1928, 64 n. 39). Stechow 1960, 180, noted that the landscape was in the style of Jan Wynants or Philips Wouwerman. Both of these paintings were probably owned by Vermeer. While the landscape listed in the inventory taken after his death cannot be specifically identified, the painting of "a cupid" must be identical with the one here depicted. See Montias 1989, 341, doc. 364.
3. Van Veen 1608, 2. The emblem is titled "Only one." The accompanying verse reads: "No number els but one in Cupids right is claymed,/All numbers els besydes he sets his foot vpon,/Because a louer ought to loue but only one./ A streame disperst in partes the force therof is maymed." The painting and the emblem were first connected by De Jongh 1967, 49–50.
4. Seth 1980, 23, 39, proposes yet another connection with an emblem from Van Veen's *Amorum Emblemata*. He suggests that the woman turned away from the light conveys a sentiment similar to that in an emblem from Van Veen 1608, 122, "Absence killeth." Van Veen writes that just as a lily turns black for want of the sun, so does a lover suffer from the absence of a loved one.
5. The Cupids were noted in Philadelphia 1984b, 104.
6. Goodman-Soellner 1989, 81–83.
7. See, for example, Cornelis de Man's *The Chess Players*, c. 1670, ill. in Philadelphia 1984a, pl. 117.
8. Biographical data derived from Centraal Bureau voor Genealogie, The Hague.
9. Gemeentearchief, Delft, ONA 3003–11, deed 375, 18r: "Een juff: spelende opde Clavecimbael door Vermeer." See also Wijsenbeek-Olthuis 1987, 266 and 392 n. 16.
10. Hoet 1752–1770, 1: 176, no. 12: "een Klavecimbael-speelster in een Kamer, van Vermeer van Delft, konstig geschildert."
11. Sale catalogue, Amsterdam, 16 August 1797, 33, no. 169: "Een Juffrouw, staande voor een Clavecimbaal te speelen; aan de Wand hangen schilderyen; zeer fraai van penceel-behandeling." (Lugt no. 5640)
12. Sale catalogue, Amsterdam, 16 August 1797, 33, nos. 167–169: see also the provenance section of cat. 17.
13. Sale catalogue, London, 11 July 1845, 4, no. 5: "From the collection of E. Solly, Esq." (Lugt no. 17853): not to be traced to one of the many Solly auctions, see: National Gallery London 1960, 438 n. 10; Hermann 1967B, 18 n. 9; on Solly, see Hermann 1967A, 229–234.
14. Sale catalogue, London, 2 May 1855, 4, no. 22 (Lugt no. 22404); the back of the panel displays references to the auctions of 1845 and 1855 (National Gallery London 1960, 438 nn. 11–12).
15. Thoré-Bürger 1866, facing 326.
16. Paris 1866.
17. Sale catalogue, Paris, 5 December 1892, 7–8 (Lugt no. 51162); on Lacroix, see GDEL, 6: 6073.
18. Heppner 1938, 21.
19. Inv. no. 605; Mauritshuis 1987, 134–139, no. 24 and ill.
20. Hofstede de Groot 1892B, 405.
21. Hofstede de Groot 1893, 119.

COLLECTION CATALOGUES

National Gallery London 1960, 436–438, no. 1383; National Gallery London 1991, 1: 466–468, no. 1383; 2: ill. 393

LITERATURE

Josi 1821, unpaginated, s.v.; Thoré-Bürger 1866, 326–328 and ill., 459–460, 467, 556–557, no. 29; Havard 1888, 37, no. 32; Hofstede de Groot 1892B, 405; Hofstede de Groot 1893, 118–119, no. 30; Rooses 1898, 356, 358–360 and ill.; Hofstede de Groot 1907–1928, 1: 597, no. 23; Alfassa 1911, 401–402 and ill.; Plietzsch 1911, 117, no. 22 and pl. 33; Delbanco 1928, 64 n. 39; Hale 1937, 154–156 and pl. 31; Heppner 1938, 142; De Vries 1939, 94, no. 41 and ill. 64; Blum 1946, 126–127 and 172, no. 29; Sulzberger 1948, 37; Swillens 1950, 50–51, no. 1, 67, 73, 79–80, 82, 86–87, 89, 102–103, 108–109, 118 and pl. 1; Gowing 1952, 155–157 and pl. 74; Goldscheider 1958, 146, no. 34 and pls. 78, 80; Gerson 1967, cols. 731, 743 and ill. 338; Hermann 1967B, 18 n. 9; De Jongh 1967, 48–50 and ill. 34; Blankert 1975, 74–75, 78, 80, 82, 84, 87, 89, 116 n. 53, 159, no. 25 and pl. 25; Blankert 1978, 10, 53–56, 59, 77 n. 64, 167, no. 25 and pl. 25; Slatkes 1981, 88–89 and ill.; Wheelock 1981, 16, 42, 76, 98, 152, 154, and pl. 45; Aillaud 1986, 128, 134, 142, 167–168 n. 58, 193, no. 25, and pl. 20; Edwards 1986, 198; Wheelock 1988, 122–123 and ill. 38; Montias 1989, 150, 191, 220–221, 256, 266 and ill. 49; Nash 1991, 19, 36, 50, 114–118, and ill.; Blankert 1992, 134, 136, 142, 146, 148, 167, 196–197, no. 25 and pl. 20; Weber 1994A, 98–99; Wheelock 1995, 157, 185, and ill. A33

22

A Lady Seated at the Virginal

c. 1675

inscribed at right, next to the lady's head: *IVMeer* (IVM in ligature)

oil on canvas, 51.5 x 45.6 (20¼ x 17⅞)

The Trustees of the National Gallery, London

PROVENANCE

(?) Diego Duarte, Antwerp, 1682 (sold before 1691) and Dissius sale, Amsterdam, 16 May 1696, no. 37 (*f* 42.10), or (?) Nicolaes van Assendelft, Delft, before 1692 and Widow van Assendelft, Delft, 1711; (?) Sale, Amsterdam, 11 July 1714, no. 12 (*f* 55); Lothar Franz von Schönborn, Pommersfelden, c. 1714–1729; Schloss Weissenstein, Pommersfelden, until 1867; Count Von Schönborn sale, Paris, 17 May 1867, no. 78 (Ffr 2,000 to Thoré-Bürger); Thoré-Bürger, Paris, 1867–1869; Paul Lacroix, Paris, 1869–1884; Widow Lacroix, Paris, 1884–1892; Thoré-Bürger sale, Paris, 5 December 1892, no. 32 (Ffr 25,000 to Sedelmeyer); [Lawrie & Co, London, 1893 (Frf 33,100 from Sedelmeyer)]; [T. Humphry Ward, London, 1894]; George Salting, London, before 1898; and by bequest to present owner, 1910

EXHIBITIONS

London 1894, 22, no. 93; Paris 1898, 102, no. 85; London 1900, 24, no. 15; London 1976, 93, no. 117 and ill.

TECHNICAL DESCRIPTION

The fine, plain-weave linen support, which has been lined, has a thread count of 14 x 14 per cm². The original tacking edges are still present.

The double ground, a warm, gray buff over a pale gray layer, extends over the tacking edges on all sides. The first layer contains lead white, chalk, and charcoal black; the second layer contains chalk, lead white, and a red-brown ocher or burnt umber.[1]

The flesh tones were built up with pink, with a pink-white mixture added in the highlights, and green earth added in the shadows. The shaded areas have a further brown-green layer. The pearls are pure white spots on a gray-brown band, which uses the brown-green of the flesh shadow as a base. The paint layers do not extend over the tacking edges. A pinhole, where Vermeer marked the vanishing point, is visible in the paint layer behind the chair.

Both the paler yellow-brown and the dark brown surface layers in the yellow skirt are affected by a white efflorescence. The paint in all the blue areas has a somewhat degraded appearance.

The chronology of Vermeer's late work is particularly hard to establish because during this period the artist turned to his compositions of the 1660s for inspiration. The pose and enticing gaze of the young woman in *A Lady Seated at the Virginal*, for example, recall that of the sitter in *A Lady Writing* (cat. 13). Vermeer also included the motif of an unattended viola da gamba in the foreground of two earlier paintings, *The Music Lesson* (cat. 8) and *The Concert* (page 17, fig. 1). On the rear wall of *The Concert*, moreover, hangs Dirck van Baburen's *The Procuress* (fig. 1).[2] Closest stylistically and thematically to *A Lady Seated at the Virginal*, however, is *A Lady Standing at the Virginal* (cat. 21), in which a wealthy young woman looks directly out at the viewer as she rests her hands on the keyboard. Indeed, the similarity of scale, subject matter, and painting technique has suggested to many that Vermeer created the two works as pendants.[3]

Several facts, however, argue against such a hypothesis. In 1682 Diego Duarte owned only one of these works (see below), and if these were pendants they almost certainly would not have been separated at such an early date. Moreover, differences in the manner of execution

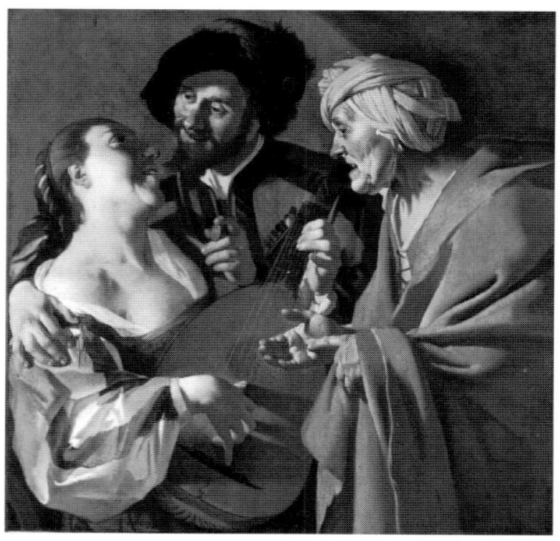

fig. 1. Dirck van Baburen, *The Procuress*, 1622, oil on canvas, Museum of Fine Arts, Boston

suggest that Vermeer completed the paintings at slightly different dates. The most obvious stylistic difference is in the treatment of the dress. While crisp accents convincingly articulate folds of stiff material in the dress of the standing lady, the light blue accents on the folds of material in *A Lady Seated at the Virginal* create flat patterns of color rather than the semblance of material.

Comparable differences in approach characterize the handling of paint on the gold picture frames. While Vermeer articulates the physical structure of the intricate frame behind the standing lady with varied impastoes, he summarily renders the frame surrounding Van Baburen's *The Procuress* with broad, flat strokes of yellow paint. This simplification of form, more pronounced than in any other of his works, indicates that Vermeer painted *A Lady Seated at the Virginal* very late in his career, probably c. 1675.[4] These two paintings should therefore be seen as variations upon a theme – the relationship of love and music – but not strictly as pendants.

Indeed, Vermeer conveys his message in each painting in a fundamentally different manner. Although he places a painting behind each woman to reinforce the thematic content of the image, these paintings-within-paintings function differently. While Cupid, signifying the purity of love, reinforces the moral tenor of *Lady Standing at the Virginal*, the inclusion of *The Procuress* in *Lady Seated at the Virginal*, implying erotic and illicit behavior, represents but one component of a composition that examines a more complex theme: the choice between ideal and profane love.

Although the presence of *The Procuress* on the back wall has led some to interpret the young woman's gaze as an invitation to profane love,[5] the virginal had associations with a far more elevated form of love than

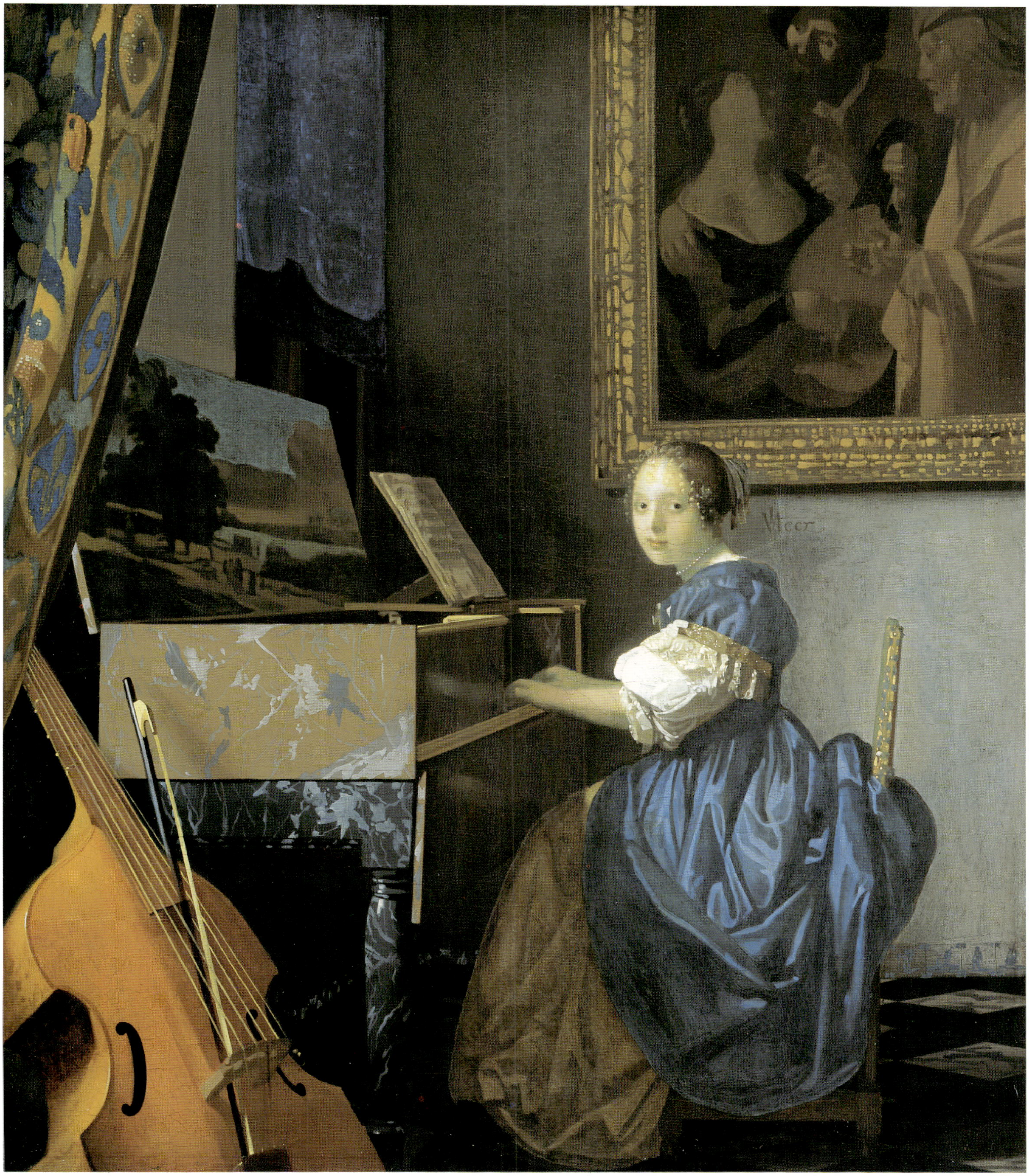

did the lute strummed by the seductive young woman in *The Procuress*.[6] The virginal, often played by a woman in a family gathering, appears most often in Dutch paintings as a symbol for harmony and concord.[7] The viola da gamba in the foreground further strengthens the association with harmony. The woman, like the male musician in Jacob Cats' well-known emblem "Quid Non Sentit Amor" (page 130, fig. 1), plays her instrument while a second lies unused.[8] The text explains that the resonance of one lute echoes onto the other just as two hearts can exist in harmony even if they are separated.

A comparable celebration of music as a metaphor for harmony in love underlies *The Concert*.[9] Vermeer joins the three figures in this musical ensemble in complete harmony as they play their instruments, keep time to the music, and sing. Thus, as in *The Concert*, the presence of Van Baburen's painting on the rear wall establishes a thematic contrast between music associated with illicit love and music associated with harmony and moderation.

Vermeer subtly reinforces the choice he advocates through his treatment of light. Although the dimly lit interior suggests an intimate and seductive environment, strong light falls upon the woman, separating her from the background. The light originates from a hidden source behind the curtain and illuminates both the viola da gamba and the front edge of the virginal, thereby reinforcing the thematic connection between these three compositional elements.

The remarkable similarity between *Lady Seated at the Virginal* and Gerrit Dou's *Woman at the Clavichord*, c. 1665 (fig. 2) may well indicate that Vermeer derived his composition from the work of this Leiden artist.[10] Not only is the woman's pose comparable, but a viola da gamba also rests prominently in the foreground. The curtain pulled to one side in both paintings, moreover, announces a symbolic or allegorical intent, in each instance concerning the relationship between music and love.[11] Like Vermeer's woman, the woman in Dou's painting appeals to the viewer to join in harmonious and binding love.[12] The comparison also reveals that at the end of his career Vermeer continued to create at once thematically complex and restrained compositions. While Dou places the young woman in a large interior space and introduces a multiplicity of elements – wineglass, music book, flute, grapevine, decanter – to elucidate the theme, Vermeer situates his figure close to the viewer, and includes only a few carefully placed and clearly articulated objects to transmit his thematic intent. As a result, Vermeer's image is at once visually more direct and iconographically more suggestive.

The whereabouts of *A Lady Seated at the Virginal* in the seventeenth and early eighteenth centuries cannot yet be determined with certainty. The painting may have left the Netherlands at an early date and have become part of the collection of Diego Duarte in Antwerp. In 1682 this prosperous collector compiled a "Register of the paintings here in our house," by which he meant his residence on the Meir in Antwerp. Among the almost two hundred Italian, Flemish, and Dutch pictures was "A work with a lady playing on the virginal with addenda by Vermeer...cost guilders 150."[13] The picture probably held particular significance for Duarte because of its subject.

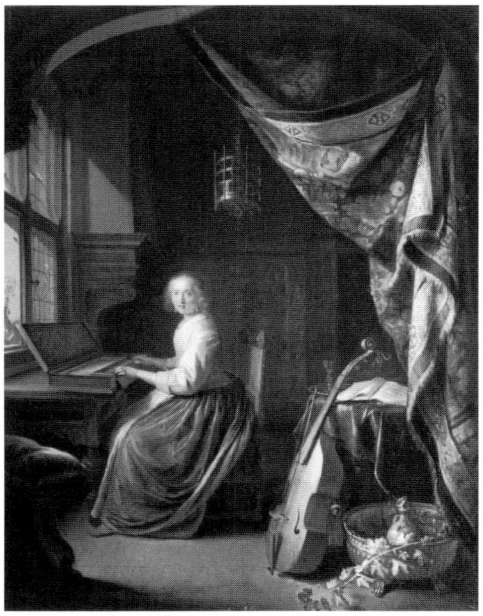

fig. 2. Gerrit Dou, *Woman at the Clavichord*, c. 1665, oil on panel, By Permission of the Trustees of Dulwich Picture Gallery, London

The Duarte family of Antwerp maintained close contacts with the Huygens family of The Hague (see page 51). Constantijn Huygens Jr. (1628–1697) and Diego Duarte (c. 1610–1691) were lifelong friends and shared a love of music. A renowned organist and composer, Duarte's house concerts were major events in Antwerp. In his capacity as Secretary to Prince William III, Huygens regularly visited the Duarte family during the campaigns of 1673 to 1678, as he mentioned in his diaries.[14] Although he did not note whether he brought the Vermeer from Holland for his musical friend, the possiblity that a Vermeer painting, presumably either *A Lady Standing at the Virginal* (cat. 21) or *A Lady Seated at the Virginal*, ended up in Antwerp because of Huygens is an attractive hypothesis.

Before his death in 1691 Duarte sold a third of his art treasures, probably among them the painting by Vermeer.[15] At that time Abraham or Jacob Dissius must have acquired the painting, adding it to the twenty Vermeers noted in the Van Ruijven/Dissius inventory of 1683.[16] The picture was sold at the Dissius sale for forty-two guilders and ten five-cent pieces (stuivers) as "A Playing Lady on the Harpsichord by dito (J. vander Meer van

Delft)."[17] It is not clear from the mentions of the work in the Duarte Collection and the Dissius sale whether these refer to the present painting or *A Lady Standing at the Virginal*.[18] Presumably, however, the latter picture is the "lady playing on the harpsichord" that was in the estate of the widow of Nicolaes van Assendelft in 1711 (see page 48).

The first certain reference to the painting occurs in 1746 when it is listed in the catalogue of the collection that was assembled by the Elector of Mainz and Archbishop of Bamberg, Lothar Franz von Schönborn (1655–1729), who built Schloss Weissenstein in Pommersfelden between 1711 and 1729. In 1867 only one copy still existed of the earliest printed collection catalogue of 1719, but it has since disappeared. We do not know, therefore, if the Vermeer was already in Pommersfelden in that year but the painting is mentioned in the catalogues of 1746 and 1857.[19]

Thoré-Bürger reported in 1866 that the painting in Pommersfelden was being attributed to "Jacob van der Meer."[20] To his great satisfaction he was able to acquire the picture one year later, when part of the Schönborn collection was auctioned in Paris. He was asked to author the sale catalogue.[21] By this time Thoré-Burger already owned *A Lady Standing at the Virginal* (cat. 21).

After the "discoverer of Vermeer" passed on in 1869, his collection came into the possession of Paul Lacroix (1807–1884) (see page 199). After the death of Lacroix, the present painting, for which Thoré-Burger had paid 2,000 francs in 1867, was sold in 1892 to the dealer Sedelmeyer for 25,000 francs.[22] In 1894 the picture was in the possession of the dealer T. Humphry Ward, who parted with it for an exhibition in the Royal Academy,[23] and must have sold it soon afterward to George Salting (1835–1909). Salting had devoted his life almost entirely to acquiring art, from Chinese porcelain to French impressionist paintings.[24] He bought the present painting before 1898. In 1910 he left the picture, along with dozens of other masterpieces of the Dutch Golden Age, to the National Gallery, London, which had already bought *A Lady Standing at the Virginal* from the Thoré-Burger Collection back in 1892.[25]

1. Kühn 1968, 202.
2. This painting was owned by Maria Thins (see page 16).
3. Gowing 1970, 155–157; Slatkes 1981, 88, 91–92; Nash 1991, 114–118.
4. This late date is also advocated by Blankert 1975, 164, cat. 31; Blankert 1978, 170, cat. 31.
5. Slatkes 1981, 91.
6. As De Jongh explains in Haarlem 1986, 285–288, the lute was often understood symbolically to represent harmony in love. Nevertheless, because the instrument's shape has female characteristics, it also was an instrument with sexual associations, particularly when depicted in a procuress scene. See De Jongh in Brussels 1971, 175. Ripa 1644, 75–76, moreover, identifies the lute as an attribute of the sanquine temperament.
7. For images of women playing a virginal, or comparable instrument, see De Jongh in Haarlem 1986, figs. 42, 43, 69a, cat. 47. This iconographic tradition almost certainly is associated with Saint Cecilia, a virgin martyr and patron saint of music who lived in Rome during the second or third century. She was renowned for her ability to play any instrument, none of which, however, sufficed to give expression to the flood of heavenly melody that filled her soul. She thus invented the organ. She is often depicted at the keyboard looking out from her instrument.
8. Cats 1627, 85, emblem 42.
9. For a further discussion of this painting, see Wheelock 1995, 112–119. Music as a representation of harmony in love is also found in paintings by other Dutch artists. See, for example, Fischer 1975, 80–82, who discusses the role of music in fusing sacred and profane love in Bartholomeus van der Helst's *Musician*, 1662, The Metropolitan Museum of Art, New York.
10. This connection was first noted by Boström 1949, 24.
11. I would like to thank Ronni Baer for sending me her text on this painting in her dissertation: Baer 1990, cat. III.1.
12. Above the woman's head hangs a closed bird cage, certainly purposefully placed there by the artist as a reference to an emblem in Hooft 1611, 66–67, emblem 28 (in Hooft 1671). The emblem, "Voor vryheyt vaylicheyt" (Instead of freedom, safety), stresses that love is strengthened when limits are placed upon it, and that with freedom comes danger. The love she seeks, thus, is faithful and true.
13. Dogaer 1971, no. 182: "Register vande schilderyen alhier in onsen huyse," "Een stuckxken met een jouffrou op de clavecingel spelende met bywerck van Vermeer...kost guld[en] 150."
14. Mauritshuis 1993A, 293–294; see also Legêne 1994, 83.
15. Samuel 1976, 306–307; the painting was not mentioned in the remnant of the Duarte Collection that was sold in Amsterdam (Dudok van Heel 1975, 110–111, no. 165).
16. The collection was expanded by one work between 1683 and 1695 (see page 53).
17. Hoet 1752–1770, 1:36, no. 37: "Een Speelende Juffrouw op de Clavecimbael van dito (J. vander Meer van Delft)."
18. National Gallery London 1960, 438–439, no. 2568; incorrect is the proposition: "Whichever it was, the other was in the Van Ruijven-Dissius Collection" (Montias 1989, 257).
19. Pommersfelden 1746, no. 60, and Pommersfelden 1857, no. 60; T. von Frimmel in Pommersfelden 1894, 8; Sale catalogue, Paris, 17 May 1867, 36, no. 78 (Lugt no. 29816). For unknown reasons, however, the 1788 and 1845 descriptions of the count's collection were silent about the Vermeer (See National Gallery London 1960, 439 n. 7).
20. Thoré-Bürger 1866, 327.
21. Sale catalogue, Paris, 17 May 1867 (Lugt no. 29816).
22. Sale catalogue, Paris, 5 December 1892, 24, no. 32 (Lugt no. 51162).
23. London 1894, 22, no. 93; Hofstede de Groot 1894, 172.
24. DNB (supplement), 1: 254–256; Roberts 1910.
25. National Gallery London 1960, 439 and 503–504.

COLLECTION CATALOGUES

Pommersfelden 1857, no. 60; National Gallery London 1960, 438–439, no. 2568; National Gallery London 1991, 1: 468–469, no. 2568; 2: ill. 394

LITERATURE

Thoré-Bürger 1866, 327 and 557, no. 30; Havard 1888, 37, no. 33; Hofstede de Groot 1907–1928, 1: 597–598, no. 25; Alfassa 1911, 401–408; Plietzsch 1911, 117, no. 25; Hale 1937, 156–157 and pl. 32; Heppner 1938, 142; De Vries 1939, 52, 94–95, no. 42 and ill. 65; Blum 1946, 173, no. 30 and ill.; Swillens 1950, 51, no. 2, 67, 73, 80–81, 86–87, 89, 103, 108–109, 116 and pl. 2; Goldscheider 1958, 146, no. 35 and ills. 77, 79, 81, 82; Gerson 1967, col. 743; Blankert 1975, 89, 116 n. 53, 164–165, no. 31 and pl. 31; Blankert 1978, 27, 59, 77 nn. 48 and 64, 170–171, no. 31 and pls. 31, 31a–b; Slatkes 1981, 90–93 and ill; Wheelock 1981, 16, 24, 33, 45, 70, 152, 154, and pl. 46; Aillaud 1986, 146, 198, no. 31, and pl. 30; Wheelock 1988, 43, 124–125 and ill. 39; Nash 1991, 114–116 and ill.; Blankert 1992, 148, 202, no. 31 and pl. 30; Wheelock 1995, 5, 117, 157, 186, and ill. A35

23

Young Girl with a Flute

probably 1665/1670
Circle of Johannes Vermeer
oil on oak, 20 x 17.8 (7 7/8 x 7)

National Gallery of Art, Washington, Widener Collection

PROVENANCE

(?) Pieter Claesz van Ruijven, Delft, before 1674; (?) Maria de Knuijt, Widow Van Ruijven, Delft, 1674–1681; (?) Magdalena van Ruijven and Jacob Dissius, Delft, 1681–1682; (?) Jacob Dissius (with his father Abraham Dissius, 1685–1694), Delft, 1682–1695; (?) Dissius sale, Amsterdam, 16 May 1696, possibly no. 39 (*f* 17) or no. 40 (*f* 17); Van Son Collection, 's-Hertogenbosch; Jan Mahie van Boxtel en Liempde and Geertruida van Boxtel en Liempde-van Son, Boxtel; bought from the estate by her daughter Jaqueline Gertrude Marie de Grez-van Boxtel en Liempde, wife of Jonkheer Jan de Grez, Brussels, by 1876 for *f* 32 (on loan to the Mauritshuis, The Hague, 1907); [Antiquar Jonas, Paris, 1911]; August Janssen, Amsterdam; [Jacques Goudstikker, Amsterdam, by 1919]; [M. Knoedler & Co., New York]; inheritance from Estate of Peter A. B. Widener by gift through power of appointment of Joseph E. Widener, Elkins Park, Pennsylvania, after purchase by funds of the Estate; and by bequest to the present owner in 1942

EXHIBITIONS

The Hague 1919, no. 131 and ill.

TECHNICAL DESCRIPTION

The vertically grained oak panel support has beveled edges on the back. The panel has a slight convex warp, a small check in the top edge at the right, and small gouges, rubs, and splinters on the back from nails and handling. A very thin, smooth, white chalk ground was applied overall, followed by a coarse-textured gray ground. A reddish-brown dead coloring exists under most areas of the painting and is incorporated in the design of the tapestry.[1]

Paint is applied moderately thinly, forming a rough surface texture in lighter passages. Still-wet paint in the proper right cheek and chin was textured with a fingertip, then glazed with a translucent green half-tone. In many areas of the whites, particularly in the proper left collar and cuff, a distinctive wrinkling is present, which disturbs the surface. Small, irregularly shaped losses over much of the surface may have resulted from abrasion to similar wrinkles that occurred during old restorations.

Young Girl with a Flute is a fascinating and problematic painting, whose place within Vermeer's oeuvre, and even century of origin, have long been disputed.[2] The panel support, the style of the costume, and the quality of execution all raise questions about the attribution. Although the discolored varnish and old repaint that distorted the image were removed during the painting's restoration in 1995, even now extensive abrasion of the paint surface hinders a conclusive assessment of artistic quality. The blue glaze that once covered the back of the chair, for example, has now mostly disappeared, leaving visible only the reddish-brown underpaint.[3] Nevertheless, the restoration and related technical examinations have provided a fuller understanding of both the complex compositional alterations and the sequence of paint layers that comprise this image, information essential for any informed judgment of attribution.

The *Young Girl with a Flute* is the only painting on panel exhibited here, other than *The Girl with the Red Hat* (cat. 14). Owing also to their similarities in scale and subject matter, scholars frequently cited these works as pendants.[4] Indeed, both girls look expectantly toward the viewer with alert eyes and half-open mouths. Each wears an exotic hat, sits before a tapestry in a chair with lion finials, and leans on one arm. Light enters from the left in both compositions, striking the left cheek, nose, and chin of both figures. A thin green glaze pulled over the flesh tone, moreover, indicates the shaded portions of both faces. Finally, colored highlights accent each mouth, turquoise in *Young Girl with a Flute* and pink in *The Girl with the Red Hat*.[5]

Despite these similarities, slight differences in both the size of the panels and the compositional arrangement of the figures indicate that the paintings are not companion pieces.[6] Differences in artistic quality prove even more significant. In *Young Girl with a Flute*, the flesh tones of the face are modulated with a lesser degree of refinement. Transitions between the shadow of the eye and the sunlit cheek, the shaded and unshaded portions of the chin, and the areas between the nose and mouth, appear abrupt. Unusually thick impasto defines the girl's thumbnail and ill-proportioned right hand, and the flute in her left hand is inaccurately rendered.[7]

A comparison of the lion-head finials in the two paintings also illustrates the relatively unrefined brushwork of the *Young Girl with a Flute*. While Vermeer modeled the right finial in *The Girl with the Red Hat* with subtle variations in the weight and thickness of brushstrokes, those in *Young Girl with a Flute* less successfully create a sense of form and volume.[8] In addition, the diffused yellow highlights enliven the blue jackets in a different manner. In *The Girl with the Red Hat* Vermeer first highlighted the blue robe with light blue strokes and then applied short dabs of thin lead-tin yellow paint. He then painted the ridges of the highlighted folds with strokes of opaque lead-tin yellow. The jacket of the *Young Girl with a Flute* is painted in a similar technique, but the colors appear less fresh and the strokes less fluid.

Many shared characteristics between these paintings, however, complicate efforts to attribute *Young Girl with a Flute*. Moreover, a judgment based on a single comparison is always ill-advised, particularly when so little is known about an artist's oeuvre. Indeed, stylistic connections exist between *Young Girl with a Flute* and other Vermeer paintings. The softly modeled yellow highlights on the blue jacket, for example, resemble those on the blue edging of the yellow material hanging from the turban in *Girl with a Pearl Earring* (cat. 15). By the

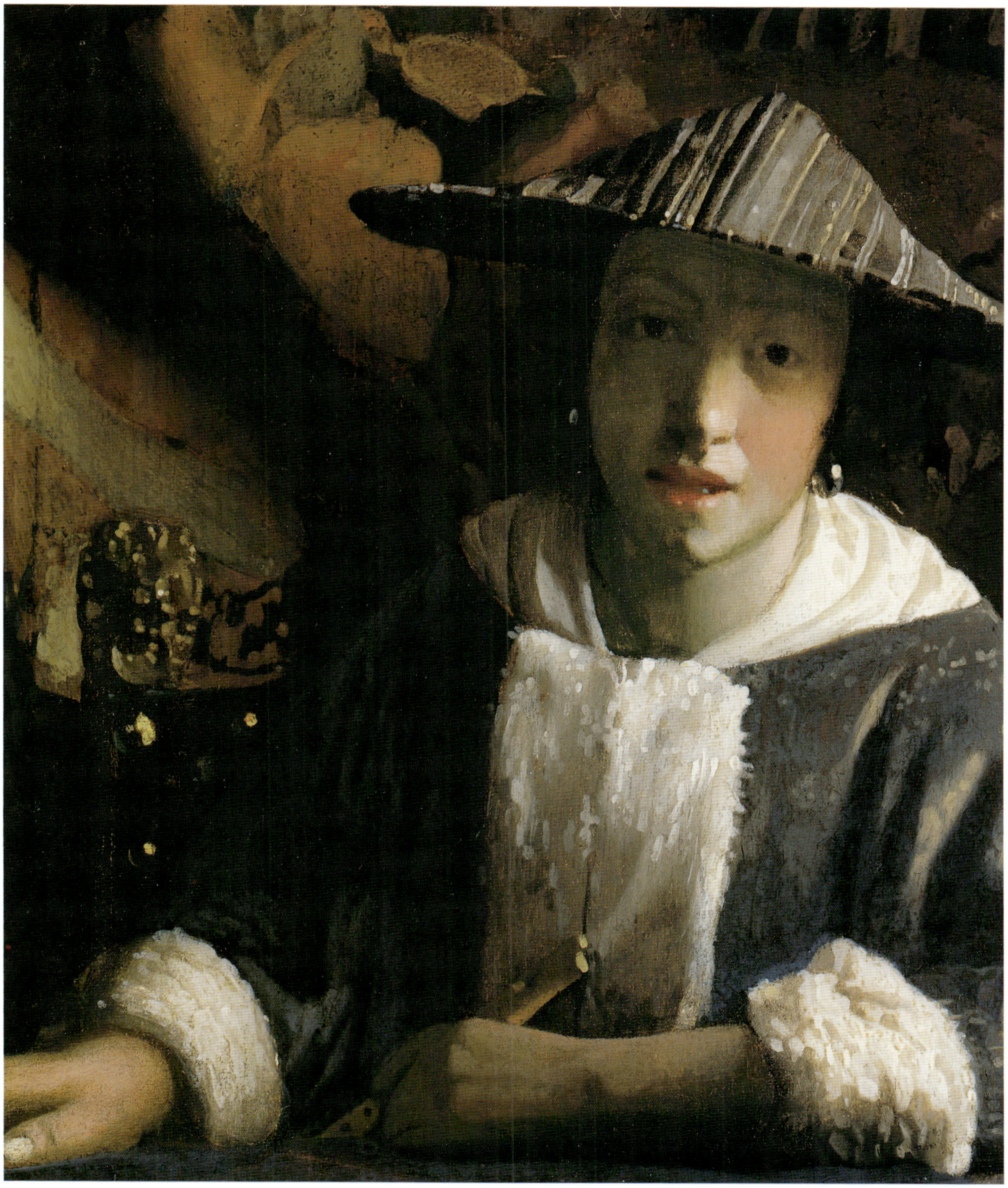

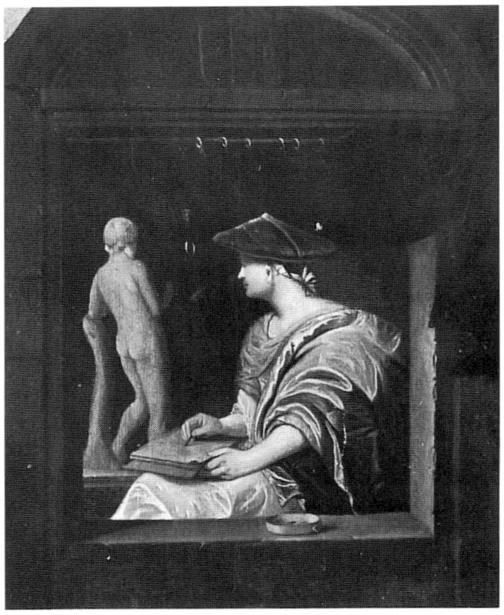

fig. 1. Follower of Frans van Mieris the Elder, *A Girl Drawing*, 1670s, oil on panel, private collection

end of the 1660s and early 1670s, moreover, Vermeer modeled forms with more abrupt transitions, similar to those that define the girl's face (page 32, fig. 1). Finally, the blocky character of the brushstrokes defining the finial compares well to the abstract modeling of the gold picture frame in, for example, *A Lady Seated at the Virginal* (cat. 22).

Technical examinations disprove doubts about the seventeenth-century origins of this work. Dendrochronology has determined a felling date for the panel from the early 1650s.[9] Moreover, a paint sample taken from a yellow highlight on the girl's left sleeve contains natural ultramarine, azurite, and lead-tin yellow, all pigments frequently used by Vermeer.[10] The costume, although unusual, parallels contemporary styles of dress. The girl's fur-lined jacket, for example, appears in other works from the mid-1660s, such as *Woman Holding a Balance* (cat. 10) and *The Concert* (page 17, fig. 1). Similar wide-brimmed hats, Chinese in style, appear in Dutch prints and drawings of working-class women.[11] This hat, however, decorated with a gray, white, and black striped material, has been made respectable for a lady of means.[12] It is similar to one worn by a female artist in a painting by a follower of Frans van Mieris (fig. 1), and owes much to the contemporary vogue for oriental fashion.[13]

The painting suffers from both poor preservation and extensive reworking in the seventeenth century. X-radiography (fig. 2) and infrared reflectography (fig. 3) reveal the following alterations: the lowering of the proper left shoulder and alteration of the pattern of folds on the left collar, the movement of the collar opening to the viewer's left, the enlargement and repositioning of the left jacket cuff to reveal more of the girl's arm, the alteration of the contour of the proper right shoulder and arm, the reduction in the size of the hat, and the addition of the fur trim on the front of the jacket to cover the lower part of the original V-shaped neck opening. Finally, the finger that rests on the recorder was added, suggesting that the flute did not exist in the original composition. Without the added finger, the flute could not be held.

These alterations appear to have been made after the blocking-in stage of the painting but before modeling had commenced. This initial design layer remains uncovered in only two areas: the figure's proper right collar and the hat. The reasons for these extensive changes remain uncertain. Perhaps they were made to enhance the composition, for by lowering the left shoulder and adjusting the position of the cuff, the young girl no longer leans to such a degree on her left arm.

While this explanation suggests a close chronological proximity between the initial design concept and the reworking of the image, this seems not to have been the case. The x-radiograph reveals unexplained losses in the underlying design layer, appearing under the white collar on the girl's left shoulder, below her left eye, between her nose and mouth, and on her cuffs and right hand. It has been suggested that the initial design was scraped down,[14] but it seems more probable that some inherent problem of adhesion existed between the paint layers and the ground, a problem that might also account for the peculiar alligatoring that occurs in the paint on the woman's cuff and in the thin blues of her jacket.

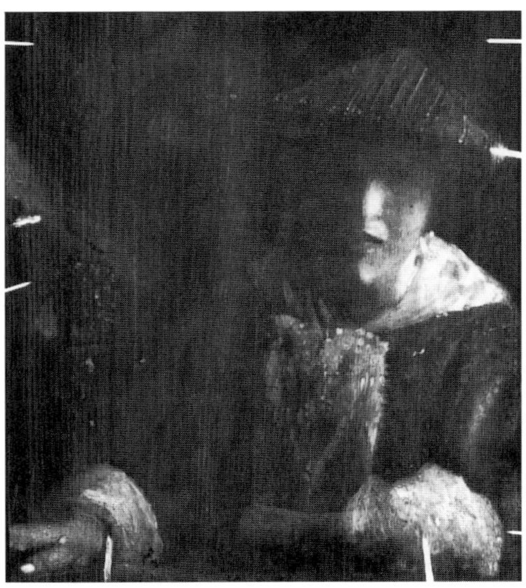

fig. 2. *Young Girl with a Flute*, x-radiograph

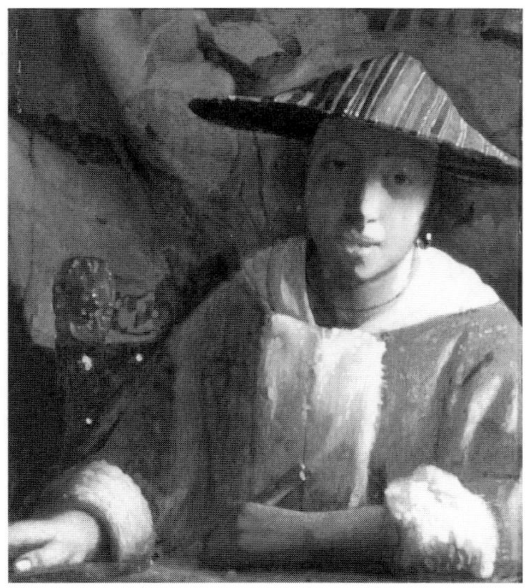

fig. 3. *Young Girl with a Flute*, infrared reflectogram

The complex issues surrounding the attribution of this painting can be summarized as follows. Technical analysis confirms that the panel was prepared in the 1650s and that the paints originated in the seventeenth century. The general character of the image, and even the painting techniques, compare well to Vermeer's, specifically to *The Girl with the Red Hat*. The image underwent extensive revisions after damages had occurred in the underlying layer, but the quality of the reworking is not consonant with Vermeer. Finally, the image has suffered from general abrasion.

Given the close compositional and stylistic similarities to Vermeer's other paintings, particularly *The Girl with a Red Hat*, it seems probable that Vermeer conceived and blocked in the composition but for some reason abandoned it. Vermeer may have left the painting largely unfinished, and it may have been subsequently worked up in his style by an unidentified follower.[15] Montias, who also arrived at this conclusion, plausibly suggests that this is the work of Jan Coelenbier, who purchased paintings in 1676 from Catharina Bolnes soon after Vermeer's death.[16] As these paintings were to be auctioned the following year, Coelenbier may have tried to improve the work to secure a higher price.[17] Whether Montias' hypothesis proves true, the second artist at work in *Young Girl with a Flute* certainly knew Vermeer's paintings from the late 1660s and early 1670s, for he incorporated a number of stylistic features from this period of Vermeer's career.

In 1906 Abraham Bredius, director of the Mauritshuis from 1889 to 1909, was invited to Brussels to study the Rembrandt drawings in the then relatively unknown De Grez Collection. Here he had an epiphany comparable to one that he had experienced in 1898, when he had stood face to face with the *Polish Rider* by Rembrandt (1606–1669).[18] "Suddenly my eye fell on a small picture, hanging up high. 'Am I permitted to take this down once, as it appears to be something very beautiful?' And yes! It was very beautiful!" Bredius thought this must be an unknown work by Johannes Vermeer, published the panel as a work by the Delft master,[19] and arranged for the panel to be lent to the Mauritshuis during the summer of 1907.[20] No one doubted the judgment of the discoverer of so many masterpieces of the Dutch Golden Age.[21]

Two later letters elucidate the provenance as the descendants of Jonkheer De Grez were able to remember it. The great-great-grandmother of J. H. L. van de Mortel (one of the letter writers) was called Geertruida van Son. She "had a rich bachelor brother Van Son, who lived off rental properties in 's-Hertogenbosch. When the tenants could not pay, he is thought to have said on occasion 'never mind, just give me that painting instead.'"[22] Geertruida van Son was the spouse of J. Mahie van Boxtel en Liempde; she died in 1876 in Stapelen Castle, near Boxtel. Her daughter Jaqueline Gertrude Marie ("Mies"), who was married to Jonkheer Jan de Grez (1837–1910), bought the small painting out of the Van Son estate for thirty-two guilders. Considering the small sum paid for the work, no one would have thought of it as an important work of art. Bredius' visit suddenly brought an end to this situation. A few years after the death of Jonkheer de Grez in 1910, the dowager sold the painting by way of her nephew Henri van de Mortel to the art dealer Jonas of Paris. The sum of the transaction was 25,000 guilders![23] Bredius *cum suis* had set the tone. In 1907 Martin had written: "After all, the work is so characteristic that it may be recognized as a Vermeer even at first sight."[24] Freise added: "Our picture is unusually warm in tone for a Vermeer."[25] In 1939 A. B. De Vries still said of the painting: "highly virtuoso painting, with many *pointillés*."[26]

We know the next owner of the Vermeer, but not the amount that he paid for it. August Janssen (1863–1918), compared by Frits Lugt to such legendary collectors of Dutch art as Six and Braamcamp, only owned the panel for a short while. "The greatest collector that our country has possessed since the middle of the past century, has gone to his maker," wrote Lugt on 20 April 1918.[27] About a year later the Amsterdam dealer Goudstikker exhibited a number of paintings, including the Vermeer discovered by Bredius, in "Pulchri Studio" in The Hague.[28] A new buyer was not easily found, however, which is hardly surprising considering the asking price of 325,000 guilders.[29] Nonetheless, the *Algemeen Handelsblad* announced on 20 April 1921 that "The 'Girl with the Flute' by Vermeer from the Goudstikker Collection, which was for some time on loan to the Alte Pinakothek in Munich, has, we have been informed, been sold to America."[30] Knoedler & Co. of New York sold the *Young Girl with a Flute* to Joseph E. Widener (1872–1943) of Philadelphia, who gave it to the National Gallery of Art in 1942.[31]

1. Kühn 1968, 194, analyzed the pigments. Robert L. Feller, Carnegie Mellon University, found chalk with perhaps a trace of yellow ocher in the ground. His report, dated 12 July 1974, is kept in the scientific research department, National Gallery of Art.
2. The attribution of this painting to Vermeer was first rejected by Swillens 1950, 64–65. Blankert 1975, 108–110, 168, considered the work to be a nineteenth-century imitation. He restricted this view in Blankert 1978, 172, and again in Aillaud 1986, 200–201. A similar opinion is held by Brentjens 1985, 54–58. Wheelock 1977B argued for the seventeenth-century origin of the painting, placing the work in the circle of Vermeer. He expanded upon this theory in Wheelock 1978, 242–257, and in Wheelock 1981, 156. Montias 1989, 265 n. 2, proposed that "the painting was begun by Vermeer and finished after his death by an

inferior painter, perhaps by Jan Coelenbier, who bought paintings from Vermeer's widow soon after his death." Liedtke in The Hague 1990, 43, on the other hand, defends the attribution to Vermeer. Since 1983, the painting has been designated by the National Gallery of Art as "Attributed to Vermeer"; see National Gallery Washington 1995, 387–393. The designation in the present exhibition catalogue as "Circle of Vermeer" reflects the divergent opinions of the coorganizers.
3. A disturbing number of paint losses also exist, such as the brass nails on the chair back, that actually extend down through the paint to the panel itself.
4. They may even have been considered companion pieces in the Dissius sale in 1696. See Montias 1989, 363–364, doc. 439. Items 38, 39, and 40 are described as "a tronie in antique dress, uncommonly artful"; "Another ditto Vermeer"; and "A pendant of the same." The unusual costumes in *The Girl with a Red Hat* and the *Young Girl with a Flute* may well have been seen as depicting "antique dress" by the compiler of the catalogue.
5. The turquoise color of the highlight in *Young Girl with a Flute* is similar to that in the eye of *The Girl with the Red Hat*.
6. *Young Girl with a Flute* measures 20 by 17.8 cm. *The Girl with the Red Hat* measures 23.2 by 18.1 cm. There is no indication that the panel has been trimmed, as was first suggested by Martin 1907A, 20, who thought the painting to be a fragment. Not only has the back of the panel been beveled at some early date along all four edges, but also the paint along the edges does not appear fractured in a way that would suggest a reduction in size.
7. I am most grateful to Helen Hollis, formerly of the division of musical instruments, Smithsonian Institution, Washington, for her observations on the nature of musical instruments in Vermeer's oeuvre and on the specific character of the flute in this painting. Although its fipple mouthpiece is correctly indicated by the double highlight, the air hole below the mouthpiece is placed off-line. As seen in the recorder hanging on the wall in a painting by Judith Leyster, it should lie on an axis with the upper lip of the mouthpiece (Nationalmuseum, Stockholm, inv. no. NM 1126). The finger holes seen below the girl's hand are turned even further off this axis, although such a placement would be allowable if the recorder were composed of two sections.
8. Microscopic examination of the chair finial reveals that the surface is filled with small particles of foreign matter imbedded in the paint. This foreign matter, whether it be dust, brush hairs, or wood splinters, is found throughout the paint. Similar foreign matter is found embedded in the paint in *The Guitar Player*, c. 1672 (page 32, fig. 1).
9. Joseph Bauch and Peter Klein of the Universität Hamburg gave the earliest possible felling dates of 1653 and 1651 respectively. See reports in the archives of the scientific research department, conservation laboratory, National Gallery of Art: Bauch, 29 November 1977; and Klein, 29 September 1987.
10. Kühn 1968, 194. These pigments were prevalent in the seventeenth century but not at later dates. Similar results have been reached by Melanie Gifford in her examination of the painting during the 1994–1995 restoration.
11. A. M. Louise E. Mulder-Erkelens, keeper of textiles, Rijksmuseum, Amsterdam, has suggested (letter in National Gallery of Art curatorial files) that the hat may have been intended to suggest some "archaic or exotic characteristics." She related it to hats seen on gypsies and shepherdesses in works by Abraham Bloemaert (1564–1651) and Carel van Mander (1548–1606). She also noted that artists often kept unusual headgear in their studios that could assist in giving chiaroscuro effects to the model's face. See Gudlaugsson 1938, 21. Similar wide-brimmed hats are frequently found in works by Rembrandt and his school. See Held 1969, 11–12.
12. Thomas Lawton, director of the Freer Gallery of Art, of the Smithsonian Institution, Washington, has been most helpful in analyzing the nature of this hat.
13. See Slive 1957–1958, 32–39. I would like to thank Otto Naumann for calling my attention to this painting by a follower of Van Mieris, which is catalogued by Naumann 1981, 2: 146, cat. C30.
14. I am grateful to Melanie Gifford for suggesting this possible explanation.
15. See note 2.
16. Montias 1989, 338, doc. 362.
17. I am particularly grateful to Meredith Hale for her comments and observations about this painting.
18. Broos 1991, 52–56.
19. Bredius 1906–1907, 385–386: "Plötzlich fällt mein Auge auf ein kleines, hochhängendes Bildchen. 'Darf ich das nicht einmal herunternehmen, das scheint ja etwas sehr Schönes zu sein?' Und Jawohl! Sehr schön war es!" Jonkheer Jan de Grez inherited a collection of old drawings from his cousin Joseph de Grez, which he augmented considerably and transferred from Breda to Brussels. Jan himself wrote a catalogue, which was published in 1913, after his widow had bequeathed the collection of more than 4000 drawings to the Belgian State (Brussels 1913, unpaginated, foreword).
20. Report Mauritshuis 1907, 90; the only documentation concerning this loan is a postcard from Mrs. De Grez, dated 15–16 May 1907, in which she gives permission to have the painting photographed (Mauritshuis documentation archives, 1907, no. 224).
21. See, for instance, Hofstede de Groot 1907–1928, 1: 610, no. 22d; Martin 1907A; Martin 1907B.
22. Letter from J. B. V. M. J. van de Mortel to John Walker, dated 18 November 1946, and from J. H. L. van de Mortel to A. B. de Vries, dated 12 February 1971 (National Gallery of Art curatorial files): "had een rijke ongetrouwde broer Van Son, die huisjesmelker in 's-Hertogenbosch was. Als de huurders niet konden betalen zou hij wel eens gezegd hebben 'laat maar zitten, geef maar in plaats daarvan dat schilderijtje.'"
23. According to the letter of 1946 (see n. 22 above) Henri van de Mortel was the father of the writer; De Grez's year of death is mistakenly specified as 1913 instead of 1910 (see *Nederland's Adelsboek* 12 [1914], 27).
24. Martin 1907B, 21: "Immers, het stukje is zóó karakteristiek, dat het reeds op het eerste gezicht als [Vermeer] te herkennen is."
25. Freise 1907, 277: "Für Vermeer ist unser Bildchen von ganz besonders warmem Ton."
26. De Vries 1939, 89, no. 28: "Zeer virtuoos geschilderd met vele pointillé's."
27. Lugt 1918, 7: "De grootste verzamelaar, dien ons land sedert het midden der vorige eeuw heeft bezeten, is ter ziele."
28. The Hague 1919, no. 131 and ill.
29. Swillens 1950, 65, no. E.
30. *Algemeen Handelsblad*, 20 April 1921, Evening Edition, 3rd section, 9: "Het 'Meisje met de fluit' van Vermeer uit de verzameling Goudstikker, dat eenigen tijd als bruikleen in de Oude Pinacotheek te München is geweest, werd, naar men ons mededeelt, naar Amerika verkocht."
31. Widener 1923, unpaginated, s.v.; Hale 1937, 143, no. 28 and ill. On the Widener gift, see Finley 1973, 93–102, 105–107.

COLLECTION CATALOGUES

Widener 1923, unpaginated, and ill.; Widener 1931, 100 and ill.; Widener 1948, 64, and ill.; National Gallery Washington 1975, 362–363, and ill.; National Gallery Washington 1985, 421 and ill.; National Gallery Washington 1995, 387–393 (with extensive literature)

LITERATURE

Bredius 1906–1907, 385; Freise 1907, 277–278 and ill.; Hofstede de Groot 1907–1928, 1: 610, no. 22d; Report Mauritshuis 1907, 90; Martin 1907A; Martin 1907B; Plietzsch 1911, 55, 78–79, 115, no. 13 and ill. 30; Hirschmann 1920, 70–71, 73 and ill. 13; Tatlock 1921, 28–33 and ill.; Barker 1925, 227; Borenius 1925, 126; Cortissoz 1925, 47; Lavallée 1925, 324; Hofstede de Groot 1907–1930, 9, no. 42 and ill.; Hale 1937, 132, 143 and ill. 28; Waldmann 1938, 341; De Vries 1939, 88–89, no. 28 and ill. 52; Comstock 1941, 166, 170 and ill.; Van Thienen 1949, 23, no. 25 and ill. 26; Swillens 1950, 64–65, no. E; Gowing 1952, 145 and 147 nn. 120, 122 and pl. 56; Goldscheider 1958, 144, no. 26 and ill. 61; Seymour 1964, 327 and ill. 1; Gerson 1967, col. 740; Blankert 1975, 108–110, 120 n. 27, 168, no. B 4 and ill.; Van Straaten 1977, 36–37, no. 44 and ill.; Brown 1977, 57; Wheelock 1977B, 439; Blankert 1978, 73–74, 79 n. 109, 172, no. B 4 and ill. B 4; Wheelock 1978, 242, 251–256 and ills. 2, 18–22; Slatkes 1981, 98–99 and ill.; Wheelock 1981, 45, 156, and pl. 47; Aillaud 1986, 200–201, no. B4, and ill.; Wheelock 1988, 126–127 and ill. 40; Montias 1989, 265; Blankert 1992, 206, no. B4, and ill. 127; Wheelock 1995, 122, 186, and ill. A36

Bibliography

Aikema 1993
AIKEMA, Bernard, and Ewoud MIJNLIEFF. "Giovanni Antonio Pellegrini 1716–1718. A Venetian Painter in the Low Countries." *Nederland-Italië. Relaties in de beeldende kunst van de Nederlanden en Italië 1400–1750. Nederlands Kunsthistorisch Jaarboek* 44: 215–242.

Aillaud 1986
AILLAUD, Gilles, Albert BLANKERT, and John Michael MONTIAS. *Vermeer.* Paris. See Blankert 1987, 1988, 1992.

Ainsworth 1982
AINSWORTH, Maryan Wynn, John BREALY, Egbert HAVERKAMP-BEGEMANN, and Pieter MEYERS. *Art and Autoradiography: Insights into the Genesis of Paintings by Rembrandt, Van Dyck, and Vermeer.* New York.

Alexandre 1906
ALEXANDRE, Arsène. "Van der Meer de Delft." *L'Art et les Artistes* 2 (October-May): 1–5.

Alexandre 1933
ALEXANDRE, Arsène. "Vermeer et l'école de Delft: Nouveaux aperçus sur Vermeer." *L'Art et les Artistes,* new series, 25: 145–173.

Alfassa 1911
ALFASSA, P. "Les Vermeers de la Galerie Nationale de Londres." *La Revue de l'Art Ancien et Moderne* 20: 401–408.

Allen 1949, 1965
ALLEN, F. L. *The Great Pierpont Morgan.* New York.

Alpers 1976
ALPERS, Svetlana. "Describe or Narrate? A Problem in Pictorial Representation." *New Literary History* 8 (Autumn): 15–41.

Alpers 1982
ALPERS, Svetlana. "In Detail: Vermeer and the Art of Painting." *Portfolio* 4 (March-April): 88–93.

Alpers 1983
ALPERS, Svetlana. *The Art of Describing: Dutch Art in the Seventeenth Century.* Chicago.

Arasse 1994
ARASSE, Daniel. *Vermeer: Faith in Painting.* Princeton.

Arnheim 1976
ARNHEIM, R., D. ASHTON, H. GARDNER, R. HELD, W. HESS, F. METELLI, E. NASH, H. SCHAEFER-SIMMERN, M. TEUBER, and W. ZUCKER. *Vision and Artifact.* New York.

L'Art 1877
"Chronique de l'Hôtel Drouot." *L'Art* 8: 117.

Ashwin 1984
ASHWIN, Clive. "The Age of Vermeer and De Hooch: Exhibition at the Royal Academy, London, 7 September to 18 November 1984." *Studio International* 197: 48.

Asemissen 1988
ASEMISSEN, Hermann. *Jan Vermeer Die Malkunst.* Frankfurt.

Athenaeum 1901
"The Newly discovered Vermeer," *The Athenaeum* (30 March): 409.

Badt 1961
BADT, Kurt. *Modell und Maler von Jan Vermeer: Probleme der Interpretation. Eine Streitschrift gegen Hans Sedylmayr.* Cologne.

Baer 1990
BAER, Ronni. "The Paintings of Gerrit Dou (1613–1675)." Ph.D. diss., Institute of Fine Arts, New York University.

Bakker 1993
BAKKER, Boudewijn. "Levenspelgrimage of vrome wandeling? Claesz. Janszoon Visscher en zijn serie *Plaisante Plaetsen.*" *Oud-Holland* 107: 97–116.

Baldinucci 1681–1728
BALDINUCCI, Filippo. *Notizie de' professori del disegno da Cimabue in qua, per le quali si demonstra come, e per chi le bell'arti di pittura, scultura, e architettura lasciata la rozzezza delle maniere greca, e gottica, si siano in questi secoli ridotte all'antica loro perfezione.* 6 vols. Florence.

Barker 1925
BARKER, Virgil. "A Trans-Atlantic Chronicle No. 1." *Arts* 8: 222–227.

Barnouw 1914
BARNOUW, A. J. "Vermeers zoogenaamd 'Novum Testamentum'." *Oud-Holland* 32: 50–54.

Batavus 1921
BATAVUS [M. D. Henkel]. "Vom holländischen Kunstmarkt. 'Die Strasse' von Vermeer für 680.000 Gulden versteigert." *Kunstwanderer:* 345.

Bauer 1988
BAUER, Linda Freeman. "Seventeenth-Century Naturalism and the Emblematic Interpretation of Paintings." *Emblematica* 3 (Fall): 209–228.

Bauer 1992
BAUER, Linda Freeman. "Vermeer's *Allegory of Temperance.*" *Source: Notes in the History of Art* 11 (Winter): 35–39.

Bear 1972
BEAR, N. S., N. INDICTOR, and A. JOEL. "The Chemistry and History of the Pigment Indian Yellow." *Conservation of Paintings and Graphic Arts* 98: 401–409.

Becker 1991
BECKER, Jochen. "Are These Girls Really so Neat?: On Kitchen Scenes and Method." In *Art in History/History in Art: Studies in Dutch Seventeenth-Century Culture.* Ed. David Freedberg and Jan de Vries. Santa Monica: 139–173.

Bedaux 1975
BEDAUX, Jan Baptist. "Minnekoorts-, zwangerschaps- en doodsverschijnselen op zeventiende-eeuwse schilderijen." *Antiek* 10: 17–42.

Bennett 1990
BENNETT, Shirley K. "Art on Netherlandish Maps, 1585–1685, Themes and Sources." Ph.D. diss., University of Maryland.

Benvenuti 1993
BENVENUTI, Marie-Dominique. "Les Derniers Mois de la vie de Vermeer de Delft, d'après le récit de Thomas Van Haag." *La Nouvelle Revue Française* (May): 51–61.

Van Beresteyn 1938
VAN BERESTEYN, E. A. *Grafmonumenten en grafzerken in de Oude Kerk te Delft.* Assen.

Berger 1988A
BERGER, Harry, Jr. "Conspicuous Exclusion in Vermeer: An Essay in Renaissance Pastoral." In *Second World and Green World: Studies in Renaissance Fiction-Making.* Berkeley: 441–461.

Berger 1988B
BERGER, Harry, Jr. "Some Vanity of His Art: Conspicuous Exclusion and Pastoral in Vermeer." In *Second World and Green World: Studies in Renaissance Fiction-Making.* Berkeley: 462–509.

Bertram 1948
BERTRAM, Anthony. *Jan Vermeer of Delft.* London and New York.

Białostocki 1975
BIAŁOSTOCKI, Jan. "Eugène Fromentin as Critic of Art of the Past." *Etudes d'art français offertes à Charles Sterling.* Paris.

Białostocki 1988
BIAŁOSTOCKI, Jan. "Mere Imitation of Nature or Symbolic Image of the World? Problems in the Interpretation of Dutch Painting of the XVIIth Century." In *The Message of Images: Studies in The History of Art.* Vienna: 166–180, 271–273.

Bianconi 1967
BIANCONI, Piero. *The Complete Paintings of Vermeer.* New York.

De Bie 1661
DE BIE, Cornelis. *Het gulden cabinet van de edel vry schilder-const.* Lier.

Biermann 1909
BIERMANN, Georg. "Jan Vermeer van Delft." *Velhagen & Klasings Monatshefte* 24: 295–304.

Bille 1961
BILLE, Clara. *De tempel der kunst of het kabinet van den heer Braamcamp.* 2 vols. Amsterdam.

Blanc 1860–1863
BLANC, Charles. *Histoire des peintres de toutes les écoles. École hollandaise.* 2 vols. Paris.

Blanc 1877
BLANC, Charles. "Une visite à San-Donato. Galerie des peintres des écoles flamande et hollandaise." *Gazette des Beaux-Arts,* second series, 17: 410–421.

Blankert 1975, 1978
BLANKERT, Albert (with contributions by Rob RUURS and Willem VAN DE WATERING). *Johannes Vermeer van Delft 1632–1675.* Utrecht and Antwerp. (English ed. Oxford and New York, 1978.)

Blankert 1987, 1988, 1992
BLANKERT, Albert, John Michael MONTIAS, Gilles AILLAUD, Rob RUURS, Willem VAN DE WATERING, and Phillipe RESCHE-RIGON. *Vermeer.* Amsterdam. (English ed. New York, 1988.)

Blankert 1991A
BLANKERT, Albert. *A Newly Discovered Painting by Hendrick ter Brugghen.* Zwolle.

Blankert 1991B
BLANKERT, Albert. "Vrouw 'Winter' door Caesar van Everdingen." *Bulletin van het Rijksmuseum* 39: 505–523.

Blankert 1994
BLANKERT, Albert. "Vermeers Gezicht op Delft." *Kunstschrift* 38: 48–49.

Blankert 1995
BLANKERT, Albert, and Louis P. GRIJP. "An adjustable leg and a book: Vermeer's *Lacemaker* compared to others." In *Shop Talk: Studies in Honor of Seymour Slive.*

Van Bleyswijck 1667
VAN BLEYSWIJCK, Dirck. *Beschryvinge der Stadt Delft.* Delft.

Bloch 1940
BLOCH, Vitale. "Vermeer." *Maandblad voor Beeldende Kunsten* 17: 4–8.

Bloch 1954, 1963
BLOCH, Vitale. *Tutti la Pittura de Vermeer di Delft*. Milan. (English ed. New York, 1963.)

Bloch 1966
BLOCH, Vitale. *Vermeer, suivi de l'Éloge de Thoré-Bürger*. Paris.

Blum 1946
BLUM, André. *Vermeer et Thoré-Bürger*. Geneva.

Blunt 1957
BLUNT, Anthony, and E. CROFT-MURRAY. *Venetian Drawings of the XVII & XVIII Centuries in the Collection of her Majesty the Queen at Windsor Castle*. London.

BNF
Biographie Nationale Française. Paris.

Bober 1986
BOBER, Phyllis Pray, and RUBINSTEIN, Ruth. *Renaissance Artists and Antique Sculpture: A Handbook of Sources*. New York.

Bode 1895
BODE, Wilhelm von. "Alte Kunstwerke in den Sammlungen der Vereinigten Staten." *Zeitschrift für bildende Kunst*, new series, 6: 13–19.

Bode 1904
BODE, Wilhelm von. *Die Kunstsammlungen des Alfred Beit in seinem Stadthause in Park Lane zu London*. Berlin.

Bode 1906
BODE, Wilhelm von. *Rembrandt und seine Zeitgenossen: Charakterbilder der grossen Meister der Holländischen und Vlämischen Malerschule im siebzehnten Jahrhundert*. Leipzig.

Bode 1911
BODE, Wilhelm von. "Jan Vermeer und Pieter de Hooch als Konkurrenten." *Jahrbuch der Königlich Preuszischen Kunstsammlungen* 32: 1–2.

Bode 1913
BODE, Wilhelm von. *Die Gemäldegalerie des weiland Herrn A. de Ridder in seiner Villa zu Schönberg bei Cronberg im Taunus*. Berlin.

Bode 1919
BODE, Wilhelm von. *Die Meister der Holländischen und Vlämischen Malerschulen*. Leipzig.

Bode 1926
BODE, Wilhelm von. "Kunsthistorische Ausbeute aus dem Deutschen Kunsthandel von heute." *Repertorium für Kunstwissenschaft* 47: 251–255.

Bodkin 1940
BODKIN, Thomas. Review De Vries 1939. *Burlington Magazine* 77 (August): 67–68.

Bodmer 1927
BODMER, F. "Vermeer-Stiftung in Edinburgh/ Londoner National Gallery." *Der Cicerone* 19: 66–67.

Boeck 1932
BOECK, Wilhelm. "Die künstlerische Abkunft Vermeers: Aus Gedanken von Emil Orlik." *Der Kunstwanderer* 14: 378–379.

De Boer 1991
DE BOER, Marjolein. "'Ze kunnen ze krijgen als ze zoet zijn'." In *Bredius, Rembrandt en het Mauritshuis*. Mauritshuis, The Hague: 49–50.

Boitet 1729
BOITET, Reinier. *Beschryving der Stadt Delft*. Delft.

Bolton 1985
BOLTON, Jaap. *Method and Practice: Dutch and Flemish Drawing Books 1600–1750*. Landau.

Bonafoux 1992
BONAFOUX, Pascal. *Vermeer*. Paris.

Boogaard-Bosch 1939
BOOGAARD-BOSCH, A. C. "Een onbekende acte betreffende den vader van Jan Vermeer." *Nieuwe Rotterdamsche Courant* (25 January): unpaginated.

Boone 1991–1992
BOONE, M. Elizabeth. "Gilded Age Values and a Golden Age Painter: American Perceptions of Jan Vermeer." *Rutgers Art Review* 12/13: 47–68.

Borenius 1923
BORENIUS, Tancred. "Vermeer's Master." *Burlington Magazine* 42 (January): 37–38.

Borenius 1925
BORENIUS, Tancred. "The new Vermeer." *Apollo* 2: 125–126.

Borenius 1929
BORENIUS, Tancred. "Dutch Painting at Burlington House." *International Studio* 92: 21–27.

Bosman-Jelgersma 1979
BOSMAN-JELGERSMA, H. A. *Vijf eeuwen Delftse Apothekers*. Amsterdam.

Bosse/Desargues 1664
BOSSE, Abraham. *François Desargues: Algemene manier tot de praktijk den Perspective gelyck tot die der meet-kunde met de kleyn voet-maat....* Amsterdam.

Bosse 1684
BOSSE, Abraham. *De Figuren en Redeneeringe tot de Praktyck der Perspective op Tafereelen of Regelloose Buyten gedaanten*. Amsterdam.

Boström 1949
BOSTRÖM, Kjell. "Peep-show or case." *Kunsthistorische Mededelingen van het Rijksbureau voor Kunsthistorische Documentatie 's-Gravenhage* 4: 21–24.

Boström 1951
BOSTRÖM, Kjell. "Jan Vermeer van Delft en Cornelis van der Meulen." *Oud-Holland* 66: 117–122.

Bots 1972
BOTS, Jan. *Tussen Descartes en Darwin: geloof en natuurwetenschap in de achttiende eeuw in Nederland*. Assen.

Bouricius 1925
BOURICIUS, L. G. N. "Vermeeriana." *Oud-Holland* 42: 271–273.

Boymans Annual Reports 1923
Verslag omtrent den toestand en de aanwinsten van het Museum Boijmans over het jaar 1923 (bijlage BB). Rotterdam.

Boymans Annual Reports 1928
Verslag omtrent den toestand en de aanwinsten van het Museum Boijmans over het jaar 1928 (no. 27). Rotterdam.

Braider 1989
BRAIDER, Christopher S. "The Denuded Muse: The Unmasking of Point of View in the Cartesian *Cogito* and Vermeer's *The Art of Painting*." *Poetics Today* 10 (Spring): 173–203.

Van den Brandhof 1979
VAN DEN BRANDHOF, Marijke. *Een vroege Vermeer uit 1937: achtergronden van leven en werken van de schilder/vervalser Han van Meegeren*. Utrecht.

Breck 1910
BRECK, J. "Hollandsche kunst op de Hudson-Fulton tentoonstelling te New York." *Onze Kunst* 17: 5–12, 41–47.

Bredius 1880–1881
BREDIUS, Abraham. "17e eeuwsche reisherinneringen." *Nederlandsche Kunstbode* 2 (1880): 403–405, 412–415; 3 (1881): 13–14.

Bredius 1882
BREDIUS, Abraham. "Ein Pseudo-Vermeer in der Berliner Galerie." *Beiblatt zur Zeitschrift für bildende Kunst* (9 November): 68–71.

Bredius 1885
BREDIUS, Abraham. "Iets over Jan Vermeer, 'De Delftsche Vermeer'." *Oud-Holland* 3: 217–222.

Bredius 1890–1895
BREDIUS, Abraham. "Het schildersregister van Jan Sysmus, Stads-Doctor van Amsterdam." *Oud-Holland* 8 (1890): 1–17, 217–234, 297–313 and 9 (1891): 137–149 and 12 (1894): 159–171 and 13 (1895): 112–120.

Bredius 1901
BREDIUS, Abraham. "Letteren en Kunst. De nieuwe 'Delftsche' (!) Vermeer te Londen." *Nieuwe Rotterdamsche Courant* (27 March): unpaginated.

Bredius 1903
BREDIUS, Abraham. *Vereeniging tot bevordering van beeldende kunsten. Verzameling 'Mauritshuis.'*

Bredius 1906–1907
BREDIUS, Abraham. "Der 36. (oder 37.?) Delfter Vermeer." *Kunstchronik* 18: 385–386.

Bredius 1910
BREDIUS, Abraham. "Nieuwe bijdragen over Johannes Vermeer (de Delftsche)." *Oud-Holland* 28: 61–64.

Bredius 1915–1922
BREDIUS, Abraham. *Künstler-inventare: Urkunden zur Geschichte der Holländischen Kunst des XVIten, XVIIten und XVIIIten Jahrhunderts*. 8 vols. The Hague.

Bredius 1921
BREDIUS, Abraham. "Waar 'het straatje van Six' van Vermeer in 1799 was." *Oud-Holland* 39: 59–62.

Brenninkmeyer-De Rooij 1992
BRENNINKMEYER-DE ROOIJ, Beatrijs. "De liefhebberij van Flora/ For Love of Flora." In *Boeketten uit de Gouden eeuw/Bouquets from the Golden Age*. Mauritshuis, The Hague: 9–46.

Brentjens 1985
BRENTJENS, Yvonne. "Twee meisjes van Vermeer in Washington: Een kostuumstudie." *Tableau* 7 (February): 54–58.

Van den Brink 1989
VAN DEN BRINK, Paul, and Jan WERNER, eds. *Gesneden en gedrukt in de Kalverstraat: De kaarten-en atlass endrukkerij in Amsterdam tot in de 19de eeuw*. Utrecht.

Brion 1962
BRION, Marcel. *Vermeer*. London.

Broer 1969
BROER, A. L. *Delft vroeger en nu*. Bussum.

Broos 1971
BROOS, Ben P. J. "De caers uut, de schaemschoe uut: een vergeten erotisch symbool." *Vrij Nederland* 31 (24 April): 25.

Broos 1984
BROOS, Ben P. J. "'Notitie der Teekeningen van Sybrand Feitama': de boekhouding van drie generaties verzamelaars van oude Nederlandse tekenkunst." *Oud-Holland* 98: 13–36.

Broos 1985
BROOS, Ben P. J. "'Notitie der Teekeningen van Sybrand Feitama', II: 'verkocht, verhandeld, vereërd, geruild en overgedaan'." *Oud-Holland* 99: 110–151.

Broos 1991
BROOS, Ben P. J. "Het mysterie van de Poolse ruiter." *Vrij Nederland* 45 (7 December): 52–56.
Brown 1976
BROWN, Christopher. *Dutch Genre Painting.* London.
Brown 1977
BROWN, Christopher. Review of Blankert 1975. *Simiolus* 9: 56–58.
Brown 1981
BROWN, Christopher. *Carel Fabritius.* Oxford.
Brown 1984
BROWN, Christopher. *Scenes of Everyday Life: Dutch Genre Painting of the Seventeenth Century.* London.
Brown 1989
BROWN, Christopher. Review of Blankert 1988. *Apollo* (November): 360–361.
Brunt 1912
BRUNT, Aty. "De Schilderijen van Johannes Vermeer in Hollandsche musea." *Morks' Magazin* XIV: 177–186.
De Bruyn 1988
DE BRUYN, Jean-Pierre. *Erasmus II Quellinus (1607–1678). De schilderijen met catalogue raisonné. Vlaamse schilders uit de tijd van de grote meesters.* vol. 4. Freren.
Bruyn 1983
BRUYN, Joshua. "Review of Albert Blankert, *Ferdinand Bol (1616–1680). Rembrandt's Pupil.*" *Oud-Holland* 97: 208–215.
Bruyn 1986
BRUYN, J., B. HAAK, S. H. LEVIE, P. J. J. VAN THIEL, and E. VAN DE WETERING. *A Corpus of Rembrandt Paintings. II. 1631–1634.* Dordrecht, Boston, and Lancaster.
Bryson 1987
BRYSON, Norman. "Herméneutique de la Perception." *Les Cahiers du Musée National d'Art Moderne* 21 (September): 103–117.
Buijs 1989
BUIJS, Hans. "Voorstellingen van Christus in het huis van Martha en Maria in het zestiende-eeuwse keukenstuk." *Nederlands Kunsthistorisch Jaarboek* 40: 93–128.
Buijsen 1990
BUIJSEN, Edwin. "The Battle against the Dollar: The Dutch Reaction to American Collections in the Period from 1900 to 1914." In The Hague 1990: 60–78.
Burke's 1963
TOWNEND, P. (ed.) *Burke's Genealogical and Heraldic History of the Peerage, Baronetage and Knightage.* London.
Burlington Magazine 1969
"Notable Works of Art Now on the Market." Supplement to *Burlington Magazine* 111: unpaginated.
Burroughs 1932
BURROUGHS, B., and H. B. WEHLE. "The Michael Friedsam Collection." *Bulletin of the Metropolitan Museum of Art* 27: 5–52.
Canfield 1974
CANFIELD, C. *The Incredible Pierpont Morgan. Financier and Art Collector.* London.
Carstensen/Putscher 1971
CARSTENSEN, R., and M. PUTSCHER. "Ein Bild von Vermeer in medizinhistorischer Sicht." *Deutsches Ärzteblatt-Ärzliche Mitteilungen* 68: 1–6.
Cats 1625
CATS, Jacob. *Houwelijck, dat is de gantsche gelegenheyt des echten-staets.* Middelburg.
Cats 1627
CATS, Jacob. *Proteus, ofte, Minne-beelden verandert in sinnebeelden.* Rotterdam.
Chantavoine 1926
CHANTAVOINE, Jean. *Ver Meer de Delft.* Paris.
Chapman 1986
CHAPMAN, Dana L. "Dutch Costume in Paintings by Dutch Artists: A Study of Women's Clothing and Art from 1600 to 1650." Ph.D. diss., Ohio State University, Columbus.
Chong 1992
CHONG, Alan. *Johannes Vermeer: Gezicht op Delft.* Bloemendaal.
Clausen 1925
CLAUSEN, George. "Vermeer of Delft and Modern Painting." In *Charlton Lectures on Art.* Oxford: 64–81.
Cohen 1905
COHEN, Walter. "De Delftsche Vermeer." *Galerien Europas* I: 5–8.
Colombier 1916
COLOMBIER, Jan. "Schilderijen uit de nalatenschap van den Delft'schen Vermeer." *Oud-Holland* 34: 160–161.
Comstock 1941
COMSTOCK, Helen. "The Connoisseur in America." *Connoisseur* 107 (May): 165–170.
Comstock 1946
COMSTOCK, Helen. "The Widener Collection at the National Gallery of Art, Washington." *Connoisseur* (December): 129–137.
Constable 1925
CONSTABLE, W. G. Review of Reiffenberg 1924. *Burlington Magazine* 47: 269.
Constable 1964
CONSTABLE, W. G. *Art Collecting in the United States of America. An Outline of History.* London.
Coremans 1949
COREMANS, Paul B. *Van Meegeren's Faked Vermeers and De Hooghs: A Scientific Examination.* Amsterdam.
Cortissoz 1909
CORTISSOZ, Royal. "Old Dutch Masters." *Bulletin of the Metropolitan Museum of Art* 4: 162–167.
Cortissoz 1925
CORTISSOZ, Royal. *Personalities in Art.* New York and London.
Couprie 1975
COUPRIE, Leendert. "Het Melkmeisje als symbool voor de Matigheid." *Cultureel Supplement NRC Handelsblad* (19 December): 2.
Cox 1909–1910
COX, K. "Art in America. Dutch Pictures in the Hudson-Fulton Exhibition." *Burlington Magazine* 16: 178–184, 245–246, 302–306.
Craven 1939
CRAVEN, Thomas. *A Treasury of Art Masterpieces from the Renaissance to the Present Day.* New York.
Cunnar 1990
CUNNAR, Eugene R. "The Viewer's Share: Three Sectarian Readings of Vermeer's *Woman Holding a Balance.*" *Exemplaria* 2 (Fall): 501–536.
DAB
Dictionary of American Biography. 29 vols. and supplement of 7 vols. New York, 1929–1981.
Dacier 1921
DACIER, E. "La 'petite rue' de Vermeer de Delft de la collection Six." *Revue de l'Art Ancien et Moderne* 39: 275–278.
Dantzig 1947
DANTZIG, H. M. van. *Johannes Vermeer de 'Emmausgangers' en de Critici.* Leiden.
Daudet 1928
DAUDET, Léon. "Vermeer de Delft." *Balcon d'Europe* I: 63–68.
DBF
Dictionnaire de Biographie Française. 16 vols. Paris 1933–1985.
Decker 1984
DECKER, Andrew. "A Legacy of Shame." *Art News* 84 (December): 54–76.
Decoen 1951
DECOEN, Jean. *Vermeer–Van Meegeren. Back to the Truth: Two Genuine Vermeers.* Rotterdam.
Delbanco 1928
DELBANCO, G. *Der Maler Abraham Bloemaert (1564–1651).* Strasbourg.
Deregowski 1988
DEREGOWSKI, Jan, and Denis PARKER. "On a changing perspective illusion within Vermeer's *The Music Lesson.*" *Perception* 17: 13–21.
Descargues 1966
DESCARGUES, Pierre. *Vermeer: Biographical and Critical Study.* Geneva.
Van Deursen 1978-1980
VAN DEURSEN, Arie Theo. *Het kopergeld van de Gouden Eeuw.* 4 vols. Assen.
DNB
Dictionary of National Biography (63 vols. and 3 vols. supplement, index, and errata. London, 1885–1904.
Dobell 1932
DOBELL, Clifford. *Anthony van Leeuwenhoek and His "Little Animals."* London.
Dogaer 1971
DOGAER, G. "De Inventaris van Diego Duarte." *Jaarboek van het Koninklijk Museum voor Schone Kunsten:* 195–221.
Dollekamp 1983-1984
DOLLEKAMP, Annelous. "'De Astronoom' van Vermeer in het Louvre." *Tableau* 6 (December-January): 54.
Dreyfous 1912
DREYFOUS, Georges. *L'Oeuvre de Jan Vermeer de Delft dit Van Der Meer de Delft (1632–1675).* Paris.
Dudok Van Heel 1975
DUDOK VAN HEEL, Sebastiaan A. C. "Honderdvijftig advertenties van kunstverkopingen uit veertig jaargangen van de Amsterdamsche Courant. 1672–1711." *Amstelodamum. Jaarboek* 67: 149–173.
Dudok Van Heel 1977A
DUDOK VAN HEEL, Sebastiaan A. C. "Ruim honderd advertenties van kunstverkopingen uit de Amsterdamsche Courant 1712–1725." *Amstelodamum. Jaarboek* 69: 107–122.
Dudok Van Heel 1977B
DUDOK VAN HEEL, Sebastiaan A. C. "Rembrandt's etsen uit de verzameling van Cornelis Ploos van Amstel J. Czn." *Amstelodamum* (Appendix, November-December) 64: 53–59.

Dumas 1991
DUMAS, Charles, and H. P. R. ROSENBERG (ed.). *Het kabinet der Koningin. Geschiedenis van het instituut en het huis aan de Korte Vijverberg.* The Hague.

Duparc 1975
DUPARC, Frederik J. *Een eeuw strijd voor Nederlands cultureel erfgoed.* The Hague.

Duveen 1935
DUVEEN, J. H. *Kunstschatten en intrige. Anderhalve eeuw kunstkoopen.* Amsterdam.

Edwards 1986
EDWARDS, JoLynn. "La curieuse histoire de l'Astronome de Vermeer et de son 'pendant' au XVIIIe siècle." *La Revue du Louvre et des Musées de France* 36: 197–201.

Van Eeghen 1958
VAN EEGHEN, Isabella H. "Amsterdamse kunstverzamelingen omstreeks 1875." *Amstelodamum. Maanblad* 45: 226–228.

Van Eeghen 1957
VAN EEGHEN, P. "Eensaem was mij Amsterdam." *Amstelodamum* 44: 150–154.

Eiche 1982
EICHE, Sabine. "*The Artist in His Studio* by Jan Vermeer: About a Chandelier." *Gazette des Beaux-Arts* 99 (May-June): 203–204.

Van Eijnden/Van der Willigen 1816–1820
VAN EIJNDEN, R., and A. VAN DER WILLIGEN. *Gesschiedenis der vaderlandsche schilderkunst.* 4 vols. Haarlem.

Eisler 1916
EISLER, Max. "Der Raum bei Jan Vermeer." *Jahrbuch der Kunsthistorischen Sammlungen des Allerhöchsten Kaiserhauses* 33: 213–291.

Elias 1903-1905, 1963
ELIAS, J. E. *De vroedschap van Amsterdam. 1578–1795.* 2 vols. Amsterdam.

Elovsson 1991
ELOVSSON, P. E. "The Geographer's Heart. A Study of Vermeer's Scientists." *Konsthistorisk tidskrift* 40: 17–25.

Emiliani 1966
EMILIANI, Andrea. *Vermeer.* Milan.

Engelbrecht 1974
ENGELBRECHT, E. A. *Bronnen voor de geschiedenis voor de van Rotterdam uitgegeven op last van het gemeentebestuur. V. De vroedschap van Rotterdam 1572–1795.* Rotterdam.

Familieblad 1976
Familieblad. Ten Cate-Ten Kate van vroeger tot heden.

Fegers 1952
FEGERS, H. "Jan Vermeer: Ruhm der Malkunst." *Der Kunsthandel*: 8–10.

Fell 1934
FELL, H. Granville. *Vermeer.* London and Edinburgh.

Fierens 1952
FIERENS, Paul. *Jan Vermeer de Delft, 1632–1675.* Paris.

Fink 1954
FINK, August. *Geschicte des Herzog Anton-Ulrich Museum in Braunschweig.* Brunswick.

Fink 1971
FINK, Daniel A. "Vermeer's Use of the Camera Obscura – A Comparative Study." *Art Bulletin* 53 (December): 493–505.

Finley 1973
FINLEY, D. E. *A Standard of Excellence. Andrew W. Mellon Founds the National Gallery of Art at Washington.* Washington.

Fischer 1975
FISCHER, Pieter. *Music in Paintings of the Low Countries in the 16th and 17th Centuries.* Amsterdam.

Fleming 1959
FLEMING, John. "Messrs Robert & James Adam: Art Dealers (1)." *Connoisseur:* 168–171.

Flint 1925
FLINT, Ralph. "Rare Dutch art in a loan exhibition." *Art News* 7 (21 November): 3.

Flocon 1962
FLOCON, A. "Une magistrale psychanalyse de l'Atelier de Vermeer." *Arts* 7 (November): 20.

Flocon 1968
FLOCON, A. "Clio chez le peintre." *Entretiens art psychanalyse*: 345–356.

Floerke 1905, 1972
FLOERKE, H. *Studien zur niederländischen Kunst und Kulturgeschichte; die Formen des Kunsthandels, das Atelier und die Sammler in der Niederlanden vom 15.–18. Jahrhundert.* Munich. (Repr. Soest, 1972.)

Flugi van Aspermont 1899–1900
FLUGI VAN ASPERMONT, C. H. C. "Mauritshuis." *Bulletin...Nederlandschen Oudheidkundigen Bond* 1: 13–14.

Fockema Andreae 1947
FOCKEMA ANDREAE, S. J. *Geschiedenis der Kartografie van Nederland van den romeinschen Tijd tot het Midden der 19de Eeuw.* The Hague.

De la Fontaine Verwey 1970
DE LA FONTAINE VERWEY, H. "De binder Albert Magnus en de verzamelaars van zijn tijd." *Amstelodamum. Jaarboek* 62: 87–110.

De la Fontaine Verwey 1976
DE LA FONTAINE VERWEY, H. et al. *Vier eeuwen Herengracht. Geveltekeningen van alle huizen aan de gracht, twee historische overzichten en de beschrijving van elk pand met zijn eigenaars en bewoners.* Amsterdam.

Ford 1990
FORD, Charles. "Portraits and Portraiture in the Literature of Art." *Dutch Crossing* 41: 110–131.

Foucart 1983
FOUCART, Jacques. "*L'Astronome* de Vermeer." *La Revue du Louvre et des Musées de France* 33: 280–281.

Foucart 1987
FOUCART, Jacques. *Musée du Louvre, Nouvelles acquisitions du Département des Peintures (1983–1986).* Paris.

Foucart 1994
FOUCART, Jacques. "Acquisitions. Barent Fabritius." *Revue du Louvre* 44 (April): 69–70.

Franits 1993
FRANITS, Wayne. *Paragons of Virtue: Women and Domesticity in Seventeenth-Century Dutch Art.* Cambridge.

Freise 1907
FREISE, Kurt. "Der neue Vermeer." *Zeitschrift für bildende Kunst*, new series, 18: 277–278.

Friedländer 1910
FRIEDLÄNDER, Max J. "Die Ausstellung holländischer Bilder im Metropolitan Museum zu New York 1909." *Repertorium für Kunstwissenschaft* 33: 95–99.

Von Frimmel 1906
VON FRIMMEL, Theodor. "Zu Vermeer van Delft." *Blätter für Gemäldekunde* 2: 183–189.

Von Frimmel 1912-1913
VON FRIMMEL, Theodor. "Notes on Various Works of Art. A Woman Weighing Pearls by Vermeer of Delft." *Burlington Magazine* 22: 48–49.

Fromentin 1876, 1976
FROMENTIN, Eugène. *Les Maitres d'Autrefois.* Paris. (Dutch trans. by H. van der Waal. Rotterdam, 1976.)

Fuchs 1978
FUCHS, Rudolph Herman. *Dutch Painting.* New York.

Fuller 1976
FULLER, Peter. "Forgeries." *Art Monthly* 1 (October): 7–9.

Gardner 1954
GARDNER, Albert TenEyck. "Metropolitan People and Pictures." *Art News* (January): 32–35, 71–72.

Garnier 1889
GARNIER, Henry. "La vente Secrétan." *Le Guide de l'Amateur d'oeuvres d'Art* 4: 145–150.

Gaskell 1984
GASKELL, Ivan. "Vermeer: Judgment and Truth." *Burlington Magazine* 126 (September): 557–561.

Gault de Saint Germain 1818
GAULT DE SAINT GERMAIN. *Guide des amateurs de tableaux pour les écoles allemande, flamande et hollandaise.* Paris.

GDEL
Grand Dictionaire Encyclopédique Larousse. Paris.

Geffroy 1900
GEFFROY, G. *Les Musées d'Europe. La Hollande.* Paris.

Geisberg 1974
GEISBERG, Max. *The German Single-Leaf Woodcut: 1500–1550.* New York.

Van Gelder 1957
VAN GELDER, Hendrick Enno. *Ikonografie van Constantijn Huygens en de zijnen.* The Hague.

Van Gelder 1948
VAN GELDER, Jan Gerrit. *Rembrandt. Saul en David. Petrus verloochent Christus.* Leiden.

Van Gelder 1951
VAN GELDER, Jan Gerrit. "Jan Vermeer's Clio." *Oud-Holland* 66: 44–45.

Van Gelder 1956
VAN GELDER, Jan Gerrit. "Diana door Vermeer en C. de Vos." *Oud-Holland* 71: 245–248.

Van Gelder 1958A
VAN GELDER, Jan Gerrit. *De schilderkunst van Jan Vermeer.* Utrecht.

Van Gelder 1958B
VAN GELDER, Jan Gerrit. "Jan Vermeer (1632–1675). De keukenmeid." *Openbaar Kunstbezit* 2: 13a–b.

Van Gelder 1970
VAN GELDER, Jan Gerrit. "Lambert ten Kate als verzamelaar." *Nederlands Kunsthistorisch Jaarboek* 21: 139–186.

Van Gelder 1974
VAN GELDER, Jan Gerrit. "Het kabinet van de heer Jacques Meyer." *Rotterdams Jaarboekje* 2: 167–183.

Gerson 1952
GERSON, Horst. *Het tijdperk van Rembrandt en Vermeer.* Amsterdam.

Gerson 1967
GERSON, Horst. "Johannes Vermeer." *Encyclopedia of World Art*, 14: col. 739–745.

Gerson 1969
GERSON, Horst. *Rembrandt. The Complete Edition of Paintings.* By Abraham Bredius. London.
Gerson 1977
GERSON, Horst. "Recent Literature on Vermeer." *Burlington Magazine* 119: 288–290.
Gibson 1926
GIBSON, W. P. "A Foreign Element in Vermeer's Art." *Apollo* 4: 202–206.
Glueck 1978
GLEUCK, Grace. "The Experts' Guide to the Experts." *Art News* (November): 52–57.
Goldscheider 1940
GOLDSCHEIDER, Ludwig. *The Paintings of Jan Vermeer.* New York.
Goldscheider 1958, 1967
GOLDSCHEIDER, Ludwig. *Jan Vermeer. The Paintings: Complete Edition.* (2d ed. London, 1967.)
Goldscheider 1964
GOLDSCHEIDER, Ludwig. "Vermeers Lehrer." *Pantheon* 22 (January-February): 35–38.
Gombrich 1970
GOMBRICH, Ernst H. *Aby Warburg, An Intellectual Biography.* London.
Goodman-Soellner 1989
GOODMAN-SOELLNER, Elise. "The Landscape on the Wall in Vermeer." *Konsthistorisk Tidskrift* 58: 76–88.
Van Gool 1750–1751
VAN GOOL, Jan. *De Nieuwe Schouburg der Nederlantsche Kunstschilders en Schilderessen.* 3 vols. The Hague.
Goudappel 1977
GOUDAPPEL, C. D. "Ondertrouw en huwelijk van Jan Vermeer." In *Delftse historische sprokkelingen.* Delft: 20–26.
Gowing 1951
GOWING, Lawrence. "Light on Baburen and Vermeer." *Burlington Magazine* 93 (May): 169–170.
Gowing 1952 and 1970
GOWING, Lawrence. *Vermeer.* London. 2d ed. New York, 1970.
Gowing 1954
GOWING, Lawrence. "Vermeer: An Artist in his Studio." *Art News* (Annual) 52: 82–97, 184–185.
Gravenkamp 1931
GRAVENKAMP, Curt. "Corot und Vermeer van Delft: Zwei Frauenbildnisse." *Die Kunst* 63: 315–318.
Graves 1913-1915
GRAVES, Algernon. *A Century of Loan Exhibitions 1813–1912.* 5 vols. London.
Gregory 1993
GREGORY, Alexis. *Families of Fortune. Life in the Gilded Age.* New York.
Greindl 1961
GREINDL, Edith. *Jan Vermeer, 1632–1675.* Milan.
Grimme 1974
GRIMME, Ernst Günther. *Jan Vermeer van Delft.* Cologne.
Grimschitz 1957
GRIMSCHITZ, Bruno. *Ferdinand Georg Waldmüller.* Salzburg.
Grundy 1925
GRUNDY, Cecil Reginald. "The Rediscovered Vermeer." *Connoisseur* 73 (October): 116–118.
Gudlaugsson 1938
GUDLAUGSSON, Sturla J. *Ikonographische Studien über die holländische Malerei und das Theater des 17. Jahrhunderts.* Berlin.
Gudlaugsson 1959
GUDLAUGSSON, Sturla J. *Gerard ter Borch.* 2 vols. The Hague.
Gudlaugsson 1968A
GUDLAUGSSON, Sturla J. "Kanttekeningen bij de ontwikkeling van Metsu." *Oud-Holland* 83: 13 42.
Gudlaugsson 1968B
GUDLAUGSSON, Sturla J. "Jan Vermeer." In *Kindlers Malerei Lexikon.* 6 vols. (1964–1971); 5: 656–664.
Gwynne 1966
GWYNNE, James Calvin. "Paintings Based on Vermeer's *Woman with a Water Jug.*" Ph.D. diss., Institute of Fine Arts, New York University.
Haak 1984
HAAK, Bob. *The Golden Age: Dutch Painters of the Seventeenth Century.* New York.
Hager 1966
HAGER, W. *Vermeer van Delft: Die Malkunst.* Stuttgart.
Hale 1913
HALE, Philip L. *Jan Vermeer of Delft.* Boston.
Hale 1937
HALE, Philip L. *Vermeer.* Ed. F. W. Coburn and R. T. Hale. London.
Hamlyn 1993
HAMLYN, Robin. "Exhibition previews. Robert Vernon's gift to the nation." *Apollo* 138: 193.
Hannema 1974–1975
HANNEMA, Dirk. "Nieuws over Johannes Vermeer van Delft." *Enkele mededelingen "Stichting Hannema-de Steurs Fundatie"*: 21–22.
Hannema 1978
HANNEMA, Dirk. "Problemen rondom Vermeer van Delft." In *Boymans Bijdragen.* Ed. J. C. Ebbinge Wubben. Rotterdam: 89–103.
Harbison 1976
HARBISON, Craig. "Reformation Iconography: Problems and Attitudes." *Print Review* 5 (September): 78–87.
Harms Tiepen 1909
HARMS TIEPEN, C. "Bij dr. Bredius." *De Hofstad* 2 (January): 2.
Harms Tiepen 1913
HARMS TIEPEN, C. "Holland waakt!" *Holland. Geïllustreerd Maandschrift* 1: 12–125.
Haskell 1963
HASKELL, Francis. *Patrons and Painters. A Study in the Relations Between Italian Art and Society in the Age of the Baroque.* London.
Hauser 1981
HAUSER, Andreas von. "Allegorischer Realismus. Zur Ikono-Logik von Vermeer's 'Messkünstler'." *Städel-Jahrbuch* 8: 186–203.
Havard 1873
HAVARD, Henry. *Les merveilles de l'art hollandais, exposées à Amsterdam en 1872.* Arnhem.
Havard 1877
HAVARD, Henry. "L'Etat-civil de Van der Meer de Delft." *Chroniques des Arts* (1877): 121–123.
Havard 1883A
HAVARD, Henry. "Johannes Vermeer (Van der Meer de Delft)." *Gazette des Beaux-Arts* 27: 389–399.
Havard 1883B
HAVARD, Henry. "Johannes Vermeer (Van der Meer de Delft)." *Gazette des Beaux-Arts* 28: 213–224.
Havard 1888
HAVARD, Henry. *Van der Meer de Delft.* Paris.
Haverkorn van Rijsewijk 1909
HAVERKORN VAN RIJSEWIJK, P. *Het Museum-Boijmans te Rotterdam.* The Hague and Amsterdam.
Haywood 1987
HAYWOOD, Ian. *Faking It: Art and the Politics of Forgery.* Brighton.
Hedinger 1984
HEDINGER, Bärbel. "Karten in Bildern. Zur politischen Ikonographie der Wandkarte bei Willem Buytewech und Jan Vermeer." In *Holländische Genremalerei im 17. Jahrhundert Symposium Berlin 1984.* Ed. Henning Bock and Thomas W. Gaehtgens. Berlin: 139–168.
Heerkens Thijssen 1948
HEERKENS THIJSSEN, H. F. "Over een weduwnaar en een weduwe." *Nederlandsch Archief voor Geneaologie en Heraldiek* 6: 7–9.
Heesakkers 1987
HEESAKKERS, C. L., ed. *Constantijn Huygens. Mijn jeugd.* Amsterdam.
Heijbroek 1983
HEIJBROEK, J. F. "De Vereiniging Rembrandt en het Rijksmuseum." *Bulletin van het Rijksmuseum* 31: 153–194.
Heijbroek 1992
HEIJBROEK, J. F,. and Wouter KLOEK. "'Het straatje' van Vermeer, een geschenk van H. W. A. Deterding." *Bulletin van het Rijksmuseum* 40: 225–231.
Held 1969
HELD, Julius S. *Rembrandt's 'Aristotle' and Other Rembrandt Studies.* Princeton.
Henkel 1932
HENKEL, M.D. "Jan Steen und der Delfter Vermeer." *Der Kunstwanderer* 14: 265–266.
Henny 1994
HENNY, Xenia. "Hoe kwamen de Rotterdamse schilders aan hun verf?" In *Rotterdamse meesters uit de Gouden Eeuw.* Ed. Nora Schadee. Rotterdam and Zwolle: 42–53.
Henze 1962
HENZE, A. *Rom und Latium.* Reclam's Kunstführer Italien. vol. 5. Stuttgart.
Heppner 1935
HEPPNER, A. "Vermeer: Seine Künstlerische Herkunft und Ausstrahlung." *Pantheon* 16 (August): 255–265.
Heppner 1938
HEPPNER, A. "Thoré-Bürger en Holland." *Oud-Holland* 55: 17–34, 67–82, 129–144.
Hermann 1967A
HERMANN, Frank. "Who was Solly? Part 1." *Connoisseur* (April), no. 662: 229–234.
Hermann 1967B
HERMANN, Frank. "Who was Solly? Part 2: the Collector and his Collection." *Connoisseur* (May), no. 663: 13– 18.

Hesius 1636
HESIUS, Guilielmus. *Emblemata sacra de fide, spe, charitate.* Antwerp.

Highsmith 1976
HIGHSMITH, Patricia. "The Trouble with Sir Harry." *TLS* (9 July): 853.

Hind 1932
HIND, Arthur M. *Rembrandt: Being the Substance of the Charles Eliot Norton Lectures Delivered before Harvard University 1930–1931.* Cambridge, Mass.

Hirschmann 1920
HIRSCHMANN, Otto. "Die Sammlung August Janssen." *Der Cicerone* 12: 17–26, 69–77.

Hoet 1752–1770
HOET, Gerard. *Catalogus of naamlijst van schilderyen, met derzelver pryzen.* 3 vols. The Hague.

Hofmann 1980
HOFMANN, Walter Jurgen. *Vermeer's Painting of Diana.* Zurich.

Hofstede de Groot 1892A
HOFSTEDE DE GROOT, Cornelis. "Schilderijen-verzamelingen van het geslacht Slingelandt." *Oud-Holland* 10: 229–237.

Hofstede de Groot 1892B
HOFSTEDE DE GROOT, Cornelis. "De veiling Bürger-Thoré." *De Nederlandsche Spectator* 1892: 405.

Hofstede de Groot 1893
HOFSTEDE DE GROOT, Cornelis. "Paris, Hôtel Drouot. Die Auction Thoré-Bürger." *Repertorium für Kunstwissenschaft* 16: 116–119.

Hofstede de Groot 1894
HOFSTEDE DE GROOT, Cornelis. "Ausstellungen und Versteigerungen. Die 25. Winteausstellung der Londoner Royal Academy." *Repertorium für Kunstwissenschaft* 17: 169–173.

Hofstede de Groot 1895
HOFSTEDE DE GROOT, Cornelis. "Johannes Vermeer." *Die Graphischen Künste* 18: 16–24.

Hofstede de Groot 1907-1930
HOFSTEDE DE GROOT, Cornelis. *Jan Vermeer van Delft en Carel Fabritius. Photogravures naar al hunne bekende schilderijen met biographischen en beschrijvenden tekst.* 3 vols. Amsterdam.

Hofstede de Groot 1907–1928
HOFSTEDE DE GROOT, Cornelis. *A Catalogue Raisonné of the works of the Most Eminent Dutch Painters of the Seventeenth Century.* 10 vols. London.

Hofstede de Groot 1907
HOFSTEDE DE GROOT, Cornelis. "Junges Mädchen Mit Flöte." *Holländischen Maler*: 610.

Hofstede de Groot 1910-1911
HOFSTEDE DE GROOT, Cornelis. "A Newly Discovered Picture by Vermeer of Delft." *Burlington Magazine* 18: 133–134.

Hollander 1990
HOLLANDER, Martha. "Vermeer's Empty Room." *Raritan* 10 (Fall): 1–17.

Holmes 1904–1905
HOLMES, C. J. "A Newly-Discovered Study for the Christ Blessing Little Children (National Gallery)." *Burlington Magazine* 6: 329–330.

Hondius 1647
HONDIUS, Hendrick. *Grondige onderrichten in de optica of de perspective konste.* Amsterdam.

Hooft 1611
HOOFT, Pieter Corneliszoon. *Emblemata Amatoria.* Amsterdam.

Hooft 1671
P. C. Hooft's Wercken. Amsterdam.

Van Hoogstraeten 1678
VAN HOOGSTRAETEN, Samuel. *Inleyding tot de Hooge Schoole der Schilderkonst: anders de Zichtbaere Werelt....* Rotterdam. Facsimile ed. Utrecht, 1969.

Hoogewerff 1947
HOOGEWERFF, G. J. *De Geschiedenis van de St. Lucasgilden in Nederland.* Amsterdam.

Houbraken 1718–1721
HOUBRAKEN, Arnold. *De groote schouburgh der Nederlantsche konstschilders en schilderessen.* 3 vols. Amsterdam.

Houbraken 1753
HOUBRAKEN, Arnold. *De groote schouburgh der Nederlantsche konstschilders en schilderessen.* The Hague. Facsimile ed. Amsterdam, 1976.

Houtman 1992
HOUTMAN, L. "De muziek in het werk van Johannes Vermeer." *Muziek en muziekinstrument in de Nederlandse schilderkunst van de zeventiende eeuw, Een bundeling van werkstukken.* Ed. R. Rausch and P. Bruyn. Utrecht.

Hubschmitt 1987
HUBSCHMITT, William Evan. "*The Art of Painting:* An Iconographic Examination of *De Schilderconst* by Johannis Vermeer of Delft." Ph.D. diss., State University of New York, Binghamton.

Huiskamp 1994
HUISKAMP, M., and C. de GRAAF. *Gewogen of Bedrogen. Het wegen van geld in de Nederlanden.* Rijksmuseum het Koninklijk Penningkabinet, Leiden.

Hultén 1949
HULTÉN, Karl G. "Zu Vermeer Atelierbild." *Konsthistorisk Tidskrift* 18: 90–98.

Huneker 1916
HUNEKER, James. "The Magic Vermeer." In *Ivory Apes and Peacocks.* New York: 141–152.

Hurley 1989
HURLEY, Ann. "*Ut Pictura Poesis:* Vermeer's Challenge to Some Renaissance Literary Assumptions." *The Journal of Aesthetics and Art Criticism* 47 (Fall): 349–357.

Huygens 1911-1917
HUYGENS, Constantijn. *De Briefwisseling (1608–1687).* 6 vols. Ed. J. A. Worp. The Hague.

Huyghe 1936
HUYGHE, René. "Vermeer et Proust." *L'amour de l'art* 17: 7–15.

H. W. 1877
H. W. "Van der Meer." *The Athenaeum* (12 May): 616.

Hyatt-Mayor 1946
HYATT-MAYOR, A. "The photographic eye." *The Metropolitan Museum of Art Bulletin* 5 (Summer): 15–26.

IBF
DWYER, H., and B. *Index Biographie Français.* 4 vols. London.

Immerzeel 1842–1843
IMMERZEEL, J. *De levens en werken der Hollandsche en Vlaamsche konstschilders, beeldhouwers, graveurs en bouwmeesters, van het begin der vijftiende eeuw tot heden.* 3 vols. Amsterdam.

Isarlo 1935
ISARLO, Georges. "Vermeer à l'Exposition de Rotterdam." *La Renaissance de l'Art* 18: 94–111.

James 1955
JAMES, Richard. *Vermeer, Dutch School.* London.

Jameson 1842
JAMESON, Mrs. *A Handbook to the Public Galleries of Art in and near London, with Catalogue of the Pictures.* 2 vols. London.

Jenkins 1992
JENKINS, Simon. "Who was the guitar player?" *London Times* (26 December): 12.

Jesse 1931
JESSE, Wilhelm. "Der Braunschweiger Vermeer." *Kunstchronik und Kunstliteratur, Beilage zur Zeitschrift für bildende Kunste* 4: 33–35.

Johansen 1920
JOHANSEN, P. "Jan Vermeer de Delft, à propos de l'ordre chronologique de ses tableaux." *Oud-Holland* 38: 185–199.

Jones 1989
JONES, Kimberly. "Vermeer's *Woman Holding a Balance:* A Secularized Vision of the Virgin Mary." Lecture delivered at the Mid-Atlantic Symposium, National Gallery of Art, Washington.

De Jongh 1967
DE JONGH, Eddy. *Zinne- en Minnebeelden in de schilderkunst van de zeventiende eeuw.*

De Jongh 1969
DE JONGH, Eddy. "The Spur of Wit: Rembrandt's Response to an Italian Challenge." *Delta*: 49–67.

De Jongh 1975/1976
DE JONGH, Eddy. "Pearls of Virtue and Pearls of Vice." *Simiolus* 8: 69–97.

De Jongh 1993
DE JONGH, Eddy. "Die 'Sprachlichkeit' der Niederländischen Malerei im 17. Jahrhundert." In Frankfurt 1993: 23–34.

Josi 1821
JOSI, C. *Collections d'imitations de dessins d'après les principaux maitres hollandais et flamands.* London.

Kahr 1972
KAHR, Madlyn Millner. "Vermeer's Girl Asleep: A Moral Emblem." *Metropolitan Museum Journal* 6: 115–132.

Kahr 1978
KAHR, Madlyn Millner. *Dutch Painting in the Seventeenth Century.* New York.

Kelch 1988
KELCH, Jan. "Gemäldeuntersuchung mit Neutronaktivierungs-Autoradiographie und -Analyse: *Jan Vermeer, 'Die Dame mit dem Perlenhalsband', Gemäldegalerie SMPK.*" Lecture delivered at symposium "Art and Non-Destructive Testing Methods" Bundesanstalt für Materialprüfung, Berlin.

Kemp 1986
KEMP, Martin. "Simon Stevin and Pieter Saenredam: A Study of Mathematics and Vision in Dutch Science and Art." *Art Bulletin* 68: 237–252.

Kenner 1990
KENNER, Hugh. "Serenity of the Seen: A Look at the

Masterpiece We Lost in Boston." *Art & Antiques* (Summer): 168.

Kettering 1993
KETTERING, Alison McNeil. "Ter Borch's Ladies in Satin." *Art History* 16: 95–124.

Keyselitz 1956
KEYSELITZ, Rudolf. "Der 'Clavis interpretandi' in der holländischen Malerei des 17. Jahrhunderts." Ph.D. diss., Munich.

Kitson 1969
KITSON, M. "Current and Forthcoming Exhibitions: Florentine Baroque Art in New York." *Burlington Magazine* 111 (June): 409–410.

Van Kleffens 1980
VAN KLEFFENS, E. N. *Belevenissen. I. 1894–1940.* Alphen aan den Rijn.

Klessman 1971
KLESSMAN, Rüdiger. *Gemäldegalerie Berlin.* Berlin, Darmstadt, and Vienna.

Klingsor 1921
KLINGSOR, Tristan. "Vermeer van Delft." *L'Amour de l'Art* (1921): 324–329.

Knipping 1939–1940
KNIPPING, John Baptist. *De Iconografi van de Contra-Reformatie in de Nederlanden.* 2 vols. Hilversum.

Knoef 1948
KNOEF, J. "De verzamelaar A. van der Hoop," In *Twee en veertigste jaarboek van het genootschap Amstelodamum.* Amsterdam.

Knoef 1948–1949
KNOEF, J. "De verzamelaars Goll van Franckenstein." *Nederlands Kunsthistorisch Jaarboek* 1: 268–286.

Koningsberger 1967, 1968
KONINGSBERGER, Hans. *The World of Vermeer 1632–1675.* New York. (Dutch ed. Amsterdam, 1968.)

Koomen 1935
KOOMEN, Pieter. "Vermeer en zijn verwanten." *Maandblad voor Beeldende Kunsten* 12: 272–281.

Koopman/Van Dijck 1987
KOOPMAN, Ton, and Lucas VAN DIJCK. *The Harpsichord in Dutch Art before 1800.* Zutphen.

Koslow 1967
KOSLOW, Susan. "De wonderlijke Perspectyfkas: An Aspect of Seventeenth Century Dutch Painting." *Oud-Holland* 82: 35–56.

Korevaar-Hesseling 1932
KOREVAAR-HESSELING, Elisabeth H. "Johannes Vermeer van Delft, 31 Oct. 1632–13 Dec. 1675." *De Delver* 6: 33–37.

Kramm 1857–1864
KRAMM, Christiaan. *De levens en werken der Hollandsche en Vlaamsche kunstschilders, beeldhouwers, graveurs en bouwmeesters.* 6 vols. Amsterdam.

Kremer 1993
KREMER, Mark. "Girls or Winning the World by Looking at it." *Kunst & Museum Journaal* 4: 49–52.

Van Kretschmar 1974
VAN KRETSCHMAR, F. G. L. O. "Voorgeslacht en aanverwanten van moederszijde van de generaal Jhr. Jan Willem Janssens." *De Nederlandsche Leeuw* 99: 232–260.

Kronig 1908
KRONIG, J. O. "Johannes Vermeer (De Delftsche Vermeer)." *Elsevier's geïllustreerd Maandschrift* 18 (July-December): 73–82.

Kühn 1968
KÜHN, Hermann. "A Study of the Pigments and the Grounds Used by Jan Vermeer." *Report and Studies in the History of Art* 2: 154–202.

Kuiper 1972
KUIPER, L. "Report on the Restoration of Vermeer's Love Letter." *Bulletin van het Rijksmuseum* 20 (November): 147–167.

Kultermann 1978
KULTERMANN, Udo. "Vermeer and Contemporary American Painting." *American Art Review* 4 (November): 114–119, 139–140.

Kuretsky 1979
KURETSKY, Susan Donahue. *The Paintings of Jacob Ochtervelt, 1634–1682.* Oxford.

Lafenestre 1898
LAFENESTRE, G., and E. RICHTENBERGER. *La peinture en Europe. La Hollande.* Paris.

De Lairesse 1707
DE LAIRESSE, Gerard. *Het groot schilderboek.* 2 vols. Amsterdam.

De Lairesse 1740, 1969
DE LAIRESSE, Gerard. *Groot schilderboek, waar in de schilderkonst in al haar deelen grondig werd onderweezen, ook door redeneeringen en prentverbeeldingen verklaard....* 2 vols. Haarlem. (Repr. Davaco, 1969.)

Lane 1925
LANE, S. *Jan Vermeer of Delft (1632–1675).* London.

Larousse 1865–1890
LAROUSSE, P. *Grand dictionnaire universel.* 17 vols. Paris.

Laurentius 1980
LAURENTIUS, T., J. W. NIEMEIJER, and G. PLOOS VAN AMSTEL. *Cornelis Ploos van Amstel. 1726–1798. Kunstverzamelaar en prentuitgever.* Assen.

Lavallée 1925
LAVALLÉE, Pierre. "Un Tableau Inconnu de Vermeer: La Jeune Femme au Chapeau Rouge." *La Revue de l'Art Ancien et Moderne* 47 (May): 323–324.

Lazarev 1933
LAZAREV, Viktor N. *Vermeer.* Moscow.

Leader 1980
LEADER, Bernice Kramer. "The Boston School and Vermeer." *Arts Magazine* 55 (November): 172–176.

Lebrun 1792
LEBRUN, J. B. P. *Galerie des peintres flamands, hollandais et allemands.* 2 vols. Paris.

Leerintveld 1990
LEERINTVELD, A. M. T. "' 'tquam soo wel te pas': Huygens' portretbijschriften en de datering van zijn portret geschilderd door Jan Lievens." *Nederlands bijdragen over de portretkunst in de Nederlanden. Portretten uit de zestiende, zeventiende en achttiende eeuw.* Leids Kunsthistorisch Jaarboek 7: 159–182.

Legêne 1994
LEGÊNE, Eva. "A 'Foolish Passion for Sweet Harmony': The Musical Instrument Collection of a Compleat Gentleman, a Monarch and an Artist, in the Seventeenth Century." In The Hague 1994: 80–110.

Legrand 1963
LEGRAND, Francine-Claire. *Les peintres flamands de genre au XVIIe siècle.* Brussels.

Lemcke 1878
LEMCKE, Carl. "Jan Vermeer (van der Meer) aus Delft." *Kunst und Künstler*: 12–20.

Van Lennep 1959
VAN LENNEP, F. J. E. "Amsterdammers in 's-Graveland." *Amstelodamum. Jaarboek* 51: 93–169.

Levey 1981
LEVEY, Michael. *The Painter Depicted.* Over Wallop.

Levey 1991
LEVEY, Michael. "Johannes Vermeer: The Spell of Stillness." *Art News* 91 (March): 77–78.

Levi D'Ancona 1977
LEVI D'ANCONA, Mirella. *The Garden of the Renaissance: Botanical Symbolism in Italian Painting.* Florence.

L. G. S. 1925
L. G. S. "Two Vermeers are Newly Discovered." *Art News* 40 (12 September): 1.

Liedtke 1979A
LIEDTKE, Walter A. "Pride in Perspective: The Dutch Townscape." *Connoisseur* 200 (April): 264–273.

Liedtke 1979B
LIEDTKE, Walter A. "Hendrik van Vliet and the Delft School." *Museum News (The Toledo Museum of Art)* 21: 40–52.

Liedtke 1992
LIEDTKE, Walter A. "Vermeer Teaching Himself." In *Rembrandt Och Hans Tid/Rembrandt and His Age.* Exh. cat. Nationalmuseum, Stockholm: 89–105.

Limentani Virdis 1981
LIMENTANI VIRDIS, Caterina. *Il quadro e il suo doppio; effetti di specularitá narrativa nella pittura fiamminga e olandese.* Modena.

Lindenburg 1992
LINDENBURG, M. A. "Het 'straatje' van Vermeer." *Delfia Batavorum Jaarboek* 1992: 680–690.

Lloyd 1991
LLOYD, Christopher. *The Queen's Pictures. Royal Collectors through the Centuries.* London.

Lloyd 1925
LLOYD, David. "The Vermeers in America." *International Studio* 82 (November): 123–128.

Loffelt 1889
LOFFELT, A. C. "Zwervers tot rust gekomen." *De Nederlandsche Spectator* 1889: 61–63.

Lucas 1922
LUCAS, Edward Verrall. *Vermeer of Delft.* London.

Lucas 1929, 1971
LUCAS, Edward Verrall. *Vermeer the Magical.* London. Repr. New York 1971.

Lugt 1907
LUGT, Frits. *Is de aankoop door het Rijk van een deel der Six-collectie aan te bevelen? Beschouwingen.* Amsterdam.

Lugt 1918
LUGT, Frits. "De kunstverzamelaar August Janssen." *De Amsterdammer. Weekblad voor Nederland* (20 April): 7.

Lugt 1936
LUGT, Frits. "Italiaansche Kunstwerken in Nederlandsche verzamelingen van vroeger tijden." *Oud-Holland* 53: 97–135.

Lyczko 1979
LYCZKO, Judith Elizabeth. "Thomas Wilmer Dewing's Sources: Women in Interiors." *Arts Magazine* 54 (November): 152–157.

MacColl 1901
MACCOLL, D. S. *A note on Vermeer of Delft and the picture 'Christ with Martha and Mary.'* London.

Maier-Preusker 1991
MAIER-PREUSKER, Wolfgang C. "Christaen van Couwenbergh (1604–1667): Oeuvre und Wandlungen eines holländischen Caravaggisten." *Wallraf-Richartz-Jahrbuch* 52: 163–236.

Malraux 1952, 1953
MALRAUX, André. *Vermeer in Delft*. Paris.

Mantz 1860
MANTZ, Paul. "Le cabinet de M. A. Dumont, à Cambrai." *Gazette des Beaux-Arts* 8: 303–313.

Margadant 1925
MARGADANT, S. W. F. *Dr. Abraham Bredius 1855–1925. Album hem aangeboden op 18 april 1925*. Amsterdam.

Mariani 1928
MARIANI, Valerio. "Vermeer de Delft." *L'Arte* 31: 62.

De Marigny 1990
DE MARIGNY, Alfred. *A Conspiracy of Crowns*. New York.

Marius 1908
MARIUS, G. H. "De Schilderijen van den Delftschen Vermeer in Hollandsche musea en verzamelingen." *Onze Kunst* 14 (November): 181–193. French version in *L'Art flamand et hollandais* 10 (1908): 215–225.

Marolois 1628
MAROLOIS, Samuel. *Perspective contenant la théorie, pratique et instruction fondamentale d'icelle*. Amsterdam.

De Marsy 1880
DE MARSY, Le Comte. *Balthasar de Monconys. Analyse de ses voyages au point de vue artistique*. Caen.

Martin 1901
MARTIN, Willem. "Jan Vermeer van Delft." *Woord en Beeld*: 3–8.

Martin 1902
MARTIN, Willem. "Jan Vermeer van Delft." *Woord en Beeld*: 150–157.

Martin 1904
MARTIN, Willem. "Jan Vermeer van Delft." *Woord en Beeld*: 1–8.

Martin 1907A
MARTIN, Willem. "La Jeune Fille à la Flute de Vermeer de Delft." *L'Art Flamand & Hollandais* 8 (July): 20–23.

Martin 1907B
MARTIN, Willem. "Jan Vermeer van Delft. Het Meisje met de Fluit." *Onze Kunst* 6 (July): 20–24.

Martin 1908
MARTIN, Willem. "'s Rijks aankoop uit de Six-collectie." *Bulletin van den Nederlandschen Oudheidkundigen Bond*, second series, 1: 5–9.

Martin 1911
MARTIN, Willem. *Gérard Dou. Sa vie et son oeuvre. Étude sur la peinture hollandaise et les marchands aux dix-septième siècle*. Paris.

Martin 1913
MARTIN, Willem. *Gerard Dou, des Meisters Gemälde. Klassiker der Kunst*. Stuttgart and Berlin.

Martin 1921
MARTIN, Willem. "Het straatje van Vermeer en de Six-stichting." *Oudheidkundig Jaarboek* 1: 107–108.

Martin 1927–1928
MARTIN, Willem. "Der neuaufgefundene Jan Vermeer van Delft." *Der Kunstwanderer*: 6–7.

Maser 1971
RIPA, Cesare. *Baroque and Rococo Pictorial Imagery*. Ed. Edward A. Maser. New York.

Mayer-Meintschel 1978–1979
MAYER-MEINTSCHEL, Annaliese. "Die Briefleserin von Jan Vermeer van Delft-zum Inhalt und zur Geschichte des Bildes." *Jahrbuch der Staatlichen Kunstsammlungen Dresden* 11: 91–99.

Mayer-Meintschel 1986
MAYER-MEINTSCHEL, Annaliese. "Vermeer's Kupplerin." *Jahrbuch der Staatlichen Kunstsammlungen Dresden* 18: 7–18.

McInnes 1990
MCINNES, Angus. "*Review of J. M. Montias, Vermeer and His Milieu: A Web of Social History (1989)*." *History* 75 (October): 492–493.

Meinsma 1896
MEINSMA, K. O. *Spinoza en zijn kring. Historisch-kritische studiën over Hollandsche vrijgeesten*. The Hague.

Mengden 1984
MENGDEN, Lida von. *Vermeer's de Schilderkonst in den Interpretationen von Kurt Badt und Hans Sedlmayr*. Frankfurt.

Menzel 1977
MENZEL, Gerhard W. *Vermeer*. Leipzig.

Meyerman 1976
MEYERMAN, A. M. "Een staartster boven Rotterdam in 1680, Lieven Verschuier (c. 1630-1680)." In *Vereniging Rembrandt, Verslag over 1976*: 52–54.

Miedema 1972
MIEDEMA, Hessel. "Johannes Vermeer's Schilderkunst." *Proef* (September): 67–76.

Miedema 1984
MIEDEMA, Hessel. "Tekst en afbeelding als bronnen bij historisch onderzoek." In *Wort und Bild in der Niederländischen Kunst und Literatur des 16. und 17. Jahrhunderts*. Ed. Herman Vekeman and Justus Müller Hofstede. Erftstadt: 7–16.

Millar 1977
MILLAR, Sir Oliver. *The Queen's Pictures*. London.

De Mirimonde 1961
DE MIRIMONDE, Albert P. "Les sujets Musicaux chez Vermeer de Delft." *Gazette des Beaux-Arts* 57 (January): 29–52.

Mistler 1973
MISTLER, Jean. *Vermeer*. Paris.

Mittelstädt 1969
MITTELSTÄDT, Kuno. *Jan Vermeer van Delft*. Berlin.

Moes 1909
MOES, E. W., and E. van BIEMA. *De Nationale Konst-Gallery en het Koninklijk Museum*. Amsterdam.

De Monconys 1677
DE MONCONYS, Balthasar. *Iovrnal des voyages de monsievr de Monconys ... seconde partie*. Paris.

De Montebello 1993
DE MONTEBELLO, Philippe. *Masterpieces of the Metropolitan Museum of Art*. New York and Boston.

Montias 1977A
MONTIAS, John Michael. "The Guild of St. Luke in Seventeenth Century Delft and the Economic Status of Artists and Artisans." *Simiolus* 9: 93–105.

Montias 1977B
MONTIAS, John Michael. "New Documents on Vermeer and His Family." *Oud-Holland* 91: 267–287.

Montias 1980
MONTIAS, John Michael. "Vermeer and His Milieu: Conclusion of an Archival Study." *Oud-Holland* 94: 44–62.

Montias 1982
MONTIAS, John Michael. *Artists and Artisans in Delft: A Socio-economic Study of the Seventeenth Century*. Princeton.

Montias 1987
MONTIAS, John Michael. "Vermeer's Clients and Patrons." *Art Bulletin* 69 (March): 68–76.

Montias 1989
MONTIAS, John Michael. *Vermeer and His Milieu: A Web of Social History*. Princeton.

Montias 1991
MONTIAS, John Michael. "A Postscript on Vermeer and His Milieu." *The Hoogsteder Mercury* no. 12: 42–52.

Montias 1993
MONTIAS, John Michael. *Vermeer en zijn milieu*. Baarn.

Moreno 1982
MORENO, Ignacio L. "Vermeer's *The Concert*: A Study in Harmony and Contrasts." *Rutgers Art Review* 3 (January): 50–57.

Morning Post 1927A
"Coats Pictures to be Sold. Vermeer Masterpiece for Scotland. Romantic History." *The Morning Post* (4 January): 9.

Morning Post 1927B
"Picture Romance. How a Vermeer Masterpiece was Discovered." *The Morning Post* (14 January): 9.

Mottola 1964
MOTTOLA, Anthony, ed. *The Spiritual Exercises of St. Ignatius*. Garden City, New York.

Murray 1819–1823
MURRAY, John. *Tour in Holland in the Year MDCCCXIX*. London.

Nagler 1835–1852
NAGLER, G. K. *Neues Allgemeines Künstlerlexicon*. 22 vols. Munich.

Nash 1972, 1979
NASH, John. *The Age of Rembrandt and Vermeer: Dutch Painting in the Seventeenth Century*. New York.

Nash 1991
NASH, John. *Vermeer*. London.

Nasse 1922
NASSE, Hermann. "Jan Vermeer van Delft, der Meister des Raumes und der malerischen Kultur." *Kunst für Alle* 38: 1–15.

Naumann 1981
NAUMANN, Otto. *Frans van Mieris the Elder (1635–1681)*. 2 vols. Doornspijk.

NDB
Neue Deutsche Biographie. 17 vols. Berlin. 1952–1993.

Nefzger 1980
NEFZGER, Ulrich. "Erwägungen zu Vermeer: Vom Halt der inneren Welt." In *Festschrift für Wilhelm Messerer zum 60. Geburtstag*. Ed. Klaus Ertz. Cologne: 251–271.

Neurdenburg 1942
NEURDENBURG, Elisabeth. "Johannes Vermeer. Eenige

opmerkingen naar aanleiding van de nieuwste studies over den Delftschen Schilder." *Oud-Holland* 59: 65–73.
Neurdenburg 1948
NEURDENBURG, Elisabeth. *De zeventiende eeuwsche beeldhouwkunst in de Noordelijke Nederlanden.* Amsterdam.
Neurdenburg 1951
NEURDENBURG, Elisabeth. "Nog eenige opmerkingen over Johannes Vermeer van Delft." *Oud-Holland* 66: 34–44.
Nicodemi 1924
NICODEMI, Giorgio. "Jan Vermeer di Delft." *Emporium* 60: 665–682.
Nicolson 1946
NICOLSON, Benedict. *Vermeer: Lady at the Virginals.* London.
Niemeijer 1969
NIEMEIJER, J. W. "Een zeventiende-eeuwse memorietafel uit het geslacht Muys van Holy." *Bulletin van het Rijksmuseum* 17: 135–139.
Niemeijer 1981
NIEMEIJER, J. W. *Cornelis Troost 1696–1750.* Assen.
Niemeijer 1981
NIEMEIJER, J. W. "De kunstverzameling van John Hope (1737–1784)." *Nederlands Kunsthistorisch Jaarboek* 32: 127–232.
Nieuwenhuys 1834
NIEUWENHUYS, C. J. *A Review of the Lives and Works of Some of the Most Eminent Painters.* London.
Nieuwenhuys-van Berkum 1987
NIEUWENHUYS-VAN BERKUM, A. "Constantijn Huygens als kunstadviseur. Schilders, aankopen en opdrachten, 1625–1652." In *Huygens in Noorder licht. Lezingen van het Gronings Huygens-symposium.* Groningen: 113–126.
NNBW
Nieuw Nederlandsche Biografisch Woordenboek. 10 vols. and index. Leiden 1911–1937. Amsterdam, 1974.
ÖBL
Österreichisches Biographisches Lexikon 1815–1950. 8 vols. Graz-Köln and Vienna. 1957–1983.
Obreen 1881–1882
OBREEN, Frederik Daniel Otto. "Iets over den Delftschen schilder Johannes Vermeer." *Archief voor Nederlandsche Kunstgeschiedenis* 4: 289–303.
O'Connor 1977
O'CONNOR, Andrew. "A Note on the Beit Vermeer." *Burlington Magazine* 119 (April): 272–275.
Olbrich 1981
OLBRICH, Harald and Helga MÖBIUS. "Wahrheit und Wirklichkeit: Zum Realismus holländischer Kunst." *Bildende Kunst* 7: 320–328.
O'Malley 1993
O'MALLEY, John W. *The First Jesuits.* Cambridge, Mass.
Overbeek 1935
OVERBEEK, J. M. C. van. "Jan Vermeer en zijn Delftsche Omgeving." *Elsevier's geïllustreerd Maandschrift* 45: 231–238.
Ovid/Miller 1966
OVID. *Metamorphoses.* Trans. Frank Justus Miller. Cambridge, Mass.
Palisca 1961
PALISCA, C. "Scientific Empiricism in Musical Thought." In *Seventeenth-Century Science in the Arts.* Ed. H. H. Rys. Princeton: 91–137.
Palmer 1989
PALMER, Frederick. "Theme and Variation: 1. Pictures within Pictures." *The Artist* (January): 29–31.
Panofsky 1968
PANOFSKY, Erwin. *Idea: A Concept in Art Theory.* Trans. J. J. S. Peake. Columbia, South Carolina.
De Pauw-de Veen 1969
DE PAUW-DE VEEN, Lydia. *De begrippen 'schilder', 'schilderij' en 'schilderen' in de zeventiende eeuw.* Brussels.
Van Peer 1946A
VAN PEER, A. J. J. M. "Was Jan Vermeer van Delft Katholiek?" *Katholiek Cultureel Tijdschrift* 2 (August): 468–470.
Van Peer 1946B
VAN PEER, A. J. J. M. "Was Jan Vermeer Katholiek?" *Katholiek cultureel tijdschrift Streven*, new series, 4: 615–626.
Van Peer 1951
VAN PEER, A. J. J. M. "Rondom Jan Vermeer: De kinderen van Vermeer." *Katholiek cultureel tijdschrift Streven*, new series, 4: 615–626.
Van Peer 1957
VAN PEER, A. J. J. M. "Drie collecties schilderyen van Jan Vermeer." *Oud-Holland* 72: 92–103.
Van Peer 1959
VAN PEER, A. J. J. M. "Rondom Jan Vermeer Van Delft." *Oud-Holland.* 74: 240–245.
Van Peer 1968
VAN PEER, A.J.J.M. "Jan Vermeer van Delft: Drie archiefvondsten." *Oud-Holland* 83: 220–224.
Pepper 1984
PEPPER, D. Stephen. *Guido Reni: A Complete Catalogue of His Works with an Introductory Text.* Oxford.
Perl 1979
PERL, Jed. "Johannes Vermeer's 'Young Woman with a Water Jug'." *Arts Magazine* 53 (January): 118–121.
Plasschaert 1924
PLASSCHAERT, Albert. *Johannes Vermeer en Pieter de Hooch.* Amsterdam.
Plasschaert 1929
PLASSCHAERT, Albert. "Vermeer van Delft." *De Stem* 9: 609–611.
Plechl 1987
PLECHL, P. M. "St. Praxedis ist eine Kopie und doch ein echter Vermeer." *Die Presse* (Wissenschaft) (2–3 May).
Plietzsch 1911
PLIETZSCH, Eduard. *Vermeer van Delft.* Leipzig.
Plietszch 1917
PLIETZSCH, Eduard. *Johannes Vermeer van Delft.* Leipzig.
Plietzsch 1939
PLIETZSCH, Eduard. *Vermeer van Delft.* Munich.
Pops 1984
POPS, Martin. *Vermeer, Consciousness and the Chamber of Being.* Ann Arbor.
Post 1992
POST, Wim. *Buitenplaatsen van Bloemendaal.* Haarlem.
Potonniée 1936
POTONNIÉE, Georges. *The History of the Discovery of Photography.* Trans. Edward Epstein. New York.
Price 1974
PRICE, J. L. *Culture and Society in the Dutch Republic during the 17th Century.* London.
Proust 1952
PROUST, Marcel, and André MALRAUX. *Vermeer de Delft.* Paris.
Pyne 1819
PYNE, W. H. *The History of the Royal Residences.* 3 vols. London.
Raupp 1984
RAUPP, Hans. *Untersuchungen zu Künstlerbildnis und Künstlerdarstellung in den Niederlanden im 17. Jahrhundert.* Hildesheim.
Réau 1955–1959
RÉAU, L. *Iconographie de l'art chrétien.* 3 vols. Paris.
Van Regteren Altena 1937
VAN REGTEREN ALTENA, I. Q. "Towards Vermeer." *Proceedings of the Anglo-Batavian Society*: 18–28.
Van Regteren Altena 1960
VAN REGTEREN ALTENA, I. Q. "Een jeugdwerk van Johannes Vermeer." *Oud-Holland* 75: 175–194.
Reiffenberg 1924
REIFFENBERG, Benno. *Vermeer van Delft. Das Bild: Atlanten zur Kunst* 10. Munich.
Reinhold 1912
REINHOLD, C. F. "Vermeer van Delft." *Hochland* 9: 318–324.
Reiss 1952
REISS, Stephen. Review of Swillens 1950. *Burlington Magazine* 94: 182.
Report Mauritshuis 1899
Verslagen omtrent 's Rijks verzamelingen van geschiedenis en kunst. XXII. 1899. The Hague, 1900.
Report Mauritshuis 1907
Verslagen omtrent 's Rijks verzamelingen van geschiedenis en kunst. XXX. 1907. The Hague, 1908.
Rérat 1993
RÉRAT, Alain. *Vermeer.* Paris.
Reutersward 1980
REUTERSWÄRD, Patrik. "Om realismen i holländsk bildtradition." *Konsthistorisk tidskrift* 49: 1–16.
Reuterswärd 1988
REUTERSWÄRD, Patrik. "Vermeer. Ett försvar för ögats vittnesbörd." *Konsthistorisk Tidskrift* 57: 55–59.
Reynolds 1781
REYNOLDS, Joshua. "A Journey to Flanders and Holland (1781)." In *The Literary Works of Sir Joshua Reynolds.* London, 1901. 2: 1–124.
Van Rhede van der Kloot 1891
VAN RHEDE VAN DER KLOOT, M. A. *De Gouverneurs-generaal en Commissarissen-Generaal van Nederlandsch-Indië 1610–1688. Historisch-Genealogisch beschreven.* The Hague.
Richard 1987
RICHARD, P. "Trying to verify a Vermeer." *International Herald Tribune* 25: 18.
Riding 1993
RIDING, Alan. "Paintings by Vermeer and Goya Are Recovered Seven Years After Theft." *The New York Times* (16 September): C11, 18.
Van Riemsdijk 1900
VAN RIEMSDIJK, B. W. F. "De collectie-Six." *Eigen Haard:* 440–443.

Rigby 1944
RIGBY, Douglas, and Elisabeth RIGBY. *Lock, Stock and Barrel. The Story of Collecting.* Philadelphia, New York, and London.
Rinder 1904
RINDER, Frank. "Jan Vermeer of Delft." *The Art Journal* 67: 255–258.
Ripa 1644
RIPA, Cesare. *Iconologia.* Amsterdam. Trans. D. P. Pers.
Roberts 1897
ROBERTS, W. *Memorials of Christie's. A Record of Art Sales from 1766 to 1896.* 2 vols. London.
Roberts 1910
ROBERTS, W. "The Salting Collection. Part I. Pictures." *Connoisseur* 26: 203–214.
Robinson 1974
ROBINSON, Franklin W. *Gabriel Metsu (1629–1667): A Study of His Place in Dutch Genre Painting of the Golden Age.* New York.
Rollenhagen 1613
ROLLENHAGEN, Gabriel. *Selectorum Emblematum Centuria Secunda.* Arnhem.
Rooseboom 1968
ROOSEBOOM, Maria. "Antonie van Leeuwenhoek, zijn ontdekkingen en het denken van zijn tijd." *Spiegel Historiael* 3: 13–21.
Rooses 1898
ROOSES, Max. "De Hollandsche Meesters in de National Gallery te Londen. Jan Vermeer van Delft. Het vrouwtje bij het klavier." *Elseviers Geïllustreerd Maandschrift* 15: 352–360.
Rosenberg 1966, 1984
ROSENBERG, Jakob, Seymour SLIVE, and Enno H. TER KUILE. *Dutch Art and Architecture 1600 to 1800.* Baltimore and London.
Roskill 1976
ROSKILL, Mark. *What is Art History?* London.
Rudolph 1938
RUDOLPH, Herbert. "Vanitas: Die Bedeutung mittelalterlicher und humanistischer Bildinhalte in der niederländischen Malerei des 17. Jahrhunderts." In *Festschrift Wilhelm Pinder zum 60 Geburtstag.* Leipzig: 405–433.
Rutter 1829
RUTTER, John. *Delineations of the North Western Division of Somerset.* London.
Ruurs 1983
RUURS, Rob. "'Even if it is not architecture': Perspective Drawings by Simon de Vlieger and Willem van de Velde the Younger." *Simiolus* 13: 189–200.
Ruurs 1987
RUURS, Rob. *Saenredam. The Art of Perspective.* Amsterdam, Philadelphia, and Groningen.
Salomon 1983
SALOMON, Nanette. "Vermeer and the Balance of Destiny." In *Essays in Northern European Art Presented to Egbert Haverkamp-Begemann on his Sixtieth Birthday.* Doornspijk: 216–221.
Samuel 1976
SAMUEL, Edgar R. "The Disposal of Diego Duarte's Stock of Paintings 1692–1697." *Jaarboek van het Koninklijk Museum voor Schone Kunsten Antwerpen:* 305–324.
Schama 1987
SCHAMA, Simon. *The Embarrassment of Riches: An Interpretation of Dutch Culture in the Golden Age.* New York.
Schendel 1972
VAN SCHENDEL, A. "The Love Letter Restored." *Bulletin van het Rijksmuseum* 20 (November): 127–128.
Schilling 1930
SCHILLING, Edmund. "Der Astronom." In *Meisterwerke Alter Malerei im Städelschen Kunstinstut.* Frankfurt: 145–147.
Schmidt 1986
SCHMIDT, C. *Om de eer van de familie. Het geslacht Teding van Berkhout 1500–1950. Een sociologische benadering.* Amsterdam.
Schneider 1993
SCHNEIDER, Norbert. *Jan Vermeer, 1632–1675: Verhüllung der Gefühle.* Cologne.
Schutte 1974
SCHUTTE, O. *Het archief van de familie Teding van Berckhout.* N. p.
Schutte 1976
SCHUTTE, O. *Repertorium der Nederlandse vertegenwoordigers, residerende in het buitenland 1584–1810.* The Hague.
Schwartz 1989
SCHWARTZ, Gary, and Marten Jan BOK. *Pieter Saenredam: De schilder in zijn tijd.* Maarsen and The Hague.
Schwartz 1966
SCHWARTZ, Heinrich. "Vermeer and the Camera Obscura." *Pantheon* 24 (May-June): 170–180.
Schwartz 1985
SCHWARTZ, Heinrich. *Art and Photography: Forerunners and Influences.* Layton.
Sedlmayr 1951
SEDLMAYR, Hans. "Der Ruhm der Malkunst. Jan Vermeer 'De schilderconst'." In *Festschrift für Hans Jantzen.* Berlin: 169–177.
Sedlmayr 1958
SEDLMAYR, Hans. "Jan Vermeer: Der Ruhm der Malkunst." In *Kunst und Wahrheit.* Hamburg: 161–172.
Sedlmayr 1962
SEDLMAYR, Hans. "Jan Vermeer: De Schilderkunst." *Hefte des Kunsthistorischen Seminars der Universität München* 7/8: 34–65.
Seth 1980
SETH, Lennart. "Vermeer och van Veens Amorum Emblemata." *Konsthistorisk Tidskrift* 49: 17–40.
Seymour 1964
SEYMOUR, Charles, Jr. "Dark Chamber and Light-Filled Room: Vermeer and the Camera Obscura." *Art Bulletin* 3 (September): 323–331.
Simpson 1988
SIMPSON, C. *The Artful Partners. The Secret Association of Bernard Berenson and Joseph Duveen.* London, Sydney, and Wellington.
Sipkes, Kees. "La restaración de 'La carta de amor'." *Ci'ónica de Holanda* 29: 10–15.
Siple 1927
SIPLE, Ella S. "Recent Acquisitions by American Collectors." *Burlington Magazine* 51 (December): 297–309.
Six 1908
SIX, Jan. "De techniek van Vermeer in 'Een meyd die melk uytgiet'." *Bulletin ... Nederlandschen Oudheidkundigen Bond,* 2d series, 1: 1-5.
Six 1918
SIX, Jan. "Een gesicht van eenige huysen van Vermeer." *Oude Kunst* 4: 32–35.
Slatkes 1981
SLATKES, Leonard J. *Vermeer and His Contemporaries.* New York.
Slive 1957–1958
SLIVE, Seymour. "A Family Portrait by Nicolaes Maes." *Fogg Art Museum Annual Report:* 32–39.
Slive 1968
SLIVE, Seymour. "Een dronke slapende meyd aan een tafel by Jan Vermeer." In *Festschrift Ulrich Middeldorf.* Berlin: 452–459.
Slive 1970-1974
SLIVE, Seymour. *Frans Hals.* 3 vols. New York and London.
Sluijter 1986
SLUIJTER, Eric Jan. "De 'Heydensche Fabulen' in de Noordnederlandse schilderkunst circa 1590–1670." Ph.D. diss., Rijksuniversiteit, Leiden.
Sluijter 1988
SLUIJTER, Eric Jan. "Een stuck waerin een jufr. voor de spiegel van Gerrit Douw." *Antiek* 23: 156–159.
Sluijter 1991
SLUIJTER, Eric Jan. "Over fijnschilders en 'betekenis'. Naar aanleiding van Peter Hecht, *De Hollandse fijnschilders.*" *Oud-Holland* 105: 50-63.
Smith 1987
SMITH, David R. "Irony and Civility: Notes on the Convergence of Genre and Portraiture in Seventeenth-Century Dutch Painting." *Art Bulletin* 69 (September): 407–430.
Smith 1829-1842
SMITH, John. *A Catalogue Raisonné of the Works of the Most Eminent Dutch, Flemish, and French Painters.* 8 vols. and supplement. London.
Snow 1979
SNOW, Edward A. *A Study of Vermeer.* Berkeley, Los Angeles, and London.
Sonnema 1990
SONNEMA, Roy Brian. "Representations of Music in Seventeenth-Century Dutch Painting." Ph.D. diss., University of California at Berkeley.
Sonnenburg 1973
SONNENBURG, Hubert von. "Technical Comments." *The Metropolitan Museum of Art Bulletin* 31 (Summer): unpaginated.
Spaans 1994
SPAANS, Erik. "Vendetta voor Vermeer." *HP/De Tijd* (13 May): 40–44.
Springell 1963
SPRINGELL, Francis C. *Connoisseur and Diplomat.* London.
Stechow 1960
STECHOW, Wolfgang. "Landscape Painting in Dutch Seventeenth-Century Interiors." *Nederlands Kunsthistorisch Jaarboek* 11: 165–184.
Steenhoff 1908
STEENHOFF, W. "De collectie Six en de aanwinst eruit door het Rijksmuseum." *Onze Kunst* 7: 205–219.
Steneberg 1957
STENEBERG, K.E. "Vermeer's Malarfilosofi." *Symbolister 1 tidskrift för konstvetenskap* 30: 125–147.

Stephenson 1909
STEPHENSON, F. G. "Great Dutch Artists." *Bulletin of the Metropolitan Museum of Art* 4: 167–173.

Stokman 1988
STOKMAN, J. "Archiefsprokkeling: de weduwe van Vermeer in Breda." *Oud-Holland* 102: 246–247.

Stone-Ferrier 1985
STONE-FERRIER, Linda. *Images of Textiles: The Weave of Seventeenth-century Dutch Art and Society.* Ann Arbor.

Van Straaten 1977
VAN STRAATEN, Evert. *Johannes Vermeer 1632–1675; een Delfts schilder en de cultuur van zijn tijd.* The Hague.

Stuckenbrock 1993
STUCKENBROCK, Christiane. *Frans Hals. Fröhliche Kinder, Musikanten und Zecher.* Frankfurt am Main.

Sulzberger 1948
SULZBERGER, Suzanne. "Ajoute à la bibliographie de Vermeer de Delft." *Kunsthistorische Mededelingen van het Rijksbureau voor Kunsthistorische Documentatie* 3, no. 2: 37.

Sumowski 1983
SUMOWSKI, Werner. *Gemälde der Rembrandt-Schuler.* 5 vols. Landau.

Sutton 1980
SUTTON, Peter C. *Pieter de Hooch: Complete Edition with a Catalogue Raisonné.* New York.

Sutton 1986
SUTTON, Peter C. *A Guide to Dutch Art in America.* Grand Rapids and Kampen.

Swillens 1929
SWILLENS, Pieter T. A. "Een perspectivische studie over de schilderijen van Jan Vermeer van Delft." *Oude Kunst* 7: 129–161.

Swillens 1932
SWILLENS, Pieter T. A. "Johannes Vermeer van Delft, 31 Oct. 1632–15 Dec. 1675." *Opgang* 12: 689–699.

Swillens 1950
SWILLENS, Pieter T. A. *Johannes Vermeer Painter of Delft: 1632–1675.* Utrecht and Brussels.

Tatlock 1921
TATLOCK, R. R. "Vermeer's 'Girl with a Flute'." *Burlington Magazine* 39: 28-33.

Taverne 1972–1973
TAVERNE, E. "Salomon de Bray and the Reorganization of the Haarlem Guild of Saint Luke in 1631." *Simiolus* 6: 50–69.

Th. 1936
Th. "Christus in het huis van Martha en Maria van Jan Vermeer van Delft in de 'National Gallery of Scotland' te Edinburgh, tentoongesteld in het Boymans' Museum te Rotterdam in den zomer van 1935." *Het Gildeboek* 19: 157–159.

Theroux 1988
THEROUX, Alexander. "The Sphinx of Delft." *Art & Antiques* (December): 84–88, 120–124.

Van Thiel 1972
VAN THIEL, Pieter J. J. "The Damaging and Restoration of Vermeer's Love Letter." *Bulletin van het Rijksmuseum* 20 (November): 129–146.

Van Thiel 1983
VAN THIEL, Pieter J. J. "Verkregen met steun van de Vereniging Rembrandt." *Bulletin van het Rijksmuseum* 31: 195–231.

Thieme/Becker
THIEME, Ulrich, and Felix BECKER. *Allgemeines Lexikon der bildenden Künstler von der Antike bis zur Gegenwart.* 37 vols. Leipzig.

Van Thienen 1939
VAN THIENEN, Frijthof. *Vermeer.* Amsterdam.

Van Thienen 1949
VAN THIENEN, Frijthof. *Jan Vermeer of Delft.* New York.

Thoré-Bürger 1858-1860
BÜRGER, William (Etienne Joseph Théophile Thoré). *Musées de la Hollande.* 2 vols. Paris.

Thoré-Bürger 1859
BÜRGER, William (Etienne Joseph Théophile Thoré). *Galerie d'Arenberg à Bruxelles avec la catalogue complet de la collection.* Paris, Brussels, and Leipzig.

Thoré-Bürger 1866
BÜRGER, William (Etienne Joseph Théophile Thoré). "Van der Meer de Delft." *Gazette des Beaux-Arts* 21: 297–330, 458–470, 542–575.

Thoré-Bürger 1868
BÜRGER, William (Etienne Joseph Théophile Thoré). "Meisterwerke der Braunschweiger Galerie. In Radierungen von William Unger. III. Das Mädchen mit dem Weinglase. Oelgemälde von Jan van der Meer." *Zeitschrift für bildende Kunst* 3: 262–263.

Thoré-Bürger 1869
BÜRGER, William (Etienne Joseph Théophile Thoré). "Nouvelles études sur la galerie Suermondt à Aix-la-Chapelle." *Gazette des Beaux-Arts* 24: 5–187.

Thoré-Bürger/Waagen 1860
BÜRGER, William (Etienne Joseph Théophile Thoré), and Gustav WAAGEN. *Galerie Suermondt à Aix-la-Chapelle, Études sur les peintres hollandais et flamands.* Paris, Aix-la-Chapelle, and Amsterdam.

Tietze 1939
TIETZE, Hans. *Masterpieces of European Painting in America.* New York.

Tietze-Conrat 1922
TIETZE-CONRAT, Erika. *Die Delfter Malerschule: Carel Fabritius, Pieter de Hooch, Jan Vermeer.* Leipzig.

Tolnay 1953
TOLNAY, Charles de. "L'Atelier de Vermeer." *Gazette des Beaux-Arts* 41 (April): 265–272.

Tomkins 1970
TOMKINS, Calvin. *Merchants and Masterpieces. The Story of the Metropolitan Museum of Art.* New York.

Trivas 1939
TRIVAS, N. S. "Oude kunst op de New Yorksche Wereldtentoonstelling." *Elsevier's Geïllustreerd Maandschrift* 49: 136–141.

Van Uitert 1968
VAN UITERT, Evert. "Interieurschilderijen uit de 17de eeuw." *Openbaar Kunstbezit TV* : 4–8

Ungaretti 1967
UNGARETTI, G., and P. BIANCONI. *L'Opera Completa di Vermeer.* Milan.

Valentiner 1910
VALENTINER, Wilhelm R. "Die Ausstellung holländischer Gemälde in New York." *Monatshefte für Kunstwissenschaft* 3: 5–12.

Valentiner 1933
VALENTINER, Wilhelm R. "Zum 300. Geburtstag Jan Vermeers, Oktober 1932: Vermeer und die Meister der Holländischen Genremalerei." *Pantheon* 5 (October): 305-324.

Vanzype 1908A, 1921
VANZYPE, Gustave. *Vermeer de Delft.* Brussels.

Vanzype 1908B
VANZYPE, Gustave. "Vermeer van Delft." *Ralliement* 33: 505–507.

Vanzype 1925
VANZYPE, Gustave. *Vermeer de Delft.* Paris and Brussels.

Van der Veen 1992
VAN DER VEEN, Jaap A. Review of Montias 1989. *Oud-Holland* 106: 99–101.

Van Veen 1608
VAN VEEN, Otto. *Amorum Emblemata.* Antwerp. Repr. New York, 1979.

Veth 1908
VETH, Jan. *Schilderijen van Johannes Vermeer in Nederlandsche Verzamelingen.* Amsterdam.

Veth 1910
VETH, Jan. "Gemälde von Johannes Vermeer in niederländischen Sammlungen." *Kunst und Künstler* 8 (November): 102–117.

Veth 1914
VETH, Jan. "Schilderijen van Johannes Vermeer in Nederlandsche verzamelingen." In *Beelden en Groepen.* Amsterdam: 95–109.

Visscher 1614
VISSCHER, Roemer. *Sinnepoppen.* Amsterdam.

Vivian 1962
VIVIAN, F. "Joseph Smith and Giovanni Antonio Pellegrini." *Burlington Magazine* 104 (August): 330–333.

Vosmaer 1868
VOSMAER, Carel. *Rembrandt Harmens van Rijn. Sa vie et ses oeuvres.* The Hague.

Vosmaer 1875
VOSMAER, Carel. "Het Mauritshuis." *De Nederlandsche Spectator* 51: 401–402.

Vosmaer 1887
VOSMAER, Carel. "Barthold Suermondt." *De Nederlandsche Spectator* (19 March): 97–98.

Voss 1912
VOSS, Hermann. "Vermeer van Delft und die Utrechter Schule." *Monatshefte für Kunstwissenschaft* 5: 79–83.

Vredeman de Vries 1604
VREDEMAN DE VRIES, Hans. *Perspective. Dat is de hoochgheroemde conste....* The Hague.

De Vries 1939, 1945, and 1948
DE VRIES, Ary Bob. *Jan Vermeer van Delft.* Amsterdam. (English ed. London, 1948.)

De Vries 1954
DE VRIES, Ary Bob. "Vermeer's Diana." *Bulletin van het Rijksmuseum* 2: 40–42.

De Vries 1965
DE VRIES, Ary Bob. "Johannes Vermeer van Delft (1632–1675). Het blauwe vrouwtje c. 1663." *Openbaar Kunstbezit* 9: 39a–b.

De Vries 1966
DE VRIES, Ary Bob. "Vijf eeuwen schilderkunst. In het licht van Vermeer." *Openbaar Kunstbezit* 10: 45a–b.

De Vries 1967
DE VRIES, Ary Bob et al. *150 jaar Koninklijk Kabinet van*

Schilderijen. Koninklijke Bibliotheek. Koninklijke Penningkabinet. The Hague.

De Vries 1900
DE VRIES, J. "Stadsgezicht van J. van der Meer." *Eigen Haard* no. 32: 504–506.

De Vries 1990
DE VRIES, Lyckle. *Diamante gedenkzuilen en leerzaeme voorbeelden. Een bespreking van Johan van Gools Nieuwe Schouburgh*. Groningen.

De Vries 1993
DE VRIES, S., and R. DE GROOT. *Vincent van Gogh in Amsterdam*. Amsterdam.

De Vries/Huyghe 1948
DE VRIES, Ary Bob, and René HUYGHE. *Jan Vermeer de Delft*. Paris.

Waagen 1854
WAAGEN, Gustav Friedrich. *Treasures of Art in Great Britain: Being an Account of the Chief Collections of Paintings, Drawings, Sculptures, Illuminated Mss. & c. & c.* 3 vols. and supplement. London.

Waagen 1858
WAAGEN, Gustav Friedrich. *Einige Bemerkungen über die Aufstellung, Beleuchtung und Catalogisirung der Koeniglichen Gemaelde zu Dresden*. Berlin.

Waagen 1862
WAAGEN, Gustav Friedrich. *Handbuch der deutschen und niederländischen Malerschulen*. 2 vols. Stuttgart.

Waagen 1863-1864
WAAGEN, Gustav Friedrich. *Manuel de l'histoire de la peinture. Écoles Allemande, Flamande et hollandaise*. 3 vols. Brussels, Leipzig, and Ghent.

Van der Waals 1992
VAN DER WAALS, Jan. "In het straatje van Montias, Vermeer in historische context." *Theoretische geschiedenis* 19: 176–185.

Wadum 1994
WADUM, Jørgen. *Vermeer Illuminated. Conservation, Restoration and Research*. The Hague.

Wadum 1995
WADUM, Jørgen. "Vermeer's Use of Perspective." *Historic Painting Techniques, Materials and Studio Practice. Preprints of a Symposium Held at the University of Leiden*. Santa Monica: 148–154.

Wagner 1982
WAGNER, Franz. "Die Sammlung Czernin und ihr Begründer." *Weltkunst* 52 (March): 770–773.

Waldmann 1926
WALDMANN, Emil. "Ein neues Bild von Jan Vermeer van Delft." *Kunst und Künstler* 24: 186–187.

Waldmann 1938
WALDMANN, Emil. "Die Sammlung Widener." *Pantheon* 22 (November): 334–343.

Walicki 1970
WALICKI, Michal. *Jan Vermeer van Delft*. Dresden.

Walsh 1973
WALSH, John Jr. "Vermeer." *The Metropolitan Museum of Art Bulletin* 31 (Summer): unpaginated.

Walsh 1978
WALSH, John Jr. "Paintings in the Dutch Room." *Connoisseur* 198 (May): 50–61.

Ward 1945
WARD, A. C. *Seven Painters: An Introduction to Pictures*. London.

Watson 1960
WATSON, F. J. B. "The Collections of Sir Alfred Beit: 1." *Connoisseur* 145: 156–163.

Weber 1993
WEBER, Gregor J. M. "Antoine Dézallier d'Argenville unf fünf Künstler namens Jan van der Meer." *Oud-Holland* 107: 300–301.

Weber 1994A
WEBER, Gregor J. M. "Johannes Vermeer, Pieter Jansz. van Asch und das Problem der Abbildungstreue." *Oud-Holland* 108: 98–106.

Weber 1994B
WEBER, Gregor J. M. "'om bevestige[n], aen-te-raden, verbreden ende vercieren'-rhetorisch Exempellehre und die Struktur des 'Bildes im Bild'." Festschrift für Prof. Dr. Justus Müller Hofstede. *Wallraf-Richartz-Jahrbuch* 55: 287–314.

Weisberg 1974
WEISBERG, Gabriel P. "François Bonvin and the Critics of his Art." *Apollo* 100 (October): 306–311.

Welther 1991
WELTHER, L. *Die Geschichte und die Herstellung des Abenländischen Künstlerpinsels*. Stuttgart.

Welu 1975
WELU, James A. "Vermeer: His Cartographic Sources." *Art Bulletin* 57 (December): 529–547.

Welu 1977
WELU, James A. "Vermeer and Cartography." Ph.D. diss., Boston University.

Welu 1978
WELU, James A. "The Map in Vermeer's Art of Painting." *Imago Mundi* 30, 2d series, 4: 9–30.

Welu 1986
WELU, James A. "Vermeer's *Astronomer*: Observations on an Open Book." *Art Bulletin* 68 (June): 263–267.

Van Westrheene 1868
VAN WESTRHEENE, Tobias. "De verzameling van schilderijen van oude meesters van den heer Neville D. Goldsmid te 's Gravenhage." *Kunstkronijk*, new series, 9: 89–94.

Van de Wetering 1993
VAN DE WETERING, Ernst. "De paletten van Rembrandt en Jozef Israëls, een onderzoek naar de relatie tussen stijl en schildertechniek." *Oud-Holland* 107: 137–151.

Van de Wetering 1995
VAN DE WETERING, Ernst. "Reflections on the Relations between Technique and Style: The use of the Palette by the Seventeenth-century Painter." *Historic Painting Techniques, Materials and Studio Practice. Preprints of a Symposium Held at the University of Leiden*. Santa Monica: 196–203.

Weyerman 1729–1769
WEYERMAN, Jacob Campo. *De levensbeschryvingen der Nederlandsche Konst-schilders en Konst-schilderessen*. 4 vols. The Hague.

Wheelock 1975–1976
WHEELOCK, Arthur K., Jr. "Gerard Houckgeest and Emanuel de Witte: Architectural Painting in Delft around 1650." *Simiolus* 8: 167–185.

Wheelock 1977A
WHEELOCK, Arthur K., Jr. *Perspective, Optics, and Delft Artists around 1650*. New York and London.

Wheelock 1977B
WHEELOCK, Arthur K., Jr. Review of Blankert 1975. *Art Bulletin* 59 (September): 439–441.

Wheelock 1977C
WHEELOCK, Arthur K., Jr. "Constantijn Huygens and Early Attitudes toward the Camera Obscura." *History of Photography* 1: 20–32.

Wheelock 1978
WHEELOCK, Arthur K., Jr. "Zur Technik zweier Bilder, die Vermeer zugeschrieben sind." *Maltechnik Restauro* 4: 242–257.

Wheelock 1979
WHEELOCK, Arthur K., Jr. "Perspective and Its Role in the Evolution of Dutch Realism." In *Perception and Pictorial Representation*. Ed. Calvin F. Nodine and Dennis F. Fisher. New York: 110–117.

Wheelock 1981, 1988
WHEELOCK, Arthur K., Jr. *Jan Vermeer*. New York.

Wheelock 1982
WHEELOCK, Arthur K., Jr., and C. J. KALDENBACH. "Vermeer's *View of Delft* and His Vision of Reality." *Artibus et Historiae* 6: 9–35.

Wheelock 1984
WHEELOCK, Arthur K., Jr. "Pentimenti in Vermeer's Paintings: Changes in Style and Meaning." In *Holländische Genremalerei im 17. Jahrhundert Symposium Berlin 1984*. Ed. Henning Bock and Thomas W. Gaehtgens. Berlin: 385–412.

Wheelock 1986
WHEELOCK, Arthur K., Jr. "*Saint Praxedis*: New Light on the Early Career of Vermeer." *Artibus et Historiae* 14: 71–89.

Wheelock 1987
WHEELOCK, Arthur K., Jr. "Girl through the Glass: How Optics Changed a Dutch Master's Art." *The Sciences* 27: 1987.

Wheelock 1989
WHEELOCK, Arthur K., Jr. "History, Politics, and the Portrait of a City: Vermeer's *View of Delft*." In *Urban Life in the Renaissance*. Ed. Susan Zimmerman and Ronald F. E. Weissman. Newark: 165–184.

Wheelock 1992
WHEELOCK, Arthur K., Jr. "Vermeer and Bramer: A New Look at Old Documents." In *Leonaert Bramer 1596–1674: A Painter of the Night*. Frima Fox Hofrichter. Milwaukee: 19–22.

Wheelock 1995
WHEELOCK, Arthur K., Jr. *Vermeer and the Art of Painting*. New Haven and London.

White 1983
WHITE, Christopher. "The Variety of Dutch and Flemish Art." Review of Slatkes 1981 and Wheelock 1981. *Apollo* (January): 64–65.

Wijbenga 1986
WIJBENGA, D. *Delft; een verhaal van de stad en haar bewoners van 1572 tot het jaar 1700 (II)*. Rijswijk.

Wijnman 1959
WIJNMAN, H. F. *Uit de kring van Rembrandt en Vondel*. Amsterdam.

Wijnman 1976
WIJNMAN, H. F., and G. ROOSEGAARDE BISSCHOP. *Vier eeuwen Herengracht. Geveltekeningen van alle huizen*

aan de gracht, twee historische overzichten en de beschrijving van elk pand met zijn eigenaars en bewoners. Amsterdam.

Wijnman et al 1974
WIJNMAN, H. F., E. WERKMAN, and J. H. VAN DEN HOEK OSTENDE et al. *Historische gids van Amsterdam.* Amsterdam.

Wijsenbeek-Olthuis 1987
WIJSENBEEK-OLTHUIS, Thera. *Achter de gevels van Delft. Bezit en bestaan van rijk en arm in een periode van achteruitgang (1700–1800).* Hilversum.

De Wilde 1959
WILDE, E. de. "Johannes Vermeer (1632–1675). Gezicht op Delft." *Openbaar kunstbezit* 3: 32a–b.

Wilenski 1929
WILENSKI, Reginald Howard. *An Introduction to Dutch Art.* New York and London.

Wilenski 1945
WILENSKI, Reginald Howard. *Dutch Painting.* London.

Winkler 1931A
WINKLER, Friedrich. "Der Tauschhandel der Museen und der Braunschweiger Vermeer." *Pantheon* 8: 488–489.

Winkler 1931B
WINKLER, Friedrich. "Der Braunschweiger Vermeer." *Kunst und Künstler* 29: 74–76, 369.

Wolf 1915
WOLF, Georg Jacob. "Jan Vermeer van Delft." *Westermanns Monatshefte* 60: 66–75.

Wolf 1950
WOLF, Abraham. *A History of Science, Technology, and Philosophy in the 16th and 17th Centuries.* London.

Woordenboek
Woordenboek der Nederlandsche taal. 25 vols. The Hague and Leiden, 1882–1991.

Wrangell 1912
WRANGELL, N. "Vermeer van Delft." *Apollo* (January): 5–11.

Wright 1976
WRIGHT, Christopher. *Vermeer.* London.

Wurzbach 1906–1911
WURZBACH, A. von. *Niederländisches Künstler-Lexikon.* 3 vols. Vienna and Leipzig.

Yetts 1925
YETTS, W. Perceval. "The Literature of Art." *Burlington Magazine* (November): 266–272.

Young 1978
YOUNG, Eric. Review of Wright 1976. *Apollo* (October): 282.

Zijderveld 1949
ZIJDERVELD, A. "Cesare Ripa's Iconologia in ons land." *Oud-Holland* 64: 113–128, 184–192.

Exhibition Catalogues

Amsterdam 1814
Lijst der kunstwerken van nog in leven zijnde Nederlandsche meesters, welke zijn toegelaten tot de algemeene tentoonstelling van 1814. Arti et Amicitiae.

Amsterdam 1867
Katalogus der tentoonstelling van schilderijen van oude meesters. Arti et Amicitiae.

Amsterdam 1872
Katalogus der tentoonstelling van schilderijen van oude meesters. Arti et Amicitiae.

Amsterdam 1892
"Rembrandt." Vereeniging tot behoud in Nederland van Kunstschatten. Arti et Amicitiae.

Amsterdam 1900
Catalogus der verzameling schilderijen en familieportretten van de heeren jhr. P. H. Six van Vromade, Jhr. J. Six en jhr. W. Six. Stedelijk Museum.

Amsterdam 1935
Vermeer tentoonstelling ter herdenking van de plechtige opening van het Rijksmuseum op 13 juli 1885. Rijksmuseum.

Amsterdam 1945
Weerzien der meesters. Rijksmuseum.

Amsterdam 1950
120 Beroemde schilderijen uit het Kaiser-Friedrich-Museum te Berlijn. Rijksmuseum.

Amsterdam 1976
DE JONGH, Eddy. *Tot leering en vermaak. Betekenissen van Hollandse genrevoorstellingen uit de zeventiende eeuw.* Rijksmuseum.

Amsterdam 1982
HEIJBROEK, J. F. et al. *Met Huygens op reis.* Rijksprentenkabinet.

Amsterdam 1985
BROOS, Ben. *Rembrandt en zijn voorbeelden/Rembrandt and his sources.* Rembrandthuis.

Amsterdam 1988
SUTTON, Peter et al. *Masters of 17th-Century Landscape Painting.* Rijksmuseum.

Amsterdam 1989A
HECHT, Peter. *De Hollandse fijnschilders: van Gerard Dou tot Adriaen van der Werff.* Rijksmuseum.

Amsterdam 1989B
Heijbroek, J. F. (ed.). *De verzameling van mr. Carel Vosmaer (1826–1888).* Rijksprentenkabinet.

Amsterdam 1991
TÜMPEL, Christian, and Jacqueline BOONEN. *Het Oude Testament in de Schilderkunst van de Gouden Eeuw.* Joods Historisch Museum.

Amsterdam 1993
Meeting of Masterpieces: De Hooch-Vermeer. Rijksmuseum.

Antwerp 1946
De Hollandsche Schilderkunst van Jeroen Bosch tot Rembrandt. Keuze van Meesterwerken uit de Nederlandsche Musea. Koninklijk Museum voor Schone Kunsten.

Berlin 1929
ERASMUS, Kurt. *Die Meister des holländischen Interieurs.* Galerie Dr. Schäffer.

Berlin 1991
BROWN, Christopher, Jan KELCH, and Pieter J. J. van THIEL. *Rembrandt: The Master & His Workshop.* Gemäldegalerie, Staatliche Museen zu Berlin.

Bonn/Bad Godesburg 1980
ZIEMKE, Hans-Joachim. *Das Städelsche Kunstinstitut-die Geschichte einer Stiftung.*

Brunswick 1978
KLESSMANN, Rüdiger. *Die Sprache der Bilder: Realität und Bedeutung in der niederlandischen Malerei des 17. Jarhunderts.* Herzog Anton Ulrich-Museum.

Brussels 1873
Exposition de tableaux et dessins d'anciens maitres organisée par la société néerlandaise de bienfaisance à Bruxelles. Musées Royaux.

Brussels 1971
Rembrandt en zijn tijd. Palaeis voor Schone Kunsten.

Caen 1986
L'Allégorie dans la peinture: la représentation de la chrité au XVIIe siècle. Musée des Beaux Arts.

Cape Town 1949
Skilderye van ou Meesters uit de Beit-Versameling. Nationale Kunstmuseum.

Chicago 1933
A Century of Progress. Exhibition of Paintings and Sculpture. The Art Institute of Chicago.

Cracow 1991
GRABSKI, J. *Jan Vermeer van Delft (1632–1675). Saint Praxedis: An Exhibition of a Painting from the Collection of Barbara Piasecka Johnson.* International Cultural Center/The Warsaw Royal Castle.

Delft 1950
Het koninklijke kabinet 'Het Mauritshuis' in het museum 'Het Prinsenhof' te Delft. Stedelijk Museum 'Het Prinsenhof.'

Delft 1952
Prisma der bijbelse kunst. Stedelijk Museum 'Het Prinsenhof.'

Delft 1981
De Stadt Delft: cultuur en maatschappij van 1572 tot 1667. 2 vols. Stedelijk Museum 'Het Prinsenhof.'

Delft 1994
TEN BRINK GOLDSMITH, Jane, et al. *Leonaert Bramer. 1596–1674. Ingenious Painter and Draughtsman in Rome and Delft.* Stedelijk Museum 'Het Prinsenhof.'

Detroit 1925
A Loan Exhibition of Dutch Paintings. The Detroit Institute of Arts.

Detroit 1939
Masterpieces of Art from Foreign Collections. European Paintings from the New York and San Francisco World's Fairs. The Detroit Institute of Arts.

Detroit 1941
Masterpieces of Art from European and American Collections. Twenty-Second Loan Exhibition of Old Masters. The Detroit Institute of Arts.

Edinburgh 1992
WILLIAMS, J. L. *Dutch Art and Scotland. A Reflection of Taste.* National Gallery of Scotland.

Frankfurt 1993
SCHULZE, Sabine, et al. *Leselust, Niederländische Malerei von Rembrandt bis Vermeer.* Kunsthalle.

Haarlem 1986
DE JONGH, Eddy. *Portretten van echt en trouw: huwelijk en gezin in de Nederlandse kunst van de zeventiende eeuw.* Frans Halsmuseum.

The Hague 1881
Catalogus der tentoonstelling van schilderijen van oude

meesters te 's Gravenhage ten behoeve van watersnoodlijdenden. Gotisch Paleis.

The Hague 1890
Catalogus der tentoonstelling van schilderijen van oude meesters. Pulchri Studio.

The Hague 1919
Catalogue de la collection Goudstikker d'Amsterdam. Pulchri Studio.

The Hague 1945
Nederlandsche kunst van de XVde en XVIde eeuw. Mauritshuis.

The Hague 1948
Masterpieces of the Dutch School from the Collection of H.M. the King of England on the Occasion of the 50-year Reign of Queen Wilhelmina. Mauritshuis.

The Hague 1966
VRIES, Ary Bob de. *In het licht van Vermeer.* Mauritshuis.

The Hague 1974
Gerard ter Borch: Zwolle 1617, Deventer 1681. Mauritshuis.

The Hague 1990
BROOS, Ben, et al. *Great Dutch Paintings from America.* Mauritshuis.

The Hague 1994
BUIJSEN, Edwin, Louis GRIJP, et al. *The Hoogsteder Exhibition of: Music and Painting in the Golden Age.* Kunsthandel Hoogsteder & Hoogsteder.

Leiden 1988
SLUIJTER, Eric Jan, et al. *Leidse fijnschilders. Van Gerrit Dou tot Frans van Mieris de Jonge 1630–1760.* Stedelijk Museum De Lakenhal.

Leningrad 1976
Paintings from American Museums. Hermitage State Museum.

London 1838
Catalogue of Pictures by Italian, Spanish, Flemish, Dutch and French Masters. British Institution.

London 1876
Exhibition of Works by Old Masters and Deceased British Masters. Royal Academy of Arts.

London 1878
Exhibition of Works by the Old Masters and by Deceased Masters of the British School. Royal Academy of Arts.

London 1894
Exhibition of Works by the Old Masters and Deceased Masters of the British School. Royal Academy of Arts.

London 1895
TEMPLE, A. G. *Catalogue of the Loan Collection of Pictures.* Art Gallery of the Corporation of London.

London 1900
Exhibition of Pictures by Dutch Masters of the Seventeenth Century. Burlington Fine Arts Club.

London 1929A
Exhibition of Dutch Art, 1450–1900. Royal Academy of Arts.

London 1929B
Dutch Art. An Illustrated Souvenir of the Exhibition of Dutch Art at Burlington House, London. Burlington House.

London 1938
Catalogue of the Exhibition of 17th Century Art in Europe. Royal Academy of Arts.

London 1946
Catalogue of the Exhibition of the King's Pictures. Royal Academy of Arts.

London 1952
Dutch Pictures 1450–1750. 2 vols. Royal Academy of Arts.

London 1964
The Orange and the Rose. Holland and Britain in the Age of Observation 1600–1750. Victoria and Albert Museum.

London 1971
Dutch Pictures from the Royal Collection. The Queen's Gallery. Buckingham Palace.

London 1976
BROWN, Christopher. *Art in Seventeenth-Century Holland.* The National Gallery.

London 1993
A King's Purchase. King George III and the Collection of Consul Smith. The Queen's Gallery, Buckingham Palace.

Milan 1951
Mostra del Caravaggio a dei Caravaggeschi. Palazzo Reale.

Milan 1954
Mostra di pittura olandese del seicento. Palazzo Reale.

Münster 1994
Christian Tümpel, ed. *Im Lichte Rembrandts: Das Alte Testament im Goldenen Zeitalter der niederländischen Kunst.* Westfälisches Landesmuseum.

New York 1909
The Hudson-Fulton Celebration: Loan Exhibition of Paintings by Old Dutch Masters. The Metropolitan Museum of Art.

New York 1912
Exhibition of Old Masters for the Benefit of the Artists' Funds and Artists' Aid Societies. M. Knoedler & Co.

New York 1925
Loan Exhibition of Dutch Masters of the Seventeenth Century. M. Knoedler & Co.

New York 1928
A Loan Exhibition of Twelve Masterpieces of Painting. M. Knoedler & Co.

New York 1939
Masterpieces of Art. New York World's Fair.

New York 1941
Loan Exhibition in Honor of Royal Cortissoz and His 50 Years of Criticism in the New York Herald Tribune. M. Knoedler & Co.

New York 1942
Paintings by the Great Dutch Masters of the Seventeenth Century. Duveen Galleries.

New York 1946
Loan Exhibition: 24 Masterpieces. M. Knoedler & Co.

New York 1954
Dutch Painting: The Golden Age. An Exhibition of Dutch Pictures of the Seventeenth Century. The Metropolitan Museum of Art.

New York 1969
NISSMAN, Joan. *Florentine Baroque Art from American Collections.* The Metropolitan Museum of Art.

New York 1984
STOLBACH, Michael Hunt. *Inaugural Exhibition.* Spencer A. Samuels Gallery.

Oslo 1959
Fra Rembrandt til Vermeer. Nasjonalgalleriet.

Paris 1866
Exposition rétrospective tableaux anciens empruntés aux galeries particulières. Palais des Champs-Elysées.

Paris 1874
Exposés au profit de la colonisation de l'Algérie par les Alsaciens-Lorrains. Palais de la Présidence du Corps léegislatif.

Paris 1898
Illustrated catalogue of 300 Paintings by Old Masters of the Dutch, Flemish, French, and English Schools Being Some of the Principal Pictures Which Have at Various Times Formed Part of the Sedelmeyer Gallery. Sedelmeyer Gallery.

Paris 1914
Hundred Masterpieces. A Selection from the Pictures by Old Masters. Sedelmeyer Gallery.

Paris 1921
Exposition hollandaise. Tableaux, aquarelles et dessins anciens et modernes. Jeu de Paume.

Paris 1946
Les Chefs-d'oeuvre des collections privées françaises. Orangerie des Tuileries.

Paris 1950
Le paysage hollandais au XVIIe siècle. Orangerie des Tuileries.

Paris 1966
Dans la lumière de Vermeer. Musée de l'Orangerie.

Paris 1970
La siècle de Rembrandt. Tableaux hollandais des collections publiques françaises. Musée du Petit Palais.

Paris 1986
BROOS, Ben. *De Rembrandt à Vermeer: Les peintres hollandais au Mauritshuis à la Haye.* Grand Palais.

Philadelphia 1984A
SUTTON, Peter. *Masters of Seventeenth-Century Dutch Genre Painting.* Philadelphia Museum of Art.

Philadelphia 1984B
Dutch Tiles in the Philadelphia Museum of Art. Philadelphia Museum of Art.

Rome 1928
Mostra di capolavori della pittura olandese (2d edition). Galleria Borghese.

Rome 1954
Mostra di pittura olandese del seicento. Palazzo delle Esposizioni.

Rome 1956
Le XVIIe siècle Européen. Réalisme classicisme baroque. Palazzo degli Esposizioni.

Rotterdam 1935
Vermeer, oorsprong en invloed. Fabritius, de Hooch, de Witte. Museum Boymans-van Beuningen.

Rotterdam 1991
GILTAIJ, Jeroen, Guido JANSEN, et al. *Perspectiven: Saenredam en de architectuurschilders van de 17e eeuw.* Museum Boymans-van Beuningen.

Rotterdam 1994
SCHADEE, Nora, ed. *Rotterdamse meesters uit de Gouden Eeuw.* Historisch Museum.

Saint Petersburg 1989
Masterpieces of Western Paintings of the XVIth–XXth Centuries from the Museums of the European Countries and USA. Hermitage State Museum.

Schaffhausen 1949
Rembrandt und seine Zeit. Museum zu Allerheiligen.

Stockholm 1967
Holländska Mästare. I svensk ägo. Nationalmuseum.

Tokyo 1968
The Age of Rembrandt. Dutch Paintings and Drawings of the 17th Century. The National Museum of Western Art.

Tokyo 1984
Dutch Painting of the Golden Age from the Royal Picture Gallery Mauritshuis. The National Museum of Western Art.

Tokyo 1987
Space in European Art: Council of Europe Exhibition in Japan. The National Museum of Western Art.

Utrecht 1952
Caravaggio en de Nederlanden. Centraal Museum.

Warsaw 1990
Opus Sacrum. Catalogue of the Exhibition from the Collection of Barbara Piasecka Johnson. Royal Castle.

Washington 1980
BLANKERT, Albert, Beatrijs BRENNINKMEYER-DE ROOIJ, Christopher BROWN, Susan Donahue KURETSKY, Eric J. SLUITER, Derk P. SNOEP, Pieter van THIEL, Astrid TÜMPEL, Christian TÜMPEL, and Arthur K. WHEELOCK, Jr. *Gods, Saints & Heroes: Dutch Painting in the Age of Rembrandt.* National Gallery of Art.

Washington 1982
Mauritshuis, Dutch Paintings of the Golden Age. National Gallery of Art.

Washington 1988
BROWN, Beverly Louise, and Arthur K. WHEELOCK, Jr. *Masterworks from Munich: Sixteenth to Eighteenth-Century Paintings from the Alte Pinakothek.* National Gallery of Art.

Washington 1989
SLIVE, Seymour, et al. *Frans Hals.* National Gallery of Art.

Zurich 1953
Holländer des 17. Jahrhunderts. Kunsthaus.

Collection Catalogues

Boymans-van Beuningen 1925
Beknopte catalogus der schilderijen, teekeningen en beeldhouwwerken tentoongesteld in het Museum Boymans te Rotterdam. Rotterdam.

Boymans-van Beuningen 1927
Catalogus der schilderijen, teekeningen en beeldhouwwerken tentoongesteld in het Museum Boymans te Rotterdam. Rotterdam.

Coats 1904
Catalogue of the Collection of Pictures of the French, Dutch, British and Other Schools Belonging to W. A. Coats. Glasgow.

Gemäldegalerie Dresden 1982
MAYER-MEINTSCHEL, Annaliese, et al. *Gemäldegalerie Alte Meister Dresden. Katalog der ausgestellten Werke. Staatliche Kunstsammlungen Dresden.* Dresden.

Herzog Anton Ulrich-Museum 1710
QUERFURT, Tobias. *Kurtze Beschreibung des Fuerstl. Lust-Schlosses Saltzdahlum.* Brunswick.

Herzog Anton Ulrich-Museum 1776
EBERLEIN, Christian N. *Verzeichniss der Herzoglichen Bilder-Gallerie zu Saltzthalen.* Brunswick.

Herzog Anton Ulrich-Museum 1836/1849
PAPE, Ludwig. *Verzeichnis der Gemälde-Sammlung des herzoglichen Museums zu Brunswick.* Brunswick.

Herzog Anton Ulrich-Museum 1870
UNGER, William. *Die Galerie zu Brunswick in ihren Meisterwerken.* Leipzig.

Herzog Anton Ulrich-Museum 1882
RIEGEL, Herman. *Die niederländischen Schulen im herzoglichen Museum zu Brunswick.* Berlin.

Herzog Anton Ulrich-Museum 1983
KLESSMANN, Rüdiger. *Die holländischen Gemälde.* Brunswick.

Louvre 1891
LAFENESTRE, Georges, and Eugène RICHTENBERGER. *Le musée national du Louvre.* Paris.

Louvre 1979
BREJON DE LAVERGNÉE, Arnauld, Jacques FOUCART, and Nicole REYNAUD. *Catalogue sommaire illustré des peintures du Musée du Louvre. I Ecoles flamande et hollandaise.* Paris.

Mauritshuis 1826–1830
STEENGRACHT VAN OOSTCAPELLE, J. *Les principaux tableaux du musée royal à La Haye.* 4 vols. The Hague.

Mauritshuis 1874
DE STUERS, Victor. *Notice historique et descriptive des tableaux et des sculptures exposés dans le Musée Royal de la Haye.* The Hague.

Mauritshuis 1877
Notice historique et descriptive des tableaux et des sculptures exposés dans le musée royal de la Haye. Supplément Août 1877. The Hague.

Mauritshuis 1879
DE JONGE, J. K. J. *Petit guide du Visiteur au Mauritshuis à la Haye.* The Hague.

Mauritshuis 1885
Catalogue des tableaux et des sculptures de Musée Royal de La Haye. The Hague.

Mauritshuis 1893
Catalogue of the Pictures and Sculpture in the Royal Picture Gallery (Mauritshuis) at The Hague. The Hague.

Mauritshuis 1895
BREDIUS, Abraham, and Cornelis HOFSTEDE DE GROOT. *Musée Royal de La Haye (Mauritshuis). Catalogue raisonné des tableaux et des sculptures.* The Hague.

Mauritshuis 1898
BREDIUS, Abraham. *Beknopte catalogus der schilderijen en beeldhouwwerken in het Koninklijk Kabinet van Schilderijen te 's Gravenhage.* The Hague.

Mauritshuis 1899
BREDIUS, Abraham. *Abridged Catalogue of the Pictures and Sculpture in the Royal Picture Gallery (Mauritshuis).* The Hague.

Mauritshuis 1903
BREDIUS, Abraham. *Beknopte catalogus der schilderijen en beeldhouwwerken in het Koninklijk Kabinet van Schilderijen (Mauritshuis).* The Hague.

Mauritshuis 1914
BREDIUS, Abraham, and Willem MARTIN. *Musée royal de la Haye (Mauritshuis). Catalogue raisonné des tableaux et des sculptures.* The Hague.

Mauritshuis 1935
MARTIN, Willem. *Catalogue Raisonné de Tableaux et Sculptures.* The Hague.

Mauritshuis 1985
HOETINK, H. R., ed. *The Royal Picture Gallery Mauritshuis.* Amsterdam, The Hague, and New York.

Mauritshuis 1987
BROOS, Ben. *Meesterwerken in het Mauritshuis.* The Hague.

Mauritshuis 1993A
Broos, Ben. *Intimacies and Intrigues. History Painting in the Mauritshuis.* The Hague and Ghent.

Mauritshuis 1993B
Mauritshuis. Illustrated General Catalogue. Amsterdam and The Hague.

Mellon 1949
National Gallery of Art. *Paintings and Sculptures from the Mellon Collection.* Washington.

Metropolitan Museum of Art 1895
The Metropolitan Museum of Art. Handbook no. 6. New York.

Metropolitan Museum of Art 1920
BURROUGHS, B. *The Metropolitan Museum of Art. Catalogue of Paintings.* New York.

Metropolitan Museum of Art 1980
BAETJER, Katharine. *European Paintings in the Metropolitan Museum of Art by Artists Born in or before 1865. A Summary Catalogue.* 3 vols. New York.

Museum Van der Hoop 1855
Catalogus der schilderijen van het Museum van der Hoop te Amsterdam. Amsterdam.

Museum Van der Hoop 1872
Beschrijving der schilderijen in het Museum van der Hoop. Amsterdam.

National Gallery Ireland 1988
LE HARIVEL, Adrian, Rosemarie MULCAHY, and Homan POTTERTON. *National Gallery of Ireland. The Beit Collection.* Dublin.

National Gallery London 1960
McLaren, Neil. *National Gallery Catalogues: The Dutch School*. London.

National Gallery London 1977
Levey, Michael, and Homan, Potterton. *The National Gallery, London*. London.

National Gallery London 1983
Brown, Christopher. *National Gallery Schools of Painting: Dutch Paintings*. London.

National Gallery London 1991
McLaren, Neil. *National Gallery Catalogues: Dutch School 1600–1900*. 2 vols. London.

National Gallery Scotland 1929
Catalogue National Gallery of Scotland Edinburgh. Edinburgh.

National Gallery Scotland 1936
Catalogue National Gallery of Scotland Edinburgh. Edinburgh.

National Gallery Scotland 1957
National Gallery of Scotland. Catalogue of paintings and sculpture. Edinburgh.

National Gallery Scotland 1978
Brigstocke, Hugh, and Colin, Thompson. *National Gallery of Scotland. Shorter Catalogue* 2d rev. ed. Edinburgh.

National Gallery Washington 1965
National Gallery of Art: Summary Catalogue of European Paintings and Sculpture. Washington.

National Gallery Washington 1968
National Gallery of Art: European Paintings and Sculpture. Washington.

National Gallery Washington 1975
European Paintings: An Illustrated Summary Catalogue. Washington.

National Gallery Washington 1985
European Paintings: An Illustrated Catalogue. Washington.

National Gallery Washington 1995
Wheelock, Arthur K., Jr. *Dutch Paintings of the Seventeenth Century* in The Collections of the National Gallery of Art Systematic Catalogues, Washington.

Pommersfelden 1746
Beschreibung des fürtrefflichen Gemähld und Bilder Schatzes, welcher in denen hochgräfflichen Schlössern und Gebäuen Deren Reichs Grafen Van Schönborn...zu finden. Ascaffenburg.

Pommersfelden 1857
Katalog der gräflich Schönbron'schen Bilder-Gallerie zu Pommersfelden. Würzburg.

Pommersfelden 1894
Von Frimmel, Theodor. *Verzeichnis der Gemälde in Gräflich Schönborn-Wiesentheid'schem Besitze*. Pommersfelden.

Rijksmuseum 1887
Bredius, Abraham. *Catalogue des peintures du musée de l'état à Amsterdam*. Amsterdam.

Rijksmuseum 1976
Van Thiel, Pieter J. J. *All the Paintings of the Rijksmuseum: A Completely Illustrated Catalogue*. Amsterdam and Maarssen.

Royal Collection 1906
Cust, Lionel. *The Royal Collection of Paintings at Buckingham Palace and Windsor Castle. Vol. II. Windsor Castle*. London and New York.

Royal Collection 1982
White, Christopher. *The Dutch Pictures in the Collection of Her Majesty the Queen*. Cambridge.

Staatliche Museen Berlin 1883
Meyer, Julius. *Königliche Museen zu Berlin. Beschreibendes Verzeichniss der Gemälde. Zweite Auflage*. Berlin.

Staatliche Museen Berlin 1891
Königliche Museen zu Berlin. Beschreibendes Verzeichnis der Gemälde. Dritte Auflage. Berlin.

Staatliche Museen Berlin 1921
Staatliche Museen zu Berlin. Beschreibendes Verzeichnis der Gemälde im Kaiser-Friedrich-Museum. Achte Auflage. Berlin and Leipzig.

Staatliche Museen Berlin 1975
Gemäldegalerie Berlin. Staatliche Museen Preußischer Kulturbesitz: Katalog der ausgestellten Gemälde des 13.–18. Jahrhunderts. Berlin-Dahlem.

Staatliche Museen Berlin 1978
Picture Gallery Staatliche Museen Preußischer Kulturbesitz Berlin: Catalogue of Paintings 13th–18th Century. Trans. Linda B. Parshall. 2d rev. ed. Berlin-Dahlem.

Staatliche Museen Berlin 1986
The Complete Catalogue of the Gemäldegalerie, Berlin.

Städelsches Kunstinstitut 1971
Verzeichnis der Gmälde aus dem Besitz des Städelschen Kunstinstituts und der Stadt Frankfurt. Frankfurt am Main.

Thyssen-Bornemisza 1989
Gaskell, Ivan. *The Thyssen-Bornemisza Collection: Seventeenth-century Dutch and Flemish Painting*. London.

Westfälisches Landesmuseum 1975
Westhoff-Krummacher, H. *Katalog der Gemälde des 19. Jahrhunderts im Westfälischen Landesmuseum für Kunst und Kulturgeschichte*. Münster.

Widener 1913–1916
Pictures in the Collection of P. A. B. Widener at Lynnewood Hall, Elkins Park, Pennsylvania. 3 vols. Philadelphia.

Widener 1923
Valentiner, Wilhelm R. *Paintings in the Collection of Joseph Widener at Lynnewood Hall*. Elkins Park, Pennsylvania.

Widener 1931
Paintings in the Collection of Joseph Widener at Lynnewood Hall. Elkins Park, Pennsylvania. Philadelphia.

Widener 1948
National Gallery of Art. *Paintings and Sculpture from the Widener Collection*. Washington.

Wrightsman Collection 1973
Fahy, Everett, and Sir Francis Watson. *The Wrightsman Collection: Paintings, Drawings, Sculpture*. New York.

Index